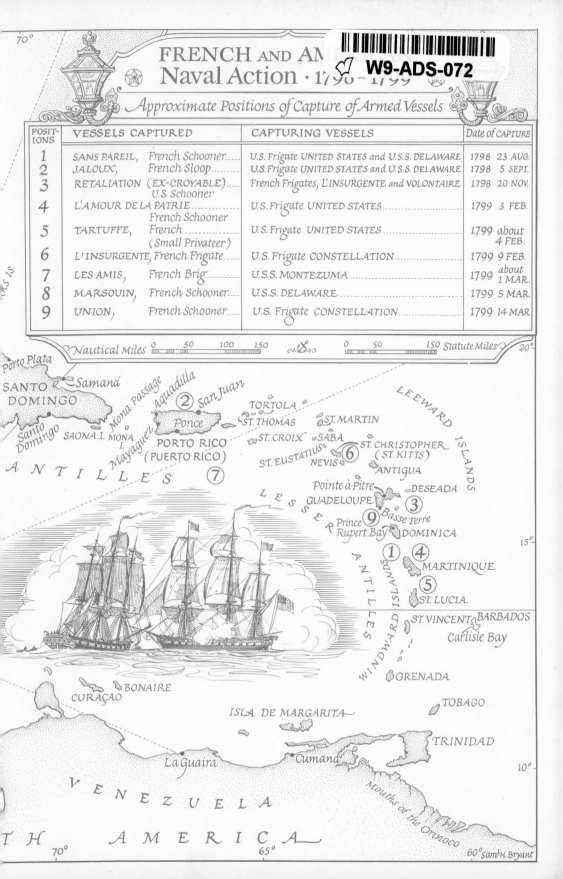

FRENCH AND AM...
Naval Action · 1798–1799

Approximate Positions of Capture of Armed Vessels

POSITIONS	VESSELS CAPTURED		CAPTURING VESSELS	Date of CAPTURE	
1	SANS PAREIL,	French Schooner......	U.S. Frigate UNITED STATES and U.S.S. DELAWARE	1798	23 AUG.
2	JALOUX,	French Sloop......	U.S. Frigate UNITED STATES and U.S.S. DELAWARE	1798	5 SEPT.
3	RETALIATION (EX-CROYABLE)...... U.S. Schooner		French Frigates, L'INSURGENTE and VOLONTAIRE	1798	20 NOV.
4	L'AMOUR DE LA PATRIE...... French Schooner		U.S. Frigate UNITED STATES......	1799	3 FEB.
5	TARTUFFE,	French (Small Privateer)	U.S. Frigate UNITED STATES......	1799	about 4 FEB.
6	L'INSURGENTE, French Frigate......		U.S. Frigate CONSTELLATION......	1799	9 FEB.
7	LES AMIS,	French Brig......	U.S.S. MONTEZUMA......	1799	about 1 MAR.
8	MARSOUIN,	French Schooner......	U.S.S. DELAWARE......	1799	5 MAR.
9	UNION,	French Schooner......	U.S. Frigate CONSTELLATION......	1799	14 MAR.

Nautical Miles 0 50 100 150   0 50 150 Statute Miles

Sam.ᴸ H. Bryant

The Quasi-War

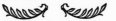

The Quasi-War

THE POLITICS AND DIPLOMACY
OF THE UNDECLARED WAR
WITH FRANCE 1797-1801

Alexander DeConde

CHARLES SCRIBNER'S SONS

NEW YORK

Copyright © 1966 Alexander DeConde

This book published simultaneously in the
United States of America and in Canada—
Copyright under the Berne Convention

All rights reserved. No part of this book
may be reproduced in any form without the
permission of Charles Scribner's Sons.

A–10.66[V]

Printed in the United States of America
Library of Congress Catalog Card Number 66-24492

PICTURE CREDITS

Bibliothèque Nationale, Paris. Cabinet des Estampes. Photographs by Ina Bandy
from France Benoit: 27, 28. Courtesy of Mrs. James Bruce, New York City: 6.
Essex Institute Collection, Salem, Mass.: 3. Courtesy of the Fogg Art Museum,
Harvard University. Louise E. Bettens Fund: 12. Photo-Hachette: 20, 21. From
the Collections of the Historical Society of Pennsylvania: 9, 32. Reproduced by
permission of The Huntington Library, San Marino, California: 11. Independence
National Historical Park Collection: 8. Library of Congress: 31. Courtesy of
Richard Coke Marshall: 13. The Metropolitan Museum of Art: Gift of William
H. Huntington, 1883: 2; Gift of Miss Josephine L. Stevens, 1908: 5. National
Gallery of Art, Washington, D.C.: Gift of Mrs. Robert Homans: 1; Andrew
Mellon Collection: 23. Courtesy of The New-York Historical Society, New York
City: 18, From *La Vie de Toussaint-Louverture,* by Dubroca. Paris. 1802; 29.
The New York Public Library: Emmet Collection, Manuscript Division: 7;
Picture Collection: 22; From *Tableaux Historiques de la Révolution Française* by
Duplessi-Bertaux. Paris. 1817: 26; Prints Division: 30. Peabody Museum of
Salem, Mass.: 14, 15, 16, 17. Radio Times Hulton Picture Library: 19. Courtesy
of The South Carolina Historical Society, Charleston, South Carolina: 10. Cour-
tesy of the University of North Carolina (Photo Laboratory): 24.

973.45
D 35

42809
**Mitchell College Library
New London, Conn.**

For My Sons

MAY THEIR GENERATION KNOW TRUE PEACE

✒ Preface ✒

THIS BOOK TELLS THE STORY OF THE LONG CRISIS OF HALF WAR AND half peace between the United States and France, 1797–1801, usually called the Quasi-War. That limited war was the first armed conflict that Americans, as citizens of an independent nation, fought. This book touches the military exploits lightly, for their story has already been told. It offers, instead, an interpretation of national and international diplomacy, of American politics, and of related ideas. On the international level it analyzes America's clash with France. On the national level it analyzes the conflict between the Federalist and the Republican parties and between two wings of the Federalist party.

The Quasi-War dwarfed all else in the administration of John Adams. So this study shows special concern for the ideas and actions of those men within the administration who made crucial decisions that shaped policy and of those men outside the administration who made decisions that affected the course of the Quasi-War. Some of those men, such as Adams himself, Alexander Hamilton, Thomas Jefferson, Charles Maurice de Talleyrand-Périgord, Toussaint L'Ouverture, and Napoleon Bonaparte, were among the most publicized, powerful, colorful, and perplexing personalities to stride across the history of the western world in the opening years of the nineteenth century.

Like those men, several of the key events in this account are among the most widely known in American history. It seems appropriate, therefore, to explain why this segment of history is being analyzed and where this book fits in historical literature.

Despite the familiarity of Americans with episodes such as the X Y Z affair, to many of them the Quasi-War itself is practically an unknown, or perhaps a forgotten, conflict. Up to this time no one has written a scholarly history of its politics and diplomacy. The one book on the war itself, Gardner W. Allen, *Our Naval War with France* (Boston, 1909), is essentially a naval history based on printed American sources. It was written at a time when materials in American, French, and British archives, and other manuscript repositories, were not as available to the scholar as they are today. The present study, then, is the first attempt, based on a variety of manuscript and printed sources, to present a full synthesis and interpretation of the diplomacy of the Quasi-War.

I try in this book to explain why peace between France and the United States was never beyond the reach of statesmen, even though most factors in the armed crisis seemed to point, almost inevitably, to full-scale war. By explaining why a particular war came, many histories have thrown light on the causes of war itself. By explaining why full-scale war did not come in 1798, or 1799, this history attempts, in a small way, to illuminate the causes of peace.

Some readers may believe, as did the English novelist Thomas Hardy, that "War makes rattling good history; but Peace is poor reading." I warn them that I disagree. Peace fascinates me. I think that peace is the best kind of history, that it is important history, and that it can make interesting reading. This study, I hope, supports my beliefs.

Although this book is a unit complete in itself, it is also a sequel to my *Entangling Alliance: Politics and Diplomacy under George Washington* (Durham, N.C., 1958). That book dealt with the origins of the Quasi-War.

ALEXANDER DECONDE

Santa Barbara, California

~ Contents ~

List of Illustrations

The Quasi-War

I

The Crisis

*My entrance into office is marked by a misunderstanding
with France, which I shall endeavor to reconcile, provided
that no violation of faith, no stain upon honor, is exacted.
But if infidelity, dishonor, or too much humiliation is demanded, France shall do as she pleases, and take her course.
America is not SCARED.*

                                    JOHN ADAMS, *March 1797*

ON HIS WAY TO PHILADELPHIA, THE NATION'S CAPITAL, IN NOVEMBER
1796 shortly before being elected President, John Adams paused
to contemplate the state of national affairs. Bitter relations with
France, he wrote to Abigail, his wife, will make the new President's task a dangerous one. Nonetheless, he continued, "Fear
takes no hold of me and makes no approaches to me that I perceive, and if my country makes just claims upon me, I will be as I
ever have been, prompt to share fates and fortunes with her."

Peering into the future, Adams explained that if he were
chosen to lead the nation, even though he dreaded war with
neither France nor England, he would not move aggressively
against either country without just and necessary cause. "If I
have looked with any accuracy into the hearts of my fellow citizens," he prophesied, "the French will find, as the English have
found, that feelings may be stirred which they never expected to

3

find there, and that, perhaps, the American people themselves are not sensible are within them." [1]

Adams won the Presidency, and in the next four years his prophecy would prove to be accurate. His administration would be dominated by a long crisis with France. The effect of the crisis would be felt throughout the nation, particularly in a violence of party spirit that would even threaten civil war. So deep would the crisis become that more than once the President would find himself on the knife-edge of decisions that could mean peace or war.

Even though Adams came to the Presidency as an elder statesman sixty-one years old with broad national and international experience, how he would react to the crisis was something of a mystery, even to men who knew him well. This puzzlement may have stemmed from his frosty temperament or from the fact that like many men long active in public affairs he had expressed various points of view on similar issues. Sometimes his ideas contradicted one another.[2] Yet Adams possessed some qualities that seemingly never changed, and he clung to a few principles that appeared always a part of him.

Adams was usually more a man of action than of reflection, yet in the twentieth century he could be considered an intellectual. He liked ideas and the play of the mind, but he disliked small talk and the bruising give-and-take of democratic politics. He had a strong, even violent temper, a thin skin, and an impulsiveness that seemed dangerous for one in high office. Benjamin Franklin, aware of a proneness to unpredictable action in the man, once remarked that "Adams was an honest man, often a wise one, but sometimes wholly out of his senses." [3]

While Adams had courage and intelligence, and convictions anchored in principle, which he would not easily sacrifice for expediency, he was not the kind of politician admired by the masses. He was vain, susceptible to flattery, inclined to retrospection, and often failed to show tact or warmth to those outside his own family. Enemies called him squeamish, cold, and unsocial. So did friends. "He can't dance, drink, game, flatter, promise, dress, swear with gentlemen, and small talk and flirt with the ladies," an old friend once remarked.[4] In short, Adams possessed the qualities of a patriot, but not those of a democratic party leader. He was usually unwilling, for example, to place party loyalty above principle.

Adams, something of a political theorist as well as a statesman, was not an original or unorthodox thinker. His political and economic ideas were conservative enough to satisfy even the most extreme members of his own Federalist party, the more conservative of the two national political parties. Like Alexander Hamilton, the principal founder of the Federalist party, he was a nationalist who favored a strong central government. Distrusting the masses, he liked the idea of a governing hereditary aristocracy, or executive. More than one critic considered him "the high priest of monarchy." As the English political philosopher James Harrington had suggested, Adams believed that power always follows property.[5]

In other aspects of his thinking Adams differed from Hamilton and those Federalists who felt that only the rich should rule. Adams was convinced that an unchecked aristocracy of wealth would pose as great a danger to life, liberty, and property as would uncontrolled democracy in the hands of the masses. In other words, he considered absolute power an evil, "tyranny delirious tyranny, wherever it is placed." He favored an aristocracy of ability and talent, which in practice meant rule by the upper classes, or men of wealth and status.

In his best-known political work, *A Defence of the Constitutions of . . . America,* Adams argued that in every society there is constant conflict between the rich and the poor, each trying to despoil the other, and that the task of statesmanship is to set bounds for the contenders. A statesman, in his view, should rise above the conflict and maintain a balance as would a moderator.[6]

Although as Vice-President Adams had been a loyal Federalist who had supported his party's program, he was not a devoted party man. He thought political parties should exist and function openly, but he felt, as did George Washington, that the Chief Executive should stand beyond the strife of partisan politics and that the parties should recognize his independence from them. As President, therefore, Adams intended to stand above party battles and pursue a national policy that would benefit all regardless of party allegiance. He would step from this path only when partisanship became so violent as to approach disloyalty to the nation.

Again like Hamilton, Adams admired the English government, writing at one time that in Europe there had never been a country more free than England, and that nowhere on earth had there been any liberty the equal of English liberty.[7] Unlike Hamilton, however, he never fully overcame his distrust of British policy, mainly towards the United States. This distrust had taken root during the American Revolution and had been kept alive by his experience as Minister to the Court of St. James's after the Revolution.

Toward France, Adams had a mixed attitude. He liked France and admired the French as individuals, but he disliked their Catholicism and their changing governments, which he never truly understood. From the beginning he had been alarmed by the French Revolution, believing that its constitutional experiments and violence endangered the balanced government he admired.[8] Even though he had lived in France for several years as a diplomat during the American Revolution, he had little confidence in French sincerity. Adams, then, cherished no special attachment either to Great Britain or to France and looked forward to a foreign policy that would treat each of those great powers with impartiality.

Even before Adams had been elected President he had reason to realize that a policy of impartiality would be difficult, if not impossible, to carry out. Britain and France were at war, and in the United States each had passionate partisans. Within Adams's own party there were those who considered commitment to England's cause practically a matter of faith. Adams did not share in this commitment, or in other dogmas of extreme Federalism, and would not allow himself to be controlled by anyone.[9] Acting as the uncrowned head of the party, Hamilton had tried, therefore, to maneuver Adams, who had served as Vice-President for eight years, out of accession to the Presidency in 1796. Hamilton had run Thomas Pinckney, a South Carolina Federalist whom he hoped he could manipulate, as an opposition candiate.

Hamilton's scheme failed, but it disturbed the elective process enough to give the Vice-Presidency to Thomas Jefferson, the presidential candidate of the opposition Republican party, and to mortify Adams. That plot, by adding to Adams's earlier distrust of Hamilton, had the effect of contributing to a split in the leadership of the Federalist party. Adams was determined that Hamilton should not gain a decisive voice in his administration.[10] In foreign affairs, especially, Adams feared Hamilton's bias in favor of Britain. Adams believed that Hamilton's bias would clash with Jefferson's partiality for France and would produce chaos in the country.

Ironically, almost immediately after his election, in an effort to promote party harmony, Adams played into Hamilton's hands. Since Adams had allied himself with no one faction within the Federalist party and had no friends among its leaders who were dedicated to him personally, he tried to gain Washington's following by retaining his predecessor's cabinet.[11] In Washington's last years in office, this cabinet had been guided by Hamilton.

Three of the department heads, Timothy Pickering, the Secretary of State; Oliver Wolcott, the Secretary of the Treasury; and James McHenry, the Secretary of War, were actually Hamilton's creatures and were devoted to his leadership. Wolcott, a handsome, gracious man, was a competent administrator rather than a statesman with ideas of his own, a politician willing to follow where others led. McHenry, a simple, gossipy, Irish immigrant, also followed rather than led, but as an administrator, he was incompetent.

The strongest of this trio was Pickering, a proud, stubborn, contentious New Englander and a thoroughly orthodox Federalist. His devotion to his own point of view, his admiration of England and hatred of France, were imbedded in an attitude of rigid self-righteousness. Yet, he could be charming, especially to those he liked, such as England's representatives in Philadelphia. Henrietta Liston, the wife of the British Minister, found Pickering attractive as a person. She considered him "an honest good Man," saying that "if he has a fault as a man, it is warmth of temper." [12]

These three executive officers were part of what came to be an extreme wing of the Federalist party. Although at first, as Pres-

ident, Adams showed no hostility to the point of view of this wing
of his party, in time he made it clear that he had little sympathy
with it. Only Charles Lee, the Attorney General, a man with
meager initiative and scanty political influence, considered himself tied to Adams by any sense of personal loyalty.

Hamilton, this restless, ambitious, versatile political genius
of the Federalist party, was now only a private citizen, a lawyer
practicing in New York. Yet through the cabinet officers, particularly through Wolcott, he planned to direct government policy as
he had under Washington. In fact, because the three department
heads, like other thoroughgoing Federalists, distrusted Adams's
devotion to party principles and did not consider themselves obligated to him personally for their posts, Hamilton's power in the
cabinet appeared to increase rather than diminish as Adams prepared to take over the Presidency. Through his influence over
Federalist leaders in Congress, furthermore, Hamilton could co-
ordinate action in the executive and legislative branches and,
thus, exercise considerable control over national policy.

Although aware that the department heads he would inherit
were close to Hamilton, Adams probably did not know the extent
of Hamilton's influence.[13] The President-elect therefore went
ahead with his plans for a national administration that would rise
above the turmoil of party.

MUTUAL GRIEVANCES

To Adams, primarily because of the crisis with France, national unity seemed imperative. After the consummation of Jay's
Treaty of 1794 with England, it may be recalled, the French had
tried to destroy a *rapprochement* between the United States and
England by meddling in America's domestic politics, by attacking
and seizing American shipping, and by breaking off normal
diplomatic relations with the United States. French privateers, or
private armed ships authorized by their government to attack
enemy shipping, made a lucrative business of raiding American
commerce, especially in the Caribbean. There, at times, they
were hardly distinguishable from pirates. The French brought

prizes, or captured ships, to their own colonial ports for condemnation. Often, the judicial proceedings against the prizes were
little more than formalities preceding confiscation of property.
Pickering reported that in 1795 French cruisers had captured 316
American ships. Spanish raiders also took American prizes.

In February 1797 the Secretary of State made a detailed list
of American grievances. In addition to raiding American commerce, spoiling it, and maltreating American seamen, he reported, the French had laid embargoes on American ships at
Bordeaux, had refused to pay bills incurred by their colonial ad-
ministrators in the West Indies, had seized American goods for
public use without paying for them, had failed to carry out contracts made by government officials for the delivery of American
supplies, and had condemned American ships and cargoes under
laws that violated treaties with the United States.

Three brief examples can illustrate Pickering's charges and
the nature of the French spoliations. On Christmas Day 1796 a
French privateer ordered the ship *Commerce*, out of Newburyport, Massachusetts, bound for Jamaica, to heave to. After the
Commerce had obeyed the order, the French ship sent a broad-
side into her that wounded four men. In the following February
the French privateer *Hirondale* captured the schooner *Zilpha*
headed for her home port of Portsmouth, New Hampshire, from
Tobago. The French raider seized all of the *Zilpha's* papers,
stripped her of sails, rigging, and provisions and forced the
captain and crew to leave her. They ultimately made their
way home on another ship. Early in March 1797 a French armed
brig captured the ship *Cincinnatus* of Baltimore. The captors
tortured the American captain with thumbscrews to force him to
declare his cargo to be English property so that they could confis-
cate it legally. He refused, so finally he and his ship were released, but only after he was robbed of most of his own property
and his ship's provisions were plundered.

The French justified their plunder of American commerce as
just reprisal and as indemnity for injuries they said they suffered
because George Washington's administration had abandoned the
principle of free ships, free goods, and had acquiesced in a broad

definition of contraband of war in Jay's Treaty. This doctrine of
free ships, free goods meant essentially that if a cargo in a ship
flying the flag of a neutral country contained no contraband, or
warlike instruments such as guns and ammunition, the vessel was
free, or not subject to capture by the cruisers of a belligerent
country. Naturally, if contraband were defined narrowly fewer
ships would be subject to capture than under a broad definition
where many items were classified as warlike. In their treaty of
commerce of 1778 France and the United States had pledged
themselves to uphold the doctrine of free ships, free goods in
their relations with each other. Now, the French argued, the
American government had violated its obligations under this
treaty.[14]

Some Frenchmen believed, in addition, that the success of a
slave rebellion against French authority in their Caribbean possession of Saint Domingue, later to be known as Haiti, could be
traced to the aid Americans had given the Negro insurgents. The
bitterness of French statesmen also stemmed from the realization
that their main hope of retaining their possessions in the West
Indies, or of seriously harassing British commerce there, lay in
support they claimed the United States was obligated by the
treaties of alliance and commerce to provide.

Many Frenchmen were convinced that the American government had betrayed them by selling out to the English. The instrument of betrayal, they insisted, was Jay's Treaty. It was, as
some called it, the Pandora's box that contained the ingredients
for a bloody war. "In vain have we hoped for some time," a
French journalist wrote of the United States, "that gratitude, or at
least self-interest, would make of that federal republic a loyal ally
of France. Now Washington has concluded with our most implacable enemies a treaty wholly inimical to our interests." As
Washington's administration drew to a close, then, anti-Ameri-
canism was growing in France, and animosity against France had
revived in the United States. France and the United States were
on the verge of war.[15]

Like Washington and other Federalist leaders, Adams never

doubted that France was wrong and the United States right, but unlike many of the leaders of his own party, he wished to resolve the conflict through diplomacy.[16] Unknown to Adams, at this time Hamilton also favored such a procedure. In fact, several weeks before Adams took office Hamilton began efforts to shape the new administration's policy toward France.

Hamilton realized that if war came without some publicized effort to heal the breach with France, the Federalists, many of whom would welcome hostilities, might find themselves leaders of a disunited country at a time when they would need the confidence and resources of all the people. In addition, a main objective of foreign policy in his thinking was to rid the nation of the entangling French alliance of 1778. Although, as Washington prepared to leave office, that alliance was practically dead, Hamilton believed that a special diplomatic mission to France might give the alliance a decent burial through mutual consent and might also avert war.

The time was right for a special mission, Hamilton thought, because the change of administration in the United States would offer the French government a chance to negotiate without losing face, as it might if it bargained with the administration that had made Jay's Treaty. "Were I Mr. Adams," he wrote to a friend who had access to the President-elect, "then I believe I should begin my Presidency by naming an extraordinary commission to the French republic." Hamilton thought the commission should explain American policy, remonstrate against French actions, seek indemnities for spoliations of American shipping, "and perhaps . . . abrogate or remodify the treaty of alliance," while negotiating a new commercial treaty.[17]

Republicans, too, urged a special mission, pointing out that in 1794, another time of crisis, such a mission had been sent to England and that now France had the right to expect similar consideration. They also believed that such a commission might gratify the French and thus prevent war. As the day for Adams's inauguration approached, therefore, the idea of the mission had become a popular topic of discussion, even in the newspapers, and the President-elect was more concerned about the matter than anyone else.

Since Adams desired national unity and considered the Republicans numerous and active enough to be treated with care, he felt that both the Federalist and Republican parties should be represented on the special commission. This bipartisan approach, he thought, would assure French respect for the commission and also Republican acceptance of its results. This idea also reflected Adams's hope of maintaining a foreign policy of neutrality and of trying to gain nonpartisan support for his administration. Jefferson and the Republicans were willing to offer such support and to go along with the President-elect's plan. They were anxious to keep the new administration from falling under the control of extremists who appeared bent on war with France.[18]

Republicans believed they could work effectively with Adams himself, particularly in matters of foreign policy. Shortly after Adams's electoral victory, in fact, Jefferson had written the President-elect a friendly letter offering cooperation.[19] The Virginian was convinced that Adams, if not his party, wished to avoid war with France, and that despite sympathy for England he would not truckle to British statesmen. Although Jefferson never sent his conciliatory letter, its substance reached Adams. In turn, Adams indicated a desire to bury past differences and to gain Jefferson's support.

Uncompromising Federalists were worried by manifestations of this reconciliation between the incoming President and Vice-President, but Hamilton expressed less alarm than most. "Our Jacobins," he wrote, "say they are well pleased, and that the lion and lamb are to lie down together. Mr. Adams's PERSONAL friends talk a little in the same way." Yet, he explained, Adams had a basic loyalty to the Federalist system, and hence the *rapprochement* with Jefferson could not last.[20] Whether or not Hamilton's skepticism was justified would depend on how Adams dealt with the special mission to France. In fact, how the new President handled that problem, and the whole question of relations with France, would determine his foreign policy and possibly the character of his administration.

PRE-INAUGURAL CONVERSATIONS

As members of both parties dribbled into Philadelphia to witness the first change in administration in the nation's history, the question of the French crisis and how Adams would deal with it seemed to be everybody's concern. Jefferson, who had not seen Adams in four years, arrived on March 2, 1797, two days before the inauguration. He immediately called on the President-elect, whose lodgings were in Francis's Hotel, a rooming house not far from his own. On the following day Adams visited Jefferson.

At this second meeting, before Adams had had a chance to discuss the idea with his cabinet, the President-elect brought up his plan for a special mission to France. He asked Jefferson to take on the negotiation as his emissary. Saying that as Vice-President he should not leave the country, Jefferson declined. According to Jefferson, Adams immediately took up the idea of sending a commission of three made up of Charles Cotesworth Pinckney, Elbridge Gerry, and James Madison. Of the three, only Pinckney, already in Europe, could at this time be considered a trustworthy Federalist. Madison shared the leadership of the Republican party with Jefferson; Gerry, a friend and neighbor of Adams from Massachusetts, was a man of shifting political allegiances, at this time a lukewarm Federalist with Republican leanings, and hence unpopular among Federalist leaders. Jefferson promised to seek Madison's acceptance; then he and Adams parted.[21]

On the following day, shortly before noon, John Adams, his round body stuffed into a pearl-gray broadcloth suit without jeweled buckles or buttons, and wearing a sword and carrying a hat with a cockade, stepped slowly into the chamber of the House of Representatives, crowded with members of Congress and spectators. While gazing at the scene before him, the incoming President fixed his eyes on George Washington, "whose countenance was as serene and unclouded as the day."

Adams imagined that Washington was enjoying a triumph over him. "Methought I heard him say," Adams told his wife,

"'Ay! I am fairly out and you fairly in! See which of us will be happiest.'" [22] Then Adams began his inaugural address, a speech that would reveal to the people his attitude toward the French crisis.

In a simple direct style Adams, an orator of considerable ability, reviewed the nation's short history, praised the Constitution, proclaimed his faith in republican government, and denounced the spirit of party. He warned against foreign meddling in domestic politics, as had been the case in his own election campaign, for with such interference it would be foreign nations "who govern us, and not we, the people, who govern ourselves." He pledged himself to maintain peace with all nations and to adhere to an impartial neutrality among the belligerent powers of Europe, mainly between France and Great Britain. He expressed "a personal esteem for the French nation, formed in a residence of seven years chiefly among them, and a sincere desire to preserve the friendship which has been so much for the honor and integrity of both nations." Through negotiation, he also promised to seek reparation for injury inflicted on American commerce. [23]

Applause mingled with weeping followed the speech, and when the noise died down Chief Justice Oliver Ellsworth administered the oath of office. John Adams had become the second President of the United States. [24]

Even though Adams had expected his address to be met with some hostility, he had been determined, he said, to appeal to posterity and foreign nations and, apparently, to unite the country behind him to meet a foreign danger. The immediate impact, particularly of his attack on party spirit, was ominous, for the inflexible Federalists were alarmed. Their reaction now betrayed what had not been clearly visible on the surface. Adams had behind him a loosely organized party divided in its sentiments toward the French crisis, a party that had previously been held together mainly by the prestige of one man. "All the federalists," the President thought, "seem to be afraid to approve any body but Washington." [25] Adams was no Washington, and his administration could not live in Washington's shadow.

Republicans, on the other hand, expected a change, particularly in foreign affairs, from Washington's policies. The fact that they received Adams's inaugural sentiments, especially the conciliatory reference to France, with satisfaction indicated that they thought their expectations were to be met. A prominent Republican editor, Benjamin Franklin Bache of Philadelphia's *Aurora,* praised the address for its wisdom and hailed Adams as a patriot, a "friend of France, of peace, and admirer of republicanism, the enemy of party. . . ." [26]

Adams's first consultation with his department heads confirmed the split in his party over foreign policy, and that he was on one side and his cabinet on the other. On the day after his inauguration he mentioned his idea of the bipartisan French mission, with Madison as a member, to Wolcott. "Sending Mr. Madison," the Secretary of the Treasury said, "will make dire work among the passions of our parties in Congress, and out of doors thro' the States." When the President objected to being overawed by fear of party passions, Wolcott offered his resignation, which Adams refused.

The President then consulted other advisers and party leaders, among them George Washington. He discovered that Federalist opposition to Madison was so intense as to endanger confirmation of the mission in the Senate. Rather than risk open turmoil in his party Adams decided to exclude Madison and to postpone a decision on the mission itself.

A few days later, probably on March 6, at a dinner party given by Washington, Jefferson told the President that Madison could not go to France. Apparently embarrassed, Adams replied that he would be unable to use Madison as an emissary anyway. Believing that the Hamiltonians were only a little less hostile to the President than to himself, the Vice-President surmised correctly that Adams had sought the counsel of his cabinet and had been diverted from his plan "to steer impartially between the parties," and had returned to his "former party views." This episode, within the first few days of Adams's administration, in effect ended the possibility of true cooperation between the President and Republican leaders. After this, Adams did not consult Jefferson on matters of policy.[27]

Some observers still hoped for cooperation between the parties. "I am much pleased," an associate justice of the Supreme Court wrote, "that Mr. Adams and Mr. Jefferson lodge together. The thing looks well; it carries conciliation and healing with it, and may have a happy effect on parties." [28] Others thought a peaceful reconciliation with France was also still possible.

Adams himself was alarmed. "The different gradations of attachment and aversion to me in different parties," he believed, proceeds from foreign attachments. "The difference between France and England occasions the differences here. This is to me a frightful consideration." The President did take solace in the thought that the "great body of the people" was like himself, not passionately attached to any party. [29]

Despite the foreign attachments of the parties, Adams at this time was one of those who believed a reconciliation with France possible and desirable. He said so several days later, when Pierre Auguste Adet, France's recalled Minister in Philadelphia who had worked for Adams's defeat in the election of 1796, visited him before returning to Paris. The President explained that he wished to maintain the good understanding which had governed relations with France until this time of crisis. Adet, who had himself been saying there would be no war, was convinced he was sincere. [30]

On the following day, apparently, Adams received news from Europe that jarred his hopes for an amicable understanding. Before leaving office, President Washington had sent Charles Cotesworth Pinckney, a moderate Federalist from South Carolina, to Paris to replace James Monroe, a Republican whom Washington had recalled because of conduct displeasing to Federalists, as America's Minister to the French republic. Adams now learned that the Directory, as France's government was then called, had not only refused to receive Pinckney, but had also driven him out of Paris as if he were in undesirable foreigner. Pinckney had retreated to Amsterdam to await further instructions. [31] From Amsterdam he tried to justify American policy and to influence French policy by sending documents to politicians and other important people in France. Even though these actions amounted to an appeal over the head of the executive branch of the French government, Pinckney believed he acted properly because if most fair-minded Frenchmen could only understand the true nature of their government's policy toward the United States they surely would demand a change.

Adams was also shocked to learn that on March 2 the Directory had issued a decree that violated the Franco-American commercial treaty of 1778 by annulling the principle of free ships, free goods. This law thus allowed warships to bring into French ports all neutral vessels caught carrying British goods. The edict also declared that any American found serving under an enemy flag would be treated as a pirate, and that all American ships which did not carry a list of crew and passengers, or *rôle d'équipage*, in a form considered proper by French officials, would be considered lawful prize.[32] American ships did not usually carry such papers, and France had not previously made such a demand even though she could, technically, under the commercial treaty of 1778.

The Directory had, in effect, launched limited maritime hostilities against Americans while France, on paper at least, was still an ally and at peace with the United States. To influential orthodox Federalists the crisis had come to a head. The Directory's policy appeared to justify the declaration of war they desired.

ADAMS'S DILEMMA

As intended, the French reprisals placed Adams in a predicament. He could, it seemed, react in one of three ways. He could ask Congress for an embargo on American shipping, mainly on cargoes destined for the Caribbean and French ports, and seek to evade difficulties; he could ask for war in defense of the national interest; or he could still try to find some means of avoiding war without surrendering national honor.

With these alternatives before him, the President acted promptly. About as soon as he was able to grasp the meaning of the disturbing news from France he turned to his advisers for their views. What preparations, he asked, should he make for war? Should the government commission privateers to attack

French shipping? Should it commission new frigates? And lastly, should he try new negotiations? [33]

Eleven days later, on March 25, 1797, the President issued a call for Congress to meet in special session on May 15. In his proclamation he asked the representatives of the people "to consult and determine on such measures as in their wisdom shall be deemed meet for the safety and welfare of the said United States." At the same time, Adams had "it at heart to settle all disputes with France" and was still willing to try everything to accomplish it. But he dreaded war less than disgrace.

During this time, as Fisher Ames, a prominent and zealous Federalist explained, "The great theme of every man's inquiries is, are we going to war with France?" He thought war should be avoided, but not at the cost of honor. Another Federalist believed that unless France changed her ways, "we must have war with her." "Many are of the opinion that we shall be compelled to go to War, and others think a partial or general Embargo will take place until we see the issue of negotiation." [34]

Other Americans, particularly Republicans, were alarmed. They openly expressed fear that the President was preparing to take the country to war. He did not, they reasoned, need the assistance of Congress to maintain a policy of peace. This fear at this time may have been groundless, for what Adams desired was congressional approval of a new negotiation with France supported by measures for national defense. He, and others, believed that a special mission's chance for success would be enhanced if the nation were placed in a posture of defense.

Jefferson, the only Republican of consequence within the government, remained skeptical. He felt that the Federalists were taking "the high ground of war" and that a special session was unnecessary. He pointed out that Pinckney's hostile reception had been known earlier. The administration, he believed, had called Congress into extraordinary session to gauge the depth of legislative support it could expect in opposing France.[35]

Adams also met resistance within his own party but for different reasons. Pickering, Wolcott, and McHenry were all opposed to any new mission to France, and many other Federalists, including Washington, shared their views. Hamilton did not. This was important because the three Secretaries sent the President's queries to Hamilton in New York asking him to outline appropriate answers. The opposition of the department heads to a special mission upset the New Yorker.

Hamilton warned Wolcott "that a suspicion begins to *dawn* among the friends of government, that the *actual* administration is not much averse to war with France," meaning not Adams's but Hamilton's own friends in the cabinet. "How very important to obviate this!" Hamilton added.[36]

Finally, Hamilton got over the point that a special mission was necessary, even if refused by France, to expose French unreasonableness in the most glaring light and to refute completely the charge "that the *actual* administration are endeavoring to provoke a war." Furthermore, since the Republicans favor the measure, he said, "'tis the strongest reason for adopting it. This will meet them on their own ground and disarm them of the argument that all has not been done which might have been done towards preserving peace." To achieve this end, he added, a Republican must be included in the commission. "It is important," he told Pickering, "that a man [who] . . . will be agreeable to France" should go. He suggested Madison or Jefferson and two Federalists, namely Pinckney and George Cabot of Massachusetts.[37]

Convinced by Hamilton's reasoning, and also because other intelligent Federalists argued with the same ideas, the three department heads made most of his ideas their own. They now responded to the President's questions, saying they opposed war and favored a special mission to France coupled with measures for defense. They advised him to arm merchant ships and to create a naval force capable of providing convoy escorts to protect the ships. Thus, if the negotiations failed, the government would be prepared for hostilities. Attorney General Lee declared himself not only in favor of a new mission, but also of doing as well by France diplomatically as had been done by Britain. In general, all recommended that Adams should make an effort to reach an agreement with France comparable to Jay's Treaty, but at the same time to prepare for the worst.

As far as some Americans were concerned matters could not

be worse. As if someone had turned a valve, the news from France opened floodgates to a torrent of party passion that spilled over into a bitter newspaper war. Insisting that the Directory's treatment of Pinckney had insulted the United States and that the maritime decree of March 2 had grievously injured it, many Federalists demanded action against France. Those who would dare speak up for the French government, ardent Federalists argued, were traitors. Even in the South, where Republicanism was strong, anti-French sentiment burst to the surface.[38]

Republicans, on the other hand, defiantly defended the Directory's actions and reaffirmed friendship for France. They publicly celebrated the victories of French arms in Italy. The only cause for concern, they maintained, was the effort of Federalists to foment war.[39]

Federalists and Republicans even took to brawling. In the Tontine Coffee House in New York in the middle of March 1797 someone, obviously a Francophile, walked in and tore down a card that carried an imprint of English and American flags. A disturbance followed, forcing the manager to prohibit the hanging of all flags in the establishment. As a result, the French and American emblems that had been on the wall of the coffee house for two years were carted away.[40]

The Directory's actions did more than arouse emotions. Its decree caused a panic among American shippers. Marine insurance jumped 10 per cent overnight. Underwriters refused to insure vessels headed for French ports, requiring "war premiums" for those bound for the British West Indies where French cruisers, or privateers, were taking a heavy toll from American shipping.[41]

Adet told Secretary of State Pickering that he thought the French government had not itself authorized the attacks against American commerce in the West Indies. It was impossible, he explained, to prevent privateers from committing excesses. But, Pickering pointed out, French civil officers condemned the ships and the cargoes carried into port by the privateers. Most depredations, the Secretary of State insisted, directly violated the Franco-American commercial treaty of 1778 and the law of nations.[42]

These French depredations strengthened ties between Britain and the United States, the very development, ironically, that French statesmen wanted to prevent. The British were keenly aware of the rising American resentment against the French government and moved swiftly to take advantage of it. Late in March, for example, Robert Liston, the British Minister in Philadelphia, received instructions to offer naval protection to American commerce against attacks from the "Common Enemy," if the United States should actually break with France.[43]

Liston himself, who felt most comfortable while moving in Federalist circles, was surprised at how rapidly and wildly a spirit of animosity toward France had spread over the United States. With some exaggeration, his wife described the changed public attitude toward France as practically an unstoppable torrent. Liston was pleased that "the men of fortune, of weight and of character begin so generally to look forward to a close connection with Great Britain as the only wise system of American politicks. . . ." Pickering certainly agreed with this view; he would have liked a British alliance, if possible. In any case, he authorized acceptance of the protection of British convoys when offered.[44]

Protection of American commerce, and other problems of defense, also occupied the President's thinking. Again he turned to his department heads for advice on dealing with France, and that he could use in preparing the message he planned to deliver to Congress. Is Pinckney's rejection, he asked, a barrier to further negotiations, "or in other words, will a fresh mission to Paris be too great a humiliation of the American people . . . ?" If we should send another mission, he inquired, how shall we instruct the emissaries? What should we demand of France? Should we try to get rid of the alliance and other treaties with France, and negotiate a new treaty?

Adams told Pickering not to confine himself merely to matters within the Department of State, but to give himself a wide latitude in supporting his opinions. The President also asked the Secretary of State to prepare instructions for an emissary to France in case "it should be deemed consistent with the dignity,

honor, and interest of the United States to send another mission
to that power." In a special note to Secretary of War McHenry he
asked for an estimate of the defensive forces needed to shield the
country from invasion and of the cost of recruitment and equip-
ment.[45]

As before, the cabinet members passed on the questionnaire
to Hamilton. To McHenry, Hamilton offered detailed advice, cov-
ering virtually all aspects of relations with France. He outlined
what Adams's speech should contain and stressed that it "should
be confined to the foreign affairs of the Country. . . ."

Hamilton pointed out that he himself wanted a new negotiation, peace, not war. The triumphs of French arms, he explained,
have confounded and astonished mankind. The principal powers
of Europe, and even England, have found it expedient to submit
to some humiliation from France. As for the United States, it had
the strongest motives to avoid war. It had much to lose and little
to gain; it could be greatly annoyed, and could annoy little. It
was even possible, he wrote, that the United States might be *"left
alone to contend with the Conquerors of Europe."* This crisis
called for prudence. Even "a considerable degree of humiliation
may, without *ignominy*," he counseled, "be encountered to avoid
the possibility of much greater and a train of incalculable evils."
After all, in rejecting Pinckney, France "has not gone to the *ne
plus ultra.*"

Hamilton also warned, as did other Federalists, that within
the country "there is a general and strong desire for peace—and,
with a considerable party, still a particular repugnance to war
with France." Public opinion, he surmised, would probably not
consider a "further attempt at negotiation as too humiliating." He
apparently expected the mission to fail. This failure would arouse
popular sentiment against France and gain wide support for his
program of cooperation with England.[46]

In his reply to the President, McHenry followed Hamilton's
advice closely, and in many sentences he used Hamilton's exact
words. McHenry also sent data on the existing state of the military establishment and gave his estimate of the force needed to
protect American cities and commerce. Like McHenry, Wolcott

recommended a new mission to France. Anticipating congressional support for such a negotiation, he suggested a commission of three.

Pickering embedded his advice to the President, taken largely from Hamilton, in an elaborate document of twenty-five pages that covered relations with France in blunt detail. He denounced French policy and actions in strong language, but he concurred in Adams's view that national honor did not forbid new advances toward France, and hence he, too, favored a fresh effort to negotiate. Europeans, he warned, will attempt "to draw us into the vortex" of their struggle, but the United States should shun the politics of Europe.[47]

As Hamilton desired, all the papers submitted by the department heads advised the same program—a new attempt at negotiation accompanied by preparations for war. They all had a similar motive in supporting the mission, namely to placate public opinion, silence Republican criticism of foreign policy, and promote Federalist unity. Since this program flowed from a single brain, the papers as a whole made a unified, cogent case.[48]

Impressed by the reasoning of his department heads, Adams went ahead with the preparation of his address. It would, he told Abigail, acquit him of the crime of being praised by Republican newspapers such as the *Aurora* of Philadelphia. Drawing heavily from Hamilton's indirect advice, the President took whole phrases and sentences from Pickering's paper, weaving them into the body of his speech. He seems also to have absorbed something of his Secretary of State's defiant attitude, though his own mood was not belligerent. "As to going to war with France lightly," he wrote at this time, "I know of nobody who is willing for it—but she has already gone to war with us lightly. She is at war with us, but we are not at war with her." [49]

Actually, the French government did not consider itself at war with the United States and did not believe that the American government would declare war. A ship captain who had just returned from Bordeaux reported, for example, "that there appeared a considerable coolness and displeasure in the French towards the Americans, but no disposition for war; that the talk of

war . . . was much more general among the Americans than by
the French." [50]

The French government felt that it lost little by the existing
situation and awaited overtures from the United States. Joseph
Philippe Létombe, the French Consul General in Philadelphia,
who claimed to have confidential relations with Jefferson, told
Adams and Jefferson at this time that France did not in the least
desire a complete rupture. The Directory would end its reprisals
and all could be put right beween the two countries, Létombe
said, if the United States would send to Paris a minister the
French could trust. This would offer proof of a change of attitude
toward France by the American government. [51]

Such a change appeared unlikely, particularly at this time
when an item from Europe indicated that the Directory still
sought to tamper with American politics. On May 2, 1797, the
New York *Minerva,* a Federalist newspaper, published a garbled
version of a private letter Jefferson had written more than a year
earlier to his friend Philip Mazzei in Italy. With the letter, the
Minerva included remarks from the *Moniteur,* considered the official newspaper of the Directory. The *Moniteur* had originally
published the letter in January. The French translator claimed
that the letter, which criticized Federalist foreign policy, offered
an explanation of American conduct toward France. Such conduct, he wrote, justified the Directory's action in breaking off
communication with "an ungrateful and faithless ally." Then he
expressed hope that the Republicans, "the friends of France,"
would gain power in the United States.

Since the letter itself also attacked Washington, and indirectly Adams too, it added heat to rising party passions. Some
Federalists called the letter treasonable and demanded Jefferson's
impeachment. As Congress prepared to convene, the Mazzei letter and the comments of the *Moniteur* aroused popular anger
against Republicans, and any supporters of France, and helped
the Federalists gain an unaccustomed favor among the masses.
Federalists were themselves impressed by "the rapidity with
which the people have come to a right way of thinking on French
politics." They concluded "that almost any measures the government may take would be approved. . . ." [52]

AN EXTRAORDINARY MISSION

Poor roads, bad weather, and other obstacles made the obtaining of a quorum difficult, but the opening of the special session of the Fifth Congress was delayed only one day because of the lack of a quorum. Adams appeared before both houses assembled in the chamber of the House of Representatives at twelve o'clock noon on May 16, 1797, and began his message. It was, as Hamilton had desired, devoted solely to the French crisis. Although the President's words were defiant, his manner was calm.

France's rejection of Pinckney and "refusal to receive him until we have acceded to their demands without discussion and without investigation," Adams said, "is to treat us neither as allies nor as friends, nor as a sovereign state." The French leaders have tried to separate our people from their government, the President went on, and thus to "produce divisions fatal to our peace." These attempts, he insisted, "ought to be repelled with a decision which shall convince France and the world that we are not a degraded people, humiliated under a colonial spirit of fear and a sense of inferiority, fitted to be the miserable instruments of foreign influence, and regardless of national honor, character, and interest."

Even though France had "inflicted a wound in the American breast," the President announced he would try to heal the injury by instituting "a fresh attempt at negotiation." He would seek an accommodation on terms "compatible with the rights, duties, interests, and honor of the nation." While he did this, he added, the country must build its defenses, especially its Navy, to protect its commerce and vulnerable coasts. "A naval power, next to the militia," he said, "is the natural defense of the United States." So he recommended the arming of merchant vessels and the enlarging of the Navy. He also suggested the formation of a provisional army, and new laws for strengthening the militia.

Although the United States should not involve itself in the "political system of Europe," it should make plans to defend its neutrality. "However we may consider ourselves," Adams warned, "the maritime and commercial powers of the world will consider the United States of America as forming a weight in that balance of power in Europe which never can be forgotten or neglected." [53]

Since the address embodied Hamilton's ideas, there was little in it that could dissatisfy even the most faithful of Federalists. Yet there were Federalist leaders who still feared that Adams would become the tool of Jefferson and the Francophiles, and those leaders needed reassurance. They obtained it from the speech, which they said met the French crisis with firmness and dignity. George Cabot, a staunch New England Federalist sometimes called the "Nestor of the Federal cause," expected the message, which charmed those like himself, to "excite the most national feeling of anything that has been published since the French disease infected the country." [54] France could not, Federalists now proclaimed, intimidate the United States.

Republicans, who considered Adams's speech warlike, were surprised, shocked, and alarmed. They were surprised because the tone of the President's exhortation was unexpected; they were shocked because they had deluded themselves into thinking that Adams shared their views on foreign policy; and they were alarmed because they believed that the President had succumbed to war hawks in his own party. His address, Republicans insisted, was bad diplomacy and an unnecessary irritant to France. Relations with France, they claimed, were not perilous; the crisis had grown out of Federalist mismanagement of foreign policy. Proper negotiations, they assumed, would restore calmness to relations with the nation's only ally.

Most Federalists, Albert Gallatin, the shrewd Swiss-born Republican leader in the House of Representatives, maintained, privately acknowledged "the propriety of treating with France," and only a few desired war. [55]

Gallatin was probably right, but the Federalist war hawks were loud and persuasive in their arguments. Robert Goodloe Harper, a skillful though blustering Federalist demagogue from South Carolina, for example, told his constituents that if war came it would bring benefits to the United States, and to Britain, too. "We can," he pointed out, "buy at a price cheap to ourselves the full co-operation of the British navy," take some of France's pressure off England, conquer New Orleans and the Floridas, and "free ourselves from a troublesome neighbour," meaning Spain.[56]

The Republican press took a completely opposite position. It now claimed that Adams was in his dotage, an inveterate enemy of the French, a tool of the British, and a creature of the Hamiltonians. Jefferson himself thought that the House and Senate might now "raise their tone to that of the executive, and embark in all measures indicative of war and, by taking a threatening posture, provoke hostilities from the opposite party." He wished to shun all preparation for war because it might further irritate the French. Adams, he feared, had embarked on a course, despite his desire for a new negotiation, "which would endanger the peace of our country."[57]

Other Republicans shared this fear. "A war with France seems to be inevitable," wrote Benjamin Rush, a leading citizen of Philadelphia and the nation's foremost physician. "Honor! Dignity! Glory!—how I hate the words when applied to kings or governments. To engage in a war in defense of either of them is nothing but duelling upon a national scale. Even the property we have lost by French spoliations is not a sufficient or just cause for war."[58]

Debate in Congress also reflected partisan reaction to Adams's words. At this time it was customary for each house of Congress to offer a ceremonial reply to a message from the President. The members of Congress usually presented their reply in a body at the President's residence. In this instance the nature of the replies led to controversy in both chambers.

Since the Federalists held a majority in the Senate, that body's reply of May 23 endorsed the President's proposals unequivocally. In the House, where Republicans were stronger, debate consumed two weeks, during which policy toward France became the central issue. Believing that the tenor of the reply might set the tone of relations with France, Republicans wanted it to be conciliatory. For similar reasons Federalists demanded that it be firm and uncompromising. Finally, after successive Republican efforts to make the address less hostile to the French than Federalists desired, the Federalists won. Nonetheless, one Federalist complained that "the apprehension of war is so great that it is difficult to bring a majority to speak a firm and energetic language." As a result, Republicans managed to soften the tone slightly, and the reply was given to the President on June 2.[59]

More important than the congressional debate in the increasingly complicated pattern of relations with France was Adams's conflict with his cabinet over the composition of the commission to be sent to Paris. Although the President had given up the idea of a truly bipartisan commission, he still wanted to place on it at least one Moderate acceptable to Republicans. He wished to give the commission a national coloring by including on it important men from the three main sections of the Union, the southern, the middle, and the northern states. He also hoped that a balanced commission would gain public support.

When Adams called his cabinet together, therefore, he said, "Gentlemen, what think you of Mr. Gerry for the mission?" The department heads objected not only to Gerry himself, but also to what they called a "piebald commission." [60] In this instance they departed from Hamilton's wishes. They insisted on a wholly Federalist mission.

Adams yielded. He agreed to name a Federalist acceptable to his advisers. The man he chose was Francis Dana, the Chief Justice of Massachusetts' Supreme Court, a friend with diplomatic experience. The other two envoys were Pinckney, a man already known to be unacceptable to the French, but who would nonetheless head the commission, and John Marshall, a prominent Federalist lawyer from Virginia. Adams submitted these names to the Senate on May 31, 1797. After some debate, the Senate confirmed the nominations.[61]

A few weeks later Dana declined to serve because of poor health. Without consulting his department heads, Adams replaced Dana with Gerry. Although it may not have been obvious at the time, the President's decision had the effect of placing a screen of suspicion between himself and his cabinet. Before making a final decision in foreign policy George Washington had usually confided in his Secretary of State and had frequently sought the views of his other department heads. Adams's advisers were, as a result, unprepared for this independent decision by their new Chief. They were alarmed, too, by the President's seeming defiance of the wishes of party leaders and other important Federalists, all of whom were opposed to Gerry.

Many Republicans were pleased by the nomination. "It was with infinite joy to me," Jefferson wrote to Gerry, "that you were yesterday announced to the Senate as envoy extraordinary." You must accept, the Vice-President advised, or a party appointment is sure to be made.

Gerry promptly accepted. Although six adamant Federalists voted against him, the Senate confirmed the nomination.[62]

Gerry's appointment threatened the unity of the mission. Yet, since neither Federalists nor Republicans felt responsible for it, the Federalists could not rightly blame the Republicans for any disunity within the commission, or for its failure, if it failed. In brief, Gerry's appointment was the President's own decision, and hence Adams took upon himself full political responsibility for the mission's success or failure.

Despite its suddenness, Gerry's appointment was not the result of haste. For several months, on Gerry's initiative, Adams had corresponded with him on matters of policy toward England and France. Gerry's own sympathies were with the French, but he treasured his friendship with the President, supported him politically, and offered him independent, balanced judgments. "I believe," Adams said, "that Gerry and I are the two most impartial men in mind or speech almost in the union." [63] The President felt that Gerry was one of the few men of Republican persuasion with whom he could still calmly discuss the issues that separated the two parties. Gerry appealed to him not only as an old, loyal friend, but also because he displayed Adams's own qualities of independence and integrity.

In their correspondence on foreign policy Gerry had complained that an anti-Gallican, pro-British faction, headed by Timothy Pickering, existed in the United States. Adams agreed that there was strong feeling against France, but he said there were sound reasons for opposing France. Gerry argued that some

Americans hated the French because they were good Republicans, and that such men were eager for a war that would stamp
out republicanism. That was not so, the President insisted, for the
French were no more capable of maintaining a republican government "than a snowball can exist a whole week in the streets of
Philadelphia under a burning sun."

Like many contemporary observers, Adams believed that the
French governmental system, whatever its form, could not endure. Other observers were convinced that a republican form of
government could not last in the United States. "I am not one of
those," Adams wrote. Yet he warned that such government would
not last "if French influence as well as English is not resisted."

After having accepted the appointment from Adams, Gerry
asked questions pertinent to his conduct on the commission. Since
the French consider us a divided people, he wrote, is it not essential that the envoys, should they differ on important points, "be
finally unanimous on those points by the minority yielding to the
majority? Without such an agreement may they not encourage an
opposition to their measures?"

The President replied that harmony and unanimity were of
the utmost necessity. He also wrote that no one could shake his
confidence in Gerry, but he warned that some had "expressed
doubts of your orthodoxy in the science of government" and
others "fears of an unaccommodating disposition."

Despite Federalist resistance to Gerry, Adams was satisfied
that on the whole he was acting properly in sending the commission. "If there is reason or justice or decorum in France," he
thought, "the measure we have taken is respectful enough to
draw it all out. But if we are again insulted we must defend ourselves." [64]

THE SPECIAL SESSION

In Congress, meanwhile, where Federalists tried to enact
Adams's recommendations into law, even limited measures for defense did not fare well. These measures were entrusted to William Smith, a Federalist from South Carolina who was chairman

of the Ways and Means committee in the House of Representatives and who acted as Hamilton's mouthpiece. On June 5, 1797, Smith introduced a series of ten resolutions that embodied the President's program, or, in other words, Hamilton's program. These and companion measures in the Senate met strenuous Republican opposition. Republicans followed the strategy of opposing all of Adams's recommendations except the mission to Paris.[65] As a result, for weeks Congress debated nothing else but foreign policy, mainly policy toward France.

Since, as Jefferson said, there was a desire "in both parties to show our teeth to France," Congress finally passed an emasculated bill that would increase the Navy and legislation that would regulate the import and export of arms, prohibit American citizens from privateering against nations at peace with the United States, allow the arming and equipping of 80,000 militia who would march in case of need, provide artillery, and authorize the construction of fortifications at harbors. The legislators refused to raise taxes immediately, but they did authorize a loan of $800,000, and salt and stamp taxes to be placed into effect at a later time. Basically, Congress provided for slight improvement in land defenses, appropriated money to complete, equip, and man three frigates already under construction, authorized the use of revenue cutters for naval purposes, and established delayed means of financing most of these measures.

This was not much of an accomplishment for a Congress that had been called into special session to deal with a national crisis. The British Minister in Philadelphia reported "that every measure of warlike preparation or internal defence has been adopted with an excess of caution, and provided for with a niggardly hand." [66] One uncompromising Federalist blamed the poor showing on Republican cowardice toward France, "*a dread of the power & vengeance of the terrible Republic,*" he said. Another grumbled about being "disgraced by the Congressional discussion of the last session." Yet the caution in Congress appeared to reflect a desire for peace, which was apparently what most people wanted.

All was not gloom for Federalists. As a result of partisan tensions stirred up by the case of William Blount, a land speculator, a former territorial governor, and now a Republican senator from Tennessee, Federalists gained at least one minor triumph against a Republican before the special session of the Fifth Congress closed. The Blount case grew out of difficulties with Spain on the southern frontier.

On June 12, 1797, the President had complained to the House that Spanish officers in Louisiana were interfering with the running of the nation's southern boundary under the terms of Pinckney's Treaty of 1795 with Spain. At this time Adams also had in his hands evidence of a plot for an assault, from United States territory, on Spain's possessions. In the bundle of documents he sent to Congress on July 3 on this subject, he therefore included an intercepted letter from Blount to an Indian interpreter that indicated the British would support Blount in a filibustering expedition against the Spaniards in Louisiana and the Floridas.[67]

Four days later, on the basis of this evidence, the Senate found Blount guilty of a very high misdemeanor and expelled him. The House appointed a committee to examine Blount's behavior with a view to possible impeachment.

Since Blount could not be defended even by his own partisans, his conduct appeared to give some basis to Federalist insinuations that Republicans were tainted with treason. Republicans, on the other hand, pointed out that Robert Liston was implicated in the Blount conspiracy. His behavior, they charged, was another instance of British meddling in America's internal affairs. They condemned Adams for not demanding Liston's recall.[68]

On June 27, 1797, while the special session was locked in debate over the French crisis, James Monroe arrived in Philadelphia directly from France. Republican leaders quickly prepared a handsome welcome, a banquet on July 1 held at Oeller's Hotel on Chestnut Street, within hailing distance of Congress Hall, so as to give public approbation of his conduct in Paris. Vice-President Jefferson, Governor Thomas McKean of Pennsylvania, and some fifty members of Congress joined in the tribute to the repudiated diplomat. Federalists, of course, were upset by these proceedings and denounced them, saying they reflected a disloyal subservience to France. One Federalist described the dinner as a motley affair. "Here you saw an american [sic] disorganiser & there a blundering wild Irishman," he said, "in one corner a banished Genevan & in another a french [sic] Spye —on one side a greasy Butcher & on the other a dirty Cobler. . . ." In listing the important guests, a Federalist gazette sarcastically called each one Monsieur. The members of the cabinet were particularly offended because, under Washington, they had initiated Monroe's recall.[69]

Almost as soon as he landed Monroe began to quarrel with Secretary of State Pickering. He demanded, in writing, an explanation of why he had been recalled. Pickering refused to state the grounds officially, maintaining that he could not do so because a new President now headed the government. Besides, he said, any President had the right to dismiss his subordinates at will without furnishing reasons. Monroe then sent Pickering an angry rejoinder, published his correspondence with the Secretary of State, and began to prepare his own vindication for publication.[70]

The Federalist attacks on Monroe's mission in Paris had angered James T. Callender, a Republican pamphleteer and hack writer. He held Hamilton responsible for the attacks. So early in July 1797, as Congress prepared to adjourn, Callender published documents that exposed the details of an illicit love affair Hamilton had had six years before with a faded beauty of easy virtue, Mrs. Maria Reynolds.[71] The woman's husband had used the affair to blackmail Hamilton.

Monroe had learned of the liaison years earlier and had promised to remain silent. Now Hamilton rushed to Philadelphia and blamed him for the exposure, a charge Monroe denied. Nevertheless, many Republicans were delighted with this low level assault on their leading opponent. Monroe's presence in Philadelphia and the airing of the Reynolds affair, it was clear, were adding to partisan tensions.

On July 8, in the midst of these tensions, after having been in session almost two months, Congress adjourned. Adams, obviously, had not achieved the national unity in foreign policy that he desired. Instead, policy toward France had divided his countrymen, and they had solidified their views according to party loyalty. There was no doubt, furthermore, that the French crisis had aroused deep feelings. "Men who have been intimate all their lives," Jefferson wrote, "cross the streets to avoid meeting, and turn their heads another way, lest they should be obliged to touch their hats." [72] Even more disturbing was the atmosphere of violence in the special session itself. Heated arguments almost resulted in several duels between members of Congress.

Many Republicans remained convinced that war against France had been the purpose behind the special session. Jefferson, who presided over the Senate, remarked that war had indeed been close. France might have declared war herself if her legislature had not been opposed to it. "Thus we see," he said, "two nations who love one another affectionately, brought by the ill temper of their executive administrations, to the very brink of a necessity to imbue their hands in the blood of each other." He attributed Federalist setbacks in the special session to the feeling that France, already triumphant over enemies such as Austria, would emerge victorious against England. That feeling, as well as news that England was suffering from internal weaknesses, he believed, had tempered Federalist enthusiasm for war. [73]

Federalists had not, in fact, retreated. Many still favored a tough policy toward France that would compel respect for the American flag and put an end to raids on American commerce. If Republicans would not support such a policy, one Federalist suggested, the New England and Middle Atlantic states should secede from the Union and leave the South to link itself with France. George Washington, for example, was disturbed by the Federalist defeats in the special session. From his retirement he wrote several letters questioning the patriotism of the Republicans in Congress.

Despite the party passions, as soon as the special session ended the members of Congress scattered. All were eager to escape Philadelphia's stifling summer heat and the yellow fever that came often at this time of year. Now the fever came in epidemic proportions. Even on the subject of the disease Americans could not escape partisanship. Although no one really knew the cause, those of British sympathy were convinced the plague came from a French ship, the *Marseilles,* and French partisans claimed it had spread from a British vessel, the *Arethusa.* Later, the Academy of Medicine published "proofs of the domestic origin of our late epidemic." [74]

The President, too, prepared to flee. John Adams gathered his family together, and eleven days after Congress had adjourned he left in a cooling shower of rain for his home in Quincy, Massachusetts. From there, although some criticized his departure in the midst of crisis, he planned to direct the government and control the crisis through correspondence with his department heads.

On the following day, July 20, 1797, John Marshall sailed from Philadelphia on the brig *Grace,* the first step on the long journey to Paris. Three days later Gerry departed from Boston. With these two men went the hope of many Americans that somehow they and Pinckney would find the means of unraveling the tangled relations with France that endangered the peace, and also the internal stability, of the American republic.

~~~ II ~~~

The X Y Z Affair

*Might I be permitted to hazard an opinion it wou'd be the
Atlantic only can save us, & that no consideration will be
sufficiently powerful to check the extremities to which
the temper of this government [of France] will carry it,
but an apprehension that we may be thrown into the arms of
Britain.*

JOHN MARSHALL, *October 1797*

WHILE JOHN ADAMS WAS TRYING TO OVERCOME PARTY DIFFERENCES
in his effort to resolve the crisis in foreign policy, events in France
were transforming that country's government and altering its attitude toward the United States. The government of the First
French Republic was moderate, constitutional, and republican.
That government was headed by an executive commission of five
men, called Directors, and, as we have seen, was known as the
Directory. The Directors, one of whom was to be elected each
year by the legislature, ruled through ministers they named who
were individually responsible to them. The legislature was divided into two chambers, one called the Council of Five Hundred
and the other the Council of Elders, or Ancients, mainly because
its members had to be at least forty years old whereas the minimum age in the Five Hundred was thirty.[1]

In keeping with the republican principles popular at that

time the Directory was designed to avoid the extreme of dictatorship or despotism. Yet it was unstable, and almost fatally dependent on the army for protection against those who wished to
overthrow it. Since the composition of the Executive Directory
changed each year, when a new member was brought in and an
old one dropped, it was often torn by internal strife, and it never
had a clear or steady policy on many important matters. It followed a vacillating, unpredictable, seesaw policy, or *la politique
de la bascule,* and steadily lost favor with the people.

In elections held in March 1797, for example, the people
changed one-third of the membership of the legislative bodies,
and gave victory to conservative groups that wanted peace and
stability, and that opposed the Directory's policy toward the
United States. So in April 1797 when France's legislative session
began it was clear that the executive arm of government held one
view toward foreign policy and the legislature another. On many
issues, in fact, the Executive Directory and the legislative majority faced each other in savage hostility.

Many Frenchmen, apparently, were disturbed by the difficulties with the United States, and blamed the Executive Directory for the troubled state of affairs.[2] Some argued that France's
naval weakness left the Americans at the mercy of the English.
They wanted the Directors to moderate their policy and to seek a
reconciliation, for they assumed that in any war with the United
States, France would lose her colonies in the New World. Without
such a change in policy, many also believed, Americans would
become bitterly anti-French. In brief, there existed a strong feeling in France that the Directory should seek peace, and try to win
and hold American friendship, not dissipate it.[3]

In the legislature itself men openly questioned the Directory's suspension of diplomatic relations with Philadelphia. On
June 20 one group began denouncing the Directory for violating
the French constitution, mainly through the creation of a state of
hostility against the United States without consulting the legislative chambers. A leader of that group, Charles Emmanuel Joseph
Pierre, Marquis de Pastoret, even defended the American government, and charged the Directory with failure in living up to its

obligations under the treaties of 1778. He predicted an Anglo-American alliance as a result of the Executive Directory's policy.

"The Directory appears to treat the Americans as enemies," Pastoret asserted, "and yet the legislature has not declared war against them." Since the constitutional power to declare war is vested in the legislature, by what right, he asked, did the Directory's agents outfit corsairs against Americans?

Another critic in the Council of Five Hundred expressed a similar complaint. "We believe we take vengeance on the English," he said. "We serve them. To embitter the United States, is that not to cause them to lean towards Great Britain? To ruin American commerce, is that not to increase the strength of Great Britain?" [4]

The Minister of Foreign Relations, Charles Delacroix de Constant, and the President of the Directory, Jean François Reubell, who had more to say about the making of France's foreign policy at this time than any other person, resented this criticism. They had carried out the hostile policy toward the United States that one official called "a little clandestine war," based on the idea of trying to inflict the greatest possible damage on American commerce without setting off a formal war. Delacroix had said, for example, that France was locked in conflict with the American government, not the American people. In one of his last acts as Minister of Foreign Relations, Delacroix prepared a report for the Directors that defended his American policy. What had caused the clash with the United States, he claimed, was not the Executive Directory's policy, or its acts such as the decree of March 2, but an accumulation of grievances against the American government, such as the Jay Treaty.

Two of the Directors, Lazare Nicolas Marguerite Carnot and François (Marquis de) Barthélemy, sympathized more with the critics than with the defenders of the Executive Directory's policy. These Directors opposed the government's policy toward the United States mainly for political reasons, not because they thought it morally wrong. [5]

Regardless of the right or wrong of the Executive Directory's foreign policy, the legislative opposition to it contributed to a crisis within the government. The French constitution provided a system of checks and balances between the legislature and the executive, but no means for avoiding, or cutting through, a deadlock between these two branches of government. Unable to act legally, the majority of the Directors decided to break the deadlock with the legislature with force. In the *coup d'état* of 18 *Fructidor,* or September 4, 1797, the Directors committed to republican principles used the army to nullify the elections, to crush royalist counterrevolutionaries, to force Carnot and Barthélemy out of office, to declare 198 seats in the legislature vacant, and to deport 18 of the legislators to French Guiana, known then as the "dry guillotine."

What remained were three firm republican Directors, Reubell, Louis Marie Larévellière-Lépeaux, and Paul Jean François Nicolas, Count de Barras. Two new Directors—Phillipe Antoine Merlin, called Merlin de Douai, and François de Neufchâteau— were soon elected to fill the vacancies. Not one of these men could be considered friendly to the United States. William Vans Murray, a Federalist diplomat at The Hague, described Merlin, formerly the Minister of Justice, as "the most bitter enemy of our rights." This new, or "second," Directory was more arbitrary and dictatorial than the "first" one. It ruled, Murray said, "as Tiberius did by the Legions, with the show of a Representative body. . . ." [6] In addition, it was bankrupt.

Thus, as John Marshall and Elbridge Gerry were on their way to join Charles Cotesworth Pinckney in Paris, the men who governed France were more hostile to America's Federalist government than had been their predecessors. As Marshall saw the situation, "all power is now in the undivided possession of those who have directed against us those hostile measures of which we so justly complain."

John Quincy Adams, the President's eldest son who served as the American Minister in Berlin, was also aware of the hostile attitude of the Directors, and warned his father about them. "Everything that envy and malice, both against our country and against you personally, can suggest," young Adams wrote, "they will attempt." Like Murray, he was most alarmed by Merlin,

whom he believed had "long since entered into an organized plan
for dismembering our union." [7]

These were not the only developments that could make for
the success or failure of the American mission. Events elsewhere
also contributed to the change in France's government. A brilliant
Corsican general, Napoleon Bonaparte, cast a shadow over the
Directory which was still the most democratic government of a
large country in the world. He had directed the *coup d'état* of 18
Fructidor, and had conquered much of Europe. As a result,
France had established a number of vassal republics, complete
with classical names, in Italy and Holland. Only England, the
leader of conservative counterrevolution in Europe and defiant
behind her channel moat and wooden ships, lay beyond the claws
of this young lion.

Bonaparte's victories gave the Directory prestige abroad, and
the spoils of conquest appeared to bring profit. This pattern of
war and expansion, despite its glory, did not strengthen the government internally. Plagued with a reputation for corruption, the
Directory lacked strong roots among the people. It could not
stand on its own feet. So it became fatally dependent on Bonaparte's support. Bribery among a few government officials gave
the impression that all were corrupt, an erroneous view of the Directory held by many Americans. Yet it was true that weak countries, such as Portugal, had to buy peace with France, or bribe
some of the venal ministers merely for the privilege of negotiating.

Since the United States, even though it was still technically
an ally, had defied France in making Jay's Treaty, it could expect
to be treated like any other power, small or large, which sought to
negotiate with the Executive Directory. The American envoys
could, in other words, anticipate having to pay before the French
ministers would consent to formal negotiations.[8] Furthermore,
unless the Americans made it clear that they were willing to
capitulate to the French demands, the most important of which
was the abrogation of Jay's Treaty, there seemed to be no compelling reason for the Directors to change their policy toward the
United States. The state of affairs late in 1797 seemed profitable

enough to those officials of the Directory who were corruptible and hungry for loot. Fat ships in America's growing merchant marine were desirable prey for such men.

TALLEYRAND

Some Americans, including the Consul General in Paris, Fulwar Skipwith, and among the commissioners, Gerry, thought that the Directory's new Minister of Foreign Relations, Charles Maurice de Talleyrand-Périgord, who had replaced Delacroix in July, wished an accommodation and would be willing to negotiate on reasonable terms.[9] They based their optimism on the fact that Talleyrand had recently returned from the United States where he had lived in exile for over two years and had been treated well. In this simple analysis, those Americans were mistaken. This man, an unscrupulous, pleasure-loving aristocrat of elegant taste and loose morals, who had once been a bishop in the Catholic Church and whose talent as a diplomat was to become known throughout the world, had in truth been uncomfortable in the United States. He still resented the fact that President Washington had refused to receive him, and he had a poor opinion of Americans. "If I have to stay here another year," he had written to the novelist Madame de Staël from the New World, "I shall die." Gold, he said contemptuously, was the American God.

Ironically, Talleyrand himself, who felt insecure in his new post, found in gold an intense attraction. Gold offered a means of strengthening his position with corrupt colleagues and of maintaining a style of living he had known before the Revolution, and beyond what his official salary could support. Through huge commissions, tips, and speculation in stocks, he used his position to enrich himself. No minister, historians have said, was ever more successful than Talleyrand at making money out of his duties.

As Minister of Foreign Relations Talleyrand had little direct power. Except for the details, the Directors usually handled foreign policy themselves. Talleyrand called himself "the editor responsible for other people's works." His own views on foreign

policy differed basically from those of the Directory, at least
when the Directory's policy was openly warlike. Opposed to war
and military conquests, he preferred peaceful means, mainly the
use of diplomacy, to achieve national objectives.[10]

Talleyrand's attitude toward the United States, on which he
considered himself something of an expert, came out in a paper
he read on commercial relations between England and the United
States on April 4, 1797, at a public meeting of a learned body
called the National Institute. Speaking without bitterness, he
pointed out that America's close relations with England since
1794, which angered France, grew out of mutual interests and a
shared language. Americans, he said, had not yet developed a
character of their own. They were still English, and subject to
English influence. "In every part of America through which I
travelled," he explained, "I have not found a single Englishman
who did not feel himself to be an American, not a single Frenchman who did not find himself a stranger." Americans, therefore,
should be held in check. He even suggested that a French establishment in America, meaning Louisiana, would probably be the
best means of restraining them.[11]

Two months after Talleyrand had presented his paper another diplomat, Louis Guillaume Otto, who had spent twelve
years in the United States in various official capacities, including
chargé d'affaires, gave his views on American affairs to the Directory. Surveying relations with the United States since 1789, he
maintained that French officials in the United States had failed to
realize that Americans were a people isolated from the politics of
Europe and concerned primarily with their own problems.
French agents were wrong in assuming that a division existed between the American people and their government. Most Americans, he had observed, placed love of their own country above
party preferences for either France or England. Such preference,
he felt, was merely a passing fancy, or just a secondary affection.
He urged this time that the Directory negotiate, and restore a
good understanding with the United States. Not to do so, Otto insisted, would be foolish and unjust, and might force the United
States into a coalition with Britain.[12]

Having, no doubt, been informed of Otto's report, Talleyrand at first expressed a similar attitude toward the coming negotiations. Although disturbed by American resentment over Pinckney's treatment in Paris, he felt that if the American envoys had the power to negotiate on terms compatible with the dignity of the French republic, then the differences would be resolved. He favored a reconciliation. Pierre Auguste Adet, the Directory's last minister to the United States, had now returned home. Although still suspicious toward the American government, he too urged the Directory to receive the envoys. He also advised a frank negotiation, saying a settlement with the United States would benefit France.[13]

In its instructions for dealing with the American emissaries the Executive Directory assumed that the negotiations would revolve around three issues. The first issue would involve the stopping of French depredations at sea, the second would concentrate on American demands for indemnities for prizes taken by French privateers, and the third would focus on a permanent settlement of differences between the two nations.

On the first two issues the Directory's stand was clear. It would not restrain its corsairs as long as Jay's Treaty remained in force, but it would be willing to give up the demand that American ships carry a *rôle d'équipage*. It would try to put off payment of the indemnities indefinitely by establishing a special commission to deal with them. The Directory insisted that the negotiations must be based on the theory that Jay's Treaty permitted France the same rights at sea that it gave Britain. If this theory were not accepted, then the terms of the Franco-American commercial treaty of 1778 would apply, and France would be obligated to pay for all ships and goods seized.

These instructions suggested, at the least, a desire for a settlement. The ideas advanced by Létombe and Alexandre Maurice Blanc de Lanautte, Comte d'Hauterive, formerly France's Consul at New York and a friend who had known Talleyrand when he was an exile in the United States, did not. They advised delay and procrastination in dealing with the American commissioners. Létombe pointed out that Adams would be President for less than four years, and then American policy would change.

The American envoys should be received, Hauterive said,

without "displays of friendship or bitterness," and with "almost silent politeness." If their behavior, or their terms, did not satisfy France, he wrote, "the negotiations can be stopped, neglected, or put off, without any danger if the Government will show a careful regard for American public opinion, for national spirit, and for the influence of the party which favors the French alliance." Hauterive considered the United States incapable of fighting a major war. So he looked upon the danger of war as so unlikely that it could be ignored.[14]

Although Talleyrand did not abandon his instructions, and wished ultimately for a settlement, he appeared to follow Létombe's and Hauterive's ideas in his relations with the American commissioners. Talleyrand thought, for example, that Pickering was carried away by "an immoderate hatred" of the French, and that "such feelings are very little apt to reassure us as to the sincerity of the negotiations which are about to take place."[15]

In contrast, the American commissioners' detailed instructions, governed by Hamilton's ideas, sought specific objectives, but offered nothing solid in return, except protestations of goodwill. Those instructions assumed that France would negotiate a new treaty to supersede, or amend, the existing agreements. The envoys were told, as matters of principle, that the United States would accept no blame for the Franco-American crisis, would give no aid, financial or military, to France in her present war, and would sign no treaty inconsistent with commitments in any prior agreement, such as in Jay's Treaty. The new treaty should have a duration of ten or twenty years.

Among the specific issues the commissioners wished to settle, that of compensation to Americans for losses suffered as a result of French depredations at sea or seizures in port was prominent. But such reparation was, the instructions said, "not to be insisted on as an indispensable condition of the proposed treaty." At the same time, the commissioners could not renounce the American claims. Although Pinckney, Marshall, and Gerry could accept no restraint on American commerce, they were permitted, in matters of contraband and seizure of belligerent goods on American vessels, to yield terms similar to those conceded to England in

Jay's Treaty. The commissioners could, therefore, as John Jay had done, abandon the principle of free ships, free goods. This would mean that the British, with their powerful navy, could seize American ships bound for France while the French, with their inferior navy, could not stop those going to British ports.[16]

In seeking a revision of all the French treaties, the commissioners were to keep two objectives in mind. They should get rid of the now annoying provision of reciprocal guaranty in the alliance of 1778. They should also cancel the concession in the consular convention of 1788 which allowed the establishment of prize tribunals in American ports. "The guaranty by France" of our independence, the instructions pointed out, "will add nothing to our security; while, on the contrary, our guaranty of the possessions of France in America will perpetually expose us to the risk and expense of war. . . ."

In summary, the instructions were conciliatory but aside from offering protestations of goodwill, were also vague about meeting French grievances. They assumed that Jay's Treaty, which irritated France most, was a closed issue. In other matters, the powers of the commissioners were broad enough to resolve most differences with France and bury the entangling alliance of 1778, notably by replacing the old French treaties with a new one.[17] From the French point of view, the Americans sought much and offered little.

Before the American envoys could even think of applying these instructions to a specific negotiating situation, they had an opportunity to observe the politics of the Directory from a close point. Marshall arrived at The Hague on September 3, 1797, forty-eight days after leaving Philadelphia, and one day before the Directory's *coup d'état*. He wrote to his wife that the *coup* might preclude negotiations and cause him to return home promptly.[18]

At The Hague, Marshall met Pinckney, and waited two weeks for Gerry's arrival. Believing that their presence in Paris at this time might be important, Marshall and Pinckney decided to tarry no longer. On September 18 they set out slowly for the French capital, hoping to be overtaken by Gerry. Nine days later the two Americans arrived in Paris where they rented quarters in the same apartment building in St. Germain, rue de la Fontaine Grenelle. Pinckney and his family took the larger apartment on the second floor, and Marshall the smaller quarters below.

UNDERCOVER AGENTS

Marshall and Pinckney immediately informed the French foreign office of their arrival, but delayed the presentation of their credentials until Gerry, who had arrived in Holland two days after they left, could join them. He did so on October 4, 1797. Four days later the three Americans met Talleyrand informally at his home. Although polite, the Minister of Foreign Relations said he could not receive them officially until after he had completed a special report on American affairs he was preparing for the Directors. He did give them "cards of hospitality" to keep the police from bothering them. Such a courtesy had been denied to Pinckney on his previous mission in Paris.

Within three days the commissioners received a letter from Thomas Paine, the propagandist of the American Revolution, then residing in Paris, that led to the first of many disagreements between Marshall and Gerry. Paine suggested that the Americans accept, for their country, the status of an unarmed neutral. Believing that Talleyrand had inspired the letter, Marshall wished to ignore it. Gerry did not. He insisted that the commission should close no channel of communication, or scorn any proposal. Pinckney took a middle position. On the following day, therefore, the commissioners sent Paine a noncommittal reply.[19]

Marshall's suspicions apparently had been well founded, for Talleyrand now assumed that the Americans were willing to negotiate on an unofficial level. On the evening of October 18 the French statesman made his second indirect approach by sending a Monsieur Jean Conrad Hottinguer, a Swiss financier acting as his private agent, to the Americans' quarters. Since Pinckney was the only commissioner who could speak French, he left the dinner table at which Marshall was seated, and talked privately with Hottinguer.

The Directory, Hottinguer said, had been offended by President Adams's unfriendly remarks in his address of May 16 to the special session of Congress. Before the envoys could expect to be received officially, he pointed out, they had to placate the Directors, most likely Barras, the most venal of the Directors. The Americans could do this, Hottinguer suggested, by disavowing the offensive parts of Adams's speech, by making a loan to France, and by paying a bribe "for the purpose of making the customary distributions in diplomatic affairs." As was the custom, the Americans should place the money at Talleyrand's disposal for his own use, for the Directors, and for other officials. At this time the Swiss agent did not specify the amount desired.

Pinckney reported Hottinguer's demands to his colleagues who showed no particular moral indignation over the idea of bribing the Directors. Yet Marshall and Pinckney wished to turn down the whole proposition, mainly because they considered a loan to France unneutral.[20] They would not, furthermore, accept the theory that the loan and bribe were merely preliminaries to negotiation. These Americans were, according to custom, willing to pay, but only after France had signed a treaty, not before.

Gerry objected to breaking off the effort to negotiate, suggesting that if they did this war would follow. Finally, all agreed that Pinckney should obtain Hottinguer's proposal in writing, which he did. The amount of the bribe astonished the Americans. The French demanded one million two hundred thousand *livres*, or approximately one quarter of a million dollars.[21]

On the evening of October 20 Hottinguer called on all three commissioners, this time accompanied by a Monsieur Bellamy, a banker of Swiss origin from Hamburg who claimed to be a confidential friend of Talleyrand's. Supporting Hottinguer's demands, Bellamy explained that even though Talleyrand considered himself a friend of the United States, the outraged Directors would not allow him to communicate directly with the American commissioners. Nonetheless, Bellamy added, he was certain that once Talleyrand's conditions were met, terms that Bellamy spelled out in greater detail than had Hottinguer, the Minister of Foreign Relations would be able to calm the Directors. Then the Executive

Directory would agree to a new treaty that would place France in
the same position toward the United States as was England.

Bellamy stressed that all must be preceded by the bribe. "I
will not disguise from you," he said, "that this situation being
made, the essential part of the treaty remains to be adjusted . . .
you must pay money, you must pay a great deal of money."

At this point the discussion ended, and began again the next
morning. Bellamy now advanced another plan. The Americans
could make the loan without violating their country's neutrality,
he suggested, by buying 32 million Dutch florins at their face
value of $12.8 million. Since the market value was half that
amount, France would take a profit of over $6 million, or more
than one hundred per cent. Ultimately the United States would
lose nothing, Bellamy insisted, for after the war the Dutch would
redeem their florins at par. He also indicated that even if the
American commissioners agreed to this "loan," they still must pay
the bribe.[22]

Deciding that these terms were unreasonable, Marshall and
Pinckney wanted to break off their informal discussions. Yet Britain's Prime Minister, William Pitt, in need of peace, almost accepted a similar proposition from the French through an American agent, probably a Federalist.[23] Gerry again objected to his
colleagues' position, arguing that Talleyrand's conditions could
be used as a starting point in the negotiations, and that perhaps
later the Directory would soften its demands. Marshall and
Pinckney were convinced that Gerry's thinking on this point was
naïve. They believed the Directory was under the influence of
those who profited from the plunder of American commerce, and
hence was opposed to any true accommodation. Nonetheless,
Marshall and Pinckney gave in to Gerry, and agreed to continue
the unofficial bargaining.[24]

The envoys then informed Bellamy that although they had
no authority to negotiate a loan, one of them would be willing to
return to the United States for fresh instructions. They would
seek such instructions only if France would immediately stop her
attacks on American shipping. The commissioners also refused to

disavow President Adams's speech of May 16, insisting that such action lay beyond the range of diplomatic discussion.

A few days later news reached Paris that on October 17 General Napoleon Bonaparte had forced the Treaty of Campo Formio on defeated Austria, confirming France's mastery of Western Europe. "England," Marshall wrote, "is threatened with invasion." Bonaparte's triumph also had the effect of increasing French threats against the United States, and of making the bargaining position of its agents even weaker than it had been.

Marshall now believed the Directors were so hostile to the United States that "the Atlantic only can save us." Nothing, he felt, could counter that hostility "but an apprehension that we may be thrown into the arms of Britain."

At about this time two American adventurers who were in Europe, John Trumbull and James C. Mountflorence, talked to Talleyrand. Mountflorence offered his services as an intermediary between the Minister of Foreign Relations and the American commissioners. Both men reported that Talleyrand wanted money to facilitate the negotiations. When Trumbull remarked that the American diplomats probably could not employ money, Talleyrand burst out, "But they must, sir." (*Mais, il le faut, monsieur.*) [25] Hottinguer also stressed the need for money. Think, he told the American commissioners, of the "power and violence of France." He indicated that war might follow if the commissioners did not meet the Directory's demands. If war came, the envoys answered, the United States would protect itself.

"You do not speak to the point," the exasperated Hottinguer said, "it is money; it is expected that you will offer money."

"We have given an answer to that demand," the commissioners retorted.

"No you have not," the Swiss responded. "What is your answer?"

"It is no, no; not a sixpence," Pinckney blurted out.[26]

Seemingly unaffected by Pinckney's outburst, Hottinguer insisted that a bribe would be money well spent.

Meanwhile, a third agent from Talleyrand, a Monsieur

Lucien Hauteval, had taken a hand in this backdoor diplomacy. First he had spoken to Gerry, and then to all three envoys, urging them to call on Talleyrand privately. Pinckney and Marshall said they would meet with Talleyrand only when he gave them an official appointment. Gerry decided to accept the invitation, assuming that he could make his visit a social one without loss of dignity since he had known Talleyrand in Boston. The French Minister of Foreign Relations snubbed him, and Gerry vowed he would not call again. Nonetheless, it had now become clear to Talleyrand that Gerry was willing to negotiate independently of his colleagues. Yet, the French Minister needed the cooperation of Pinckney and Marshall to gain the money he desired.

Hottinguer, therefore, urged the envoys to make one more effort to see Talleyrand, and also pressed them to advance the bribe. Since his colleagues would not budge, Gerry, despite his vow, on October 28 sought to break the impasse by once again informally visiting Talleyrand, who this time had Hauteval at his side. Talleyrand repeated his agents' terms, but did not demand a bribe. Gerry returned to his apartment and reported to Pinckney and Marshall that within one week the Directory would take additional hostile measures against the United States if the commissioners did nothing to appease it.

Talleyrand's pressure did have some effect on Pinckney and Marshall. When Hauteval told the envoys that if they paid the bribe the Directory would allow them to remain in Paris and Talleyrand would receive two of them while the third returned home for new instructions that would allow the desired loan, Pinckney and Marshall appeared interested. They replied that if France were "disposed to do us justice . . . we might not so much regard a little money, such as he stated to be usual, although we should hazard ourselves by giving it." [27]

The Americans then asked if the attacks on their shipping would, in the meantime, end. No, Hauteval answered. Since the bribe would not abate French hostility, the commissioners said, in effect, they saw no reason why they should pay.

After that Hottinguer and Bellamy again approached the Americans, hinted at personal violence, and once more threat-

1. *Abigail Adams by Gilbert
Stuart. She reflected her
husband's views on the
Quasi-War but at times appeared
more belligerent than he.*

2. *John Adams by Charles
Févret de Saint-Mémin. He
was the first President to
face the problems of
fighting an undeclared war.*

3. *Alexander Hamilton by John Trumbull. His desire for military glory helped wreck the Federalist party.*

THOMAS JEFFERSON
Rembrandt Peale 1800

4. *Thomas Jefferson by Rembrandt Peale (White House Collection).*
He was the only Republican to hold high office during the Quasi-War.

5. *Albert Gallatin by James Sharples. He led the Republican opposition to war in the House of Representatives.*

6. *James McHenry by Charles Févret de Saint-Mémin. As Secretary of War, he echoed Hamilton's views in meetings of Adams's Cabinet.*

7. *Robert Goodloe Harper by Charles Févret de Saint-Mémin, 1799. This Federalist from South Carolina spoke for the war hawks.*

8. *Timothy Pickering by Charles Willson Peale. Anything that could injure the French appeared to please this violently anti-Jacobin Secretary of State.*

9. *George Logan by Gilbert Stuart. The personal peace mission of this Quaker and Jeffersonian Democrat led to Logan's Law against personal diplomacy.*

10. *Charles Cotesworth Pinckney, from a portrait by Edward Malbone. Ironically, the failure of the X Y Z mission and words he did not utter made him a national hero.*

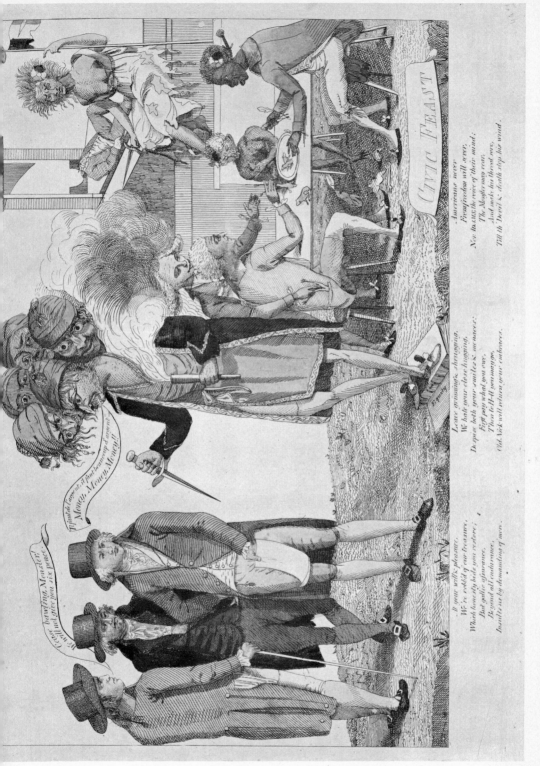

11. "Cinque-tetes, or the Paris Monster." An American cartoon representing the X Y Z affair, the print shows Gerry, Pinckney and Marshall turning down demands of a five-headed monster which symbolizes the Directory.

12. *Elbridge Gerry by John Vanderlyn, 1798. He desired peace so strongly that he risked the loss of friends and reputation to seek it.*

13. *John Marshall by J. W. Jarvis. The X Y Z mission made him a national hero but he did not become an extreme Federalist.*

ened war. They warned that the "French party in America,"
meaning the Republicans, would throw the blame for the failure
of the mission on the British party, or the Federalists. The commissioners explained, as they had previously, that they could
make a treaty to restore friendship but had no authority to meet
the French demands. Talleyrand's agents urged them to assume
the power to negotiate a loan.

Then, on November 1, 1797, the commissioners decided to
have nothing more to do with unaccredited agents but discovered
that only the unofficial channels of communication were open to
them. Ten days later they sent Talleyrand a formal note, signed
by all three of them, demanding official recognition. It, too,
proved futile, for Talleyrand did not even answer it.

Marshall now sensed impending failure. "My own private
opinion," he wrote, "is that this haughty ambitious government is
not willing to come to an absolute rupture with America during
the present state of the war with England but will not con-
descend to act with justice or to treat us as a free and independent
nation."

The French Minister of Foreign Relations now persisted in
trying to divide the commission by flattering Gerry with special
attention, and even with dinner invitations that excluded Pinckney and Marshall. A group of Americans residing in Paris, "American Jacobins," Pinckney called them, also courted Gerry. Both
Pinckney and Marshall deplored this, and what they termed
Gerry's acquiescence in the "old reprobated system of indirect
unauthorized negotiation." [28]

Despite these vexations and the frequently expressed determination to demand their passports, the Americans lingered.
Each time they considered leaving they decided, on second
thought, to remain just a little longer, and the weeks slipped into
months. Paris, after all, was pleasant, offering diversion in entertainment and attractive feminine company. Moreover, there was
always the hope of some improvement in their situation.

One of the women the envoys came to know well, a Madame
de Villette, the niece and adopted daughter of Voltaire and ru-
mored to have been his mistress, was another of Talleyrand's

agents. Late in November, in an effort to economize, Marshall and Gerry had taken rooms in a hotel at 54–56 rue de Vaugirard run by Madame de Villette. She dined regularly with "the two *batchelors*" and made "their situation very agreeable." Marshall, the youngest of the commissioners, found this widow of about thirty-two years of age so captivating that he broke an engagement with Pinckney to take her to the theater. "What could I do," the Virginian said in apology, when Madame "invited me to accompany her?" [29]

On one occasion Madame de Villette attempted to wheedle diplomatic concessions from Pinckney. "Why will you not lend us money?" she asked. "If you were to make us a loan, all matters will be adjusted. When you were contending your Revolution we lent you money."

The two situations were not comparable, Pinckney answered. Americans had merely requested a loan, but the French now demanded one. When Madame de Villette persisted, the South Carolinian replied that the envoys might as well leave immediately. The widow countered with the warning that they should avoid a final rupture because France had a considerable party in America working in her interest. [30]

MARSHALL'S MEMORIAL

By the end of the year Marshall and Pinckney were drained of patience. Convinced that the mission had failed, Marshall prepared a long memorial recounting the difficulties between France and the United States. He stressed America's grievances against France and the American desire to avoid war. He also defended Jay's Treaty, arguing that it neither violated American obligations to France nor granted special favors to Britain. At the end, he asked the French government to allow him and his fellow commissioners to present their case for an accommodation, otherwise they would go home.

Marshall believed that even though the memorial might have no effect on the Executive Directory, it would show the American people that the Adams administration had earnestly sought a reconciliation with France. Pinckney agreed with the note's sentiments, but Gerry objected and insisted on some revisions. Although the memorial was dated January 17, 1798, Gerry did not sign it until a week later. It did not go to the French foreign office until January 31.[31]

On January 18, while the memorial was being polished, the Directory published a harsh new decree on neutral trade intended mainly to strike at American shipping. France would, the decree said, seize all ships having English goods on board, regardless of who owned them. A ship's cargo, not its flag, would now determine whether the vessel would be treated as a neutral or an enemy. Anything that had once been English, a jug of rum or metal buttons on the skipper's jacket perhaps, on board a ship could provoke its seizure. American captains even filed the manufacturers' names off their English compasses and sextants so that these instruments could not be used as a pretext for capture of their ships. That law also forbade any ship which had touched at a British port, except in distress, to enter French ports.[32]

As far as the commissioners were concerned the new decree, which went into force without preliminary warning, sealed the failure of their mission. "There is not the least hope of an accommodation with this government," Pinckney wrote. "We sue in vain to be heard." [33]

In addition to the United States, other neutrals—Sweden, Denmark, and Prussia—protested the decree. By driving neutral trade away from French ports that law harmed France far more than it did Britain. The decree had the effect of imposing a self-blockade on France. It was, therefore, foolish. Many Frenchmen realized this and soon demanded its repeal.

These developments did not dispel the despair of the envoys. Gerry became increasingly the center of French attention. Marshall and Pinckney now feared that Gerry might succumb to Talleyrand's flattery, and on his own arrange for a bribe, or a loan. In February 1798 they learned that Gerry planned another of his private meetings with Talleyrand. Pinckney then told Gerry that "a prompt, immediate, & decisive negative should be given to any proposition that may be made, or insinuation given to obtain money from us in any shape or under any pretence." [34]

This advice was appropriate, for Talleyrand had analyzed the pertinent portions of the commissioners' instructions, and he convinced Gerry that the envoys had the authority to grant France a loan. Talleyrand also persuaded Gerry to keep the subjects of their discussions secret. Gerry agreed, for he believed that on the outcome of those discussions "probably depended peace or war."

Since Marshall and Pinckney could not stop Gerry's independent diplomacy, they hoped some good would come from it. "We shall both be happy," they said, "if by remaining without us, Mr. Gerry can negotiate a treaty which shall preserve the peace without sacrificing the independence of our country. We will most readily offer up all personal considerations as a sacrifice to appease the haughtiness of this Republic."

On February 10 Gerry broke his silence by revealing the Directory's renewed demand for a loan. This led Gerry into an argument with Marshall. Relations between the commissioners became even more strained when Gerry refused to sign a note to Talleyrand in which the Americans asked for their passports. This request was not necessary, for Talleyrand had already decided to force Marshall and Pinckney out of France and to persuade Gerry to remain.

Marshall assumed that the Directory's main reason for insisting on a loan was to prolong the unofficial discussions while French cruisers preyed on American commerce. Exasperated by this view, Gerry accused Marshall of allowing his anti-French bias to warp his judgment. This led Marshall to suggest a personal meeting with the Minister of Foreign Relations so that the commissioners could hear from Talleyrand's own lips the threat that if no loan were made there would be war.

At last, on March 2, 1798, the three commissioners had a conference with Talleyrand. The Americans uncovered nothing new, but they now understood that the success or failure of their mission depended on the loan, whereas two months before the fate of the mission had appeared to rest on the payment of a bribe. Gerry had argued earlier that he would take no responsibility for war if a loan were refused. He had also advanced the view that though the envoys' instructions prohibited a loan to France during the war with England, the instructions implied that arrangements could be made for a loan immediately after the war had ended.

Now, to break the deadlock, Gerry suggested that the Americans apologize for the statements by George Washington and John Adams that the Directory considered offensive. Admit that the President's complaints "had been founded in mistake," Gerry urged, and the Directory might become more reasonable on the issues at stake. Marshall objected. Gerry retorted "that he wished to God Marshall would propose something which was accommodating."

Four days later, in another interview, Talleyrand let the commissioners know once more that the loan was the crucial issue. Without it there could be no treaty. This widened the split in the American commission. Talleyrand then moved to take advantage of it by putting pressure on Marshall and Pinckney to leave France and to allow Gerry to remain.

Now Talleyrand made use of Pierre Augustin Caron de Beaumarchais, poet, playwright, skilled musician, and accomplished intriguer, in pressuring the Americans. Known to posterity mainly as the author of the comedies, *The Barber of Seville* and *The Marriage of Figaro*, Beaumarchais had also earned a reputation as a friend of the United States for aid he had given during the Revolution against England. At this time he had a suit before American courts to recover payment for some of the supplies he had furnished during the Revolution, and Marshall was his American attorney.

Beaumarchais urged Marshall, his lawyer, to meet Talleyrand's demands. "France," Beaumarchais said, "thought herself sufficiently powerful to give the law to the world and exacted from all around her money to enable her to finish successfully her war against England." Still, Marshall and Pinckney stood firm. You are considered, Beaumarchais explained, "as being sold to the English." Finally, he hinted that if Marshall did not cooperate he would find himself in political trouble at home.[35]

These tactics reflected Talleyrand's own views of what French policy toward the United States should be.[36] The Americans' memorial of January 17 had given him an opportunity to outline his plan to the Executive Directory and to seek its support.

In reporting to the Directory, Talleyrand explained that he had resorted to unofficial negotiations with the American commission and had suggested payment of an indemnity for Adams's speech to the special session of Congress. Since payment could not be arranged through normal diplomatic channels, he had proposed a loan, mainly under the guise of the American purchase of depreciated Dutch florins. As a matter of policy, he favored a permanent settlement with the United States, but only after punishing its government. The only true difficulty in such a policy, he felt, arose from French spoliations of American commerce. Since France had amply avenged herself on the United States in the past two years, those depredations could now stop.[37]

"I have operated on the principle that the Directory did not wish to carry things to extremities," Talleyrand reported, "and that it would be impossible even with a declaration of war to avenge ourselves on the American government more than we have done." We should, he advised, "prevent a forced rupture which would inevitably throw the United States into the arms of England."

Since in Talleyrand's mind Pinckney and Marshall were firm Federalists, he considered them hostile emissaries and obstacles to a successful negotiation. So he requested permission to deal only with Gerry. This would be possible, he argued, because all three of the Americans were accredited as ministers plenipotentiary. The Directory approved Talleyrand's conduct and adopted his plan. In the policy toward the American mission, therefore, the Minister of Foreign Relations now managed to become an author as well as the editor.[38]

Talleyrand now proceeded to deal with the American commissioners according to plan, and on the principle that France would recognize her debts to the United States and pay damages for American ships and goods seized before the signing of Jay's Treaty. She would also take measures to iron out defects in the treaties with the United States.

With this program in mind Talleyrand prepared his answer to the American memorial. That answer reached the commissioners on March 19, 1798, more than six weeks after they had sent their memorial. Talleyrand's reply was not really a diplomatic document. It was, instead, propaganda addressed to the American people with the purpose of separating them from their Federalist government. For example, he sent a copy to Joseph Philippe Létombe in the United States with instructions to give it wide publicity.

Talleyrand listed French grievances, and accused the American government of violating its treaties with France and of being partial to Britain. To support this charge he pointed out that at this critical time the American government had assigned hostile envoys to France, but in 1794 they had sent a friendly emissary to negotiate a treaty with England. France, he insisted, merited the same consideration, particularly since Jay's Treaty impaired the alliance of 1778 which had contributed to American freedom. Since Pinckney and Marshall were partisans of England, he concluded, the Directory would treat only with the friendly envoy, meaning Gerry.[39]

Marshall, it was agreed, should answer Talleyrand's complaints. Before Marshall could prepare a reply, he and Pinckney quarreled with Gerry over what should be done. Marshall and Pinckney, who had been threatened with expulsion from France, now decided to leave Paris, but not Gerry. "To prevent war," Gerry declared, "I will stay." He complained privately that his colleagues' "conduct to me has not been of that frank and friendly description which I expected." [40]

Despite these differences, Gerry signed the note, dated April 3, 1798, which Marshall prepared. It rebuffed Talleyrand's charges, and said that the opinions the envoys had advanced were "purely American, unmixed with any particle of foreign tint." Not

one of them, the note stated, had the power "to take upon himself
a negotiation." They still hoped, nonetheless, that negotiations
might begin, but if talks did not start immediately, they desired
their passports, which they had to obtain from the French before
they could leave.[41]

This demand for passports did not include Gerry. He stuck to
his decision to remain in Paris. Talleyrand had told him that his
staying would prevent an irreparable rupture between France
and the United States. Gerry believed this, but indicated that
since he had no power to negotiate on his own, he would stay
only as a private citizen. Nonetheless, Gerry expected to receive
full power from President Adams to negotiate a treaty acceptable
to Talleyrand. Gerry had convinced himself that he alone stood
between a decision on war or peace, that Talleyrand sincerely desired an accommodation, and that eventually he, Gerry, would return home with a satisfactory treaty. Regardless of Gerry's stubborn courage in clinging to what he considered the last chance
for peace and in absorbing the abuse of his fellow negotiators, his
attitude and decision to remain in Paris meant that Talleyrand
had succeeded in dividing the commission.[42]

The American commission, as a result, broke up in dissension
with Marshall and Pinckney not speaking to Gerry. Marshall told
Pinckney that he was happy to "bid an eternal adieu to Europe (I
wish to add) & to its crimes.—Mark I only mean its political
crimes, for those of a private nature are really some of those so
lovely that it required men of as much virtue & less good temper
than you & myself to hate them." He sailed from Bordeaux on
April 24 on the ship *Alexander Hamilton,* which he said was "a
very excellent vessel but for the sin of the name." He also remarked that his passage on this ship made his return home seem
almost criminal to the French.[43]

Pinckney had a daughter sick with fever. He asked and obtained permission from the government to remain in the south of
France so that she might, as directed by physicians, regain her
health. He and his family, therefore, remained in France until
August.

As Marshall and Pinckney left Paris, contemporaries, either in

France or the United States, were not aware of what had happened. As the result of misunderstanding, miscalculation, or just plain blundering in diplomacy, one of mankind's recurring tragedies—unwanted and purposeless war—was in the making. On the American side, Pinckney and Marshall were convinced that they could not deal with the French and that the Executive Directory was determined to have war, or at least to subject the United States to unbearable humiliation. Yet in fact Talleyrand, despite his personal greed and arrogant demands, wanted peace. He saw no profit for France in war with the United States.

On the French side, Talleyrand mistakenly believed he could keep the American commissioners dangling for months without a final rupture that would precipitate war. Like his predecessors in the foreign office, he based his actions on reports from agents in America, such as Létombe, who wrote that Republicans were gaining strength. On this basis Talleyrand assumed that procrastination in dealing with the commissioners would divide them, discredit President Adams, and help the Republicans come to power. He even tried to encourage firmer Republican opposition to Adams by letting Republicans know that France would not declare war even if the commissioners made no treaty. Mistakenly, he also believed that no section, outside New England, was alarmed by the crisis with France. How badly Talleyrand miscalculated the temper of the American people can be seen in their reaction to the treatment given their commissioners in Paris.[44]

THE WAITING CONGRESS

The American people and their government had been waiting anxiously for news from their envoys. By the end of October 1797 the yellow fever had disappeared, and the citizenry and government officials had begun to filter back into Philadelphia.[45] John Adams and his family had left Quincy, Massachusetts, late in September, but because of fear of the plague they did not enter the national capital until the middle of November. Ironically, as he arrived, the President caught cold and had to remain in bed for a week. Like everyone else he had been wondering what was happening in Paris, but, unlike others, he doubted that France wanted war. She would, he felt, profit more by maintaining an appearance of anger and continuing to despoil American shipping.

Adams could only conjecture as to the French attitude, for no word had arrived from the commissioners. They had sent their first dispatches from Paris on October 22 and had mailed others at regular intervals. The war between France and England, and a desire to keep the dispatches from falling into unfriendly hands, had forced the envoys to send their reports home by circuitous channels. As a result of these tactics, as well as of west winds, the dispatches were *en route* for months.[46]

It was in this atmosphere of uncertainty over whether there would be war or peace with France that Philadelphia prepared for the second session of the Fifth Congress. The Congress was slow in assembling because its members approached the city cautiously to ascertain if the yellow fever had abated. By November 15, 1797, the House had a quorum, but the Senate did not, so Congress did not convene for another week. By this time Adams had received news of the *coup d'état* of 18 *Fructidor,* and he now feared his mission might flounder.

On November 23 Adams delivered his opening address, written basically by Secretary of State Pickering, to Congress. It reflected the prevailing spirit of uncertainty. After announcing that Marshall and Gerry had landed safely in Holland and that he had no other news from the commissioners, he warned that too much must not be expected from the mission.

Whatever the result, or even if peace came to Europe, Adams declared, "I hold it most certain that permanent tranquility and order will not soon be obtained." He saw no reason why the French depredations would stop as long as American shipping remained exposed and unprotected. The nation must, he insisted, protect its commerce and place itself "in a suitable posture of defence" with the measures he had recommended in the previous session. The House, for instance, should levy taxes adequate to provide for naval and military defense.[47]

Adams, it seemed clear from the speech, intended to continue resistance to France, a logical extension of the policy he had launched in the special session, and that he had inherited from George Washington. This policy, which he considered necessary for national independence and for securing redress from the Directory, pleased Federalists and alarmed some Republicans.

Nonetheless, the task of drafting replies did not set off harsh debate in Congress, as it had in the special session. The Senate, with its solid Federalist majority, agreed with the President's sentiments. After a week's discussion, the House replied that the country should remain neutral and that it would cooperate with the President to avoid war.

Congress took up the President's recommendations, but passed no important legislation while tensely awaiting news from Paris. During this period, a prominent Federalist wrote, "the mind of Congress" seemed suspended until the fate of the negotiation was known.[48] Party bitterness showed itself in the Senate in arguments over the impeachment of William Blount, who had been brought to trial after a House committee had presented articles of impeachment against him; in six weeks of intermittent debate over a Foreign Intercourse Bill for a substantial diplomatic establishment; and in a quarrel in the House between Roger Griswold, an acid-tongued Federalist from Connecticut, and Matthew Lyon, a fiery Republican from Vermont.

Griswold insulted Lyon, and the Vermonter spit a stream of tobacco juice into his face. Later, Griswold pummeled Lyon with a heavy hickory stick, and Lyon grabbed a pair of fire tongs to fight back, setting off a small riot in the House chamber. Attempts were made to expel the brawlers from Congress, but both retained their seats without even a reprimand.

Federalists were particularly upset by the fact that "the Spitting Lyon" of Vermont had gone unpunished. "I feel grieved," a Bostonian wrote, "that the saliva of an Irishman should be left upon the face of an American & He, a New Englandman." [49]

Investigation of the unimportant Lyon-Griswold affair held the attention of the House until the end of February 1798. By the first week in March Congress had been in session almost three months without acting on the President's recommendations. Without news from Paris nothing seemed urgent, and the legislators waited. Albert Gallatin told his wife, "My greatest leisure time is while Congress sits, for we have nothing of any real importance before us. . . ."

Since Republicans believed, as Gallatin himself wrote, that the extreme Federalists sought to provoke war with France, and the Republicans were strong enough in the House to delay action on almost any matter, it became clear that nothing decisive would pass. Yet, Gallatin was fearful. "Our situation grows critical; it will require great firmness to prevent this country being involved in a war should our negotiations with France meet with great delay or any serious interruption," he wrote. "We must expect to be branded with the usual epithets of Jacobins and tools of foreign influence." [50]

Federalists, on the other hand, gave up hope of overcoming the Republicans in the House. Oliver Wolcott, who considered the situation in Congress humiliating, despairingly predicted that the Directory was "too wise and politic to do anything which would rouse and unite the country." [51]

Such despair was premature. Rumors were already seeping into Philadelphia indicating failure of the Paris mission, and of the possibility of war. One story said, in effect, that several Republican members of Congress had written to the Directors urging them to reject Pinckney, Marshall, and Gerry. Yet, almost everyone was concerned over the lack of news from the commissioners themselves. George Washington asked, "Are our commissioners guillotined, or what else is the occasion of their silence?" [52]

Jefferson, too, expected the worst. Although Vice-President, he did not know much more about developments within the executive branch of the government than did any alert ordinary citizen. Like Jefferson, James Madison was in the dark and felt pessimistic about peace.

In view of the almost insuperable difficulties imposed by the "insidious" Jay Treaty, Madison wrote, success of the mission seemed improbable. Americans could resolve the differences with France, he thought, by dissolving the Jay Treaty or by allowing France to plunder us "as we have stipulated that Great Britain

may plunder us." Since Adams's government could not accept
either of these alternatives, he believed the President would try to
avoid formal hostilities but would go to war indirectly by using
frigates as convoy escorts and by resorting to other belligerent
tactics. In doing this, Madison pointed out, the nation would be
defending the British treaty, which itself had been adopted to
prevent war.[53]

The President himself was also still in the dark as to the fate
of his emissaries, but he, too, had heard the rumors. So he decided to prepare for the worst. On January 24, 1798, he sent another inquiry to his department heads. What should he do,
Adams asked, if the French refused to receive the commissioners
or forced them to return empty-handed? Should he recommend
war, or an embargo, to Congress? What policy should he adopt
toward England? Should the United States seek an alliance with
her? Perhaps it would be best, he suggested, to remain silent on
this matter and wait for Britain's overture. If England fell, might
not an alliance increase the possibility of civil war in the United
States? [54]

At this time the possibility of England's fall seemed real. In
the spring of 1797 the Bank of England had stopped cash pay-
ments, and government bonds had fallen to unprecedentedly low
levels. In concerted action with the Directory, Irish leaders, such
as Theobald Wolfe Tone, a revolutionary and friend of James
Monroe, fought the English. In April the Irish even launched a
revolt that failed. Sailors at the home bases of Spithead and Nore
had rioted, and the Royal Navy had to deal with a massive
mutiny, one that involved 50,000 men and 113 ships. An alliance
between France, Spain, and Holland even gave the Directory the
possibility of bringing together a fleet larger than Britain's. For
the first time in two centuries England's tight island seemed insecure and in serious danger of invasion.

Across the channel, at Boulogne, Napoleon Bonaparte had
brought together a formidable force of veterans, the *Armée
d'Angleterre,* and was reported poised for a cross-channel attack. In
the United States some Republicans hoped the attack would succeed.[55] One of these was Andrew Jackson, a young senator from

Tennessee. "Do not . . . be surprised," Jackson wrote to a friend,
"if my next letter should announce a revolution in England.
Should Bonaparte make a landing on the English shore tyranny
will be humbled, a throne crushed, and a republic will spring
from the wreck, and millions of distressed people [will be] restored to the rights of man by the conquering arm of Bonaparte." [56]

From another point of view, perceptive Federalists were
rightly pointing out that England held the critical position in
France's attitude toward the United States. "In order to understand the policy of *France,* as it relates to maritime affairs,"
George Cabot explained, "it is necessary always to keep in our
eye the object at which she aims. This object undoubtedly is the
destruction of the naval power of *England,* for it is *England* alone
that prevents *France* from establishing the same absolute empire
on the sea which she now exercises over many nations by land.[57]

Harrison Gray Otis, another prominent New England Federalist, used stronger words. "Should Great Britain be compelled to
yield," he wrote, ". . . our liberties would fall a sacrifice. She is
the only barrier to the dreadful deluge, and when that is broken
down, it will be time for us to prepare to be good and dutiful subjects to the French."

John Marshall, too, thought that France would step up hostilities against the United States once she overcame England. On
the outcome of France's war against Britain, he wrote, "is staked
the independence of Europe and America." [58]

Meanwhile, two days after receiving President Adams's queries, Secretary of War McHenry had forwarded them to Hamilton.
The undercover strategist then replied with an outline of the
policy he thought should now be followed toward France. The
people, Hamilton said, held a strong aversion to war, particularly
against France. So, if the mission in Paris failed, the government
should not seek a formal declaration of war. "A mitigated hostility," he suggested, would leave "a door open to negotiation" and
avoid the extremities of full-scale war. The United States, moreover, could not profit from an unlimited conflict. France had no
trade or territory within reach worth attacking. It would be best,

therefore, to pursue a vigorous plan of defense while still being willing to negotiate.

In its details, Hamilton's plan repeated earlier suggestions. Allow the merchant ships to arm, he wrote; acquire twenty sloops of war, and in case of an open rupture, ten ships of the line; complete as rapidly as possible the three frigates that were under construction; suspend the treaties of alliance and commerce with France; increase the regular army; create a provisional one; and devise a system of taxation and raise a loan to support the increased expenditures. France's defeat of England and then an invasion of the United States, he thought, were possible. The American government should, in fact, prepare for just such a contingency, but he advised against an embargo. He also advised against an alliance with England. "Mutual interest," he said, "will command as much from her as a Treaty." He felt, as did Adams, that " 'twill be best not to entangle," even with England.

As for the President himself, he should, Hamilton suggested, tell Congress with calm, manly firmness, but "without strut," of the breakdown of the attempted negotiations. He should also deplore the failure of his peace mission.

On February 15, 1798, McHenry sent Hamilton's plan to Adams as his own, but with a few modifications. That report also represented the views of Pickering and Wolcott, though Pickering was willing to form an alliance with England, and he wished to take Louisiana from Spain before France could reacquire it. Attorney General Charles Lee also opposed an embargo, or an alliance with England. He recommended recall of the commissioners, an immediate declaration of war, and seizure of New Orleans if Spain should join France in hostility against the United States.[59]

By this time the British Foreign Office had heard that the Executive Directory would soon promulgate a new decree, that of January 18, against American shipping, and that the commissioners in Paris would be dismissed. William Wyndham Grenville, Lord Grenville, the British Foreign Minister, explained "this new Situation of Affairs" to Robert Liston in Philadelphia. Grenville said that England wished to improve relations with the American government and to prove that the interests of the American people should "lead them to look to Great Britain as their Most Natural Friend and Support." [60] Foreseeing war between France and the United States, he even offered Rufus King, the American Minister in London, the use of a swift packet to relay the news from France to Philadelphia.

THE DISPATCHES

By the time King's report reached Philadelphia, the first word had arrived from Pinckney, Marshall, and Gerry themselves concerning their treatment. Late in the evening of March 4 Secretary of State Pickering received a bundle of dispatches from the commissioners and immediately read what was not in code. As he read his anger rose, and then he rushed to the President. Although it would take days to decipher most of the dispatches, the few uncoded letters revealed enough to convince Adams and Pickering that the climax of the French crisis had come.

On the next day, in a belligerent mood, the President informed Congress that the first dispatches from the envoys had arrived. Although he could not pass on more information until the documents were deciphered, he felt that one of the dispatches in plain English, dated January 8, was of such importance that his duty compelled him to transmit it at once. In that letter the commissioners said, "we can only repeat that there exists no hope of our being officially received by this Government, or that the objects of our mission will be in any way accomplished." [61] Since the mission had failed, Adams explained, Congress must pass measures to protect commerce. On that same day a Federalist gazette in Philadelphia printed the dispatch, as well as some other letters from abroad, which exposed the "most shameful neglect" of the commissioners.[62]

This news, as well as ominous information in private letters from Pinckney which said the French government was preparing the "public mind" for hostilities against the United States, was enough to cause alarm, but not to satisfy curiosity. Many in Congress wondered if the ciphered passages hid even more alarming intelligence.

While Congress and the nation waited apprehensively, the dispatches were slowly deciphered, laying bare the story of solicited bribes and covert threats. The President himself now inclined toward war and felt that the country must prepare for a long, hard struggle. If the entire episode were made public, it seemed obvious, it might arouse such emotion among the people as to drive the nation immediately into war. Albert Gallatin was so alarmed by the thought of impending conflict that he closed a letter to his wife with these words, "May God save us from a war!" [63]

On March 13 Adams again queried his department heads, all of whom had seen the story unfold. Should he disclose the details, including the demands for a bribe, to Congress? he asked. Then, should he recommend "an immediate declaration of war?" [64]

Lee, who answered first this time, now opposed a quick declaration of war, but once the envoys were safely out of France, he advised disclosure of the details with a recommendation for war. To him there appeared "no alternative between actual hostilities . . . or national ruin." As he had before, McHenry recommended stronger defensive measures and "a qualified hostility." Wolcott vaguely suggested similar measures.

Pickering advised a declaration of war. He also sent Hamilton a detailed summary of the dispatches. Hamilton replied, "I am delighted with their contents," but warned against immediate war. He told the Secretary of State, who collaborated with High Federalists in Congress, that the independence of the United States was at stake. As he had to McHenry earlier, he suggested that the President send a firm but temperate message to Congress and urge the passage of defensive measures. Pickering himself now considered Britain "to be the only bulwark against the universal domination of France by sea, as well as by land." [65]

At this point Adams appeared more bellicose than the Hamiltonians, believing a formal declaration of war an economic necessity, and a moral obligation the nation would have to meet if its honor were to be preserved. So he went to his desk and began drafting a belligerent message, intended for Congress, denouncing the Directory. If Americans were to defend their commerce against the Directory's decree of January 18, he wrote, "every effort and every resource should be called into action, which cannot be done, unless there be a formal declaration of war. To proceed no farther, than the plan of arming vessels under regulations and restrictions is too inefficient of itself, and more dangerous to the lives of our seamen in cases of capture than in a State of declared war."

The President went on, saying he saw no alternative between actual hostilities and national ruin. No American would hesitate in preferring the hostilities. "All men will think it more honorable and glorious to the national character when its existence as an independent nation is at stake," Adams wrote in his draft, "that hostilities should be avowed in a formal Declaration of War." [66]

In other rough notes Adams denounced France's "unexampled arrogance" and claimed that she had piled up such outrage and insult that "no nation which is not sunk below the Character of Man, ought or can Submit to." So he wanted immediate nullification of all treaties with France and prohibition of commerce and correspondence with her people. The Directory's conduct, in his opinion, demanded "on the part of Congress an immediate Declaration of War against France." [67]

With his temper honed to a fighting edge, Adams wanted to send Pinckney, Marshall, and Gerry's dispatches to Congress. With the full story of French intrigue spread before it, Congress might give him the declaration of war he desired. On second thought, he realized that if he released the documents he might endanger the lives of the commissioners. He also had to take into account another important condition. Congress' reaction to the failure of the peace mission had been heated, but the composition of that legislative body was such that it probably would not vote a declaration of war. So, even though it pained him to do so, he held back the dispatches, putting aside the draft of his biting war message, at least its most belligerent passages. [68]

As the President revised his message he even cut out this passage: "If the measure recommended by the Executive Directory to the two Councils of the French Legislature which has been communicated to you has been adopted, as there is every reason to believe, I see not a possibility of avoiding war." [69]

The nation would now have to wait in a state of undeclared, or unofficial, war while the people achieved unity behind Adams's policy of resistance to France. In time, Adams thought, there would be incidents on the seas, more insults, and growing animosity that would spark an enlarged war. Then he would have his declaration from Congress.

The French Consul General in New York, Jean Antoine Rozier, among others, saw through Adams's strategy. Adams, he reported, is doing everything he can to arouse Americans against France. Federalist journalists picture France "as the devastator of Europe," and England as the only possible savior of the continent. Partisans of the government want war, but many Americans hesitate to go that far because war would be costly and would cripple their commerce. The Consul advised against a French declaration of war, saying the Republican party would eventually gain control of the American government, and France's difficulties would then end. Not knowing what had happened in Paris, he suggested that Talleyrand prolong the negotiations there and "make such peaceful offers that the President could not find any pretext to declare war, or if he does, everything will fall back on him." [70]

In keeping with his strategy of waiting for war, Adams on March 19 sent Congress a milder message than he at first had in mind. Even though it did not call for a formal declaration of war, it answered the Directory's decree and announced a state of limited hostilities against France. After studying the envoys' dispatches, the President said, "I perceive no ground of expectation that the objects of their mission can be accomplished on terms compatible with the safety, the honor, or the essential interests of the nation." This failure did not result from any lack of moderation, or effort, on the part of the American government to preserve peace.

"I can discern nothing," Adams added, "which could have insured or contributed to success, that has been omitted on my part, and nothing further which can be attempted. . . ." He then reiterated his recommendations, made at the opening of Congress, for defense of shipping, protection of coastal areas, manufacture of arms, and provision of revenues to pay for these measures. In conclusion, he announced he was revoking an order that had been issued by President Washington forbidding the arming of American ships.[71]

On March 23 Pickering took the next step toward open hostilities when he wrote to the commissioners saying he presumed they had closed their mission "by demanding passports to leave the territories of the French republic." If they had not, then the President directed them to do so, unless they had been received officially and were engaged in negotiations with authorized agents of the Directory.[72]

In these few days the President's message made its impact on the politicians. Republicans responded with cries of anguish. Jefferson called it "insane," or almost so. The leading Republican journal, the *Aurora* of Philadelphia, as well as others, claimed that the President had asked the people to draw the sword on the side of England. He had, it insisted, declared war without consulting Congress and the people. Republicans were apparently convinced that France could not seriously consider war against the United States. If that were so, the President was planning on his own to bring the country into the European conflict on the side of England.[73]

Adams's words also divided the Congress against itself. The House, meeting as a committee of the whole, discussed the address behind closed doors. Denouncing the "war message," Republicans tried to prevent the arming of merchant ships and in other ways sought to embarrass the President. Federalists retorted that the Republicans, not they, comprised the war party because Republican actions would bring on a civil war. Some Republican members, believing that Adams had withheld the dispatches because they would reveal that France stood ready to negotiate, wanted to see the documents.

Adams, it seems, had misjudged popular sentiment. He had not anticipated, at this point, intense opposition even to measures of defense.[74]

On March 27, 1798, as the result of a caucus of Republican members, three resolutions were introduced into the House with the object of blocking the President's policy. The first proposal said it was inexpedient to resort to war against France, the second that Congress should restrict the arming of private ships, and the third that measures should be taken for the protection of the sea-coast and for internal defense. These resolves, known as the Sprigg Resolutions, led to heated debate but to no action. Federalists opposed them.[75]

Irritated by the intensity of such Republican opposition, and by charges that her husband was deliberately concealing evidence that might prevent war, Abigail Adams expressed her feelings to her sister. "What benefit can war be to him?" she asked. "He has no ambition for military Glory. He cannot add by war to his peace, comfort, or happiness. It must accumulate upon him an additional load of care, toil, trouble, malice, hatred, and I dare say revenge." [76]

Regardless of Adams's own views on war or peace, the pressure for submission of the dispatches to Congress increased. Pickering was convinced that they had to be published immediately, for, he said, "until the insupportable conduct of the French government as therein described shall be fully displayed, the opposition to efficacious measures of defense will be continued." He believed that the dangers of publication must be hazarded to expose the true character of the French government to the American people.

On March 30, as if to satisfy the Republican demands for disclosure, John Allen of Connecticut, "the most virulent Federalist in the House," presented a resolution calling on the President to submit the dispatches, or such parts of them as the public safety would permit.[77] Samuel Smith, a Republican from Maryland, moved that the qualifying proviso be struck out. After a fierce debate, the Republicans forced through Smith's amendment. So, on Monday, April 2, by a vote of 65 to 27, the House demanded the commissioners' dispatches without deletions, and the original instructions as well.[78]

An analysis of the vote shows that this was not truly a party decision, that the Republicans alone did not insure passage of the demand. Extreme Federalists, who had gained some knowledge of the damaging content of the communications, voted with the Republicans to override moderate Federalists. That this action had the makings of a trap can also be seen in the disclosures of another uncompromising Federalist who desired publication of the papers. "The Jacobins want them," he had written. "And in the name of God let them be gratified; it is not the first time they have wished for the means of their destruction."

Two weeks earlier Theodore Sedgwick had reported that "orders will be given immediately to withdraw these envoys from France and there will be told a tale at which every ear will tingle; and unless I am mistaken will give a most fatal blow to the Jacobins." [79]

Suspecting a trap, Gallatin, for one, had refused to join in the call for the papers. Another Republican leader, William B. Giles of Virginia, was overheard saying to colleagues, "You are doing wrong to call for those dispatches. They will injure us." [80]

Adams relished this opportunity to confound his political enemies. On the following day, April 3, he promptly met the House's demand, sending all the deciphered dispatches, including recent ones that brought the story of the Paris commission into the year 1798. To protect the commissioners, he withheld the names of Beaumarchais, Hottinguer, Bellamy, and Hauteval, substituting the letters W, X, Y, and Z for them. He told Congress to reflect carefully on what the consequences might be if the documents were published. [81]

The House immediately locked and guarded its doors, went into secret session, and spent three days examining the correspondence. As the tale unfolded, Republican members were astounded. [82] They recognized that a wider disclosure would probably arouse the public to such frenzy as to precipitate the very war they sought to avoid. Knowing now that the President had not exaggerated the crisis, they stilled the clamor of their own followers for publication. But on April 6, after considerable argument, the House voted to print 1200 copies for use of the members and their constituents. [83]

Three days later, in the Senate, where the documents were also examined, the Federalist majority passed a concurring resolution directing publication. Of course, the contents of the documents, which came to be known as the X Y Z dispatches, were widely known through the gazettes before official publication. Nonetheless, one of the Hamiltonian Federalists, Robert Troup, admitted that Congress' action was without precedent "and a novel and extraordinary act in diplomatic concerns." [84]

This decision to publish, obviously, was a Federalist triumph. Yet, the crisis John Adams had faced a year earlier when he took office was still unresolved; it still overshadowed all else in his administration; and it was more dangerous than ever.[85] Since the worst had happened in Paris, the reaction in the United States might determine whether there would be war or peace. Much would depend, too, on how the Federalists would exploit their triumph.

~~~~~ III ~~~~~

The Black Cockade Fever

It is too late to preach peace, and to say we do not think of war; a defensive war must be waged, whether it is formally proclaimed or not. That, or submission, is before us.

FISHER AMES, *April 1798*

WITH THE X Y Z AFFAIR EXPOSED TO ALL AMERICANS, AND TO THE world, Republicans almost lost hope in trying to block a Federalist program they thought would lead to war.[1] Like other Republicans, Thomas Jefferson insisted that France's refusal to receive the three commissioners, and the revelations in their dispatches, did not "offer a single motive for going to war." The only obstacle to an amicable negotiation with France, he claimed, was the President's speech to the special session of Congress. If Adams were to disavow truculence, the Vice-President asserted, the Directory would negotiate and arrange a peaceful settlement of its differences with the United States.

As Jefferson himself knew, his was a minority view. As a result of the X Y Z disclosures, he feared that "wavering characters" in his own party would "go over to the war measures so furiously pushed by the other party" in order to "wipe off the imputation of being French partisans."

The Vice-President's assumption was sound. Like an electric

current, the disclosures had sent a charge of anger through Congress. "The publication of the instructions to our envoys to the French Republic and their dispatches, is operating admirably," Secretary of State Pickering wrote. "The Democrats in neither House of Congress make much opposition; and out of doors the French Devotees are rapidly quitting the worship of their idol." [2]

Although the people at first appeared too stunned to reveal any decisive change in their general attitude toward France, or toward Adams's foreign policy, Pickering's observation proved accurate enough. As the humiliation suffered by the mission in Paris became clear, many Americans became outspokenly anti-French. Even in western Pennsylvania, where Republicans were numerous and farmers had been sympathetic to the French Revolution, people were swept off their feet by the news from Paris. In New Hampshire when the chaplain in the state legislature was foolish enough to pray for the success of Fench armies, and failed to recommend Adams to divine favor, the young preacher was dismissed. [3]

In Philadelphia there seemed to be no doubt about the reaction. "The public opinion," Abigail Adams observed, "is changing here very fast, and the people begin to see who have been their firm unshaken friends, steady to their interests and defenders of their Rights and Liberties." After all, she pointed out, "the olive Branch, tendered to our Gallic Allies, by our Envoys; has been rejected with scorn." The tricolor cockade of France that many, mostly Republicans, had been wearing a few days before, now practically disappeared. Those who still dared to flaunt these cockades ran the risk of being mobbed and having the tricolor torn from their hats.

Amazed by this depth of public feeling against France, Mrs. Liston reported that "the Democrats are silent, some indeed seem to recant, whether convinced, or waiting a fit moment to rally, I know not." Men spoke with "a degree of violence," she said, "at which I often stare with astonishment." [4]

From other parts of the country came similar reports. Those reports stressed that the dispatches had "the most magical effects" on public opinion. "The effect of the publication . . . on the people," an orthodox Federalist wrote, "has been prodigious. The leaders of the opposition . . . were astonished and confounded at the profligacy of their beloved friends, the French." [5]

Englishmen, too, reacted with astonishment to the X Y Z embroglio. "SHAKESPEARE calls Z an unnecessary letter," one journalist commented. "Our immortal Bard surely would have retracted this contemptuous epithet, had he lived to see this identical letter make a very conspicuous figure in an important negociation." [6]

All during the French crisis Hamilton had been writing essays for the press to warn the people of the danger they faced from the Directory. Now, with the tide of emotion flowing in his direction, he stepped up his efforts to shape popular opinion and to win support for Federalist policy. At the end of March 1798, under the pseudonym "Titus Manlius," and running through April, he wrote a series of newspaper articles called "The Stand." In these he attacked France, outlined his program, and implied that its Republican opponents were subversive. As he had done privately in letters to Adams's department heads, he called publicly for arsenals, an army, a navy, the licensing of privateers, the borrowing in anticipation of new tax revenues, and a suspension of the alliance and other treaties with France by act of Congress.

"The election," Hamilton wrote, "is between tame surrender of our rights or a state of mitigated hostility." Since he believed that his program would not lead to full-scale hostilities, what he sought at this time was commitment to a limited war against France. In his view, expressed earlier, it was "important to avoid war if we can—if we cannot, to strengthen as much as possible the opinion that it proceeds from the Unreasonableness of France. . . ." [7]

Federalists in Congress wasted no time in taking advantage of favorable public sentiment. On April 9, 1798, before Hamilton completed his series of articles, and only a few days after the decision to publish the X Y Z dispatches, Samuel Sewall, a Massachusetts lawyer on the Committee of Defense, upon recommendation of the Secretary of War, introduced the administration's program in the House of Representatives. Sewall's proposals repeated what Adams had sought earlier, including the creation of a provisional army. Since these measures fell below what Hamilton had advised, extreme Federalists tried to substitute Hamilton's program for that of the President.

This action by the Hamiltonians in Congress suggested that they might have serious differences with the President and with those Federalists who looked to his leadership on the nature of the measures needed to meet this latest development in the French crisis. Those who committed themselves to the Hamilton program have often been called High Federalists. Those who disliked aspects of that program, or who preferred to go along with the President's policies when clearly discernible, have been known as Moderate, or Adams, Federalists. But the differences between High and Moderate Federalist were not precise. Some Federalists shifted from one side to another, and many defied classification. Since almost all Federalists at this time, whether or not they wanted it, considered war with France virtually inevitable, this developing difference in the two wings of the party at first caused no difficulty in the war program.[8]

Fisher Ames, a former Federalist leader in the House, told his successor what many in the party probably felt. "It is," he said, "too late to preach peace." Whether or not formally proclaimed, a defensive war must be waged. "The President and his ministers," he pointed out, "are decidedly popular, and if a strong impulse should be given to the people, by the measures of the government, the disorganizers would fall."

This assessment was true, for previously Adams had always suffered in public esteem when compared to Washington. Now he appeared to rank with the Virginian in the public mind, a status that pleased the President, and especially his wife.

Federalists such as Ames, who feared the rise of Republicanism, had welcomed the war crisis and were delighted with Adams's sudden popularity. They saw in these developments the means by which their party could retain power. Foreign policy, they believed, could be used as a weapon against domestic adversaries as well as against the French. They wished to keep patriotism at fever pitch and to identify their own program so closely with patriotism as to make the two appear synonymous. "To be lukewarm after reading the horrid scenes" in the X Y Z letters, one Federalist gazette announced, "is to be criminal—and the man who does not warmly reprobate the conduct of the French must have a soul black enough to be *fit* for *treasons stratagems and spoils.*" [9]

Some belligerent Federalists were even willing to accept civil war to achieve their ends. "The President Shines like a God in the Declaration of his sentiments," the former Secretary of War wrote. "They must and will electrify all the good people of the U S—but all are not good. We must have some short but sharp internal conflicts." [10]

Many Federalists, of course, were convinced that the nation was truly in danger and hence did not view the idea of war with France as merely an excuse, or even the means, for smiting Republicans. Yet war had a particular appeal to extremists because it would help in purging the government of domestic Jacobins and alleged traitors. High Federalists, therefore, adopted the strategy of questioning the loyalty of those who refused to support their war program, while exalting their own patriotism. For a time, this became practically the credo of President Adams himself. Abigail Adams described "those whom the French boast of as their Partizans" as wicked men who would be "adjudged Traitors to their Country." [11]

By repeating similar views, Federalist newspapers kept the people angry and built up a mood for war. Some extremists, arguing that the best defense is the offense, urged preparations for an offensive war against France and Spain, but at the minimum, reprisals against France.

In this mood, and under the guise of patriotism, Federalists tried to muzzle criticism of the government, and were reasonably successful in doing so. They organized vigilance committees to trace the movements of prominent Republicans, even of Vice-President Jefferson. Pickering studied the political loyalties of newspaper editors and favored those who used "all the arts and retrick Hell can invent to blackguard the Republican printers and all they print."

Newspapers which had been politically neutral, or at least had been considered so, became open supporters of the administration. Some three quarters of the press heartily endorsed Adams's policy against France. Moreover, most papers relied almost exclusively on English sources for European news, which meant that American readers saw world affairs as filtered through English lenses.

The Philadelphia *Aurora,* as did lesser Republican journals, staggered from losses in circulation and advertising. Two weeks after publication of the dispatches, the *Aurora* was near financial collapse.[12] Nonetheless, it and other Republican gazettes opposed the Federalist war program, urging the administration to comply with French demands. Compliance, it argued, would be cheaper and would involve less risk for the nation than would war.

Benjamin Franklin Bache, the *Aurora's* editor and grandson of the famous Dr. Benjamin Franklin, described by his enemies as "the greatest fool and the most stubborn sansculotte in the United States," pointed out that the administration had purchased peace with the Barbary pirates of North Africa and had confirmed the purchase with a treaty. He suggested that Adams follow the same principle in dealing with the Directory. Federalists retorted that it would be unthinkable to adopt such a policy toward France, and they charged Bache with being a hireling of the French.

Later, mobs attacked "Benny" Bache's home. Two prominent Federalists, on separate occasions, assaulted him. Adams appointed one of the assailants, Abel Humphreys, who was convicted and fined fifty dollars for attacking Bache, to carry diplomatic dispatches to Europe. Despite the physical danger, Bache refused to be silenced and continued to criticize the administration's policy toward France. So did other Republicans. Some gathered in town meetings, "remonstrating to Congress against war with France!"[13]

There seemed to be only one aspect of foreign policy upon which Republicans, such as Bache, and Federalists agreed. Both agreed that America was in peril. Republicans argued that the danger lay in the Federalist desire for war, and Federalists insisted that the danger lurked in France's aggressive policy toward the United States, abetted by subversive Americans.

THE TRUCULENT PRESIDENT

Many Republicans were convinced that Adams wanted to provoke war, and they protested. Some revived the Revolutionary practice of erecting liberty poles as symbols of protest against the administration's measures. These poles stirred Federalists, who called them "emblems of sedition," to fury.

According to Robert Liston, who would have been pleased with war between France and the United States, the charge that Adams wanted war was false. In his view the administration did not desire war, but did think it practically unavoidable, and did not dread the conflict. After all, some felt, American trade could suffer no greater loss after hostilities began than at present. If forced into war, Adams expected to gain the support of all the people, and eventually the cooperation of the British. Neither the American public nor Britain, Liston believed, would want a closer connection at this time.

Adams told Liston that probably Americans would have to battle the French alone for a year or two and "then Great Britain will help them out of the scrape." Americans, Liston said, eye the conquest of Louisiana, Florida, Saint Domingue, or modern Haiti, and other French islands. The American government's greatest anxiety, he reported, was the possibility of a peace between France and Britain that would leave the Directory free to devote its entire attention to the United States and wreak the vengeance it had threatened. Administration leaders, he felt, "are now convinced that Great Britain is the only bulwark remaining against the oppressive power and the destructive principles of the French Republick. . . ."

Despite the nature of Adams's comments to Liston, to the American public the President gave the appearance of a leader eager for war. George Logan, a Philadelphia Quaker, warned that "wars created by ambitious executives have been undertaken more to their own aggrandizement and power than for the protection of their country." [14]

Adams's warlike attitude seemed most striking in his reaction to formal addresses framed by towns, societies, militia companies, and associations of merchants in support of his stand against France. These resolutions became the most widespread means used by Federalists to express patriotism. Many of these groups sponsored public meetings in which they condemned France and gained numerous signatures in support of their resolutions. An address from New York, for instance, contained four thousand signatures. These resolutions poured into the President's office in a steady flow.

From May until the middle of August 1798 Adams apparently devoted much of his time to the preparation of answers to these addresses.[15] Since the addresses and their replies were published in newspapers over the country, Adams was able through this means to spread his views before the people more effectively than through any other channel. In his replies the President denounced the French, attacked the loyalty of Republicans, and stimulated demands for war. One theme that ran through many of his answers was that the people had to decide whether they or the French would control the American government.

Invariably, Adams identified his political opponents with the French enemy. In a typical statement in May he linked "foreign hostility" with "domestic treachery," and denounced both. In August he explained to a Vermont regiment that the French Directory was trying to obtain control over the American government. "Rather than this I say with you—let us have war." At another time he told a crowd, "The finger of destiny writes on the wall the word: War." [16]

When twelve hundred young men in Philadelphia marched to the President's home to offer their services against France, Adams addressed them in full military uniform, including a sword dangling at his side. On another occasion he told the youth of Boston, "To arms, then, my young friends,—to arms, especially by sea." A Republican newspaper lampooned the eagerness of Boston's young men, who claimed to number five hundred, to defend their country when the frigate *Constitution* lay in Boston harbor lacking half of its crew.[17]

When a delegation from Philadelphia called on the Presi-

dent, according to one story, Mrs. Adams, who insisted on re-
ferring to the Republican opposition as the "French party," presented the Philadelphians with a black cockade, essentially a rose
of black ribbon of about four inches in diameter as had been worn
by American soldiers during the Revolution. As if to replace the
tricolor cockade, worn by Republicans, with an anti-French symbol of patriotism, Federalists quickly adopted the black ribbon as
their own, showing it "as the open and visible sign of Federalism."
Their leaders declared that every true American should sport the
black emblem on his hat, for it would add cement to the Union.
"Every cockade," an editor wrote, "will be another Declaration of
Independence. . . ." Federalist members of Congress, eager to
vaunt their Americanism, were conspicuous in conforming to the
principle of wearing the black cockade. Ironically, as Republicans pointed out, the English cockade was also black.[18]

The spirit of the black cockade, or what a Republican later
lampooned as "COCKADEROPHOBIA," was evident everywhere, even
in churches and places of public entertainment. From pulpits
throughout the land preachers thundered against France as though
urging a crusade.

In one of Philadelphia's fashionable playhouses, the New
Theatre on Chestnut Street, audiences now refused to listen to
French revolutionary airs, such as the "Marseillaise," "Ça Ira,"
and the "Carmagnole." Instead, they turned to "American tunes
and American sentiments." Two of those new popular favorites,
"Hail Columbia" and "Adams and Liberty," were written by Federalists, an editor and a lawyer, it was said, in spurts of patriotism. A foreign visitor remarked that *"Hail Columbia* exacts not
less reverence in *America,* than the Marsellois [*sic*] Hymn in
France, and Rule Britannia in *England."*

Deborah Logan, the wife of a prominent Republican, described life in Philadelphia as a veritable reign of terror, "a state
of society destructive of the ties which in ordinary times bind one
class of citizens to another." She observed that "friendships were
dissolved, tradesmen dismissed, and custom withdrawn from the
Republican party . . . Many gentlemen went armed. . . ."[19]

Even the women wore cockades as badges of party attachment. In later years one congressman recalled seeing women "meet at the church door and violently pluck the badges from one another's bosoms."

By proclamation, the President had set aside May 9, 1798, "as a day of solemn humiliation, fasting, and prayer" throughout the United States. Republicans reacted with defiance. One of their gazettes published a "Psalm for the Federal Fast" that expressed their attitude toward the government's policy. It opened with these lines:

> YE Federal states combine
> In solemn Fast and Prayer
> And urge the powers divine
> To drive us into war [20]

When the day of fast arrived, in the national capital and elsewhere, it began with solemn observances in churches and meeting houses where sermons dwelt on the duties of loyal Americans and on the horrors of French atheism. One preacher in Boston's New North Church shocked his parishioners with a story of French perfidy. Agents from a secret organization in Europe, an offshoot of Freemasonry called the Society of Illuminati, he announced, had invaded the United States. This organization, he claimed, had kindled the French Revolution, aided French armies in their recent successes, and had dedicated itself to the destruction of all civil and ecclesiastical authority. This kind of preaching turned many of the clergy into allies of the Federalists during the French hysteria, and after.[21]

On that same afternoon in Philadelphia the wearers of the black cockade clashed with defiant Republicans, many of whom had replaced the tricolor emblem with a red cockade as the badge of Republicanism. The trouble began as a scuffle between the reds and blacks in the State House yard. It frightened the authorities to such an extent that they called out the light horse soldiers to maintain order. They also posted a guard before President Adams's house and had the streets patrolled all night. The President himself became so alarmed by what he called this terrorism that he ordered chests of arms from the war office brought to his house through back lanes and back doors. He was, he said later,

determined to defend his home at the cost of his life and the lives
of his few servants.[22]

INVASION JITTERS

On the following morning Jonathan Dayton of New Jersey,
Speaker of the House and an opportunistic recent convert to Federalism, added to the climate of fear in Philadelphia. He announced that troops known to be massed in French ports were
not preparing to invade England as had been thought; instead
they were destined for an assault on the United States. Although
Republicans ridiculed the idea of a French invasion as "a mere
bugbear," a month later the leading Federalist gazette, citing "authentic information" from Europe, confirmed this ominous an-
nouncement.[23]

This story tended to support another Federalist rumor, that
of a Negro uprising in the South incited allegedly by the spread
of French revolutionary ideas among slaves. After he had received the X Y Z dispatches Secretary of State Pickering had told
Robert Goodloe Harper of South Carolina that France was secretly fomenting a slave rebellion in the South, and would launch
an invasion of the Southern states from Saint Domingue. Former
Secretary of War, Henry Knox, urged Adams to raise an army for
protection against a possible attack by "ten thousand blacks" re-
cruited by the French. He feared that the invaders would land at
"the defenceless ports of the Carolinas and Virginia," where
slaves would join them in a march of conquest.

Rumors spread saying that special Negro agents were dis-
tributing arms among the slaves in preparation for the French attack. These rumors were repeated in a Federalist pamphlet published in April. "Take care, take care, you sleepy southern fools,"
a Federalist gazetteer warned. "Your negroes will probably be
your masters this day twelve month." [24]

Partly as a result of these rumors, the black cockade fever
rushed southward. In Charleston the people became so fearful of
an attack by the French that they maltreated foreigners and
placed this port city in a state of emergency. On May 5, at a mass

meeting in St. Michael's Church, called to endorse Adams's policy toward France, Charlestonians decided to supplement federal funds with contributions of their own for protection of their city. Eventually, the citizens of Charleston raised about $100,000, but did not use the money to beat off invaders. Instead, they built a sloop of war which they christened, appropriately, the *John Adams*. To protect the harbor, they also erected a small fort, which they named "Fort Pinckney" in honor of their "late envoy to France" who had written that war was "very, very probable."

Fear of invasion by the French enhanced the desire of Federalists to cooperate with Britain. Some even talked of an agreement whereby the United States would take Louisiana and the Floridas, and Britain would seize Saint Domingue. To military men this appeared logical. "Indeed we are vulnerable in the Southern States to an alarming degree," Henry Knox told the President. "The British navy is the only preventative against an invasion of those States from the West India Island." [25]

So concerned were Federalists about the politics of the South, where Republicanism was strong, that they tried to pull George Washington out of retirement at Mount Vernon to help them in stirring up anti-French sentiment. In May 1798 Hamilton suggested that his old chief make a trip through the South, ostensibly for reasons of health but in fact to stimulate demonstrations of loyalty to the government. Replying that he did not think war inevitable, Washington refused. Yet a month and a half later the former President declared that "if the French should be so *mad* as openly and formidably to invade these United States, in expectation of subjugating the Government, laying them under contribution, or in hopes of dissolving the Union, I conceive there can hardly be two opinions respecting their Plan, and their operations will commence in the Southern quarter."

To forestall invasion some High Federalists wanted to strike first with a declaration of war against France. War would also serve another purpose. It would expose the disloyalty of the opposition party and allow Federalists, as patriots, the chance to crush internal opposition in the name of national security. Republicans, they charged, were tools of France and enemies of American society, enemies who would aid the invaders. Jeffersonians were nothing more than domestic Jacobins who threatened the stability of the nation, traitors who had contributed to America's humiliation. With the assistance of French and Irish aliens in the country, it was alleged, the Republicans were plotting to subvert the government. One rumor that reached the President himself said that Frenchmen in Philadelphia had plotted to destroy the city by fire and to massacre the people.[26]

As a result, a nativist frenzy became part of the black cockade fever. Harvard College even omitted the French oration from its commencement exercises to forestall a storm of protest. Among the first foreigners to feel Federalist wrath were French royalist refugees, particularly those in Philadelphia. Most of those refugees probably detested the French republic, yet alarmed Federalists were convinced that in case of war the loyalty of those aliens to their mother country would be stronger than their political prejudices, hence they must be harried out of the country or made harmless.

When Congress began to consider legislation against those and other aliens, Frenchmen prepared themselves to flee the United States. Jefferson reported that "the threatening appearances from the Alien bills have so alarmed the French who are among us, that they are going off. A ship, chartered for themselves for this purpose, will sail within a fortnight for France, with as many as she can carry. Among these I believe will be Volney, who has in truth been the principal object aimed at by the law." [27]

A month later, as if more than mere coincidence, William Cobbett, an English expatriate and a violently anti-French, anti-Jeffersonian, pro-English, and pro-Federalist editor, using the pseudonym "An American," charged that the country had become the resort "of abominably seditious foreigners of every distinction." He singled out Constantin-François Chasseboeuf, Comte de Volney, the French scientist and author who Jefferson said had been marked for Federalist vengeance, as a particularly dangerous carrier of French revolutionary ideas. "Americans!" Cobbett warned, "Beware—at this moment beware of the diplomatic skill of the French republic." [28]

Volney could not be touched. On June 7, nearly three weeks before the first alien bill became law, he left for France on the cartel ship *Benjamin Franklin*. Fearing that Frenchmen who had fled to escape Federalist persecution would be so irritated that their resentment would increase the anger of the Directory against the United States, Jefferson was pleased to learn that Volney at least was not hostile. "He is most thoroughly impressed with the importance of preventing war," the Vice-President wrote, "whether considered with reference to the interests of the two countries, of the cause of republicanism, or of man on the broad scale." [29]

Among those who had sailed with Volney was Victor Marie DuPont, who early in 1798 had been appointed Consul General for the French Republic in Philadelphia to replace Létombe. DuPont had arrived in May, in the midst of the black cockade frenzy, to take up his duties, but President Adams had refused to accept his credentials. The diplomat had decided, therefore, to return home promptly with his countrymen who were fleeing. Since most of the French consuls who had been stationed in the United States were on that ship, France was left without adequate consular representation in America at a time when some kind of open diplomatic connection might be vital in the prevention of full-scale war.[30]

Secretary of State Pickering was delighted with the departures and asked naval authorities for unmolested passage for the *Benjamin Franklin*. Later, a permit guaranteeing safe passage was issued to another ship carrying Frenchmen to Bordeaux. In July and August, after passage of the alien laws, more than a dozen ships loaded with anxious French refugees sailed for France, or Saint Domingue. Not all fled the alien acts. Some feared war; some could not stand living as objects of suspicion and antagonism; and some were merchants forced to return home because Congress had suspended commercial intercourse with France.[31]

Nativist hysteria, roused as though to resist an invading foe, appeared to reach a climax on July 4, 1798. On that Independence Day the native born by the thousands sported the black cockade. In town after town Federalist patriots burned Talleyrand in effigy, and seemingly at every public rally orators praised Adams and damned the French. In one of these orations on the evils of "illuminatism" and French infidelity, Timothy Dwight, Congregational clergyman and Federalist president of Yale College, solemnly warned his fellow Americans that "we may see our wives and daughters the victims of legal prostitution; soberly dishonoured; speciously polluted. . . ." So intense did anti-French sentiment become after warnings such as this that Abigail Adams predicted that if the Directory were to send a new minister to the United States, he would be unable to find a resting place for twenty-four hours.

Like Mrs. Adams, High Federalists rejoiced in the bellicose demonstrations of the people. They were pleased, too, by the President's strong stand against France. The violent and often warlike language in his public addresses, they realized, had probably done more to whip up popular hysteria in favor of war than anything they themselves had done, or could do.

"All men whose opinions I know," one such Federalist wrote, "are unbounded in their applause of the manly, just, spirited, and instructive sentiments expressed by the President in his answers to the addresses." Another High Federalist claimed that Adams's words "have elevated the spirit, and cleared the filmy eyes of many. The people have risen *gradatim;* every answer was a step up stairs." [32] To keep the anti-French fever high, the President's speeches of the spring and summer of 1798, hailed by Federalists as "the scriptures of Political Truth," were collected and promptly published as a book.

Skeptical of the strident patriotism of the black cockade, Republicans believed that the President's addresses insulted France unnecessarily and crippled whatever opportunities there remained to save the peace. "Perhaps it is a universal truth," Madison commented, "that the loss of liberty at home is to be charged to provisions against danger real or pretended from abroad."

Jefferson agreed, and Madison then observed that "the answers of Mr. Adams to his addressors form the most grotesque scene in the tragi-comedy acted by the government." [33]

There was considerable truth to the Republican charges, yet it was also true that in his replies to the citizenry Adams did not insist on full-scale war. Despite his bellicose words he left the door unlocked, though not open, for a diplomatic accord, saying he would willingly settle differences with France on an honorable basis. This attitude appeared to reflect the President's changing views on whether or not war was desirable. Shortly after informing Congress of the X Y Z letters he had put aside the idea of recommending a declaration of war. On the basis of information from his son John Quincy in Berlin, he concluded that the Directory would not itself declare war on the United States.

Yet the President, under pressure from some High Federalists to ask Congress for a declaration of war against France, wavered in his decision against such action. As weeks passed and the envoys did not return, he became uneasy. Their absence and rumors that Gerry was negotiating alone in Paris gave new hope to Republicans in their resistance to the administration's program of mitigated hostility and brought dismay to Federalists.

As for Adams, in trying to wage a defensive war with uncertainty as to the extent of presidential powers and without a formal declaration, he encountered one frustrating problem after another. He learned, as High Federalists pointed out, that in dealing with Congress "half measures are much harder to carry, and to support, than such as great perils call for." This experience and the intensity of the popular response of the X Y Z disclosures led him to believe that the real resources of the nation could be mobilized only by a declaration of war, which in May and June he again began to consider seeking.[34]

WAR FOOTING

It was against this domestic background of the patriotic fervor of the black cockade, of High Federalist desires for a declared war, of Republican resistance to any warlike measures, and of Adams's uncertainty about a declared war that Congress debated and acted on a program that placed the nation in a state of limited, or Quasi-War. With majorities, in both houses, Federalists voted bill after bill that put the country on a war footing. Impatiently eager to adopt the war measures, the Senate even suspended the rule requiring the lapse of a day between the several readings of a bill. From the end of March to the middle of June, Congress enacted some twenty laws for waging the Quasi-War.

If the threat of expanded war were real, the Federalists were justified in their desire for haste. In almost every category the country's defenses were lamentably weak. Since there was no navy, and the coastal forts were practically useless, America's shores seemed open to invasion. Only at Philadelphia was there a fort capable of offering resistance to a determined attacker. Other forts, at New York and Baltimore, had been stripped of their guns to provide armament for three frigates not yet ready for action. The army, numbering only 3,500 men, could hardly hurl back a raid in force, let alone an invasion. On top of these inadequacies, the country suffered from a shortage of cannon and small arms.[35]

Since preparation had to begin somewhere, and the Quasi-War was being fought at sea, several of Congress' first measures after publication of the X Y Z dispatches augmented the naval establishment and created the Department of the Navy. Until the end of April 1798, when Adams signed the law establishing the department, naval affairs were under the control of the War Department. As tension mounted with France this proved unsatisfactory because Secretary of War McHenry was considered a bungler. Federalists argued, in addition, that a separate department for naval affairs was necessary to impress Europe. For the first Secretary of the Navy, Adams nominated George Cabot of Massachusetts, who declined. The President then appointed Benjamin Stoddert, a moderate Federalist and prosperous shipping merchant from Georgetown, Maryland, known as "a true American" and a man of sound judgment and active mind, qualities that Adams sorely needed in his cabinet at this time.[36]

Increases in naval power were authorized by a law of April 27, 1798, which permitted the President to obtain twelve ships of not more than twenty-two guns each, and an act of May 4 which enabled him to procure cannon, arms, and ammunition. At the end of the month, on May 28, another law, directed against French privateers and commerce raiders, authorized him to use the Navy to "seize, take, and bring into port" French ships found hovering on America's coast with the intent of attacking American shipping and to retake vessels captured by the French. On this same day, in response to the President's request, Congress gave him discretionary power to increase the strength of the regular army.

When Federalists forced the first of these measures through the House, a Republican, speaking in opposition, said: "Let no man flatter himself that the vote which has been given is not a declaration of war. Gentlemen know that this is the case." [37]

Regardless of the nature of these measures, Federalists wanted to go further. They wished to destroy whatever remained of the old friendship with France, for after all she was now the enemy. They tried, accordingly, to gain support for a bill that would void all treaties with France, the alliance and the commercial treaty of 1778, and the consular convention of 1788. Since Republicans opposed the measure, and no one yet knew whether or not the commissioners had safely left France, it was thought wise at this time to postpone such action. "To annul the French treaty," Federalists still felt, "is indispensable. Every day's delay is perilous."

Other action against France could be, and was, taken. Federalists in Congress voted an embargo, to go into effect on July 1, on all commerce with France and her dependencies. This act, signed on June 13, also prohibited all French ships, armed or unarmed, from entering American ports, unless in distress. If the French government were to acknowledge American grievances, then the President could suspend the law before its date of expiration, which was the end of the next congressional session. [38]

As this legislative program advanced, Republican leaders became more firmly convinced than ever that Federalists were determined to have war and to replace "representative republican government with a military or executive despotism." "By Peace, we shall stand," one Republican announced, "by *War*, we may fall."

Since the Republicans were unable to stem the anti-French

legislation, their representatives adopted the strategy of agreeing to measures of internal defense while opposing those seemingly designed for war. Jefferson, who thought that the decision for war or peace lay with his own country, believed that if war could be put off until the end of the congressional session, it might be avoided altogether. "The question of war and peace," he asserted, "depends now on a toss of cross and pile."

Secretary of State Pickering saw no choice between war or peace. He considered war with France inevitable. Henrietta Liston wrote, "This country is preparing for War," and expressed amazement at how suddenly a whole nation could switch its sentiments toward France and England with its politics. There were moments, she said, "when I can almost impute it to Magic. . . ."

Since the Federalists were approaching war step by step, the Vice-President believed that Republicans in Congress could defeat the more drastic measures if only they would act together. Instead, enough Republicans left Congress while it was in session to give Federalists decisive majorities, even in the House of Representatives where Federalism had been weakest.[39]

Albert Gallatin tried to rally his minority forces to block the war program. As a result, he bore the brunt of Federalist vilification. He insisted that war was unnecessary, was in itself a humiliation, and that French dominance of the United States was not the only alternative to war. Americans should accept the losses they had suffered from French depredations and seek to avoid new injuries, he argued, for war would bring even greater loss. Patience, he maintained, should be the theme of American foreign policy. Americans should wait for the war in Europe to end, for when that happened the attacks against their shipping would cease. Republicans also pointed out that the British were as guilty of despoiling American shipping as were the French, but Federalists did not wish war with Britain.

On June 16, 1798, at the height of this congressional debate and war fever, John Marshall, without anyone knowing beforehand of his coming, landed in New York. Two days later, as he approached Philadelphia, Secretary of State Pickering and three corps of the city's cavalry in full regalia went out to greet him. Within the city ringing bells announced the diplomat's return, and crowds lined the streets. Marshall had returned to a welcome for a national hero. Senators, representatives, and just plain citizens swarmed around the Virginian to praise him and to congratulate him on his safe return.[40]

That evening, to show their "affection, approbation and respect," the Federalist members of Congress entertained Marshall with a banquet at Oeller's Hotel, Philadelphia's finest. There, some one hundred and twenty distinguished guests, including members of the President's cabinet and justices of the supreme court, paid tribute to his "patriotic firmness" in Paris. Admirers drank sixteen toasts in his honor. Of these, the thirteenth, "Millions for defense, but not one cent for tribute," received the loudest applause. It quickly became the slogan of Federalist patriots. Marshall himself seemingly gave substance to that war cry by declaring that an accommodation with France on terms compatible with American independence was practically impossible. Yet he had said privately that he thought France did not want war with the United States.

If, before this, any Federalist had doubted that the mission to France had failed and that America's ally had now become an enemy, Marshall's return and the events accompanying it dispelled all such remnants of uncertainty. War hysteria seemed to rise to a higher level than before. Many Americans now thought war would come at any moment.[41]

On the day Marshall had arrived in New York, and before the Department of State had released the official text, the Philadelphia *Aurora* had published a letter from Talleyrand to the envoys in Paris. This was the note in which Talleyrand ignored Pinckney and Marshall, and offered to discuss Franco-American problems only with Gerry. Federalists charged that Bache's "French paper" had printed the letter at the order of the Directory, and that publication itself was proof of a direct link between the French government and disloyal Americans who acted as its agents. Bache denied any sinister connection, defending his action as serving the cause of peace. The Adams administration, he

claimed, had withheld the letter from the public so that Federalist efforts to bring on an unnecessary war with France would not
be impeded.

Up to this point, in addition to his bellicose speeches, Adams
had been contributing to the black cockade fever by sending
newly arrived dispatches from the commissioners, accompanied
by special messages, directly to Congress. He had done so on May 4
and June 5. Now, on June 18, the day of Marshall's entry into
Philadelphia, he forwarded the eighth dispatch, a document that
contained Talleyrand's note, which the *Aurora* had printed, and
the commissioners' response.

Federalists in Congress immediately claimed that this correspondence offered an incontrovertible answer to the Bache publication. The dispatch, Federalists insisted, should itself be published to counteract the machinations of the Directory and its
American agents. Four days later a joint congressional resolution
ordered the Secretary of State to print ten thousand copies of the
latest X Y Z correspondence "to be distributed *gratis* throughout
the United States, and particularly in such parts thereof, wherein
the dissemination of information through the medium of newspapers, is the most obstructed." [42]

On June 18, 1798, also, the President signed the Naturalization Act, the first of four laws that were to be known collectively
as the Alien and Sedition Acts. Based on the assumption that a
French faction within the country threatened national survival,
these laws constituted a far-reaching program to destroy Republicanism and to force internal conformity to Federalist war aims.
They were the fruit of an unchecked Federalist extremism, of a
paranoiac fear of ill-defined conspiracies against the established
order, and of a superpatriotism committed to the crushing of
dissenters. This package of legislation stands as an early example
of a political intolerance that has threaded its way through America's history. Although mainly the work of High Federalists, these
laws won wide support in the party.

Formerly, five years of residence had been required before
an alien could qualify for citizenship. The Naturalization Act
raised this period to fourteen years, required aliens, under pen-

alty of imprisonment, to register with designated government officials, and subjected foreign residents to a system of surveillance. Since most immigrants, particularly the Irish, who hated England and sympathized with France, became Republicans, this law was designed to cut off one source of Jeffersonian political strength. This was proper, Federalists maintained, for abusive aliens were in fact agents of France.[43]

Three days later the President sent a special message to Congress expressing pleasure over Marshall's arrival "at a place of safety where he is justly held in honor." Adams also included a letter from Gerry that explained Gerry's conduct, intentions, and prospects. "I presume," Adams said, "that before this time he has received fresh instructions . . . and therefore the negotiation may be considered at an end." Then the President offered a pledge. "I will never," he announced, "send another minister to France without assurances that he will be received, respected, and honored as the representative of a great, free, powerful, and independent nation."

A declaration of war was now widely anticipated. High Federalists even blocked efforts to adjourn Congress early so that they could help keep the war spirit strong. "To separate Congress now," Jefferson observed, "will be withdrawing the fire from under a boiling pot." [44]

The reasoning of the High Federalists was logical enough. "The impulse given by the Despatches to the people is excellent, and is yet strong," one of them explained; "but it is too much to expect that any popular impulse will last long, and not only go right, but keep government right."

Marshall himself, who had been publicly belligerent, had already privately caused a change in the government's position that would displease extreme Federalists. To the President and Secretary of State he reported his own conviction that the Directory did not want full-scale war. Instead, it believed it could, with other means, coerce the United States into complying with its demands. This led Adams, who had been prepared to ask Congress for a declaration of war, to postpone his decision. If France saw that he could not be intimidated, and that he had the support of the masses, perhaps she might be willing to end the Quasi-War on reasonable terms. It was on the basis of this reasoning that he had left an opening for a possible diplomatic accommodation in his special message to Congress.[45]

On June 22, the day following Adams's special message, Congress empowered him to appoint commissioned officers for an "Additional Army" of 10,000 men. Earlier, on May 28, Congress had authorized increases in the army, but had made no arrangements for recruiting, or the commissioning of officers. In other words, the law provided only the framework for an army. The soldiers of the Additional Army were to serve "during the continuance of the existing differences between the United States and the French Republic, unless sooner discharged."

On July 16 Congress authorized the President to increase the regular military establishment with twelve regiments of infantry of 700 men each and with six troops of light dragoons. These regiments, planned mainly on paper, were to be part of what came to be known as the "Provisional Army." This Provisional Army of 50,000 men was not to be formed until full-scale war began, or when the President decided that national security, such as defense against a threatened invasion, required it. In addition, the President was authorized to call 80,000 militia to active duty.

Adams was never happy with the idea of an expanded army. To him the creation of a standing army was only one of the defensive measures in the Quasi-War, and a secondary one at that. The nation's main weapon, he felt, should be a strong navy.[46]

Everyone in the government expected George Washington to emerge from retirement to take command of the new Army and to repel a French invasion if it should come. His name still carried political magic and would bring additional strength to the administration in the war crisis. On the day Congress passed the army officer bill Adams wrote to Washington saying that "if the French come here, we must learn to march with a quick step, and to attack, for, in that way only, they are said to be vulnerable," and he added, "we must have your name."

Twelve days later, without further word, Adams submitted the former President's name to the Senate as Commander in Chief with the rank of lieutenant general. Previously Washington had been a major general. The Senate promptly and unanimously confirmed the nomination. Adams then ordered Secretary of War McHenry to go to Mount Vernon with the appointment and to obtain the general's advice on the organization of the army, especially on the appointment of other high-ranking officers. Since Washington's bitterness against the French now equaled that of the High Federalists, he accepted the appointment, but with two conditions. He asked that he not be called to assume active command until or unless war began, and that he have the privilege of selecting his own general officers, men "such as I can place confidence in." [47]

This seemingly minor question of the selection and rank of the staff officers for the Provisional Army immediately became a crucial one in the politics of the Federalist party and indirectly in the conduct of the Quasi-War. Driven by restless ambition and dreams of military glory he had long cherished, Hamilton wanted the Army's second post, that of Inspector General. Since Washington would not take command until absolutely necessary, the second ranking officer would become the true head of the Army, and most likely even military operations in the field would fall under his direction. To gain the second position Hamilton had the active support of three of Adams's department heads, as well as of Washington himself.

Through McHenry, Washington gave the President his choice of general staff officers, with three major generals at the top of the list in this order: Hamilton, as Inspector General, Charles Cotesworth Pinckney, and Henry Knox. Adams, who detested and distrusted Hamilton, would not advance him over Pinckney and Knox, who outranked the New Yorker in the old army. "That man," Abigail Adams said of Hamilton, "would in my mind become a second Buonaparty if he was possessed of equal power."

Indignant and hurt, Knox refused to serve under Hamilton. Nonetheless, Pickering, McHenry, and Wolcott, insisted that the President give Hamilton the second command. So determined were they to have Hamilton that when Congress, on July 16, passed a bill increasing the Army to twelve regiments, McHenry immediately asked Hamilton to make plans for the organization of those forces. While expressing a willingness to do so, Hamilton said he would form full plans only "after receiving an official communication of my appointment." [48]

This effort to make Hamilton the ranking major general in the Provisional Army began to awaken the President to the significance of the fact that he did not possess the full loyalty of his cabinet, and that Hamilton sought to exercise control over foreign policy. This issue, like the edge of a knife, also began to cut into the unity of the Federalist party, particularly on policy toward France.[49]

REPRESSION AT HOME

While the question of rank in the Provisional Army was being debated, Federalists in Congress stepped up the pace of their war program. On the theory that the government need not wait for a declaration of war before expelling French agents and taking action against their American collaborators, Congress passed, and the President signed, two alien acts and a sedition law. In part at least, the continuing fear of a French invasion, aided and supported by domestic Jacobins, contributed to the passage of these laws.

Staunch Federalists, such as the handsome, elegant, and eloquent Harrison Gray Otis of Massachusetts, argued in Congress that "French apostles of sedition" had prepared the way for the fall of Holland and Switzerland to revolutionary forces. "Do we not know," he added, "that the French nation . . . [has] organized bands of aliens as well as their own citizens, in other countries, to bring about their nefarious purposes. . . . By these means they have overrun all the republics in the world but our own. . . . And may we not expect the same means to be employed against this country? We certainly might," Otis said in reply to his own question.[50]

Gallatin responded for the Republicans, arguing that the Federalist fear of a domestic conspiracy designed to place the government under a French yoke was imaginary, based on a misreading of history and not on any existing danger in the United States. The revolutions in Holland and Switzerland, he explained, had not been designed by resident French aliens as Federalists claimed. In both countries an invading French army, as well as local citizens, had overthrown the government. Moreover, he insisted, Federalists had to do more than contend that because events had fallen into a certain pattern in other republics, developments in the United States would follow a similar course.

Federalists continued, nonetheless, to argue by analogy. They claimed, for instance, that the reason why the French and their revolutionary doctrines had not succeeded in overthrowing England's government was that the English had passed anti-alien laws. "Unless we follow their example," the Federalist leader in the House warned, "we shall not, like them, escape the scourge which awaits us." [51]

The army issue, too, was tied to the Alien and Sedition laws. When High Federalists called for a standing army to repel the purported invasion, the opposition charged that the talk of a French attack amounted to nothing more than subterfuge to cover the actual design of using the army to enforce the sedition act and silence the opposition. The administration intended, one critic said, "to arm one half of the people, for the purpose of keeping the other in awe." [52]

Regardless of the Republican arguments, Federalists went ahead with their repressive legislation, and not one prominent Federalist, neither Adams, nor Washington, nor Hamilton, opposed it, though Marshall spoke out against the laws after they had been enacted. The first of these laws, the Alien Friends Act of June 25, 1798, dealt with the problem of alleged French agents. Some 30,000 Frenchmen reputedly resided in the United States, and each was suspected of being devoted to the mother country. The act gave the President extraordinary power over aliens by allowing him to deport those "dangerous to the peace and safety of the United States." Limited to a period of two years, this act was designed to cope only with the French crisis. It made every alien liable to arbitrary arrest and deportation, in peace or war, and climaxed a wave of nativism in Federalist areas, notably in New England, that had been set off by publication of the X Y Z correspondence.

The second alien act, or Alien Enemies Act of July 6, would apply only in case of a declared war or invasion, and after a presidential proclamation. It permitted the President to restrain, arrest, or deport enemy aliens on terms he might see fit to impose in order to preserve the public safety. Since methods of enforcement were defined, even Republicans supported this measure.

As the capstone for their internal war program, the Federalists enacted the Sedition Act, a law of July 14 called by Republicans a "Gag Law," which attempted to define sedition and prescribe punishment. The intensity of Federalist feeling against France can be seen in the original draft of the bill. That version declared that France and her people, "in consequence of their hostile conduct toward the United States," were enemies and that anyone convicted of aiding the French would suffer the penalty of death.

Since these drastic terms aroused heavy opposition, Federalists were forced to revise their bill. In its final form the sedition law prescribed punishment, by fine and imprisonment, for conspiracies against the government and for scandalous statements uttered against it, the Congress, or the President. This law, based on the Federalist assumption that there would be a declared war against France, was to expire on the last day of Adams's term. One of its objects was to intimidate or silence Republicans and other critics and thus to force a united front against France.[53]

The Alien and Sedition Acts, Adams admitted in later years, "were war measures, and intended altogether against the advocates of the French and peace with France." Under these laws, with Secretary of State Pickering as their chief enforcement officer, and Hamilton a leading advocate of their enforcement, the spirit of the black cockade became one of intolerant, oppressive, and, at times, hysterical native Americanism. "It is patriotism to write in favor of our government," a Federalist journal announced, and "it is sedition to write against it."

A short time later, after yellow fever had once again taken

possession of Philadelphia, a Republican pamphleteer commented acidly that the fever was "justly deserved by all the male inhabitants," and might prove "a happy check to a much worse one; the Black Cockade Fever—I mean the fever, that under pretense of defending us from a foreign war, aims at provoking a *civil* one." [54]

Republicans were equally bitter about foreign policy, believing that the administration had done everything it could to turn France against the United States. Under Adams, "our present Viceroy," some charged, the country had become a client of Britain, and hence Republicans persisted in their fight against the Federalist armament program. Since the Federalist majorities were too large to be stopped, Congress continued to enact anti-French legislation in support of the program.

After long debate Congress passed a law, signed on June 25, 1798, allowing American merchant ships to arm and defend themselves, but only against France, by resisting and capturing any armed French vessel that attempted to search them or attacked them. Federalist merchants had long wanted this right so that they could arm their ships that sailed from England to the United States. Since all carried British goods, those ships were subject to obnoxious French decrees, and hence needed protection.

Proceeds from the disposal of vessels captured under this law were to go in equal halves to the crew of the capturing ship and to its owners. A similar procedure for the disposition of ships captured by the Navy itself was enacted on June 28. This law allowed condemnation of captured ships, stipulated that the proceeds, in most instances, would be divided equally between the crew of the capturing vessel and the federal government, and that captured crews might be jailed.

Two days later another act designed to strengthen the Navy was approved. It allowed the President to accept as many as twelve ships from private individuals. In exchange, he would give the shipowners United States bonds bearing interest not to exceed 6 per cent. The President could also accept ships as gifts.

Next, Congress provided for detachments of Marines to be

employed in the armed ships and galleys of the United States. Although fighting men called Marines had been on duty in the
Treasury Department's revenue cutters for a number of years,
they were not part of the military establishment. Each unit was
commanded by the captain of the ship on which it served. Now,
an act of July 11 established a Marine Corps with a table of
organization of its own and authorized the President to form the
Marines into detachments.[55]

To pay for this expanded war program Congress voted a direct property tax, approved on July 14, of two million dollars. In
anticipation of the tax revenues, and so that the program could be
launched quickly, Congress authorized the President to borrow
the two million at a rate of interest not to exceed 6 per cent. In
addition, Adams was given power to borrow five million dollars in
any way he could.

This tax fell on two kinds of property, houses and slaves. On
houses the tax graduated. For example, on a dwelling with
the market value of two hundred dollars the tax was forty cents,
but when the value reached five hundred dollars the rate became
thirty cents per hundred dollars of valuation. For every slave,
from twelve to fifty years old, the tax was fifty cents.

In principle Republicans favored a direct tax. They did not,
therefore, resist enactment of this law, and hence it did not pass
as wholly a Federalist measure. If Republicans had opposed it,
they would have exposed themselves to the charge that they were
bent on crippling all measures of defense. Since they did attempt,
with some vigor, to change the mode of levying the tax, they were
able later to profit from its widespread unpopularity.[56]

On July 7, almost a week before the direct tax became law,
and even though Pinckney and Gerry were still in France, Adams
had signed an act formally abrogating all treaties with France.
Under the Constitution treaties were the supreme law of the land.
Some of the war measures conflicted with provisions in the
French treaties. This left the possibility that part of the Federalist
program might be considered unlawful. To avoid this difficulty
and to bury the alliance of 1778 as Federalists desired, Congress
had voted this law. The measure passed the Senate by a vote of

14 to 5, with more than a third of the members, mostly Republicans, absent. Six days later, stressing French hostilities against Americans as the reason, the President revoked the exequaturs of Consul General Joseph Philippe Létombe and of all other French consuls remaining in the United States. Formal ties with France were now practically severed.[57]

Several weeks earlier a step had been taken to break the last informal connection. On June 25 Secretary of State Pickering, on the President's instructions, had sent Gerry a stinging rebuke for remaining alone in Paris. He ordered Gerry to break off discussions with Talleyrand and to return immediately to Philadelphia.[58] Although Federalists scoffed at Gerry's reports, Republicans had hailed his efforts to preserve peace as the only worthwhile activity carried on under Adams. Republicans were, therefore, unhappy over Pickering's instructions to Gerry.

"It is a curious fact," Bache wrote, "that America is making war with France and *not* treating, at the very moment the Minister for Foreign Affairs fixes upon the very day for opening a negotiation with Mr. Gerry. What think you of this, Americans?"

On July 3 Edward Livingston, a Republican from New York, introduced a resolution in the House calling on the President to authorize Gerry to negotiate a treaty with Talleyrand. Livingston had based his motion on the idea that Gerry had the power to negotiate alone because the commission of the three envoys had been joint and several. Talleyrand had interpreted Gerry's power in the same way. Federalists attacked Livingston's proposal as infamous, scandalous, and even treasonous, and it was defeated by a vote of 51 to 30.[59]

THE ELUSIVE DECLARATION OF WAR

What many Federalist leaders wanted and anticipated, including the President himself at this time, was a declaration of war against France. Articles in the leading Federalist gazettes urged naked war, and High Federalists insisted that Congress must declare it.[60]

Perhaps typical of High Federalist thinking were the views

of Theodore Sedgwick, a politician of limited talent and conservative views often associated with a clique of ideological con-
servatives within the Federalist party. The group was called the
Essex Junto because earlier most of the members had lived in
Essex County, Massachusetts. Sedgwick believed that a declaration of war was necessary to prevent Republicans from recovering
ground they had lost as a result of the X Y Z exposures, meaning
to keep the Federalist party in power. Every Federalist senator
but one, he wrote, favored an immediate declaration. Unless defeat appeared certain, Sedgwick reported, the Speaker thought
the House would vote on war by July 4.[61]

Believing also that Congress would soon declare war, George
Cabot, an Essex County Federalist, wrote, "It is true that we shall
do little more at first than provide for our own defense, but we
are capable of greater efforts after we are fully engaged, and a
variety of considerations unite to render our association in the
war extremely favorable to G[reat] B[ritain]; we are at least sufficient for a make weight where the scales are so nearly even." He
was convinced that in concert with Britain the United States
could command the seas in opposition to virtually all of Europe.
As a result, those two nations would "enjoy exclusively" the commerce of most of the world, including that of the French colonies.[62]

High Federalists saw other advantages in a formal declaration of war. It would, they thought, rouse the spirit of the people,
facilitate the collection of taxes, quicken the military preparations, and cut off the correspondence of Republicans with France
by making such correspondence a crime punishable by law.

Despite these alleged advantages, and the pressure they
exerted on Congress, High Federalists were uncertain of majority
support in the House for a declaration of hostilities. Some
claimed that sentiment for war in Congress was "far behind the
people" and that "the members still talk too much of peace." On
the evening of July 4, dependable Federalists from both houses of
Congress held a caucus to determine if they had the votes to force
a declaration of war. After heated debate, and after "counting
noses," the leaders were mortified to find that the moderates

would not go beyond an undeclared naval war against France.[63]

Still, the extremists persisted. On the following day that violently partisan Federalist, John Allen of Connecticut, introduced a resolution in the House calling for a committee "to consider the expedience of declaring, by Legislative act, the state and relation subsisting between the United States and the French Republic." High Federalists had no doubt about that relation. "We are," one of them declared, "now in a state of war." When the resolution was debated the next day it became clear it could not pass. The House voted down the motion without a roll call.[64]

The crucial position of the moderates could also be seen in the votes on a bill that allowed the Navy to take French ships beyond American waters and permitted the commissioning of privateers. On June 30, when the House began consideration of this bill, Peleg Sprague, a New Hampshire Federalist, moved to expand the proposal by allowing the capture of all French ships, whether armed or unarmed. Such a law would have abolished the essentially defensive character of the Quasi-War. Sprague's proposal was defeated 32–41.

Two days later debate focused on the privateering section of the bill. Federalists made it plain that they wished to do more than defend American commerce, the stated original purpose of the bill. They wanted to injure France. Republicans could and did point out that the measure was avowedly belligerent. Furthermore, since few French merchant ships sailed the seas, disappointed American privateers would be tempted to prey on neutrals. What Federalists were after, Republicans asserted, was a test vote on whether or not a declaration of war would pass the House.

According to Robert Goodloe Harper of South Carolina, the United States did not have to decide on war or when it would come. "War is made upon us," he exclaimed. There was also a legal issue involved, he said. Without privateering commissions the crews of American merchantmen would not be treated as prisoners of war, but as pirates. The privateering section, therefore, was not killed.

Sprague then renewed his motion, which in effect called for

offensive war without a formal declaration. The roll call thus indicated the sectional strength of the war party in the House. The middle states refused to go along with the measure, the South stood firmly against it, and even New England weakened by failing to give it full support. In the final vote Sprague's proposal met defeat with 31 for and 52 against it. This was, in a sense, the closest the House came to taking a test vote on full-scale war.

One moderate Federalist who voted against the measure explained not only his attitude, but that of others also. He thought "we should have war; but he did not wish to go on faster to this state of things than the people of this country, and the opinion of the world would justify."

As finally passed by Congress, and signed by Adams on July 9, this "Act further to protect the commerce of the United States" extended naval operations to the seven seas. It permitted the Navy to take armed French ships anywhere and authorized the President to commission privateers. This law was based on the theory that the miscarriage of justice in French ports nullified the usual rights of visit and search of neutral merchantmen. Adams sent out the naval order to capture in all seas on July 10.[65]

As this extraordinary session of the Fifth Congress drew to a close, High Federalists—men such as George Cabot, Stephen Higginson of Massachusetts, Philip J. Schuyler of New York, Fisher Ames, and Timothy Pickering—regretted that no declaration of war had been voted. John Adams shared this regret. "Indeed we are all but at war," Abigail Adams explained. "All we need is a declaration of war . . . one undoubtedly would have been made—ought to have been made—but for Mr. Gerry's unaccountable stay in France." [66]

When Congress adjourned on July 19 still another objective of the High Federalists was unattained. Hamilton had not yet obtained the second position in the Provisional Army. The President was thus in the paradoxical position of opposing the leaders of his own party on the army question, and welcoming their support on the war issue. At this point Adams apparently believed that the people favored war, and that only disloyal obstructionists blocked it. "The people throughout the United States, with a few exceptions," his wife reported, "would have wholeheartedly joined in the most decided declaration which Congress could have made . . . but the majority in Congress did not possess firmness and decision enough to boldly make it." [67]

Robert Goodloe Harper explained the decision against war with less emotion. "Many persons were of opinion that we ought to go the last lengths, and declare war," he wrote, "which they deemed the most manly and honourable course, as well as the safest; but others thought it best to confine ourselves to defence and preparation, and leave the French either to discontinue their attacks, or to declare war, as they might think best. This course was finally adopted." [68]

This attitude made it clear to Adams that he could not obtain unity and broad support for full-scale war. In Virginia there were hostile demonstrations against him, and John Marshall was publically insulted. Under these circumstances it would have been folly for Federalists, with a slender majority in Congress, to rush the country into open war. This policy of waiting for the French to enlarge the war had the merit of maintaining Federalist unity.[69]

Although disappointed in this course of action, neither Adams nor the High Federalists had compelling reasons for despair over the work of Congress. They had aroused the martial spirit of the people, gained support for at least a partial war, and had freed the nation formally, if not legally, from the entangling alliance of 1778, which practically all Federalists detested.

"I never reflect upon the recent conduct of France towards us," one representative Federalist wrote, "without an ejaculation to Heaven for its special favor in giving us cause to dissolve our connection with her. It was a connection pregnant with the most destructive poison to our morals. . . . I consider the act of Congress which rescinded the treaties as a new declaration of our freedom and independence; and if my wishes were to be gratified, the day in which the act finally passed would be celebrated as a great anniversary festival." [70]

As summer began to fade it seemed obvious to most Federalists, and to other Americans, too, that France was an enemy state.

The Attorney General even advanced this view as an official opinion. He announced "that there exists not only an *actual* maritime war between France and the United States, but a maritime war *authorized* by both nations." [71]

Nonetheless, the question of a declared war was still a live one. "Wage war and call it self-defence; forbear to call it war," another High Federalist had advised. Arouse the people to danger, and bring them to full-scale war gradually.[72] Such men believed that the measures voted by Congress would provoke further French hostility, which would be as welcome to them as rain to farmers caught in a drought. Then moderate Federalists, and even Republicans, would be forced to acquiesce in a declaration of war.[73] Republicans could then oppose war at the risk of political suicide.

Disappointed over Congress' failure to declare war, George Cabot lamented that "it is impossible to make the people feel or see distinctly that we have much more to fear from peace than war." He believed that "war, open and declared, would not only deprive our external enemy of his best hopes, but would also extinguish the hopes of internal foes."

Pinckney reported that France herself, in time, would probably launch unlimited war against the United States. "If we would have peace with France," Pinckney advised, "it must be obtained, not by negotiation, but by the sword . . . I am convinced we must fight for its preservation." [74] In the late summer and autumn of 1798, therefore, the leaders of the Federalist party had to wait for overt acts from France, which many felt were certain to come, before they could obtain the full-scale war, supported by a united people, that they desired.[75]

❧ IV ❧

Neither Peace nor War

*Congress have left the country neither in peace nor in war!
& france [sic] is too skilfull not to profit from this ambiguity
of situation.*

RUFUS KING, *September 1798*

LIKE ALMOST EVERYONE ELSE WHO COULD, JOHN AND ABIGAIL ADAMS
wished to flee Philadelphia before yellow fever started taking its
yearly toll.[1] As soon as Congress adjourned they tried to dash for
Quincy, but their trip northward was not as swift as desired. The
President had to pay a price for his new popularity. At almost
every point on his route he met cheering crowds, and when he
stopped the people greeted him with dinners and receptions he
could not gracefully turn aside. Invariably, he responded with
speeches of his own that struck a patriotic note and breathed defiance of France.

All this activity, the rigors of travel, and the fact that the
weather turned hot, was too much for Abigail. She became exhausted, and by the time the Adamses arrived in Quincy she was
dreadfully sick. The doctors her husband summoned from Boston
to attend her soon ran through their stock of remedies without
improving her condition. So concerned was the President that
during much of August 1798 he neglected affairs of state to watch
over her.

One problem Adams could not ignore, even in his Quincy household surrounded by the silence of sickness, was that stemming from Hamilton's desire to gain the second command in the Provisional Army. On July 30 Hamilton asked Secretary of War McHenry to call him and Henry Knox to active duty. The Secretary then requested such authority from the President.[2]

Adams replied on August 14 that he did not wish to order Knox and Hamilton into service until the question of rank had been settled. "In my opinion, as the matter now stands," the President said, "General Knox is legally entitled to rank next to General Washington; and no other arrangement will give satisfaction." Pinckney, too, must rank before Hamilton. If George Washington consents to the arrangement, Adams went on, then you may call these officers into active service "when you please." Any other plan would cause delay and confusion.[3]

Alarmed, McHenry replied that the order of ranking he had recommended, with Hamilton the senior major general, had proceeded "originally and exclusively" from Washington. Adams countered that he would gladly resign the Presidency to Washington, but in this matter "the power and authority are in the President. I am willing to exert this authority at this moment, and to be responsible for the exercise of it." Then he went on, "There has been too much intrigue in this business with General Washington and me; if I shall ultimately be the dupe of it, I am much mistaken in myself."

Taking offense at this reference to intrigue, McHenry offered to resign if the President had lost confidence in him. Adams did not take up the offer, saying "I have no hard thoughts concerning your conduct in this business and I hope you will make your mind easy concerning it." Yet the President remained firm. "I am not and never was of the opinion," he stated, "that the public opinion demanded General Hamilton for the first, and I am now clear that it never expected nor desired any such thing."[4]

The other members of the cabinet, Pickering, Wolcott, and Stoddert, each wanted to urge the President to reverse his decision, but they finally decided that the Secretary of the Treasury alone should make the last appeal for Hamilton. Wolcott then outlined the course of the quarrel over rank and argued that perfect confidence must exist between the President and the commander of the Army, which would be the case if Hamilton were made Inspector General. Wolcott stressed that Washington wanted Hamilton to have the second command, that Congress had assumed Hamilton would have it, and that the public expected he would have it.

Other Federalists, too, using their strongest arguments, urged Hamilton's appointment to the second post. George Cabot, for example, explained that "most enlightened men through New England" favored Hamilton over Knox.[5]

If Adams had not realized the nature of his dilemma before this time, it now became obvious that this was not merely a quarrel over the personal precedence of two generals. It was a conflict of personalities that touched the power of the Presidency itself, and, as a consequence, the policy of the government in a time of crisis. If Hamilton gained control of the Provisional Army his influence over the government might be such as to make him its *de facto* leader. It was apparently galling to Adams, at the height of his popularity, to find the members of his official family and the leaders of his own party determined to force him to defer to Hamilton, a private citizen.

Next, the President heard from General Washington himself. What Washington said came as the crowning blow to Adams in the quarrel over rank. In words that left little room for misunderstanding, the General implied that he would resign his own commission if Hamilton were not appointed the senior major general as he, Washington, had recommended.[6]

If Adams stood firm against Hamilton's appointment to the second position and Washington resigned, the President's own party would turn against him. In addition, he would probably lose much of the popular support he had worked hard to cultivate. In short, he would become a President without party or popular following. As such, he could offer no effective leadership against France.

Unwilling to accept these consequences, Adams capitulated. On October 9, 1798, he conceded that Washington would determine the ranking of the generals. Hamilton was then commissioned first, and Knox second. When Henry Knox refused the third position, it went to Charles Cotesworth Pinckney.[7]

Humiliated by the defeat, Adams now lost much of his enthusiasm for a call to arms against France. If Hamilton had no army to command, the President seemingly reasoned, his drive for power might be curbed, or at least slowed. Adams, therefore, became reluctant to convert the paper army into a real one.[8]

Adams made this attitude clear when the Secretary of War complained that recruiting was too slow and warned that "the ardor of the country may soon subside to a temperature unfavorable to the attainment of soldiers." "Regiments are costly articles everywhere, and more so in this country than any other under the sun," the President answered. "If this nation sees a great army to maintain, without an enemy to fight, there may arise an enthusiasm that seems to be little foreseen. At present there is no more prospect of seeing a French army here, than there is in Heaven." [9]

This attitude, in fact the whole wrangle over rank, brought to the surface Adams's and Hamilton's conflicting ideas as to the proper means of defending the country, and the kind of war that should be fought against France. Convinced that any struggle against France must be fought mainly at sea, Adams favored a navy and a defensive war. Hamilton wanted a large army, or a respectable professional army that could be easily expanded, and a war of conquest.

"I have always cried Ships! Ships! Hamilton's hobby horse was Troops! Troops!" Adams wrote in later years. "With all the vanity and timidity of Cicero, all the debauchery of Marc Anthony and all the ambition of Julius Caesar," Adams explained, "his object was the command of fifty thousand men. My object was the defense of my country, and that alone, which I knew could be affected only by a navy."

High Federalists sided with Hamilton in this conflict. They wished to use the Army as a political instrument, particularly to keep their party in power. This could not be done with a navy. Furthermore, they maintained, a navy was unnecessary because the British fleet would protect American shipping.[10]

Dependence on the British navy, the creation of a large army, the constraining of political adversaries, and the waging of a war of conquest seemingly were part of a grand Hamiltonian design that High Federalists embraced as a matter of patriotic commitment. According to this design, the path of conquest ran southward. Federalist leaders, and other Americans too, had long been attracted to adjoining Spanish provinces, particularly to Louisiana and the Floridas.

Spain, it may be recalled, in the wars of the French Revolution had been an ally of England against France. In 1795 Spain reversed her foreign policy and sought to withdraw from the war against France. Fearing English reprisals, perhaps an Anglo-American assault on Louisiana, Spanish statesmen sought to forestall such an attack by purchasing American friendship. In October of that year they signed the Treaty of San Lorenzo with Thomas Pinckney which settled a dispute over the southwest boundary of the United States and gave Americans unrestricted navigational rights on the Mississippi River.

Within a year Spain abandoned her conciliatory policy toward the United States. First, she deserted England. Then, on August 19, 1796, she concluded the first Treaty of San Ildefonso which made her an ally of France and an enemy of England. Next, Spain joined France in protesting Jay's Treaty and America's acquiescence in British maritime practices. In addition, Spain, supported by France, delayed the execution of Pinckney's Treaty by refusing to give up forts in the American Southwest. When John Adams became President, therefore, France had a strong influence in Spanish foreign policy; Spain was hostile to the United States; and there appeared to be substance in rumors that Spain would retrocede Louisiana to France.[11]

ALLURING LOUISIANA

If French statesmen had been able to have their own way, they would have regained Louisiana, "this superb territory," before Adams came to office, for the Directory wished to reconstruct France's colonial empire in the New World. In that empire

Louisiana would be the sun and the smaller colonies in the Caribbean and South America would be its planets in orbit. In the politics of Europe, therefore, one of the goals of French diplomacy was the recovery of Louisiana from Spain.[12]

In dealing with the United States, Talleyrand, like other French statesmen familiar with America, apparently had always had Louisiana in mind. He sought first to protect that province against Britain and the United States and then to acquire it before frontiersmen in the Southwest, who were already encroaching upon Spain's lands, would wrench the province from Spain's feeble grip. This concern was important in shaping Talleyrand's conduct toward the United States.

American statesmen did not know of France's precise plans, but they had long suspected that she wished once again to entrench herself in Louisiana. Even before Adams was inaugurated, Secretary of State Pickering had tried to investigate rumors that Spain had ceded Louisiana and the Floridas to France. "The Spaniards," he wrote, "will certainly be more safe and quiet neighbors." The British, too, had heard such rumors, and were alarmed.[13] A few months later the Secretary of State expressed the conviction that France intended to regain Louisiana, "and to renew the ancient plan of her Monarch of *circumscribing* and encircling what now constitutes the Atlantic States."

As the months passed these rumors became more frequent. In Berlin John Quincy Adams also suspected that France had formulated a scheme for regaining Louisiana. "There must certainly be," he wrote, "some project of momentous magnitude carried on for several years past by the French, and of which our Government is not well informed." [14]

French statesmen, on the other hand, now feared that in retaliation for the spoliations committed by their corsairs the United States might join Britain in an alliance, invade Spain's colonies in the Americas, and destroy France's opportunity to recover Louisiana. General Dominique-Catherine Pérignon, France's Ambassador in Madrid in 1797, was in fact instructed to play up the danger of an Anglo-American assault when applying pressure on Spain for a prompt cession of Louisiana. Although aware of the danger, the Spaniards could not truly protect the province. "You can't," their chief minister remarked, "lock up an open field." [15]

The British, too, had their eyes on Louisiana. When France and England began peace negotiations in July 1797 at Lille, they discussed the colonial spoils the British had taken from France and her allies. Although William Pitt, Britain's Prime Minister, did not demand Louisiana, he desired it. Lord Malmesbury, the English negotiator, was instructed to point out that his government saw considerable advantage in obtaining "the town and port of New Orleans with a sufficient territory to be annexed to it." The negotiators talked of exchanging Gibraltar for Louisiana, among other possibilities. Malmesbury even suggested this to Pitt, but such plans were carried no further, for in October these peace talks collapsed.[16]

France's next Ambassador at Madrid, Ferdinand-Pierre Guillemardet, a former physician turned politician, had as his main task a negotiation for the acquisition of Louisiana. He was cautioned to pursue this objective with renewed urgency, for after the publication of the X Y Z dispatches Létombe in Philadelphia reported on the warlike measures before Congress. He warned that "already they talk about the conquest of Louisiana" and of an American alliance with Britain.[17] Létombe advanced the idea of guarding Spain's provinces by placing a French barrier between them and the United States.

As though stimulated by Létombe's reports, Talleyrand told the Spaniards in May 1798 that the Americans planned to make themselves the masters of the North American continent. Instead, he suggested, they should be confined behind the Appalachian Mountains. Since Spain could not "do this great work alone," he noted, she should allow France to take over Louisiana and the Floridas. France would make those territories "a wall of brass forever impenetrable to the combined efforts of England and America." In July Talleyrand observed that Spain appeared willing to give in partially to his pressure by allowing French troops to go to America to help repel expected British and American invasions of Spanish colonies.[18]

At the same time, Létombe submitted a report to the Executive Directory that contained the recommendations of General Victor Collot, a former governor of Guadeloupe who had reconnoitered the Mississippi Valley and had then lived with the Consul General while writing on what he found. Collot said the American government wanted France to declare war. So he advised the Directory "not to seem to pay attention to John Adams's insults, nor to his hostilities." Instead, France should acquire Louisiana and the Floridas through negotiation and take Canada by force. Such action, he believed, offered the only means of keeping the United States at peace, of breaking its ties to England, and of preserving France's colonies in America. With this policy, he suggested, France would recover that preponderance in the New World "which the nature of things gives to us." [19]

To thwart such plans, which he assumed existed, Hamilton began to shape a project of his own for an attack on Louisiana and the Floridas. The Quasi-War with France, he realized, offered a unique opportunity for such an assault. If France were to regain Louisiana her presence there might bring strength to Republicans, and perhaps revive secessionist agitation in the West. If the United States took Louisiana, he reasoned, it could check the secessionist sentiment, dampen the enthusiasm of Westerners for France and Republicanism, and strengthen the Union. So he and other Federalists envisaged a crusade against Spain as well as France, one linked to territorial conquests. It could make a full-scale war, when it came, popular in the South and West. In those sections there existed serious opposition to the idea of a war against France alone.

One gazetteer summed up what was probably the view of many extreme Federalists. "A war with Spain," he wrote, "is absolutely necessary to the salvation of this country, if a war with France takes place, or if the Spaniards have ceded Louisiana to France. They must both be driven into the Gulf of Mexico, or we shall never sleep in peace. Besides, a war with Spain would be so convenient!" The wealth gained from Spanish America "would be the cream of the war." [20]

This idea of an expanded war and close collaboration with England also had roots in the mind of Francisco de Miranda, a soldier of fortune born in Venezuela who became the first of the Latin American revolutionaries. He had fought in the American Revolution and later had become embroiled in the politics of revolutionary France, where he was thrown into prison. In January 1798 he escaped and crossed the channel to England. A visionary and a plotter, he now devoted himself to schemes for freeing his homeland from the grip of Spain.

Since Miranda had cherished this dream of liberation for years, he had talked about it to many people. When he was in the United States he had described the project to Hamilton, who "expressed ideas favorable to the object and perhaps gave an opinion that it was one to which the United States would look with interest—." [21]

Miranda's plan, as he explained it early in 1798 to British and American officials, called for an alliance of Britain, the United States, and the Spanish-American colonies against France and Spain. He wished to merge the Anglo-French war and the Quasi-War into one conflict that would lead to the liberation of Spanish America. He envisaged a joint Anglo-American expedition against Spanish America, with Britain furnishing the fleet and the United States the troops. For the United States the reward would be Louisiana and the Floridas.

The British were willing to go along with the scheme. Prime Minister William Pitt told Miranda, "We should much enjoy operating jointly with the United States in this enterprise." Rufus King, the American Minister in London, also liked the plan, as did the Secretary of State. Pickering, who quarreled bitterly with Carlos Martinez de Yrujo, the Spanish Minister in Philadelphia, over navigation of the Mississippi and Spain's retention of posts in the Southwest, was eager for a rupture with Spain and, of course, for an alliance with England.

Hamilton urged cooperation with England on the Miranda project, but without an alliance, and made his ideas known to the President through McHenry. "All on this side of the Mississippi must be ours," Hamilton said, "including both Floridas." [22]

Adams stood in the way of this plan. He wished to follow an independent course, one that required a navy to keep the United States from becoming fatally dependent on Britain. In the spring of 1798, when Robert Liston tried to exploit the war spirit in Congress by suggesting naval cooperation between England and the United States, the President refused the offer. Pickering therefore told Rufus King, that "threatening as is the aspect of our affairs with France, the President does not deem it expedient at this time to make any advances to Great Britain."

At this point Adams did not appear adamantly opposed to collaboration or even to an alliance with Britain. Yet he apparently accepted Hamilton's view, as advanced to him through McHenry and other department heads, that public opinion would not support so close a connection.

At the same time, Adams and other Federalist leaders feared that if France and Britain made peace the United States would be diplomatically isolated. "It is pretty certain that, if Britain yields," a prominent Federalist commented, "we shall have the weight of the whole European world to oppress us." [23] The British knew of this fear and wished to make use of it for a closer connection with the American government. The greatest object of American anxiety, Liston reported, "is the possibility of our concluding a peace with the French Republic and allowing the Directory to devote their whole attention and force to the vengeance they threaten to take on this country."

Asserting that the American apprehension was "certainly solid and well-founded," Lord Grenville in June 1798 renewed his government's offer of an alliance. As a basis for discussion, he indicated that England would be satisfied with an American conquest of Louisiana and Florida, if England, in turn, could acquire Saint Domingue. The British were also willing to lend, or sell, ships, and to loan the services of naval officers to the United States.

In July, after Congress had adjourned, Liston formally approached Pickering with Grenville's proposal for an alliance. Although he himself favored such a connection, Pickering said, he could not speak frankly in support of it because the Republican party was bitterly opposed to any tie with England, and the President had given him no instructions on the matter.[24]

A month later, at Quincy, the President obtained details on Miranda's idea for a triple alliance. Through Rufus King, Mi-

randa had, in fact, sent papers outlining his whole liberation
project. Concerned about Abigail's illness, Adams did not react
immediately, and Pickering was still left without instructions on
the matter of any alliance.[25] Hamilton, who corresponded with
Miranda through Rufus King, also felt constrained by Adam's in-
action on Miranda's proposal.

"With regard to the enterprise in question," Hamilton confided to King and Miranda, "I wish it much to be undertaken,"
and that the United States should furnish the whole land force.
"The command in this case would . . . naturally fall upon me,
and I hope I shall disappoint no favorable anticipation." Hamilton also pointed out that he could not participate in the project,
despite his desire to do so, unless it were "patronized by the Government of this Country."

Pleased, Miranda answered that his plan was progressing as
Hamilton desired. Then he said, "we await only the fiat of your
illustrious Pres. to leave like lightning. . . . Let us save America
from the frightful calamities that, in upsetting a large part of the
world, threaten with destruction the parts which are still
whole." [26]

Unknown to Miranda, when the President finally discussed
the Venezuelan's letter with Pickering, he reacted negatively.
"We are friends with Spain," Adams said. "If we were enemies,
would the project be useful to us? It will not be in character for
me to answer the letter. Will any notice of it, in any manner, be
proper?"

In effect, Adams wished to cultivate Spain's neutrality, regardless of her alliance with France, and would not embrace
Miranda's scheme, which he officially ignored. In later years he
claimed that what had happened in revolutionary France had led
him to shrink from "engaging myself and my country in most
hazardous and expensive and bloody experiments to excite similar
horrors in South America." [27]

COOPERATION WITH ENGLAND

Liston, who thought that war between the United States and
France was inevitable, meanwhile had gone north to Quincy to

take up the matter of the alliance directly with the President. In this meeting, which took place before Adams had capitulated in the dispute over rank in the Army, the President spoke freely. He acknowledged that it would be in the interest of the United States, as well as of Britain, to agree to a temporary alliance for the joint conduct of war against France. He also expressed an awareness of danger to the United States if the Directory should offer terms of peace so attractive that England could not refuse them. Then the United States would be left to struggle alone against the whole power of France.

If all depended on him, Adams said, he would enter into a temporary alliance, as Liston suggested, without scruple or loss of time. The nature of the Constitution, however, compelled him to wait until such a commitment could gain the approbation of the people, who were now deliberating over it.[28]

Adams had not, in fact, waited for a decision from the public before embarking on a limited collaboration with Britain. That summer, during the early naval hostilities of the Quasi-War, he took advantage of British assistance. Since American manufacturers were few and could not produce military and naval supplies in quantity, the United States obtained what it needed from England. It even accepted the loan of cannon from British forces at Halifax, Nova Scotia. The British also allowed American merchantmen and privateers to arm themselves in English ports, gave convoy protection to American merchant ships, and exchanged naval recognition signals with American warships. American naval vessels, in turn, escorted some British convoys in the West Indies.[29]

Yet, all was not serene in relations with England. British naval officers stopped and searched American ships at sea, and, despite vehement protests, impressed American sailors. Even when England had offered the United States convoy escorts, and an alliance, she insisted on the right of visit and search. She also made it clear that she would continue to impress from the decks of American ships.[30]

To some historians, nonetheless, Federalist cooperation with England at this time amounted to a quasi-alliance. It seems logical to assume that this cooperation might have gone further than it did if it were not for the divided state of American public opinion over foreign policy, and the cooling of Adams's martial ardor after his defeat in the army issue. Liston attributed his own failure to gain an alliance to the "bias of the public mind" produced by "the violent and artful declamation of the French Party," meaning the Republicans. The Federalist party itself was split. Federalists, Liston pointed out, "are by no means unanimous in their wish for the adoption of engagements with England whether of a temporary or a permanent nature." [31]

Despite this division in his own party, Hamilton, driven by his desire to lead an army southward, became increasingly anxious for collaboration with Britain. Previously he had opposed aggressive war, believing apparently that sooner or later France herself would make full-scale war inevitable. Now he was willing to put his plan of conquest into motion, and to strike before France did. His reasoning, as he now expressed it, was logical enough, based on the simple military principle of hitting the enemy when and wherever possible. "If we are to engage in war, our game will be to attack where we can," he explained in December 1798. "France is not to be considered as separated from her ally. Tempting objects will be within our grasp."

A month later, Hamilton hoped the new session of Congress would empower the President to use the land and naval forces against France and her allies. If France should attempt to seize Louisiana and the Floridas, which he considered "essential to the permanency of the Union," the United States should thwart the move by taking those provinces for itself.

Then Hamilton summarized his larger objective. If France still sought a universal empire what could better defeat that purpose, he said, "than to detach South America from Spain, which is only the channel through which the riches of *Mexico* and *Peru* are conveyed to France?" The President should take steps to effect that separation. "Tis to be regretted," the Inspector General asserted, "that the preparation of an adequate military force does not advance more rapidly." [32]

While waiting for Adams to build the Army, Hamilton went

ahead with his own military plans, just in case the enlarged war
he now desired should come. Early in 1799 he called General
James Wilkinson, the commander of the western army, East to
confer with him. The Inspector General wanted to discuss "the
best mode (in the event of a rupture with Spain) of attacking the
two Floridas."

After a tedious trip from New Orleans Wilkinson arrived in
New York early in August 1799. He gave his superior officer a
long report on the frontier army. In conversations over a period of
several months Hamilton was so forceful that Wilkinson gained
the clear impression military action would come soon. Hamilton
ordered him to gauge the feelings of settlers and Indians in the
Southwest toward the projected attack on Spain's provinces, to
chart the disposition of Spanish troops and their fortifications,
and to investigate how an army in the field could be supplied
with provisions, ammunition, and forage. He also directed Wilkinson to stockpile ammunition and guns, especially heavy cannon
and mortars for use in siege warfare. Then the two generals
worked out plans for transporting three thousand men down the
Mississippi River.

At the same time, the Inspector General pressed the President to prepare for war in the Southwest by urging him to appoint
distinguished men from Natchez and other settlements in that region as officers in the Provisional Army. "It is obviously a powerful means of conciliating the inhabitants," he told Adams, in what
might prove to be the most important theater of the war.[33]

If Hamilton had been willing to carry out—on his own—his
idea of invading Louisiana and the Floridas before anyone declared
war, he needed the support of his immediate military superior for
such an attack. General Washington, however, refused such help.
He opposed all offensive operations against Spanish territory
without a declaration of war. When Wilkinson wanted to station
a detachment of troops at Natchez, for example, he turned the
plan down because it might alarm the Spaniards, prompt them to
reinforce their own troops in Louisiana, and bring Spain and the
United States much closer to war than they were. So Hamilton's

plan for a frontier war, which neither Adams nor the Westerners, nor Washington, were willing to support, faded into failure.[34]

While Hamilton was working out these war plans he received a letter and a manuscript from a friend in London, Christopher Gore, which made a case for immediate war against France. A Federalist lawyer and gentleman farmer from Massachusetts, Gore was serving on a special commission, authorized by Jay's Treaty, which was attempting to settle Anglo-American differences over compensation to be paid for American ships seized by the British. Although Gore's essay, called "The Present State of the United States, and the Consequences of not adopting vigorous . . . measures of war against France," was never published and distributed widely, as he desired, it is noteworthy because it brought together most of the Hamiltonian arguments for full-scale war.

An immediate unlimited war, Gore argued, would prevent Republicans from defending France and attacking the Federalist party. It would permit the government to move from defensive actions, which bring no profit, to offensive operations against French and Spanish possessions. Victory would be cheap and easy. Not more than ten-thousand troops would be needed for such an offensive. There would be other advantages too. Offensive war would break the chains of tyranny in South America, lead to an American hemisphere united and strong enough to resist future invasions from Europe, open a profitable trade to American shippers and manufacturers, and assure the United States the security of friendly neighbors and allies to the south.[35]

Demands such as Gore's for an enlarged war reflected the disappointment of extreme Federalists over the failure of limited hostilities at sea, particularly of the retaliatory blows of the new American Navy against French cruisers, to provoke the Directory to a declaration of war. This reluctance of the French government to expand the fighting at sea into a larger conflict stemmed from various reasons, such as fear of putting Louisiana beyond reach, but can be seen clearly in the nature of the Quasi-War.

THE NAVY IN ACTION

From the beginning of the crisis chance rather than deliberate policy gave France the opportunity to damage American shipping in the Caribbean, where most of the undeclared naval war was fought. To a large extent, the islands of the West Indies were dependent on the American mainland for provisions. While France and England were at war most of the trade to those islands fell to the United States. By 1796, a French diplomat pointed out, the United States had more than six hundred ships engaged in trade with Saint Domingue alone.[36] Consequently, as the West Indian trade grew in volume, American shipping became increasingly vulnerable to attacks from French privateers. These privateers, essentially private armed ships devoted to offensive action in war, and not French naval cruisers, caused most of the damage to American shipping. As the crisis with France became more intense, the privateers stepped up their assaults.

In 1797, because of pressing commitments in other parts of the world, the British eased their harassment of French shipping in the West Indies, contenting themselves with the defense of their own shipping in those waters. This British retreat allowed raiders, based in the French West Indies, or in the island possessions of Spain and Holland, allies of France, to plunder American shipping almost at will. This plunder, because the British navy prevented goods from France from reaching the French islands, supplied those islands with desperately needed provisions.

American losses were heavy. In the summer of 1796, before French raiders had struck hard, the insurance rate for a Caribbean voyage from a port in the United States was about 6 per cent. Within six months this rate doubled. In the following year the cost of premiums ran from 15 to 25 per cent of the value of ship and cargo. Within a year's time the French took several hundred American merchant ships. By the spring of 1798 insurance rates on American shipping had climbed to a peak of 30 to 33 per cent, and sometimes went higher. This amounted to a fivefold increase in two years. Insurance on a voyage from the Atlantic sea-board to Jamaica, for example, claimed as much as 40 per cent of the value of ship and cargo.[37]

French captors, as has been indicated, looted ships, some-times committed atrocities against crew members and passengers, and frequently condemned vessels illegally. Technically, the French government was obligated to pay for the ships its officials condemned, but if it paid it did so in depreciated paper currency. Prize courts, which often acted in collusion with the owners of privateers, even condemned provision ships sent to French islands by French consuls in the United States. The Directory simply found itself unable to control many of the greedy privateers which flew the flag of France.

In 1797 the American government could do nothing to stop the French raids. It had no navy. Except for a few small revenue cutters, each manned by crews of six men, it did not have a single national vessel in commission. As a consequence, privateers be-came so bold that they attacked shipping within sight of the American shore. French corsairs worked off Long Island Sound and swarmed around the entrance of Delaware Bay in search of prey. The British navy was far more active in American coastal waters than were ships of the American government. Not until after the publication of the X Y Z dispatches and the enactment of the war measures, did the government hasten to equip and send a naval force to sea.

Fortunately, as the result of earlier laws, several American shipyards held the nucleus for a naval force. In 1794 Congress had authorized the building of six ships for a navy. The Secretary of War at that time, Henry Knox, had decided to make these ships super-frigates, that is vessels faster and more powerful than any European frigate. Work on the frigates had started slowly and had stopped in 1795 with the signing of a peace treaty with Algiers. A supplementary naval act in April 1796 had authorized completion of three of the frigates, the *United States,* forty-four guns; the *Constitution,* forty-four guns; and the *Constellation,* thirty-six guns, but they were still unfinished when the hostilities of the Quasi-War broke out.[38]

Finally, by the spring of 1798, officers had been assigned to the frigates and these officers went ahead with the recruiting of crews. In addition, the government had purchased merchant vessels, and had them armed and fitted for naval service. These ships, aided by Treasury Department revenue cutters, went to sea as soon as ready as a small anti-privateer patrol. So by early summer the United States had a small Navy ready for action.

The only extended American naval operation before the end of June was the cruise of the sloop of war *Ganges*, a former merchant vessel converted to naval service, which sailed from Philadelphia on May 24. She patrolled American coastal waters between Long Island and the Virginia capes. Although Richard Dale, the captain, made no captures on this mission, the Secretary of the Navy claimed that he "frightened the French Cruisers from our Coasts. . . ." [39]

By the end of June the *United States* and the *Constellation* were at sea patrolling coastal waters, but the *Constitution* was not even launched until October. The Navy, as a result, did not exert a strong influence on the Quasi-War until late in 1798.

To supplement the naval establishment Congress authorized letters of marque for merchant ships. These commissions allowed private ships to carry guns for the purpose of repelling French privateers or cruisers, or for capturing other armed French vessels. Neither American private armed vessels nor warships could take or sink unarmed French ships, as would be permissible in a regular war. Even if the American Navy had been capable of doing more, by law it could not fight more than a half war.

The measures Congress had passed permitted American commanders to capture French privateers and warships. These captures were, in effect, warlike actions without a formal declaration of war. The laws themselves were half measures, as we have seen, because they did not call for the defeat of the French. These laws, then, were basically defensive, and were to expire when the commanders of French ships stopped their depredations against American commerce. This was why, from the American point of view, the clash with France was a quasi-war. It was a limited war that Americans fought only at sea under self-imposed restrictions.

Although more than a thousand armed American merchantmen were commissioned and many of them clashed with French privateers, the restricted nature of the sea warfare made the American privateer, armed for offensive action, a negligible factor in the fighting of the Quasi-War. Privateers usually did their most effective work in destroying an enemy's merchant marine, but American privateers were prohibited from molesting ordinary French merchantmen. Moreover, the British navy had practically swept French commerce from the seas, leaving afloat only a few unarmed French ships, such as interisland traders, canal boats, and shoal drafters. Since the Quasi-War offered little chance for personal profit, few American privateers were engaged in it.

French privateers, on the other hand, found plenty of profit in attacking American shipping in the Caribbean. While deadly menaces to unarmed merchant ships, these corsairs could not stand up against a warship. Secretary of the Navy Benjamin Stoddert, therefore, concentrated the infant Navy in coastal waters and in the Caribbean. President Adams desired such concentration. He ordered the Navy to "sweep the West India seas" and to capture French seamen.[40]

The new Navy took its first prize off Egg Harbor, New Jersey, early in July 1798 when the *Delaware*, a small merchant packet converted to a sloop of war of sixteen guns, captured the *Croyable*, a French private schooner of twelve guns. The French skipper argued that he knew of no war between his country and the United States. He had tried to flee from the *Delaware*, he said, because he thought she was British.

"The French have been making war on us for a long time," the American captain, Stephen Decatur, Sr., replied. "Now we find it necessary to take care of ourselves."

Since the *Croyable* had taken several American ships, she was condemned, turned over to the Navy, and then placed in service under the name *Retaliation*. Four months later the French recaptured the ship.[41]

By the winter of 1798 French corsairs had stopped their depredations in American coastal waters and had fallen back on their bases in the West Indies. The Navy, at some risk, then expanded operations, basing most of its ships in the enemy's waters in the Caribbean. It maintained two regular stations there, one off Guadeloupe and the other off Saint Domingue.

In December the Navy Department could issue an order that said with truth, "The French can have no force in the West Indies this winter equal to ours, which is thought to be sufficient to rid those seas as well of French commissioned armed vessels as of the pirates which infest them. . . ." As the new year began the United States thus had a respectable naval force patrolling the Caribbean. In convoys protected by naval escorts, American merchantmen once again carried on a busy commerce in the West Indies. The rapid growth and display of maritime skill of the infant Navy had quickly impressed Europeans.[42]

The strength of the American Navy also impressed Edmé Etienne-Borne Desfourneaux, France's governor-general at Guadeloupe. He suggested a scheme for the neutralization of his two small islands. In January 1799, when he released the captain of the *Retaliation* and the American seamen he held as prisoners, he sent President Adams a letter professing friendship for the United States. Guadeloupe's privateers, he said, would cruise only against France's enemies. They would treat Americans, whose trade he desired, as allies.[43]

A month later, on February 9 off the island of Nevis, occurred the first important engagement of the Quasi-War between a regular warship of the French navy and one from the American Navy. In this battle the more heavily armed *Constellation*, under the command of Thomas Truxtun, who had commanded a privateer during the Revolution and who was to become the most notable military figure of the Quasi-War, captured the French frigate *Insurgente*. Under orders from Desfourneaux not to fire on American ships, the French captain had tried to avoid battle. When captured, he asked, "Why have you fired on the national flag? Our two nations are at peace." Truxtun merely replied, "You are my prisoner." [44]

Later, Truxtun expressed dissatisfaction with the state of half war and half peace. In his report on the battle he explained,

"The french Captain tells me, I have caused a War with France, if so I am glad of it, for I detest Things being done by Halves."

When Desfourneaux learned of the naval battle he sent his secretary to Basseterre, St. Kitts, where the *Insurgente* had been taken, to demand the return of the warship. This must be done, he insisted, because France and the United States were at peace. Truxtun refused, pointing out that he had captured the frigate under orders from his government.[45]

Although Desfourneaux pretended to believe that Truxtun had acted without orders, the captain's action was a true expression of American policy. Since privateers out of Guadeloupe had continued to harass American shipping when they could, Americans concluded that Desfourneaux's desire for neutrality was insincere, and that he sought private gain rather than peace.

The continued suffering of imprisoned Americans, some of whom the French treated as pirates, from cold, hunger, disease, and maltreatment, and the impressment of some into the French naval service, caused such resentment that Congress passed a special act. A law of March 3, 1799, required the President "to cause the most rigorous retaliation to be executed on any such citizens of the French Republic" as might fall into American hands.[46] American hands were not entirely clean, for French prisoners in the United States complained of their own suffering and maltreatment.

After his failure to regain the *Insurgente*, Desfourneaux saw that American hostility was firm. On March 14, 1799, therefore, he issued a declaration of war of his own against the United States. Since Americans had rebuffed his friendly overtures, he announced, their ships thenceforth were to be seized, sent to Guadeloupe, and condemned. If not liable to condemnation, those ships were to be sold and the proceeds paid to the captors, or to the owners, according to orders from the Directory. Desfourneaux's various pronouncements apparently had little effect on American policy, for he was only a minor public servant. Furthermore, Americans were not aware that privateering out of Guadeloupe had ever ceased as a result of French initiative.

American, not French, initiative had curbed the privateers. In less than a year the new Navy, it seemed to many, had redeemed honor and had restored national confidence. It also paid for itself by making possible a revived and flourishing merchant marine and by forcing down insurance rates. According to one estimate, in the Navy's first year of operation American shippers saved more than $8.5 million in insurance. In the first six months of 1799 insurance rates dropped to almost half of what they had been at their peak in the previous year. They now fluctuated between 15 and 20 per cent. By the beginning of the following year, the rate had fallen to about 10 per cent.[47]

By demonstrating that the United States was capable of placing a stronger force in American waters and the Caribbean than France could, the new Navy may also have contributed to the Directory's desire to terminate the Quasi-War. Yet it was French forbearance more than the actions of the American Navy that kept the limited hostilities at sea from spreading into a real war. Even Federalists who were disappointed because the Directory had not declared war, or had not forced Congress to do so, saw in naval actions, such as Truxtun's against the *Insurgente,* no sign of peaceful intent. They viewed the battles of the American Navy as evidence of the administration's desire for full-scale war.[48]

One specific advantage Federalist leaders, particularly Hamiltonians, envisaged in an enlarged war was that the United States would cooperate with Britain to drive the French from the West Indies. In particular, such cooperation would probably free Saint Domingue, the western third of the island of Santo Domingo, from French control. Fear of losing that island possession was also a reason why the French wished to contain the Quasi-War, for Saint Domingue became the main object of American interest in the Caribbean during the war.

SAINT DOMINGUE

Profit from trade, primarily in sugar had first attracted Americans to Saint Domingue. Before 1793, when former slaves drove French planters from the island, Saint Domingue was considered one of the richest colonial possessions in the world; it had produced as much sugar as all the British West Indies. The revolt of the slaves ended the export trade, but not the desire of Americans to gain entry into what was potentially still an important source of cheap sugar.[49]

Saint Domingue was also a source of considerable harm to American shipping. Its ports that were under French control swarmed with armed ships that regularly ran a British blockade of the island. From these ports, under orders from French commissioners in the colony, privateers and warships raided American commerce. The dispatches of Jacob Mayer, the American Consul at Cap Français, were filled with descriptions of ships taken by French corsairs. It was against these raiders in the Caribbean that the second session of the Fifth Congress had enacted its laws of reprisal.[50]

Although many Americans wanted to strike directly at their French tormentors and drive them from Saint Domingue, few favored independence for the colony. Southerners in particular were horrified by the idea of an independent Negro country, believing that such a nation would offer standing encouragement for their own slaves to revolt.

British policy, too, stood in opposition to an independent Saint Domingue. Late in 1793, at the invitation of French planters with royalist sympathies, British forces invaded and tried to conquer the colony. They failed to overcome native resistance led by two generals, Benoit Joseph Rigaud, a mulatto, and François Dominique Toussaint, a Negro usually known as Toussaint L'Ouverture. He was born a slave, the son of a petty African chieftain who had been brought to Saint Domingue from Guinea as a slave. Toussaint, a small, ugly man of remarkable ability and intelligence, had been a trusted slave who had not suffered ill-treatment. He was not a bloodthirsty revolutionary. He was, instead, a gifted leader who wielded virtually independent power, but who still professed loyalty to France.[51]

In 1796 Britain's inability to conquer the French colony led to a rivalry between Rigaud and Toussaint for actual control of Saint Domingue. Still hoping to retain the loyalty of the colony, the Directory in May sent a civil commission of five to the island, headed by Léger Félicité Sonthonax, the leader of an earlier commission in the colony. Under Sonthonax's influence this new commission favored Toussaint L'Ouverture and sided with the blacks against the mulattoes.

Toussaint's power now grew to such an extent that General Desfourneaux, at this time commander of the few French troops in the colony, reported that "San Domingo can be saved to France only by Republican bayonets. Our moral influence here has become absolutely *nil.*" Pride, he said, has given birth to schemes of independence.[52] This attitude of independence expressed itself in a bold stroke in August 1797 when Toussaint, having no further use for Sonthonax, forced the commissioner to flee to France.

Alarmed by Toussaint's attitude, the Directory now sent one of its ablest servants, General Marie Joseph Gabriel, Theodore Count d'Hédouville, to the colony to reestablish French control on a firm basis. This special agent arrived at Cap Français in April 1798 and soon realized that his mission was hopeless. Toussaint, who had been made General-in-Chief with military command over all of Saint Domingue, was so strongly entrenched in the north and west that only overwhelming force could dislodge him. Since Hédouville had no such force, and the Directory could send no army through the British blockade, Hédouville could do little other than to cooperate with Toussaint in a common effort to expel the English.[53]

At this time the British held a few key points in the western part of the colony, Rigaud ruled in the south, and Toussaint controlled elsewhere. Having lost more than seven thousand troops and facing opposition from both Rigaud and Toussaint, the British had already given up plans for conquest. Before leaving Saint Domingue, however, the British hoped to injure France by widening the breach between Toussaint and the Directory.

In April 1798 a young lieutenant colonel, Thomas Maitland, assumed command of the British forces in Saint Domingue. On his own authority he quickly decided to withdraw his troops from advanced positions and to concentrate them at two ports, Môle

St. Nicolas and Jeremie. This operation, the result of direct negotiation with Toussaint, was completed by May 10.

Several months later, on August 31, Maitland signed a secret
convention with Toussaint providing for Britain's complete evacuation of Saint Domingue. In return, the Negro leader promised
not to support armed attack or political intrigue against Jamaica
and to open ports under his control to British shipping. Since
Toussaint was technically still a French general without authority to sign a treaty with his country's enemy, he had acted as
though he were the actual ruler of a Negro state. In the negotiations he virtually ignored Hédouville.[54]

These developments in Saint Domingue coincided with the
rising demand in the United States for war against France. Some
Federalists wished to attack, capture, and hold the French West
Indies as an indemnity for the spoliations of American commerce.
Federalist leaders, who followed events in the Caribbean, realized, however, that neither French, nor British, nor American
control of Saint Domingue was likely. Jacob Mayer, for one, believed that the colony was ready for separation from France.[55]

Pleased by this state of affairs, many Federalists now began
to think that an independent Saint Domingue might be good for
the United States. Wishing to strike at the French wherever possible, Hamilton raised the question of the colony's independence
in a memorandum to Oliver Wolcott. "Is not the independence of
the French Colonies under the guarantee of the United States, to
be aimed at?" Hamilton asked. "If it is, there cannot be too much
promptness in opening negociations for the purpose."

Secretary of State Pickering now took the view that the
germs of freedom would not necessarily spread from the French
colony and infect slaves in the United States. He told Liston that
there could be advantages for the United States in an independent Saint Domingue. This attitude so alarmed Lord Grenville that he expressed his horror over the idea of self-government
for Negroes to Rufus King. Nonetheless, many Americans apparently preferred an independent state connected to the United
States "by alliance and friendship rather than by subjection" to a

colony controlled by Europeans. Commerce between the United States and the West Indies, Liston reported, "opens prospects to the speculating and enterprizing that are irresistably alluring."

The President, Liston learned, shared Pickering's views on Saint Domingue. Adams believed that France had very little chance of regaining true control of her colony. For this reason, he felt, the United States should make "some kind of agreement" with the blacks. His hesitancy in initiating such a move immediately stemmed from his desire not to offend Britain, who still opposed independence for Saint Domingue.[56]

Regardless of the British attitude, Toussaint continued to behave as though he were the absolute ruler of an independent state, while still admitting a general allegiance to France. After the British troops had been evacuated he decided to get rid of Hédouville. Early in October 1798 Toussaint's agents galloped through the north plain of Saint Domingue shouting, "Hédouville wants to restore slavery!" When resentment against the Directory's agent reached a high point, Toussaint suddenly approached Cap Français at the head of an army. Aware that all power was in Toussaint's hands, Hédouville gathered the whites, the mulattoes, and the few Negroes who feared Toussaint and on October 22 sailed for France.

Before leaving, Hédouville issued a proclamation saying that "General Toussaint Louverture is about to put into effect his plan for independence, agreed upon in concert with the Court of Saint James and the Government of the United States." Hédouville also instructed Rigaud to resist Toussaint, "who has sold himself to the English, the emigrés, and the Americans."

All that remained of French authority was P. R. Roume de Saint-Laurent, one of the commissioners who had spent the last two years in Spanish Santo Domingo. Since Roume's authority was nominal, his ultimate return to Saint Domingue as the Directory's agent did nothing to change the balance of power on the island.[57] The stage had already been set for war between Toussaint and Rigaud. Before launching his campaign against Rigaud, the Negro general turned to the United States for assistance. He needed American food and munitions to maintain his army.

On November 6, 1798, Toussaint wrote to President Adams expressing surprise and sorrow over the fact that American ships had practically abandoned the ports of Saint Domingue. He offered, in violation of French decrees against American shipping, to guarantee protection to American commerce, to give full payment for cargoes Americans brought to his ports, and to respect the United States Navy as that of a powerful friend and ally. In addition, he explained, orders had been given to French corsairs to return to France, and steps had been taken for payment for cargoes they had seized. He hoped the United States would now renew trade with Saint Domingue.[58]

Toussaint's bid for American goodwill proved effective. Pickering now considered him "amiable and respectable" and sent new instructions to Mayer. The Secretary of State pointed out that Congress had prohibited trade with French possessions only where the power of the mother country was recognized. "If the inhabitants of St. Domingo have ceased to acknowledge that power," Pickering said, "there will not, as I conceive, be any bar to the prompt and extensive renewal of trade between the United States and the ports of that Island. Our merchants, I understand, are already preparing to renew that commerce."

Pickering also expected Toussaint to restrain all privateers, or at least to keep them from touching Americans. In effect, if Hédouville's expulsion meant that French authority in Saint Domingue was dead, American cargoes would be forthcoming.

To strengthen his case for obtaining American goods, especially to explain the advantages renewed trade would bring to American shippers, Toussaint sent a personal representative, Joseph Bunel, to the United States. Accompanied by Jacob Mayer, Bunel arrived in Philadelphia on December 19. He dined with the Secretary of State, talked to several senators, and was invited to visit the President.[59]

Adams responded promptly and favorably to Toussaint's overtures. Within a few weeks Captain John Barry, the senior officer of the Navy, was instructed to show himself "with the greatest part of the fleet at Cape Francois, to Genl. Toussaint, who has a great desire to see some Ships of War belonging to

America." The President also wished Barry "to cultivate a good understanding" with the Negro general.[60]

Following the administration's lead, Congress took the next step. It passed a bill, the fourth section of which authorized the President to proclaim a reopening of commerce with Saint Domingue whenever he was satisfied that such action would serve the interest of the United States. Jefferson called this "Toussaint's clause." Its object, "as is charged by the one party and *admitted* by the other," he wrote, "is to facilitate the separation of the island from France." Even though this was also a British objective, Adams approved the act on February 9, 1799, only after he had satisfied himself that it would not offend the British government.[61]

STEVENS, MAITLAND, AND TOUSSAINT

To ascertain the precise state of affairs in Saint Domingue and to learn if American ships should be permitted to go there, the President decided to send Edward Stevens of Philadelphia, a distant relative of Hamilton, who had been born and had lived in the West Indies, to Cap Français as Consul General. Stevens, Jefferson wrote, "may be considered as our Minister to Toussaint." There was some truth to this observation, for Stevens had diplomatic powers.

Pickering informed Toussaint of Stevens's appointment in a reply to the Negro leader's letter of November 6. The Secretary of State said that renewal of trade would come only after privateers based in Saint Domingue ended their depredations. "On this condition the President will cheerfully allow a renewal of commerce," Pickering asserted, explaining that Congress has empowered the President to act on these terms. When Stevens reports that the terms have been met, the Secretary said, trade will be quickly resumed.[62] Pickering thought Stevens would have no difficulty securing approval of these terms from Toussaint.

Stevens arrived at Cap Français on April 18, 1799, with a cargo of supplies, which delighted Toussaint. His people were suffering from a lack of provisions as a result of the British blockade. Stevens's instructions reflected an American policy which sought to separate France and Toussaint, to suppress privateering, to extend trade, to enable the Negro leader to crush Rigaud, and to encourage, or aid, Toussaint in achieving independence.[63]

Hamilton, who had urged American support for an independent Saint Domingue, saw such support as part of the larger policy of war against France. He was puzzled, therefore, when Adams appointed Stevens, and at approximately the same time decided to send a peace mission to Paris. "How," Hamilton asked, "is the sending of an agent to Toussaint to encourage the independency of Saint Domingo, and a minister to France to negotiate an accommodation reconcilable to consistency or good faith?" [64]

If contradictory on the surface, Adams's policy did have the internal consistency of serving the national interest. While willing to discuss peace, he also wished to continue to keep France off balance in the Caribbean, mainly by depriving her of her major colony there. At the same time, he also sought profit from trade with Toussaint, in part as compensation for American losses to French corsairs. This might be the only way of obtaining some kind of indemnity from France.[65]

The new Consul General immediately began talks with Toussaint that would lead to an arrangement for opening Saint Domingue to American shipping. As these talks progressed he and Toussaint became friendly, but before a binding agreement could be reached relations with England came to require Stevens to work out a joint policy with the British concerning trade in Saint Domingue.

Although Britain and the United States both wished to detach Saint Domingue from France, they differed over commercial policy toward the colony. For example, when the American government learned of the secret convention of August 1798 between Maitland and Toussaint, Rufus King asked the British government if this meant it had recognized Toussaint as the head of an independent state. If it had, the United States had an equal right to trade with Toussaint. If it had not, British ships could not be permitted to carry cargoes from the United States to Saint Domingue, for American law forbade trade with French possessions.

Since the British would give no clear answer, and Maitland's

unauthorized diplomacy was not legally binding, King asked
them to reject the convention with Toussaint or to amend it so as
to give American commerce the same protection from privateers
based in Saint Domingue as it gave to British commerce. Henry
Dundas, the British Secretary of State for War, agreed to this
proposal.[66]

Lord Grenville, the Secretary of State for Foreign Affairs,
then suggested a more inclusive policy. The best way to restrain
privateers and the dangerous doctrine of Negro freedom, he said,
was to limit Toussaint's contacts with the outside world. This
could be done by establishing an Anglo-American monopoly to
trade with Saint Domingue. Pointing out that this was not legally
possible in the United States, King suggested instead that the
trade be opened to British and American merchants in general,
who would be watched by their own governments. The British
agreed.[67]

To work out detailed agreements on a common policy the
British appointed Maitland, who had returned to England and
was now a brigadier general, a confidential agent to negotiate
with the United States and with Toussaint. Maitland was instructed to accede to American desires as long as the principle of
limited, supervised intercourse with Saint Domingue was maintained.

Maitland arrived in Philadelphia on April 2, 1799, after
Stevens had departed for Saint Domingue. At first Maitland made
no progress. The views of the British and American governments,
he reported, are extremely different. "Our Policy is to protect,
theirs to destroy, the present Colonial System. Our views only go
to a partial, theirs to a compleat opening of the Saint Domingo
Market."

Maitland and Liston, who was also one of the negotiators,
realized that Stevens might conclude an agreement with
Toussaint that would give the United States exclusive trading
privileges. As a result, the British diplomats decided to go beyond
the letter of their instructions and try quickly to reach an accord
with the Americans.

On April 20, with Pickering and Wolcott representing the

United States, the negotiators adopted an informal agreement called "Heads of Regulations" to be proposed by Maitland to Toussaint, and to which the American government would assent. Under this arrangement the direct trade with Saint Domingue would be opened to British and American ships but would be limited to one or two ports of entry. Only persons of French or other nationality who had passports acceptable to Britain, to the United States, or to Toussaint would be allowed to travel to or from Saint Domingue on British or American ships.

Since the agreement at Philadelphia was a compromise that took into account the existing situation in Saint Domingue, the war against France, and the interests of Britain and the United States, it aroused varying degrees of enthusiasm. Liston expressed delight with the accord, seeing in it a significance beyond the commercial status of an island in the Caribbean. "We draw the Government of the United States closer to Great Britain," he reported, "and give consistency to measures which tend to widen their breach with France."

Maitland, who had a low opinion of Americans, considered Liston's policy a mistake. "It appears to me," he wrote, "that we wish by conciliation on our part to lead the Americans into war with France, and into a closer connection with us." This is wrong, he explained, for conciliation will only lead the Americans to expect further concessions. Profit is their only motive. They would make the "most disgraceful Peace" for the smallest of profits, and "it would be impossible for the Government to carry on the War for a Moment if so inclined." [68]

Pickering liked the agreement. Trade with Saint Domingue, he explained to Stevens, would be governed by Britain's naval power. The United States was, therefore, bound by considerations of commerce as well as of political safety against "what may justly be called a common enemy, to act in perfect concert with Great Britain in all this business respecting St. Domingo." [69] As a consequence, Pickering directed Stevens to suspend his own negotiations until Maitland, accompanied by an American official, arrived to present the "Heads of Regulations" to Toussaint.

French statesmen were alarmed over this growing accord between England and the United States. They feared that the Anglo-Saxon powers would combine forces to conquer coveted Louisiana and to separate Saint Domingue and other Caribbean colonies from French control.[70] These concerns for territories in the New World contributed to a French desire for peace and for some kind of an accommodation with the United States. In the autumn of 1798 diplomatic and other evidence indicated that France, despite earlier belligerence, would not force an enlarged war upon the United States.

France, as Talleyrand saw clearly, had little to gain and much to lose if hostilities at sea were expanded into a full-scale war with the United States. Since England had driven most of her ships from the sea, France needed the American merchant marine to maintain contact with the world outside Europe. American ships brought goods, such as sugar and tobacco, an important source of government revenue, which France could obtain in practically no other way because of the British blockade.[71] Furthermore, the United States was a rich market for French wines, vinegar, ribbons, silks, linens, and porcelains. So dependent were the French colonies in the West Indies on American ships that after June 1798, when Congress had enacted its embargo against trade with France and her possessions, those colonies suffered genuine distress. This distress persisted even though traders from Baltimore and elsewhere defied the law and smuggled provisions to the French islands.

Continuance of the Quasi-War also threatened ruin to the Netherlands, a satellite country now called the Batavian Republic and bound to France by an offensive and defensive alliance. The mere prospect of an enlarged war between France and the United States dismayed Dutch merchants. With most of their commerce destroyed and their colonies seized by England, the Dutch relied on trade with the United States as one of their few remaining sources of profit. Under the stimulus of the war in Europe this business with the United States had increased from slightly more than three million dollars in 1793, to nearly nine million dollars in 1797. So valuable was this commerce that William Vans Murray, the American Minister at The Hague, thought the Dutch would plead with France to allow them to remain neutral in an enlarged Franco-American war.[72]

Such a war would also jeopardize the commercial interests of the Spanish empire, which France regarded with a maternal interest. All these factors had a part in shaping Talleyrand's thinking and conduct. Yet, as events had shown, he had miscalculated the depth of American nationalism, the extent of anti-French feeling in the United States, and the influence of the Republican party in the conduct of foreign policy.

V

Talleyrand's Overtures

France has a double motive, as a Nation and as a Republic, not to expose to any hazard the present existence of the United States. Therefore it never thought of making war against them; and every contrary supposition is an insult to common sense.

CHARLES MAURICE DE TALLEYRAND-PÉRIGORD, *August 1798*

ALTHOUGH TALLEYRAND HAD REACTED WITH HUMILIATING INDIFFER-ence to American efforts to seek peace, he himself wanted peace, not war. Even before the eruption of the black cockade fever in the United States he had taken steps to prevent a final rupture with Americans. In March 1798, for instance, he had instructed Létombe to assure members of Congress who were friendly to France, other Americans, and especially Jefferson, that the Directory would not be tricked into war with the United States. "The Executive Directory," he wrote, "is always disposed to discuss amicably the questions in dispute between the United States and the Republic." [1]

Early in May 1798 Talleyrand assured Elbridge Gerry that the Directory bore no ineradicable ill will toward the United States. Yet on May 15 the Executive Directory issued a decree forbidding American ships, "under any pretext," to enter France's military ports. Regardless of such a law, which was based on military precautions rather than on increased hostility toward Americans, the knowledge that the Directory considered peace possible had been the main reason why Gerry had remained in Paris after Pinckney and Marshall had departed. A few weeks later, actually on May 28, the French government received copies of the published X Y Z dispatches. This marked a turning point in Talleyrand's attitude and in the Directory's relations with the United States.[2]

At this point, too, the Directory's position changed once more, and this change affected its outlook on foreign policy. In elections held in March 1798 throughout France the Directors again suffered defeat. This time democrats, or liberals hostile to the Directors and their policies, won a large number of seats in both chambers of the legislature. Once again, therefore, the legislative and the executive branches of the government of the First French Republic faced a constitutional deadlock.

Like George Washington, John Adams, and most other believers in constitutional government in these years, the Directors considered party politics an evil. Like the ruling Federalists in the United States, they had had no experience with a system of government in which one party should govern while another led an organized, legal opposition. To the Directors active opposition meant that constitutional government could not function properly. Like the High Federalists in the United States, they could not stand the public criticism and attacks from the "democrats," whom they now considered enemies of the republic. So, as it had a year earlier, but this time with greater speed, the Executive Directory moved to break the constitutional deadlock.

On May 11, in the *coup d'état* of 22 *Floréal*, the Directory annulled 106 of the elections and illegally obtained a majority in the legislature with which it could work. Previously the Directors had crushed danger from the right; now they had stamped out opposition from the left. With virtually no friends but generals, whom it could not control effectively, the Executive Directory had now become what constitutionalists had sought to prevent—a kind of dictatorship. To make the constitution work, the Directors had violated it twice. Yet France was still a republic, and the Directory still showed some respect for constitutional principles.[3]

Up to this juncture Talleyrand, who managed to survive the convulsions of the Directory, had prolonged his negotiations with Gerry in their "half friendly, half hostile condition" for several reasons, none of which included the possibility of full-scale war. Owners of privateers and corrupt officials in Paris were enriching themselves from the loot gathered in raids on American commerce. Since the naval depredations were profitable, Talleyrand had implied, they would continue as long as there was no diplomatic accord with the American government.

Talleyrand also wished to delay earnest negotiations with the Americans until the next presidential election in the United States, believing that the Republicans would then come to power. His desire for Louisiana, for booty, and for a friendly administration in Philadelphia precluded a declaration of war against the United States. Such a declaration, he told the Directors on June 1, would lead France into an "Anglo-Federalist trap." To enable the French party, or Republicans, to win the next election, he advised, the Executive Directory should follow a temporizing policy in dealing with the United States.[4]

Although Gerry proved less pliant than Talleyrand had anticipated, he might have served the Foreign Minister's purpose well enough in this temporizing policy if the furor in the United States and the war measures passed by Congress had not threatened to force a declaration of war. The publication of the X Y Z dispatches, news of which reached Paris from New York and London newspapers, caused a great scandal in France and apparently placed Talleyrand in "extreme peril" in his relations with the Directors.[5] He quickly disowned his subordinates, pointing out that no foreign minister could maintain a tight control over secret agents whose success depended on a certain amount of freedom from such supervision. He pleaded ignorance of the activities of W, X, Y, and Z, insisting that the American commissioners had been made the dupes of imposters.

Talleyrand published an unsigned disavowal in the Parisian press. This refutation, he maintained, did not offend Gerry but nettled Adams, whose policy it allegedly unmasked, and encouraged the friends of France in America. "I believe this was required," he later asserted.

From Gerry, in an effort to save face with the Executive Directory, Talleyrand demanded to know who the intriguers were. Gerry knew perfectly well that Talleyrand knew the names of his own agents. In fact he had sat at Talleyrand's dinner table with them. Yet Gerry went through the game of confidentially disclosing the names of the agents who had approached him and his colleagues. He also furnished the Minister of Foreign Relations with a statement saying that neither Talleyrand himself nor anyone employed in his office had solicited a bribe. Talleyrand then published Gerry's admissions.[6]

In an elaborate defense of his conduct submitted to the Executive Directory, Talleyrand called the whole X Y Z story "ridiculous," and denied any wrongdoing. He assailed the leaders of the Federalist government as British puppets who were trying to provoke the Directory's anger. He blamed the American commissioners, "picky men, shy and stubborn," for the failure of their mission. "They twisted around the meaning of honest conversations," he complained. They had "to be warned of what was expected of them." It was not, he wrote, "easy to make use of the negotiators who, angered at not being received officially, neglected the opportunity of meetings in society and nowhere presented themselves to the minister." Other Frenchmen suggested that the entire episode was part of a British scheme designed to involve the United States in the war against France.[7]

Despite Talleyrand's professions of innocence, the evidence more than suggests that the demands for money had come from him. Hauteval told Gerry that he, too, had been duped by Hottinguer and Bellamy. On the other hand, Bellamy admitted that he neither wrote, said, nor did anything without the express orders of Talleyrand.

Talleyrand now saw that he had overreached himself, and that the war he did not desire might come suddenly from the United States. Admitting that "this state of things does not resemble peace," he asked Eustache Bruix, the Minister of the Navy and Colonies, what should be done. In a letter to the Executive Directory on the same day Bruix declared, "We should order our warships to pursue the ships of this ungrateful and treacherous nation." [8] Talleyrand disliked such advice, for he was now willing to make humiliating concessions to prevent an Anglo-American entente.

Talleyrand, who had clothed the Directory's policy toward the United States with whatever stability it had, now also realized that Gerry provided one of the few remaining channels to President Adams. Gerry had become more important than ever, if war were to be prevented. Yet Gerry was restless. When the news of the published dispatches had reached France, he feared for his own safety and tried to leave Paris. Moreover, he had been ordered home by Pickering, had not obtained the additional diplomatic powers he desired, realized he could do little on his own, and knew that his official talks with Talleyrand had become a vexing political issue in the United States. Nonetheless, the Minister of Foreign Relations pleaded with him to remain.

In a lengthy memoir Talleyrand examined the dispute between the United States and France. Then he asked Gerry to request the necessary powers from his government to conclude a treaty and, hence, to prevent war. Although conciliatory, Gerry insisted on returning to America where he thought he might help to overcome the demands for war. Gerry's confidants in Paris, Richard Codman, Nathaniel Cutting, the American Consul at Le Havre, and Thomas Paine, all wanted him to stay. There seemed to be little doubt about French friendliness and desire for peace.[9]

"Did you not come, Monsieur," Talleyrand asked Gerry, "to re-establish amity between the two republics and determined to spare nothing to attain this end equally desirable for the United States and France? Can you leave after what has happened at Philadelphia? Should you leave when the French government, superior to all resentment and heeding only justice, shows itself anxious to conclude an accord solid and mutually satisfactory? . . . I cannot reconcile your language with the avowed object of your mission, with your plenipotentiary powers, and with the

14. *The* Constellation *capturing the* Insurgente, *February 9, 1799.*

15. *"Truxton's Victory," another view of action between the* Constellation *and the* Insurgente, *February 9, 1799.*

16. *The American merchant ship Planter in action with a French privateer, July 10, 1799.*

17. *The American armed merchant ship* Mount Vernon *engaging French privateers off Gibraltar, July 31, 1799.*

18. *Toussaint L'Ouverture,
from a portrait by François
Bonneville. By keeping Saint Domingue
practically independent
of France, this brilliant
Negro leader made possible
America's ultimate
acquisition of Louisiana.*

19. *William Wyndham,
First Baron Grenville,
by John Hoppner. He was
England's Secretary of
State for Foreign Affairs
during the Quasi-War.*

20. *Charles Maurice de Talleyrand-Périgord, from a portrait by F. Gérard.*
This brilliant and unscrupulous diplomat contributed as much as any man
to the peaceful resolution of the Quasi-War.

21. *Napoleon as First Consul, in the*
Parc at Malmaison, from the
portrait by Jean-Baptiste
Isabey, 1803. He tried to use
peace with the United States
to advance a grand design in European
diplomacy and politics.

22. *Joseph Bonaparte. He led*
the French negotiations in
discussions that culminated in
the Treaty of Môrtefontaine.

23. *William Vans Murray by Mather Brown. He was the key figure in the secret diplomacy that led ultimately to Franco-American peace negotiations.*

assurances you do not cease to give of the sincerity of your government." [10]

On July 1 Gerry explained Talleyrand's new tactics. "My frequent applications for a passport, letter of safe conduct for the vessel & her exemption from the embargo at Havre," he wrote, "have been altogether unnoticed." The French Minister of Foreign Relations then stated frankly that if Gerry departed his act would be interpreted by the British as evidence of a final rupture between France and the United States.[11]

At the same time, the Directory's anger against the United States, which had not entirely subsided, flared up again in reaction to the war measures the American Congress had enacted. Some French statesmen, such as Talleyrand himself, believed that America's hostile measures, such as the pursuit of French ships by naval vessels, constituted virtually a declaration of war.[12] On July 9, 1798, therefore, the Directory ordered an embargo on American ships in French ports.

MURRAY AND PICHON

During this time Talleyrand did not let up in his policy of conciliation. While Gerry was still in Paris, the Foreign Minister decided to send a young man of about twenty-eight who worked in the Foreign Office, Louis André Pichon, to the French legation at The Hague. Talleyrand instructed Pichon to cultivate William Vans Murray, the American Minister Resident to the Batavian Republic, and engage him in confidential peace talks.

This approach was shrewd and logical. Pichon, a secretary in the Foreign Office, had spent several years in the United States as secretary to two former French Ministers there, the turbulent Edmond C. Genet and the politically alert Joseph Fauchet. During his years in Philadelphia, Pichon had become acquainted with Murray. Like Gerry, Murray had direct access to the President, being one of John Quincy Adams's closest friends and his successor at The Hague post. The President's son and Murray carried on an intimate and extensive correspondence, much of which reached John Adams, for John Quincy acted as his father's personal observer of European affairs and wrote directly to him without going through Secretary of State Pickering.[13] Unlike Gerry, Murray, a lawyer and politician from Maryland's Eastern Shore, was considered a firm Federalist.

Pichon met Murray again socially at The Hague on June 26, 1798, and warmed up the old friendship by complimenting the Marylander. Then he quickly indicated that France desired peace and an accommodation with the United States. "Mr. Pichon as I said before is often talking about conciliation," Murray wrote in his diary. "He is a friend & a sincere one of U.S.—& of me." So Murray encouraged the overtures, pointing out as the conversations progressed, that he could not act officially. He could express himself, he said, only as a person who wished peace with France.[14]

Pichon reported this attitude to Talleyrand, saying that Murray was not a blind Federalist partisan. Like the mass of Americans, Pichon commented, Murray only wanted to defend his country. He did not want war. Murray even gave Pichon a copy of the American commissioners' instructions, which Pichon forwarded to Talleyrand. The Minister of Foreign Relations considered them conciliatory and expressed surprise that the conduct of the commissioners, at least from his point of view, did not fully reflect those instructions.

Several days after his first talks with Pichon, which were kept secret from the French Minister at The Hague, Murray wrote to John Quincy Adams about them. From these unofficial conversations, Murray wrote, he sensed that the French were afraid of war with the United States. Pichon asserted that war with the United States would be unpopular in France. Such a war, moreover, would endanger France's colonies.[15]

At this juncture, on July 6, after almost a month at sea, Victor Marie DuPont arrived at Bordeaux. In his first report to Talleyrand he said Adams was "hoping the Directory will declare war," and he advised against such a declaration. Jefferson and other friends of France, he reported, have their "hopes in you, and in the wisdom, dignity, power, and moderation of the Direc-

tory." On July 16 Talleyrand wrote to DuPont asking about the
activities of French cruisers in the Caribbean and along the
North American coasts which had led to bitter complaints from
the American government. He also inquired about the proceedings of colonial tribunals and French consuls in America and how
the Directory's measures against neutrals were being carried out,
particularly against the United States.[16]

DuPont, who brought documents and information from
Létombe, answered Talleyrand's questions in a report of July 21
to the Directors. He explained that the piracy, brigandage, and
acts of violence by cruisers sailing under the French flag formed a
principal cause for the American hostility against France. Not
only did the corsairs prey on American commerce in the West Indies, but they also attacked ships within American territorial
waters.

The widespread anger those raiders aroused, DuPont declared, served as the pretext for those "hostile measures which the
Government of the United States has promised England to adopt
against us." The violations of American territory, he pointed out,
were even alienating France's friends, for the Republicans, as
much as the Federalist merchants, were "proud of their independence as a nation." These excesses, which transcend sane
policy, he said, instead of being repressed were actually stimulated by French agents at Saint Domingue and Guadeloupe.
Those agents protected the corsairs.[17]

Apparently Talleyrand and the Directors, while aware of
these unsavory facts, did not know the details until this time. At
least DuPont and Létombe believed they were unknown in Paris,
and Létombe claimed that DuPont's report was made at his suggestion. This may be true, for the Directory's bureaucracy was
disorganized and, to a degree, corrupt. DuPont thought that most
employees at the ports and in the maritime service desired full-
scale war with the United States. Open hostilities would give
them free rein to pillage American commerce. Talleyrand frequently complained that the Executive Directory's decrees were
not properly executed.[18]

Before leaving the United States, DuPont had talked with

Jefferson and other Republicans who had expressed deep concern over the injuries suffered by the Republican party as a result of the Directory's tactics. This situation, DuPont insisted, should impress the Directors. If the Directory did not curb the corsairs, there would be a "long and cruel war between the two republics," and the United States would unite with England in the conflict.

DuPont claimed that full-scale war with the United States would strengthen the British navy, imperil Saint Domingue and France's other Caribbean possessions, invite American frontiersmen to invade Spain's neighboring colonies, and hence deprive France of the opportunity of regaining Louisiana. Furthermore, Jefferson had warned that his party would lose whatever opportunity it had of winning the forthcoming elections and of gaining control of the American government if France did not change to a conciliatory policy. He urged, as DuPont reported, that the Directory recall all the commissions to corsairs in the West Indies, revise the decrees of which neutrals complained, and let the American government know it would negotiate with a mission sent to Paris, Holland, or Spain.[19]

Other French diplomats familiar with American affairs offered similar advice. Pierre Auguste Adet, a former Minister to the United States, said he corresponded with Republicans who told him that President Adams had added considerably to his influence because many Americans were convinced "that France wants to declare war on them." The English, he claimed, had spread this idea. To counteract it and to show the peaceful intentions of the Directory, he suggested the lifting of the embargo on American ships in French ports.

Another diplomat pointed out the need for increased trade with the United States, suggested the sending of a well-known minister to Philadelphia, and urged the government to forbid privateers from indiscriminately capturing American ships. Those measures, he advised, should be followed by the appointment of commissioners to consider the claims of both France and the United States.

Since DuPont's report indicated that French plans for a revived colonial empire in America were in danger, it redoubled

Talleyrand's zeal to reach an accommodation with the United States. To achieve this end he followed DuPont's and Jefferson's suggestions, and some of those from his own diplomats who knew America.[20]

DuPont's warning came at a time when Talleyrand believed success was near in his negotiations with Spain for the retrocession of Louisiana. On July 10 the Minister of Foreign Relations had reported that Spain was yielding. He and other French statesmen did not wish to jeopardize the attainment of this prize with an enlarged war against the United States.

On July 15 Talleyrand had again told Gerry that France desired a reconciliation. The United States, the Foreign Minister said, was perpetuating the friction between the two countries by ordering attacks on French warships and by breaking off all commercial relations. Since the Directory could not endure its suffering much longer, it would have to retaliate by carrying out its temporary embargo on American ships. Then he nullified this threat by saying the Directory would wait until "irresistably forced" into hostilities because of its "repugnance to consider the United States as enemies." "Since you will depart, sir," he told Gerry, "hasten, at least, to transmit to your Government this solemn declaration." [21]

At The Hague, two days later, Pichon approached Murray with a letter from Talleyrand dated July 9 in which the Minister of Foreign Relations deplored Gerry's determination to leave Paris and also made overtures to Adams for a reconciliation. At first Murray was reluctant to forward the letter to the President, saying to himself, "much as I wish for Peace I will not be the instrument of such uncertain advances to it." [22] Talleyrand's desire to avoid war seemed so obvious and Pichon's acknowledgement that the United States had true grievances and a right to take defensive measures appeared so frank that Murray apparently changed his mind. He sent the information directly to President Adams.

Murray reported that America's defensive measures had alarmed the French. They claimed that the Americans had prematurely broken off the X Y Z negotiation and had even blocked the possibility of negotiation with Gerry. Pichon said that as a result just as Talleyrand had persuaded the Executive Directory to negotiate with the United States he was unable to find an American in Paris with the authority to do so. Murray wrote that the French wished to reestablish proper diplomatic relations with the United States.

Then Murray went on to explain that he did not write to Pickering because the letter Pichon had given him might not have come from Talleyrand himself. Besides, too many people were looking at the State Department's correspondence, and some men might use his letter "to foolish or wicked ends." He might, moreover, be going beyond the purposes of the government as they had been developing since he had received his last set of instructions. As for his own feelings, he was certain the letter Pichon had presented had come from Talleyrand.[23]

Within a week, on July 22, Talleyrand made a final plea to Gerry, asking him to resume negotiations in Paris. There need be no loan to the Directory, the Minister of Foreign Relations said, nor explanations about President Adams's speeches. He explained that the Directory had learned that "violence has been committed on the commerce and the citizens of the United States in the Antilles and on their coasts." Steps were already being taken, he added, to curb that violence.

These concessions appeared to meet Gerry's desires, for he had told Talleyrand that the basic causes of friction, as far as Americans were concerned, were France's desire for a loan and the spoliations at sea. If France truly desired peace, Gerry had indicated, she could so demonstrate by stopping her attacks on American commerce. He said he was pleased to learn of the Directory's willingness to negotiate peace. The United States had always been willing to do so.[24]

During this time Murray had, however, added another condition for France to meet before there could be peace and the resumption of diplomatic relations. He urged the Dutch government to persuade the Directory to offer the assurances Adams had demanded in his message to Congress on June 21, 1798.[25] The Dutch said they would try.

Pinckney, who was now in Bordeaux awaiting passage to America, also heard from Talleyrand that the French government's attitude toward the United States had changed. But Pinckney was skeptical. He reported Talleyrand's friendly gestures to Secretary of State Pickering, saying that he thought those overtures "are intended only to amuse us, till they are in a state of better preparation to attack us than they are at present, or as an insidious attempt again to divide us. . . ."

Talleyrand's overtures were not at all as diabolical as Pinckney thought they were. On July 27 the Minister of Foreign Relations used DuPont's report as the basis of an appeal to the Executive Directory for a policy of restraint and reconciliation toward the United States. This appeal apparently succeeded. Four days later the Directory issued a new decree that revoked the commissions of privateers in the West Indies, ordered the recall of judges suspected of having a personal interest in the pillaging of commerce, and demanded respect for the ships of allies and neutrals.[26]

Gerry had left Paris for Le Havre on July 26, but on August 3 Talleyrand sent him a copy of this new decree of July 31 and another to Fulwar Skipwith, the American Consul General, with the wish that "the conduct of the Federal government should correspond to that of the Directory. In this case amicable relations between the two peoples should soon be re-established." The French government would also lift the temporary embargo imposed on American vessels as retaliation for the acts of Congress, and it repealed that part of the decree of March 2, 1797, requiring the *rôle d'équipage*.

Five days later, on August 8, Gerry sailed from Le Havre convinced that a new negotiation would be successful. He carried with him French proposals for a *rapprochement*. "The aspect of affairs between the two countries is very pacific at present, on this side of the atlantic," he wrote. "God grant it may be so, on my arrival the other side of it." But trouble awaited him at home. Furthermore, the French government aggravated his difficulties by forwarding all of his correspondence with Talleyrand to Létombe for publication in the United States.[27]

After Gerry had left Paris, Talleyrand continued to stress his desire for a *rapprochement* in his indirect approaches to Murray. Believing the French were sincere in seeking a negotiation, the Maryland diplomat now forwarded information from some of his conversations with Pichon to Secretary of State Pickering. Murray pointed out that the French were taking great pains to promote a negotiation. "This is," he wrote, "a natural consequence of the energy and power of the United States combined in a view of the *present* state of Europe." He felt that his countrymen, by capturing French colonies, could hurt France more than she could injure the United States.[28]

"Continue unostentatiously to see Mr. Murray," Talleyrand told Pichon, "and endeavor to learn the views of his own government as well as to convince him of the good disposition of the French government. It is important to make some impression on the men devoted to the administration of Mr. Adams and to make them doubt at least the justice of the measures he continues to enact in the legislative Body of the United States." [29]

In keeping with its conciliatory policy toward the United States, the Directory on August 16 issued another decree that raised the embargo that had been directed against American ships in French ports, with the hope that the American government "would take measures conformable to the pacific disposition of the French Republic." [30] Three days later Murray reported to President Adams that the French had received, "with satisfaction," a Dutch offer to mediate their quarrel with the United States. Murray believed that this receptive attitude proved France's desire for peace. It was at Murray's suggestion that the Dutch had informally and confidentially offered to mediate. He and others thought that France and the United States could use the Dutch as a channel for sounding out each other on the possibility of an accommodation.[31]

PRIVATE PEACE SEEKERS

On August 22 Skipwith reported to Pickering that those American seamen who had been arrested as Englishmen were being released from French prisons. Different people gave different reasons for this act by the French and for the lifting of the embargo. Murray claimed that the retaliatory laws passed by Congress, especially the abrogation of the French treaties, were the cause. The Dutch attributed the French actions to their own mediation efforts, and Pichon to his conversations with Murray. Others assumed that the French had acted in response to the pleas of Tadeusz A. Kosciuszko, the Polish soldier who had fought in the American Revolution by the side of General Washington, and to the private peace mission of Dr. George Logan of Philadelphia. The Polish patriot, who had undertaken his mission to Paris at the suggestion of Vice-President Jefferson, had frequent secret talks with the Directors urging them to make peace with the United States.[32]

Logan, a Quaker idealist and a Republican, aroused more controversy than did Kosciuszko. The Quaker had left the United States secretly, to evade Federalists who had been assigned to watch him, on June 12, 1798, and had arrived in Paris on August 7. Federalists had denounced him as a traitor disloyally in correspondence with Jacobins, but his motive was peace. Fearing that the Adams administration would drag the country into war, he had gone to France on his own to do what he could to prevent an irreparable break. Some Federalists accused him of going to Paris with the purpose of making arrangements for a French invasion of the United States. When Logan arrived in Amsterdam, for example, Murray commented, "Peace his object. . . . What sort of Peace! submission?—" To Murray, Logan was an "incendiary physician."[33]

In Paris, Logan received a warm welcome from a colony of American expatriates headed by Joel Barlow, the poet and publicist from Connecticut who had gone to Paris in the 1780's and had stayed on to become a warm supporter of republican France. Although merely a private citizen, Logan sought to reopen negotiations between France and his own country. With this in mind, he brought with him letters from Létombe addressed to Merlin de Douai, the new president of the Executive Directory, and to Talleyrand. He also had letters from Thomas McKean, Chief Justice of Pennsylvania and a prominent Republican, and from Vice-President Jefferson. McKean's and Jefferson's letters merely certified Logan's citizenship and character, a common procedure at this time.

Secret agents, apparently acting on instructions from Talleyrand, quickly visited Logan and sought to ascertain the background of his mission. They tried, for instance, to obtain Létombe's letter to Merlin, which Logan refused to surrender.

Logan's private diplomacy stressed that the French protestations of goodwill would be more effective with Americans if the Directory would support them with deeds. The Executive Directory could release imprisoned American sailors and raise its embargo against American ships as a tangible expression of goodwill. Logan's pleas alone, however, did not cause the Directory to lift the embargo. The Directors apparently reached that decision, as the result of various pressures, before Logan arrived in Paris. The first order for the release of the American sailors was dated only four days after Logan's arrival—probably before he had seen any of the Directors.

To Logan, Talleyrand appeared cool and evasive. The Directors, on the other hand, were noticeably friendly, and openly feted him. Later, they acted as though they had been influenced by his suggestions. This friendliness stemmed from the fact that Logan was a prominent Republican, untainted by any record of pro-English sentiments. Larévellière-Lépeaux expressed warm feeling for France's sister republic across the sea, but he felt that it had temporarily fallen under evil leadership. He told Logan the Executive Directory would do all that it could, through any legitimate action a foreign government could employ, to help elevate Jefferson to the Presidency. In this way, he said, the Directory would attempt to overcome the obstacle of the Federalist leaders to peaceful relations.

Merlin, on the other hand, told the Quaker that France did not wish to interfere in America's internal affairs. She had, he explained, violated the rights of neutral shipping because England had done so first. France's violations, he promised, would soon stop.[34]

As for Talleyrand, he apparently was playing a complicated

game in which he tried to please his superiors and sought to gain peace regardless of which party held power in the United States. So, he was trying to placate the Adams administration and obtain a reconciliation through Murray, while also attempting to maintain close ties with the Jeffersonians whom he soon expected to assume power. If the Minister of Foreign Relations appeared too friendly in his dealings with Logan, whom the Federalists detested, he might jeopardize his peace overtures.

During his three weeks in Paris, Logan associated mainly with the small circle of Americans, all of them Jeffersonians, that had greeted him upon his arrival. This group, in addition to Barlow, included Robert Fulton, the inventor and former printer of miniatures in Philadelphia who was trying to sell his newly devised submarine to the Directory, Nathaniel Cutting, and Fulwar Skipwith. Many of those in the American colony in Paris were speculators whose property would have been seized as soon as full-scale war began.[35] So they had a selfish stake in peace.

Logan left Paris for Bordeaux on August 29 and sailed for home two weeks later, carrying with him dispatches from the Consul General to the President and the Secretary of State. These letters contained official notification that France had lifted her embargo and had freed her American prisoners. A duplicate set of dispatches was entrusted to Joseph Woodward, a Federalist from Boston, who was to reach America before Logan.[36]

Gerry, Murray, Logan, and the Americans in Paris were not the only ones who concluded that the French professions of a desire for peace were sincere. From Berlin in this summer of 1798 John Quincy Adams sent letters to Pickering, to his mother, to his father, and to others, indicating that he had evidence the French government wished to avoid war with the United States. Newspapers also suggested that the "good sense of the American people" would prevent war.[37]

Young Adams knew of the conversations between Murray and Pichon and of the assurances Murray sought from the French. Murray said that Pichon now stressed "that a great change had taken place in the mind of his government on American affairs, that it was now clear to them that they had been deceived by men who meddled on both sides of the water."

Pichon repeated, Murray added, "as he had often done the interests which France had in not going to war with us—loss of colonies, junction with England, future fortune of America as a powerful nation. . . ." [38]

On August 28 Talleyrand had addressed a letter to Pichon to be shown to Murray, who was to be permitted to retain a copy if he agreed to keep it secret from everyone except President Adams. In it Talleyrand stressed the economic and commercial rivalry between France and Britain. On the other hand, he saw "no clashing of interests, [nor] any cause of jealousy" between France and the United States. The cause of misunderstanding, he suggested, was that "the Government of the United States has thought that France wanted to revolutionize it. France has thought that the Government of the United States wanted to throw itself into the arms of England. . . . Let us substitute calmness for passion, confidence for suspicions, and we shall soon agree." [39]

In this letter Talleyrand also rejected the idea of Dutch or Spanish mediation, apparently preferring a direct settlement. He disavowed any disposition to dictate the choice of an American envoy to France, but he said the Directory would naturally have more confidence in a minister who had not expressed hatred of the French republic, or a predilection for England, than one who had.

On the night of September 6 Pichon showed Murray the letter. It had Talleyrand's signature and was marked with an official seal. On the following day Pichon gave Murray a copy, warning him not to have the letter published.[40] Murray received the document in a friendly spirit and forwarded it to Adams.

News of France's desire for peace was spreading. James C. Mountflorence, who worked with Murray at The Hague, reported that Americans lately from Paris were saying that the Directors had declared "that they will not go to War with us, and that even should the U.S. issue a Declaration of War, they will not engage in it, but use all their efforts to negotiate." [41]

By this time the British, too, were convinced that France would not wage war against the United States. British observers maintained that the vigor and firmness of the American government in all probability had prevented full-scale war with France. Without support from American Jacobins, it was pointed out, the French were impotent against the United States. They were disappointed in the amount of support they had received from the Republican party in America. With war, moreover, the French could do no greater harm than they had already inflicted with their cruisers.[42]

Leading Federalists were also becoming convinced that the Directory desired peace. "You will have no war!" Rufus King told Hamilton. "France will propose to renew the negotiation upon the basis laid down in the President's instructions to the envoys." He pointed out, however, that this was merely conjecture. Nonetheless, Hamilton was convinced. "France will treat, not fight; grant us fair terms and not keep them," he wrote in the margin of King's letter. "Meantime our election will occur & bring her friends into power." [43]

Although pleased with the French assurances of desire for peaceful negotiation, Murray thought that Talleyrand had not gone far enough. The rejection of envoys on previous occasions, Murray told Pichon, gives the American government the right to an explicit declaration, such as President Adams had demanded on June 21, that any envoy sent to France will be received and treated with the respect due to the representative of a great, powerful, free, and independent nation. Such a reception is a right which was twice refused. Hence, Murray insisted, it ought to be "expressly declared & with a Handsomeness equal in Degree to the Harshness with which it was deny'd—" [44]

On the next day, September 24, 1798, Pichon left for Paris. Although surprised that the Americans would require any further guarantee, Talleyrand complied with Murray's request. Two weeks later, on October 7, the French military postmaster brought Murray the original of a letter from Talleyrand to Pichon dated September 28. This was not the direct public statement that Murray had demanded, but otherwise it met his stipulations for a renewed negotiation.

Talleyrand's letter contained almost the same words used by President Adams. "You were right," the Minister of Foreign Relations wrote, "to assert that, whatever plenipotentiary the Government of the United States might send to France, to put an end to the existing differences between the two countries, would be undoubtedly received with the respect due to the representative of a free, independent, and powerful nation." [45]

Murray was pleased by this diplomatic victory. He attributed it to his country's defiance, which he felt had shed ridicule on the Directory. "The United States," he asserted, "tore off the mask, and spoke out to all the world. . . ." [46]

At about this time, actually on October 1, Gerry arrived in the United States. As he walked up Boston's State Street, Federalists, by agreement, ignored him. No one offered a friendly greeting. While he had been gone his family had suffered. At night ruffians had milled around his house, hung effigies of him in the elms, shouted obscenities, and placed a miniature guillotine smeared with blood under Mrs. Gerry's window. As for Gerry himself, he was now a marked man. His movements were watched and his mail was tampered with. Orthodox Federalists ostracized him and his family.

Gerry immediately wrote to Pickering, forwarding the correspondence he had had with Talleyrand in Paris. In his long report of 44 pages, virtually a history of the mission to France, Gerry explained how Talleyrand had tried to prevent his departure, hoping thereby to ascertain if the United States would be willing to negotiate another treaty. The Directory, he said, was "very desirous of a reconciliation." He concluded that "if the door is still open to peace, the establishment of it must be a happy event to the United States." If, on the other hand, "the national pulse beats high for war" and the government considers it "the only safe and honourable alternative," may the Lord protect the nation. [47]

Then Gerry went straight to Adams at Quincy. There he dispelled the President's concern about his conduct in Paris and explained the French desire for peace and a new negotiation. Adams treated him kindly and advised him to bear Federalist abuse in silence.

This intimacy between Gerry and the President alarmed the High Federalists. They feared that Gerry had cast a spell over Adams, and that Gerry's pleas for peace might subvert their own plans for war. Pickering even denounced Gerry publicly as a man steeped in duplicity and treachery who deserved to be impeached. Except for the President's intervention, Pickering would even have deprived Gerry of his pay for the period he had remained alone in Paris.[48]

In later years Adams claimed that Gerry had "saved the peace of the nation; for he alone discovered and furnished the evidence that X. Y. and Z. were employed by Talleyrand; and he alone brought home the direct, formal, and official assurances upon which the subsequent commission proceeded. . . ." Adams also stated that "Gerry's negotiations were more useful and successful than those of either of his colleagues." [49]

These statements, written when Adams was an old man, exaggerated Gerry's role. Adams received other evidence from other sources. While he and Gerry were conferring, in fact, Murray's first letters telling of Talleyrand's overtures arrived in the United States.

At this juncture, also, news of British triumphs and of French setbacks gave encouragement to Americans, to those who wanted peace as well as to those who desired war. The Irish rebellion had failed, and on August 1, 1798, Admiral Horatio Nelson had caught and destroyed the French fleet off the shoals of Aboukir Bay, east of Alexandria. This victory in the Battle of the Nile had cut off Bonaparte and his army, which had invaded Egypt instead of England as originally planned, from France. In addition, Turkey had declared war against France.

Murray called Nelson's triumph grand news for the United States as well as for Britain. It was important to Americans because Nelson's guns had eliminated much of the limited naval force France could use to hurt the United States and, hence, diminished the possibility of any French effort to enlarge the Quasi-War.[50]

Jubilant over the British victories, High Federalists did not see them as serving the cause of peace. They denounced those "skulking half-measures" which left the initiative to the enemy and demanded unrestricted war against France.

THE PEACE FEELERS

Ironically, on October 9, 1798, just as Adams tasted bitter defeat in the quarrel over Hamilton's rank in the Provisional Army, two of Murray's private letters reached him at Quincy. Admonished by the President to keep the contents secret, Pickering deciphered the two dispatches in Philadelphia and returned them to Adams on October 18.

Murray's first letter, dated July 1, 1798, explained the Directory's concern over the possibility of an Anglo-American alliance, a fact that impressed the President. Most impressive, however, was the basic message. These letters indicated quite clearly that Adams could succeed in ending the French raids on American commerce without resorting to full-scale war. Since the problem of Louisiana's future could wait, this news suggested that there was no need for a war of conquest that would add to Hamilton's glory.[51]

Two days after receiving Murray's ciphered dispatches, Adams indicated a new drift in his thinking. He wrote to Pickering directing him to obtain the advice of the other department heads on two questions. First, should the President in his second annual message to Congress in December call for a declaration of war if France had not already declared war against the United States? Secondly, could he safely make any further proposals for negotiation?

Adams explained that he still held to the sentiments of his message of June 21 that he would send no ministers to France without prior assurances they would be received honorably. Nonetheless, he thought it might be wise to tell Congress he would be willing to send an envoy so as to keep open the channels of communication if France were to offer assurance of his proper reception. Adams now preferred the second course to a declaration of war. He even mentioned possible candidates for a new mission, among them Patrick Henry of Virginia and William Vans Murray, moderate Federalists who were not obnoxious to the French.[52]

Instead of accepting the President's conciliatory lead, Pickering called the other members of the cabinet together with the purpose of forcing Adams into committing himself to a continuation of the Quasi-War. Hamilton and other Federalist leaders, such as George Washington, Charles Cotesworth Pinckney, and the high command of the Army, also attended this meeting, held in Trenton, New Jersey, the temporary national capital while yellow fever raged in Philadelphia. Fearing "the instability" of Adams's attitude, the department heads began, at Hamilton's insistence, to draft a belligerent message.

At this juncture, on the evening of October 28, Harrison Gray Otis, a Hamiltonian Federalist who had now broken with the extremists, called on the President with news from Richard Codman, a Boston friend and firm Federalist who was in Paris on business. Codman's letter supported what Adams had been hearing from his own son, from Murray, and from Gerry about France's changed attitude toward the United States. Codman attributed the change to the advice offered the Executive Directory by Victor Marie DuPont, Constantin-François Chasseboeuf Volney, and other Frenchmen who had returned from the United States.

"I hope to God that on the arrival of the dispatches which Mr. Skipwith sends, by the Vessel that carries this," Codman wrote, "no declaration of War will have taken place or alliance with great Britain, if not & the desire for Peace still continues with our Government I think they may count on an equal desire on the part of France, & a reconciliation yet be brought about, which ought to be desired by all true friends to both countries." [53]

Codman also told how Logan had informed the Directors and Talleyrand that they could not count on the support of any party in America. Every American, the Quaker had said, would rally to the government and resist a foreign invasion. A few days later, on November 1, Joseph Woodward brought Adams a copy of the memorial Logan had presented to Talleyrand.

All this additional evidence substantiated Adams's view that Gerry's conduct in Paris had been proper, had been motivated by a genuine desire for peace, not by a partisan political commitment, and that he had been unjustly maligned by the High Federalists. Pickering, for example, had recklessly condemned Gerry in letters to friends, and even in a public letter of October 16 to petitioners from Prince Edward County, Virginia. Taking exception to the Secretary's accusations, Gerry wrote to the President defending his actions.

Adams forwarded Gerry's letter to Pickering, suggesting that in fairness to the accused it should be published. The Secretary of State defied the President, saying on November 5 that if Gerry took to the press, he himself would go further in exposing "not his pusillanimity, weakness and meanness alone, but his duplicity and treachery as well." Pickering claimed that testimony from Pinckney and Marshall would support his charges, and that Gerry would be impeached except for political expediency.

This defiance sprang from frustration, for the President's defense of Gerry had the effect of undermining the contentions of High Federalists that the French overtures to Gerry had been insincere, and that he had been duped. Seeing no advantage in making an issue of Pickering's defiance at this time, Adams retracted his request and persuaded Gerry not to publish.[54]

Pickering's reliance on Pinckney, who had now returned to the United States as something of a hero, was not misplaced. High Federalists tried to use Pinckney's popularity to keep the indignation against France boiling and to stimulate the martial spirit. Pinckney cooperated by making belligerent speeches denouncing "Gallic despotism." At Trenton, for example, he asserted that if "we would have Peace with France, it must be obtained, not by negociation, but by the sword."[55]

At this time, or about November 10, Logan arrived in Philadelphia with his message from Merlin de Douai expressing friendship for the United States. A few days later, in Trenton, Logan approached Pickering with his words of peace, saying the Directory would soon make further conciliatory gestures, such as the curbing of its corsairs. The Secretary of State replied that he placed no faith in these assurances. As he showed Logan to the door he announced coldly, "Sir, it is my duty to inform you that the government does not thank you for what you have done."

On November 13, accompanied by the Reverend Robert Blackwell of St. Peter's Church, who by chance arrived at the same time, Logan called on General Washington who happened to be in Philadelphia. As the Quaker spoke, the General remained impassive, cold, and unbelieving. Washington, who directed most of his conversation to Blackwell, pointed out that it was truly remarkable that Logan, an unknown private citizen, should succeed in a mission of reconciliation when "gentlemen of the first respectability in our Country, specially charged under the authority of the government," had failed.[56]

Washington's attitude was not unusual; it merely reflected the general High Federalist skepticism toward France's overtures. William Smith, now a Federalist diplomat in Europe, suggested that the peaceful gestures stemmed from the belief of French statesmen that they could no longer injure the United States, and that their cause was losing ground in America. Yet, Smith said, "deceived by their intolerable vanity & by the false intelligence of their partizans . . . they still assert that the opposition to them is merely that of a party headed by J.[ohn] A.[dams]." [57]

As Smith wrote these lines, Adams was traveling toward Philadelphia after some three months in Quincy, where the sick Abigail had been in bed for eleven weeks. The President now had a different attitude toward the Quasi-War than he did when his carriage had taken him away from the capital city. Then he had regretted that Congress had not declared war. Now, suspicious of the loyalty of his advisers and fortified by evidence of the authenticity of the French overtures, he was ready to act independently for peace. If necessary, he was also ready to defy the war hawks of his own party.

The President arrived in Philadelphia on November 25 and on the following day saw Logan, who repeated the story he had told, with little effect, to Pickering and Washington. Adams responded with unexpected graciousness. He served tea and asked many questions about the desire of the French authorities to receive an American envoy and to negotiate an accommodation. Apparently he was impressed with Logan's message.[58]

Only once did the President blow up. When Logan insisted that the Directory would now receive an American minister, Adams jumped from his chair, gesticulated, and said, "Yes, I suppose if I were to send Mr. Madison or Mr. Giles or Dr. Logan, they would receive either of *them*. But I'll do no such thing; I'll send whom I please."

"And whoever you do please to send," the Quaker answered, "will be received."

By this time Adams had apparently decided to reopen negotiations if genuine acceptance of his terms were to come from the Executive Directory. The information he had from his son, John Quincy, from Murray, Gerry, Codman, and Logan all indicated that such assurances were on the way.[59]

After conferring with his department heads, the President reviewed their recommendations for his address to Congress. McHenry urged an immediate declaration of war against France, but then hedged. Since the President was engaged in a game of skill with the Directory and domestic Jacobins, the Secretary of War suggested, he should not now show his cards to these opponents of his administration. It would be better for Congress to take the initiative in declaring war. Adams's speech should simply provide the materials for such action by Congress. He should, the Secretary said, leave no doubt about refusing to send another minister to France until the Executive Directory itself gave him definite assurances it would receive the envoy.

McHenry also advised Adams to request in his address "such full powers . . . as would enable him to take effectual measures to counteract or render the designs of France to possess themselves of Louisiana and the Floridas as little injurious as possible to the United States." In effect, he wished the President to accept Miranda's project and also those who had associated themselves with it.

Stoddert, with whom Adams discussed the content of the address at some length, also considered a recommendation for a declaration of war desirable in theory. Congress, however, might turn down the request. Then confusion and rancor would result, and the administration would lose prestige and weaken its authority. Pickering, too, doubted the willingness of Congress to declare war, saying "the people of the United States are not yet convinced of the necessity of war." Time and more provocation, he felt, were needed to arouse popular anger. He insisted that the Directory must send an envoy to the United States.

Wolcott's reply to the President's inquiry was not his own, but the work of the Federalist chieftains whom Pickering had called together at Trenton, or what Jefferson called a military conclave and Adams himself later described as a war caucus. In any case, Hamilton's incisive mind had shaped the response, and as a result it went to the President as the ablest of the cabinet members' recommendations.

After weighing the advantages and disadvantages of the Quasi-War, Wolcott advised against its immediate enlargement, saying that a declaration of war was "inexpedient and ought not to be recommended." Adams should continue his present foreign policy and should prevent the political opposition, or Republicans, from gaining a "rallying point." The sending of another minister to France would be so humiliating that the nation should not commit itself to such an act except under the most extreme necessity. Such a necessity, Wolcott insisted, did not now exist. He also advised against negotiation unless France first sent an envoy to the United States to assure the President of her sincere intentions.

The wording in this draft meant that the French government had to humble itself with a public acknowledgment of past error before the American government would even consider serious diplomatic probings toward peace. Then the French had to fulfill American terms for the reopening of negotiations precisely as they, the Americans, had prescribed them. Wolcott did not spell out the manner of receiving such assurances from the French. Yet the Hamiltonians made it clear that they wanted to prevent a new negotiation and to keep the nation on a war footing. Renewed explorations for peace might destroy their program. They apparently wanted the President himself to take the initiative in recommending a declaration of war.[60]

When the Hamiltonians learned definitely that the President would not ask Congress for a declaration of war in his message, they called Federalist members from both houses of Congress to a secret caucus to see if they could obtain a declaration of war over Adams's head. The war hawks failed to obtain majority support.

Adams, who had now, in effect, received a vote of confidence, took Wolcott's draft as the basis of his message, modifying it to fit his own changing views. Basically, he altered the Hamiltonian statement that he would not send another mission to France. Since none of his department heads had told him clearly whether they were for or against a declaration of war, the President chose to interpret their advice as a vote against peace. It indicated, he realized, the cabinet's wish to continue the undeclared war until a new crisis or some emotional incident converted it into the unrestrained conflict the war hawks desired.[61]

THE PRESIDENT'S TERMS

The third session of the Fifth Congress was scheduled to convene on December 3, 1798, but a quorum did not form until the eighth, when Adams delivered his message. The High Federalist legislators, bitter over their inability to control Congress, were still in a belligerent mood. Those who had opposed them, they believed, were enemies of order and government, mongers of sedition, and traitors. Journalists, such as William Cobbett, castigated "the small federalists," or moderates. First, he predicted that Congress would declare war within a week. Then, his mood changed to gloom. "They will," he wrote of the members of Congress, "seek nothing but *peace* and safety," as if such a quest were a crime.[62]

Adams proved Cobbett correct. The President told Congress that even though the Directory appeared anxious to avoid a complete rupture and had "in a qualified manner declared itself willing to receive a minister from the United States for the purpose of restoring a good understanding," nothing in France's conduct so far should encourage Americans to relax their measures for defense. Even though we demonstrate that we do not fear war, he said, "we shall give no room to infer that we abandon the desire for peace." Then he stressed,

> It is peace that we have uniformly and perseveringly cultivated, and harmony between us and France may be restored at her option. But to send another minister without more determinate assurances that he would be received would be an act of humiliation to which the United States ought not to submit. It must therefore be left with France (if she is indeed desirous of accommodation) to take the requisite steps.

Adams also pledged that "the Executive authority of this country still adheres to the humane and pacific policy which has invariably governed its proceedings." Whether or not it negotiated with France, it would continue vigorous preparations for war. "These alone," he insisted, "will give to us an equal treaty and insure its observance." [63]

Although willing to negotiate, Adams seemed not yet fully satisfied that the French had reformed. So his message had faced two ways. High Federalists considered it weak because it was conciliatory and left the final decision for war or peace to France. Their leaders in the government knew, moreover, that Adams favored peace and that their war program was in trouble. Upset by this threat to Hamiltonian aspirations, Pickering blamed Gerry for the President's stand. Another prominent Federalist lamented that Congress had not itself grasped the reins of foreign policy in the last session and declared war. Now a "general stupor" had fallen over the country, and men were pleased that there would probably not be expanded hostilities.

Having seen the President deliver his message from a platform where he was flanked by the generals of the new Army—Washington, Hamilton, and Pinckney—and seeing in it no firm gesture toward France for a new mission, many Republicans considered it uncompromising, provocative, and warlike. Jefferson, among others, held this view.

Yet some Republicans were pleasantly surprised, saying the address was "more moderate than we expected." Adams, they believed, had left an opening for negotiations "which was not perhaps desired by all his faction." Another Republican remarked that "the tone of the president is much changed, and that we may still hope for peace. What has produced this, or how far he is sincere we cannot yet determine." Outside observers agreed with this view. In Paris Adams's speech was received with a good deal of satisfaction, and the government there continued to stress its desire for peace and an accommodation.[64]

In the formal answers to the President's speech the House expressed approval of the conciliatory attitude, but the Federalist Senate evinced hostility. The senators claimed that the government had done a great deal to assure France of its sincerity. So, if the Directory still refused to meet the American terms and tried "to prescribe the political qualifications" of any American minister sent to France, such action, they advised, "ought to be regarded as designed to separate the people from their Government and to bring about by intrigue that which open force could not effect." The Senate also attacked Logan's private diplomacy, saying it should be rebuffed. James Madison thought the upper house wanted to goad France into a war the senators themselves were unwilling to declare.

When Adams accepted the Senate's reply, publicly he seemed as far from a firm policy of peace as he had been before he gave his speech. He told the Senate on December 12 that he had "no real evidence" of change in France's attitude toward the United States. Taking up the reference to Logan, he condemned "officious interference of individuals without public character" and asked for measures to prevent the intrusion of such persons into foreign affairs. Nonetheless, the President also indicated that he stood ready to act upon French overtures which met the conditions he had announced to Congress on June 21. In this he acted logically, for, as Jefferson had pointed out a few weeks earlier, the reports of French willingness to negotiate honorably had become too well known for Federalists to continue to dismiss them as duplicity.[65]

As a consequence, Harrison Gray Otis, chairman of the House Committee on Defense, asked Hamilton for advice on how to proceed on this matter of war or negotiations. I would be grateful, Otis wrote, if you can "devote an hour to my instruction." Hamilton, who prepared legislation for Otis to introduce, which Otis did, said he hoped that Congress would pass a law empowering the President, "at his discretion . . . to declare that a state of war exists between the two countries" if negotiations with France did not begin by August 1, or if started, should they fail. It was at this time, too, that he repeated suggestions for the acquisition of Spanish lands to the south.

Adams apparently heard of Hamilton's ideas, for he wrote to Otis about them. "This man is stark mad, or I am," the President said of Hamilton. "He knows nothing of the character, the principles, the feelings, the opinions and prejudices of this nation. If Congress should adopt this system, it would produce an instantaneous insurrection of the whole nation from Georgia to New Hampshire." [66]

With Hamilton probably in mind, the President now also expressed distaste for those Americans who "grow amazingly fearless and valiant in proportion as they hear the English beat the French. . . . I don't like this bravery," he admitted, "which grows in proportion as danger appears to lessen." [67]

In keeping with the President's suggestion, Congress took up the Logan mission as its first order of business in the new session. This action upset the plans of Republican leaders in Congress. They had decided to proceed cautiously in the new session by trying to avoid "all questions of foreign relations" so that they, the Republicans, could not "be charged with being agents of France." Whatever resistance they would offer, they decided, would be in domestic issues.

When debate over Logan's mission opened, handsome Robert Goodloe Harper, the leading orator in Congress, sprang to the attack, holding the floor of the House for four hours. He flayed Republicans by arguing the existence of a "pro-French party" in the nation that had used an American agent to conspire with the Directory, and particularly with Talleyrand, to lull the American people into a false sense of security with signs of peaceful intent. That party, he asserted, sought to regain prestige lost as a result of the X Y Z disclosures, win the election of 1800, and then with the government in its hands, welcome godless revolutionary troops from France to America's shores.

These charges forced the Republicans to give up their plan of caution. Their leader in the House, Albert Gallatin, speaking in his thick Genevan accent, hotly denied Harper's elaborate thesis. But the Republican resistance could not stop the Federalist majority from censuring Logan and from passing a bill, known as Logan's Act, intended to embarrass the Republicans. This law, signed by Adams on January 30, 1799, provided a fine and imprisonment for any American who on his own corresponded with a foreign government on a matter in dispute with the United States with the intent of influencing the conduct of that government.

From the Republican point of view the law made it a crime for a private citizen to use his own resources for peace in any quarrel the United States had with another country, but it ignored those actions by private citizens that would stir up war. Federalists saw the law as a means of stopping self-appointed diplomats from meddling in delicate international matters or from sabotaging the government's foreign policy.[68]

During the debate over Logan's law the President's third son, Thomas Boylston Adams, after almost five years in Europe as secretary to his older brother John Quincy, was on his way home. Thomas reached New York on January 11, 1799, posted his dispatches and letters, took care of his baggage, and then rushed on to Philadelphia. Four days later, with tears in his eyes, the President embraced his son and said, "I thank my God that you have returned again to your native country." [69]

Father and son talked all night long, and in addition to family and personal matters they discussed the state of Europe and the prospects for peace. Thomas brought important documents from Murray and John Quincy and, equally important, his own evaluation of the views of both. Thomas reiterated what his father already knew, that both diplomats were convinced that the mood of France had changed in favor of peace.

Thomas stressed that John Quincy endorsed Murray's judgments wholeheartedly. Even if France was bluffing in her intimations of peaceful intent, Thomas suggested, it would be better to call her bluff than to risk the danger of being maneuvered into the position of seeming unwilling to repair the breach between the two countries. The administration's policy of firmness and resolution, it appeared, had succeeded. Now the time had come to gather the fruits.

This news conveyed by Thomas, when placed beside other evidence the President had been receiving since October, indicated the formation of a pattern that spelled peace. The more President Adams thought about the situation, the clearer his course seemed. The only intense opposition to new negotiations would come from the High Federalists. These men could not be counted upon in any event. To his department heads and to the High Federalists he owed nothing. They danced to Hamilton's tune and were committed to his policy. This, as his sons and others advised, seemed the appropriate time to act.

On the very day of Thomas's arrival, the President asked Pickering to draft a plan for a new treaty and a consular convention, such as might be acceptable to the United States if France proposed such agreements. He asked the Secretary of State to work in secret, to seek the advice of the other department heads, and to complete the work quickly. Since Pickering saw no sign that France was preparing to send a mission to the United States, he concluded that Adams was planning to send one to France.

Three days later Adams sent Gerry's diplomatic correspondence to Congress.[70] On the following day the President himself answered the objections Pickering had raised to Gerry's reports. Although Adams stood firm against his Secretary's views, on January 21, 1799, he did forward to Congress a report that Pickering had prepared on his own summarizing negotiations with France. The French government, the Secretary of State warned, plotted to throw the blame for war on the United States. He also attacked Talleyrand's overtures for a new negotiation as insincere and as "pretences for unlimited depredations." He warned against deceit in the French offer of reconciliation, saying "I hope we shall remember that 'the tiger crouches before he leaps upon his prey.' "[71]

Pickering had apparently devoted more of his time to the preparation of his report and of charges against Gerry, than he had to the draft treaty. This made little difference to Adams who "wanted no report." He already had convincing evidence that the French overtures were genuine, and more such evidence had arrived from Europe that same day, mainly in new dispatches from William Vans Murray.

THE CRUCIAL PEACE BID

Earlier Murray had written privately to the President that France favored a mediation of her dispute with the United States. Pichon, Murray said, had admitted that full-scale war with the United States would be unpopular in France and would endanger her colonies. Now another letter from Murray, dated August 20, 1798, reinforced this view.

A week later, apparently on February 1, Adams received decisive evidence, or Murray's dispatch of October 7. It told how the Maryland Federalist had insisted that a reconciliation with France must be on Adams's terms and how Talleyrand had agreed to meet those terms, but not through outside mediation. As proof of French sincerity Murray had enclosed Talleyrand's letter of September 28 to Pichon in which the Minister of Foreign Relations agreed to accept an American envoy in the words Adams had used in his message of June 21 to Congress.

There now seemed to be no doubt that despite Talleyrand's earlier verbiage and insults, as Murray explained, the French government had a genuine desire to reach a settlement with the United States. Murray's own analysis, coupled with the views of John Quincy and Thomas Boylston Adams, apparently impressed the President as much or more than did Talleyrand's words. Another of Murray's dispatches, this one dated October 12, reiterated that France stood ready to receive an American minister on honorable terms if he were neither unfriendly to France, nor "an advocate of Royalty." [72]

Adams now began to act on the basis of the information he had been receiving from Europe. He informed Congress that the French had rescinded the most obnoxious of their decrees against American shipping. He decided against employing Holland's offered mediation because that country was a French satellite.

"*What indeed could be more farcical,*" Pickering wrote,"*than such a mediation in the known state of dependence of the Batavian on the French government?* This considered, the *proposition partakes of the nature of an insult,* rather than an act of friendship. . . ." [73]

At the same time the President received important assistance from George Washington. From Paris on October 2, 1798, Joel Barlow had written a sensible letter saying "the French Directory is at present sincerely desirous of restoring [peace] . . . on terms honorable and advantageous to both parties." Neither France nor the United States, he wrote, really wants war, though "each believes the other determined on war, and ascribes all its conduct to a deep-rooted hostility." So, why is it, he asked, "that a calamity so dreadful must be rendered inevitable because it is thought so?" Both governments can talk, listen, negotiate. The Directory would negotiate with any American envoy who was sent with a real intention of talking peace. For some unclear reason, he explained, the Directors did not believe the last envoys were sincere. Then Barlow listed other steps toward peace the Directory had taken. Full-scale war, in his view, would be a tragedy. "In a war," he pointed out, "there is clearly nothing to be *gained* by us, not even honor." [74]

In confidence, Washington forwarded Barlow's plea to Adams on February 1, 1799. The retired President, now acting as an indirect peacemaker, explained that although he had little confidence in Barlow himself, he believed Barlow had written with the approval of the Directory and should be heeded, particularly since the American people were "very desirous of peace." The General indicated that he was himself ready to support Adams if new negotiations would lead to an accommodation with France on honorable terms. Peace, he said, was "the ardent desire of all the friends of this rising empire." [75]

At this time Adams could dismiss the services of Barlow as those of "a more worthless fellow" than Tom Paine. Yet later he admitted that he had weighed Barlow's letter carefully, looking "for suspicion of any ill design," and had concluded that it had been written with good intentions. Even if the President had been unable to overcome his distrust of Barlow, he could not easily ignore Washington's sentiments. Although Adams could not make public use of Barlow's and the General's letters, he knew now that Washington would not throw his immense prestige on the side of the High Federalists in their disapproval, which was bound to come if he, Adams, were to accept the French overtures.

In Paris, meantime, the Directors continued to receive news of weakness in the Federalist party and pleas for a resumption of diplomatic relations with the United States.[76] Talleyrand summarized the state of relations with the United States along these lines, submitting his analysis to the Directors on February 14. The crisis with the United States, he maintained, had passed its most critical stage in the summer of 1798. Since that time the assurances he had given to Gerry and Murray had begun to take effect. Now Americans were more occupied with bitter internal strife over the Alien and Sedition laws than with French problems. Létombe, Jefferson, Americans in France, and the Spanish Ambassador in Philadelphia, he said, had all contributed to the creation of a spirit of moderation toward France in the United States.

Apparently Talleyrand learned and remembered that his country could gain little by meddling in American politics. Although it appeared that the Federalist party was in decline, he thought it would be a mistake to interfere in American politics to take advantage of the loss of power of France's enemies. The birth of a French party, he assumed, would stimulate the growth of a British one. In overcoming its present crisis with the United States, he advised, the Executive Directory should not create new ones. It should keep hands off American politics.

The most difficult problems in liquidating the Quasi-War, Talleyrand pointed out, now lay with his own countrymen rather than with the American government. French nationals were ignoring the repeal of the Executive Directory's maritime decrees. Corsairs from Guadeloupe and Cayenne, in French Guiana, had not changed their conduct, and French cruisers were still stopping American ships in European waters. The attitude of France's two legislative bodies, moreover, aggravated the difficulties with all neutrals, but particularly with the United States.

Through its overtures the Executive Directory had gained
time in dealing with the United States. This was valuable. "But,"
Talleyrand wrote, "the moment will come when justice alone will
consummate the work begun, when facts will be placed in opposition to promises. The minister cannot see without anxiety the future resources which our corsairs leave to the English Cabinet." [77]

Talleyrand's analysis of American politics was perceptive.
Through renewed activity of the Republican press the public had
become increasingly aware of France's overtures, of Logan's mission, and of Gerry's views. In the newspapers under its control,
such as the *Rédacteur,* the Executive Directory planted articles
that proclaimed its desire to extend a friendly hand to the United
States. The Jeffersonians spread this message in the United States.

When Gerry's correspondence was released to Congress on
January 18, 1799, Philadelphia's *Aurora,* now edited by William
Duane, printed it in full a few days later. From January 24
through 28 that journal published letters from Americans in Europe indicating that France wanted peace. Duane also produced
figures showing that the shipping losses suffered by Americans
were greater at the hands of the British than those of the French.
Even Pickering acknowledged that the *Aurora's* figures were reliable. Merchants trading with the French West Indies, many of
them Federalists, were among the consistent advocates of
peace.[78]

All this agitation for a peace that now seemed probable
tended to draw public sentiment toward the Jeffersonians. Jefferson himself was convinced that public opinion was "about to fall
into the Republican scale." [79]

Observing the resurgence of the Republicans, Adams noted
that they had found an effective issue in the Alien and Sedition
Acts, which they opposed. He himself chafed under the pressure
from Pickering and his other department heads to hold steady on
a hostile course against France. He watched, unhappily, the continuing and even growing emphasis on the Army.

One of the Army's ranking generals, Charles Cotesworth
Pinckney, was on his way south to prepare the defenses of that
region. On his return to Charleston he was given a hero's recep-

tion comparable to that given John Marshall in Philadelphia. A great banquet in City Hall on the night of February 8, 1799, topped the honors for Pinckney. Prominent in the hall's elaborate decorations were the now patriotic slogans "No, No! not a six pence" and "millions for defense, not a cent for tribute." These words no longer seemed to arouse violent emotions, and this celebration, far from the national capital, did not have the impact on government that Marshall's welcome had had earlier. Even at this time of rejoicing there was evidence that prominent South Carolina Federalists were not satisfied with the administration's war program. Pinckney and others disliked the Alien and Sedition Acts, and they said so.[80]

As for the President, he could delay no longer. The moment had come for him to step up the war, as the Hamiltonians desired, or to accept the French overtures for a negotiation.[81] In assessing the political situation, he apparently realized that the popularity of his administration had grown during the war crisis because the people had felt that France had been wholly to blame. They believed his administration had not resorted to hostile measures until practically all hope for peace had been exhausted. Republican strength was again rising, it seemed, because the people knew that France had offered to negotiate peace.

Taking this analysis into account, as well as the cumulative effect of all the reports he had been receiving from Europe, the President decided on a momentous act. He would no longer resist the public sentiment for peace that Republicans and moderate Federalists had helped to arouse. He would not wait for France to send a new minister to the United States, nor for the direct assurances from the French government that he had earlier demanded.

On February 18, 1799, three days after obtaining confirmation that France had retracted her onerous maritime decrees, and just after Congress had provided for raising an army of thirty thousand men, Adams nominated Murray, as suggested by Gerry, by Talleyrand, by John Quincy Adams, and by Americans in Paris, as Minister Plenipotentiary to the French Republic. The President would not, however, allow Murray to enter France until Talleyrand offered direct and unequivocal assurances he would receive Murray properly and would appoint a minister of equal grade to negotiate with him. With his message the President sent to the Senate, as a secret communication, Talleyrand's letter of September 28 to Pichon.[82]

As presiding officer of the Senate, Jefferson read the message. As he did so, he could not disguise his own astonishment. He also noted the looks of dismay on the faces of many of the Federalists in the chamber. Adams, who had not consulted his department heads or sought outside advice on this decision, had kept his secret well. In a sense he had to do so, for he knew beforehand that the majority of his department heads and important leaders in his own party were hostile to the very idea of the peace mission he had proposed. He also knew that as long as public opinion was opposed to war, it would be on his side. He realized, too, that as long as General Washington stood by him, he had little to fear from his advisers and the war hawks.

As soon as Adams had sent his message, he wrote to Washington. The main factor in his decision, he explained, was Talleyrand's letter, supported by "a multitude of other letters and documents, official and unofficial. . . . Tranquility upon just and honorable terms," was undoubtedly the "ardent desire" of all good Americans. Adams had been, in the words of Henrietta Liston, "induced by an overture from the cloven footed Devil Talleyrand. . . ."[83]

Now the President told Washington that he only hoped that "the babyish and womanly blubbering" for peace at any price would not persuade Americans to conclude a treaty that was less than honorable. All this "cant about peace," he added, lacked sincerity, for "those who snivel for it now were hot for war against Britain a few months ago and would be now, if they saw a chance." Washington responded by assuring Adams of his faith in Adams's decision and choice of emissary.

French observers did not believe that the President had suddenly been transformed from a hawk to a dove. Only three days before Murray's nomination, Létombe had reported that Adams wanted France to declare war. Ten days later the Consul General altered his views a bit, saying that the "intrigues of MM. Liston,

Hamilton and Jay" had not been able to force the President into a coalition with Britain. Adams refused to go along with these men, Létombe explained, because he sought reelection and something in Saint Domingue.[84]

Regardless of the merit of such conjecture, Adams's act of nomination, by making clear to all that war with France was not inevitable, placed him on the side of peace and destroyed the basis of High Federalist policy. Knowing that the mission would cut across the deeply embedded convictions of many and stir the partisan passions of others, he had in effect challenged the extreme wing of his own party to battle.[85]

✹ VI ✹

Decline of the Martial Spirit

> *Mr. Adams from the time of his being placed at the head of the Administration of this Country has uniformly endeavoured to strengthen and increase its political connections in Europe, and has combated on all occasions the erroneous and impracticable theory maintained by some speculators here, that America is sufficient to herself, is independent of the rest of the world, and ought to reject foreign treaties and negotiations of every sort.*
>
> ROBERT LISTON, *February 1799*

SINCE ADAMS'S NOMINATION OF MURRAY AS MINISTER TO FRANCE, even though provisional, represented a striking departure from his own previously belligerent attitude as well as from his party's policy, High Federalists were stunned by it and puzzled by its motivation.[1] Some of them believed the nomination would "palsy" important warlike measures pending in the House, excite suspicion in Britain, and above all delude the American people. In their view, French intrigue had been checked, but now, they feared, Murray's appointment would revive it.[2]

Stephen Higginson, a Federalist merchant from Boston, said of the nomination, "there is not a Sound mind from Maine to Georgia that has not been shocked at it. . . ." Adams, he thought, must have been duped by "the wiles of french diplomacy, and the folly of Gerry." Theodore Sedgwick, the Federalist leader in the Senate, denounced the nomination as "the most embarrassing and ruinous measure" that could have been adopted and called Murray "feeble, unguarded, credulous, and unimpressive." Men wagered that the Senate would not confirm Murray.

One Federalist became so angered by Adams's action that he threatened the President's life. "*Assassination* shall be your lot," wrote a man who signed himself "*a ruined merchant, alas! with ten children !!! made beggars by the French.*" [3]

High Federalists recognized that the nomination took from them their foremost issue in forthcoming political campaigns, because, they argued, "the half informed & the feeble see no harm in any measure which professes to have peace for its object. . . ." Now Federalists, the "friends of order," could no longer pose as patriots defending the national honor against an uncompromising foe unwilling to listen to the voice of reason." This appointment declares to every American," one Federalist wrote, that in the President's opinion the French were sincere in their desire for peace, and that peace was attainable and in the national interest. Thomas Jefferson saw the appointment in a similar light. "It silences all arguments against the sincerity of France," he said, "and renders desperate every further effort towards war." [4] High Federalists thought that the mere possibility of peace with France could cut across the land like an arctic wind and freeze popular support for Federalism.

This fear colored the thinking of Secretary of State Pickering. Vigorous policy, he maintained, had brought popularity to the Federalist party. Now the growth, even the support, of the party had come to depend on a continuation of the Quasi-War. Furthermore, information he had received from observers in Europe had convinced him that France's tone toward the United States had improved in ratio to the degree of firmness and independence displayed by the American government. He also disapproved of new negotiations because he so distrusted the French that he believed any treaty with them would be valueless.

Particularly galling to Pickering was the fact that the President had made this crucial decision without consulting him. The Secretary of State said that "every Federalist was astonished."

Among them was Harrison Gray Otis. He called on Pickering and asked, "How is all this? the nomination of Mr. Murray to treat with the French republic?"

"I know nothing of it," the Secretary of State replied, "but the fact [is] I hear that the President has so nominated him."

"Why, is the man mad?" Otis exclaimed.[5]

Not all Federalists felt this way. Many of them, particularly moderates, approved the idea of a new peace mission. High ranking party leaders such as Washington, John Marshall, Henry Knox, Patrick Henry, and John Jay went along with the President. Washington hoped that Adams's action would permit the country "to pass this critical period . . . without being involved in the horrors and calamities of war." Knox thought most Federalists favored what Adams had done. He acclaimed the action as "one of the most dignified, decisive, and beneficial ever adopted by the Chief Magistrate of any nation, soaring above all prejudice, and regarding the happiness of the nation as the primary object of his administration," even at the risk of his reputation.

Two of the department heads, Benjamin Stoddert and Charles Lee, supported the President's decision. "I cannot conceive," Stoddert told Adams in later years, "how you could have avoided instituting a negotiation on the receipt of Mr. Murray's letter." [6]

Republicans, too, were startled by Murray's nomination. Most of them stopped criticizing and even praised Adams. Jefferson, although critical of Adams, reported the nomination as a great event, the "event of events." "Whatever sentiments men may entertain of the President's attachment to English modes of government or to English connexions," one Republican gazette announced, "every one must applaud his appointment of Mr. Murray to go to Paris." A Republican congressman saw the nomination as momentous. He explained it to his North Carolina constituents as action taken to avoid a "desolating war."

Thomas Boylston Adams probably summarized the popular reaction as well as anyone. "Englishmen & Anglo-Americans are universally mortified at it," he explained, "and frenchmen [*sic*] as well as French Americans extol it as a most *glorious event*." [7]

Abigail, who had been almost a war hawk in her sentiments

toward the French, was pleased. She called the appointment of Murray a master stroke that showed the people their government wanted peace. Nothing he had done as President, she told her husband, "has so universally electrified the public." It was so unexpected that the whole community reacted "like a flock of frightened pigeons." [8]

Unlike pigeons, High Federalists not only complained bitterly about Adams's action, but they also sought some means of combating it. On the evening of Murray's nomination the Federalist members of the Senate had met to discuss it. At first the extremists thought of blocking the appointment openly, but the moderates balked at such procedure.[9] To reject Murray, it appeared, would drive public opinion to the support of the President. After consulting Hamilton, the High Federalist leaders decided to try to defeat the nomination by indirection.

Three days after the President had submitted Murray's name, a committee of five senators, headed by Theodore Sedgwick, discussed the nomination and decided to solicit an interview with Adams. Two days later they called on him to persuade him to withdraw the nomination. Adams greeted the group politely but said, "Gentlemen, I am glad to see you, as friends and members of the Senate; but as a committee interfering, as I think you are, with my executive duties, I cannot consent to receive you, and I protest against all such interference."

One of the senators asserted that the sending of a minister to France so soon after he, Adams, had told Congress he would not do so until he had received satisfaction for past insults would be humiliating. If France were sincere she would appoint a minister to the United States.[10]

"Here you are all wrong, gentlemen," Adams replied. "I know more of diplomatic forms than all of you. It was in France that we received the insult, and in France I am determined that we shall receive the reparation." [11]

When the committee shifted tactics, saying Murray lacked the stature for so important a mission and expressed determination to report against confirmation on that basis, Adams threatened to resign the Presidency. The party leaders, as Hamilton had suggested, then came up with a compromise that would at least maintain the façade of party unity. They urged the President to appoint two additional envoys to work with Murray, staunch Federalists who could keep him in check. Adams refused. "I have, on mature reflection," he announced, "made up my mind, and I will neither withdraw nor modify the nomination."

The Federalists then caucused and decided to reject Murray's nomination. Oliver Ellsworth, Chief Justice of the United States, then spoke to the President, and he persuaded him to enlarge the mission to a committee of three "so as to embrace more of the confidence of the country." Adams, who had heard of the caucus, wisely took this suggestion but refused to accept Hamilton and George Cabot of Massachusetts, as the Senate Federalists had urged. Instead, he insisted that Ellsworth himself head the commission.

Seeing this as a call to duty, the Chief Justice reluctantly agreed. Then on February 25, 1799, the President nominated Ellsworth and Patrick Henry, formerly an anti-Federalist but now a firm Federalist, as envoys to work jointly with Murray.[12] Adams announced that the commission, with representatives from each of the three main sections of the country, the North, the Middle, and the South, was a concession to "public opinion." He also explained that Ellsworth and Henry would not embark until he, the President, received authentic assurances from the French government that it would receive the commissioners properly.

The Senate then grudgingly confirmed all three nominations. If it had rejected them, it would probably have brought about an open break in the Federalist party in an election year. Extreme Federalists, some of whom called the commissioners an unimpressive group, remained bitter. Fisher Ames wrote that the mission "disgusts most men here. Peace with France they think an evil, and holding out the hope of it another, as it tends to chill the public fervor." Adams, in Ames's view, had betrayed the principles of Federalism.

Several days later, on March 3, 1797, Congress adjourned *sine die*. For the first time since Adams had taken office Congress closed a session without fear that open war with France might come soon. For the first time since the beginning of the crisis some visible progress had been made toward a relaxation of tension. Even High Federalists admitted that the mission, "which professes to have peace for its object," was popular, especially with "temporizers, trimmers, and Federal hypocrites with Jacobin hearts. . . ." [13]

On March 6, as directed by the President, Pickering sent Murray his commission as Minister to the French Republic, instructing him to notify the French government that the other two commissioners would not depart until the President received direct and unequivocal assurance that the Executive Directory would receive them officially, and that a minister of equal grade had been appointed to negotiate with them. In addition, the Secretary of State directed Murray not to communicate informally with French agents on the problems of the Quasi-War. [14]

At about this time Pickering also finally completed the draft of the treaty Adams had requested in January. On Friday, March 9, the President asked his cabinet members to meet with him at 5:00 P.M. the next day. When the department heads assembled at the President's home the subject of discussion was Pickering's draft. With Adams showing surprising agreement, all quickly decided to demand severe terms from the French.

All agreed that France had to meet three conditions. First of all, the French must pay indemnities for spoliations of American commerce; secondly, they must recognize that American ships were not bound to carry a *rôle d'équipage;* and thirdly, they must concede that the United States would no longer have to guarantee France's possessions in the West Indies as called for in the alliance of 1778. The instructions given to Pinckney, Marshall and Gerry, it may be recalled, had not made payment of spoliation claims, as was now the case, an indispensable condition.

These terms pleased Pickering. He believed that France would refuse to accept them and that the new mission, like the earlier one, would fail. Upon the basis of these principles, as agreed on, Adams ordered the Secretary of State to compose detailed instructions for the commissioners. Then, on March 12, despite the desire of the cabinet officers to have him remain at the seat of government, the President rushed off for Quincy to be with Abigail. "In the midst of the great Executive business arising out of the late session, and with an Insurrection [Fries Rebellion] begun," Pickering commented, "the President has left the seat of government." Adams was to be gone seven months.

Shortly after, Patrick Henry, pleading advanced age and increasing debility, declined his appointment.[15] For a replacement Adams sought another Southerner. Ellsworth suggested William Richardson Davie, the governor of North Carolina, a brigadier general in the Provisional Army, and a Federalist with correct political opinions. "I believe he would readily accept the commission," Ellsworth wrote.

Adams followed the Chief Justice's advice. When Pickering, acting for the President, offered Davie the post he stressed that it was "yet uncertain whether any negociation will take place." The Secretary of State therefore did not ask for an immediate acceptance but only whether acceptance *"may be expected."* [16] When Davie, as Ellsworth had indicated he would, took the post, the composition of the commission was completed.

Although Adams had expected a strong reaction from the Hamiltonians, he had failed to see that his decision to negotiate had not only deepened the split in the Federalist party, but it had also widened the rift between himself and his department heads. Continued opposition to his decision, furthermore, caused Adams to bristle. "If any one entertains the idea, that, because I am a President of three votes only, I am in the power of a party," he commented, "they shall find that I am no more so than the Constitution forces upon me." He would, he insisted, resist the pressure of any "combinations of senators, generals, and heads of department" to force him to adopt measures against his will.[17]

OPPONENTS OF WAR

Opposition to France had been practically the only issue on which Federalists from all sections and from all walks of life had concentrated. Some, like Pickering, had thought they could use the Quasi-War to retain power almost indefinitely. A few, such as

Uriah Tracy, a harsh, even bigoted, Federalist senator from Connecticut who despised the masses, threatened to resign "if all must be given up to France and our Democrats." [18]

The Federalist party had no other issue of broad appeal to take the place of the French crisis. Its leaders had built their program on that one foundation. The Alien and Sedition Acts, the new Army, the Navy, and the direct taxes, all rested on it. If this foundation gave way, the whole structure might crumble.

The cement that held this foundation together was President Adams. Although critical of him, Republicans realized that his attitude, more than that of any other single American, could determine if the nation would reach for the olive branch or wield its sword without restraint. As one of them, Joel Barlow, pointed out from Paris at this time, "peace & reconciliation with France on terms advantageous & honourable to the U.S. are completely in the power and at the option of John Adams & have been so for 18 months, and he has always known it." The Directors had seen through his "whole stratagem," Barlow said. "They know he is mad for war, & that his object is to provoke them to declare it, but they are determined to disappoint him." [19]

Although Adams had not suddenly become a dove, his desire for unqualified war certainly had cooled. His steps toward peace, though unintentionally, had helped the Republicans immeasurably. To many Americans the Republican party had appeared to be in league with the enemy and committed to a foreign ideology. Now, as High Federalists said, the President had lifted its head from the mire.

Adams, moreover, did not try as he might have to rally to his support all of those who, regardless of party affiliation, desired peace.[20] Nor did he strike out at the war hawks. Even though he had reason to believe that several of his department heads were disloyal, when he left Philadelphia he relied on them to follow the course he had set.

Several of those cabinet officers, like many extreme Federalists, believed that Adams's one act had destroyed the nation's martial spirit. "We have," one Federalist wrote, "experienced a sad reverse in the temper, ardor and zeal of our fellow citizens."

Few could deny that nomination of the peace mission crippled the hawks and gave hope to the doves, but it was more the result than the cause in the dampening of martial ardor.

The American people, "still holding the rejected Olive Branch in one hand, but a sword in the other," were tired of being stranded between peace and war. The bellicose spirit which had been strong and lusty in the spring and summer of 1798 had begun to decline in the winter. By the beginning of the new year it had noticeably faded. If it could be had honorably, the people desired peace.

Various signs indicated that Americans were weary of Federalist war measures, that they would welcome an end to standing armies, an elimination of direct taxes, and a cut in government spending. Business was deranged. For a year the people had lived in constant expectation of war. Now they showed evidence of a letdown that frequently follows a state of high public excitement.[21] It was, as one High Federalist had predicted, "too much to expect that any popular impulse will last long, and not only go right, but keep government right." [22]

One bit of evidence in this letdown was the denouement of a story about a nefarious French plot to subvert the government, usually known as the "Tub Plot." The story began early in 1799 when Secretary of State Pickering learned from Joseph Pitcairn, the American Consul in Hamburg, that a Matthew Salmon, who had been a deputy to France's National Convention, was on his way to Charleston, South Carolina, on board the *Minerva*, a Danish ship. Pitcairn warned that Salmon might be carrying dispatches from the Executive Directory concealed in tubs with false bottoms.

Eager to keep the war spirit alive, Pickering rashly assumed that now he would uncover firm evidence of a French plot to destroy the government. Since Salmon was a mulatto, the Secretary of State assumed that he had been sent to the South to ignite a slave rebellion among the Negroes there. So Pickering quickly wrote to Governor Edward Rutledge of South Carolina, to General Charles Cotesworth Pinckney, and to other officials, asking them to arrest the plotters when they arrived.

On February 22, as soon as the *Minerva* dropped anchor in Charleston's harbor, a boatload of officials clambered aboard. They found Salmon and four other French citizens, white and mulatto, all traveling on Swiss passports. Two in the party were mulatto women. The South Carolinians also found tubs with false bottoms and in them documents written in French. The officials took the documents and threw the supposed agents of the Directory into jail.

Now the Federalist gazettes announced that Rutledge and Pinckney, by uncovering the tub plot, had saved the nation from subversion, racial rebellion, and bloodshed of the worst kind. The press exhorted the people to unite, "rally round your government," and to prepare to smite its French enemies "with the sword."

Despite these and other exhortations, the Republicans remained calm. They denounced the "Tale of the Tubs" as nonsense, "founded on a *false bottom*." They even claimed that one of the arrested women was the "lady" of the X Y Z dispatches. Out of this supposition they wove a story of illicit passion in Paris boudoirs. Pinckney, they said, had made the woman pregnant and then deserted her, and she had followed him to Charleston seeking justice. Her former lover had become so callous that he had shut her up in prison with "a helpless infant, the only known benefit procured to the United States from the embassy of Pinckney, Marshall and Gerry." [23]

Republicans had no evidence for these slanderous charges, but neither did Federalists have evidence of a French plot. When Pinckney questioned the prisoners he learned that instead of being agents of the Directory, they were its enemies. They were, in fact, trying to make their way from Charleston to Saint Domigue to add fuel to the rebellion on the island against the French by bringing documentary proof to the colored people there that the Directory intended once again to make them slaves.

Since Adams's government had been trying to cultivate good relations with Toussaint L'Ouverture, and was now also considering peace with the Directory, it could not use all these details to refute the Republican slanders. So the "Tale of the

Tubs" backfired. Instead of producing proof of French perfidy, it made Federalist fire-eaters like Pickering appear ridiculous. It also added to the feeling that the various Federalist measures, such as the building of the Army, were not really necessary.[24]

Enlistment in the Additional Army did not begin until the spring of 1799. Few who volunteered would take up arms as common soldiers. "The army," one Federalist commented, "is progressing like a wounded snake." General Washington complained that "none but the riff-raff of the country, and the Scape gallows of the large cities" would enlist. Hamilton tried to recruit a force of ten thousand as allowed by the laws of the Fifth Congress. In addition, more than enough officers were commissioned to command the thirty thousand provisional troops which would be called to the colors when, or if, the President declared a full wartime emergency.

Since most of the applicants sought commissions in the Additional Army, which never reached more than a third of its authorized strength, the ratio of officers to enlisted men was seven to one. Even so, both the officers and the enlisted volunteers for the new regiments waited impatiently, and at some personal loss, to be called into active service. Many were unwilling to accept further sacrifice.

The federal budget for the period 1796 to 1800 reflected the cost of maintaining a heavy military establishment by an agrarian nation of five million people. In 1796 Congress had approved a total budget of $5.8 million. In 1797 it increased that figure by only $200 thousand. For 1798, however, the expense of supporting the national government rose to $7.6 million. In the following year the figure reached $9.3 million, though Jefferson reported to Madison that the cost of the proposed military and naval establishment alone for 1799 was $11.5 million. In three years the cost of government had doubled, even though Adams had stifled the growth of the Army.[25]

Even the effort to borrow money from Federalist bankers ran into difficulty. Congress had authorized the President to borrow $5 million to pay for the Army. When Wolcott reported that he could not obtain the loan for less than 8 per cent interest, Adams

objected. That rate, the President said, was extravagant and unnecessary. Wolcott, who insisted that 8 per cent was fair, did not
want to publish proposals for the loan at a lower rate. Then
Adams exploded. "This damned army will be the ruin of this
country," he shouted; "if it must be so, it must; I cannot help it.
Issue your proposals as you please." [26]

Spending and taxes were not the only sources of dissatisfaction. From the beginning there were those who had protested the
Federalist war program, feeling that it was unnecessary and
wrong. In New York City Republicans raised their glasses to this
toast: "May the old Tories and all who wish to engage the United
States in a war with any nation, realize the felicity they anticipate
by being placed in the front of the first battle." [27]

Even in the President's own state opponents of his foreign
policy had long been vocal. In March 1798 the people of Roxbury
and Milton had held town meetings to protest the arming of merchant ships. So violent were the Miltonians that at least one Federalist took it upon himself to spout "against the policy of the
people interfering with those measures of defence wh. government may find it necessary to adopt." In Virginia college students
at William and Mary burned the President in effigy as a protest
against war.

New England's leading Republican journal, the Boston *Independent Chronicle,* second only to Philadelphia's *Aurora* nation-
ally, had consistently opposed measures which might lead to war.
Even after the exposure of the X Y Z affair its editor, Thomas
Adams, had urged renewed negotiations with France. As the Federalist measures against France had unfolded, editor Adams had
attacked them and had criticized the President.[28] Opposition such
as this, apparently, had been a factor in causing President Adams
to hesitate in asking Congress for a declaration of war.

Opponents of war had frequently petitioned the President;
their petitions had become more numerous as the crisis dragged
on. In August 1798 the freeholders of Prince Edward County,
Virginia, had sent Adams an address expressing opposition to his
policy toward France. It called his speech of June 21 a "rash resolution." The war program Congress had enacted, the petitioners

said, was part of a design to overthrow the rights and liberties of the people.

This petition had so infuriated Pickering that he had refused to pass it on to the President. The Secretary of State called the address insulting, and in September he sent the freeholders a stinging reply through the newspapers. This appeared to be proper retaliation, for the freeholders had previously published their petition. Pickering reviewed relations with France, praised the administration's foreign policy, and defended the Alien and Sedition Acts.[29]

Some of this opposition to the administration was politically motivated. Yet the taxes, the increased national debt, and the war program gave substance to Republican charges. Without full-scale war the government's measures seemed unnecessary, and the Federalists were burdened with a political handicap. The French contributed to this handicap and to the decline in the martial enthusiasm with their peaceful overtures. If the goal of the American government had been a declaration of war, one of their agents reported, the favorable moment had now escaped it.[30]

"In the opinion of many intelligent men," Harrison Gray Otis wrote in April 1799, the Fifth Congress should have declared war during its second session. Owing to this "fatal and impolitic omission," he went on, "the popular zeal and enthusiasm" had subsided "for want of impulse." He suggested that Federalists could rectify this mistake "by convincing the people that no occasion of preserving peace has been omitted, and by affording to them another instance of the duplicity and perfidy of France." Then, he added, "Can we make war with success, if we reject overtures apparently pacific?" [31]

Republicans insisted that the commotion over war and subversion had been politically inspired. Federalists, they asserted, sought political gain and had raised their voices "in perfect unison for war" and against "Peace, Liberty and the equal Rights of Man." Many people apparently accepted this interpretation of Federalist actions. Jeffersonians also pointed out that Hamilton had taken advantage of the crisis in foreign affairs to advance a

system of military government. Jefferson himself declared that
government by this means had become "what the French call a
monarchie masquée." [32]

In the Alien and Sedition Acts Jefferson and the other leaders
of the Republican party, such as James Madison, had seen a trend
toward tyranny, especially an effort to muzzle political opposition. They felt that if they could expose the danger and properly
exploit it, they might melt some of the public support Adams had
gained as a result of the Quasi-War. The Alien and Sedition laws
had the effect of diverting public attention away from the Jeffersonians' unpopular defense of France, giving them a broad issue
in domestic politics. During the furor over the X Y Z dispatches
many Republicans had defected to the Federalist position, but on
the issue of the Alien and Sedition laws the Republican party expressed virtually unified opposition. "The alien and sedition acts,"
Jefferson said in January 1799, "have already operated as powerful sedatives of the X Y Z inflamation."

Jefferson secretly drew up a plan for an attack on the Alien
and Sedition laws that would publicize the Republicans as defenders of liberty and furnish them with a statement of party
principles. In the fall of 1798, after consulting with friends, he
decided to introduce his ideas to the public through Kentucky's
state legislature. John Breckinridge, a staunch Jeffersonian and
the speaker of Kentucky's assembly, agreed to present Jefferson's
principles to the legislature in the form of nine resolutions.[33]

Basically, the Kentucky Resolutions declared the Alien and
Sedition laws void and unconstitutional and demanded their
repeal. If the federal government persisted in arrogating to itself
such illegal power, the resolves said, it would drive the states into
"revolution and bloodshed." In conclusion, the resolutions called
on all the states to take similar action. None did so.

Breckinridge's resolutions were approved, with only one dis-
senting vote, by both houses of the Kentucky legislature. The
governor signed them on November 16, 1798, and ordered a
thousand copies to be printed for distribution to the members of
Congress and the governors of the states.

About a month later John Taylor of Caroline, a thorough-

going Republican and political theorist, introduced a set of similar resolutions into the Virginia legislature. Drafted by James
Madison, these resolutions were less specific in content and more
moderate in expression than those of Kentucky. Nonetheless, they
met a fierce resistance in the lower house, where they passed by a
vote of 100 to 63. On December 24, 1798, after the Virginia senate had also approved them, the governor signed the resolves, and
they were printed and distributed.

Jefferson sought to use the Kentucky and Virginia Resolutions as a means of dividing the friends of the Alien and Sedition
laws, most of them High Federalists, from the enemies of those
laws. His strategy worked, in part at least. The ardent Federalists
in the various state legislatures defended both the constitutional-
ity of the laws and the principles behind them.

Federalists attacked the resolutions whenever they could.[34]
Frequently, when they wished to arouse public passions, they
charged that the resolves had grown out of a French plot. They
were part of a grand design whereby France would detach Kentucky from the Union and tie it to Louisiana which she, France,
was trying to wrench from Spain. Virginia approved of that design, Federalists argued, because she favored the breakup of the
Union.[35]

Some Hamiltonians wished to counter the threat of disunion
allegedly posed by the Kentucky and Virginia Resolutions with
force. They were willing to fight a civil war, if necessary, to
achieve their ends. To gain support for the new Army they
argued the necessity of being prepared for the danger of a civil
uprising, as well as for a French invasion. The Jeffersonian resolutions seemed to stiffen the determination of High Federalists to
have war with France and to use it as a means of tightening their
grip on the nation.

Alarmed by the resolutions, a Virginia Federalist maintained
that "it requires only some great energetic measure like open war,
to bring those *deluded* and *imposed* upon, of our fellow citizens
to a just sense of their weakness and folly. We now appear to
have a most favorable opportunity to give a decided blow to
French ambition & cruelty—*War.,*—ever brings *peace.*"

Federalists could not sustain their charge of a French plot, for most people saw the Alien and Sedition laws as the central issue in the Kentucky and Virginia Resolutions. Petitions flooded the third session of the Fifth Congress urging a repeal of those laws, and of other war legislation. Typical of many was a petition of January 1799 addressed to the President by citizens of York County, Pennsylvania, a Federalist section of that state. "While we are warmly attached to the Union," the petitioners said, "we cannot but express our concern at several acts passed in the two last Sessions of Congress: the law for erecting a standing army, the Sedition and Alien Laws, the Stamp Act, the Direct tax on land, and great increase in Revenue officers." [36]

Despite these and similar doubts raised by many Federalists, the extremists remained unmoved. Arguing that the legislation was part of the system of national defense against France, they defended their now unpopular program. In the South the debate over the Federalist war measures became so harsh that Republicans and Federalists charged each other with fomenting civil war.

A similar comment was made in Massachusetts. "House and land tax of Congress goes on heavily, causing great uneasiness," a Dedham Republican wrote. "Some refuse and then to avoid the penalty have to conform. . . . Silent indignation hath not yet exploded—tho' hard threatened. I fear civil war be the result of Government measures." [37]

FRIES REBELLION

Public discontent against the war program, particularly against the direct tax, came to a head in Pennsylvania where it did touch off a civil commotion. The tax on land and houses, levied to pay for the Army and Navy and called the window tax because one basis of assessment was the counting and measuring of windows, was particularly obnoxious to the German farmers in the counties north of Philadelphia. Although an old English practice adopted without sinister intent, the counting of windows reminded the Germans of oppressive hearth taxes in the old country from which their fathers had fled.[38] Hence they considered the tax illegal and opposed it.

Wherever the Germans gathered, in taverns and ale houses, they damned the President and the Congress. But the tax agents encountered no open defiance until John Fries, a Bucks County auctioneer about fifty years old and a father of ten children, gathered fifty or more armed horsemen and galloped from township to township harrying assessors. Since *hausfrauen* defended their homes and aided their men by pouring hot water on assessors from upper-story windows, some observers called this the "hot water insurrection."

In Northampton County eighteen of the demonstrators were arrested and, on March 6, 1799, were thrown into jail in Bethlehem. On the following day Fries and his farmers, about 140 of them armed with rifles and swords, rode to the rescue. Some were drunk, and some flaunted the tricolor cockade. Without firing a shot they frightened the federal marshal into releasing his prisoners. News of the incident, magnified into an insurrection against the federal government, reached Philadelphia just as Adams was preparing to depart for Quincy. On March 12 he issued a proclamation denouncing the rioters as rebels who had committed acts of treason.[39]

The President then asked Governor Thomas Mifflin to order militia into the disaffected counties. Mifflin handed over responsibility to the state legislature, where political maneuvering by Republicans and Federalists delayed action. Impatient, Adams ordered the governor to raise militia forces throughout southeastern Pennsylvania and to send them into the rebellious counties. To ensure compliance, the President ordered five hundred regulars from the new Army to help hunt down the rebels.

These rebellious counties had all been Federalist strongholds. Fries himself was a confirmed Federalist and a supporter of the Adams administration. Believing themselves the victims of oppression by the government, the Germans now deserted Federalism for Republicanism.

Hamilton believed that "Whenever the government appears

in arms, it ought to appear like Hercules, and inspire respect by
the display of strength." [40] His federal Army, a formidable force,
marched into Bucks County, captured Fries, clapped him in
irons, and carried him off to Philadelphia to stand trial for treason.

In suppressing the uprising the Army used unnecessary bru-
tality. In Philadelphia, where High Federalists believed the
"rebellion" was the beginning of the Jacobin anarchy they had
long predicted, wearers of the black cockade swaggered about in
uniform, insulting and bullying the citizenry. They crashed into
the print shop of William Duane, editor of the *Aurora,* and beat
him so savagely they almost killed him. "And now," a Republican
commented, "we see the effects of a standing army in time of
peace." In later years Adams recalled that the public reacted as if
the Army were "a ferocious wild beast let loose upon the nation to
devour it."

In May 1799, after a second trial of nine days, in which Fries
had no counsel, a federal court pronounced the Bethlehem riot
treason against the United States. The judge admonished Fries to
"look up to the Father of Mercies, and God of Comfort," and sen-
tenced him to be hanged. Hamiltonians had tried to make Fries's
trial a means of turning public opinion against Adams's peace policy toward France. Refusing to see any connection between the
Fries uprising and the Directory, the President asked his department heads in late summer if he should pardon the rebels. The
cabinet said no. [41]

After further deliberation, Adams decided it was wrong to
stretch the definition of treason so as to cover what was nothing
more than a riot, though "highhanded, aggravated, daring, and
dangerous indeed." On May 21, 1800, the day before the date set
for execution, he pardoned Fries and those implicated in the uprising. [42]

This act widened the split in the Federalist party. Pickering
called it "an outrage on decency, propriety, justice and sound policy. . . ." Also, the pardon came too late to do much good with
the people of Pennsylvania who were appalled by the overwhelming display of military strength used to suppress the simple farm-

ers. The Fries Rebellion dealt Federalism a sharp blow in Pennsylvania.[43]

Another factor that reacted against Federalism and contributed to the decline of the martial spirit, was the revival of popular animosity against England. In molesting American shipping the British in many ways equaled the French. The Federalist press was silent about British seizures of American ships, a Republican gazette complained, but if the French take a ship "it is blazoned from one end of the continent to the other." [44] A Boston newspaper regularly printed a column, entitled "Evidences of British Amity," that listed the American ships seized by British warships and privateers.

To prevent France from continuing her peacetime trade with her colonies through the use of neutral carriers, such as American ships, the British government had invoked the Rule of the War of 1756. It declared that trade closed to neutral nations in time of peace could not be opened to them in time of war.

Even though the United States refused to recognize the Rule of 1756 as legal, the British navy forced American ship captains to acquiesce in its application. British Admiralty courts in Bermuda and the West Indies condemned hundreds of American vessels seized while attempting to carry produce from France's colonies to Europe. Yet the British did permit indirect trade between the French islands of the Caribbean and Europe via the United States, if the cargo in an American ship was at least nominally owned by Americans. This practice was called broken voyage.

In 1799 Sir William Scott, England's leading maritime lawyer, attempted to resolve some of the difficulties British sea captains encountered in applying the Rule of 1756 while trying also to respect the practice of broken voyage. In the case of the American ship *Polly,* carrying a cargo of sugar and cacao from Marblehead, Massachusetts, to Bilbao, Spain, he laid down the principle that when a cargo, even though of enemy origin, was landed in an American port and duties were paid on it, the captor had to consider it neutral property unless he could prove it was not. Under this doctrine the American reexport trade mushroomed. The good relations between the mercantile interests of

New England, which were largely Federalist, and Britain grew even stronger.[45]

Since France's navy could not protect American shipping against British naval power if the United States had chosen to challenge England, one way to prosperity for American shippers lay in cooperation with the British. The British navy not only frequently protected American shipping, but Britain also relaxed her navigation laws and opened much of her empire to American traders. For these concessions Americans acquiesced in the infringement of neutral rights that interfered with Britain's warfare against France.

To many American shippers this price seemed small, for despite the British maritime restrictions, their commerce had never been in such flourishing condition. Many a New England fortune was founded on the trading of this period. Taking advantage of war conditions, American merchant ships carried goods for practically anyone all over the world, ran blockades, and eluded frigates and privateers. Despite laws against it, New England merchants even carried on a lucrative trade in smuggled goods to French colonies.

Some of these traders, particularly rising Republican entrepreneurs in seaboard towns in Massachusetts, feared that full-scale war would endanger their economic ties to the French. They greedily sought more, not less, trade with the French. The plunge toward unrestricted war, therefore, alarmed them, and they added their influence to other groups which demanded peace.[46]

To most merchants neutrality meant prosperity. They did not want clashes, with either Britain or France, to end that prosperity. At sea there was always the possibility of a clash with one of the belligerents, even with the friendly British. Some American ship captain might resist when a British naval officer attempted to seize his vessel if it were suspected of violating British maritime restrictions.

Concerned over this danger, the Adams administration ordered American naval officers not to interfere with the capture of American merchant vessels by the warships of any nation except those of France. In cases of capture, the administration informed American commanders, it was to be presumed that the admiralty courts of the offending nation would do justice to the ships and cargoes brought before them for adjudication.

RESENTMENT AGAINST ENGLAND

The most important single cause for the revival of resentment against England was probably the impressment of seamen from the decks of American ships. To meet what was a critical manpower shortage in the Royal Navy, press gangs roamed through England's port towns and delivered hundreds of men into the naval service. Repelled by the brutal conditions on British warships, many of these recruits deserted and sought berths on American merchant ships where food was better, pay higher, and life more comfortable.

To recover the deserters the British boarded and searched American ships. If the searchers found British seamen they forced them back into the Royal Navy, often only long enough to be tried and hanged. At first the British had restricted this practice to those American vessels in British ports, but by 1797 they had extended the use of press gangs to ships on the high seas. As Rufus King, the American Minister in London, observed, the British officers entrusted with the delicate task of boarding and searching American ships were "men of more nautical than political skill." If their need for deckhands was great, any likely looking seaman suddenly became an English subject. Unless he could prove otherwise, he found himself in the Royal Navy. Impressments from American ships became so common, a gazette reported, that even cabin boys were not exempt.[47]

Although the British never asserted the right to impress natural born Americans, they held firmly to the doctrine of indefeasible allegiance, meaning once an Englishman always an Englishman. They refused to recognize the right of expatriation. They insisted, therefore, upon the right to impress Americans who had at one time been British subjects. Furthermore, it was almost impossible for a British naval captain to determine whether an individual in question was an Englishman, or, as he invariably claimed to be, an American citizen.

The American government tried giving certificates of citizenship to American crews, and American consuls abroad had authority to grant those documents to *bona fide* citizens. In 1796 Congress had even passed an Act for the Relief and Protection of American Seamen which the Republican majority in Congress had regarded as the final word on the controversy.

Fraud had quickly vitiated the whole system. Americans in coastal towns aided and protected British sailors who jumped ship. Lord St. Vincent of the British Admiralty asserted that for a single dollar any English deserter might become an American citizen. As a result, his Lordship declared, the American merchant marine was manned largely by British subjects.

The exasperation of one British captain over desertion in American ports illustrates the frustration that many naval commanders apparently felt. "I tell you, sir," he explained to Robert Liston, "that I have not got an American subject on board, but I will not say how long it will be so." [48]

Although there were many instances of conflict over impressment, the most humiliating case during the Quasi-War occurred on November 16, 1798. John Loring, captain of the H.M.S. *Carnatic*, stopped the American sloop of war *Baltimore*, Isaac Phillips commanding, and prevented it from entering the harbor at Havana while it was escorting a convoy. Loring ordered Phillips to stand by for examination and Phillips complied. Then the British captain compelled Phillips to call all hands and furnish a list of the crew. Loring removed fifty-five men, whom he suspected of being British subjects, from the *Baltimore's* deck. When Phillips protested that he now did not have enough seamen left to man his ship properly, Loring returned fifty of the men.

Since Loring had impressed sailors from a ship of the United States Navy, and not from the usual merchant vessel, he had violated American sovereignty. So Pickering lodged a strong protest with the British government. Embarrassed by Loring's behavior, the Admiralty then transferred him to another station.

As for Phillips, he paid a quick and drastic penalty for his timid behavior. The President himself dismissed him from the naval service, without benefit of a hearing or a trial, for dereliction of duty in assisting in the impressment. After this episode American commanders received instructions not to permit impressment from their ships unless threatened by overwhelming force.[49]

This *Baltimore* affair infuriated Americans and created a sensation in the gazettes. A young Englishman residing in the United States was astonished at the depth of feeling it aroused. Speaking of Americans as a whole, he said, "They really talk of war with France, or indeed with England, with as much unconcern as if they risqued nothing in the event." In the matter of the *Baltimore* impressment alone, he wrote, "the Feds even say, they would rather go to war for ten years than put up with such indignities." This observation reflected an American tendency to exaggerate, for the case did not seriously impair the cooperation between Britain and America.[50]

Continued impressment of American seamen and more British insults to the flag, on the other hand, did again arouse American resentment and ill will. The British never entirely overcame such feelings. Americans were pleased when they learned of instances when their Navy defied the British as well as the French, as in an episode in March 1799.

An officer from the English frigate *Surprise*, forty-four guns, boarded the sloop of war U.S.S. *Ganges*, a former merchant vessel fitted with twenty-four guns, and demanded surrender of all Englishmen on board and to see the protections, or credentials, of the American seamen. Captain Thomas Tingey of the *Ganges* replied: "A PUBLIC SHIP CARRIES NO PROTECTION BUT HER FLAG. I DO NOT EXPECT TO SUCCEED IN A CONTEST WITH YOU, BUT I WILL DIE AT MY QUARTERS BEFORE A MAN SHALL BE TAKEN FROM THE SHIP." Unwilling to fight for dead men, the *Surprise* left.[51]

Republicans played up the "British atrocities" in their gazettes just as Federalists had exaggerated French depredations. Critics magnified the extent of British impressments, accusing Adams of lacking concern for the plight of American seamen.

The President opposed the British searches of American ships and impressments from their decks. He instructed Rufus King to protest such insults to the flag. Yet Pickering softened these instructions by adding that King should also acknowledge the "general friendly and polite behavior" of British naval officers toward the United States and their readiness to protect American merchant ships. "You cannot too strongly express the desire of the President," he said, "to maintain a perfect harmony between the two countries, and his regret at every incident tending to disturb it." Such incidents, he pointed out, hurt Federalists and furnish "a topic of popular clamour to others whose enmity to their own Government is equalled only by their hatred to Great Britain."

Several months later Adams directed King to protest, "with all the decision which may be consistent with decency and politeness," the right of "British men-of-war to take from our ships of war any men whatever, and from our merchant vessels any Americans, or foreigners, or even Englishmen." There was, he believed, "no principle under heaven" which could justify such measures.[52]

King protested, but reported that there seemed "no prospect of a favorable change in the general system of England towards Neutral Nations." British impressments thus continued. The American government's agent for seamen at Kingston, Jamaica, reported in September 1799 that there were more than two hundred and fifty impressed Americans serving on ships of the British squadron in the West Indies alone.[53] While the Adams administration sought the release of these and other impressed Americans, it did nothing that would cause embarrassment to the British government or weaken the Royal Navy.

Adams maintained this policy even though in 1799 the question of impressment became an embarrassing political issue as a result of the case of Jonathan Robbins, a British deserter whose true name was Thomas Nash. This case also helped to maintain popular feeling against England.[54]

Nash had been a petty officer on the British frigate *Hermione*, whose crew had mutinied in 1797 and had murdered most of the ship's officers. Members of the crew scattered, many making their way into the American merchant marine. Knowing this, agents of the British government watched carefully for the appearance of the mutineers on American ships. Early in 1799 the British Consul in Charleston discovered Nash on an American ship and demanded that he be surrendered for trial under the extradition clause in Jay's Treaty. Nash, a boastful, hard-drinking sailor, admitted having been on the *Hermione,* but swore that he was an American who had been impressed by the British captain, and that he had not taken part in the mutiny. To support his claim he produced an affidavit showing that he was Jonathan Robbins, born in Danbury, Connecticut.

At the request of Robert Liston, Adams himself looked into the case. The evidence convinced him that Nash was not in fact an American citizen. So the President directed the federal authorities in South Carolina to turn him over to the Royal Navy. Nash was tried, found guilty, and hanged.

Other mutineers from the *Hermione* had been arrested in the United States on the demand of British consuls. One of them, William Brigstock, proved his American citizenship. Pickering refused to surrender him. Others, when evidence against them proved insufficient, were set free.

Ignoring the case of Brigstock and the others, and also the evidence, Republicans insisted that Nash was Robbins, an American whom the government had supinely surrendered to British vengeance. To many he became a martyr whom Adams, by his act of intervention, had callously murdered.

Everywhere, in Congress and in the gazettes, debate swirled around the Robbins case. "I think," Jefferson wrote, "no circumstance since the establishment of our government has affected the popular mind more." He believed it gave a boost to Republican politics in Pennsylvania.

In Congress the wrangling continued for months, developing into a full-scale attack on the President. Republicans charged that Adams's action constituted "a dangerous interference of the executive with judicial decisions." Not until March 1800, partly as a result of a powerful speech by John Marshall in defense of the President, did the House, by a vote of 61 to 35, defeat a resolution of censure.[55]

Despite the evidences of popular resentment against England, and the possibility of an accommodation with France, cooperation with Britain remained basic American policy in the West Indies. "Our operations and preparations by sea and land are not to be relaxed in the smallest degree," Adams explained. "On the contrary, I wish them to be animated with fresh energy. St. Domingo . . . , and all the parts of the French dominions, are to be treated in the same manner as if no negotiation was going on." Adams now pursued a double policy toward France. He continued to aid Toussaint while negotiating for peace in Paris.

COOPERATION WITH TOUSSAINT

Late in April 1799, while General Maitland was on his way from Philadelphia to Saint Domingue, the American Consul there, Edward Stevens, had persuaded Toussaint to exclude armed French ships commissioned elsewhere from his ports, and to protect American commerce. After securing these concessions, which implied the end of privateering attacks on American ships from Toussaint's ports, Stevens thought that trade with Saint Domingue could "be renewed with the utmost safety." He urged his government, therefore, to reopen this commerce "as quickly as possible." [56]

Stevens then used his influence in Saint Domingue to aid the British. He prevented Roume, the Directory's agent, from placing language offensive to the English in Toussaint's proclamation on the protection of American shipping. He also persuaded Toussaint to renew negotiations with the representative of the British government.

When Maitland arrived at Cap Français on May 14, with instructions from Pickering for Stevens to negotiate with Toussaint on the basis of the arguments made in Philadelphia, he assumed that Toussaint would treat British commerce the same as he would American trade. On this basis Maitland was ready to conclude an armistice with Toussaint. If the Negro general were not agreeable, the British blockade of Saint Domingue would continue. Then, in spite of Britain's friendly relations with the United States, no American ships would be permitted to land cargoes.[57]

Stevens had gone aboard Maitland's ship, the H.M.S. *Camilla*, to discuss the terms of an arrangement with Toussaint. Stevens then accompanied Maitland to Gonaives, where Stevens went ashore to persuade Toussaint to accept the British terms. Toussaint had no love for the British. They had embarrassed him by publishing his secret treaty with Maitland. He wished, moreover, to quash rumors that said he would sell Saint Domingue to the British who would bring back slavery. For these reasons, he would not deal openly with the British. So Maitland stayed in the background while Stevens negotiated.

The agreement, reached on May 22, 1799, took the form of a secret convention between Toussaint and Britain, but Stevens had shaped it, and it applied equally to American and British commerce. In this agreement Toussaint promised not to attack American or British possessions in the Caribbean and to surrender American or British ships brought into his ports by French privateers.

Still acting for Maitland as well as for the United States, Stevens now pushed for a more comprehensive arrangement, one that would commit Toussaint to the suppression of all privateering in the waters of Saint Domingue. It was agreed, finally, that Cap Français and Port-au-Prince should be opened to American and British commerce on August 1, 1799.

Since Toussaint was not ready to break all ties to France, he flatly refused to receive a British diplomatic agent. Such a reception would give the appearance of an alliance with England. It would, moreover, amount to a declaration of independence from France.

Maitland then consented to an arrangement whereby Stevens would watch over Britain's commerce with Saint Domingue until Toussaint became ready to admit a British agent. After this compromise had been worked out Maitland and Toussaint quickly concluded another secret treaty, signed on June 13. This agreement was in effect an extension of the armistice of the previous year that contained substantially the same terms as the "Heads of

Regulations" agreed to in Philadelphia by Maitland and Pickering. The new agreement contained modifications, however, that
permitted Toussaint to avoid the appearance of disloyalty to
France. Although Stevens did not sign this treaty, all understood
that the American government would be bound by it.[58]

Protection for American and British commerce had been a
foremost objective of the Anglo-American negotiators. They
achieved that, but the British basically wished to go further. They
wanted to prevent any amicable arrangement between Toussaint
and Rigaud. Their policy, as Maitland saw it, should be to keep
Toussaint "in rebellion against the Directory [more] than in any
other Character." So Maitland instructed the British resident
agent on the island to "act hand in hand with the American Consul General. You are to consult with him upon every occasion,
and in all your transactions with General Toussaint, you are previously to concert with him the line of conduct fitting to adopt for
the interest of the two Nations." [59]

President Adams matched this attitude with a cooperative
policy of his own. "It is my earnest desire," Adams explained,
". . . to do nothing without the consent, concert and cooperation of the British government in this case. They are so
deeply interested that they ought to be consulted, and the commerce of the island is not worth to us, the risk of any dispute with
them." [60] Pickering shared this view.

On June 23, 1799, as the result of the convention signed by
Maitland and Toussaint, Adams issued a proclamation lifting the
embargo on American trade with Saint Domingue. On this same
day the Secretary of the Treasury sent a circular to all collectors
of customs in the United States that contained regulations governing this commerce. These regulations allowed American ships
to bring cannon, guns, powder, and provisions to Toussaint, but
not to Rigaud.

Since Toussaint lacked all kinds of supplies, food, munitons,
and clothing, Adams's renewal of trade gave him invaluable help
in his struggle against Rigaud. This help and Stevens's friendly attitude even led Toussaint to address a personal appeal to the President. The Negro general asked for warships to blockade the

coastal waters under Rigaud's control and to cut off supplies Rigaud was receiving from American sources despite the government's embargo. Through Pickering, Stevens had made a similar appeal, arguing that "Rigaud was privately supported by the French government. . . ." But some Frenchmen thought that now their colony was lost forever.[61]

Although the President did not meet this specific request, he later decided on open cooperation with Toussaint, mainly because the Negro general was an enemy of France. American warships began to capture vessels headed for ports controlled by Rigaud, and soon Americans were engaged in open warfare against such ships. The United States Navy thus took part in a struggle which in a sense, because it injured France, was part of the Quasi-War. Fundamentally, however, it was a civil war.[62]

At the same time, in keeping with Adams's policy of constant pressure on the French, the American Navy continued its hunt for French ships elsewhere in the West Indies, particularly near Guadeloupe. Captain Thomas Truxtun, a saltwater Federalist who wanted "to have another touch at these Frenchmen," now commanded the American squadron on the Guadeloupe station, and had taken over as his own the *Constellation*, which now carried thirty-eight guns and 320 men. Early Saturday morning, February 1, 1800, he sighted a heavy French frigate, *La Vengeance*, of fifty-four guns and 320 men. In addition, she was transporting eighty military passengers and thirty-six American prisoners from Guadeloupe to France.

Truxtun immediately started chasing *La Vengeance*, and the French captain tried to avoid battle, mainly because of his passengers and the money he was carrying as cargo. The *Constellation* steadily closed the gap between the two ships and finally forced the French frigate to fight a running defensive action that lasted five hours. Both sides suffered heavy damage and casualties, but the losses of *La Vengeance* were greater. At least twice, witnesses reported, the French captain, from his deck slippery with blood, struck his colors and asked for quarter, but darkness and the intensity of the battle obscured his actions. In any case, this last major naval battle of the Quasi-War, although indecisive in that both ships survived, was greeted by many Americans as a great victory. Truxtun had inflicted greater damage than he received on a ship superior to his own. Congress voted him a gold medal for the engagement.

The Republican press deplored the battle and the honors showered on Truxtun for it, saying that this "hideous transaction" defied the will of the people, who wanted peace. Frenchmen, too, were upset by the continuing naval hostilities. One of them asked Jefferson, for example, "Whence comes this madness for killing foreigners and for getting one's fellow countrymen killed, when it is evident that both nations are reconciled or arbitrating?" Despite the swelling sentiment for peace, the fighting at sea did not stop. In fact, 1800 was a peak year for the new American Navy in the capture of armed French ships.[63]

In Saint Domingue, too, the killing continued, and the American Navy became increasingly involved in it. Adams's government virtually insured Rigaud's defeat when it permitted American naval commanders to go beyond blockade in assisting Toussaint by bombarding the forts guarding the entrance to Jacmel, Rigaud's stronghold.

Stevens urged such intervention, saying that Toussaint was certain to cut his ties to France. "If he is not disturbed," Stevens predicted, "he will preserve appearances a little longer; but as soon as France interferes with this colony, he will throw off the mask and declare it independent." This American intervention forced Rigaud's forces to evacuate the forts and allowed Toussaint's troops to take the city on March 11, 1800. A month later Adams proclaimed the areas of Saint Domingue newly under Toussaint's control open to American trade.[64]

Toussaint, meantime, had asked Roume, the Directory's agent, to aid in the campaign against Rigaud and to authorize his occupation of Spanish Santo Domingo. When Roume refused, Toussaint threw him into jail and assumed civil as well as military authority. Two terms of imprisonment compelled Roume to cooperate. When three more commissioners arrived from France with instructions to mediate a truce between Toussaint and Rigaud, the Negro leader showed them scant respect, shipping one back to France.

Then Toussaint pressed his attack against Rigaud. Neither side thought of quarter. The only prisoners taken were those reserved for torture. Finally Toussaint drove Rigaud from the island, and on August 1, 1800, he entered Les Cayes in triumph. Toussaint L'Ouverture had conquered all of Saint Domingue, and in this conquest he had had the cooperation of the Adams administration. On September 6 President Adams issued another proclamation on trade with Saint Domingue. This time he declared "every part of the said island" open to American commerce.[65]

While Adams's cooperative policy was unfolding in the Caribbean the decline in the martial spirit in the United States affected not only policy toward France, but also the course of domestic politics. The public reaction against the Federalist war program, it may be recalled, was gradual and hence did not immediately bring the Republicans into favor.

In the elections for the Sixth Congress, extending from the spring of 1798 to the spring of 1799 because election dates varied from state to state, Federalist candidates did well. Various factors contributed to the Federalist victories, but as important as any was the public indignation against France and against Republicans as a result of the X Y Z disclosures. Most of the balloting, moreover, took place in a climate of crisis before the people had felt the impact of such measures as the direct tax and the Alien and Sedition laws. In some instances the threat of disunion implied in the Kentucky and Virginia Resolutions created an adverse effect against Republicans and helped to elect moderate Federalists.

The importance of the foreign policy issue can be seen in New Jersey where Federalists stressed that the contest was one between French and American politics, between foreign subjugation and American independence, prosperity, and happiness. As a result of such appeals in the various states the elections gave the Federalists sixty-three seats and the Republicans forty-three in the House of Representatives. Federalists were elated with the efficacy of the foreign policy issue, for some had expected losses. One of them commented from aboard that "the Elections had exceeded our most sanguine expectations." [66]

Although Federalists won impressive victories in big northern states, such as New York and Massachusetts, they made their most striking gains in the South where they captured twenty-two of thirty-seven congressional seats. In Virginia and North Carolina more Federalists were elected than at any time since the birth of national political parties. North Carolina's leading Federalist, William R. Davie, in an effort to link Republicans, those "partisans of the French faction," with the humiliation of Pinckney, Marshall, and Gerry, distributed copies of the X Y Z papers to key men throughout the state.

In Virginia, George Washington took an active part in Federalist campaign strategy. When John Marshall had returned from his Paris mission Washington had urged him to seek a seat in the Congress, arguing that in the crisis with France the welfare of the country would depend on the character of the ensuing Congress. Marshall ran and won, but only because of the support of such men as Washington and Patrick Henry, who violently attacked France.[67]

Federalists rejoiced in Marshall's unexpected victory over a staunch Republican incumbent, John Clopton. They were also pleased by the election of seven of their other candidates. Those victories gave pleasure not only because they added to the Federalist congressional majority, but also because they were "Evidence of a Reform in the Politicks of the very reputable State of Virginia."

In some respects the Federalist sweep was deceptive, for it was offset by losses in areas that had previously returned Federalist majorities, and by the fact that some of the new Federalists were moderates who would not go along with the war program of the extremists. Both New York and Pennsylvania sent Republican majorities to the House, and in New Jersey and Maryland the Republicans gained ground. These were pivotal states.

In Pennsylvania the former Chief Justice, Thomas McKean, headed the ticket that swept the state into the Republican fold for the first time. McKean won the governorship with a platform that opposed every defense measure the Federalists had taken. Local issues played only a small part in the contest; peace, the Army, and federal taxes seemed to be the crucial issues. A Federalist

newspaperman admitted that "the President's appointment of
Ambassadors to make peace with France" were used with great
effect against the Federalist candidate. "The Government, it was
said, is friendly to Peace. Mr. McKean's attachment to peace is
notorious." Another disgruntled Federalist remarked that now the
state was in the hands of Jacobinical scoundrels, "United Irishmen, Free Masons, and the most God-provoking Democrats this
side of Hell." [68]

Even in the South the foundation of the Federalist victories
was shaky. There the voters reacted against measures such as the
Virginia and Kentucky Resolutions, which they considered a
threat to the Union, and returned moderate Federalists rather
than Republicans to Congress. Consequently, when the scope of
the High Federalist program began to be felt, the popular support for it, won when crisis had filled the air, dwindled.

Events in Europe, as well as the nature of the public reaction
to the war program, now played a direct part in the diplomacy of
the Quasi-War. Murray, who notified Talleyrand on May 5, 1799,
of the President's decision to reopen negotiations and his terms
for doing so, thought Adams's timing was good.[69] The United
States, Murray maintained, had grown strong and held a solid
position. France's situation, on the other hand, was bad and her
ministers were discontented.

Pickering disagreed with this analysis. The French endured
American defiance, he said, not because they respected America's
strength, but because they were busy elsewhere. The President's
appointment of another peace mission, he explained, was as unexpected in the United States as it was in Europe, where it caught
many by surprise. Every real patriot was "thunderstruck" by it.

Later, Murray defended Adams's action, saying that High
Federalists talked boldly but did not dare open the true question,
that of war, because public opinion would not support it. Moderates and the people, he observed, seemed to favor defensive measures, but in a spirit of preparation far less intense than one
necessary for war. The national pulse, he maintained, was up to
nothing stronger than halfway, temporary measures.[70]

Talleyrand replied quickly to Murray's note of May 5, giving assurances in the terms Adams required. The Minister of Foreign Relations also expressed regret that the negotiation should be delayed merely for confirmation of what he had repeatedly told Gerry.

While awaiting the arrival of the American commissioners Talleyrand continued his conciliatory policy. On May 15, 1799, he asked the Minister of the Navy and Colonies to carry out the decrees of the Directory forbidding the imprisonment of Americans taken from ships brought into French ports. Talleyrand was declared to have said that neither the French nor the American governments desired peace, *"but that the public mind forced both."*

On July 7 Talleyrand instructed the Minister of Police to liberate American prisoners at Orleans and elsewhere in France. "The Republic," he pointed out, "up to now has happily avoided a declaration of war between itself and the Federal government." More than a month later he pleaded with Pierre Alexandre Laurent Forfait, the newly appointed Minister of the Navy and Colonies, for action in freeing the unfortunate Americans. "Their government," Talleyrand wrote, "is sending new plenipotentiaries to settle their differences with France. The liberation of the citizens of the United States should be, without doubt, the first step toward a reconciliation." [71]

By this time Talleyrand, still tainted by the X Y Z scandal, was on the way out of the Foreign Office. Military reverses had weakened the Executive Directory. Earlier in the year Russia had raised an alliance of Britain, Austria, Portugal, Sardinia, Naples, and the Ottoman Empire, known as the Second Coalition, against France. At first the allies swept all before them. An expedition of English and Russian troops landed in the Netherlands; Austrian forces drove the French out of Switzerland and the Rhineland; and an army of Austrians and Russians pushed them out of most of northern Italy. The Executive Directory appeared to be collapsing.

As a result, on June 18, 1799, in a *coup d'état* called the 30th *Prairial,* the legislators purged all the Directors except Paul François Nicolas Barras. Talleyrand, who wanted to get off what was now obviously a sinking ship, offered his resignation on July

13. It was turned down. About a week later, on July 20, he tried again; this time the new Directors accepted his resignation.[72]

The new Minister of Foreign Relations, Count Karl Friedrich Reinhard, was a friend and disciple of Talleyrand, so he continued the conciliatory policy toward the United States. Yet Reinhard brought some new ideas into the Foreign Office. For example, he preferred a negotiation in the United States rather than in France and suggested that the Executive Directory send a minister to Philadelphia to make peace. In drawing up tentative instructions for such a minister, he took a stiffer attitude toward the United States than had Talleyrand. His instructions demanded an explanation of American conduct toward France, a statement on relations between Britain and the United States, a revision of Jay's Treaty, and complete execution of the Franco-American commercial treaty of 1778.

Reinhard, apparently, would have tried to gain compliance from the United States by applying pressure. He would have reminded the American government of France's alliances with Spain and Holland and of the influence France would have in the American West once Louisiana was retroceded to her. This blunt use of Louisiana stood in contrast to the secrecy with which Talleyrand had tried to cloak French policy in the Mississippi Valley.

Reinhard's plan was never carried out. He held office for only a few months.

RELUCTANT PEACE EMISSARIES

All was not functioning smoothly within the American government either. Although aware that he did not have the allegiance of all his department heads, Adams insisted that they could and should carry out his policies as he directed from Quincy. Friends warned him, nonetheless, that several of his advisers would attempt to scuttle his peace policy. "I speak the truth," Uriah Forrest wrote, "when I say that your real friends wish you to be with your officers, because the public impression is, that the government will be better conducted."

Adams, however, wished to be with Abigail, and was convinced that he could administer the government, as he had the previous summer, from Quincy. "The Secretaries of State, Treasury, War, Navy, and the Attorney-General," he replied, "transmit to me daily by the post all the business of consequence, and nothing is done without my advice and direction. . . ." He saw no need, therefore, to return to Philadelphia, "the chief seat of the synagogue." [73]

Adams might well have heeded the advice of his friends, for he was wrong about the extent of his control over his cabinet and even over the execution of policy. Hamilton still called the tune for three of the department heads. At this time, in June 1799, he even urged them to seize control of the government, or at least to take the making of policy decisions into their own hands. Since, in his view, the President had virtually abdicated his office, seemed incapable of formulating proper policy, meaning war with France, and refused to budge from Quincy, the Inspector General advised those who were capable of using power wisely to do so. He even offered to go to Philadelphia to take a hand in the palace revolution.[74]

The President, however, clung tenaciously to his constitutional power over the making of decisions and barged ahead with his own peace policy. To the disgust of Hamiltonians that policy now grew stronger, especially after July 30, when Talleyrand's renewed assurances, relayed through Murray, arrived in the United States. Those messages reached the President at Quincy on August 6.

"The business is well enough done by Mr. Murray," Adams said, "& now let citizen directors chicane if they will, or be candid if they can." He no longer feared French diplomatic skill; its magic was over in America. So his policy toward France would be candid, peaceful, and friendly. "In this spirit I shall pursue the negotiation," he told Pickering, "and I expect the co-operation of the heads of departments." [75]

Then, in spite of the known opposition of his cabinet officers, who did not consider Talleyrand's assurances satisfactory and who felt Murray had exceeded his instructions, Adams ordered Ellsworth and Davie to prepare immediately for embarking.[76]

He also asked Pickering to complete, and then to send him, a draft of their instructions. Final preparation of the detailed instructions had been delayed deliberately by Pickering and accidentally by disease. The reappearance of yellow fever in Philadelphia had compelled the removal of the public offices to Trenton and hence had disrupted government business.

Before the instructions were completed news arrived in the United States of the *coup d'état* of 30th *Prairial.* The Directory appeared to be crumbling, and to many it looked as if the Bourbon monarchy might be restored in France. This news heartened Pickering and his colleagues, who had not given up hope of blocking the mission. They and others, such as Hamilton, had tried to induce Ellsworth to resign his commission. They apparently succeeded in convincing Ellsworth he should not go to Paris.[77]

Earlier, French officials had thought of using the Marquis de Lafayette as an instrument of reconciliation by sending him as Minister Plenipotentiary to the United States. High Federalists had opposed his coming, for the masses would consider his mission proof of a sincere and amicable disposition on the part of the Directory.

As an old friend Lafayette had written to Hamilton asking if such a mission could succeed and if he could, with propriety, accept the post. Hamilton, and Washington too, advised Lafayette not to come.[78]

Hamiltonians were also active in spreading the idea that on the eve of a possible counterrevolution in France, Ellsworth and Davie should not be allowed to depart. Murray's recent dispatches all suggested collapse of the republic. Some extreme Federalists thought that perhaps the new Directors might not consider themselves bound by the assurances offered by the purged ones. Pickering, therefore, took it upon himself to postpone the carrying out of the President's order to send off the commissioners.

Benjamin Stoddert and Charles Lee, the two department heads favorable to the peace mission, then wrote to the President asking him to come to Trenton to talk to the commissioners before they left for France. The two cabinet officers thought that Adams's presence in Philadelphia might thwart the plotters who wished to destroy the mission.

Adams still refused to leave Quincy, saying "the terms of accommodation with France were so minutely considered and discussed by us all, before I took leave of you at Philadelphia, that I suppose there will be no difference of sentiments among us." Moreover, he was himself willing to postpone the date of Davie and Ellsworth's departure, if the cabinet believed events in Europe warranted such action. He wanted more details on France's political upheaval. "France," he said, "has always been a pendulum. The extremist vibration to the left has always been suddenly followed by the extremist vibration to the right." [79]

On September 14, 1799, Adams received the detailed instructions for the commissioners from Pickering, but without the views of the department heads concerning the state of the mission as now affected by the events in France. He asked Pickering to send him those opinions so that he could consider them and reach a sound decision. High Federalists were now convinced that the Ellsworth mission would be called off. Pickering himself suggested indefinite suspension. [80]

All during these exchanges Adams turned over in his mind the various arguments for and against sending the new mission to France. The upheaval within the Directory might just as easily bring a government to power in France that favored a friendly settlement with the United States as one that was hostile. While the President was deliberating, Stoddert had again written urging him to come to Trenton.

"On the subject of the mission to France, . . . it may not be believed that the instructions to the ministers will wear exactly the same complexion if you are at Quincy, when they are delivered," Stoddert explained, "as they would have done, had you been on the spot." Then the Secretary warned that "artful designing men might make use of your absence from the seat of government" to thwart your peace effort and injure your chances for reelection.

This time the President grasped that all was not well in his official family. So he decided to go to Trenton. He told Stoddert of his decision and said, "I have only one favor to beg," and that is that the question of the election of 1800 be left out of the deliberations concerning the peace mission. "I know the people of America so well," Adams wrote, "and the light in which I stand in their eyes, that no alternative will ever be left to me" but to be President in fact as well as in name.[81]

On that same day Adams notified Pickering that he would arrive in Trenton in a few weeks and ordered him to do nothing about the departure of the commissioners until he could himself confer with the department heads. "We must all be together," Adams wrote, "to determine all the principles of our negotiations with France and England."

Adams's decision to leave for Trenton did not please the Secretary of State. Pickering suggested to the President that if the news from Europe had persuaded him to abandon the mission for the time being, he need not leave Quincy. This suggestion made Adams more determined than before to go to Trenton. On the way south the President stopped at Windsor, Connecticut, to talk for about a half hour with Ellsworth. After Adams left, Ellsworth, as he had before, advised suspension of the mission, but in a manner that would not offend the President.[82]

When Adams arrived in Trenton on October 10, 1799, he was surprised at what he found. Hamilton, who had left troops that were stationed in Newark, was there, as well as Davie and the department heads. Charles Lee told the President that he could see no impressive reasons for suspending the mission. Such a suspension would disappoint the American people and cast doubts on Adams's sincerity in nominating the envoys in the first place. Stoddert took a similar position. It required no crystal ball to show that if Adams suspended the mission he would create a storm in the country, the consequences of which no one could predict.[83]

Pickering, Wolcott, and McHenry vigorously opposed the mission, insisting that its purpose was inconsistent with sound policy. Hamilton himself called on the President to urge him to delay the mission. Speaking, according to Adams, in a "style of

dogmatical confidence," Hamilton warned that if peace negotiations began with France the British would be so resentful they
would declare war on the United States. This prediction did not
upset Adams. *"Great Britain could not hurt us!"* he retorted. Then
he added, "in a just and righteous cause I shall hold all her policy
and power in total contempt." Hamilton also argued that the upheaval in the Directory would lead to the restoration of the monarchy in France by Christmas, and that this development would
make the peace mission useless.

"I should as soon expect that the sun, moon, and stars will
fall from their orbits," the President answered, "as that events of
that kind take place in any such period; but suppose such an
event possible, can it be any injury to our country to have envoys
there? . . . And if France is disposed to accommodate our differences, will she be less so under a royal than a directorial government? Have not the Directory humbled themselves to us more
than to any other nation or power in contest with her? If she
proves faithless, if she will not receive our envoys, does the disgrace fall upon her or upon us? We shall not be worse off than at
present. The people of our own country will be satisfied that
every honorable method has been tried to accommodate our
differences." After several hours of argument, Hamilton realized
that Adams would not yield. So he withdrew.[84]

Adams's decision was now firm. He would not turn back.
That evening, October 15, 1799, in a session lasting until eleven
at night, the President and his advisers agreed on the final wording of the instructions for the peace mission. Adams said nothing
about Ellsworth and Davie, and Pickering left the conference believing that there would be no immediate decision as to their time
of departure.

On the next morning, after awaking earlier than usual,
Adams wrote the Secretary of State a short note which Pickering
received before breakfast. The President asked him to deliver
copies of the instructions to Ellsworth and Davie and to notify
them they were to embark on the frigate *United States*, then lying
off Newport, Rhode Island, by November 1 or sooner if the ship
were ready. Adams added that "as their visit to France is at one of

the most critical, important, and interesting moments that ever have occurred, it cannot fail to be highly entertaining and instructive to them, and useful to their country, whether it terminates in peace and reconciliation, or not." [85]

Pickering, McHenry, and Wolcott were startled, for again Adams had refused to take the cabinet into his confidence in the making of a major decision. Pickering pointed out that Adams deliberated on the subject, made up his own mind, and presented his advisers with an unalterable decision. The Secretary of State made it clear to all Federalists that "the great question of the mission to France has been finally decided by the *President alone.*" It was, in Pickering's judgment, "a measure of magnitude surpassing, in the actual state of things, at home and abroad, every other since the formation of the federal government." [86]

Wolcott and McHenry deprecated the departing mission as "fraught with mischief." They declared that it added to America's humiliation, that it would bring new life to radical French principles, and that it would give more strength to the opposers of government. Worst of all, McHenry commented, "whether the President will think it expedient to dismiss any, or how many of us, is a problem."

Republicans and moderate Federalists were not upset. John Jay, whose Federalism was beyond reproach, believed that since Adams had already nominated the envoys and had received the assurances he had demanded, his insistence on the departure of Ellsworth and Davie was proper. Another Federalist declared that since the French had given the necessary assurances it was Adams's "duty to meet the advances which they had made. . . . If we are not to negotiate with them until they become virtuous I am afraid a perpetual State of Warfare might be expected." [87]

In a last minute effort to wreck the peace policy, Hamilton pleaded with Ellsworth, who still disliked the idea of the mission, to refuse to sail for Europe. Although willing to go to the President to seek an indefinite postponement of the mission, the Chief Justice would not openly refuse to carry out his assignment. If he did so, he feared, Adams might replace him with a Republican, perhaps with Aaron Burr or Madison. So Hamilton consoled himself with the thought that the Ellsworth commission would at least be made up of "safe persons to be intrusted with the execution of a bad measure."

Although the two envoys sailed on November 3, 1799, High Federalists still would not give up their fight against the possibility of peace. A group of them, mostly members of Congress, met at the home of Jonathan Mason, a Boston lawyer and senator from Massachusetts, to discuss the mission and to find some means of insuring its failure. They were aware that the mission had displeased the British, and might impair Anglo-American relations.[88]

Pickering, on his own, took steps to prevent damage to those relations. In confidence, he gave the substance of Davie and Ellsworth's instructions to Robert Liston and elaborated on matters that touched British interests. Pickering convinced Liston that France would gain no privileges which would impair rights Britain had acquired through Jay's Treaty.

Pickering's action indicated the depth of feeling over the peace mission, which, McHenry said, "is become an apple of discord to the Federalists." The breach in the Federalist party made by the appointment of the envoys, a South Carolina Federalist observed, "has been widened by their departure." [89]

~~~~ VII ~~~~

The Ellsworth Mission

It is in vain to say we are as much insulated from the events that affect Europe, as we are geographically. We are not; we are in political contact, because we are a nation, keeping up a perpetual relation and sympathy with Europe and her dependencies, by commerce; and our political views must be governed by that contact.
WILLIAM VANS MURRAY, *July 1800*

ON NOVEMBER 27, 1799, AFTER A COLD, STORMY, AND NERVE-SHATtering voyage of twenty-four days the frigate *United States* arrived at Lisbon. The two diplomats on board were exhausted. Ironically, Oliver Ellsworth and William R. Davie had chosen to land at this Portuguese city to avoid the rigors of a winter crossing of the North Atlantic, but more important, they thought it prudent to approach France indirectly. Before proceeding to Paris, they wished to gather information on the state of Europe and on internal conditions in France.[1]

The envoys had acted wisely, for almost as soon as they landed they learned that while they had been at sea the politics of France had undergone another, this time drastic, change. On November 9, in the *coup d'état* of 18 *Brumaire*, troops with levelled bayonets had routed the legislators of France; General Napoleon Bonaparte had overthrown the divided and unpopular Directory; and he had then replaced it with a new government known as the Consulate. Technically, three men called Consuls now ruled France. In fact, the real power was in the hands of the First Consul, Bonaparte, who held office for ten years and who wielded greater authority than had the Directors or any king of France.

This evidence of continuing political instability caused uneasiness in Ellsworth and Davie because they thought that their credentials, made out to the Executive Directory, might not be acceptable to the new government. After waiting in Lisbon for several weeks while trying to discern what policy Bonaparte would follow toward the United States, they decided to go to Holland to confer with their colleague, William Vans Murray, before entering France, but winter weather blocked this plan. Murray considered the change of *Brumaire* a good one, for he believed the Consulate would be more susceptible to reason than the Executive Directory had been.[2]

According to Murray, Bonaparte was anxious for peace and would accept almost any form of credential, for "he could not do a thing which would unite the banking, mercantile, and manufacturing interests more in his favour, than to make a treaty with the United States; and for him it would indeed be a great thing." Murray also believed that the First Consul was anxious to gain the confidence of European neutrals, such as Denmark and Sweden, who viewed the American negotiation as a touchstone of his sincerity. This moment, therefore, struck Murray as a good one for negotiation.

Murray's analysis was sound. In newspapers and elsewhere the new government took the position that the quarrel with the United States, which was unpopular in France, had been the fault of the discredited Directory. Now a friendly settlement could be easily arranged.[3]

Satisfied that they would not be rebuffed, Ellsworth and Davie sailed for France on December 21, 1799. After being buffeted by "ten days of tempestuous weather," the Americans' ship landed them at a Spanish port near La Coruña. From there they journeyed tediously, over nine hundred miles in midwinter, overland to Paris where on March 2, 1800, they met Murray.

In Paris the three Americans, like their predecessors of the X Y Z mission, had to face Talleyrand. Reinhard had resigned. So, about a fortnight after grasping power, Bonaparte had appointed Talleyrand Minister of Foreign Relations.

"The place was naturally due to Talleyrand," Bonaparte explained later, "but in order not too much to shock public opinion, which was very antagonistic to him, especially on account of American affairs, Reinhard was kept in office for a short time." The First Consul knew what Talleyrand's qualities were, the good and the bad, but he felt he needed the man. "He has what is needed in the negotiations," Bonaparte wrote, "worldliness, familiarity with the courts of Europe, cleverness that keeps him from saying too much, facial immobility which nothing can change, and finally, a great name." [4]

Talleyrand's return to power alarmed some Federalists. They expected another round of humiliating undercover diplomacy similar to that encountered by Pinckney, Marshall, and Gerry. This fear was unnecessary, for Bonaparte took command of France's foreign policy, and Talleyrand himself wished to continue the policy of peace toward the United States that he had inaugurated under the Directory. He, more than anyone else, gave that policy continuity.

Americans who resided in Paris, such as Fulwar Skipwith, the former Consul General, knew that Talleyrand desired an accommodation. Within a week of Talleyrand's reappointment Skipwith wrote to him expressing pleasure that he had returned to the Ministry of Foreign Relations before the arrival of the American envoys. [5]

In one of his first acts under the Consulate, Talleyrand prepared a review of recent relations with the United States. He attributed the American difficulties to England and boasted of his own diplomatic strategy. Instead of reacting harshly against Federalist measures, as "Mr. Adams hoped," he explained, the policy of the previous French government had been to respond with "acts of gentleness." "We have succeeded," he said, "in dividing the party of Mr. Adams himself." After the publication of the X Y Z dispatches in the United States, Talleyrand went on, it was extremely difficult to reestablish favorable relations with the American government. "One can consider as a master achievement in diplomacy," he bragged, "the success of the various measures which have been able to paralyze all the efforts of the English faction to start war and force the president to start negotiations again." [6]

After expressing concern over the delayed arrival of the Ellsworth commission, Talleyrand urged the Consulate to receive the American envoys "with a friendly dignity," and to assure them that France intended to treat them justly, and to end the controversy with their government. In arguing for a friendly reception, Talleyrand stressed that such a reception would help the Republican party in the United States, would block a possible alliance between Britain and the United States, and would deter Americans from going to war against Spain and seizing the Floridas and Louisiana. France needed a reconciliation, he said, to gain security for her own and Spain's insular possessions, to develop trade with Americans, and to deprive England of profit from her own trade with the United States. With this friendly policy, moreover, France would help in building up a rival to Britain. The United States, with its vast territory and rapidly growing population, he prophesied, would ultimately be more populous than any European state.

Talleyrand's attitude echoed knowledgeable opinion in France, much of which favored an understanding with the United States. Bonaparte, who quickly tried to learn something about his country's quarrel with the Americans, fell in with this attitude of moderation. He even wanted to send a new minister to the United States immediately, but Talleyrand persuaded him to wait.

At the same time, Talleyrand increased the privileges Americans were allowed in France. He asked the Minister of Police to permit individual Americans to enjoy all the favors that were commonly allowed them in the other countries of Western Europe. [7]

Before the negotiations began, the Consulate wished to prepare the people of France for the change of climate in relations with the United States. The death of George Washington on December 14, 1799, offered Bonaparte a means of making the change public in a magnanimous way, of identifying his regime with American republicanism, and also of identifying himself with Washington, a symbol of the republican soldier. Since 1793 Washington had been a fallen idol in France, but now French leaders again acclaimed him as a great man. On February 9, 1800, the First Consul ordered ten days of mourning in the armies of the republic in honor of Washington.[8] At Talleyrand's suggestion he also decreed that a bust of Washington would be placed in the Grand Gallery of the Tuileries alongside those of Hannibal, Caesar, Turenne, Condé, Mirabeau, and other heroes.

One eulogy for Washington went on to praise the United States as "the wisest and happiest nation on the face of the earth." In a special funeral oration held at the Temple of Mars in Paris on February 8 the speaker praised Washington and stressed that his were qualities shared by Bonaparte. "It often happens," the orator explained, "that after great political crises there arises an extraordinary man who by sheer power of his character restrains the excesses of all parties and brings order out of chaos."[9]

It was in this climate of goodwill that Talleyrand immediately, and cordially, greeted the American envoys. Their credentials, made out to the Executive Directory, posed no problem. Bonaparte had waived all objection to them. Three days later, on March 7, the First Consul himself, described by Oliver Ellsworth, Jr., his father's private secretary, as "a middle-aged man, thin, spare body, and pale face, dark eyes and short hair of black color," received the envoys with pomp and honors at the Tuileries Palace in the hall of the ambassadors.[10]

Talleyrand suggested as negotiators for France experienced diplomats who were familiar with the United States, but Bonaparte wanted to reward his political supporters. So he ignored his Foreign Minister's suggestions and appointed three commissioners with no direct knowledge of the United States to negotiate with the Americans. He named Joseph Bonaparte, his eldest brother, head commissioner. Murray later characterized Joseph as a man of "excellent character," amiable and mild in manner, learned, and possessed of "a correct but not very active mind." The other two commissioners were Pierre Louis Roederer, Counsellor of State, politician, economist, and Idéologue who admired Americans; and Charles Pierre Claret Fleurieu, also a Counsellor of State, a Minister of Marine under Louis XVI, and a prominent author. Both were enthusiastic supporters of the new regime.[11]

Among the American commissioners the only one who spoke French, and who had had diplomatic experience, was Murray. He was also the youngest and lacked the political stature of his colleagues. Ellsworth, the head of the commission, according to Murray, had a neat and accurate mind, one "that works with the precision of a mill. If he knew literature and spoke French," Murray believed, "he would be a giant among the diplomats of Europe." Davie, in Murray's estimate, was "a firm, soldierly & well informed man."

Later, however, Murray changed his mind about his fellow commissioners. He called them "men of sense—but exceedingly rude and raw." They came to Paris, he became convinced, prejudiced against him because of his part in originating the mission. In any case, he remarked that the three commissioners disliked each other and got along only "on terms of decent civility." [12]

Two days after Ellsworth, Davie, and Murray had had their audience with the First Consul, Talleyrand informed them of the appointment of the French commissioners. Despite this prompt action and the eagerness of the Americans to begin, the negotiations were delayed for almost a month by an illness of Joseph Bonaparte. Bargaining began on April 2 when the two commissions exchanged credentials. They decided to treat most matters in writing and placed Pichon, now secretary of the French commission, in charge of the exchange of correspondence.

The Americans immediately explained that they considered the powers of the French plenipotentiaries, who could only conclude a settlement of *"the existing differences"* between the two countries, inadequate. By contrast, the Americans were empowered to "settle by a treaty all controversies between the United States and France." [13]

Three days later Bonaparte enlarged the powers of his commissioners so that they could sign a treaty. After this, negotiations began in earnest, continuing for nearly six months.

THE INSTRUCTIONS

During this time the commissioners alienated the American community in Paris. Thomas Paine, who hobnobbed with Americans, considered Adams's emissaries three "useless mortals" whose presence in France was more of "an injury than a benefit" to peace. As soon as they arrived, he said, they consciously snubbed those Americans in Paris, such as Skipwith and Barlow, who were known Republicans on the theory that "they had not the confidence of the executive." [14]

The American commissioners stuck to business as they saw it. When they insisted on an equality of powers, they had reflected the demands of their instructions, written in strong language by Pickering, for a "speedy decision." The Secretary of State said that the "conduct of the French republic would well have justified an immediate declaration of war on the part of the United States." So he advised the envoys not to appear "warm and eager" for a restoration of peace and friendship. "Your country," he stressed, "will not submit to any new indignity or neglect." Indeed, the envoys were required to begin negotiations within twenty days of their arrival in Paris and to complete them by April 1, 1800.[15]

Since Congress had declared all treaties with France null and void, the instructions required the negotiation of a new treaty to replace them. The "indispensable condition" for such a treaty, the instructions insisted, was settlement of the question of claims for losses suffered by Americans as the result of French depredations at sea. France must pay an indemnity to compensate Americans for their injuries. Regardless of the merits of the American demand, this issue seemed destined to create difficulty because up to this point no nation had been able to exact indemnification from any of the French governments since the Revolution of 1789.[16]

Once the question of claims had been resolved, the negotiators could take up matters related to commerce and neutral rights. The articles in the commerical treaty of 1778, which had

allowed either France or the United States to equip and bring enemy prizes into the ports of the other, had been a source of difficulty for the United States in relations with both England and
France. As a consequence, the American government did not wish
to renew those privileges or to include them in a new agreement.
Furthermore, it now considered a renewal impossible because of
Jay's Treaty. In that treaty the United States had agreed to deny
Britain's enemies the right to arm privateers in American ports or
to bring British prizes into them. Since Congress had abrogated
the French treaties, commitments in Jay's Treaty, in the American
view, would take precedence over those in any new agreement.

At the same time, the United States was willing to acquiesce
in France's denial of freedom of the seas, or the right of neutral
ships to sail the oceans without being molested by the cruisers of
warring nations, a right which both countries had pledged themselves to uphold in 1778. This was not much of a concession because the American government had already abandoned that
principle in Jay's Treaty and in a treaty with Prussia.[17] In effect,
the United States sought a new treaty in which there would be no
definition of troublesome neutral rights.

To guard against another X Y Z fiasco, the instructions forbade the American envoys to promise aid or loans in "any form
whatever." They could sign no agreement inconsistent with commitments in Jay's Treaty, could guarantee none of France's
dominions, and could make no engagement that was "in the
nature of an alliance." They were also to deny the privileges of
the French consular courts in the United States as allowed under
the convention of 1788. Americans considered these privileges in-
compatible with their nation's sovereignty. Finally, the new
treaty could not run more than twelve years, except for agreements on debts, invested funds, and compensation for contracts
and past injuries to the United States.

Implicit in the instructions was the desire of the American
government to rid itself legally of the French alliance and related
treaties. The envoys were to accomplish this by persuading
France to acknowledge the congressional abrogation of the treaties as being valid in international practice. At the same time, the

American commissioners were expected to obtain compensation for France's violation of the very principles, such as free ships, free goods, they now wished to abandon.

Ironically, in December 1799 Bonaparte's government had repealed the Directory's harsh decrees that remained in force, such as the notorious law of January 1798 against neutral shipping that had violated freedom of the seas and had injured American shipping. The Consulate even eliminated the worst abuses in the French prize courts by establishing a Supreme Prize Court in Paris, where it could be watched and controlled.[18] Other new rules the Consulate had recently proclaimed committed France once again to the principles of broad neutral rights.

The French now favored the freedom of neutral ships to trade in noncontraband goods to and between ports of belligerent nations, and a restricted list of contraband, one that would exclude food and naval stores. These were the principles of free ships, free goods that the British had never been willing to accept, and which they certainly would not now accept in their war against France.

It was this English attitude, in fact, that had caused the First Consul to embrace freedom of the seas. England's maritime policy had also been an important factor in his decision to continue the peace policy he had inherited and to negotiate with the United States. He desired a friendly America that he could use as a weight in the balance of power against England.

Talleyrand's instructions to the French commissioners reflected Bonaparte's desire to strike at British sea power. The commissioners were to look at the negotiations from the perspective of the past, the present, and the future. They should use the past to remind the American government of its obligations to France. In the present they should end the depredations at sea and heal the bad feelings between the two countries.

Most important of all was the future. The commissioners had orders to drive a wedge between England and the United States. If they could, they were to try to provoke rivalry between the two countries. Finally, the plenipotentiaries were to attach the United States to France politically so that the French nation could secure the advantage of American sympathy and neutrality in future wars.

Another factor, one that Talleyrand did not make explicit, gave the negotiations a worldwide significance. This was Bonaparte's scheme to use them to gain favor with the neutral powers of Europe. Talleyrand's terms were in keeping with the First Consul's objective, for they emphasized the traditional liberal principles of neutral rights which the European neutrals, as weak naval powers, favored. A short time later Talleyrand took the next step in support of the Corsican's grand plan when he informed the Prussian Ambassador in Paris that France favored the forming of a league of neutrals in northern Europe to end British maritime "tyranny."

In view of France's naval weakness in her war against England, Talleyrand's attitude was logical. France needed neutral ships to carry her trade. Her own ships were either destroyed or blockaded, and the illiberal maritime system of the Directory had not only driven neutral shipping away from French ports, but it had also failed to harm Britain. That system, as has been seen, had had the effect of a self-blockade, so that was one reason why the Consulate changed it.

Bonaparte's government now sought to extend the free status of neutral ships to the goods they carried. Since Britain's merchant marine transported an unusually large proportion of her own cargoes, the French government also wanted to apply the belligerent status of British merchantmen to the products they carried, whether or not those goods belonged to neutrals. Thus the dictum of free ships, free goods with its corollary of enemy ships, enemy goods, an important principle in the Franco-American commercial treaty of 1778, had again become vital to France. This principle, if supported by the United States, might encourage the formation of another combination of neutral powers against Britain, as had been the case in 1780, to resist her denial of freedom of the seas.

In addition to these considerations, three basic conditions were to guide the French commissioners in the negotiations. They were instructed to revive the treaties of 1778 and 1788, reestablish the jurisdiction of French consuls in the United States, and revise the treaties so that France would enjoy the same advantages the United States had allowed England in Jay's Treaty.[19]

If these issues could be resolved, all that would remain would be the question of payment for damages suffered by Americans and Frenchmen. Talleyrand listed grievances for which the United States should pay compensation and acknowledged that French corsairs and maritime restrictions had injured Americans. In balancing the two sets of claims, the Minister of Foreign Relations admitted that the Americans could justifiably demand greater payment for losses than could the French.[20]

As instructed, the American diplomats brought up first the question of compensation for losses suffered by their countrymen at the hands of the French. The negotiations in April stressed this point. In these discussions the Americans quickly ascertained that they probably could not obtain what their instructions directed, for the French negotiators insisted that national claims, or losses suffered by either government, should be settled first. The French commissioners also asked if Congress had repealed the laws against French commerce as the Consulate had revoked the Directory's measures against Americans.

Since the American laws were still in force and Congress on February 24, 1800, had extended the suspension of commercial relations with France until March 3, 1801, the American envoys were embarrassed by the query. They answered that since their country's laws were retaliatory, they would end with the removal of the French provocation. The envoys then offered to send copies of the Consulate's decrees to their government in Washington.

In support of their demands for indemnity, the American commissioners offered a project, actually the first six articles of a draft treaty, for handling the claims.[21] The French ministers accepted the draft as a basis for discussion of principles. They also agreed to the principle of compensation but argued that payment hinged on the treaties of 1778. So, they said, the negotiators should set aside discussion of payment until after they had concluded a new treaty. The Americans pointed out that they had no authority to make a treaty before the claims had been settled.

This matter of claims linked to the status of the old treaties upset the American diplomats. "We find," Murray wrote of the French, "they are extremely hurt at the dissolution of Treaties & that it will be difficult to claim [damages] at all under these up to their dissolution & that it will be no easy thing to conciliate their [French] reasoning & their pride with our doctrine, that though the Treaties be dissolved yet we are not in war." [22]

The attitude and methods of the two commissions also complicated the negotiation. The Americans approached their task as would lawyers trying to prove their client in the right. They painstakingly sought to document every point they raised and fought for each point. In addition, they talked a great deal about morality and justice, and seemingly assumed that on the strength of such argument their case would prevail.

While the French believed in the righteousness of their case, and also talked of good faith and justice, they regarded their meetings with the Americans as bargaining sessions where there would be give and take. They did not seek to establish justice in the abstract but to adjust the interests of the two countries. In effect, they wished to strike what might be considered a mutually acceptable bargain. Their diplomacy, as a result, was more flexible and sophisticated than that of the Americans.[23]

These differences, and other developments, stretched out the discussions. From the middle of April 1800 to the middle of May, Talleyrand was sick and took no part in the discussions. The First Consul, who left Paris on May 6, became deeply involved in military campaigns in Italy. Since the existence of his regime depended on the outcome of the war against Austria, he concentrated on it and did not press the American negotiation. Yet little could be done without him, for he kept his mind constantly active and insisted on knowing everything. In May and June, therefore, the commissioners made little progress. "Our success," they reported, "is yet doubtful." [24]

During these months the cause of difficulty, but not the means of breaking it, was clear. The French argued that as a prerequisite to any payment for spoliations the Americans had to recognize the continuing validity of the treaties of 1778 and 1788.

"They admit," Murray explained, "that old treaties, IF EXIST-
ING will oblige them to pay, but they are not bound to *pay as a
preliminary to a new one.*" [25] Furthermore, the French denied
that the American Congress had the right to abrogate the treaties
by simple legislative act. Under existing international law this
was a sound argument. Treaties could be spurned, violated,
broken unilaterally, or abrogated by invoking the terminal date,
but otherwise they could not be abrogated without the consent of
all parties involved.[26]

Even under their own Constitution the position of the American negotiators was dubious. The American Constitution had
granted the treaty-making power to the President and to the Senate, but it did not specify the means of invalidating treaties. It
was, therefore, an open question as to whether or not Congress
had the power, even with the consent of the President, to cancel,
unilaterally, a contract with another nation. This, at least, appeared to be the case in 1800.

Congress, of course, had the exclusive constitutional power
to declare war, and by this means had the authority to break the
obligations of an international contract. Attorney General Lee, as
we have seen, had even advanced the opinion that the United
States and France, by their own actions, were at war. On the part
of the United States, he had argued, war existed by reason of the
legislation against France. Neither Adams nor Pickering had accepted this interpretation. They held that no actual war existed
because Congress, as required by the Constitution, had not declared it. The American commissioners took the position of their
President. "Our demands," Murray explained later, "were surely
bottomed on an interruption [of peace], not war." [27]

Ellsworth, Davie, and Murray could not even admit that
Congress, by its measures, had virtually declared war, for to make
such an admission might release France from obligations under
her old contracts with the United States. The American government wanted France to acknowledge the validity of its claims
against her, to pay for damages to American property, and to accept as legal the view that the United States had no obligations
under the old treaties. This American repudiation of treaty com-

mitments became a subject of heated dispute, a central factor in the negotiation. If the old treaties were still in force they carried obligations binding on the United States as well as on France, and a new agreement would not be a treaty of peace.

The French negotiators insisted not only that the alliance and the other treaties were still binding, but also that these agreements took precedence over all other obligations of the United States to foreign powers. In part, the French fought for this point because they wanted the United States to refuse asylum to the privateers and prizes of any nation unless that privilege were given first to France. Of all the privileges in the old treaties, this was the most difficult for the French to give up. They said that in losing the right of asylum, they would surrender the principal advantage they had gained in the treaties as compensation for giving up, during the American Revolution, claims to American territory. What particularly bothered them was that their enemy, England, had that advantage.[28]

Roederer, who drafted all the notes for the French commissioners, pointed out that their instructions were grounded on the principle of revising, not destroying, the alliance and related treaties. The refusal of the Americans even to acknowledge those treaties, he explained, came up as an unforeseen problem. In his judgment the American argument that Britain's privileges in American ports, as a result of the abrogation of the French treaties, had priority over those of other nations, was not valid. Since the abrogation was an act of the American government alone, and therefore could be retracted in the same way, Britain had nothing to do with the status of the treaties.

The Americans contended that the annulling was authorized by the rights of nations because France had violated the treaties. As a result, Jay's Treaty became binding in all its contingent promises the moment the treaties with France ceased to exist. The United States could not legally break the English treaty and call the violation a legislative act, and France could not demand of the United States, as a preliminary to payment of claims, action that violated international law.[29]

This argument failed to move the French commissioners.

They maintained that if the United States had not broken its obligations to France by making war on her, it was still bound by the treaties of 1778 and 1788. In addition, they asserted that the right of asylum for privateers and prizes was an obligation the United States could not compromise in any subsequent agreement with an enemy of France without the consent of France. In their view, the American government had done this in Jay's Treaty.

In keeping with Bonaparte's design, the French commissioners expressed a keen interest in retaining commitments to the principle of free ships, free goods. As far as the American envoys were concerned that obligation had caused nothing but trouble with France, Spain, and Britain. They were not, therefore, interested in renewing it. Since the American government held that the French treaties had been abrogated legally by Congress, in the American view the commitment to the principle of free ships, free goods had been discarded.

STALEMATE

Before the end of May, as a result of these conflicting views, the French commissioners realized that the instructions of the two commissions were so far apart the negotiations had become stalemated. If the negotiations were not to be broken off, the French diplomats concluded, they must seek new instructions. Roederer confessed that he and his colleagues had exhausted their powers. They reported that the Americans did not have the necessary power to recognize the validity of the old treaties as required by Talleyrand's instructions. So the French commissioners asked their superiors two questions. Were the treaties of 1778 and 1788 truly abrogated? Secondly, did France have a strong interest in maintaining or reestablishing them? [30]

The answer to the first question was no. If, however, France stood firm against unilateral abrogation, the American envoys would have to seek new powers. Then negotiations would be delayed for months longer.

As for the second question, France would suffer little if the treaties were annulled. Benefits from the alliance and commercial treaty, such as in the American guarantee of French colonies and in the French right to outfit privateers in American ports and to use those ports for asylum, had proved illusory. These provisions, if carried out, would have destroyed American neutrality. Since France desired the United States to retain its status as a neutral, she had never tried to execute all these treaty provisions. All that France really needed in a new commercial treaty were privileges in American ports equal to those enjoyed by Britain.

Finally, if France accepted the annulment of the old treaties she would gain the right to oppose payment of indemnities to American citizens, for she could then argue that by abrogating the treaties the United States had forfeited any privileges they conferred. The French commissioners then asked if they should continue to insist on the reestablishment of the old treaties, or obtain new powers which would allow them to replace those treaties with a new one.

Both Talleyrand and Joseph Bonaparte had reported the state of the negotiations to the Premier Consul, and Joseph went to Italy to explain the details in person. Talleyrand told General Bonaparte that he had accepted the principle of indemnity for losses of private citizens, but that the negotiations had deadlocked on the status of the old treaties. He felt that the abrogation of the treaties would give a hostile character to the past misunderstanding with the United States, and hence would relieve France of the necessity of paying indemnities. At this point the French commissioners, with Talleyrand's approval, suspended the negotiations until the First Consul responded.[31]

Despite the impasse, Murray thought the French would yield. The Consulate had announced to the world that it would conduct itself with moderation and justice. Since the American government was the first to bring these professions to the test of negotiations, the world had its eyes on the bargaining in Paris. Murray therefore expected Bonaparte's government to heal with justice the wounds the Directory had inflicted.

In a private conversation on the evening of May 23, 1800, however, Roederer had said that he would never surrender a privilege which had belonged to France, essentially the right to use

American ports, to England. Then he proposed that the United States allow France and England that privilege on an equal basis. Murray objected, stressing that France had held the right exclusively but had lost it. Now, through Jay's Treaty, Britain had that right for herself for at least two years after the end of her war.

Roederer replied that France did not wish to involve the United States in a war with England; the American Navy was too weak. He added that since he and his fellow commissioners must insist on revival of the old treaties, they could do nothing more until fresh instructions came from the Premier Consul. He, himself, he said, did not favor the policy of restoring the treaty of alliance. Alliances without the pledge of specific force, he maintained, were practically valueless.

The American envoys considered this conversation important because it revealed that for France the revival of the treaties had been an indispensable condition. Believing, nonetheless, that the French ministers wished to cut through difficulties, particularly since they did not close the negotiation on the basis of their instructions, the Americans decided to make a concession.

Two days after Murray's conversation with Roederer the Americans offered, as an addition to their draft treaty, equal naval privileges for France and Britain in American ports, the idea proposed by Roederer. The French commissioner responded that Murray had overrated the value of the proposition.[32]

While the negotiators bargained privately, Bonaparte himself did nothing to break the deadlock. He apparently agreed with the estimate of Pichon, that if the Americans were left to themselves they would become more tractable. He may also have sought to prolong the negotiations while working secretly to acquire a new colonial empire in Louisiana as soon as he could make peace with Britain. His defeat of the Austrians at the Battle of Marengo on June 14, 1800, had assured him control of attractive territory in Italy that Spain seemed likely to accept in exchange for Louisiana.

Within six weeks of this battle Bonaparte ordered Talleyrand to reopen secret negotiations in Madrid for the retrocession of Louisiana to France.[33] Since the French had often argued that

Louisiana in their possession would guarantee Spain's other colonies in the New World against American encroachment, the Premier Consul may have been tempted to delay a settlement with the United States so as to frighten Spain into giving up Louisiana from fear of an American thrust against it.

At this juncture the American envoys were deeply impressed by Bonaparte's victories and the rising power of France. They no longer entertained the notion that the Consulate, like the Directory, would collapse and that the Bourbons would return. They apparently became convinced that almost any arrangement with France which did not violate national honor would be preferable to expanded war.[34]

On July 3, 1800, the Premier Consul returned to Paris, followed a few days later by Joseph Bonaparte. Shortly after, the Americans requested another meeting with the French commissioners. It was held on July 11 at Joseph's home, preceded by a pleasant dinner. Joseph said he thought the cause of his brother's hesitation was the American refusal to place France on equal footing with England.[35] Roederer added that the old treaties could be broken only by war, and that France had never desired to go to war against the United States. Ellsworth answered that under the law of nations one party could renounce a treaty whenever it believed itself injured by the way the other party executed it.

The Americans supported their doctrine that a nation may rightfully dissolve a treaty which is violated, and yet not resort to war, by citing the Swiss jurist, Emeric de Vattel. The French buttressed their position, which stated that nothing but mutual consent and war could annul treaties, with the opinions of Cardinal Arnaud d'Ossat and Gabriel Bonnot, Abbé de Mably, a *philosophe* who had commented extensively on law and government. These men, in the American view, were not proper authorities because both were French.[36]

At this time Talleyrand submitted a number of reports to the First Consul on the state of the negotiations, hoping to elicit a decision on the points in dispute with the American envoys. He also reported on public opinion in the United States, stressing

Adams's break with the High Federalists, the Republican successes in state elections, and the prospect of Jefferson succeeding Adams in the Presidency. Jefferson's accession, he pointed out, would strengthen American friendship with France, but he warned that "we should not forget that we have improved our position by moderation and by complete non-intervention in their internal affairs."

These developments in the United States, Talleyrand said, offer additional reason for terminating the quarrels with the American government on a generous basis. "I am persuaded," he wrote, "that it is our liberality and conciliation that has produced the division in the cabinet and in the nation. Not to persist in this policy is to run the risk of uniting all the parties against us and of justifying all the aggressive measures followed up to the present day."

News from the United States also seemed to have an effect on the American commissioners. "They show," Talleyrand asserted, "with an appearance of true conviction, a desire to end their mission in a manner that would satisfy equally both peoples." [37]

On July 20 Roederer told Murray that Talleyrand, Joseph Bonaparte, and himself had all spoken to the Premier Consul. The general refused to accept the American proposal or any terms short of equality of privileges with England. Since this would be the first peace under his administration, he was resolved that it should not be a disgraceful one for France. Roederer said the United States could have peace but not amity. Hostilities may cease on both sides without a treaty, he pointed out, and the rights and duties of nations may exist without it. Murray replied that this then could be considered the end of the negotiation.

At a *levée* on the following day the Premier Consul informed Murray that republican France could not accept less than what had been the right of monarchical France. He also spoke of British depredations and asked if the British seized American vessels. Murray replied yes, they did. Bonaparte then observed that it was to the interest of all maritime states to raise American sea power as a counterpoise to that of Britain. He commented that the tyranny of the British at sea seemed to have excited an armed neutrality against them.[38]

On the next day Ellsworth learned of a dramatic change in France's position. Although the French still demanded equality of privilege, they now refused to pay indemnities, but were willing in return to give up the old treaties. To put an end to hostilities, they wanted a treaty of amity.

This change, Murray thought, reflected an armistice in Vienna and the preliminaries of a French peace with Austria. If a general European peace followed, Murray feared, he and his fellow commissioners would be in the embarrassing position of having broken the negotiation with France on irreconcilable grounds and of having an unfinished quarrel on their hands with no chance for peace. The defect in the American position, he believed, lay in the indispensable demand that payment of indemnities must precede a treaty. It would be to America's honor, he thought, to retreat from the quarrel by negotiating simply for a treaty of peace. The United States could, in this circumstance, consider the property losses of its citizens the price of liberation from the old treaties.

On July 25 Pichon said France would accept a proposition that included the portion of the old commercial treaty that granted asylum to French vessels in American ports. The rights under this item, he added, would not have to be absolute. They could be limited to those permitted the most favored nation, meaning that any favor the United States granted another country in this matter would automatically accrue to France. Murray thought his colleagues would accept this offer and that it would not violate the Jay Treaty.[39]

Two days later the Americans agreed among themselves to accept Pichon's proposal. The state of affairs in Europe had compelled the American commissioners to agree to break their instructions on this point, but this was nothing new, for they had already violated those instructions by negotiating beyond April 1. The envoys believed that if their government knew of the situation in Europe it would itself have altered their instructions.

"If we can preserve compensation & make peace on these

24. *William R. Davie, from a portrait by Gilles-Louis Chrétien. This North Carolina Federalist helped negotiate the peace of 1800.*

25. *Oliver Ellsworth by John Trumbull, 1792 (Yale University Art Gallery). This Chief Justice of the United States led the American peace mission in Paris in 1800.*

26. *An audience conducted by the five members of the Directoire in the Palais du Luxembourg, 30 Brumaire of the Year IV.*

27. *Signing the Treaty of Môrtefontaine, October 3, 1800.*

28. *The Château of Môrtefontaine, a contemporary view.*

29. *Congress Hall and New Theatre on Chestnut Street, Philadelphia, 1800.*

30. *"Preparation for War to defend Commerce,"* an engraving of 1800 showing the construction of the frigate *Philadelphia, with the Swedish Church, Southwark, Penn...*

31. The Capitol in Washington as it appeared in 1800.

32. *An 1800 engraving of High Street, Philadelphia, showing the funeral procession of George Washington, December*

terms," the Americans reasoned, "we shall do better than let the state of hostility [with France] continue while Europe . . . may have made peace." We should, they thought, get our government out of this increasingly embarrassing dispute. This fear of a friendless future had bothered Murray ever since he had heard of the armistice at Marengo.[40]

Developments in Europe had also led Bonaparte to renew efforts to reach a settlement with the United States. His victory over the Austrians, combined with Russia's growing antipathy toward her Austrian and British allies, had weakened the Second Coalition against France and had left Britain as the most formidable opponent to his ambitions. Concerned over the difficulties of invading England or even of occupying Louisiana without control of the seas, the First Consul stepped up his plans to unite continental Europe against England, or as he put it, "to conquer the sea by the land." [41] He could take a big step toward this goal if he could persuade the Baltic states to combine their navies against British sea power. Deteriorating relations between Britain and the neutral powers of northern Europe seemed to play into his hands.

Denmark's disposition to resist Britain's practice of visiting and searching neutral merchantmen under convoy was attracting support from Russia and Sweden. Danish convoy commanders had orders telling them that "violence must be opposed by violence." [42] John Quincy Adams, the American Minister in Berlin, reported that though the northern countries were not yet prepared to force a rupture with Britain, they would probably take joint action aganst her maritime system if they could do so "without danger of being crushed by the contest."

The key to any effective northern combination was Russia, still a member of the coalition against France. To ingratiate himself with Tsar Paul I, and to divide Russia and Britain, Bonaparte had made plans to offer the Tsar the island of Malta, which he had seized from the knights of Malta (known also as the Order of St. John of Jerusalem) on his Egyptian campaign in 1798. The knights had earlier elected Paul their Grand Master. Even though Paul was the head of a rival church, he accepted the leadership of this Catholic order. The title of Grand Master apparently pleased him more than did that of Emperor. So, as Grand Master and as a ruler anxious to push Russian influence into the Mediterranean, Paul coveted Malta. Since besieging British forces threatened the French hold on the island, Bonaparte went ahead with his plans and offered the island to Paul on July 4, 1800, before it fell. Two weeks later, in a further effort to win over the Tsar, the First Consul announced that he was releasing, and reequipping with the uniforms of their sovereign and with arms at his own expense, some seven thousand Russian prisoners taken by French armies in Switzerland.

Five days later, on July 25, an incident at sea fanned the discontent of the northern neutrals against Britain and offended Paul, who considered himself the arbiter of the North. The commander of a British squadron attempted to search a convoy of six merchantmen being escorted in the English channel by the Danish frigate *Freya*. Arguing that a belligerent had no right to visit or search neutral vessels under the escort of a warship of their own flag, the Danish captain said he would resist. Since the British regarded resistance to search as a hostile act, a battle ensued, with loss of life on both sides. In about a half hour the Danes yielded to superior force, and their ships were brought into a British harbor.[43]

BONAPARTE'S BROAD VIEW

Agitation in northern Europe over this latest British naval action increased the international significance of the Franco-American discussions in Paris. By using those negotiations to emphasize the identity of France with the cause of neutral rights, the First Consul might encourage the Baltic powers to stand firm against British domination at sea.

These wider European considerations, in part at least, as well as the desire to separate the United States and England, had led Bonaparte and Talleyrand to shift their position in the negotiations. Up to this point, as has been seen, France had expressed willingness to pay indemnities for violations of the old treaties with the United States, but only if the Americans accepted those

treaties as still binding.[44] Talleyrand also deviated from an
earlier position by deciding that a new treaty would be necessary,
and he submitted a draft for one to the First Consul. It treated
the dispute with the United States in a worldwide context.
France, the Minister wrote, should continue her traditional role
as protector of neutral commerce. She should not accept the
American proposal that required her to sacrifice the principle of
free ships, free goods.

Bonaparte's changed attitude on the payment of indemnities
led the American commissioners to reexamine their position in
the light of their instructions and of the state of European politics. They had not only argued that their government had the
right to dissolve the old treaties, but also that the dissolution was
an accomplished fact. The French denied the right because they
had not consented, and questioned the fact becase neither country recognized the existence of war. They agreed only that there
had been a dispute.

Without mentioning their instructions, the Americans had
tried to make the most of their case by advancing the theory that
they could not restore the old treaties because this would affect
obligations to Britain under Jay's Treaty. The French countered
with their own theory that even if there had been a rupture, the
parties could revive the old treaties if they chose. This led the
Americans to ask themselves what the effect of restored treaties
would be on the operation of an anterior treaty with a third
power, such as Britain in the case of the Jay Treaty?

The Americans agreed that to replace an old agreement was
not to make a new one, and that a third party could expect neither gain nor loss from a quarrel between two allies. They also
decided among themselves that unilateral abrogation was not as
strong as war, which meant dissolution by both sides, and that
the abrogation of the French treaties by Congress was the principal subject of negotiation.

To find an answer to their own question the Americans
searched through old European peace treaties. They found that
in negotiations between England and France at Lille in 1797
Lord Malmesbury, the English plenipotentiary, had offered to renew the Treaties of Utrecht of 1713. Although these negotiations

at Lille did not result in a peace treaty, this example proved, to
the satisfaction of the American commissioners, that Britain had
not considered her proposed renewal of old treaties, which im-
pinged on the Jay Treaty, an act of bad faith against the United
States. "We thus are convinced," the Americans said, "that we
may, with good faith, do what G.B. offered to do." They concluded that they could rightfully restore the privilege of asylum
in American ports to French ships without violating the Jay
Treaty.

Yet the American position remained ambivalent. Ellsworth,
Murray, and Davie admitted that their country was "not in open
declared war" but in a state of hostilities with France. The United
States had fought, and it now negotiated to gain respect for its
commerce in the future and payment of an indemnity for past injuries. This status, while France and Britain were themselves at
war, was not that of an ordinary neutral power.

If the United States had been strong enough to compel respect for its flag, France would have been the plaintiff in the
negotiations. "We can defend ourselves," the American envoys
admitted, "but not bear down—not yet." Since the United States
had not entered the European war, its problems would not be
considered at a general peace conference. This could prove upsetting, the commissioners reasoned, "as nations treat best when the
opponent is embarrassed by the other more powerful opponents
—and there is such a thing as being left in the lurch at a Peace."

The state of Europe, since the Battle of Marengo, suggested
that soon there would be a general peace in Europe. This, the
Americans thought, would be followed by peace between France
and England.

"We naturally ask ourselves," the envoys wrote, "what is the
position of the U.S.?" It would be, they decided, in a state of hostilities against France without the aid of allies. They decided,
therefore, that it would be to America's advantage to terminate
its hostilities quickly. They should avoid negotiation at a time
when they had no possible ally to turn to or in the moment of
France's triumph. The United States should not negotiate while
"impelled by any apparent necessity or force."

Although the United States had begun its negotiation voluntarily, Ellsworth, Davie, and Murray realized, circumstances had changed. France was now much stronger than she was a year ago. If they broke off the negotiation and started a new one later, it would probably be less dignified than this one. Besides, they reasoned, if they were to settle the dispute on honorable terms, they would give *éclat* to the entire Adams administration. On the other hand, if they refused to grant the French equality with the British, a new commission would only be ordered to do so, and the government would lose status.

"It is our duty some times to depart from instructions where the state of things is greatly changed & time presses," the commissioners concluded. The interests of the nation and the situation in Europe demanded such a departure.[45]

Unaware of the decision of the American commissioners, observers in Paris wrote that there appeared little likelihood the negotiations would be renewed with success. Three months, it was pointed out, had been lost in waiting for fresh instructions for the French diplomats. France would prefer not to treat with the United States at all, it was reported, than to acquiesce in advantages for her enemy.[46]

France hoped the northern European powers would adopt the principles of freedom of the seas and force the United States to do so also. On August 10, 1800, Talleyrand instructed the French commissioners to induce the Americans to accept those principles. "When the neutral powers are reconciling themselves with us and talking of forming among themselves a league against British pride," he advised, "that is not a moment for deviation from the principles which made us so many friends among them during the American Revolution, and to return to those which have made for us almost as many enemies in the past five years."[47]

NEW TERMS

On the following day the French commissioners sent the American envoys a note that embodied their new instructions. They now offered the Americans the choice of renewing the old treaties with privileges for France that took priority over those England had acquired, and with stipulations of mutual indemnities, or of signing a new treaty that assured equality of privileges for France with the most favored nation, and no payment of indemnities.[48]

Murray wanted to break his commission's instructions again by signing a treaty of equal privileges. Ellsworth and Davie would not abandon the demand for indemnities. Murray argued that financially the indemnity was not worth a struggle. To make a peace without being forced to recognize the old treaties, he said, would be a solid achievement. It would also be good for the country, which was tired of the treaties, and be a mark of American strength, for the agreements were doubtless precious to the French. It was the commission's duty, he asserted, to snatch the government from an awkward and unforeseen state of affairs. The United States would never retire with so much grace and so little expense from this situation, as with this relinquishment of indemnities. With these terms, he pointed out, this commission would do better than the X Y Z commission had been ordered to do. The old commission was permitted to relinquish compensation and yet let the old treaties remain in force.[49]

Technically, the Americans could not accept anything in the nature of an alliance. Nor could they give up compensation for losses, an indispensable condition for any agreement. "We are reduced then," Murray wrote, "to a choice of what part of our instructions we shall violate."

Murray preferred to relinquish money rather than replace painful treaties. He considered it sound policy to give up a burdensome and litigious promise of payment, which might never be executed, to obtain agreement from France that the alliance and related treaties were dead. His colleagues, still determined to obtain compensation, rejected his reasoning.[50]

So, the commission adopted a proposal advanced by Ellsworth. It called for:

1. The renewal and confirmation of the old treaties. They would have the same effect as if no misunderstanding had intervened, except as modified by a new treaty.

2. The limitation of France's claim of privileges for privateers and prizes in American ports to such as the most favored nation would enjoy. For this concession the United States would pay France three million francs within seven years.

3. Allowing both countries the right to modify the guarantee in their alliance by paying one million francs. Either side could free itself from the guarantee by paying the other party five million francs within seven years.

4. Replacement of the articles of commerce and navigation by new ones containing the principle of the most favored nation. These new articles would run for twelve years.

5. Restoration of, or payment for, public ships taken by either side. Indemnities would be limited to the claims of individuals.

6. Restoration of all property seized and not yet condemned by either side.

In this new proposal the American commissioners, in effect, offered to accede to the first French alternative—renewal of old treaties with mutual indemnities—on the condition that France relinquish her exclusive privileges under the treaties if the United States paid five million francs in seven years. The French were not to use the privileges until the end of seven years.[51]

The American commissioners thus tried to break the deadlock by going beyond their instructions. They did this by recognizing the validity of the old treaties, or at least by accepting the embarrassing provisions of those treaties as live issues. At the same time, they tried to purchase release from those obnoxious provisions. Their offer did not apply to the claims against France.

Murray thought that if France had not been eager for a triumph over the British navy, she would have refused the American demands. As it was, Bonaparte's maritime policy required her to be on good terms with the United States.[52]

Nonetheless, the French negotiators demurred. They did not wish the kind of financial offset the Americans had proposed. With it France would still be liable for payment of the spoliations of her raiders. Moreover, American claims would most likely be higher than the five million francs the United States would have to pay to be released from its treaty commitments. The French, however, did not advance this argument.

Instead, on August 25, 1800, Bonaparte's commissioners proposed the reestablishment of the old treaties, the nomination of two commissions to liquidate the damages suffered by each country, and the abandonment by the United States, within seven years, of its obligation under Jay's Treaty to admit Britain's privateers and prizes into its ports. If the United States did not succeed in freeing itself from its commitment to Britain, then France would not have to pay indemnities.

Furthermore, the United States would have to drop the obligation in Jay's Treaty regardless of whether or not Britain and France were still at war. If Britain and France should make peace before the end of seven years, this new American obligation to France would fall due within the life of Jay's Treaty. That treaty had stipulated that the right of asylum for privateers and prizes should endure for twelve years. In effect, the commissioners wished the United States to accept the suspension of what had formerly been an exclusive French right as a substitute for a cash indemnity.

The French negotiators also revised the American suggestion on guarantees. They wanted a "promise of succor" in the amount of two million francs and to increase the price of redemption from five to ten million francs.[53]

The Americans now balked. Whatever the price, they dared not accept as a basis for negotiation any proposal that would endanger Jay's Treaty.

The French then offered to relinquish their privileges under the old treaties if the United States would assume the responsibility of paying its own citizens for damages claimed. The French negotiators pointed out that one way of avoiding the problem of indemnities was to leave each government to treat its own nationals as it chose after a new treaty was concluded. This would be comparable to the situation after the signing of a peace treaty at the end of a war.

Basically, the French contended that if their country had to give up treaty rights, such as the American guarantee of her possessions in the West Indies and exclusive privileges for her privateers and prizes in American ports, she would not pay indemnities for having raided American shipping, even if she had done so in violation of obligations under the treaties of 1778. On these points the negotiation again deadlocked.

Finally, the Americans decided that regardless of their instructions, the deadlock must be broken. "We must depart from our Instructions, whether we get compensation by absolute renewal; or make a new Treaty on their principle," Murray wrote. "Our effort has been to make the departure with as much conformity to the spirit of our orders as possible & for their main object i.e. compensation."

The Americans hoped to obtain compensation for losses and to avoid the question of exclusive privileges for France by limiting her right to equality for at least seven years. In that time it seemed likely that the article in question in the Jay Treaty would expire, and the United States would have an opportunity to free itself from both the French and British treaties.

"We find no instance of a nation's doing better," the Americans concluded in assessing their plan, "except in the case of humiliation by great superiority of military force. The General routine is war—peace with restoration of Treaties & payment for vessels seized before the war. That is very different from ours, if we can obtain our object in the way proposed. . . ." [54]

The chance of some concessions by Bonaparte was good because he still desired American friendship and still wished to make use of the United States as a rival to Britain on the seas. Perhaps equally important, the Corsican was now more anxious than ever to safeguard liberal principles of neutral rights as the basis for a naval combination among neutrals. Such a combination could be decisive in defeating Britain and in freeing the oceans for French ambitions in Louisiana.

At this juncture Tsar Paul I, who had been deeply offended by the attack on the *Freya* and was furious with the British, came to France's aid. In a declaration of August 27, 1800, he had invited Denmark, Sweden, and Prussia to join Russia in a Convention of Armed Neutrality designed to defend freedom of the seas against Britain. Denouncing Britain's seizure of the *Freya* and decrying her illiberal maritime system, the Tsar acclaimed the principles that had been announced by his mother, Empress Catherine the Great, in her Declaration of Armed Neutrality in 1780. Two days later he issued a *ukase*, or decree, sequestrating all British property. This was an act of war, which he was persuaded to withdraw a few weeks later.[55]

Although the Tsar had softened a bit and the British had agreed to return the *Freya* to her owners, England's relations with the Baltic powers remained critical. Her high-handed treatment of a Swedish vessel, the *Hoffnung*, drew Sweden into the quarrel. The Royal Navy's seizure of the *Triton*, a ship carrying timber from Emden to Amsterdam, led to protests from Prussia. Finally, Britain's capture of Malta on September 5, 1800, before Bonaparte could turn it over to Paul, increased the Tsar's animosity. He demanded Malta's return to the Knights.

Meanwhile, the First Consul manipulated the negotiations with the United States so as to portray France as the champion of freedom of the seas. Now, he hoped, the northern powers would screw up their courage and support the Tsar's project for a new league of neutrals.

Joseph Bonaparte berated the Prussian Minister for Prussia's tameness in the quarrel between Denmark and England. Joseph said that all the neutral powers in Europe ought to join against the tyranny of England at sea and, addressing Murray, added, "the U.S. also."

"Put us in a state to chuse," Murray answered, "and then we can judge the better of it."

Joseph smiled.

Several days later, on September 11, 1800, the French and American commissions held a conference. Roederer explained that the French knew the high value the United States placed on getting rid of the alliance and its guarantee of French possessions. Consequently, the French would sell the alliance as dearly as possible, meaning that they would accept nothing less than America's surrender of indemnities for it.[56]

This, after almost six months of bickering, was the state of the negotiations. The French said, in effect, we wish to settle the dispute without paying indemnities, indeed that we cannot afford to pay them. We are sure you do not want to revive the alliance. We know, in fact, that you consider its revival as onerous, yet that is the price we ask for indemnities.[57]

THE CONVENTION OF MÔRTEFONTAINE

The American commissioners now met alone to decide what to do. Their mission, at least in terms of its original objectives, had ended in failure. They could ask for their passports, go home, and receive an honorable discharge. On the other hand, if they could not secure reparation for past injuries, they could perhaps prevent a recurrence of like molestations in the future. So they decided on a proposal that would, at minimum, smother the danger of a full-scale war.[58]

"We met," Murray wrote on September 13, "and agreed to a note stating the discussion on Treaties and indemnities to be closed for the present and to be resumed at a more convenient time—then offering them 4 propositions to serve as a basis of a temporary arrangement. . . ." Then he added, "It is our duty to try to settle something that shall end hostilities—and draw our Govt. out of the dispute.—"

In their note, Ellsworth, Davie, and Murray proposed postponement of discussion of the old treaties and of indemnities. Putting aside their treaty project, they suggested instead a temporary accord that would restore normal political and commercial relations. The French accepted this suggestion, and the two commissions now moved rapidly toward a settlement. As agreement neared Murray commented, "our whole negociation has proceeded on the principle of No Open War—and our settling must go on that principle—we defer—not abandon indemnity (tho' Lost in fact forever!!). . . ."[59]

The American proposal appealed to the First Consul because deferment of indemnities would relieve France from the possibility of another financial burden. The American commissioners and their government did not know of Spain's negotiations with

France. So peace might also help to mollify the United States when this Spanish transaction became known and Bonaparte was ready to take over Louisiana.

"We all dined today at my house and after dinner proceeded to business," Murray wrote on September 24. "They proposed if we wished the option to have, or not, the principle of 'free bottoms free goods,'—we said we did not hesitate in chusing that free bottoms shd. free the cargo—That it was the interest of F. & U.S. that the principle shd. be agreed to between them." Ellsworth then drew up a line or two, "saying it was understood by the parties that free ships shall [make] free goods.—" [60]

As it worked out, the settlement included most items covered in the old treaties and, hence, became more comprehensive than the American envoys had intended. Most important, it was a peace settlement. The first sentence of the first article stressed this. Secondly, the agreement postponed debate over the troublesome issues of indemnities and of the status of the alliance of 1778 and related treaties while recognizing that the treaties were not in operation. The French agreed not to require American ships to carry papers other than those customary in the United States, and the Americans consented to a restoration of naval vessels captured by either party. Measures were agreed to for the payment of debts due in each country. In return for French concessions, the American commissioners accepted maritime stipulations similar to those in the commercial treaty of 1778. Those articles repeated, almost word for word, principles the Tsar had just invoked in his declaration. [61]

Of the four leading principles to which the Tsar subscribed, the new agreement stipulated three: the right of a neutral to trade in noncontraband to and between the ports of any belligerent; a narrow list of contraband, not including naval stores; and free ships, free goods, excepting contraband.

On the fourth point, that of blockade, the treaty provisions differed from the Russian description in words, but not in purpose. The Russians defined a blockaded port as one where the attacking power's ships were stationed so as to make access obviously dangerous. The French and Americans simply said that the right of a neutral to trade between belligerent ports did not apply when such ports were "actually blockaded, besieged, or invested." Both definitions ran counter to Britain's practice of declaring a blockade and not effectively maintaining it, a procedure called paper blockade.

A fifth principle of maritime freedom, that naval officers of a belligerent power could not visit and search neutral ships in a convoy when escorted by a neutral naval vessel flying the same flag, had been the central issue in the *Freya* affair. In a convention of August 29, 1800, Britain and Denmark had deferred this question to future discussion. In their agreement the French and Americans accepted Denmark's interpretation. They agreed that if a convoy commander said the ships under his protection were from the nation whose flag he flew, and carried no contraband, this declaration would be sufficient to free them from visit and search.[62]

Difficulty arose over the title of the new agreement. The French wished to call it "a treaty of amity and commerce" and to make it more than a temporary arrangement. "They said it must be a *Treaty* not a Convention." Ellsworth, Davie, and Murray opposed this, pointing out that they had agreed to go ahead only on the basis of a temporary pact. Finally, the Americans expressed a willingness to consider the document as the substance of a treaty and to call it a "provisional treaty." That was as far as they would go.[63] They favored the word provisional because they had gone beyond their instructions and wished, therefore, to reserve the right to make changes in the settlement. The French commissioners accepted the American proposal.

Later, Murray wrote of the night of September 25, or rather of two in the morning of the 26th when the final difficulties were overcome: "We touched a port—at least were on soundings, after a voyage of fog." [64] Such late hours were not exceptional, for the commissioners usually held their conferences at night after dinner.

Except for copying and signing, the work on the treaty was finished on the night of September 27, 1800. Murray considered the completed agreement fair and honorable to both sides. "If we have not accomplished every object of the government of the United States," he wrote, "we have done all in our power—all I believe which any others would have done, all that could be expected in the present state of our relations, and of the world's affairs! We, at all events, put an end to the equivocal state of things, draw the government of the United States out of the quarrel with honour, and establish honourable rules for the future." Then he added, "We have, I dare think, made a better treaty than the last mission might according to their instructions have made. . . ." [65]

All three commissioners were convinced that given the nature of their demands, the power of France, and the state of Europe it was their duty to conclude a treaty rather than return home empty-handed. Their decision, they felt, served the interest of their government and of their people.[66]

The Provisional Treaty of Amity and Commerce was signed at Ellsworth and Davie's hotel, the Maison des Oiseaux, rue de Sevres, at 2:00 A.M., October 1, 1800. Since copies bore the date of September 30, this was left as the official time of signature.

Bonaparte immediately looked over the treaty, for late on October 1 Roederer and Fleurieu called on the American Ministers to gain acceptance for two changes requested by the First Consul. At his suggestion the document was changed from a "provisional treaty" to a "convention," and was drawn in the name of the Premier Consul of the French Republic and the President of the United States, rather than in the names of the governments of the two countries.[67] The full title of the long agreement of twenty-seven articles was Convention of Peace, Commerce and Navigation.

Bonaparte had insisted upon calling the accord a convention, he explained cryptically in private, because he knew when to observe forms and when to discard them. He apparently felt that the pact would have greater influence with the northern neutrals if its title gave it an appearance of permanence. Those powers would easily see the distinction between a treaty and a provisional one but probably would discern little difference between a treaty and a convention. The First Consul's assumption was sound because treaties and conventions were equally binding and the difference between them was slight. Bonaparte's comment on this detail suggests that he had neglected little in trying to make his relations with the United States fit his strategy of raising another armed neutrality.

Since the document had been revised, the commissioners decided that it required new signatures. The second signing took place at 6:00 P.M. on October 3, at Château Môrtefontaine, Joseph Bonaparte's country estate about eighteen miles north of Paris. With an eye on the effect their actions might have on Britain as well as on the northern powers, the French celebrated the consummation of the convention with a magnificent fête, which had to be prepared hurriedly because Ellsworth and Davie would not delay their departure for Le Havre later than October 4.

The American commissioners were the guests of honor. The Premier Consul, his family, and practically all the important officials in the French government were present. Bonaparte gave Ellsworth an expensive Gobelin tapestry, offered all three American Ministers costly Roman medals of gold, which they refused, and told them he was pleased with the convention. He declared that the misunderstanding between their two nations would leave no more traces of anger than would a family quarrel. He also expressed hope that the United States would unite with the northern powers to enforce freedom of the seas.[68]

The Americans thought the celebration, friendly and complimentary, was held mainly to publicize the reconciliation of France and America. "I tell you of a fête," Murray wrote, "because our last commission was so terribly treated. Its being done after the treaty was signed was the more agreeable. Toasts to perpetual peace between France and the United States, to neutrals who armed in defense of freedom of the seas, and to the successor of Washington, were drunk to the sound of cannon." [69]

A sumptuous dinner served to one hundred and eighty people in three separate halls, an elaborate display of fireworks in the garden—intended to depict Franco-American amity—a concert, and two short plays in one wing of the château, were offered to the guests as the climax to the long negotiation. As the French had intended, this celebration caught the popular imagination, and the Convention of 1800 became known to many as the Treaty of Môrtefontaine.

The French were satisfied with the compromise settlement. Some of them thought that the convention, as far as the maritime war was concerned, gave France one more ally and England one more enemy.[70] The Americans were also pleased, Murray more so than Ellsworth or Davie. Ellsworth admitted that he and his colleagues did not get all that was desired but, he pointed out, they did extricate the United States from a difficult conflict. "Our country is disentangled from former connections," he wrote. "Be assured, more could not be done without too great a sacrifice, and as the reign of Jacobinism is over in France, and appearances are strong in favor of a general peace, I hope you will think it was better to sign a convention than to do nothing." [71]

☙ VIII ❧

Peace and the Election of 1800

*I shall leave the State with its coffers full, and the fair pros-
pects of a peace with all the world smiling in its face, its
commerce flourishing, its navy glorious, its agriculture un-
commonly productive and lucrative. O, my country! May
peace be within thy walls, and prosperity within thy palaces.*
JOHN ADAMS, *December 1800*

WHILE ELLSWORTH, DAVIE, AND MURRAY WERE NEGOTIATING IN PARIS,
the American people were immersed in a bitter presidential campaign. Leaders of both parties, the Federalist and the Republican,
sought to use peace, if not the negotiations themselves, as one
means of attracting votes. Within the Federalist party peace became so controversial an issue that it attracted trouble as well as
votes. This part of the campaign of 1800, the emphasis on peace,
had started early.

Rebellious because of John Adams's decision to send a second mission to France, High Federalists in the summer of 1799
had adopted the attitude that he must be replaced as the party's
candidate in the coming presidential election.[1] Hoping once more
to use George Washington's prestige to advance the party's cause,
they turned first to him. In June they asked him to give up his
retirement and to run for a third term, asserting that at this time
the country was so divided by faction that only he was big

enough to reunite it. Reiterating that only an actual enemy attack could bring him back into public service, Washington refused. Hamiltonian leaders then began weighing the possibility of some other replacement for Adams.

After Adams had insisted that Ellsworth and Davie sail for Europe, High Federalists had become almost impassioned in their determination to block him as the party's candidate.[2] Pickering expressed their point of view as well as anyone. The sending of the peace mission, he wrote, "will subvert the present administration & with them the government itself. Mr Adams has not by this mission gained one friend among the democrats; to their former *hatred* will now be added *another sensation:* while among the Federalists he has forfeited the support of his best friends and our most estimable citizens." As a result, Pickering maintained, only Adams's refusal to seek a second term "can unite the federalists and save our country." [3]

Another member of the cabinet, James McHenry, felt the same way. "I see rocks and quicksands on all sides," he wrote, "and the administration in the attitude of a sinking ship. It will, I imagine, depend very much on the President whether she is to weather the storm or go down." McHenry feared that as a campaign issue the peace mission might nullify Federalist accomplishments and bring the Republicans to power. Gouverneur Morris told Washington that "leading characters, even in Massachusetts, consider Mr. Adams as unfit for the office he now holds," and he urged the retired hero to run.[4]

Moderate Federalists maintained that the Ellsworth mission should be accepted as an accomplished fact. "Opposition to or condemnation of it," one of them wrote, "can certainly now render no benefit to our country." [5]

Adams himself took an uncompromising position. He denounced Hamilton and the war faction in his own party. A few weeks after Ellsworth and Davie had departed, he bluntly told Oliver Wolcott that he intended to create a third party by drawing support from the independent thinkers in the other two parties.

The attitude of the country and the composition of the Sixth

Congress, underscored the uncertainty of the political outlook. As members of the Congress gathered in Philadelphia for the convening of the first session, scheduled to open on December 2, 1799, and to run until May 1800 when the seat of government would be transferred to the city of Washington, peace seemed to be in the air. Men who a year earlier had been hailed as vindicators of national honor were now regarded by many of their contemporaries as warmongers.

In this new Congress, because most elections for it had been held during the period of intense resentment against France following the X Y Z disclosures, Federalists for the first time since 1793 held majorities in both houses. Yet Congress could not escape the new peaceful mood of the country. In the House of Representatives Federalists held a nominal majority of about twenty. As the party program unfolded this majority faded.

The core of the High Federalist group, made up of New Englanders, appeared as solid and as unyielding as in the previous session. The large number of new Southern Federalists, however, were moderates who would not accept the leadership of Hamilton and Pickering. Instead, they looked to John Marshall, who had gained the President's support and had become the administration leader in the House. High Federalists, as a result, could not count on a steady majority. Strong party measures, in fact, seemed less likely to pass in this Congress than in the preceding one. The split in party councils had the effect of shattering the Federalist majority, at least on the issue of foreign policy.

Furthermore, Republican opposition had become more effective than in the past. The repressive internal policy of the High Federalists had forced the Republicans to discipline themselves, to draw tightly together, and to consolidate their position in Congress. This Republican solidarity alarmed Federalists. "Let that party set up a broomstick," George Washington exclaimed, "and call it a true son of liberty—a democrat—or give it any other epithet that will suit their purpose, and it will command their votes *in toto.*" [6]

Although the elections had brought some change, the Senate, unlike the House of Representatives, had retained a character similar to that of the preceding session. The Senate stood firm for harsh measures against France. Its grim Federalist majority, made solid by a band of extremists, was determined to carry out a war program regardless of public wishes, or the desires of the administration.

On December 3, 1799, the day after Congress had assembled, the President delivered his third annual message. With the exception of his inaugural address, most of Adams's messages to Congress had bristled with defiance of France, but this one struck a calm, even peaceful, note. Abigail remarked that some people would not like it "because it will not disclose enough about the mission to France. Others will growl because war is not waged against England, in words at least. They will grumble at all events and under all circumstances, and so let them." [7]

Adams spoke of his commitment to "a pacific and humane policy," stressed the disposition of the French government "to accommodate the existing differences between the two countries," and explained that duty compelled him to meet the French overtures, but he reminded the legislators that the outcome of the negotiations in Paris was uncertain. In conclusion, he advised continued defense efforts to maintain the nation's rights but also urged economy in government and an examination of expenditures for "beneficial retrenchments." Instead of asking specifically for more armaments, for increases in the Navy, and for additional protection of commerce and honor, he requested a "system of national defense commensurate with our resources and the situation of our country." [8]

Even though members of the House received the message "with more applause and approbation than any speech which the President has delivered," as Abigail had predicted, High Federalists were alarmed. Some assumed that Adams had switched his foreign policy so as to offer peace to France and hostility to Britain. They disliked his references to the Ellsworth mission because, in part at least, they assumed that a *rapprochement* with France would produce a rupture with Britain. Aside from a desire for close relations with England, some Federalists felt that England would be a more dangerous enemy than France because she could inflict greater damage on the United States in case of war.[9]

Republicans, on the other hand, were pleased with the President's peaceful references to France. They wished to indicate strong approval of the speech but did not do so because such approbation might increase Adams's popularity.

The President himself was as concerned with this factor of popularity as were the Republicans. Some of the more doctrinaire Republicans took the view that despite Adams's hostility to France, popular opinion had forced him to send the Ellsworth mission to Paris. "They admit, however," Wolcott wrote, "that considering all circumstances, the President has shown such respect for the voice of the people, as justly to entitle him to an increase of their confidence."

There appeared to be truth in this observation. Adams had complained about the mounting expenses of government. His unwillingness to issue recruiting orders for the Army had stemmed from a knowledge that the Army and the expense of maintaining it had cost the administration much of the popularity it had gained with the publication of the X Y Z dispatches.[10]

The statement of the Secretary of the Treasury at the opening of the congressional session reinforced the President's plea for economy. Wolcott showed that customs revenue for the past fiscal year had fallen off nearly one million dollars, and that an expenditure exceeding the standing revenue of the government by five million dollars annually would have to be incurred to maintain the operation of the federal government at its present standard. With returns from the direct tax yet to come, with the revenues from internal sources and customs precarious, and with loans already contracted at high rates of interest, it made political sense for a President who sought reelection to ask Congress to reconsider the extent of the war emergency. None could escape the fact that preparations for war were costly and were particularly onerous at a time when revenues were decreasing.

These factors, as well as Adams's message, set the tone for the Sixth Congress. That Congress would be, it seemed, as peaceful as its predecessor had been warlike.

Before Congress could attack the various problems confronting it, word reached Philadelphia of Washington's death. Immediately, on December 18, Congress adjourned. Neither the country nor the Federalist party had been prepared for his demise, which came suddenly after a brief illness. To the High Federalists it fell as another blow to their program. During the course of the Quasi-War Washington's support had been invaluable to the party. Whatever policy the Federalist party followed, whatever charges might be made against it, there were men who believed it could not endanger liberty as long as Washington had a voice in its councils. His passing removed whatever restraint he may have imposed upon Hamiltonians for the sake of party unity.[11]

Hamilton himself felt Washington's death deeply in two ways. He suffered a personal loss and the loss of an irreplaceable political champion. He could say truthfully that the departed Washington had been *"an Aegis very essential to me."* [12]

If Adams had entertained a jealousy of Washington, the General's death eliminated or softened such feeling. The President delivered an official eulogy that mingled praise with personal grief. "I feel myself alone," Adams admitted, "bereaved of my last brother." [13]

REPUBLICAN RESURGENCE

Even before Washington's death Federalist leaders had realized that the days of the Provisional Army were numbered. Theodore Sedgwick had concluded on his own that the Army would have to go. "Good men in New England, where tranquility generally prevails," he declared, "cannot easily be led to understand for what purpose the Army can be necessary, provided a peace be made with France." [14]

It seemed clear that the party held responsible for the cost of keeping up this unemployed military force would become as unpopular as the Army itself. Even those who hated France "could not agree to carry their resentment as far as to keep up such extraordinary expenses and systems when there was no real danger."

Washington's death triggered action to do away with the

Army. The general was hardly buried when John Nicholas of Virginia, one of the best Republican speakers in the House, stood up and pointed out the desirability of "lopping off all unnecessary expenses in the army establishment." He proposed the repeal of the act of June 16, 1798, authorizing the appointment of a commander of the Army and the "raising of twelve regiments of infantry."

John Marshall replied that the United States faced real danger, and that it was in fact, if not in form, at war with France.[15] For the time being the repealer was laid on the table. Yet with the passing of the Army's nominal commander and with the reluctance of Adams to appoint Hamilton in Washington's place and to build up the Army, it had become obvious that the war party had lost prestige and much of its public appeal. Popular passions could no longer be aroused with reports or rumors of French outrages.

High Federalist speakers now found themselves unable to persuade Congress that subversive French ideas were destroying the nation's morals and institutions, or that Jacobins would crush liberty in America as they allegedly had done in Holland and Switzerland. This hue and cry seemed to indicate that Federalists were frightened. They realized their popularity was dependent on the crisis with France, and now that popularity was in danger of dying.

As the Republicans became more conscious of their strength and of popular support, they took up one by one the measures adopted during the war hysteria of 1798. They even tried to repeal the Alien and Sedition Acts, but they were unsuccessful. Yet George Cabot, among others, admitted regretfully that "popular passions had already evaporated." He insisted, nonetheless, that national security and self-defense required retention of the laws.[16]

To the distress of the High Federalists, a combination of Republicans and moderate Federalists on February 20, 1800, passed an act suspending further enlistments in the Army until the next session of Congress or a declaration of war. That act was followed by a supplementary law authorizing the discharge of officers and men, who had already enlisted, at an early date. So favorable did news from Paris seem that on May 14, the last day of the session, Adams signed this act. This marked the end of the controversial Provisional Army, which was soon disbanded.[17]

News from Paris was not favorable enough, however, to kill the Non-Intercourse Act against France, which had been placed on an annual basis. When that law came up for renewal in the House it was passed. In the Senate Charles Pinckney, a Republican from South Carolina, declared the act an unconstitutional delegation of power to the President, and in itself evidence of the increasing influence of the Executive. Pinckney believed, moreover, that it was unfair to single out France for retribution when other nations had been guilty of the same, or worse, offenses. Nonetheless, the Senate renewed the act by a vote of 19 to 10, and thus the ban on commercial relations with France continued for another year.[18]

At the end of the session the military appropriation was reduced from over four million dollars to approximately three million dollars. Basically, the expenditures were cut by postponing the construction of heavy frigates and by stopping the Army enlistments. The President was authorized to borrow three and a half million dollars at 8 per cent interest. On May 7, to meet the interest on this and on the previous loan, additional duties were laid on various articles.[19] A separate act required the Secretary of the Treasury to present estimates of the revenue to the Congress at the beginning of each session.

Republican critics interpreted the actions of Congress and of the President, as electioneering efforts to court popular favor. Jefferson pointed out that "on the whole, the federalists have not been able to carry a single strong measure in the lower house the whole session." Another Republican remarked that Adams "seems a while to retract from high-handed explosions against France and Democrats." [20]

High Federalists, on the other hand, were disturbed by the state of politics. Fisher Ames wrote that he perceived "a want of accordance between our system and the state of public opinion. *The Government is Republican; opinion is essentially Demo-*

cratic." He and Oliver Wolcott thought that the President had ingratiated himself with a large part of the public by showing too much "respect for the voice of the people." [21]

The department heads were also concerned about the President's state of mind. He had learned of the intrigue surrounding him and his office, particularly of his advisers' allegiance to Hamilton, and of the desire of the Hamiltonians to replace him as the Federalist candidate for President. This knowledge, like the heated matter within a volcano, smoldered within him. "He considers Col. Pickering, Mr. McHenry, and myself as his enemies," Wolcott wrote of the wrathful Adams; "his resentments against General Hamilton are excessive; he declares his belief of the existence of a British faction in the United States." [22]

Despite his inward rage, Adams retained his disloyal department heads. If he removed them he feared he would destroy party unity, or what remained of such unity, and would jeopardize his reelection. The full support of his own party seemed vital because of the mood of the country and of the growing strength of the Republican party. Furthermore, he apparently did not wish at this time to reveal differences within the administration over foreign policy. [23]

Most Americans, it seemed clear, were unwilling to sacrifice prosperity and to assume the burdens of an enlarged war with France that no longer seemed necessary. This attitude, plus the action of the first session of the Sixth Congress in stripping the Hamiltonians of their offensive armaments, destroyed the warlike program from which the Federalists had profited for the past two years.

Even in New England, Republicans began to show surprising strength. In Massachusetts Elbridge Gerry ran for governor in the spring of 1800 as a Republican against an extreme Federalist and the "war hawks." He carried Boston and almost won the entire state. An impressive feature in Gerry's loss by only two hundred votes was that he campaigned as a friend of Adams, of the people, of the rights of man, and of peace. On this program he attracted the friends of the President and other moderate Federalists as well as Republicans.[24]

More important were the local elections in New York in the spring of 1800. At stake were seats in the state legislature. Since, by a recent change, the legislature would choose New York's presidential electors, the political complexion of that body could be decisive in the coming presidential election.

Both parties looked upon New York as the pivotal state. They assumed, that the presidential contest would be close and that the votes of the New York electors would most likely decide who would be President. Within the state, the city of New York held the balance of power. Federalists and Republicans, consequently, threw themselves into the contest there, and Americans everywhere were concerned with the balloting in that city.

Adams, who had been selected by a caucus of party leaders in December 1799, was the Federalist candidate, but his enemies within his own party were numerous and powerful. They had not retreated in their determination to replace him but to get rid of him was not easy. Moderate Federalists, particularly in New England, were still loyal to Adams and would resent any Hamiltonian attempt to displace him.[25] The plan of substitution therefore could not be publicly disclosed. It went underground and took on the characteristics of a plot.

Hamilton was the Federalist chieftain in New York. Responsibility for party fortunes there rested with him, but he was also the prime mover in the plot against Adams.

Robert Troup, Hamilton's henchman and a tireless worker against "democrats" in New York, explained the plan succinctly. There was, he said, "a decided and deep rooted disgust with Mr. Adams" and a general belief that "the preservation of the federal cause essentially depends on removing Mr. Adams and appointing a more discreet man to the Presidency." In New York this attitude required Hamiltonians to make "every possible exertion to have a decided majority of sound electors."[26] Hamilton had to nominate men who would, when elected to the state legislature, vote obediently for the slate of presidential electors he would hand them.

In its essentials this plan seemed foolproof. In the past New

York City had been consistently Federalist, and Hamilton expected it to continue to be so. He therefore chose as Federalist candidates in the city men who would prove amenable to his desires, but who were mediocrities.

In carrying out his plan, Hamilton had failed to take into account the ambition and subtle political talent of Aaron Burr, the Republican boss in New York City. Jefferson was the Republican presidential candidate, but at the time of the New York elections the vice-presidential candidate had not yet been chosen. He would probably come either from Pennsylvania or New York. In New York Burr and George Clinton, an "old Revolutionary character" and a former governor of that state, were the leading contenders. Since each commanded an important faction within the Republican party, the party chiefs had decided to await the election returns before choosing between them.

Aware of the importance of the election, Burr purposely delayed the picking of a Republican slate until he learned whom the Federalists had nominated. Then he reversed Hamilton's tactics. He persuaded some of the Republican party's best men, those with national as well as local reputations, to run for the legislature.

To everyone's surprise, when the votes were counted on May 1, it was found that the Republicans in New York City had brought their entire ticket into office. This victory, as well as gains upstate, tipped the political scale sufficiently in the state legislature's lower house, even though the upper body remained Federalist, to give the Republicans a majority in the combined houses by one vote. That was enough to insure a solidly Republican slate of presidential electors casting 12 votes.[27]

The French Consul in New York immediately wrote home explaining the significance of the Republican victory. He attributed it to the peaceful gestures of the French government, "to the certitude of a coming reconciliation between the two Republics," and to public resentment against the seizure of American ships by the British navy.[28]

Burr's lieutenants took advantage of the New York City tri-

umph to push his claim to the Republican vice-presidential nomination. That claim could not now be denied. In May, a Republican caucus chose him as Jefferson's running mate.

News of the reverse in New York sped southward and
reached Federalists in Philadelphia while Congress was still in
session. Realizing that the loss of New York, which Adams had
carried in 1796, meant that the party would have to find new
sources of electoral votes if it were to save the Presidency, the
Federalist members of Congress on Saturday night, May 3, 1800,
held a secret caucus.[29] This second caucus reaffirmed the choice of
Adams and selected Charles Cotesworth Pinckney of South Carolina to run with him as the Federalist candidate for Vice-President. Political strategists expected Pinckney's presence on the
ticket to strengthen the party in the South, especially in his home
state, and offset the loss of New York.

This ticket represented merely a surface unity, for Hamiltonians hoped to slip Pinckney in ahead of Adams. They based their
plan on the expectation that Adams and Pinckney would receive
an equal number of electoral votes in all states except South
Carolina, where the electors would cast their ballots for Jefferson
and Pinckney. Pinckney, as a result, would come out ahead of
Adams and become President. Then Hamilton could hope to
guide the nation's foreign and domestic policies.[30]

A PURGED CABINET

Already gloomy over his chances for reelection, Adams saw
the New York results as tending to confirm his apprehensions. He
attributed the defeat to Hamilton's maneuvers against him. This,
as well as knowledge of the plot to drop him, apparently convinced the President that continued deference to the Hamiltonians in his official family could do him no good. Even at the risk
of revealing the split in his party during the election campaign, it
seems, he decided to reconstruct his cabinet with men he could
trust while he returned to Quincy during the approaching recess
of Congress.

Unable to restrain his anger, Adams erupted first against

McHenry who came to see him on May 5 on routine business concerning the War Department. After a hot exchange of words, the President declared that Hamilton had been opposing the administration in New York. McHenry denied this.

"I know it, sir, to be so," the flushed President retorted. "You are subservient to him."

Adams went on. He would rather serve as Vice-President under Jefferson, he said, than be indebted "to such a being as Hamilton for the Presidency." Three of his department heads, passed on to him by Washington, he asserted, were incompetent in the important area of foreign policy. "How could such men," the increasingly irate Adams demanded, "dictate to me on such matters, or dare to recommend a suspension of the mission to France." [31]

Shaken by the President's violent emotions, the unhappy Secretary of War withdrew. On the following day McHenry submitted his resignation. Adams accepted it.

Next, Adams turned on his Secretary of State, who had plotted with Hamilton to have Adams replaced. Pickering had long been defiant of his Chief, believing that duty compelled him to save the country from the policies and actions of a wrongheaded President. This defiance had earlier led Adams to consider Pickering's removal, but until this time he had always hesitated.

Several months earlier Abigail had described Pickering as a man "whose manners are forbidding, whose temper is sour and whose resentments are implacable," one who sought to dictate every measure in the cabinet. "I am mistaken," she added, "if this dictator does not get himself ensnared in his own toil. He would not now remain in office, if the President possessed such kind of resentments as I hear from various quarters, he [Pickering] permits himself to utter—from this fountain have flowed all the unpopularity of the Mission to France, which some of the federalists have been so deluded as to swallow large draughts of." [32]

Four days after McHenry's resignation Adams sent Pickering a curt note asking him to resign. Two days later the Secretary of State explained that for financial reasons he had expected to remain in office until next March when Jefferson, who would probably win the election, would become President. Until that time, Pickering concluded, "I do not feel it to be my duty to resign."

This continued defiance infuriated Adams. In a note even more peremptory than his first he immediately told Pickering, "you are hereby discharged from any further service as Secretary of State." [33]

Although brutal, Pickering's dismissal was popular, certainly among Republicans. "If ever a man went out of a public station loaded with the universal execration of an injured country," a Republican gazette announced, "it is Mr. Timothy Pickering." [34]

Wolcott had been as subservient to Hamilton as had McHenry and Pickering. He believed, for example, that "We shall never find ourselves in the straight path of Federalism while Mr. Adams is President." Yet Adams allowed him to remain in the cabinet. The President immediately nominated moderate Federalists to replace the dismissed department heads. Samuel Dexter, a senator from Massachusetts whose Federalist friends called him "Ambi" Dexter, took over as Secretary of War, and John Marshall became Secretary of State. The Senate confirmed Marshall's appointment within twenty-four hours and on the following day, May 14, 1800, Congress adjourned. [35]

Marshall appeared to be a good choice for several reasons. He was loyal to Adams, he was experienced in diplomacy, he had served in Congress, he was a personal friend of almost all Federalist leaders, and being from Virginia he would strengthen the Federalist party in the South. Even though Marshall had disapproved of the Alien and Sedition Acts, had dissented from High Federalist plans in Congress, and had supported the Ellsworth mission, Federalist leaders trusted him.

Even Republicans seemed reasonably satisfied with Marshall. "In genuine federal principles," the *Aurora* said, "General Marshall is as inflexible as Mr. Pickering; but in the negotiation with France, the General may not have imbibed so strong prejudices—and, having been one of the Envoys to that Republic, he may be supposed to be more conversant with some of the points in dispute than Col. Pickering, and consequently to be preferred."

Since some Federalist leaders were not yet convinced of Marshall's political orthodoxy, Charles Cotesworth Pinckney offered reassurance. Pinckney wrote that the party could "rely on his federalism, & be certain that he will not unite with Jefferson & the Jacobins." [36]

Marshall's appointment could not, however, overcome the increasing Hamiltonian distrust of Adams. The President's previous actions had challenged the program and views of the Hamiltonian Federalists. Now, in dismissing McHenry and Pickering, he had in effect issued a declaration of war against them.

Hamiltonians charged that when Adams realized that his own party planned to replace him with Pinckney, he concluded that he could save himself only by seeking a coalition with Jefferson. Pickering claimed that Adams had made a "corrupt bargain with the Democrats to secure his second election," and that the bargain explained the new "negotiation with France." George Cabot said "there is a good understanding" between Jefferson and Adams on the basis of which they would "make a joint-stock of their influence in the next election." When Adams denied reports of the alleged coalition, Pickering commented: "I will only say that the President is not always consistent or accurate in his remembrance."

James A. Bayard, a Delaware Federalist, reported that Adams "has contrived to forfeit the affection of most federal men whom I meet with." Then speaking of his own state, Bayard said that "if events should justify it, there will be no difficulty in keeping him out of the tickets of this State." [37]

Out of this tangle of politics, foreign policy, and personal feuds, Adams tried to hold the majority of his party to his own program, and to resist the demands of the Hamiltonian wing. He thought the public, as well as the moderate leaders of the Federalist party, would approve his policy of peace, and that now the party stood to gain by supporting it. The "great Body of Federalists, as well as the whole of the other Party," he was convinced, wanted to avoid full-scale war.

The Federalist state committee in Virginia agreed with Adams's view. It appealed to the voters with the theme of peace.

"We forget," the committee wrote, "that our government has preserved us from two impending wars, the foundation of which was laid before its existence, with the two most powerful nations of the world, armed to the full extent of their power; and that, without any sacrifice to the national interest, or of the national honor. We forget that we have been preserved from a close alliance with either of those nations, which would have been the worst, and the most inevitable consequences of a war with the other; and that we remain, if we will, completely free and independent." [38]

Republicans in Virginia and elsewhere also considered the peace issue an asset. They claimed that they represented the party of peace. James Callender, a Republican journalist, published a book at this time called the *Prospect Before Us*. In it he argued that "the object of Mr. Adams was to recommend a French war, professedly for the sake of supporting American commerce, but in reality for the sake of yoking us into an alliance with the British tyrant." He denounced Adams and those around him as war hawks and warned that disunion and a war with France faced the nation unless Adams were turned out of office. "Take your choice, then," Callender advised, "between Adams, war and beggary, and Jefferson, peace and competency." [39]

High Federalists, on the other hand, felt that their greatest burden was the fact that the Quasi-War had not expanded into the full-scale war they desired. For this they now blamed Adams.

In any case, Adams's insistence on carrying out his policy of peace in defiance of the Hamiltonians helped turn the campaign of 1800 into a fierce, mudslinging battle in which the two wings of the Federalist party became more bitter in their denunciations of each other than in their attacks on the Republicans. Thomas Boylston Adams summarized the grievances of High Federalists against his father. They were many, but none appeared as galling as the decision to send off Ellsworth and Davie "contrary to the wishes and opinions of all the Federalist party, by which the strength of the democratic party has been increased and the hopes of the Federalists totally blasted."

As the campaign went into the summer so acrimonious did

the feeling of the Hamiltonians become toward the President that they thought his reelection might be as great a misfortune as the success of the Republican party. Furthermore, they saw Adams attract more support than they had anticipated. Many people seemed to look upon him as a patriot devoted to peace. Local political leaders in New England, which was the strongest Federalist section of the country, were for Adams. Everywhere, it appeared, the party's rank and file, though irritated and perplexed, were standing by the President. His statesmanship apparently had made an impression on the masses, if not on the leadership, of his party.[40]

Knowledge of this popular mood led Hamilton to make a tour of New England, ostensibly to inspect military bases. Adams, he explained, was weak and ineffective, and could not win at the head of the Federalist ticket. Hamilton's indiscreet speeches brought him a torrent of abuse, for now he had himself carried the controversy between the two Federalist factions into the open.

On July 1, 1800, after returning to New York, Hamilton wrote his own analysis of his party's mood. "The greatest number of strong-minded men in New England," he said, "are not only satisfied of the expediency of supporting *Pinckney* as giving the best chance against Jefferson, but even prefer him to *Adams,* yet in the body of that people there is a strong personal attachment to this gentleman, and most of the leaders of the second class are so anxious for his reelection that it will be difficult to convince them that there is as much danger of failure as there unquestionably is."

George Cabot later told Hamilton that most Federalists preferred Adams to Pinckney, and that this should be admitted. Adams, he warned, could not be discarded without courting defeat in New England.[41]

As the campaign gathered heat, Adams, who had returned to Quincy in July, began to think aloud that the extreme Federalists posed a greater threat to the nation than did the Republicans. Remarks to this effect were attributed to him. Hamilton and his coterie, the President insisted, did not represent the Federalist party. They comprised "a damned faction" of "British partisans" led by Hamilton, he said, that he had long been combating.[42]

Hamiltonians found this charge of being pro-British difficult to bear, for relations with Britain were no longer as cordial as they had been early in the Quasi-War. The differences, over such things as debts owed to Britain, impressment of American seamen, and interference with American commerce, were old ones. Recent developments, however, had aggravated these difficulties.

At the end of the War of American Independence, it may be recalled, British creditors had been unable to obtain payment for prewar debts because state governments had blocked collection. Under the Jay Treaty the United States agreed on payment of those debts in the amount to be determined by a joint commission. This commission, composed of three Englishmen and two Americans, met in Philadelphia and failed to agree because the Americans believed the British majority had imposed unfair rules.

So indignant did the American negotiators become that they boycotted commission meetings. In retaliation, the British government withdrew its members from another commission sitting in London which had been set up under the Jay Treaty to pass upon claims of Americans for property the British had destroyed during the War of American Independence. Despite various efforts to break this deadlock, it continued into the period of the presidential campaign.

As before, impressment even irritated Federalists such as Hamilton. He reported that a sea captain from Jamaica "states that the British capture all American vessels that afford the slightest pretext for condemnation, and impress all their seamen without discrimination." Americans could not forget these maritime humiliations, he said, because they caused a shortage of merchant seamen, increased shipping costs, and seemingly never slackened.[43]

Some Federalists, such as James A. Bayard, hoped the United States would "be found as ready to resist the aggressions of England as of France." Not even the dread of war, he asserted, "would induce me to submit to any acts of a foreign government which tended to degrade the character of the nation." George Cabot thought Adams was willing to "hazard a war with Great Britain." [44]

Adams's appointment of the Ellsworth mission and its departure for France had added to the difficulties with England. Just as France had earlier regarded the Jay mission and treaty as offensive, Britain now looked upon the negotiations in Paris with suspicion. The American government, some Englishmen believed, was now unfriendly.

HAMILTON VERSUS ADAMS

This state of affairs, as well as various political disappointments, roiled Hamilton to such an extent that on August 1 he sent the President a note demanding to know if he had spoken "on different occasions of the existence of a *British faction* in this country. . . . and that you have sometimes named me as one of this description of persons." [45] Enraged by the letter, Adams refused to reply. Hamilton then cast off all restraint and decided to denounce Adams publicly.

With the aid of Pickering, McHenry, and others who enjoyed his confidence, Hamilton gathered materials purporting to show that Adams was unfit for the Presidency. With this data, much of it taken from confidential files, he wrote a long letter excoriating Adams. "I hope from it two advantages," Hamilton explained to Wolcott, "the promoting of Mr. Pinckney's election, and the vindication of ourselves." Although the letter was sent out too late to influence the choosing of electors, Hamilton apparently believed it might sway the electors themselves. [46]

Hamilton had intended the letter, which he had had printed, for private circulation among his friends only, but in October a copy fell into the hands of Aaron Burr. He made it available to Republican editors over the country, who published extracts from it. Then, to guard against the letter's unauthorized publication, Hamilton took out a copyright on it and had it published as a pamphlet entitled a *Letter from Alexander Hamilton, Concerning the Public Conduct and Character of John Adams, Esq., Presi-*

dent of the United States. Instead of being angry at Burr, Hamilton took the position that the country had better learn the truth about John Adams, and that publication "would be productive of good." The colossus of Federalism was wrong.

Republicans were delighted, but most Federalists were shocked. "I am bound to tell you," George Cabot wrote Hamilton, "that you are accused by respectable men of egotism. . . ." [47] Even other High Federalists were disappointed, for they believed that Hamilton's charges were not sufficiently convincing to warrant the attack. In one of his main charges Hamilton had accused Adams of damaging the honor of the country by initiating and carrying through the Ellsworth mission. This, coupled with similar charges from Federalist journalists such as John Fenno and William Cobbett, gave the impression that Federalist leadership wanted war when peace appeared within reach.

Friends of Adams rushed out with pamphlets of their own attacking Hamilton. Noah Webster, the Federalist journalist and philologist, pointed out that Americans had long known that Hamilton "attempted to direct the principal measures of our national councils." Adams's peace mission defeated Hamilton's design, particularly for a permanent military force. Indeed, the mission "removed the pretext for such an establishment." In most instances, assaults such as these merely aggravated the intraparty strife. "We must soon search for common sense among the old women of our nation," William Vans Murray remarked when he heard of the Hamiltonian attack. [48]

Whatever chance the Federalist ticket may have had now seemed shattered. "I cannot describe . . . how broken and scattered your Federal friends are!" one Federalist wrote to another. "We have no rallying point; and no mortal can divine where and when we shall again collect our strength. . . . Shadows, clouds, and darkness rest on our future prospects." [49]

While the Federalists fought among themselves, the Republicans moved to consolidate their gains. Jefferson, who was conducting his campaign from his estate at Monticello, hailed the Federalist dissensions as "wonderful" and conferred with Madison as to the best means of taking advantage of them. In particular, Republicans now hammered away at the peace issue, believing, as one of them asserted, that "a spirit of moderation and mutual forbearance begins to revive among our citizens." By forcing Adams to send the Ellsworth mission to France, they contended, they had "saved the country from war." [50]

"In plain truth," a Republican gazette announced as the campaign drew to a close, "the question is now come to this issue—Whether Adams or Pinckney were president, we should have war. —With Jefferson we shall have peace, therefore the friends of *peace will vote* for Jefferson—the friends of war will vote for *Adams* or *Pinckney*." [51]

Federalists, too, stressed the issue of peace, but from a different perspective. John Rutledge, Jr., one of South Carolina's leading Federalists, was convinced that at stake in the election was the preserving of "our Country in peaceful and prosperous neutrality, against the efforts of those who would yoke us to France and plunge us into War." [52]

Five days later a statement of party principles, or what was in effect the Republican party platform, emphasized the peace issue. Under the Federalists, the statement pointed out, there had been "the *Nation* in arms without a foe, and divided without a cause." Under the Republicans there would be "the *Nation* at peace with the world, and united in itself." The real difference between parties, another Republican pointed out, was that Republicans were "the friends of Peace and their own country," and Federalists were "the partizans of war and foreign nations." [53]

Regardless of Republican propaganda, no one knew whether or not there would be an honorable peace with France. News of what was taking place in Paris was infrequent and took a long time in reaching the United States. One reason for this lack of news, which made everyone impatient, was the attitude of the commissioners toward correspondence.[54]

Up to August 1, 1800, the envoys had written only three short letters to the Department of State, and on the nature of these the envoys had differed. Ellsworth wanted to be brief. He and Davie did not wish to write until they could report effectual action. They appeared to believe that their views and motivations could be inferred from their decisions. Murray, on the other hand, thought that their letters should constitute a journal that would record the motives behind what they did, or did not do. This diplomatic journal would explain why they departed from their instructions. He felt that the government was entitled to know, step by step, what the commissioners did and why, and their views on future action. If Murray had had his way, they would have written once a week, or at the least, once a fortnight.[55]

Since Murray did not have his way, it is not surprising that dispatches the commissioners sent on May 17, and which did not reach Secretary of State Marshall until nearly seven weeks later, were perplexing. Marshall thought the French were stalling in the hope that the elections would bring Jefferson to power and "place them on higher ground than that which they now occupy." Many Federalists felt this way. One of them remarked that "few doubt or deny that the delay is a finesse to influence our great election." [56] Marshall, nonetheless, wrote cautiously to Hamilton that the dispatches contained nothing "on which a positive opinion respecting the result of the negotiation can be formed."

The commissioners were acutely aware that their negotiations could affect the outcome of the presidential election. In fact their instructions emphasized that speed was necessary so that Congress could act on the new treaty before the election. Murray was so conscious of the political importance of the negotiations that on August 11, 1800, he wished to inform Americans of a probable treaty, hoping that the news would arrive in the United States in time "to serve the friends of Gov't at the next election," and that "so honourable a termination would raise the spirits of the good men & overset the bad." [57]

Nine days later Murray told John Quincy Adams that the commissioners were quite conscious that a successful negotiation would contribute to John Adams's reelection. "We have all along felt it and worked to get along," he wrote, "but events have been very much against speed and success." [58]

High Federalists, on the other hand, hoped that the Ellsworth mission might fail. A failure, they reasoned, would fulfill their dire predictions, lead to increased hostilities, and make their program popular again. In effect, failure could salvage their political fortunes. Some Federalists circulated rumors saying the mission had failed.[59] Others argued that the negotiations could be safe only in Federalist hands, for Jefferson was so much a Francophile that if he became President he would forfeit American interests to French demands. Still others, who considered the mission "an ill judged and unlucky measure," thought that the dignity of the government required that it should be supported in "a spirit of fairness & liberal good faith." [60]

Since the negotiations in Paris could have a decisive influence on his reelection, and were to have been concluded by April 1, Adams was understandably disturbed by the lack of news. It seemed likely that the French were protracting their diplomacy, as Secretary of State Marshall suggested, to profit from expected Republican victories in the American elections.

"I cannot," the President commented, "account for the long delay of our envoys. We cannot depart from our honor, nor violate our faith, to please the heroic consul." Concerned also about the military and political developments in Europe, which might "give great spirits and a high tone to the French," he considered the possibility of the mission's failure. Then, he assumed, it would be the nation's destiny "to fight the French republic alone."

Sharing the President's concern, the Secretary of State warned of the possibility of failure. "We ought not to be surprised," Marshall wrote on August 25, 1800, "if we see our envoys in the course of the next month, without a treaty. This produces a critical state of things, which ought to be contemplated in time." He wondered, as a consequence, if the President should expand the Quasi-War?

In acknowledging Marshall's advice Adams went a step further than his Secretary. We must, he said, face the question that surely will arise, of "whether the President ought not at the opening of the Session to recommend to Congress an immediate and general declaration of war against the French republic. Congress has already, in my judgment, as well as in the opinion of the judges at Philadelphia," he explained, "declared war within the meaning of the Constitution against that republic, under certain restrictions and limitations. If war in any degree is to be continued, it is a serious question whether it will not be better to take off all restrictions and limitations."

On this great question of expanded war, the President's own mind was not made up. He wanted his advisers to probe the subject "and view it in all its lights." One thing he did know. Indecision was bad. "We have wonderful proofs," he said, "that the public mind cannot be held in a state of suspense." Yet it seems the public opinion must prevail, "whether in the right or not." [61]

Although in private correspondence Marshall appeared apprehensive, fearing that Bonaparte's victories in Europe would "render ineffectual our endeavors to obtain peace," as Secretary of State he counseled patience and moderation. Indeed, he finally expressed hope for an accommodation.

The Secretary of State told the President that the French government now seemed willing to correct past abuses, particularly its "haughty and hostile conduct to neutrals. Considerable retrograde steps in this respect have already been taken, and I expect the same course will be continued." If so, "there will exist no cause for war, but to obtain compensation for past injuries." This, Marshall maintained, is not "a sufficient motive" for war.[62]

Adams agreed, explaining that he had new information showing that the French were trying to curb their privateers. Then, he added, this news fits in with your own idea that "the present French government is much inclined to correct, at least in part, the follies of the past." [63]

At this point the negotiations in Paris gave no cause for war, for they were drawing to a close. "I dare anticipate the pleasure," Murray wrote after work on the treaty was practically finished, "which he [John Adams] and the vast majority of the nation will receive the treaty, as a great *political* measure in the present times it must be well received." Despite Murray's concern, the treaty had little effect on the political situation. When the citizens in the various states voted for presidential electors on October 14 the negotiations in Paris were still clothed in uncertainty.[64]

JEFFERSON AND BURR

Even the election returns added to the uncertainty of the times. Since the electors in the different states were chosen in a variety of ways, there was room for considerable maneuver and even chicanery. Many of the electors had been selected for their personal popularity rather than for their commitment to a particular candidate. So the election could be won or lost in the consciences of the individual electors.

It was during this state of political uncertainty that news of the Treaty of Môrtefontaine, published prematurely in October by the French, reached the United States. The front page of the Baltimore *Telegraph and Daily Advertiser* carried the "Glorious News" on November 7, 1800, but the official version of the treaty would not reach the United States for another five weeks.[65] In the interval those who were disappointed in its provisions attacked the manner of its negotiation. Murray resented the attacks. He felt that critics could appreciate the convention only if they took into account the development of the commissioners' motives while they bargained, their reasoning as influenced by the situation in Europe, and the difficulties they encountered.[66]

During this time of tense uncertainty men began to gather in the new, raw federal capital at Washington for the second session of the Sixth Congress. There the White House, half finished, stood virtually isolated in a field overlooking the Potomac River. The nation's representatives lived huddled together in rooming houses. "Around the Capitol are seven or eight boarding-houses, one tailor, one shoemaker, one printer, a washing woman, a grocery shop, a pamphlets and stationery shop, a small dry-goods shop, and an oyster house. This," a congressman wrote, "makes the whole of the Federal city as connected with the Capitol." [67]

That second session had been scheduled to begin on November 17, but bad weather and poor roads delayed many legislators so that enough of them to make a quorum did not arrive until November 21. On the following day, in the unfinished Capitol building, John Adams delivered his fourth annual message, written by Marshall. The President informed the joint session of Congress that the First Consul had received the American commissioners "with the respect due to their character," but otherwise he touched lightly on the progress achieved in the negotiations at Paris. As of "the date of the last official intelligence," he explained, the negotiations had not terminated, so the outcome was not yet known. Even though he hoped the talks would be successful, he thought it would be imprudent at this point to abandon the measures taken for self-protection. The United States, he insisted, must maintain a naval and military establishment "adapted to defensive war." [68]

Both houses responded with the usual formal statements, but like the people, Congress remained absorbed in the election until the returns were all in and beyond dispute. Its members were in no mood for work. Senator Charles Pinckney, for example, stayed at home in South Carolina to campaign for Jefferson's election rather than go to Washington. When critics suggested that he should be in the Senate for the discussion of the French treaty, he commented, "I who know that the President's Election is of more consequence than any Treaty and who feel my presence here to be critically important, mean to remain. . . ." [69]

Pinckney had analyzed his situation correctly on one point; his presence in South Carolina was important. Federalists had fought tenaciously to regain the ground lost in the New York elections, and had done well, even though a renewal of British seizures had injured their cause.

Time and again Liston had urged his government to ameliorate its policy, but without visible effect. He warned that if the Republicans should win the election the result could be attributed to the continued British captures of American merchantmen and to the decisions of the courts of vice-admiralty at Kingston, Jamaica, and Halifax, Nova Scotia, where the prizes were taken for adjudication and condemnation. He called the seizures "perhaps the most efficient of all causes of the approaching triumph of the Democratick interest," for they had provoked an intensified resentment against England which rubbed off on the Federalists. Liston returned home at this time. On December 2, 1800, he was succeeded by Edward Thornton, who became England's *chargé d'affaires.*

On the following day, called election day, the electoral colleges assembled in each state and the electors cast their ballots. As the returns came in, all saw that South Carolina, with 8 electoral votes, was the pivotal state. Those votes went to Jefferson and Burr.[70] News of the South Carolina results arrived in Washington on December 16. It confirmed what had been suspected, that the Federalists were unable to make good the loss suffered in New York. Furthermore, the Republicans had gained majorities in both houses of Congress.

Adams had, nonetheless, come close to victory. An analysis of the election returns indicated that the Republicans did not ride to power on the shoulders of an outraged populace which had thoroughly repudiated Federalist policies. There was not, as has often been claimed, a new revolution in 1800. The switch of a few hundred votes in New York City, as has been seen, would have brought Adams's reelection. Aside from New York, he was stronger in 1800 than he had been four years earlier.

Later, in thinking over the causes of his defeat, Adams concluded that his decision to send the Ellsworth mission to France had been a key factor. Even before the results from either the election or the negotiations in Paris were known, he had been convinced that the opposition of the High Federalists to the mission had benefited the Jeffersonians. That opposition, he wrote, had "done more to shuffle the cards into the hands of the jacobin leaders, than all the acts of administration, and all the policy of the opposition [Republicans], from the commencement of the government." The mission itself, he felt, was politically sound. What had alienated the voters, he thought, were the intemperate attacks of the extreme Federalists on merely the effort to seek peace. Adams himself had always been willing to fight France if necessary. But he had refused, after getting over his emotional and belligerent reaction to the failure of the X Y Z mission, to lead the country into an unnecessary war because extremists in his own party wanted it, or because they thought full-scale war would keep Federalism in power. So he claimed in retrospect.[71]

Perhaps if the Ellsworth mission had been concluded successfully before the election took place, the results might have
been different. At least this is what some moderate Federalists
thought. Murray, who had expected the mission to aid Adams's
reelection, and who had believed its success a political necessity,
was disappointed. "Deeply shall I always regret that it [the con-
vention] could not be done sooner," he wrote, "and time enough
for its influence to have been auxiliary to him [Adams] in this
election! All was done—all—that could hasten it; in vain." [72]

Accustomed to power, Federalists were bewildered and
alarmed. Many were convinced that a revolution along French
lines would follow and would destroy the nation.[73] One thing, at
least, consoled them. As the result of a constitutional flaw,
Thomas Jefferson and Aaron Burr were tied for first place. In
1800 the electors did not make a distinction between President
and Vice-President when they voted. The man who received the
highest number of electoral votes became President, and the one
with the second highest total became Vice-President.

The tie vote meant that the election would be thrown into
the House of Representatives where the members, voting not as
individuals but as part of a state unit with each state having one
vote, would decide who would be President and who Vice-President. This legislative body, where the power of decision lay, was
not the newly elected House where the Republicans would have a
clear majority, but the expiring lame-duck legislature where the
Federalists held control. Despite this control, the Federalists in
the House did not have enough votes to elect a President, but
their votes could be decisive in the choice of a Republican.

Everyone knew that the Republicans had intended Jefferson
to have first place. Nonetheless, two possibilities unfolded before
the Federalist leaders in the House. They could choose between
Jefferson and Burr, and then obtain substantial favors as the price
of their support. They could, as the alternative, create an impasse
in which neither man would be elected. In this case the Senate,
which was also Federalist, would name the acting President. In
this way the Federalist party could hope for another year of
power. It would rule during the interregnum, or the period before

a second general election could be held. The extremists advocated this latter plan, but were unable to do much about it. So the idea of placing Burr, who was considered less friendly to France, ahead of Jefferson spread rapidly among them.[74]

Hamilton opposed this step, denouncing Burr as a Francophile at heart who would quickly plunge the country into war against England. "I have myself heard him speak with applause of the French system," Hamilton said. But Hamilton's advice and exhortations were disregarded. Some Federalists, such as Fisher Ames, wished to protect themselves against a *rapprochement* with France by exacting a pledge from Burr for their support that "the country must not be sold, given, or lent to France." [75]

On February 11, 1801, when the two houses of Congress gathered in joint session, and the electoral ballots were opened, the official count showed what everyone already knew, that Jefferson and Burr were tied for the Presidency with 73 votes each. As provided by the Constitution, the choice was left to the House. There the Federalists nearly succeeded in giving first place to Burr.

Finally, after 33 ballots and after all hope for electing Burr seemed lost, James A. Bayard, the single Representative from Delaware, a Federalist who had been consistently voting his state for Burr, decided he would no longer block Jefferson. He changed his state's vote, he said, because he could not go along with the extremists who were willing "to risk the constitution on a civil war." So, on February 17, on the 36th ballot, Jefferson was chosen President.[76] Only four diehard Federalist New England states stood by Burr to the end. This was only a gesture, for with control of both the legislative and the executive branches of the government in their hands, the Republicans now had a complete victory.

News of the election results had a decided impact on foreign policy. The French were delighted, especially with Jefferson's victory. They considered him not only the friend of liberty, but also of France and her people.

The British, on the other hand, reacted with alarm. Reports of the Republican victory, forwarded to London by the British *chargé* in a specially chartered vessel, caused a decline in government funded securities, or "consols," which had already been shaken by bad news from Europe. One London journal, the *Anti-Jacobin Review,* predicted the collapse of the American government. The *Times* commented that "the result is certainly unpleasant towards this Country, as Mr. JEFFERSON is the life and soul of the French faction in America." [77]

THE SENATE'S RESERVATIONS

Meanwhile, on December 11, 1800, one day before Adams had learned of the returns from South Carolina and of his defeat, Davie had arrived in the United States with the official text of the Convention of Môrtefontaine. Five days later the President sent the convention, three manuscript volumes containing the journal of the commissioners, and a special message asking approval of the agreement, to the Senate.

Reaction to the treaty was mixed. Republicans and moderate Federalists considered it satisfactory, though Jefferson at first grumbled about a "bungling negotiation" and another Republican critic commented that "it barely makes peace between the two republics." Nonetheless, Jefferson, Madison, and other Republicans favored ratification, but with qualifications. [78]

A Federalist diplomat expressed what seemed to be a view characteristic of the moderates. "I am pleased with the Convention," he wrote; "all the great points concerning navigation are settled to our advantage; they are extremely liberal & contain all we could require." What judicious American, he asked, would not willingly pay a few million dollars to exchange the treaties of 1778 for this convention? It is an excellent bargain. [79]

High Federalists, of course, did not share this view. One of them called it "another chapter in the book of humiliation" and predicted its rejection. Another was so disgusted that he assumed Ellsworth had been "rendered feeble by disease" because he had negotiated the treaty. Those Federalists in the Senate, many of whom were now lame ducks, considered the convention more a triumph for Adams than for the party. Within three days of receiving the diplomatic documents from the President the Senate studied them, implied dissatisfaction, and then asked for a copy of the envoys' instructions. These, and other tactics, indicated there would be a struggle over approval.[80]

Since the convention was controversial, the Federalists at first could not decide how to handle it. Consideration of the Convention of Môrtefontaine, in fact, led the Senate to adopt its first set of rules formally setting forth the procedure to be followed when the President laid a treaty before it.[81]

"The French treaty is yet before the Senate," one Federalist critic wrote, "and I believe they do not know what is best to do with it." He considered the stipulation requiring both sides to return captured national, or government, ships as degrading because only the United States would have to restore them. France had taken no American warships. Furthermore, this provision implied that the United States was the aggressor. The French diplomats, he believed, "certainly have been an over match for our Envoys, but I believe they are so for all the World in Negociation and intrigue." [82]

Influential Federalist senators turned to Hamilton for advice. He expressed distaste for the convention, saying that in "the general politics of the world" it "is a make-weight in the wrong scale," but he favored its approval because in view of the present state of public opinion its rejection would "utterly ruin the federal party and endanger the internal tranquility." Furthermore, he felt "it is better to close the thing where it is than to leave it to a Jacobin to do much worse."

Even though "far, very far, from approving" the convention, Secretary of State Marshall also desired acceptance.[83] Unwilling to accept the document as it stood, some Federalists wished to amend it rather than kill it. For instance, Gouverneur Morris, the New York Federalist who had served as a Minister to France, at first found the treaty "very bad," but later said that if it were modified, "I shall think it no bad bargain." [84]

Federalist leaders were aware that Bonaparte wished to use the treaty as a diplomatic weapon against Britain. "One part of the treaty abandons all our rights, and the other part makes us the dupes of France in the game she means to play against the maritime power of England," one of them commented. "We lose our honor, by restoring the ships we have taken, and by so doing, perhaps, make an implicit acknowledgement of the injustice of our hostile operations." [85] Nonetheless, among the acts of this final session of the Sixth Congress was one that reduced the naval establishment to a peacetime footing. Congress did this because of the favorable turn in foreign affairs and because of economy.

Some Federalists argued that good faith with England demanded rejection of the convention. Actually, the British government, which was itself negotiating with France and hoping to make peace with Bonaparte, found the agreement unobjectionable. In October 1800, as soon as the English newspapers had published the convention, Rufus King tried to discern the British government's reaction. He sounded out several of the ministers, and even found an opportunity to discuss the convention with Lord Grenville, the Secretary of State for Foreign Affairs, and George III. Instead of encountering protest, the American Minister found "no animosity nor unusual prejudice against us." King's informaion, forwarded to the Senate by Adams, blunted the argument of those who predicted that an accord with France would precipitate war with England.[86]

Edward Thornton in Washington examined the treaty and reported that "the United States seem to have acquired no advantage but that of being freed from the burthensome stipulations of the Treaties of 1778, particularly the guarantee of the French West India possessions. Thinking men may allow this advantage to have been cheaply purchased by the abandonment of the claim of indemnity for the depredations of French Privateers."

Then *chargé* Thornton offered, as proof of "how much public opinion has recovered its French bias," the observation that the convention was received throughout the country with tranquility. He also stressed "the impatience with which at least the Merchants await its ratification, that intercourse with France may be renewed." [87]

Despite the impatience of merchants and of Republicans, High Federalists saw no reason for hurrying the treaty through the Senate. They had not abandoned their antipathy toward Adams, saying for example, that his conduct exhibited "such debility or derangement of intellect" as to make him unfit to lead the government. For weeks the convention absorbed the Senate's interest, and then the senators referred the document to a select committee to report, finally, on the form of approval.[88]

On January 21 Adams gave the Senate a report from the Secretary of State and later sent the official correspondence of the envoys. "Although our right is very clear to negotiate treaties according to our own ideas of right and justice, honor and good faith," he remarked in reference to international jurists and to British approval of the convention, "yet it must always be a satisfaction to know, that the judgments of other nations, with whom we have connection, coincides with ours."

Adams's pressure did not work. Two days later the Senate rejected the convention. Although the agreement received 16 favorable votes as opposed to 14 nays, it failed to obtain the required two-thirds majority.[89] Gouverneur Morris reported that the treaty had been defeated "by the intemperate passion of its friends," but others maintained party differences had caused the defeat. Within three days, Morris added, there was a general desire in the House of Representatives "to recede from the vote as it stands on the convention. As I all along suspected, it will be reconsidered."

The rejection of the convention upset John Adams, and his eldest son also. "For although it did not secure us what we ought by good right to have obtained," John Quincy Adams wrote, "I am afraid we shall never get anything better, and that the longer settlement is delayed, the greater our damage will be." Murray expressed similar disappointment.[90]

Since popular sentiment, according to Republican and even some Federalist sources, favored the treaty, the defeat was only temporary. "However bad it is," one Federalist critic wrote, "a worse one may be made by the approaching administration; and no better one can be obtained by any administration." Within a few days Adams resubmitted the convention. On February 3,

1801, enough Federalist senators reversed their previous action so that by a vote of 22 to 9 it gained the necessary two-thirds approval.

Apparently the strongest influences in causing the Federalist legislators to change their votes were the general popularity of the convention, and the pressure of the mercantile interests which wanted to end the Quasi-War because it injured business. International trade and shipping pumped life blood into American economic development at this time, and had been at the heart of an unparalleled prosperity which the Quasi-War had interrupted. Merchants wished to resume this trade but needed peace to do so.[91]

Despite the pressure from merchants, the Federalist senators had voted approval only with broad reservations. In particular, they had reacted against the Ellsworth commission's failure to obtain indemnities and a definite abrogation of the alliance of 1778 and related treaties. So the Senate's reservations struck out the second article that called for further negotiation "at a convenient time" over those two troublesome issues. The reservations also demanded an indemnity and limited the convention, which was to have been perpetual, to a duration of eight years from the exchange of ratifications.

No one expected real difficulty from France because of the changes, though Létombe, who did not like the changes, attributed them to England's partisans in the Senate.[92] The expunging of the second article closed the question of indemnification, it was thought, and the eight-year term carried the convention beyond the duration of the Jay Treaty. "It is important to us," one senator said in explaining his colleagues' views, "to get clear as fast as possible from an intimate connection with any of the powers of Europe. . . ."[93]

The President disliked the Senate's modifications. He even considered the possibility of vetoing the conditional approval. Finally, he informed the Senate that he would have preferred an unconditional consent but considered it "more consistent with the honor and interest of the United States to ratify it [the convention] under the conditions prescribed than not at all." Although conditional, Adam's ratification finally set in motion the machinery to end the fighting at sea. A naval vessel, the *Herald*, was sent to the West Indies with news of the peace and with word to recall the American warships cruising among the islands.

Adams nominated James A. Bayard to go to Paris as Minister Plenipotentiary "to negotiate the exchange of ratifications." Bayard declined the appointment because he would have to serve under Jefferson. Then he would be open to the charge that he had acted to bring about Jefferson's elevation to the Presidency for the selfish purpose of obtaining the post in Paris. So, Adams told the Senate, "I shall take no further measures relative to this business, and leave the convention, with all documents, in the office of State, that my successor may proceed with them according to his wisdom." [94]

On the following day Adams told Edward Thornton "that from the period of the peace of 1783 it had been the most anxious wish of his heart to get rid of the Treaties of 1778 with France, which had hung like a dead weight on this Country, had involved it in undue partialities, and rendered it a party in all the disputes between Great Britain and France. In that object, the wicked and foolish conduct of the French had at length enabled him to succeed; the Treaty was destroyed, he hoped, forever." [95]

Adams's hope could be fully realized only after the French gave consent to the Senate's reservations. It was now up to Thomas Jefferson to gain this consent and thus to conduct the final negotiations over the Convention of Môrtefontaine.

IX

Bonaparte and Jefferson

So long as the power was held by the Federalists, their principles were better calculated to promote the national prosperity than those of their opponents. But if they had adopted for a maxim that a foreign war must be fostered for the sake of maintaining an army and increasing the public debt, it was time that they should be removed from the management of affairs.

JOHN QUINCY ADAMS, *March 1801*

WHILE AMERICANS WERE IMMERSED IN THE POLITICS OF THEIR PRESI-dential election, Napoleon Bonaparte had gone ahead with plans to use the reconciliation with the United States as one of his instruments in gaining ascendancy in the politics of Europe and in rebuilding a French empire in the New World. After the signing of the Convention of Môrtefontaine, Talleyrand stressed this important international aspect of the agreement. "You have rendered a real service to the French nation and to its government," the Minister of Foreign Relations told his commissioners, "by putting an end to the misunderstanding which deprived France of one of the most important branches of its commercial communications and by re-establishing between the two peoples that good will and attachment which nothing should have altered."

As a tangible expression of its satisfaction, the Consulate rewarded the commisssioners handsomely for their work. A decree of the Consuls gave Joseph Bonaparte 150,000 francs, Roederer and Fleurieu 30,000 each, and Pichon 20,000.[1]

Talleyrand also quickly took steps that would assure the United States his government was acting, as well as talking, in a spirit of reconciliation. He explained the provisions of the new convention to his country's Council of Prizes and asked the Council to allow no vessel to be condemned in violation of the principle free ships, free goods while he awaited ratification of the pact by the United States. He also urged the Minister of Navy and Colonies to execute the fourth article of the treaty, which required France to curb her privateers, immediately. If this were not done, he pointed out, it might be impossible to keep the peace with the United States.

This curbing of privateers also had another practical objective. It sought to save money. During the period between the signature and ratification France had promised to pay for American ships seized in violation of the principles of freedom of the seas.

More important than this immediate practical concern were the First Consul's long range objectives, built on the theory that he could force Britain to submission and then proceed to consolidate his empire in North America. France's efforts to regain Louisiana had lagged; Bonaparte revived them. While his agents were negotiating with the Ellsworth commission in Paris, he had other diplomats bargaining with Spain for the retrocession of Louisiana to France. His conciliatory attitude toward the United States stemmed, in part at least, from his desire to avoid renewed American resentment. He wanted to play down words or actions that might arouse suspicions and jeopardize the regaining of Louisiana.[2]

At one point the sensitiveness of Americans to the fate of Louisiana almost ruined Bonaparte's plan. In August 1800 the American Minister in Madrid, David Humphreys, saw a brief item in a Paris newspaper announcing the purpose of the mission of General Louis-Alexandre Berthier, Bonaparte's special emissary, to Spain. "This article had produced a deplorable effect," the French Ambassador complained; "the American Minister had meddled in the affair." [3] The Ambassador and the Spanish Minister of Foreign Relations both tried to calm Humphreys by denying that a treaty of retrocession was being negotiated.

These denials were mere camouflage, for on October 1, the day after the consummation of the Convention of Môrtefontaine, Berthier signed at San Ildefonso, the summer palace of Spain's king, a secret treaty that ceded Louisiana and promised six warships to France. In exchange, Bonaparte promised a kingdom in Italy for the Spanish king's son-in-law. [4] If Bonaparte could actually take possession of Louisiana, he would control four hundred miles of North America's coastline, would be able to dominate American commerce on the Mississippi, would strengthen his position in the Caribbean, and would make France a major power in the Western Hemisphere. Secrecy and American goodwill were important, for if the Americans found out about the cession and were angered, they might take over Louisiana before Bonaparte could send troops to defend it. [5]

At the same time, the First Consul strove to consolidate France's position in Europe. As part of his plan, as has been seen, he tried to show the neutral powers of the continent that his government, unlike its predecessor, had firmly committed itself to the principles of freedom of the seas. He worked to project an image of himself as the defender of neutral rights against the arbitrary maritime policies of Britain.

This careful planning, Bonaparte hoped, would at last bring together the northern neutrals, Russia, Prussia, and the Scandanavian states, into a League of Armed Neutrality against Britain, his main foe. The American convention, he assumed, would serve as a model for agreements between and with those powers who would join the League. [6]

Ellsworth, Davie, and Murray had been aware of Bonaparte's elaborate design. France, they knew, "wished by a great example to chalk out the line of treaty principles" and rights of neutral navigation which Sweden and Denmark should imitate and ask Britain to adopt. The commissioners also realized that in the pact of Môrtefontaine France had agreed to other principles "which were laws for Denmark & Sweden." [7]

Through the convention, the French thought, the members of the proposed Armed Neutrality might consider the United States an affiliate, or even an ally, of their projected organization. This idea had come up at the fête at Môrtefontaine, for example, when Charles François Lebrun, the Third Consul, had raised a toast "to the union of America with the powers of the North for freedom of the seas."

In his farewell to the American commissioners the Premier Consul himself had invoked the liberal maritime principles written into the convention as one basis for the *rapprochement* with the United States. "It is becoming in present circumstances," he said, "more important than ever for the two nations to adhere to them." In brief, Bonaparte looked upon the Convention of Môrtefontaine, whose principles amounted to an attack upon British maritime doctrine, as a weapon in his war against England.[8]

Within a few weeks after the convention had been signed, Talleyrand did use it against England. On October 3, 1800, the same day as the fête at Môrtefontaine, the semiofficial newspaper, the *Moniteur*, announced the convention. On the twenty-second it published the complete text, as though to inform the northern neutrals that here France and the United States had pledged themselves to uphold maritime principles held dear by neutral nations.[9]

This publication upset Murray. "The 4th article alone was to be made known," he wrote, "because its operation is from the date of signature. The other articles were to be kept unpublished till ratified."

The American diplomats had wished to delay publication for at least a while longer so that the convention and explanatory documents would have time to reach the United States. Now, Murray complained, the treaty "may get to U.S. & be published & become a subject of popular discussion even before the Govt. has it officially! This is intolerable conduct."

Later, Murray tried to explain on his own why the French had published the text of the convention "contrary to agreement." He supposed, correctly, that the motive was "to give eclat & popularity to Bonaparte—to help him also with the northern powers

—& give weight with Vienna." [10] This last item alluded to Austria, Britain's only remaining active ally on the continent, who, despite the defeat at Marengo, was still holding out against Bonaparte's demands.

That same issue of the *Moniteur* that published the convention carried a long essay outlining the benefits all of Europe would gain if the neutrals of the continent would raise an armed league against Britain's rule of the seas. This plea called for action from "Paul I and to all princes who, like him, by honour and interest, desire the freedom of the seas." [11] It also formed part of a larger strategy. Once the League of Armed Neutrality became a reality, Bonaparte hoped to bring the United States and the European neutrals into the final phase of a war that would crush England and enable him to take over Louisiana in peace.

To advance his plan Bonaparte had ordered Alexandre d'Hauterive, now an Undersecretary of the Ministry of Foreign Affairs, to prepare a manifesto to the neutral and belligerent powers pointing out that they and France had a common enemy in England. D'Hauterive did so, arguing that the interests of the continental powers and of France were the same. He suggested, therefore, that all the countries, neutrals and belligerents, should join France in destroying English domination of the seas. Then all nations would enjoy the privileges of freedom of the seas.

This manifesto appeared in Paris as a book in October 1800, shortly after the signing of the Treaty of Môrtefontaine, under the title *L'État de la France à la fin de l'an VIII*. Although written and printed in six weeks, the manifesto was a masterful piece of propaganda, eloquent and logical in its arguments. Despite the book's anonymous publication, all knew the identity of its author and that it represented a bid by Bonaparte for a continental alliance against England. It created a considerable stir in Europe's capitals and provoked widespread discussion.[12]

Tsar Paul I was attracted by the First Consul's strategy. At about this time he sent a peace emissary to Paris with the message that Russia and France were geographically so distant from one another they "could never be in a position to injure each other." They should, therefore, work together harmoniously to prevent other powers from injuring their interests. According to Paul's plan a Swedish general acting as his agent, Baron Joram von Sprengporten, was to receive the Russian prisoners from Bonaparte and then use them to garrison Malta. When Britain, anxious to keep the island for herself, refused to surrender it, Paul struck back. On November 18 he placed an embargo on British ships in Russian ports.[13]

THE ARMED NEUTRALITY

The embargo, followed by the seizure of some three hundred British ships and the sequestration of British property in Russia, quickly led to a clash between Russian troops and the crews of two British vessels at Narva. The British escaped to sea after sinking a Russian ship. The Tsar then burned a third British vessel that had remained in the harbor. Russia and Britain were now practically at war.

Since Britain refused to ease her policy toward neutral commerce, the First Consul continued to publicize his attachment to the principles of freedom of the seas. In Berlin, John Quincy Adams, who was carefully following these events, felt that the formation of an armed neutrality by the northern states awaited only the final success of French arms against Austria. He assumed that Bonaparte would soon compel the Austrians to make peace. Britain's subsequent isolation would then embolden the Scandanavians to accept an invitation from the Tsar to join a league of armed neutrality.

Meanwhile, Talleyrand's pressure on French naval authorities to show respect for neutral shipping and to restrain privateers, brought results. Conditions in the Caribbean caused him particular concern. Saint Domingue had practically allied itself with the United States, a condition he disliked. Along with the Premier Consul he wished to regain control of that island. Edward Stevens, they felt, stood as an obstacle to such control. Talleyrand maintained that the Ellsworth commissioners had assured him Stevens would be recalled from Saint Domingue.[14] Although the American government did not act immediately, not long after the signing of the Convention of Môrtefontaine it withdrew its support from Toussaint.

As soon as Toussaint had heard of the Treaty of Môrtefontaine, he had feared such a change in American policy. News of the signing of that convention, Stevens reported, had struck Toussaint with the impact of a thunderbolt. The Negro general realized that the United States no longer needed him as a means of injuring France, though he apparently believed Americans still wanted the profit from trade with his ports.[15]

Shortly after the signing of the Convention of Môrtefontaine, Talleyrand wrote to Toussaint, explaining that the end of the Quasi-War would mean restoration of the status in Saint Domingue that had prevailed earlier. In effect, Talleyrand suggested that at last France found herself in a position to make Saint Dominque behave as a loyal colony should. A short time later the First Consul warned the black general not to interfere in Spanish Santo Domingo.

These warnings did not deter Toussaint. He sent two armies into the Spanish colony, overwhelmed the populace, and in February 1801 he himself triumphantly marched into the Spanish capital. At last, Toussaint had made himself master of the entire island, but as a rebel against French authority and in defiance of Napoleon Bonaparte.[16]

Other French possessions, such as Guadeloupe and Guiana, presented a different problem. They were practically in a state of hostilities against the United States. Talleyrand therefore called special attention to conditions in Guadeloupe, telling the maritime authorities that they must give strict orders to stop the depredations of French corsairs there, as well as in Europe. On October 10, 1800, the naval authorities issued such orders. Those orders also called for the immediate release of any American ships detained in French ports.

At about the same time, Talleyrand took another step toward the resumption of friendly relations with the United States. By the same ship that carried William R. Davie home, Talleyrand sent a copy of the Convention of Môrtefontaine to Philippe Létombe in America with instructions to put French commercial agents in the United States to work as soon as possible. Since France had not withdrawn the exequaturs of American consuls on her soil, Talleyrand thought that commercial relations with the United States might be resumed even before the exchange of treaty ratifications.

The French government had promised Létombe, an old man failing in health, that he could soon go home. Talleyrand, therefore, had to find someone who could serve in his place as *chargé d'affaires* until a minister plenipotentiary could be sent to Washington. The Minister of Foreign Relations nominated Louis André Pichon, the man who had made the peace overtures to Murray and who had served as secretary to the French commission which had negotiated the Convention of Môrtefontaine, as Consul General and *chargé d'affaires*. Pichon's conduct in Paris had won praise from his associates, and from the American commissioners as well.

"This citizen is well known in the United States," Talleyrand explained in recommending Pichon's appointment, "where he has served the Republic as secretary to two successive legations. He knows perfectly the persons and interests of the states and the lines which unite these interests to those of France. This information is combined with great wisdom and a conciliatory character ideally suited to assure the execution of the measures of union and conciliation which the First Consul has adopted toward the United States." Bonaparte made the appointment on October 26, 1800, and four days later Pichon received official notification of it.[17]

Even though the French did not know whether the American government would ratify or reject the Convention of Môrtefontaine, the immediate danger of war had disappeared when it was signed.[18] Pichon's mission, therefore, had broader objectives than peace alone. He was to bind old wounds and to go beyond merely a reconciliation. The Consulate wanted Pichon to overcome whatever resistance there might be toward France's recovery of Saint Domingue and other possessions in the Caribbean, to ascertain the American government's attitude toward Britain, to draw the United States into the projected League of Armed Neutrality, and to explore the American attitude toward the status of Louisiana. If this last matter became sticky, his instructions told him to assure the American government that France had given up all designs on Louisiana.[19]

In keeping with the general objective of reconciliation, Pichon had authority to stop French corsairs in the West Indies from preying on American shipping. Talleyrand pointed out that "the majority of government agents and shipowners in the Antilles had exceeded and even misunderstood the instructions of the government." To strengthen his standing with Americans, Pichon brought with him copies of Talleyrand's letters to the Minister of Navy and Colonies and that Minister's orders to colonial agents. With those documents Pichon could show tangible evidence of France's peaceful desires and could impress the American government.

Talleyrand knew of the resentment aroused by the conduct of other French representatives in the United States, such as Citizen Edmond C. Genet, an impetuous young diplomat who had defied American neutrality regulations and had dabbled in domestic politics. The Minister of Foreign Relations urged Pichon to try to dissipate distrust of France by "not meddling in local questions and by affecting no marked preference in his relations with the influential persons of one or the other party." In turn, the *chargé* had the responsibility of recommending the same manner of conduct to all French officials, and even to private French citizens in the United States.

Since Talleyrand felt the British showed little respect for the American flag on the high seas, he was reluctant to send Pichon on an American ship. He therefore asked the Minister of Navy and Colonies to equip a frigate for the voyage to the United States, one that could also carry supplies for outfitting the *Insurgente*, the French naval vessel captured by the Americans. The United States was expected to return the ship under the terms of the Convention of Môrtefontaine. Pichon sailed from the naval port of L'Orient aboard the frigate *La Sémillante*, arriving in Norfolk on March 1, 1801. Three weeks later he and his new young wife took up quarters in Washington.[20]

During this period of preparation for Pichon's mission, the Premier Consul had devoted most of his attention to plans for gaining mastery of Europe. Beginning late in October 1800 his agents negotiated terms of peace with Austria at Lunéville in Lorraine. When Bonaparte discovered that the Austrians were stalling to please their ally, England, he decided to strike. At the end of November, with the formal termination of the armistice, France and Austria resumed their war. On December 3, at Hohenlinden near Munich, Bonaparte's generals won the bloodiest and most decisive battle in the War of the Second Coalition. With the road to Vienna now wide open to the French, the Austrians asked for an armistice, and seemingly had no choice but to come to terms with the First Consul.

The pleased Bonaparte then instructed Talleyrand to inform all friendly powers that France would make no peace with England until she agreed to respect the neutral rights of Russia, Prussia, Denmark, Sweden, and the United States. A league of armed northern European neutrals now seemed certain. This league became a reality on December 16, 1800, when the plenipotentiaries of Sweden, Denmark, and Norway signed separate conventions with Russia at St. Petersburg. Two days later Prussia also signed a similar convention. All the signatories professed a "disinterested desire to maintain the inalienable rights of neutral nations." Several days later the monarchs of the various countries ratified the agreements.

A month later, on January 14, 1801, Britain retaliated with an embargo on all Swedish, Danish, and Russian ships in her ports. The British had excluded Prussia from the embargo because they hoped to detach her from the League, but failed to do so. John Quincy Adams believed that these small powers, who had been forced into the League by Paul, would suffer most from it. Paul, Adams said, had committed *"rape by seduction"* on the small northern nations.[21]

These developments, on the other hand, made Bonaparte exuberant. "Your sovereign and I," he told the Tsar's representative in France, "have been called upon to change the face of the world!" [22]

As the Premier Consul had planned, the Convention of Môrtefontaine served as a model for this new neutral combination. Those pacts of armed neutrality echoed the liberal maritime principles reaffirmed in the Franco-American convention, and were more stringent than those in the Armed Neutrality of 1780.[23] In support of these principles the contracting neutral powers made arrangements for the possible use of mutual convoys and agreed to back each other's claims against belligerents who violated the League's rules. In each treaty Russia and the other state pledged themselves to reprisals against any power who refused justice for acts that had damaged their rightful commerce. An attack on any of the signatories "because of or in contempt of" the three conventions could be cause for the treaty powers to take concerted action for mutual defense.

Despite the fact that the League championed principles the United States had long favored, and that were in the Convention of Môrtefontaine, American diplomats were skeptical. France and the neutrals, Murray wrote, used "Tyranny of the Seas" as an epithet against England, but "were we possessed of a large fleet it would be also against us." He thought it foolish of "the silly powers of the north" to bind themselves "to this interested & politic cry of France against Great Britain."

Murray doubted, furthermore, that the Armed Neutrality could sustain its doctrine "that a convoy frees the merchant vessels from search by the general Laws of Nations. This may be and is often a point yielded by convention—but can not be claimed without this concession expressly made. . . . It is an attempt by force to deprive the Belligerent of a right which he has immemorially enjoyed." [24] Another Federalist diplomat, William Smith, found it ironical that Russia, "a power not possessed [of] as many commercial ships as our Salem," should head the League and attempt to establish a commercial maritime code.[25]

As the skeptics had anticipated, the League of Armed Neutrality failed to tame British sea power. Although the northern powers could in theory bring together a naval force superior to their own, the British realized from experience in past wars that leagues of maritime neutrals threatened their interests more in

principle than in practice. When faced with the choice of surrendering strategic Malta, which Bonaparte called "the apple of
discord in the hands of our enemies," to the Tsar, or retaining the
island and antagonizing him and the League, Britain decided that
the anger of the banded neutrals was the lesser of two evils. She
retained Malta.

The most serious damage the northern powers could inflict
on Britain was strategic. They could cut off her usual source of
naval stores in Europe, namely in the Baltic area, and help Bonaparte shut the continent to British goods. Even this was a limited
threat. Britain could supply her fleet from existing stocks of naval
stores and could replenish them with timber, tar, and other pine
products from her North American possessions and possibly from
the United States.

In theory, this situation increased Britain's need for American friendship, for British North America was vulnerable to overland attack from the United States. Seemingly, the British would
be foolish to do anything that could antagonize the United States
when the states of northern Europe were actively hostile. Conflict
with both the United States and the Baltic powers would jeopardize the building and outfitting of the Royal Navy and would play
into the hands of the First Consul.

James Madison, soon to become Secretary of State, was well
aware of this situation and saw it as advantageous to the United
States. Britain, he told Jefferson, "is more dependent every day on
our commerce for her resources" and must "look in a great degree
to this Country, for bread for herself, and absolutely for all the
necessaries for her islands." The Northern Confederacy of Neutrals, he went on, cannot fail "to inspire caution & management
toward the U.S. especially as, in the event of war or interruption
of commerce with the Baltic, the essential article of naval stores
can be sought here only." [26]

As far as Britain was concerned the possibility of a clash
with the United States had advanced beyond the realm of the
theoretical, for she treated the declarations of the Armed Neutrality as equivalent to announcements of war. The conventions establishing the League of Armed Neutrality included provisions for

the adherence of other neutral powers, thus leaving the way open
for American participation. If Bonaparte could, as he hoped,
bring the United States into the combination of neutrals, he
would succeed in virtually isolating Britain. Some Frenchmen
thought that if and when Jefferson became President the United
States might be induced to join the League of Armed Neutrals.

THE NEW PRESIDENT

News of Jefferson's electoral victory, acting as though it were
a shot of adrenaline, stimulated French hope for the League and
became a comforting factor in the Consulate's assessment of relations with the United States. In reporting the Republican party's
triumph to Talleyrand, Victor Marie DuPont, the consular official
who had returned to France from the United States, hailed it as "a
happy revolution which operates in our favour." [27]

Jefferson's first actions as President appeared to bear out
DuPont's estimate. At the inaugural dinner on March 4, 1801,
more than thirty of the one hundred fifty guests were Frenchmen.
"I sat at the right of Pennsylvania's governor," Létombe reported,
"and cordiality between the people of the two nations was very
vivid." [28] A week later Levi Lincoln, the Attorney General who
acted as Secretary of State until James Madison could take over,
informed Létombe that the new President was ready to receive
the commissions of French consuls or commercial agents and to
give them exequaturs.

Understandably, when Pichon arrived in Washington he had
reason to believe that the chances for success in his mission were
good. It seemed possible that he might even be able, as Bonaparte
and Talleyrand desired, to bring the United States into the Armed
Neutrality.

Americans should realize, Talleyrand had explained, that the
recently formed League of Armed Neutrality offered protection
for their expanding commerce against Britain's attempt to control
the seas. Unless the United States joined the League it could not
gain all the advantages that the organization offered. Only
through common action with the other maritime neutrals, the

French maintained, could the United States hope to enjoy true freedom of the seas. By associating itself with the League, the United States could crown its political independence with economic freedom from England as well.

Pichon must, his superiors said, persuade the Americans to join the Armed Neutrality. "It will be honorable for you," Talleyrand concluded, "to succeed in this negotiation. Besides, success can hasten the end of France's war against England by creating new embarrassments for a power [Britain] hostile or jealous of all the others." [29]

The French were not alone in thinking that Jefferson would lead the United States into the League of Armed Neutrals. Within the Federalist party and within the British government there were men who also thought this would happen, and who shuddered at the possibility. In asking us "to vindicate our neutral rights by arms," an ultra Federalist warned, France would require the United States "to fight her enemy in her cause." [30] After all, some men commented, if Jefferson joined the League he would merely be carrying out what had been expected of him—a pro-French foreign policy.

So fearful were the British of Jefferson's policy that Rufus King in London had felt it necessary to give Lord Grenville, Britain's Foreign Secretary, a long explanation on America's determination to continue her independent neutrality. King predicted that "unless farther & new causes of complaint should arise, . . . the good understanding between the U.S. & Eng. would [suffer] no diminution" under the new regime.

A short while later the British received assurance that King's estimate had been a correct one. Aware of the mistrust Englishmen felt toward him and his party, Jefferson quickly tried to show that no real basis existed for this attitude. Before his inauguration he talked several times with Edward Thornton, the British *chargé* in Washington, assuring him that the new administration would be as friendly as the Federalist governments had been. Jefferson admitted that Republican campaign speakers had insulted England, but explained that "he hoped henceforward that language would be used no longer, . . . [since] there was nothing to which he had greater repugnance than to establish distinctions in favour of one nation against another."

This point of view seemed so practical that the day after the inauguration Thornton managed another interview with Jefferson to discuss specific problems, such as the status of the Anglo-American commission on revolutionary debts, impressment, seizure of American ships, and trade with Saint Domingue. At the end of the conversation the President, whose reaction to these problems was moderate, said he hoped the British government would ignore reports of "newspaper *trash*" that he was anti-British and pro-French. Jefferson admitted a warmth for republican France, but he emphasized that "there was assuredly nothing in the present Government of that country, which could naturally incline him to show the smallest undue partiality to it at the expense of Great Britain." [31] Secretary of State James Madison shared these feelings.

Ironically, Bonaparte hoped to exploit Jefferson's predilection for France, particularly his attachment to French philosophers. Even before Jefferson's election had been assured, his reputation as a thinker whose views were congenial to those of French liberal thinkers, known as Idéologues, suggested that he might be receptive to proposals from two old friends, Thomas Paine and Joel Barlow, who were prominent in French intellectual circles. Perhaps by coincidence, or at the urging of French officials, these two literary exiles let Jefferson know at the time the Convention of Môrtefontaine was signed that they thought the United States should join the northern neutrals in checking British aggression on the seas. A month later, when Jefferson accepted nomination to the Class of Moral and Political Sciences of the National Institute of France, he appeared to give his blessing to France of the Consulate.

At this point Bonaparte apparently still appeared attractive to Jefferson, as he did to many of the French friends of America.[32] He seemed almost one of them, a relative liberal in politics, a student of science, and an advocate of revolution through reform. He, too, was a member of the National Institute, a leader possessing progressive ideas who had shown favor to scientists and men of letters during the years he had led armies in Egypt and Italy. Many of these Idéologues, therefore, mistakenly regarded Bonaparte's seizure of power as the rescue of liberty from the corrupters in the Directory.

At first the Premier Consul acted as though to foster the illusions of the intellectuals, for he needed the support of respectable republicans. Even later, as Bonaparte arrogated more and more power to himself, the liberals persisted in their republican illusions. Even the most prominent of these men had become too closely identified with the constitution that legitimatized the General's usurpations to make repudiation of him easy. Those who could not accept the strong man as a republican could at least regard him as heir of the Revolution, remedying with his strength the evils of the Directory.

Among those friends of the United States who were indebted to Bonaparte was Lafayette. Although Lafayette received no public office, the First Consul did give him back his freedom after long years of prison and exile. While admitting that the Corsican had overthrown the republic, Lafayette nonetheless assured Jefferson of Bonaparte's goodwill toward the United States. Thus, Jefferson's friends in France helped indirectly in keeping him in ignorance of Bonaparte's desire to use the United States as an instrument in furthering his own plans of empire.[33]

Pichon, too, tried to conceal Bonaparte's plans. Like the British, however, he quickly learned that the new President's ideological attachment to France did not transcend the practicalities of America's own interests in international politics. Jefferson and Madison greeted Pichon cordially, which delighted him. Soon, however, the French emissary discerned that he was dealing with tough-minded, practical politicians.

Pichon told Talleyrand that some Federalists feared that Jefferson would lead the United States into the Armed Neutrality against England. He did not agree, for if the President favored the League he would do no more than rejoice in its success. "He will be," Pichon explained, "like his predecessors, very pacific, and will be as much so towards England as towards us; towards us he will be so with the deepest sincerity."[34] In this message

Pichon, in effect, admitted failure in one aspect of his mission, but he showed a keen knowledge of American realities.

A short time later Pichon again pointed out that the hope of Frenchmen, or of others, that the United States would join the northern neutrals was based on wishful thinking. Jefferson's own neutrality, he said, was passive. This attitude stemmed from many reasons, but most of all from the basic fact of Britain's preponderant power on the seas. According to the Consul General, Jefferson approved of the principles of the League, but he thought the armed neutrals would be unable to force Britain to accept those principles. Only a concert of all commercial powers suspending all communications with England, the President maintained, was likely to succeed.

For such cooperation, Pichon concluded, America was too far away. Moreover, he assumed with some wisdom, that in a crisis the United States was too likely to make a "counter-league with England."

Pichon's analysis was sound. John Adams had opposed the idea of joining any league of armed neutrality. So did Jefferson. He wanted to avoid entanglement in any of Europe's quarrels.[35]

Soon, however, the question of American adherence to the League of Armed Neutrality became academic for other reasons. Late in March 1801 Rufus King reported from London that Britain's parliament had been debating the rights of neutrals on the seas. The ministry and the opposition party both denied the right of free ships, free goods. Two weeks earlier, apparently to take advantage of the spring thaw, a formidable fleet of eighteen battle ships of the line, accompanied by a larger number of frigates and smaller vessels, had sailed from Yarmouth, England, for the Baltic Sea. Everyone expected, King wrote, that Denmark and Russia would soon be detached from the League.[36]

King's report proved accurate. The first blow against the League of Armed Neutrality was struck in the new Mikhailovsky Palace in St. Petersburg by the assassins who strangled the demented Tsar in his bedroom on the night of March 23. Paul, the "all-powerful lunatic," had been the main force behind the League, or as Admiral Horatio Nelson saw it, the League was a tree "of which Paul was the trunk and Sweden and Denmark the branches." [37] The second blow fell a week later when the British demanded that the Danes either disarm or abandon the League of Armed Neutrality. On April 2, after the Danes refused this demand, the British fleet, led by Admiral Sir Hyde Parker with Nelson second in command, smashed the Danish navy at Copenhagen. This defeat forced Denmark, and later Sweden, to withdraw from the League.

Paul's death and the Battle of Copenhagen destroyed any chance that the northern powers might unite their navies against Britain. In Murray's eyes these developments also tended to strengthen America's motives for peace.[38]

Paul's son and successor, Alexander I, recognized the consequences of Nelson's stroke against the Armed Neutrality. In addition, the new Tsar had no obsession for Malta, though he accepted the title of Protector of the Knights of St. John. He therefore abandoned the League and entered into negotiations with the British. Out of these discussions emerged the Convention of St. Petersburg of June 17, signed first by Russia and later by Denmark and Sweden, which for the most part contained provisions favorable to Britain.[39] With this convention the northern neutrals ended their efforts to win freedom of the seas. The League of Armed Neutrality fell apart, and so did Bonaparte's most serious diplomatic challenge to British sea power.

PEACE

These dying gasps of the League of Armed Neutrality were in the background of the final round of negotiations on the terms of the Convention of Môrtefontaine. When Pichon had arrived in Washington he did not know of what was happening to the League, but he quickly learned of the Senate's conditional approval of the convention. Since he found that most informed Americans were satisfied with the treatment their commissioners had received in Paris and with the improved state of relations with France, he was not seriously disturbed by the Senate's reservations. Furthermore, he thought the Senate majority agreed fun-

damentally with the foreign policy of peace as recently advanced
by Adams, and now by Jefferson. Therefore Pichon advised his
government to accept the convention as approved by the Senate,
pointing out that otherwise relations with the United States
might return to their former disorder.

As far as Jefferson's government was concerned, the hostilities and animosities of the Quasi-War were in the past. "We have
passed through an awful scene in this country," he wrote. "The
convulsion of Europe shook even us to our centre." Now, he
added, I hope the United States "is getting back to the state in
which we knew it." [40]

Jeffersonian leaders had immediately told Pichon that they
were ending all hostilities. On March 23, 1801, they recalled all
warships and sent out instructions to agents in the French colonies to cease activities there against the mother country. Jefferson's government discontinued all retaliatory measures passed in
the Adams administration. Since the law suspending trade with
France had expired on March 3, the United States also resumed
commercial relations. [41]

France had already rescinded her decrees against American
shipping. Thus, even while the fate of the Convention of Môrten-
fontaine remained unknown, the United States and France had
gone far toward the resumption of normal relations. Jefferson
took another step in this direction shortly after his inauguration
by appointing Robert R. Livingston of New York, who had served
with him on the committee to draft the Declaration of Independence, as Minister Plenipotentiary to France. This appointment
pleased Pichon and other Frenchmen because of Livingston's past
friendly attitude toward France. The President made it clear to
the French, however, that Livingston would not leave the United
States until a courier had returned with the First Consul's ratification of the convention. Jefferson and Madison told Livingston
that the United States would remain aloof from the Armed Neutrality. [42]

This attitude meant that Jefferson had accepted Adams's
work, and expected Bonaparte to approve the Senate's reservations. It also indicated that Jefferson was going to hold to the ad-

vantage, however slight, which the United States had gained from Talleyrand's assurances that France sincerely desired a reconciliation.

Through Thomas Paine the President let the French know that he wanted to avoid "war and destruction" and foreign entanglements, saying "we shall avoid implicating ourselves with the Powers of Europe, even in support of principles which we mean to pursue." He thought this possible "now that we are likely to have our public councils detached from foreign views." Furthermore, Americans had returned "from the phrenzy into which they have been wrought, partly by ill conduct in France, partly by artifices practised upon them. . . ."[43] This notice indicated that the words of Jefferson's inaugural address, "peace, commerce, and honest friendship with all nations, entangling alliances with none," had real meaning as policy, even toward France.

To finish up the business of the Convention of Môrtefontaine, Jefferson quickly sent word to Oliver Ellsworth, and to William Vans Murray at The Hague, directing the one who could do so most promptly to go to Paris to negotiate on the points modified by the Senate and to exchange ratifications. Ellsworth had spent the winter in England because he was too sick to risk the rigors of another winter voyage across the Atlantic and because "he does not speak ten words of French," but he had left England before Jefferson's message arrived, and was unable to return to Paris. So the full responsibility for the final negotiation fell upon Murray.[44]

Murray had anticipated the appointment. "Tell me," he had asked earlier, "what are the exact steps of an *exchange of ratifications*, as it is possible I may be ordered to Paris on such business, though I hope not."

Later, when Murray received what he thought was a casual note from John Dawson, the Republican courier Jefferson had sent to Europe with the modified convention, and instructions for the negotiator, he objected. "I wrote him [Dawson]," Murray explained, "I would not go till I received some official orders!"[45]

Those instructions, which Murray received four days later,

told him to go to Paris to gain acceptance of the modified convention and to negotiate nothing else. If the French attempted to discuss America's joining the League of Armed Neutrality, for example, he was to stand fast against such involvement. "To con-
nect ourselves with the complicated combinations of the interests
of Europe," the instructions said, "would be to relinquish the
most precious gift of nature, insulation from the power and politics of that continent."

Since the convention had stipulated that ratifications were to
be exchanged within six months of signature and that period had
expired, the delay in the appointment of a negotiator nettled the
French. They were also unhappy because the United States did
not send a permanent minister.[46]

In the United States Pichon busied himself with the French
prisoners Americans had taken during the hostilities at sea, and
were now releasing, and with the resumption of commercial relations. At first his only cause of complaint had been the leisurely
pace of the Jefferson administration. Both the President and the
Secretary of State were absent from Washington much of the
time, and so the work of government was slow.[47]

Nonetheless Pichon expressed pleasure over Jefferson's attitude toward Saint Domingue. He even reported that the new
President would be willing to support Bonaparte against Toussaint. In an apparent reversal of Adams's policy, Jefferson's government did indicate it would do nothing in Saint Domingue contrary to France's rights there. Acting Secretary of State Levi Lincoln admitted that American agents on the island had violated
the principles of strict neutrality, but he promised Pichon that the
agent who replaced Stevens would be instructed "to respect the
rights and interests of your nation and to avoid just causes of
complaint."

A short time later, when Madison took over the Secretary-
ship of State, he replaced Stevens with Tobias Lear, formerly a
private secretary to President Washington. As Pichon had suggested, Madison did not designate Lear Consul General, only as
General Commercial Agent without diplomatic powers. Lear's
credentials were addressed to a locality, Cap Français, not to

Toussaint.[48] The appointment offended the general, who complained that Lear brought no personal letter to him from Jefferson. Lear explained that the American government did not send such letters with commercial agents. Brushing this explanation aside, Toussaint exclaimed in disgust that his color had caused this neglect.[49]

While these changes were taking place in Saint Domingue, Pichon learned that disturbing rumors were reaching the new President. On March 21, 1801, Lucien Bonaparte, another of Napoleon's brothers, signed the Convention of Aranjuez with Spain that confirmed the terms of San Ildefonso. Later that month Jefferson learned, at least as a persistent rumor that was appearing in European newspapers, of the retrocession of Louisiana. With this knowledge his attitude, and that of his government, toward France changed. "There is considerable reason to apprehend that Spain cedes Louisiana and the Floridas to France," he wrote. "It is a policy very unwise to both, and very ominous to us." [50]

Pichon noted this concern and reported that another rumor was spreading to the effect that the French fleet was headed for Guadeloupe or Saint Domingue. If the fleet came, he explained, it would be "one of the most delicate operations" that France could attempt. Furthermore, France could gain "no safety or advantage" in taking over Louisiana. There were two reasons for this, he asserted. First of all the Americans wanted freedom of the port of New Orleans, and secondly they had their eyes on the Floridas.

In response to American queries, Pichon said, he treated the news of Louisiana's transfer with indifference and even commented that it was "a thing *entirely unlikely*." Yet he did let Talleyrand and Bonaparte know that Americans would be hostile toward French reoccupation of New Orleans. This information reached Paris before the peace of the Quasi-War had been sealed. Later, in a conversation with Madison, Pichon asked, surely the United States would not consider it a crime for France to recover lost territory? [51]

Murray, too, heard that France had regained Louisiana. He

assumed that this would give the French another reason for seeking a friendly accord with the United States. "They may," he believed, "make a small sacrifice of pride to a solid & extensive plan, of which that cession, if made, will be the basis!" [52]

Murray arrived in Paris from The Hague on May 28, 1801, and two days later saw Talleyrand, who received him politely. The Minister of Foreign Relations asked him to confer with Joseph Bonaparte, Fleurieu, and Roederer, and promised the early settlement that Jefferson desired. Nonetheless, since Joseph Bonaparte was involved in his brother's reorganization of Germany growing out of the Treaty of Lunéville of February with Austria, which dissolved the Second Coalition, Murray feared delay.

The American diplomat expected the French to accept the qualified ratification. "The Defeat of the Northern Coalition," he reported, "will doubtless operate in our favour—Had that succeeded or even continued new conditions would probably have been held up as the Price of their Acceptance of the Ratification." [53]

THE FINAL ROUND

On June 6, 1801, at a public audience, Murray presented his letters of credence to the First Consul who "did not appear much pleased with the provisional Ratification." Yet Bonaparte intimated that the exchange of ratifications "would not meet with insurmountable Difficulties," and expressed great regard for Jefferson's administration.[54] Two days later Murray began conversations with the French commissioners.

The French negotiators did not object to the Senate's action which had placed a limitation of eight years on the convention, but they were unwilling to accept the simple abolition of the old treaties of 1778 and 1788, as required by the expunging of the second article of the convention. Why, they asked, did the Senate suppress that article?

"This is tough for me," Murray confessed privately, "as I was for that article & my instructions are silent upon the motives of its suppression! But I must make the best of it. . . ." Later, in a conversation at a dinner party with Roederer, Murray made another confession. "I told him that we had stretched our powers a little in putting in that article." [55]

At another audience a few days later Bonaparte asked Murray if he had full powers. The American said he had. Later, Roederer also questioned Murray's powers and remarked that he and his colleagues would always negotiate at a disadvantage "as long as the Senate had a veto on a Treaty." Murray objected to this criticism, insisting that all over the world a signed treaty was considered an unfinished act until ratified. [56]

One reason why the French had questioned Murray was that they felt his inability to explain why the Senate had made the reservations left no basis for negotiation over differences on the items expunged. Murray soon learned of another reason why the French had questioned his powers. Under the terms of the American ratification France would still be held liable for payment of indemnities. Therefore, the French diplomats would not accept a simple suppression of the second article. They thought that their country should agree to a removal of that article only if the United States would renounce its claim to indemnities. This attitude brought the whole question back to where it had been months earlier when the treaty itself was being negotiated.

Through Talleyrand the commissioners suggested two courses of possible action to the Premier Consul. France might open new negotiations with American plenipotentiaries who would have to obtain fresh instructions, or she might, as the American President and Senate had done, give a conditional ratification. Talleyrand advised acceptance of the second alternative. Bonaparte could add an article of his own to the convention stating that he ratified with the second article expunged, as had the Americans, provided that within a year the United States would agree to abondon its demand for indemnities.

This plan, basically, was why Bonaparte and Talleyrand had expressed direct concern over Murray's powers. They wanted to know, in effect, if his instructions permitted him to accept a conditional ratification by France. On June 27 Murray told them that he could. [57] The French then explained their terms.

Even though France could no longer hope to use the United States in a naval combination against Britain, one reason why Talleyrand strove anxiously to preserve the body of the convention rather than negotiate a new agreement was the favorable effect it had had on French policy in Europe. "It is not without interest for the honor and policy adopted by the government of the Republic," he wrote, "to preserve the first treaty in which liberal principles on the laws of neutrality have been generously and voluntarily stipulated by France. The rules which this treaty consecrates have not been without influence on the efforts which have been made in the north to free neutrality from the yoke of England. This consideration assures the convention of September 30 an honorable place in the history of international law." [58]

Although Murray believed that "it is of great importance to obtain their declaration that the Treaties [of 1778] cease!" he could not accept the conditional ratification proposed by the French because his instructions insisted that they must agree to pay indemnities. He did suggest, however, that they accept the American ratification, and then order Pichon in Washington to negotiate the points at issue under article two.

Determined to avoid payment to the United States, the French opposed Murray's proposal. Under it, they pointed out, France would abandon her claims to the old treaties while the United States retained its claims to indemnities.[59]

By this time the French were aware that they could not expect preferential treatment from Jefferson's government. "We know," Roederer told Murray, "that though Mr. Jefferson is an excellent & great man with good views for this country, yet some of his party are violent democrats [who] can not & do not love the present govt. of France wh. is an aristocracy in the philosophical sense of the term. . . ." [60]

Now, as Murray had feared, the negotiations dragged. Joseph Bonaparte spent much of his time in the country immersed in Austrian affairs, but the other two commissioners carried on without him. Poor health forced Talleyrand to take the baths for a month some hundred and eighty miles from Paris. The First Consul, too, became sick and contributed to the delay in diplomacy. All the while Murray persisted in his objective of trying to obtain a simple exchange of ratifications on his government's terms, "or something very near it." [61]

At this point members of the American colony in Paris, most of them Republican in sympathy, expressed dissatisfaction over Murray's handling of the negotiation. One of them, Joshua Barney, a sea captain who had commanded a French privateer, charged him with deliberately delaying the exchange. "Mr. Murray does not like what has been done in the U.S.," Barney wrote. "Every man who knows him, knows also his attachment to the British & his dislike to France." [62]

Aware that his diplomacy was being criticized, Murray had thought of giving up "the present little negociation" but decided finally not to do so. A failure, he reasoned, might "be imputed to me partly as a splenetic man adverse to the present administration. . . ." [63]

Murray himself wished that he had been empowered to sign away American claims because he did "not consider the indemnities as worth a farthing in the pound." He knew that the treaties of 1778 no longer existed, yet, he wrote, "I believe it may be very important *in the course of the Four following years* to have their [the French] declaration also that they no longer claim them!" Furthermore, he believed that the French "claim is in theory worth about as much as ours is in fact & in the chances of success." [64]

Talleyrand finally returned to Paris, and then he told Murray the bargaining would have to stop. He proposed a simple ratification of the convention with the abolition of the second article and the retention of the limitation of eight years, if the American government would interpret the removal of the article as a "reciprocal renunciation of the respective pretensions which are the object of the said article." This meant, as before, that in exchange for France's acceptance of the abrogation of the old treaties the United States would have to give up its claim for indemnities.

Once again Murray found himself in a dilemma. He had no authority to abandon indemnities, but if he did not compromise he knew there would be no treaty. Once more, therefore, he felt compelled to violate instructions, this time on his own, to break a stalemate. He accepted Talleyrand's proposition. "Convinced Sir as I am that nothing can be gained," he wrote to Secretary of State Madison, "& confiding in a liberal judgment in Government upon the situation in which I am placed, I shall exchange upon these terms."

Ratifications were exchanged on the evening of Friday, July 31, 1801, at Roederer's home. Several days later Murray reported the details to the Department of State. "Perfectly in the Dark as I am on the Views of the Senate in repressing the Second Article, I can not know the Extent of the Responsibility which I have assumed in accepting the French Ratification. . . . I concluded it for the best to exchange, rather than break off—" [65]

On the following day Murray reported to William R. Davie that Spain had ceded Louisiana to France. "Yet," he commented with Jeffersonian isolationism obviously in mind, "our people say we have no connection wh. European politics."

BONAPARTE AND TOUSSAINT

Murray also discussed the cession with French officials. One of them suggested that with Louisiana in her possession France would have a deeper interest in seeking a relationship of harmony with the United States. He considered it good for France to have her Caribbean islands independent of the United States. [66]

In the United States, meanwhile, Jefferson had become agitated by stories of France's recovery of Louisiana. "Should France get possession of that country," he explained, "it will be more to be lamented than remedied by us, as it will furnish ground for profound consideration on our part, how best to conduct ourselves in that case." France's delay in ratifying the Convention of Môrtefontaine also upset him, so much so, that he decided Livingston should wait no longer. He should go to Paris immediately. [67]

Perhaps, the President now thought, it might be better to let the convention lapse. This denouement, he suggested, "will only begin the work of placing us clear of treaty with all nations."

Unlike Murray, or John Adams, Jefferson believed the United States should isolate itself politically and avoid treaties which might involve it in European affairs. "The day is within my time as well as yours," the President told a diplomat in Europe, "when we may say by what laws other nations shall treat us on the sea. And we will say it. In the meantime, we wish to let every treaty we have drop off without renewal." [68]

A few days earlier news of the exchange of ratifications had arrived in the United States.[69] Even so staunch a Federalist as Gouverneur Morris was pleased. The amendments to the convention, he pointed out, "have the great and salutary effect of terminating our intimate alliance with France." From this result he concluded "that the affairs of the First Consul are not very splendid. He would not otherwise let go his hold of us, for though we are but a feather in the great scale of power, yet when that scale is nearly poised the weight of a feather is something." [70]

Actually, Bonaparte had ratified the convention not because he was weak, but because—even though the Armed Neutrality had collapsed—ratification still suited his plans for empire. In addition to the reconquest of Saint Domingue, his occupation of Louisiana depended, in part at least, on American friendliness and on peace with England.[71] Consummation of the pact seemingly would assure American goodwill.

This concern for American friendship, revived by the Consulate, had again aroused among the French people a mild interest in the United States. For the first time in years a Frenchman produced a play on an American theme. The play, a pantomime by Mayeur de Saint Paul, called *L'Héroine de Boston,* was performed in October 1801. It told the story of two French officers and two American girls who fell in love during the American Revolution. As usual in French dramas of this level, the villain who menaced this love was a lascivious English officer.[72]

Ironically, while the French people were absorbing doses of anti-English propaganda and Bonaparte was bargaining over the ratification of the Convention of Môrtefontaine, he was also carrying on secret peace negotiations in London. Peace with Britain seemed assured when his agent, Louis Guillaume Otto, signed

preliminary terms with Robert Banks Jenkinson, Lord Hawkesbury, the new young English Secretary of State for Foreign
Affairs, on October 1. Five months later, this agreement would
become the Treaty of Amiens. This agreement, or armistice, between the French and the English to stop hostilities changed the
position of the United States in international politics. Now
France would no longer need American support at sea and would
no longer have to fear that the United States might ally itself with
England.[73]

Yet if Bonaparte were to carry out his design of empire in the
New World without terrible difficulties, he could use American
friendship. In the spring of 1800 he had planned to reassert
French authority in Saint Domingue with a small expedition and
to garrison it with a few thousand French troops. Later, after he
had regained Louisiana, Saint Domingue grew to a new importance in his eyes. He worked out a new plan, though the basic
idea was an old one the Directory had adopted, that called for an
armada to carry a large expeditionary force to Saint Domingue to
conquer it. Then the First Consul would use the island as the
base for occupying, supplying, and exploiting Louisiana. Before
sending his troops to Saint Domingue, he had to wait for peace
with England.[74]

Another factor that had led Bonaparte to think of an enlarged expedition were rumors that Toussaint, who he called that
"gilded African," was planning to declare Saint Domingue independent of France. Toussaint had imprisoned Roume, and was reported to be holding white inhabitants as hostages against a possible French attack. In May 1801 he had given Saint Domingue a
new constitution in which he assumed all political power for life
and the right to name his own successor. Although Toussaint still
professed a nominal allegiance to France, he placed his island in a
state of defense and imported quantities of arms and ammunition
from the United States. In view of these developments, Pichon reported that only an imposing military expedition, assured of
American cooperation, could prevent Toussaint from declaring
independence.[75]

Jefferson and Madison indicated that they wished to see France regain Saint Domingue and that they were opposed to independence. Yet, they also explained that trade with Saint Domingue was important to the United States, and hence they were unwilling to "risk falling out with Toussaint." Such a falling out would affront American public opinion. Madison seemed to suggest that if Bonaparte wanted American support in Saint Domingue, he should abandon plans to take over Louisiana.

When Pichon asked if Jefferson would cooperate in quickly restoring French sovereignty in Saint Domingue, the President alluded to the difficulties such a restoration would create between France and Britain. ". . . in order that this concert may be complete and effective," Jefferson suggested, "you must make peace with England, then nothing will be easier than to furnish your army and fleet with everything and to reduce Toussaint to starvation." Pichon interpreted this as a promise of American help to a French expedition of conquest. Without American aid, Pichon believed, France would be unable to recover Saint Domingue.[76]

As Pichon had interpreted Jefferson's views, the American government stood ready to form a triple concert with France and England to prevent the independence of a Negro, and allegedly pirate, state in the Caribbean. This interpretation apparently influenced Bonaparte's decision to attempt to conquer Saint Domingue.

During the peace negotiations in London, Talleyrand had expressed the hope that Britain would view "with pleasure an expedition whose aim is to restore the colony of St. Domingo to a state of organization such that it will no longer be a dangerous neighbor to the European colonies in the Antilles." The British indicated a willingness to permit a French fleet to sail against Toussaint and even to help supply it.[77] Bonaparte thought, therefore, that he could rely on the cooperation of Britain and the United States when he launched his attack on Saint Domingue.

On October 23, 1801, slightly more than three weeks after the signing of the preliminaries of peace in London the First Consul placed his brother-in-law, General Victor E. Leclerc, in com-

mand of the expedition headed for Saint Domingue and, according to rumors, ultimately for Louisiana. Leclerc, married to lovely
Pauline Bonaparte, was considered one of the most important
members of the Premier Consul's family. "I know from a variety
of channels that the armament, destined in the first instance for
Hispaniola," Livingston reported, "is to proceed to Louisiana provided Toussaint makes no opposition." Although Bonaparte may
have planned to send some of Leclerc's soldiers to Louisiana and
at this time had gathered another force for Louisiana, Leclerc's
instructions said nothing about Louisiana.[78]

Several weeks later, by the middle of December, most of the
20,000 troops and the main squadron assigned to the conquest
sailed from Brest. This force, one of the largest ever to have sailed
from France and which came within sight of Saint Domingue at
the end of January 1802, encountered troubles from the beginning. Weary of nine years of war, anxious for discharge, and fearful of new trials, some of the French seamen mutinied. Several
were executed.[79]

This mutiny turned out to be only the first of a series of troubles that dogged the First Consul's efforts to carry out his grand
design for a North American empire. In Saint Domingue fierce
Negro resistance and a raging yellow fever took the lives of thousands of French soldiers, including that of General Leclerc. These
losses, as well as other factors, forced Bonaparte to abandon his
plans for the exploitation of Louisiana, a province he never occupied. Finally, in April 1803, he sold Louisiana to the United
States for fifteen million dollars. That purchase not only brought
the United States its first territorial acquisition since independence, it also doubled the nation's national domain.

Before Leclerc's armada had sailed, and as the news that
England and France were at peace spread to America, Robert R.
Livingston, who was destined to negotiate the purchase of Louisiana, arrived in France. He had sailed from New York in the
middle of October 1801 after word had reached the United States
that Murray had exchanged ratifications. While en route he heard
of the peace in Europe. On December 6 the First Consul received
him in a formal audience. He asked if Livingston had been in

Europe before and commented, "You have come to a very corrupt world." [80]

While Livingston was traveling east the copy of the Convention of Môrtefontaine that Bonaparte had ratified was on its way to the United States, but it did not reach the Department of State until late in November. On December 11, 1801, after hesitating a month over the proper constitutional procedure in this matter, Jefferson sent the convention to the Senate for approval. This was the third time that body had an opportunity to study the agreement, but now Republicans rather than Federalists were in control. The President believed he should resubmit the document because the Senate's original terms of approval had been changed. Bonaparte's ratification, he pointed out, was not "pure and simple, in the ordinary form." Since, in addition, merchants were unhappy over the loss of indemnities, he wanted to leave the treaty "on the shoulders of the senate to accept." [81]

Although the senators did not think formal advice and consent was again necessary, they referred the convention to a committee, which advised acceptance. Some considered the President's action foolish, commenting that it had merely aroused idle talk.[82] Thus, even though Murray had gone beyond his instructions and Bonaparte had introduced a substantial change, the Senate, with 22 yeas and 4 nays, resolved on December 19 that the convention was fully ratified.[83] Two days later, and just six days after Bonaparte had proclaimed the convention as ratified, Jefferson proclaimed it as law of the land.

At last, the first entangling alliance in the history of the United States, with the approval of both Federalists and Republicans, was formally buried. Regardless of the larger implications of Bonaparte's policy toward the New World, this could be considered in itself an impressive diplomatic accomplishment for American statesmanship. The British representative in Washington thought it was. "The abolition of the treaties of 1778," he wrote, "however beneficial it may be to this country [the United States], is but a matter of speculative advantage to the French. . . ." [84]

At last, too, after four years of quarreling mixed with warfare

at sea, with heated exchange of insults, and with prolonged negotiations, the United States and France resumed the political and
economic relations considered normal between friendly states.
The Quasi-War, a conflict that had smoldered and sputtered but
had never burst into full flame, had officially ended.

In Perspective

It must always happen, so long as America is an independent Republic or nation, that the balance of power in Europe will continue to be of the utmost importance to her welfare.

THOMAS BOYLSTON ADAMS, *October 1799*

A CONCLUSION TO AN HISTORICAL STUDY, BY SUMMING UP SIGNIFICANT points, by cutting through detail here and there, and by stressing or reiterating interpretations, may aid the reader in looking back and gaining perspective on the work as a whole, as does the man who climbs a mountain, gazes back, and realizes there is a unity in sky, mountain, river, and valley. Such historical perspective may in turn suggest that what the reader has just experienced, like the man on the mountain, while unique in time and particulars, is connected to a larger pattern. This conclusion, therefore, in addition to summing up, seeks to remind the reader that the history he has just read is not a fragment drifting alone in a world inhabited by academicians, but is part of a large, almost universal theme in the experience of civilized man, that of conflict, and especially of war and peace.

In this conflict with France we have had the example of a nation, the United States, perched on the brink of full-scale war, of stumbling toward, but not falling into, the inferno. The decisions

327

that drove America and France—at the time the two most democratic large nations in the world—toward unqualified war were
not thoughtfully planned, were not founded on all the available
evidence, and were not the result of the careful weighing of various alternatives. Those decisions often flowed from the heated
emotions, the irrational attitudes, and the disorderly thinking of
excited and opinionated men.[1]

Full-scale war, as we have seen, could not have brought
profit to either nation. When emotions cooled, many statesmen on
both sides of the Atlantic saw this. Peace ultimately prevailed for
selfish, rational reasons. Men could gain more from it than from
war. During the Quasi-War there was time, as there has not always been in acute international crises, for the rational to gain
ascendancy over the irrational.

Unless a conqueror ruthlessly imposed peace, the diplomacy
of peacemaking has always been complicated and time consum-
ing. So it was during the long, and even tedious, Quasi-War, or
what John Adams himself called "the half war with France."

One reason why the complicated peacemaking in this conflict
has not previously attracted careful attention from scholars is
that the Quasi-War was not a true war. Although both France
and the United States were hurt by their hostilities, neither had
proclaimed the other country a national enemy. Even at the
height of the crisis France treated the United States more as a
hostile neutral than as an enemy state.[2]

In many ways this conflict proved more frustrating than a
war fought by massed battalions and organized naval squadrons.
It placed the Adams administration and the American people in a
state of almost perpetual crisis. They found themselves caught in
a wave of political agitation and hysterical patriotism that
brought neither the emotional outlet of war nor the satisfactions
of peace. The very nature of this struggle with France, like the
head of Janus facing two ways, contributed to the turbulence of
Adams's Presidency.

Extremists in the President's own party embraced the conflict
with France, tried to expand it, and wanted to use it politically as
a partisan, one-party crusade. They considered France a land of

wild-eyed Jacobins, and looked upon those Americans who opposed their program as domestic Jacobins or, at best, dupes of
foreign Jacobins. The irrational antipathy of these Federalist extremists to France led them to believe that the war they favored
would serve, not injure, the national interest.

Occupying positions of leadership in the Federalist party
and in the government, these men wanted an unqualified declaration of war against France. In their view, and in that of later writ-
ers who approved of their actions, if ever "there existed a righteous and good ground for war since the institution of nations, it
existed in the year 1798." [3] The extreme Federalists tried to, and
did, use their party's control of foreign policy as a weapon against
Republicans. Anything that kept Jacobins out of office, even war,
they seemed to think, was proper and patriotic.

These war hawks found it easy to assume the role of patriots
seeking to avenge national honor. Justice appeared to be on their
side. Other Americans could join them in their hatred of a foreign
country and, of course, add to their own sense of "belonging" to a
national cause. Such identification was satisfying, for one did not
have to be an extremist or a war hawk to take pride in his young
country's defiance of powerful France in 1798. These Federalist
patriots of 1798 were among the new nation's first powerful,
noisy, flag-waving, and intolerant nationalists. [4]

The unyielding resistance of the United States to France
not only swelled national pride, as a British observer commented,
but it also raised America's status "in the estimation of foreign
powers." All Europe, according to William Vans Murray, viewed
America's resort to naval combat with astonishment and respect.
Then, with a chauvinism befitting any dedicated nationalist, he
claimed that the United States "appears in the Splendour of a
great nation," its reputation exalted. [5]

Republicans, while probably no less patriotic, or nationalis-
tic, but at this time less chauvinistic, from the beginning opposed
the Federalist program. Even as the crisis mounted and American
seamen fought French sailors, Republicans denied that the country was at war, pointing out that only Congress had the right to
declare war, and that it had never done so against France. High

Federalists, on the other hand, claimed that the battles at sea had grown into actual war, and they tried to justify their measures against France, and even those against fellow Americans, such as the Alien and Sedition laws, on the basis of a wartime emergency.

Political feeling on the nature of the Quasi-War ran deep, so much so that in 1800 the Supreme Court, when faced with problems arising out of French spoliations of American commerce and retaliatory legislation passed by Congress, chose to define what kind of an enemy France was. In the case of *Bas v. Tingy* the court held that a state of "limited, partial war" existed, and that hence France was legally an enemy nation. Since this decision sustained the view of Federalists, they applauded.[6]

Republicans, however, reacted with a withering hostility. They argued, apparently for the first time in the nation's history, that a judge could or should be impeached for rendering so partisan a decision. Philadelphia's *Aurora* stated, for instance, that in this case the decision was "most important and momentous to the country, and in our opinion every Judge who asserted we were in a state of war, contrary to the rights of Congress to declare it, *ought to be impeached.*"[7]

Regardless of partisan debate and judicial opinion, it is clear that those who clamored for unlimited hostilities, and who were determined to keep the door bolted against peace, never gained full command of both the executive and legislative branches of government at one time. Not even at the height of the X Y Z frenzy did diplomacy between France and the United States altogether stop, or hostilities completely take over. The reasons for this, and hence why full-scale war did not come, are woven into a web of international and domestic politics.

WHY PEACE CAME

Some contemporaries, mainly Federalists and foreign observers such as the British, summarized the reasons why actual war did not break out in a simple concept of force met by counterforce. "The firmness and vigor of the United States, in all probability, has prevented a war with France," an anonymous British commentator explained. "The French calculated upon their party in America, and they were disappointed. This was the scourge of war which they threatened. Without this they are impotent. By entering into a war with America, they can do no more mischief than they have already done by their cruisers." [8]

The French, on the other hand, believed that their forbearance and their military strength had prevented the United States from allying itself with Britain in a full-scale war. The "brilliant [military] situation of France," Létombe maintained, had kept Adams from being pushed into an unrestricted war against France, and against Spain too.[9]

It is true that the French had changed their policy toward the United States when Talleyrand took office and had become very conciliatory after the X Y Z fiasco. According to their theory of wise forbearance and patience, their careful diplomacy had thwarted English plans to involve the United States in an enlarged war with France, had defeated the scheme of High Federalists to bait them into declaring war and hence stigmatize them as aggressors, and had succeeded in changing American policy so that Adams became willing to send the Ellsworth mission to Paris. Talleyrand, who gave French policy continuity despite upheavals within the government, stressed his country's forbearance in contrast to American belligerence. "I do not know why it is that at each step towards reconciliation," he wrote, "a cause of irritation intervenes and that these are always begun by the United States." [10]

On the American side the question of war or peace had become a central issue in the party politics of an emerging modern democracy. That issue, therefore, became less susceptible to central control than in France, and in America the reasons why unrestricted war failed to erupt became more complex than in France. Three of the more important of these American reasons were public opposition to unrestrained hostilities, expressed politically through Republicans and through moderate Federalists in Congress, the changed attitude of President Adams himself, and the patient diplomacy of negotiators in Paris.

Adams's own policies had not led to the Quasi-War. He had
inherited the crisis from President Washington and had tried immediately to resolve it through negotiation. When this effort
failed Adams aligned himself with the extremists of his own party
and went along with their war program. Yet Adams did not, as
many party leaders wanted him to do, ask Congress for a declaration of war. He hesitated not because he believed in peace at all
costs, but because a part of him recoiled at the thought of leading
a disunited country into unlimited hostilities. Wishing to have behind him a popular sentiment strong enough to overcome Republican opposition to war, he wanted to be sure Congress would
vote for a declaration of war before he asked for one. He realized
that the internal opposition to an enlarged conflict was so widespread that revolution, with American pitted against American,
might follow if public support could not be built up for a declaration of war.[11]

Even Hamilton, whose attitude toward full-scale war, over a
period of three years, swung like a pendulum, finally recognized
that public opinion so strongly favored peace that the government could not ignore this sentiment. "Of one thing I am sure," he
wrote when he learned that peace was probable, "if France will
slide into a state of Peace *de facto,* we must meet her on that
ground. The actual posture of European Affairs and the opinions
of our people demand an accommodating course." [12]

Even at the height of the X Y Z crisis, with public sentiment
toward France heated and belligerently hostile, the people were
divided in their attitude toward naked war. Later, Federalists realized that the masses would sympathize with Adams's peace
moves. So moderate Federalists, at least, bowed to public opinion.

Ironically, many of the merchants and shipowners who bore
the brunt of French spoliations were among those most opposed
to war. Despite the French attacks on their property, while Britain and France fought and the United States remained technically neutral, these merchants prospered.

Like the merchants, American diplomats were willing to endure much for peace. First Marshall, Pinckney, and Gerry, and

especially Gerry, then Ellsworth, Davie, and Murray, and finally Murray alone, stretched their powers rather than risk the loss of peace. Although Federalists, these diplomats were never as unbending or irrational toward the French as were the High Federalists, such as Pickering. This willingness of American negotiators to compromise and not seek refuge in the letter of instructions made possible the Convention of Môrtefontaine, and later its ratification by Napoleon Bonaparte. In these years American diplomats abroad were more willing to make decisions on their own when confronted with unexpected situations than would be negotiators in later years.

The success of the diplomats in obtaining peace upset the plans of High Federalists. These High Federalists had been disappointed, but not dismayed, when John Adams had not obtained a declaration of war from Congress. They, and the President himself at more than one point, had expected France to declare war, or at least, to commit acts so intolerable as to make full-scale hostilities inevitable. A war declared or forced by France, they reasoned, would unite the country in a crusade against Jacobinism, abroad and at home, and hence would be more desirable than one declared under presidential initiative.[13] Although extreme Federalists waited impatiently, France never declared war or committed the final provocative act.

While Federalists waited for enlarged hostilities, animosities within their party became uncontrollable, and the drive toward war began to decelerate. These differences among party leaders, with Adams on one side and the Hamiltonians on the other, were not openly discernible when the President sent his first mission to France, but they were beneath the surface of party unity. Adams wanted the mission to succeed; the Hamiltonians expected it to fail. They wished to make use of that failure to discredit the Republican party and ultimately to obtain war. At more than one point Hamilton wanted to turn the defensive maritime struggle into a war of conquest. With some consistency, High Federalists tried to make war with France a key factor in their party's policy.

As President, Adams was crucial to this policy. Without his

request for a declaration of war, High Federalists realized, they had practically no chance of carrying a majority in Congress for it. Congress has never declared war without a request from the President.

Not until after Adams broke with the Hamiltonians over the issue of rank in the Army did he become willing to listen to overtures for peace. Later, when he became fully aware of the extent of High Federalist opposition to him, he even became willing to risk strife within his party in an effort to obtain an honorable peace.

After recovering from the shock of the American reaction to the X Y Z imbroglio, Talleyrand offered Adams a means of retreating gracefully from the brink of war. Talleyrand and other French statesmen did this and refused to take the final step into war, not because they loved the United States, but because full-blown hostilities could bring no advantage to France and possibly much harm. Within France, moreover, the idea of war against the United States had no popular support. In the French view unlimited war with the United States would have been a stinging nuisance, would have benefited only England, and would in no important way have served France's national interest.

When Talleyrand had control over foreign policy, therefore, he never allowed a complete rupture in diplomatic relations with the United States. He deliberately and carefully avoided giving the High Federalists a further pretext for war. His was a dangerous game, but it worked.[14]

Talleyrand had not had a hand in the policy that had precipitated the Quasi-War. The French statesmen who had touched off the undeclared war had misjudged the extent of their country's influence in the United States, had underestimated the strength of the Federalist tie to England, and had misunderstood the emerging American national temper. As they had ever since the American Revolution, French statesmen had sought to use, to manipulate, or to take advantage of American politics to advance their own foreign policy. In 1797, to be specific, men such as Delacroix and Reubell had tried to destroy the Jay Treaty and to turn the United States against England. In 1798, when Talleyrand and others saw that this policy of threats and humiliation had merely united former friends of France in the United States with enemies, even to the point of war, the French government shifted its policy.

Persistence in this hostile course, the new men of the Directory had realized, would drive the United States into the arms of England. Later, after Napoleon Bonaparte became First Consul, took over the Directory's foreign policy, sought to build a maritime coalition against England, and planned to reconstruct an empire in North America, the friendship of the United States became important to French policy in a positive way.

France's effort to use the United States in the international politics of Europe and the American reaction to this policy, as well as to British policy, illustrates another historically significant point about the Federalist era. Leaders such as Adams realized that the politics of Europe's rulers, particularly of France and Britain, could vitally affect the United States. Adams, and those close to him, therefore, were not isolationist in their thinking. Isolationism, in the sense of the Amercan government seeking to sever political, and even diplomatic, connections in Europe, became government policy after Jefferson took office.

THE END OF AN ERA

Jefferson's victory in 1800 and Bonaparte's triumphs in France and Europe, instead of bringing France and the United States closer together, as many Americans assumed would happen, actually kept the two countries apart on fundamental issues. In America the democratic experiment continued and expanded. In France the democratic experiment of the First Republic had failed. The coming to power of these two men may not have signified the completion of a great revolution in the Western World, but it marked the end of the democratic agitation and counteragitation that the great revolution had set in motion. The Quasi-War, with its complicated diplomacy and turbulent politics at home for Americans, can be considered one of the last episodes in that revolution in the Western World.[15]

Thomas Boylston Adams may not have seen the events in Europe in the context of a worldwide revolution, but, like his father and unlike the Jeffersonians, he considered the developments in Europe, especially the actions of Britain and France, important to American security. As long as the United States remained independent, he prophesied, "the balance of power in Europe will continue to be of the utmost importance to her welfare." There existed, he added, a substantial reason for this involvement. "We are of too much consequence in the scale of nations, to be left in the peaceable enjoyment of our commerce & gaining in proportion as others are losing it, without a struggle at least to draw us into the vortex of War & waste." [16]

William Vans Murray, too, deplored Jeffersonian isolationism. When the new League of Armed Neutrality was dissolved he maintained that its demise benefited his country, "though there are men who study newspapers in the United States who eternally babble with a triumphant chuckle that we are out of European politics while we are perpetually affected by them!" [17]

This dilemma posed by Murray was later to become common in the nation's history. So too was the dilemma that Adams as President had to face. His office and his duty to his people obligated him to maintain an honorable peace and, in the case of the French crisis, to accept a tolerable reconciliation. At the same time, he was also obligated to prepare measures of defense, and even of offense, which could contribute to victory if war should come, but which would most likely aggravate the crisis.[18] His task was further complicated by the knowledge that if he openly challenged the war policy of High Federalists and sought peace, he risked the disruption of his party and its defeat at the polls.

When Adams nominated Murray as Minister to France, and later when he sent off the Ellsworth mission, he consciously challenged the extremist leadership in his own party. These decisions in foreign policy, despite efforts of extremists to reverse them, disrupted the Federalist party to such an extent that it never recovered its unity. In this sense, these decisions made possible the so-called "revolution of 1800" and changed the orientation of American politics. Ironically, these decisions also opened the way to the outstanding achievement of his administration, the Convention of Môrtefontaine, and the peace it signified. Yet Adams's successor, not he, profited from that accomplishment.

Contemporary observers were aware of this irony. Shortly after Adams had left office, Edward Thornton pointed out "that almost every step which he took has turned to the advantage, and increased the triumph of his antagonists. The measure of appointing Commissioners to France without the concurrence of his Ministers, while it produced the pacification with that country, divided his adherents into two irreconcilable parties and enabled his enemies to enter at the breach and to snatch from him all the glory of a reduction of taxes, which now gives so much splendour to the first acts of Mr. Jefferson." [19]

While it may be disputed, as it has been, that Adams acted as he did in seeking an accommodation with France knowing that the negotiation would injure his party, the fact is that peace, with all the discord it aroused, did contribute to the demise of Federalism. Adams, of course, was not the sole contributor. Hamilton and his followers also merit recognition as wreckers of the Federalist party.[20]

Adams's success in diplomacy, furthermore, was not entirely of his own doing. As has been seen, the French, for reasons of their own, desired peace as much as did the United States. This desire oiled the machinery of the diplomacy that led to the consummation of the Convention of Môrtefontaine. For France that agreement marked the first step toward a general pacification inaugurated by Bonaparte after he became First Consul, and, of course, a step toward a new empire in North America.

Pierre Louis Roederer stressed this aspect of the convention when appraising it before the French legislature. "The United States," he announced, "are too near our colonies for it not to be useful to us to have them as friends." He, too, maintained that the United States could not truly isolate itself from Europe. It had, he said, "a powerful interest in the liberty of the seas" and "the equilibrium of the powers of Europe." [21]

The Convention of Môrtefontaine, however, was more important to the interests of the United States than to those of

France. In the sense that the President had indicated that the
Ellsworth mission would be his last effort at conciliation and if it
failed there seemingly would be no alternative to actual war, it
prevented full-scale war. That resolution of a frustrating conflict,
despite the fact that the convention did not settle all the questions
at issue with France to the satisfaction of many Americans, was in
itself a major achievement.[22]

In addition, the Convention of 1800 laid to rest the dispute
over neutral rights with France that had risen out of the Jay
Treaty. Before the Quasi-War France had been the most favored
nation in America's treaty obligations, but now France accepted
the loss of that status, and even accepted the Jay Treaty as a fact.
This in itself constituted a considerable diplomatic accomplishment for the United States. The new convention removed the
causes of irritation imbedded in the treaties of 1778 and the consular convention of 1788. It rescued all the ships and other property the French had taken but had not yet definitely condemned.
More important, that treaty legally freed the United States from
its first entangling alliance, an obligation that had seemingly
grown more onerous with each passing year. Finally, the convention helped secure the goodwill of Bonaparte, and thus laid the
groundwork for the acquisition of Louisiana two years later.

When Bonaparte sold Louisiana he stated, possibly with exaggerated emphasis, that he did so because, among other reasons,
he wished to prevent misunderstandings with the United States.
He and other French statesmen professed to regard the Louisiana
Treaty, styled simply an act of amity between two friendly countries, as complementing the Convention of 1800.[23] Regardless of
the true depth of these sentiments, they do indicate that the convention was important in French policy, and that without it the
United States might not have acquired Louisiana peacefully and
cheaply, as it did in 1803.

For all this, the United States gave up claims against France
which might never have been paid anyway.[24] By almost any
standard of measurement this peace settlement was a significant
accomplishment for a young nation not yet able to place the inde-

pendent weight on the scale of international power its own patriots, with exaggerated national pride, thought it could or should.

Under more difficult circumstances than in the negotiations in London in 1794 the Convention of Môrtefontaine secured more from France than England had conceded in the Jay Treaty, though John Jay did obtain compensation for shipping losses suffered at the hands of the British. No American, despite Adams's bellicosity, his desire several times to seek a declaration of war against France, his vacillating attitude toward peace overtures, his loose control over subordinates, and his feeling that his own people had repudiated him and his policies at the polls, contributed more to this diplomatic feat than did John Adams. As his son John Quincy pointed out, the elder Adams proved "that in your administration you were not the man of any party but of the whole nation." [25]

John Adams recognized the importance of this contribution, for out of his many achievements near the close of his long life he chose, with strained simplicity, to stress this one. "I will defend my missions to France, as long as I have an eye to direct my hand, or a finger to hold my pen. They were the most disinterested and meritorious actions of my life. I reflect upon them with so much satisfaction, that I desire no other inscription over my gravestone than: 'Here lies John Adams, who took upon himself the responsibility of the peace with France in the year 1800.'" [26]

Adams has often, and sometimes with exaggerated justification, been praised as the peacemaker, but another man whose contribution to peace in the period of the Quasi-War was greater, has seldom been thought of as the peacemaker. This is the sinuous Talleyrand, whose reputation for honesty is just the opposite of that of flinty John Adams. Perhaps this reputation for unscrupulousness has clouded everything Talleyrand touched. Yet in the crisis of the undeclared war Adams more often than he surrendered to emotions and strutted like a warrior. Both men, nonetheless, strove for peace over great obstacles before it was too late. Both were peacemakers.[27]

As for the United States itself, peace with France, the escape from imperialistic ventures in the West Indies and Latin America, the dissolution of the alliance of 1778, and the ultimate acquisition of Louisiana, are among the most enduring diplomatic achievements of the republic. All flowed, in one way or another, from the Convention of Môrtefontaine. From the perspective of a century and three quarters it seems fair to conclude that perhaps no peace settlement has brought the nation greater benefits for so little cost.

ᵰᵰᵰᵰᵰ᷾ Chronology ᷾᷾᷾ᵰᵰᵰ

1797

March   2 The French issue a decree that permits attacks against American shipping

  3 John Adams and Thomas Jefferson discuss a peace mission to France

  4 Adams is inaugurated as the second President of the United States

  5 Adams discusses the peace mission with his cabinet officers

14 Adams learns that the French have rejected Charles Cotesworth Pinckney

14 Adams asks his cabinet officers for advice on the French crisis

25 The President issues a call for Congress to meet in special session on May 15

April 14 Adams sends a second inquiry on the French crisis to his department heads

May   2 Jefferson's letter to Philip Mazzei, which criticizes George Washington, is published in America

16 Adams addresses the Fifth Congress on the French crisis

31 Charles Cotesworth Pinckney, John Marshall, and Francis Dana are nominated as ministers to France

June   5 The Federalist defense program is introduced in Congress

20 Elbridge Gerry replaces Dana on the peace commission for France

27 James Monroe returns from France and confers with Republican leaders

July   1 Monroe is honored by Republicans at a special dinner

  3 Adams sends papers to Congress that stir up talk of the Blount Conspiracy

  4 The Senate expels William Blount

  8 Congress adjourns

July 10 Pierre Auguste Adet urges the Directory to make a peaceful settlement of differences with the United States

18 Charles Maurice de Talleyrand-Périgord is appointed France's Minister of Foreign Relations

20 Marshall sails for Europe from Philadelphia

23 Gerry sails from Boston

September 4 In the *coup d'état* of 18 *Fructidor* in France the Executive Directory illegally uses force against the legislature

27 Pinckney and Marshall arrive in Paris. Gerry arrives later

October 8 The American commissioners have their first informal meeting with Talleyrand

11 Thomas Paine writes to the American commissioners in Paris

17 General Napoleon Bonaparte forces the Treaty of Campo Formio on Austria

18 Jean Conrad Hottinguer, Talleyrand's agent, demands a bribe from the American commissioners

22 The commissioners send their first dispatches to the United States

November 11 The American commissioners demand official recognition from Talleyrand

23 Adams delivers a message to the second session of the Fifth Congress. He urges preparations for defense

1798

January 18 The Directory publishes a new decree against American shipping

24 Adams sends an inquiry to his cabinet asking advice on war measures

31 The commissioners send a long memorial on American grievances to Talleyrand

February 10 Gerry quarrels with Pinckney and Marshall

March 4 The commissioners' first dispatches arrive in Philadelphia

6 The commissioners have their last interview with Talleyrand

13 Adams asks his department heads if he should seek a declaration of war

c. 15 Adams prepares a war message, but abandons it

19 Talleyrand answers the American memorial

19 Adams sends Congress a message reporting failure of the peace mission and announcing limited hostilities against France

23 Pickering directs the peace commissioners to demand their passports

27 Republicans introduce the Sprigg Resolutions to block Federalist war measures

April Count d'Hédouville arrives in Saint Domingue

April   2 The House of Representatives demands the peace commissioners' dispatches

      3 Adams sends Congress the dispatches, substituting the letters W X Y and Z for the names of Talleyrand's agents

      6 The House of Representatives votes to publish the X Y Z dispatches

      9 The administration's war program is introduced in the House

   24 Marshall sails for the United States from Bordeaux. Gerry and Pinckney remain in France

   30 The Navy Department is created

May   9 Adams had set this day aside for fasting and prayer, but French and English partisans clash in the streets

   10 The Speaker of the House reports that French troops will invade the United States

   10 Thomas Maitland of England completes negotiations with Toussaint L'Ouverture to end fighting in Saint Domingue

   11 In the *coup d'état* of 22 *Floréal* the Directory annuls elections

   15 The Directory issues a decree keeping American ships out of military ports

   24 The first American warship, the *Ganges,* goes on patrol against the French

   27 Increases in the Navy are authorized

   28 The French government receives copies of the published X Y Z dispatches

   28 Congress authorizes an increase in the Army

   28 Congress authorizes the use of force against the French at sea

June   7 Frenchmen, such as the Comte de Volney, flee hostility in the United States

   13 Congress votes an embargo against French ships

   13 Dr. George Logan of Philadelphia leaves the United States on a personal peace mission to France

   16 John Marshall returns home to a hero's welcome

   18 The Naturalization Act becomes law

   21 Adams sends a special message to Congress announcing the end of the peace mission and saying he will not send another mission to France

   22 More X Y Z dispatches are ordered published

   25 The Alien Friends Act becomes law

   25 Pickering orders Gerry to return home

   26 Louis André Pichon, under instructions from Talleyrand, has his first conversation with William Vans Murray at The Hague

   30 Congress has a test vote on a declared war

July   2 Federalist members of Congress hold a war caucus

    4 The black cockade fever reaches a climax

July 6 The Alien Enemies Act becomes law

6 Victor Marie DuPont arrives at Bordeaux

7 Congress abrogates the French treaties of 1778 and 1788

9 Congress authorizes naval operations on all the seas

9 The Directory places an embargo on American ships in French ports

9 Talleyrand makes overtures to Adams, through Pichon and Murray, for a reconciliation

13 Exequaturs of the French consuls in the United States are revoked

13 Pichon approaches Murray with Talleyrand's overtures

14 The property tax and the Sedition Act become law

15 Talleyrand tells Gerry that France desires a reconciliation

16 Talleyrand asks DuPont about American grievances

16 Congress authorizes further increases in the Army

19 Congress adjourns

21 DuPont submits a report urging a reconciliation with the United States

22 Talleyrand makes a final plea to Gerry for negotiations

27 Talleyrand urges the Executive Directory to adopt a policy of reconciliation toward the United States

31 The Directory repeals obnoxious restrictions on American shipping

August 1 Horatio Nelson defeats the French at Aboukir Bay

7 Dr. George Logan arrives in Paris, and is greeted by Republicans

8 Gerry sails for home from Le Havre

14 Adams opposes Alexander Hamilton's appointment as Inspector General in the Provisional Army

16 The Directory lifts its embargo on American ships

21 Attorney General Charles Lee announces, as an official opinion, the existence of a maritime war

28 Talleyrand, via Pichon, urges negotiations upon Adams

29 Logan leaves Paris carrying a message of peace

31 Toussaint and Maitland sign a secret convention for British evacuation of Saint Domingue

September 6 Pichon shows to Murray Talleyrand's letter urging negotiations

27 Adams favors a temporary alliance with Great Britain

28 Talleyrand writes a letter that indirectly meets Adams's terms for negotiations

October 1 Gerry arrives in the United States

2 Joel Barlow writes to Washington on French desires for peace

3 Adams turns down Francisco de Miranda's scheme for the liberation of Spanish America

October   7 Murray receives Talleyrand's letter that meets Adams's terms for peace talks

         9 Adams capitulates to George Washington's pressure and allows Alexander Hamilton to become Inspector General of the Army

         9 Two of Murray's letters telling of Talleyrand's overtures for peace reach Adams

   20 Adams asks his cabinet's advice on a declaration of war or peace negotiations

   22 Hédouville leaves Saint Domingue for France

   28 Harrison Gray Otis brings the President evidence of the French desire for peace

November   6 Toussaint writes to Adams asking him to renew trade with Saint Domingue

   13 George Logan talks to George Washington

   16 The governor signs the Kentucky Resolutions

   16 The British naval officer, John Loring, humiliates the U.S.S. *Baltimore*

   26 Logan brings his peace message to the President

December   8 Adams delivers his second annual message to the third session of the Fifth Congress. He leaves an opening for peace negotiations

   19 Joseph Bunel, Toussaint's agent, arrives in Philadelphia

   24 The governor signs the Virginia Resolutions

1799

January 15 Thomas Boylston Adams brings words of peace to his father

   15 John Adams asks Timothy Pickering to draft a new treaty for possible use in negotiations with France

   18 Adams sends Gerry's diplomatic correspondence to Congress

   30 As passed by Congress, Logan's law prohibits private diplomacy

February   1 Washington forwards Joel Barlow's letter of France's desire for peace to Adams

  c. 1 Adams receives Talleyrand's assurances—through Murray—for an honorable peace negotiation

    8 Pinckney is honored at a banquet in Charleston

    9 The *Constellation* captures the French frigate *Insurgente*

    9 Congress passes and the President signs a law authorizing trade with Toussaint

   18 Adams nominates Murray as Minister to France to seek peace

   18 Federalist senators meet and decide to block Murray's nomination

February 25 Adams bows to High Federalist pressure and enlarges his second peace mission

March 3 Congress enacts law of retaliation against the French

3 Congress adjourns *sine die*

c. 6 The uncovering of the "Tub Plot" of alleged French agents is announced

7 The Fries Rebellion erupts in Bethlehem, Pennsylvania

10 Adams discusses the nature of the instructions for the Ellsworth commission with the cabinet officers

12 Adams issues a proclamation against the Fries rebels

12 Adams leaves Philadelphia for Quincy

April 2 Maitland arrives in Philadelphia for negotiations on Saint Domingue

18 Edward Stevens, the American Consul, arrives at Cap Français, Saint Domingue

20 American and British diplomats adopt a special agreement, "Heads of Regulations," on policy toward Saint Domingue

May 5 Murray informs Talleyrand of Adams's decision to reopen negotiations

14 Maitland returns to Saint Domingue for new negotiations with Toussaint and Edward Stevens

23 Robert Liston, the British Minister, asks John Adams to investigate the case of Jonathan Robbins

June 13 Toussaint and Maitland sign another secret treaty

18 The *coup d'état* of 30 *Prairal* purges the Executive Directory

20 Talleyrand resigns as Minister of Foreign Relations, and is replaced by Karl Friedrich Reinhard

23 Adams, as a result of the Toussaint-Maitland agreement, lifts the embargo on trade with Toussaint

August 6 Talleyrand's final assurances for an honorable negotiation reach Adams at Quincy

September 14 Adams receives Pickering's instructions for the Ellsworth mission

October 10 Adams arrives in Trenton, New Jersey, to confront his cabinet on what is to be done with the Ellsworth mission

16 Adams ignores his department heads and orders Oliver Ellsworth and William R. Davie to depart for Europe

November 3 Ellsworth and Davie sail for Europe

4 Pickering informs Liston of the Ellsworth commission's instructions

9 The *coup d'état* of 18 *Brumaire* overthrows the Directory and brings Napoleon Bonaparte to power

22 Talleyrand again becomes Minister of Foreign Relations

27 Ellsworth and Davie arrive at Lisbon

December The Consulate repeals remaining harsh decrees against American commerce

December 3 Adams delivers a calm message concerning the French crisis to the first session of the Sixth Congress

14 George Washington dies, and the nation mourns

18 Congress adjourns in Philadelphia

1800

February 1 The *Constellation* defeats *La Vengeance*

7 First Consul Bonaparte orders ten days of public mourning for George Washington

20 Congress votes to suspend Army enlistments

24 Congress extends prohibition on trade with France

March 2 Ellsworth, Davie, and Murray meet in Paris

7 Bonaparte receives the American envoys

April 2 Negotiations with the French begin

May 1 Republicans win the crucial New York elections

3 A Federalist caucus chooses Adams and Charles Cotesworth Pinckney as candidates for President and Vice-President

6 Adams forces James McHenry to resign as Secretary of War

6 Bonaparte leaves Paris for military campaigns in Italy

11 A Republican caucus selects Aaron Burr to run for Vice-President while Jefferson runs for President

12 Adams dismisses Timothy Pickering as Secretary of State

14 Adams signs an act that ends the Provisional Army

14 Congress adjourns

21 Adams pardons Fries and other "rebels"

24 The French commissioners seek new instructions to break a stalemate in the peace negotiations

June 14 Bonaparte defeats the Austrians at the Battle of Marengo

July 3 Bonaparte returns to Paris to take a hand in the peace negotiations

4 Bonaparte offers Malta to Tsar Paul I

20 Bonaparte releases Russian prisoners with honors of war

22 The French peace negotiators dramatically change their terms

25 The British capture the Danish frigate *Freya*

27 The American peace negotiators agree among themselves to break their instructions

August 1 Toussaint triumphs in Saint Domingue

25 The French commissioners offer a compromise settlement in the peace negotiations in Paris

27 Tsar Paul issues invitations for a League of Armed Neutrality

September 5 The British capture Malta

26 After the American peace negotiators suggest a temporary accord, the French and Americans reach an agreement

October 1 The Convention of 1800 is signed in Paris

October   1 The second Treaty of Ildefonso, transferring Louisiana from Spain to France, is signed

        3 The Convention of 1800 is signed for the second time at Môrtefontaine amidst great ceremony

    10 French authorities order their corsairs to stop all attacks on Americans

    14 The voters in the United States choose presidential electors

    22 Parts of Hamilton's letter denouncing Adams are published in Republican gazettes

The text of the Convention of Môrtefontaine is published in the *Moniteur*

    26 Pichon is appointed *chargé d'affaires* in the United States

November   7 News of the Convention of Môrtefontaine reaches the United States

    21 The second session of the Sixth Congress convenes in Washington, D.C.

    22 Adams tells Congress that the outcome of the negotiations in Paris is not yet known

December   2 Edward Thornton becomes British *chargé d'affaires*. Liston returns home

    3 Bonaparte's generals, at Hohenlinden, win the most decisive battle of the War of the Second Coalition

    3 Electors in the various states meet to choose a President and Vice-President

    11 Davie arrives in the United States with the official text of the Convention of Môrtefontaine

    16 Adams submits the convention to the Senate

    16 The League of Armed Neutrality comes into existence

1801

January 23 The Senate rejects the Convention of Môrtefontaine

February 3 After Adams submits the Convention of Môrtefontaine for the second time, the Senate approves it with reservations

    11 The electoral ballots are counted. Jefferson and Burr are tied for the Presidency

    17 After 36 ballots, the House chooses Jefferson as President

March   1 Pichon arrives at Norfolk, Virginia, to begin his duties as *chargé*

    4 Jefferson is inaugurated President of the United States

    5 Jefferson talks with Edward Thornton and assures him that his anti-British sentiments have been exaggerated

    21 The Convention of Aranjuez confirms the transfer of Louisiana to France

    23 Assassins strangle Tsar Paul I

    23 Orders to American cruisers for ending naval hostilities are entrusted to the warship *Herald*

April 2 Admiral Horatio Nelson smashes the Danish fleet at Copenhagen. This is a blow to the League of Armed Neutrality and to Bonaparte

11 The *Herald* sails from Boston harbor

May 26 Jefferson expresses alarm over the rumor of Louisiana's transfer to France

28 William Vans Murray arrives in Paris to negotiate the exchange of ratifications of the Convention of Môrtefontaine

June 6 At a public audience, Murray presents his diplomatic credentials to First Consul Napoleon Bonaparte

17 Russia and Britain, and later Denmark and Sweden, sign the Convention of St. Petersburg that marks the end of the Armed Neutrality

July 4 Tobias Lear, as General Commercial Agent, arrives in Saint Domingue

19 Jefferson and Madison say they are not opposed to France's reconquest of Saint Domingue

23 Murray once again violates his instructions to break a diplomatic stalemate

31 Ratifications of the Convention of 1800 are exchanged in Paris

September 29 News of the exchange of ratifications of the Convention of Môrtefontaine reaches the United States

October 1 The British and French sign an armistice, or preliminary articles to a peace treaty

16 Robert R. Livingston sails for Europe to take up duties as Minister to France

November

late—The ratified Convention of Môrtefontaine reaches the Department of State

December 6 The First Consul receives Robert R. Livingston

11 Jefferson submits the ratified Convention of Môrtefontaine to the Senate for approval

14 Most of the forces for Bonaparte's reconquest of Saint Domingue sail from Brest

19 The Senate resolves that the Convention of Môrtefontaine is fully ratified

21 Jefferson proclaims the convention as the law of the land

1802

January

latter part—General Victor E. Leclerc's armada arrives off Saint Domingue

Convention of Môrtefontaine

Convention signed at Paris September 30, 1800, with additional article and with provisos. Orginal in French and English.
Submitted to the Senate December 16, 1800. (Message of December 15, 1800.) Resolution of advice and consent, with proviso, February 3, 1801. Ratified by the United States February 18, 1801. Ratified by France, with proviso, July 31, 1801. Ratifications exchanged at Paris July 31, 1801. Resubmitted to the Senate December 11, 1801. Resolution of the Senate December 19, 1801, declaring the convention fully ratified. Proclaimed December 21, 1801.

Convention entre la République française et les Etats-unis d'Amérique.

Le Premier Consul de la République française, au nom du Peuple français, et le Président des Etats-unis d'amérique, également animés du désir de mettre fin aux différens qui sont survenus entre les deux Etats, ont respectivement nommé leurs Plénipotentiaires; et leur ont donné pleins pouvoirs pour négocier sur ces différens et les terminer; c'est à dire, le premier Consul de la République française, au nom du Peuple français, a nommé pour Plénipotentiaires de la dite République les Citoyens Joseph Bona-

Convention between the French Republic, and the United States of America.

The Premier Consul of the French Republic in the name of the People of France, and the President of the United States of America, equally desirous to terminate the differences which have arisen between the two States, have respectively appointed their Plenipotentiaries, and given them full power to treat upon those differences and to terminate the same, that is to say, the Premier Consul of the French Republic, in the name of the People of France has appointed for the Plenipotentiaries of the said Republic, the Citizens, Jo-

parte ex Ambassadeur de la République française à Rome et Conseiller d'Etat; Charles-Pierre Claret Fleurieu, Membre de l'Institut national et du Bureau des Longitudes de France, et Conseiller d'Etat, Président de la Section de la Marine; et Pierre Louis Roederer, Membre de l'Institut national de france et Conseiller d'Etat, Président de la Section de l'Intérieur—

Et le Président des Etats-unis d'Amérique, par et avec l'avis et le consentement du Senat desdits Etats, a nommé pour leurs plenipotentiaires, Oliver Ellsworth, chef de la justice des Etats-unis; William, Richardson, Davie, cidevant Gouverneur de l'Etat de la Caroline Septentrionale; et William Vans-Murray, Ministre résident des Etats-unis à la Haye.

Lesquels, après avoir fait l'échange de leurs pleins pouvoirs, longuement et mûrement discuté les intérêts respectifs, sont convenus des Articles Suivans.

seph Bonaparte, Ex-Ambassador of the Republic at Rome, and Counsellor of State, Charles Pierre Claret Fleurieu, member of the national Institute, and of the Board of longitude of France, and Counsellor of State—President of the section of the Marine, and Pierre Louis Roederer, member of the national institute of France; and Counsellor of State—President of the Section of the Interior: and the President of the United States of America by and with the advice, and consent of the Senate of said States, has appointed for their Plenipotentiaries, Oliver Ellsworth, Chief Justice of the United States William Richardson Davie, late Governor of the State of North Carolina, and William Vans Murray, Minister Resident of the United States at the Hague, who after having exchanged their full powers, and after full and mature discussion of the respective interests have agreed on the following articles.

ARTICLE 1 ᵉʳ

Il y aura une Paix ferme, inviolable et universelle et une amitié vraie et Sincère entre la République française et les Etats-Unis d'Amérique, ainsi qu'entre leurs pays, territoires, villes et places et entre leurs Citoyens et habitans, sans exception de personnes ni de lieux.

ARTICLE I

There shall be a firm, inviolable, and universal peace, and a true and sincere Friendship between the French Republic, and the United States of America, and between their respective countries territories, cities, towns, and people without exception of persons, or places.

ART. 2.

Les Ministres plénipotentiaires des deux parties ne pouvant, pour le présent, s'accorder relativement au Traîté d'alliance du six février mil sept cent soixante dix huit, au

ARTICLE II

The Ministers Plenipotentiary of the two Parties, not being able to agree at present, respecting the Treaty of Alliance of 6ᵗʰ February 1778, the Treaty of Amity and Com-

Traité d'amitié et de commerce de la même date et à la Convention en date du quatorze Novembre mil sept cent quatre vingt huit, non plus que relativement aux indemnités mutuellement dues ou réclamées; les parties négocieront ultérieurement sur ces objets dans un tems convenable et jusqu'à ce qu'elles se soient accordées sur ces points, les dits Traités et Convention n'auront point d'effet et les relations des deux Nations seront règlées ainsi qu'il suit.

merce of the same date, and the . . . Convention of 14th November 1788, nor upon the indemnities mutually due, or claimed, the Parties will negotiate further on these subjects at a convenient time, and untill they may have agreed upon these points, the said Treaties, and . . . Convention shall have no operation, and the relations of the two Countries shall be regulated as follows.

ART. 3.

Les Bâtiments d'Etat qui ont été pris de part et d'autre, ou qui pourraient être pris avant l'échange des ratifications, seront rendus.

ARTICLE III

The Public Ships, which have been taken on one part, and the other, or which may be taken before the exchange of ratifications shall be restored.

ART. 4.

Les Propriétés capturées et non encore condamnées définitivement, ou qui pourront être capturées avant l'échange des ratifications, excepté les Marchandises de Contrebande destinées pour un port ennemi, seront rendues mutuellement sur les preuves suivantes de propriété, savoir:

De part et d'autre les preuves de propriété relativement aux Navires marchands, armés ou non armés, seront un passeport dans la forme suivante:

A tous ceux qui les présentes verront soit notoire que faculté et permission a été accordée à ......
...... Maître ou Commandant du Navire appelé .... de la ville de .... de la capacité de .... tonneaux ou environ, se trouvant présentement dans

ARTICLE IV

Property captured, and not yet definitively condemned, or which may be captured before the exchange of ratifications, (contraband goods destined to an Enemy's port excepted) shall be mutually restored on the following proofs of ownership, viz, The proof on both sides, with respect to Merchant Ships, whether armed, or unarmed, shall be a Passport in the form following

To all who shall see these presents. Greeting: It is hereby made known that leave, and permission has been given to .... Master, and Commander of the Ship called .... of the town of ....
.... burthen ...... Tons, or thereabouts, lying at present in the

le port et havre de .... et
destiné pour .... chargé
de .... qu'après que son
navire a été visité, et avant son
départ, il prêtera serment entre les
mains des officiers autorisés à cet
effet, que le dit Navire appartient à
un ou plusieurs sujets de ....
.... dont l'acte sera mis à la fin des
présentes, de même qu'il gardera et
fera garder par son équipage les
Ordonnances et règlements mari-
times, et remettra une Liste signée
et confirmée par témoins, contenant
les noms et surnoms, les lieux de
naissance et la demeure des personnes composant l'Equipage de son
navire, et de tous ceux qui s'y embar-
queront, lesquels il ne recevra pas à
bord sans la connaissance et permission des officiers autorisés à ce; et
dans chaque port ou havre où il en-
trera avec son navire, il montrera la
présente permission aux officiers à
ce autorisés, et leur fera un rapport
fidèle de ce qui s'est passé durant son
voyage, et il portera les Couleurs,
Armes, et Enseignes de (la République française ou des Etats-Unis)
durant son dit voyage, en témoin de
quoi nous avons signé les présentes,
les avons fait contresigner par......
.... et y avons fait apposer le
Sceau de nos armes.
      Donné à .... le ....
.... de l'an de grace le ......

Et ce passeport suffira sans
autre pièce, nonobstant tout règlement contraire. Il ne sera pas exigé
que ce passeport ait été renouvellé
ou révoqué, quelque nombre de
voyages que le dit navire ait pu
faire, à moins qu'il ne soit revenu
chez lui dans l'espace d'une année.
      Par rapport à la Cargaison, les

port, and haven of ....
and bound for .... and
laden with .... after that
his ship has been visited, and before sailing, he shall make oath before the Officers, who have the jurisdiction of maritime affairs, that the
said Ship belongs to one, or more of
the subjects of .... the act
whereof shall be put at the end of
these presents; as likewise that he
will keep, and cause to be kept by
his crew on board, the marine or-
dinances, and regulations, and enter
in the proper Office a list, signed, and
witnessed, containing the names, and
surnames, the places of birth, and
abode of the crew of his Ship, and of
all who shall embark on board her,
whom he shall not take on board,
without the knowledge, and permission of the Officers of the Marine;
and in every port, or Haven, where
he shall enter with his ship, he shall
shew this present leave to the Officers, and Judges of the Marine, and
shall give a faithful account to them,
of what passed, and was done during
his voyage, and he shall carry the
colours, arms, and ensigns of the
(French Republic or the United
States) during his voyage. In witness
whereof we have signed these presents, and put the seal of our arms
thereunto, and caused the same to be
countersigned by .... at
.... the .... day
of .... A. D. ....
      And this Passport will be suffi-
cient without any other paper, any
ordinance to the contrary notwithstanding: which Passport shall not be
deemed requisite to have been renewed, or recalled, whatever number
of voyages the said Ship may have
made, unless she shall have returned
home within the space of a year.

preuves seront des Certificats contenant le détail de la Cargaison, le lieu d'où le Bâtiment est parti et celui où il va, de manière que les Marchandises deffendues et de contrebande puissent être distinguées par les certificats, lesquels certificats auront été faits par les Officiers de l'endroit d'oùle Navire sera parti, dans la forme usitée dans le Pays; et si ces passeports, ou certificats, ou les uns et les autres ont été détruits par accident ou enlevés de force, leur défaut pourra être supplée par toutes les autres preuves de propriété admissibles d'après l'usage général des Nations.

Pour les Bâtiments autres que les Navires marchands, les preuves seront la Commission dont ils sont porteurs.

Cet article aura son effet à dater de la signature de la présente Convention, et si, à dater de la dite signature, des propriétés sont condamnées contrairement à l'esprit de la dite Convention avant qu'on ait connaissance de cette stipulation, la propriété ainsi condamnée sera, sans délai, rendue ou payée.

Proof with respect to the cargo, shall be certificates containing the several particulars of the cargo, the place whence the Ship sailed, and whither she is bound, so that the forbidden, and contraband goods may be distinguished by the Certificates: which certificates shall have been made out by the Officers of the place, whence the ship set sail, in the accustomed form of the country. And if such passport or certificates, or both, shall have been destroyed by accident or taken away by force, their deficiency may be supplied by such other proofs of ownership as are admissible by the general usage of nations. Proof with respect to other than Merchant ships, shall be the commission they bear.

This article shall take effect from the date of the signature of the present Convention. And if from the date of the said signature, any property shall be condemned contrary to the intent of the said Convention before the knowledge of this stipulation shall be obtained, the property so condemned shall without delay be restored or paid for.

ART. 5.

Les Dettes contractées par l'une des deux Nations envers les particuliers de l'autre, ou par des particuliers de l'une envers des particuliers de l'autre, seront acquittées ou le payement en sera poursuivi comme s'il n'y avait eu aucune mésintelligence entre les deux Etats. Mais cette clause ne s'étendra point aux indemnités réclamées pour des Captures ou pour des Condamnations;

ARTICLE V

The debts contracted by one of the two nations, with individuals of the other, or by the individuals of one, with the individuals of the other shall be paid, or the payment may be prosecuted in the same manner, as if there had been no misunderstanding between the two States. But this clause shall not extend to indemnities claimed on account of captures, or confiscations.

ART. 6.

Le Commerce entre les deux parties sera libre: Les Vaisseaux des deux Nations et leurs Corsaires, ainsi que leurs prises, seront traités dans les Ports respectifs comme ceux de la Nation la plus favorisée; et, en général, les deux parties jouiront dans les Ports l'une de l'autre, par rapport au Commerce et à la navigation, des Priviléges de la Nation la plus favorisée.

ARTICLE VI.

Commerce between the Parties shall be free. The vessels of the two nations, and their Privateers, as well as their prizes, shall be treated in the respective ports, as those of the nation the most favoured; and in general the two parties shall enjoy in the ports of each other, in regard to commerce, and navigation, the privileges of the most favoured nation.

ART. 7.

Les Citoyens et habitans des Etats-unis pourront disposer par testament, donation ou autrement de leurs biens meubles et immeubles possédés dans le territoire Européen de la République française, et les Citoyens de la République française auront la même faculté à l'égard des biens, meubles et immeubles possédés dans le territoire des Etats-Unis, en faveur de telles personnes que bon leur semblera. Les Citoyens et habitans d'un des deux Etats qui seront héritiers des biens meubles ou immeubles situés dans l'autre, pourront succéder *ab intestat,* sans qu'ils ayent besoin de Lettres de naturalité, et sans que l'effet de cette stipulation leur puisse être contesté ou empêché, sous quelque prétexte que ce soit; et seront les dits héritiers, soit à titre particulier, soit *ab intestat,* exempts de tout droit quelconque chez les deux nations. Il est convenu que cet article ne dérogera en aucune manière aux loix qui sont à présent en vigueur chez les deux Nations ou qui pourraient être promulguées à la suite contre l'émigra-

ARTICLE VII

The Citizens, and inhabitants of the United States shall be at liberty to dispose by testament, donation, or otherwise, of their goods, moveable, and immoveable, holden in the territory of the French Republic in Europe, and the Citizens of the French Republic, shall have the same liberty with regard to goods, moveable, and immoveable, holden in the territory of the United States, in favor of such persons as they shall think proper. The Citizens and inhabitants of either of the two countries, who shall be heirs of goods, moveable, or immoveable in the other shall be able to succeed *ab intestato,* without being obliged to obtain letters of naturalization, and without having the effect of this provision contested or impeded under any pretext whatever: and the said heirs, whether such by particular title, or *ab intestato,* shall be exempt from every duty whatever in both countries. It is agreed that this article, shall in no manner derogate from the laws, which either State may now have in force, or hereafter may enact to prevent emigra-

tion; et aussi que dans le cas où les loix de l'un des deux Etats limiteraient pour les Etrangers l'exercice des droits de la propriété sur les immeubles, on pourrait vendre ces immeubles ou en disposer autrement en faveur d'habitans ou de citoyens du pays où ils seraient situés, et il sera libre à l'autre nation d'établir de semblables loix.

tion: and also that in case the laws of either of the two States should restrain Strangers from the exercise of the rights of Property with respect to real estate, such real estate may be sold, or otherwise disposed of, to citizens, or inhabitants of the country where it may be, and the other nation shall be at liberty to enact similar laws.

ART. 8.

Pour favoriser de part et d'autre le Commerce, il est convenu que si, ce qu'à dieu ne plaise, la guerre éclatait entre les deux Nations, on allouera de part et d'autre aux Marchands et autres Citoyens ou habitans respectifs six mois après la déclaration de guerre, pendant lequel tems ils auront la faculté de se retirer avec leurs effets et meubles qu'ils pourront emmener, envoyer ou vendre comme ils le voudront sans le moindre empêchement. Leurs effets et encore moins leurs personnes ne pourront point pendant ce temps de six-mois, être saisis. Au contraire, on leur donnera des passeports qui seront valables pour le temps nécessaire à leur retour chez eux; et ces passeports seront donnés pour eux ainsi que pour leurs bâtiments et effets qu'ils desireront emmener ou renvoyer: ces passeports serviront de sauf-conduits contre toute insulte et contre toute capture de la part des Corsaires, tant contr'eux que contre leurs effets; et si dans le terme cidessus désigné, il leur était fait par l'une des parties, ses Citoyens ou ses habitans, quelque tort dans leurs personnes ou dans leurs effets, on leur en donnera satisfaction complète.

ARTICLE VIII

To favor commerce on both sides, it is agreed that in case a war should break out between the two nations, which God forbid, the term of six months after the declaration of . . . war, shall be allowed to the Merchants and other citizens and inhabitants respectively, on one side, and the other, during which time they shall be at liberty, to with draw themselves, with their effects, and moveables, which they shall be at liberty to carry, send away, or sell, as they please, without the least obstruction; nor shall their effects, much less their persons be seized during such term of six months; on the contrary Passports which shall be valid for a time necessary for their return, shall be given to them, for their vessels, and the effects which they shall be willing to send away, or carry with them; and such Passports shall be a safe conduct against all insults, and prizes, which Privateers may attempt against their persons and effects. And if any thing be taken from them, or any injury done to them, or their effects, by one of the parties, their citizens, or Inhabitants, within the term above prescribed, full satisfaction shall be made to them on that account

ART. 9.

Les Dettes dues par des individus de l'une des deux Nations aux individus de l'autre ne pourront, dans aucuns cas de guerre ou de démélés nationaux, être sequestrées ou confisquées, non plus que les actions ou fonds qui se trouveraient dans les fonds publics ou dans des banques publiques ou particulières.

ARTICLE IX

Neither the debts due from individuals of the one nation, to individuals of the other, nor shares, nor monies which they may have in . . . public funds, or in the public, or private banks, shall ever, in any event of war, or national difference be sequestered, or confiscated

ART. 10.

Les deux parties contractantes pourront nommer pour protéger le Négoce, des Agens commerciaux qui résideront en france et dans les Etats-Unis; chacune des parties pourra excepter telle place qu'elle jugera à propos, des lieux où la résidence de ces Agens pourra être fixée; avant qu'aucun agent puisse exercer ses fonctions, il devra être accepté dans les formes reçues, par la partie chez laquelle il est envoyé; et quand il aura été accepté et pourvu de son *exequatur,* il jouira des droits et prérogatives dont jouiront les Agens semblables des Nations les plus favorisées.

ARTICLE X

It shall be free for the two contracting parties to appoint commercial agents for the protection of trade, to reside in France, and the United States. Either party may except such place as may be thought proper, from the residence of these agents. Before any Agent shall exercise his functions, he shall be accepted in the usual forms, by the party to whom he is sent, and when he shall have been accepted and furnished with his exequatur, he shall enjoy the rights, and prerogatives of the similar Agents of the most favored nations.

ART. 11.

Les Citoyens de la République française ne payeront dans les ports, hâvres, rades, contrées, isles, cités et lieux des Etats-unis, d'autres ni de plus grands droits, impôts de quelque nature qu'ils puissent être, quelques noms qu'ils puissent avoir, que ceux que les Nations les plus favorisées sont ou seront tenues de payer; et ils jouiront de tous les

ARTICLE XI

The Citizens of the French Republic shall pay in the ports, havens, roads, countries, islands cities, and towns of the United States, no other or greater duties, or imposts, of what nature soever they may be, or by what name soever called, than those, which the nations most favored are, or shall be obliged to pay, and they shall enjoy all the rights, liberties,

droits, libertés, priviléges, immunités et exemptions en fait de négoce, navigation et commerce, soit en passant d'un port des dits Etats à un autre, soit en y allant ou en revenant de quelque partie ou pour quelque partie du monde que ce soit, dont les Nations susdites jouissent ou jouiront.

Et réciproquement, les Citoyens des Etats-unis jouiront dans le territoire de la République française en Europe, des mêmes priviléges, immunités, tant pour leurs biens et leurs personnes que pour ce qui concerne le Négoce, la Navigation et le Commerce.

priviledges, immunities, and exemptions, in trade, navigation and commerce, whether in passing from one port in the said States, to another, or in going to, and from the same, from, and to any part of the world, which the said nations do, or shall enjoy. And the Citizens of the United States shall reciprocally enjoy in the territories of the French Republic, in Europe, the same priviledges, and immunities, as well for their property, and persons, as for what concerns trade, Navigation, and Commerce.

ART. 12.

Les Citoyens des deux Nations pourront conduire leurs vaisseaux et marchandises (en exceptant toujours la Contrebande) de tout port quelconque dans un autre port appartenant à l'ennemi de l'autre nation. Ils pourront naviguer et commercer en toute liberté et sécurité avec leurs navires et marchandises dans les pays, ports et places des ennemis des deux parties, ou de l'une ou de l'autre partie, sans obstacles et sans entraves, et non seulement passer directement des places et ports de l'ennemi sus-mentionnés, dans les ports et places neutres; mais encore de toute place appartenant à un ennemi, dans toute autre place appartenant à un ennemi, qu'elle soit ou ne soit pas soumise à la même juridiction, à moins que ces places ou ports ne soyent reéllement bloqués, assiégés ou investis.

Et dans le cas, comme il arrive souvent, où les vaisseaux feraient voile pour une place ou port apparte-

ARTICLE XII

It shall be lawful for the Citizens of either Country to sail with their ships and Merchandize (contraband goods always excepted) from any port whatever, to any port of the enemy of the other, and to sail, and trade with their ships, and Merchandize, with perfect security, and liberty, from the countries ports, and places, of those who are enemies of both, or of either party, without any opposition, or disturbance whatsoever, and to pass not only directly from the places and ports of the enemy aforementioned to neutral ports, and places, but also from one place belonging to an enemy, to another place belonging to an enemy, whether they be under the jurisdiction of the same power, or under several, unless such ports, or places shall be actually blockaded, beseiged, or invested.

And whereas it frequently happens that Vessels sail for a port or place belonging to an enemy without

nant à un ennemi, ignorant qu'ils sont bloqués, assiégés ou investis, il est convenu que tout navire qui se trouvera dans une pareille circonstance sera détourné de cette place ou port sans qu'on puisse le retenir ni confisquer aucune partie de sa Cargaison (à moins qu'elle ne soit de contrebande ou qu'il ne soit prouvé que le dit navire, après avoir été averti du blocus ou investissement, a voulu rentrer dans ce même port); mais il lui sera permis d'aller dans tout autre port ou place qu'il jugera convenable. Aucun Navire de l'une ou l'autre nation, entré dans un port ou place, avant qu'ils ayent été réellement bloqués assiégés ou investis par l'autre, ne pourra être empêché de sortir avec sa Cargaison; s'il s'y trouve lorsque la dite place sera rendue, le Navire et sa Cargaison ne pourront être confisqués mais seront remis aux propriétaires.

knowing that the same is either beseiged, blockaded, or invested, it is agreed that every vessel so circumstanced may be turned away from such port, or place, but she shall not be detained, nor any part of her cargo if not contraband be confiscated, unless after notice of such blockade or investment, she shall again attempt to enter: but she shall be permitted to go to any other port or place she shall think proper. Nor shall any vessel of either, that may have entered into such port, or place, before the same was actually beseiged, blockaded, or invested by the other, be restrained from quitting such place with her cargo, nor if found therein after the reduction and surrender of such place, shall such vessel or her cargo be liable to confiscation but they shall be restored to the Owners thereof.

ART. 13.

Pour règler ce qu'on entendra par Contrebande de guerre, seront compris sous cette dénomination la poudre, le salpêtre, les pétards, mêches, balles boulets, bombes, grenades, carcasses, piques, hallebardes, épées, ceinturons, pistolets, fourreaux, selles de Cavalerie, harnois, canons, mortiers avec leurs affuts, et généralement toutes armes et munitions de guerre et ustensiles à l'usage des troupes. Tous les articles ci dessus, toutes les fois qu'ils seront destinés pour le port d'un ennemi, sont déclarés de contrebande et justement soumis à la confiscation. Mais le batiment sur lequel ils étaient chargés, ainsi que le reste de la Cargaison, seront regardés comme libres et ne

ARTICLE XIII

In order to regulate what shall be deemed contraband of war, there shall be comprised under that denomination, Gun-powder, salt-petre Petards, match, ball, bombs, grenades, carcasses, Pikes, Halberds, swords, belts, Pistols, holsters, cavalry saddles, and furniture, Cannon, Mortars, their carriages, and beds, and generally all kinds of arms, ammunition of war, and instruments fit for the use of Troops, all the above articles whenever they are destined to the port of an enemy, are hereby declared to be contraband, and just objects of confiscation: but the vessel in which they are laden, and the residue of the cargo shall be considered free, and not in any manner infected by

pourront en aucune manière être vi-
ciés par les Marchandises de Contrebande, soit qu'ils appartiennent à
un même ou à différens propriétaires.

the prohibited goods, whether belonging to the same or a different
Owner.

ART. 14.

Il est stipulé par le present
traité, que les Bâtiments libres as-
sureront également la liberté des
Marchandises, et qu'on jugera libre
toutes les choses qui se trouveront à
bord des Navires appartenant aux
Citoyens d'une des parties contractantes, quand même le chargement ou partie d'icelui, appartien-
draient aux ennemis de l'une des
deux; bien entendu néanmoins que
la contrebande sera toujours exceptée. Il est également convenu que
cette même liberté s'étendra aux personnes qui pourraient se trouver à
bord du bâtiment libre, quand même
elles seraient ennemies de l'une des
deux parties contractantes; et elles
ne pourront être enlevées des dits
navires libres à moins qu'elles ne
soyent militaires et actuellement au
Service de l'ennemi.

ARTICLE XIV.

It is hereby stipulated that free
ships shall give a freedom to goods,
and that every thing shall be deemed
to be free, and exempt which shall
be found on board the ships belonging to the citizens of either of the
contracting parties, altho' the whole
lading, or any part thereof should
appertain to the enemies of either,
contraband goods being always excepted. It is also agreed in like manner, that the same liberty be extended to persons, who are on board a
free ship, with this effect, that altho'
they be enemies to either party, they
are not to be taken out of that free
ship, unless they are soldiers and in
actual service of the enemy.

ART. 15.

On est convenu, au contraire,
que tout ce qui se trouvera chargé
par les Citoyens respectifs sur des
Navires appartenant aux ennemis de
l'autre partie, ou à leurs sujets sera
confisqué sans distinction des marchandises prohibées ou non prohibées, ainsi et de même que si elles
appartenaient à l'ennemi; à l'exception toutefois des effets et marchandises qui auront été mis à bord
desdits navires avant la déclaration
de guerre, ou même après la dite

ARTICLE XV.

On the contrary, it is agreed,
that whatever shall be found to be
laden by the citizens of either party
on any ship, belonging to the enemies
of the other, or their Citizens, shall
be confiscated without distinction of
goods, contraband, or not contraband, in the same manner, as if it
belonged to the enemy, except such
goods, and merchandizes as were put
on board such ship before the declaration of war, or even after such declaration, if so be it were done, with-

déclaration, si au moment du chargement on a pu l'ignorer; de manière que les marchandises des Citoyens des deux parties, soit qu'elles se trouvent du nombre de celles de contrebande ou autrement, lesquelles, comme il vient d'être dit, auront été mises à bord d'un vaisseau appartenant à l'ennemi avant la guerre ou même après ladite déclartion, lorsqu'on l'ignorait, ne seront en aucune manière sujettes à confiscation, mais seront fidèlement et de bonne foi rendues sans délai à leurs propriétaires qui les réclameront; bien entendu néanmions qu'il ne soit pas permis de porter dans les ports ennemis les marchandises qui seront de contrebande. Les deux parties contractantes conviennent que le terme de deux mois passé, depuis la déclaration de guerre, leurs citoyens respectifs, de quelque partie du monde qu'ils viennent, ne pourront plus alléguer l'ignorance dont il est question dans le présent article.

out knowledge of such declaration, so that the goods of the citizens of either party, whether they be of the nature of such as are prohibited, or otherwise, which as is aforesaid were put on board any ship belonging to an enemy, before the war, or after the declaration of the same, without the knowledge of it, shall no ways be liable to confiscation, but shall well, and truly be restored without delay to the Proprietors demanding the same; but so as that if the said Merchandizes be contraband it shall not be any ways lawful, to carry them afterwards to any ports belonging to the enemy. The two contracting parties agree, that the term of two months being passed after the declaration of war, their respective citizens, from whatever part of the world they come, shall not plead the ignorance mentioned in this Article.

ART. 16.

Les Navires marchands appartenans à des Citoyens de l'une ou l'autre des deux parties contractantes, lorsqu'ils voudront passer dans le port de l'ennemi de l'une des deux parties, et que leur voyage, ainsi que les effets de leur Cargaison pourront donner de justes soupçons, les dits navires seront obligés d'exhiber, en pleine mer comme dans les ports, ou rades, non seulement leurs passeports; mais encore leurs certificats prouvant que ces effets ne sont point de la même espèce que ceux de contrebande spécifiés en l'article treize de la présente Convention.

ARTICLE XVI.

The Merchant ships belonging to the citizens of either of the contracting parties, which shall be bound to a port of the enemy of one of the parties, and concerning whose voyage, and the articles of their cargo, there shall be just grounds of suspicion, shall be obliged to exhibit, as well upon the high seas, as in the ports or roads, not only their passports, but likewise their certificates, shewing that their goods are not of the quality of those which are specified to be contraband in the 13th Article of the present Convention.

ART. 17.

Et afin d'éviter des Captures sur des Soupçons frivoles, et de prévenir les dommages qui en résultent, il est convenu que quand une des deux parties sera en guerre et l'autre neutre, les Navires de la partie neutre seront pourvus des passeports semblables à ceux spécifiés dans l'article quatre; de manière qu'il puisse par là apparaître que les navires appartiennent véritablement à la partie neutre. Ces passeports seront valides pour un nombre quelconque de voyages, mais il seront renouvellés chaque année, si le navire retourne chez lui dans l'espace d'une année.

Si ces Navires sont chargés, ils seront pourvus, non seulement des passeports sus-mentionnés, mais aussi de certificats semblables à ceux mentionnés au même article, de manière que l'on puisse connaître s'il y a à bord des marchandises de contrebande. Il ne sera exigé aucune autre pièce, non obstant tout usage et règlement contraires; et s'il n'apparait pas par ces certificats qu'il y ait des marchandises de contrebande à bord, les navires seront laissés à leur destination. Si au contraire il apparait, par ces certificats, que les dit navires ayent des Marchandises de contrebande à bord et que le Commandant offre de les délivrer, l'offre sera acceptée et le Navire sera rèmis en liberté de poursuivre son voyage; à moins que la quantité des marchandises de contrebande ne soit trop grande pour pouvoir être prise convenablement à bord du vaisseau de guerre ou Corsaire; dans ce cas le navire pourra être amené dans le port pour y délivrer ladite marchandise.

Si un Navire est trouvé sans

ARTICLE XVII

And that captures on light suspicions may be avoided, and injuries thence arising be prevented, it is agreed, that when one party shall be engaged in war and the other party be neuter, the ships of the neutral party shall be furnished with passports similar to that described in the fourth Article, that it may appear thereby that the ships really belong to the citizens of the neutral party: they shall be valid for any number of Voyages, but shall be renewed every year, that is if the ship happens to return home in the space of a year. If the ships are laden they shall be provided not only with the passports above mentioned, but also with certificates similar to those described in the same article, so that it may be known whether they carry any contraband goods. No other paper shall be required, any usage or ordinance to the contrary notwithstanding. And if it shall not appear from the said certificates that there are contraband goods on board, the ships shall be permitted to proceed on their voyage. If it shall appear from the certificates that there are contraband goods on board any such ship, and the commander of the same shall offer to deliver them up, the offer shall be accepted, and the ship shall be at liberty to pursue it's voyage; unless the quantity of the contraband goods be greater than can conveniently be received on board the ship of war, or privateer, in which case the ship may be carried into port for the delivery of the same. If any ship shall not be furnished with such passport, or certificates, as are above required for the same, such case may be exam-

avoir le passeport ou les Certificats cidessus exgés, l'affaire sera examinée par les juges ou tribunaux compétens et s'il conste par d'autres documens ou preuves admissibles par l'usage des Nations, que le Navire appartient à des Citoyens de la partie neutre, il ne sera pas condamné et il sera remis en liberté avec son chargement, la Contrebande exceptée, et aura la liberté de poursuivre sa route.

Si le Capitaine nommé dans le passeport du Navire venait à mourir ou a être ôté par toute autre cause et qu'un autre fût nommé à sa place, le Navire et Sa Cargaison n'en seront pas moins en Sûreté et le passeport demeurera dans toute sa force.

ined by a proper judge, or tribunal, and if it shall appear from other documents, or proofs, admissible by the usage of nations, that the ship belongs to the citizens of the neutral party it shall not be confiscated, but shall be released with her cargo (contraband goods excepted) and be permitted to proceed on her voyage.

If the Master of a Ship named in the passport should happen to die, or be removed by any other cause, and another put in his place, the ship, and cargo shall nevertheless be equally secure, and the passport remain in full force.

ART. 18.

Si les Bâtiments des Citoyens de l'une ou l'autre nation sont rencontrés le long des Côtes ou en pleine mer, par quelque vaisseau de guerre, ou Corsaire de l'autre; pour prévenir tout désordre, les-dits vaisseaux ou Corsaires, se tiendront hors de la portée du Canon, et enverront leur canot à bord du navire marchand qu'ils auront rencontré: ils n'y pourront entrer qu'au nombre de deux ou trois hommes et demander au patron ou capitaine du dit navire, exhibition du passeport concernant la propriété dudit navire, fait d'après la formule prescrite dans l'article quatre ainsi que les certificats sus-mentionnés relatifs à la Cargaison. Il est expressement convenu que le neutre ne pourra être contraint d'aller à bord du Vaisseau visitant pour y faire l'exhibition demandée des papiers, ou pour toute autre information quelconque.

ARTICLE XVIII

If the ships of the citizens of either of the parties, shall be met with, either sailing along the coasts or on the high seas, by any ship of war, or privateer of the other; for the avoiding of any disorder, the said ships of war, or privateers shall remain out of Canon-shot, and may send their boats on board the Merchant ship, which they shall so meet with, and may enter her to the number of two, or three men only, to whom the Master or commander of such ship, shall exhibit his passport concerning the property of the ship made out according to the form prescribed in the fourth Article. And it is expressly agreed that the neutral party shall in no case be required to go on board the examining vessel for the purpose of exhibiting his papers, or for any other examination whatever.

ART. 19.

Il est expressément convenu par les parties contractantes, que les Stipulations ci dessus relatives à la conduite qui sera tenue à la mer par les Croiseurs de la partie belligérante envers les Bâtiments de la partie neutre, ne s'appliqueront qu'aux bâtiments naviguans sans convoi: et dans le cas où les dits bâtiments seraient convoyés, l'intention des parties étant d'observer tous les égards dûs à la protection du pavillon arboré sur les vaisseaux publics, on ne pourra point en faire la visite; mais la déclaration verbale du Commandant de l'escorte, que les navires de son Convoi appartiennent à la Nation dont ils porte le pavillon, et qu'ils n'ont aucune contrebande à bord, sera regardée par les Croiseurs respectifs comme pleinement Suffisante; le deux parties s'engageant réciproquement à ne point admettre sous la protection de leurs convois des bâtiments qui porteraient des marchandises prohibées à une destination ennemie.

ARTICLE XIX

It is expressly agreed by the contracting parties, that the stipulations above mentioned, relative to the conduct to be observed on the sea by the cruizers of the belligerent party, towards the ships of the neutral party, shall be applied only to ships sailing without convoy; and when the said ships shall be convoyed, it being the intention of the parties to observe all the regard due to the protection of the Flag displayed by public ships, it shall not be lawful to visit them: but the verbal declaration of the commander of the convoy, that the ships he convoys belong to the nation whose flag he carries, and that they have no contraband goods on board shall be considered by the respective cruizers as fully sufficient: the two parties reciprocally engaging not to admit under the protection of their convoys, ships which shall carry contraband goods destined to an enemy.

ART. 20.

Dans le cas où les bâtiments seront pris ou arrêtés sous prétexte de porter à l'ennemi quelqu'article de Contrebande, le *Capteur* donnera un reçu des papiers du bâtiment qu'il retiendra; lequel reçu sera joint à une liste énonciative desdits papiers. Il ne sera point permis de forcer ni d'ouvrir les écoutilles, coffres, caisses, caissons balles ou vases trouvés à bord du dit navire, ni d'enlever la moindre chose des effets, avant que la Cargaison ait été débarquée en présence des Officiers compétens qui

ARTICLE XX.

In all cases where vessels shall be captured, or detained, under pretence of carrying to the enemy contraband goods, the Captor shall give a receipt for such of the papers of the Vessel as he shall retain, which receipt shall be annexed to a descriptive list of the said papers: and it shall be unlawful to break up, or open the hatches, chests, trunks, casks, bales, or vessels found on board, or remove the smallest part of the goods, unless the lading be brought on shore, in presence of the

feront un inventaire desdits effets: ils ne pourront, en aucune manière être vendus, échangés ou aliénés, à moins qu'après une procédure légale, le juge ou les juges compétens, n'ayent porté contre les dits effets sentence de confiscation (en exceptant toujours le Navire et les autres objets qu'il contient).

competent officers, and an inventory be made by them of the said goods. Nor shall it be lawful to sell, exchange or alienate the same, in any manner, unless there shall have been lawful process, and the competent judge or judges shall have pronounced against such goods sentence of confiscation, saving always the ship and the other goods which it contains.

ART. 21.

Pour que le bâtiment et la Cargaison soyent surveillés avec soin, et pour empêcher les dégâts, il est arrêté que le Patron, Capitaine ou Subrécargue du Navire *capturé,* ne pourront être éloignés du bord, soit pendant que le navire sera en mer après avoir été pris, soit pendant la procédure qui pourra avoir lieu contre lui, sa Cargaison, ou quelque chose y relative.

Dans le Cas où le Navire appartenant à des Citoyens de l'une ou l'autre partie, serait pris saisi et retenu pour être jugé, ses officiers, passagers et équipage seront traités avec humanité. Ils ne pourront être emprisonnés, dépouillés de leurs vêtemens, ni de l'argent à leur usage, qui ne pourra excéder pour le Capitaine, le Subrécargue, et le Second cinq cens dollars chacun et pour les matelots et passagers cent dollars chacun.

ARTICLE XXI.

And that proper care may be taken of the vessel and cargo, and embezzlement prevented, it is agreed that it shall not be lawful to remove the master or commander or Supercargo of any captured ship, from on board thereof, either during the time the ship may be at sea, after her capture, or pending the proceedings against her, or her cargo, or any thing relative thereto. And in all cases where a vessel of the citizens of either party shall be captured, or seized, and held for adjudication, her officers, passengers, and crew shall be hospitably treated. They shall not be imprisoned, nor deprived of any part of their wearing apparel, nor of the possession, and use of their money, not exceeding for the captain super cargo, and mate five hundred dollars each and for the Sailors and Passengers, one hundred dollars each.

ART. 22.

Il est de plus convenu que dans tous les cas les tribunaux établis pour les causes de prises dans les pays où les prises seront conduites pourront seuls en prendre connaissance, et quelque jugement que le tribunal de

ARTICLE XXII.

It is further agreed that in all cases, the established courts for Prize Causes, in the Country to which the prizes may be conducted, shall alone take cognizance of them. And whenever such tribunal of either of the

l'une ou de l'autre partie prononce contre quelque navire, ou marchandises ou propriétés réclamées par des Citoyens de l'autre partie, la sentence ou décret fera mention des raisons, ou motifs qui ont déterminé ce jugement, dont copie authentique, ainsi que de toute la procédure y relative, sera, à leur réquisition, délivrée sans délai au Capitaine ou agent du dit Navire moyennant le payement des frais.

ART. 23.

Et afin de pourvoir efficacement à la Sureté respective des Citoyens des deux parties contractantes, et prévenir les torts qu'ils auraient à craindre des Vaisseaux de guerre ou Corsaires de l'une ou de l'autre partie, tous Commandans des Vaisseaux de guerre et des corsaires et tous autres citoyens de l'une des deux parties s'abstiendront de tout dommage envers les citoyens de l'autre et de toute insulte envers leurs personnes. S'ils faisaient le contraire ils seront punis et tenus à donner dans leurs personnes et propriétés satisfaction et réparation pour les dommages avec intérêts, de quelqu'espèce que soyent les dits dommages.

A cet effet, tous Capitaines de Corsaires avant de recevoir leurs Commissions, s'obligeront devant un juge compétent, à donner une garantie au moins par deux Cautions responsables, lesquelles n'auront aucun intérêt sur le dit Corsaire, et dont chacune ainsi que le Capitaine s'engagera particulièrement et solidairement pour la Somme de Sept mille Dollars ou trente six mille huit cent vingt francs et si les dits vaisseaux portent plus de Cent cinquante matelots ou Soldats, pour la Somme de

parties, shall pronounce judgement against any vessel, or goods, or property, claimed by the citizens of the other party, the sentence or decree shall mention the reasons, or motives on which the same shall have been founded, and an authenticated copy of the sentence or decree and of all the proceedings in the case shall if demanded be delivered to the commander, or agent of the said vessel without any delay, he paying the legal fees for the same.

ARTICLE XXIII

And that more abundant care may be taken for the security of the respective citizens of the contracting parties, and to prevent their suffering injuries by the men of war, or privateers of either party, all commanders of ships of war, and privateers, and all others of the said citizens shall forbear doing any damage to those of the other party, or committing any outrage against them, and if they act to the contrary, they shall be punished, and shall also be bound in their persons, and estates, to make satisfaction and reparation for all damages and the interest thereof, of whatever nature the said damages may be.

For this cause all commanders of Privateers before they receive their commissions shall hereafter be obliged to give, before a competent judge, sufficient security, by at least two responsible sureties who have no interest in the said Privateer, each of whom together with the said commander, shall be jointly, and severally bound in the sum of seven thousand dollars or Thirty Six Thousand eight hundred and twenty Francs, or if such ships be provided with above one hundred and fifty seamen or

quatorze mille dollars ou Soixante treize mille six cent quarante francs qui serviront à réparer les torts, ou dommages que les dits Corsaires, leurs officiers, équipages, ou quelqu'un d'eux auraient faits ou commis, pendant leur *croisière* de contraire aux dispositions de la présente Convention ou aux loix et instructions qui devront être la règle de leur conduite: En outre les dites Commissions seront révoquées et annullées dans tous les cas où il y aura en aggression.

soldiers in the sum of Fourteen thousand dollars or Seventy three Thousand six hundred and forty francs, to satisfy all damages, and injuries, which the said privateer, or her officers, or men, or any of them may do or commit, during their cruize contrary to the tenor of this convention or to the laws, and instructions for regulating their conduct; and further, that in all cases of aggressions, the said commissions shall be revoked, and annulled.

ART. 24.

Lorsque les Vaisseaux de guerre des deux parties contractantes ou ceux que leurs Citoyens auraient armés en guerre, seront admis à relâcher avec leurs prises dans les ports de l'une des deux parties, lesdits Vaisseaux publics ou particuliers, de même que leurs prises, ne seront obligés à payer aucuns droits, soit aux officiers du lieu, soit aux juges ou à tous autres; lesdites prises entrant dans les hâvres ou ports de l'une des deux parties, ne pourront être arrêtées ou saisies, et les officiers des lieux ne pourront prendre connaissance de la validité desdites prises, lesquelles pourront sortir et être conduites en toute franchise et liberté aux lieux portés par les Commissions dont les Capitaines desdits Vaisseaux seront obligés de faire apparoir. Il est toujours entendu que les Stipulations de cet article ne s'étendront pas au delà des priviléges des Nations les plus favorisées.

ARTICLE XXIV.

When the ships of war of the two contracting parties, or those belonging to their citizens, which are armed in war, shall be admitted to enter with their prizes the ports of either of the two parties, the said public or private ships, as well as their prizes, shall not be obliged to pay any duty either to the officers of the place, the judges or any others: Nor shall such prizes, when they come to, and enter the ports of either party, be arrested or seized, nor shall the Officers of the place, make examination concerning the lawfulness of such prizes; but they may hoist sail at any time, and depart, and carry their prizes, to the places expressed in their commissions, which the commanders of such ships of war shall be obliged to shew. It is always understood that the stipulations of this article shall not extend beyond the priviledges of the most favored nation.

ART. 25.

Tous Corsaires étrangers ayant des Commissions d'un Etat ou prince

ARTICLE XXV.

It shall not be lawful for any foreign Privateers who have commis-

en guerre avec l'une ou l'autre Nation, ne pourront armer leurs Vaisseaux dans les ports de l'une ou l'autre nation, non plus qu'y vendre leurs prises, ni les échanger en aucune manière: il ne leur sera permis d'acheter de provisions que la quantité nécessaire pour gagner le port le plus voisin de l'Etat ou prince duquel ils ont reçu leurs Commissions.

sions from any Prince, or State, in enmity with either nation, to fit their ships in the ports of either nation, to sell their prizes, or in any manner to exchange them; neither shall they be allowed to purchase provisions, except such as shall be necessary for their going to the next port of that Prince, or State, from which they have received their commissions.

ART. 26.

Il est de plus convenu qu'aucune des deux parties contractantes non seulement ne recevra point de pirates dans ses ports, rades ou villes, et ne permettra pas qu'aucun de ses habitans les reçoive, protége, accueille ou recèle en aucune manière; mais encore livrera à un juste châtiment ceux de ses habitans qui seraient coupables de pareils faits ou délits. Les Vaisseaux de ces pirates, ainsi que les effets et Marchandises par eux pris et amenés dans les ports de l'une ou l'autre nation, seront saisis partout où ils seront découverts, et restitués à leurs propriétaires ou aux agens ou facteurs duement autorisés par eux, après, toutefois, qu'ils auront prouvé, devant les juges compétens, le droit de propriété.

Que si les dits effets avaient passé, par vente, en d'autres mains, et que les acquéreurs fussent ou pussent être instruits ou soupçonnaient que les dits effets avaient été enlevés par des pirates, ils seront également restitués.

ARTICLE XXVI.

It is further agreed that both the said contracting parties, shall not only refuse to receive any pirates into any of their ports havens, or towns, or permit any of their inhabitants to receive, protect, harbour, conceal, or assist them in any manner, but will bring to condign punishment, all such inhabitants, as shall be guilty of such acts, or Offences.

And all their ships, with the goods, or merchandizes taken by them, and brought into the port of either of the said parties, shall be seized as far as they can be discovered, and shall be restored to the owners, or their Factors, or agents, duly authorised by them, (proper evidence being first given before competent judges for proving the property) even in case such effects should have passed into other hands by sale, if it be proved, that the Buyers knew, or had good reason to believe, or suspect, that they had been piratically taken.

ART. 27.

Aucune des deux Nations ne viendra participer aux Pêcheries de

ARTICLE XXVII.

Neither party will intermeddle in the Fisheries of the other on it's

l'autre, sur ses Côtes, ni la troubler dans l'exercice des droits qu'elle a maintenant ou pourrait acquérir sur les côtes de Terre-Neuve, dans le Golfe de St Laurent ou partout ailleurs, sur les Côtes d'amérique au Nord des Etats-Unis: mais la pêche de la baleine et du Veau Marin sera libre pour les deux nations dans toutes les parties du Monde.

Cette Convention sera ratifiée de part et d'autre en bonne et due forme, et les ratifications seront échangées dans l'espace de Six mois ou plutôt s'il est possible.

En foi de quoi les Plénipotentiaires respectifs ont signé les Articles ci dessus, tant en langue française qu'en langue anglaise, et ils y ont apposé leur Sceau; déclarant néanmoins que le Signature en deux langues ne sera point citée comme exemple et ne préjudiciera à aucune des deux parties.

Fait à Paris, le huitième jour de Vendémiaire de l'an Neuf de la République française et le trentième jour de Septembre dix huit cent.

coast nor disturb the other in the exercise of the rights, which it now holds or may acquire on the coast of Newfoundland, in the Gulph of Saint Lawrence or ellswhere on the American coast, northward of the United States. But the whale and seal Fisheries shall be free to both in every quarter of the world.

This Convention shall be ratified on both sides in due form, and the ratifications exchanged in the space of six months or sooner if possible.

In faith whereof the respective plenipotentiaries have signed the above articles both in the French and English languages, and they have thereto affixed their seals, declaring nevertheless that the signing in the two languages, shall not be brought into precedent nor in any way operate to the prejudice of either party.

Done at Paris the eighth day of Vendemiaire of the ninth year of the French Republic, the thirtieth day of September, Anno Domini Eighteen Hundred.

[Seal]	JOSEPH BONAPARTE
[Seal]	C. P. CLARET FLEURIEU
[Seal]	ROEDERER
[Seal]	OLIV. ELLSWORTH
[Seal]	W. R. DAVIE.
[Seal]	W. V. MURRAY.

[Seal]	JOSEPH BONAPARTE
[Seal]	C. P. CLARET FLEURIEU
[Seal]	ROEDERER
[Seal]	OLIV. ELLSWORTH.
[Seal]	W. R. DAVIE
[Seal]	W. V. MURRAY.

[The United States Instrument of Ratification]

John Adams, President of the United States of America.
To all and singular, to whom these Presents shall come Greeting:

Whereas a certain Convention between the United States of America and the French Republic was concluded and signed between their Plenipotentiaries, The Honorable Oliver Ellsworth, William Richardson Davie and William Vans Murray Esquires, their Envoys Extraordinary and Ministers Plenipotentiary to the French Republic, and the Plenipotentiaries of the French Republic, the Citizens Joseph Bonaparte, Charles Pierre Claret Fleurieu, and Pierre Louis Roederer, at Paris, on the 30th day of September last past, which convention, is word for word, as follows to wit:

[Here follows the English text of the convention.]

And whereas the Senate of the United States did by their resolution, on the 3ᵈ day of this present month of February (two thirds of the Senators then present concurring) consent to and advise the ratification of the said Convention; Provided the second article be expunged, and that the following article be added or inserted: "It is agreed that the present Convention shall be in force for the term of eight years from the time of the exchange of the Ratifications" Now therefore, I John Adams, President of the United States of America, having seen and considered the convention and additional Article above recited, do, in pursuance of the aforesaid advice and consent of the Senate of the said United States, by these presents accept, ratify and confirm the said Convention and additional Article and every clause and article thereof, as the same are herein before set forth, saving and excepting the second Article of the said Convention, which I hereby declare to be expunged and of no force or validity: and I do moreover hereby declare, that the said Convention (saving the second article as aforesaid) and the said additional Article form together one instrument and are a Convention between the United States of America and the French Republic, made by the President of the United States, by and with the advice and consent of the Senate thereof.

In Testimony whereof I have caused the seal of the United States of America to be hereto affixed.

Given under my hand at the City of Washington this 18ᵗʰ day of February in the year of our Lord one thousand (L. S.) eight hundred and one, and of the Independence of the said States the Twenty fifth.

Signed, JOHN ADAMS

By the President
Signed JOHN MARSHALL
Acting as Secretary of State

[The French Instrument of Ratification]

[Translation]

Bonaparte, Premier Consul, au nom du Peuple Français, les Consuls de la République ayant vu et examiné la Convention conclue, arrêtée et signée à Paris le Huit Vendémiaire an neuf de la République Française (Trente Septembre Mil huit cent), par les Citoyens Joseph Bonaparte, Fleurieu et Roederer, Conseillers d'Etat, en vertu des pleins pouvoirs qui leur avaient été conférés à

Bonaparte, First Consul, in the name of the French people—the Consuls of the Republic having seen and examined the convention concluded, agreed to, and signed at Paris the 8th Vendémiaire, 9th year of the French Republic (30th September, 1800), by the Citizens Joseph Bonaparte, Fleurieu, and Roederer, Counsellors of State, in virtue of the full powers which have been

cet effet, avec Messieurs Ellsworth, Davie et Murray, Ministres Plénipotentiaires des Etats-unis, également munis de pleins-pouvoirs, de laquelle Convention la teneur suit:

[Here follows the French text of the convention.]

Approuve la Convention ci-dessus en tous et chacun des articles qui y sont contenus; déclare qu'elle est acceptée, ratifiée et confirmée et promet qu'elle sera inviolablement observée.

Le Gouvernement des Etats-unis ayant ajouté dans sa Ratification que la Convention sera en vigueur l'espace de huit années, et ayant omis l'article second, le Gouvernement de la République française consent à accepter, ratifier et confirmer la Convention ci-dessus, avec l'addition portant que la Convention sera en vigueur pendant l'espace de huit années, et avec le retranchement de l'article second: bien entendu que par ce retranchement les deux Etats renoncent aux prétentions respectives qui sont l'objet du dit article.

En foi de quoi sont données les présentes, signées, contresignées, et scellées du grand Sceau de la République.

A Paris le douze Thermidor an neuf de la République (trente un Juillet Mil Huit cent un).

BONAPARTE

Le Ministre des Relations Extérieures,
CH. MAU. TALLEYRAND.

Par le Premier Consul:
Le Secrétaire d'Etat
HUGUES B MARET

given to them to this effect, with Messieurs Ellsworth, Davie, and Murray, Ministers Plenipotentiary of the United States, equally furnished with full powers, the tenor of which convention follows:

Approves the above convention in all and each of the articles which are therein contained; declares that it is accepted, ratified, and confirmed; and promises that it shall be inviolably observed.

The Government of the United States having added in its ratification that the convention should be in force for the space of eight years and having omitted the second article, the Government of the French Republic consents to accept, ratify, and confirm the above convention with the addition importing that the convention shall be in force for the space of eight years and with the retrenchment of the second article: *Provided,* that by this retrenchment the two states renounce the respective pretentions which are the object of the said article.

In faith whereof these presents are given, signed, countersigned, and sealed with the Great Seal of the Republic.

At Paris the 12th Thermidor, 9th year of the Republic (31st July, 1801).

BONAPARTE

The Minister of Exterior Relations
CH. MAU. TALLEYRAND.

By the First Consul
The Secretary of State
HUGUES B MARET

Acknowledgments

IT IS IN THE NATURE OF THINGS FOR THOSE WHO ATTEMPT WORKS OF scholarly synthesis to owe many debts. Since I am no exception to this rule, I am pleased to express my gratitude to the many—colleagues, student assistants, and typists—who have helped me. In particular, I am indebted to Professors Thomas A. Bailey of Stanford University, Marvin R. Zahniser of Ohio State University, and Wilbur R. Jacobs and Morton Borden of the University of California, Santa Barbara, for perceptive readings of the manuscript. Their knowledgeable suggestions and critiques saved me from a number of serious errors. Geoffrey S. Smith compiled the Index.

I am also grateful for assistance from librarians and custodians of historical collections ranging from the Massachusetts Historical Society in Boston to the Huntington Library in San Marino, California, and from the Public Record Office in London to the *Archives de France* in Paris. Dr. Percy C. Powell of the Manuscript Division of the Library of Congress was particularly gracious in allowing me extended use of valuable photostatic reproductions of documents from the *Archives des Affaires Étrangères, Correspondance Politique, États Unis,* the originals of which are in Paris, for the years 1797–1801. Dr. Donald C. Davidson, Librarian, Mrs. Martha H. Peterson, Head, Acquisitions Department, University of California, Santa Barbara, and their staff, practiced patience beyond the requirements of duty in obtaining filmed copies of materials in scattered libraries and historical societies for my use. At the William L. Clements Library of The University of Michigan Dr. Howard H. Peckham, the Director, and Mr. William S. Ewing, the Curator of Manuscripts, provided space and resources for quiet research. Dr. Ullane Bonnel, a close student of early relations between France and the United States, merits special thanks because she took time from her own pressing schedule to arrange introductions for me to custodians of documentary collections in Paris.

Three organizations helped subsidize the research and writing of this history. The John Simon Guggenheim Memorial Foundation granted me a fellowship in 1960 which made possible freedom from academic obligations; the American Philosophical Society of Philadelphia provided funds for travel and research in France and England in the summer of 1963; and the Research Council of the University of California, Santa Barbara, financed some of the research and other necessary assistance. To each of these I offer thanks for a generosity that has been extended to many, but which, as I experienced it, retained the graciousness of a personal concern for the individual scholar.

                                                                                    A.D.

References

FOR THE QUOTATIONS AT THE HEADS OF CHAPTERS

I. To John Quincy Adams, Philadelphia, March 31, 1797, in Charles Francis Adams, ed., *The Works of John Adams . . .* (10 vols., Boston, 1850–1856), VIII, 537.

II. To George Washington, Paris, October 24, 1797, quoted in Albert J. Beveridge, *The Life of John Marshall* (4 vols., Boston, 1916–1919), II, 271.

III. To Harrison Gray Otis, Dedham, April 23, 1798, in Seth Ames, ed., *Works of Fisher Ames . . .* (2 vols., Boston, 1854), I, 225.

IV. To William Vans Murray, London, Sept. 17, 1798, William Vans Murray Papers, Manuscript Division, Library of Congress.

V. August 28, 1798, quoted in George A. King, "The French Spoliation Claims," *American Journal of International Law*, VI (April 1912), 375.

VI. To Lord Grenville, February 18, 1799, quoted in Charles C. Tansill, *The United States and Santo Domingo, 1798–1873* (Baltimore, 1938), p. 69 n.

VII. To Samuel Dexter, Paris, July 12, 1800, in Worthington C. Ford, ed., "Letters of William Vans Murray to John Quincy Adams, 1797–1803," *Annual Report of the American Historical Association for the Year 1912* (Washington, 1914), p. 650.

VIII. To T. F. A. Vanderkemp, Washington, December 28, 1800, in Adams, *Works of John Adams*, IX, 577.

IX. To John Adams, Berlin, March 24, 1801, quoted in Samuel F. Bemis, *John Quincy Adams and the Foundations of American Foreign Policy* (2nd printing, with corrections, New York, 1956), p. 107 n.

X. To Joseph Pitcairn, Germantown, October 23, 1799, in "Letters of Thomas Boylston Adams to Joseph Pitcairn," *Quarterly Publication of the Historical and Philosophical Society of Ohio*, XII (January-March, 1917), 29.

Comment on Sources

THIS BOOK RESTS HEAVILY ON MANUSCRIPT AND OTHER ORIGINAL SOURCES scattered in archives and other depositories in the United States, France, and Great Britain. Yet I could not have written it without using the interpretive, narrative, and edited works of others. So, in addition to exploiting the records left by participants in the events analyzed, I have stood on the shoulders of scholars who have labored before me in the same fields, and am pleased to acknowledge my debt to them.

The notes which follow are unusually full because they serve several purposes. As is traditional, they acknowledge the sources of quotations and of especially significant facts or interpretations. In addition, these notes serve as bibliographical guides, or as keys to additional literature on particular points. Occasionally they contain elaborating comment on a point or scholarly issue. Such comment is always important but often does not belong in the mainstream of the narrative because it would interrupt the flow of thought. In the notes such comment can offer some enrichment to those who are interested, and may be ignored by others whose main interest is the story.

Practically all of my quotations refer back ultimately to an original source from a participant, in the events analyzed, or to a source roughly contemporary to him. Sometimes these quotations may give the impression of conversation, but all of them are from written records. Whenever possible, I have referred the reader to a printed version of a letter, dispatch, or other document.

In the diplomatic negotiations of 1800 and 1801, in addition to the official documents and other sources, I have made extensive use of William Vans Murray manuscripts. I have done so because Murray's papers are rich sources and have never before been fully exploited. Most other original sources in this period have. Furthermore, Murray's letters and diaries are free from the inhibitions frequently found in official documents, are filled with fresh and provocative insights, are crisp and incisive in expression and reasoning, and carry the ideas of one of the key men in this story.

For those who may wish to use the notes as a bibliography, or just to trace my scholarship, the first entry of any source contains the full title, listed by author or editor. The interested reader may easily obtain the number of the page where the full title is cited by consulting the index wherein the first entry of every source is listed by author. In the case of manuscript sources, the place of each depository is listed with the first entry of such a source. When there is a possibility of confusion because similar manuscript collections are housed in separate places, the depository is repeated in each citation.

The quotations from the Adams Papers are from the microfilm edition, by permission of the Massachusetts Historical Society.

Notes

Chapter I

1. John Adams to wife, Stratford, Conn., Nov. 27, 1796, in Charles Francis Adams, ed., *Letters of John Adams Addressed to His Wife* (2 vols., Boston, 1841), II, 230. Philadelphia was the national capital from 1790 to 1800.
2. Page Smith, *John Adams* (2 vols., New York, 1962), p. 273.
3. Franklin is quoted in James Schouler, *History of the United States of America under the Constitution* (7 vols., New York, 1880–1913), I, 497. See also Rudolph Marx, *The Health of Presidents* (New York, 1960), pp. 29, 32, and 37, and John R. Howe, Jr., *The Changing Political Thought of John Adams* (Princeton, 1966), p. xv.
4. Jonathan Sewall to Judge Lee, Sept. 21, 1787, quoted in Richard B. Morris, *The Peacemakers: The Great Powers and American Independence* (New York, 1965), p. 451.
5. Clinton Rossiter, in "The Legacy of John Adams," *Yale Review*, XLVI (Summer, 1957), 528–550, stresses Adams's conservatism. See also Richard Beale Davis, *Intellectual Life in Jefferson's Virginia, 1790–1830* (Chapel Hill, N.C., 1964), p. 246, and Smith, *Adams*, p. 259. Adams read and was influenced by Harrington's writings. See Theodore W. Dwight, "Harrington and His Influence upon American Political Institutions and Political Thought," *Political Science Quarterly*, II (March 1887), 1–44. Anson D. Morse, "The Politics of John Adams," *American Historical Review*, IV (Jan. 1879), 310, points out that until Adams became President his views coincided with those of most Federalists. Howe, in *Changing Political Thought of John Adams*, p. iv, explains that Adams's political thinking grew out of his practical involvement in politics.
6. See Correa M. Walsh, *The Political Science of John Adams* (New York, 1915), p. 56; Charles F. Adams, ed., *The Works of John Adams* (10 vols., Boston, 1850–1856), IV, 228, 271 ff., and 284–86; John Adams, *A Defence of the Constitutions of Government of the United States of America . . .* , 3rd ed. (3 vols., Phil., 1797), I, 9 and elsewhere; Manning J. Dauer, *The Adams Federalists* (Baltimore, 1953), pp. 40–43;

Charles A. Beard, *Economic Origins of Jeffersonian Democracy* (New York, 1915), pp. 316–317; Sidney H. Aronson, *Status and Kinship in the Higher Civil Service: Standards of Selection in the Administrations of John Adams, Thomas Jefferson, and Andrew Jackson* (Cambridge, Mass., 1964), pp. 3–7, 194; and Adrienne Koch, *Power, Morals, and the Founding Fathers* (Ithaca, N.Y., 1961), p. 88.

7. One critic maintained that "Mr. Adams never was consistently a federalist." George Gibbs, ed., *Memoirs of the Administrations of Washington and John Adams, Edited from the Papers of Oliver Wolcott, Secretary of the Treasury* (2 vols., New York, 1856), I, 456. Hereinafter cited as Gibbs, *Wolcott Papers*. Adams looked upon the English constitution with special reverence. See Edward Handler, *America and Europe in the Political Thought of John Adams* (Cambridge, Mass., 1964), p. 49.

8. Dauer, *Adams Federalists*, p. 86, and Handler, *America and Europe*, pp. 98–99. In later years Adams said that "France is the natural ally of U.S. if we must have any Ally. We ought not to war with her, but in the last Necessity." To Benjamin Waterhouse, Quincy, March 16, 1813, in Worthington C. Ford, ed., *Statesman and Friend: Correspondence of John Adams with Benjamin Waterhouse, 1784–1822* (Boston, 1927), pp. 92–94. See also Adams to Jefferson, Quincy, Aug. 15, 1823, in Lester J. Cappon, ed., *The Adams-Jefferson Letters: The Complete Correspondence Between Thomas Jefferson and Abigail and John Adams* (2 vols., Chapel Hill, N.C., 1959), II, 595.

9. "I am not enough of an Englishman," Adams told his wife, "nor little enough of a Frenchman, for some people." Dec. 12, 1796, in Adams, *Works of John Adams*, I, 495.

10. Hamilton's plot, Adams wrote, "filled me with apprehensions for the safety of us all." To Henry Knox, Phil., March 30, 1797, in *ibid.*, VIII, 535. The antagonism between Adams and Hamilton was both personal and political. See Lynn H. Parsons, "Continuing Crusade: Four Generations of the Adams Family View of Alexander Hamilton," *The New England Quarterly*, XXXVII (March 1964), 44. See also John C. Miller, *Alexander Hamilton: Portrait in Paradox* (New York, 1959), p. 45, who suggests that the French crisis prevented an open break between Adams and Hamilton in 1797.

11. "When I came into office," Adams explained later, "it was my determination to make as few removals as possible," and none for personal or party considerations. To General Benjamin Lincoln, Phil., March 10, 1800, in Letterbook, Adams Papers, Massachusetts Historical Society, Boston (microfilm copy, reel 120). Hereinafter cited as the Adams Papers. Stephen G. Kurtz in *The Presidency of John Adams: The Collapse of Federalism, 1795–1800* (Phil., 1957), pp. 268–270, argues that Adams retained Washington's cabinet because he could not obtain first-rate men to become department heads.

12. Henrietta Liston to James Jackson, near Phil., July 14, 1797, Liston Papers, National Library of Scotland, microfilm copy from the Library of Congress.

13. Dauer, *Adams Federalists*, p. 122; Leonard D. White, *The Federalists* (New York, 1948), pp. 237–240; and John Quincy Adams and Charles Francis Adams, *The Life of John Adams* (2 vols., Phil., 1871), II, 215–217. Hamilton's chief lieutenant in the Senate was Theodore Sedgwick. See Richard E. Welch, Jr., *Theodore Sedgwick, Federalist: A Political Portrait* (Middletown, Conn., 1965), p. 167. Elbridge Gerry had warned Adams of Hamilton's power, but the President-elect replied, "Pickering and all his colleagues are as much attached to me as I desire. I have no jealousies from that quarter." To Gerry, Phil., Feb. 13, 1797, Adams, *Works of John Adams*, VIII, 523. Yet Claude G. Bowers, in *Jefferson and Hamilton, The Struggle for Democracy in America* (Boston, 1925), p. 315, likened Adams's position to that of Ali Baba among his forty thieves.

14. For Pickering's report of June 22, 1797, see Walter Lowrie and Matthew St. Clair Clarke, eds., *American State Papers: Class I, Foreign Relations* (6 vols., Washington, D.C., 1832–1861), II, 28, and 55–62 for a list of American ships captured by the French from Oct. 1796 to June 1797. Hereinafter cited as *ASP FR*. For Pickering's report to Congress of Feb. 28, 1797, see Dudley W. Knox, ed., *Naval Documents Related to the Quasi-War between the United States and France* (7 vols., Washington, D.C., 1935–1938), I, 1–2. Hereinafter cited as Knox, *Quasi-War Documents*. See also Gardner W. Allen, *Our Naval War with France* (Boston, 1909), pp. 31–39; Brooks Adams, "The Convention of 1800 with France," *Massachusetts Historical Society Proceedings, 1910–1911*, XLIV (Boston, 1911), 395–399; and James W. Gerard, "French Spoliations before 1801," *Magazine of American History*, XII (July 1884), 29–45, a popular summary of the problem.

15. The quotation is from *Décade philosophique* (Paris) April 19, 1797, cited in Durand Echeverria, *Mirage in the West: A History of the French Image of American Society to 1815* (Princeton, 1957), p. 218. The origins and development of the war crisis are analyzed in Alexander DeConde, *Entangling Alliance: Politics and Diplomacy under George Washington* (Durham, N.C., 1958). See also Bernard Faÿ, *The Revolutionary Spirit in France and America*, trans. from the French (New York, 1927), p. 382, and Albert H. Bowman, "The Struggle for Neutrality: A History of the Diplomatic Relations between the United States and France, 1790–1801" (unpublished Ph.D. dissertation, Columbia University, 1954), pp. 286–296. In "Jefferson, Hamilton and American Foreign Policy," *Political Science Quarterly*, LXXI (March 1956), 39, Bowman argues that the Jay Treaty made war with France "inevitable." Some leaders of the French government wanted to declare war but feared that the United States would then ally itself with England. See Ossian Larévellière-Lépeaux, ed., *Mémoires de Larévellière-Lépeaux* (3 vols., Paris, 1895), II, 258.

16. At this point Adams thought humility should come before honor. Adams to John Trumbull, Phil., Jan. 19, 1797, in Adams Papers, reel 117.

17. To Theodore Sedgwick, Feb. 26, 1797, in John C. Hamilton, ed., *The Works of Alexander Hamilton* (7 vols., New York, 1850–1851), VI, 209.

Earlier, on Jan. 22, Hamilton had written to George Washington suggesting a special mission. See p. 194. Hamilton's views, as expressed to several people in Jan. and Feb. 1797, are summarized in Arthur B. Darling, *Our Rising Empire, 1763–1803* (New Haven, 1940), p. 277. Darling also gives a detailed account of the origins of the crisis.

18. The considerations in these two paragraphs are discussed in Robert Liston to Lord Grenville, Phil., March 18, 1797, No. 10, and July 13, 1797, No. 33, Public Record Office, Great Britain, Foreign Office 5, in transcripts in the Library of Congress. Hereinafter cited as PRO GB FO. See also Edward H. Phillips, "The Public Career of Timothy Pickering, Federalist, 1745–1802" (unpublished Ph.D. dissertation, Harvard University, 1950), p. 281, and Nathan Schachner, *The Founding Fathers* (New York, 1954), p. 417.

19. Jefferson to Adams, Monticello, Dec. 28, 1796, in Paul L. Ford, ed., *The Writings of Thomas Jefferson* (10 vols., New York, 1892–99), VII, 95.

20. Hamilton to Rufus King, Feb. 15, 1797, in Hamilton, *Works of Hamilton*, VI, 206.

21. Henry Knox, the former Secretary of War, favored the idea of sending Jefferson to France. Knox to Adams, Boston, March 12, 1797, The Henry Knox Papers, 1770–1825, Massachusetts Historical Society, Boston (microfilm copy). See also the entry of March 2, 1797, in Franklin B. Sawvel, ed., *The Complete Anas of Thomas Jefferson* (New York, 1903), pp. 184–185; Dumas Malone, *Jefferson and the Ordeal of Liberty* (Boston, 1962), p. 296; and John A. Carroll and Mary Wells Ashworth, *George Washington: First in Peace* (New York, 1957), pp. 440–441 n. This is the seventh volume of the biography started by Douglas S. Freeman.

22. Phil., March 5, 1797, in Adams, *Letters of John Adams Addressed to His Wife*, II, 244.

23. For a readily accessible printing of the inaugural address of March 4, 1797, see James D. Richardson, comp., *A Compilation of the Messages and Papers of the Presidents* (20 vols., New York, 1897–1917), I, 218–222. In stressing his commitment to republican government, Adams sought to dispel a suspicion held by many that he leaned toward monarchism. See Louise B. Dunbar, *A Study of "Monarchical" Tendencies in the United States from 1776 to 1801* (Urbana, Ill., 1923), p. 121.

24. For descriptions of the inaugural see *Claypoole's American Daily Advertiser*, Phil. (May 6, 1797); Kurtz, *Presidency of John Adams*, pp. 223–224; Carroll, *Washington*, pp. 436–437; Robert Goodloe Harper to his constituents, Phil., March 13, 1797, in Elizabeth Donnan, ed., "Papers of James A. Bayard, 1796–1815," *Annual Report of the American Historical Association for the Year 1913* (2 vols., Washington, D.C., 1915), II, 29–30. Hereinafter cited as Donnan, "Bayard Papers." See also Malone, *Jefferson and the Ordeal of Liberty*, pp. 296–298.

25. To Abigail, Phil., March 17, 1797, in Adams, *Letters of John Adams Addressed to His Wife*, II, 252.

26. The Philadelphia *Aurora*, March 14,1797. The British Minister in Philadelphia was cynical. Adams, he said, "has been accused of an antipathy to France and Frenchmen:—and he has taken care by an ambig-
uous phrase to endeavour to persuade the mass of his hearers that he
bears to that nation a greater degree of regard than those who are best
acquainted with his real sentiments choose to give him credit for."
Liston to Grenville, Phil., March 18, 1797, No. 5, PRO GB FO 5. The
recalled French Minister, on the other hand, was pleased with the
friendly reference to his country. See Pierre Auguste Adet to Minister
of Foreign Relations, Phil., March 10, 1797, in Frederick J. Turner, ed.,
"Correspondence of the French Ministers to the United States, 1791–
1797," in *Annual Report of the American Historical Association for the
Year 1903* (2 vols., Washington, D.C., 1904), II, 993–994.
27. Dauer, *Adams Federalists*, p. 125; Malone, *Jefferson and the Ordeal of
Liberty*, p. 299; Kurtz, *Presidency of John Adams*, p. 229; Sawvel,
Complete Anas, p. 185; Adams to Gerry, Phil., April 6, 1797, Adams,
Works of John Adams, VIII, 538–540. Thomas Paine reported that
Madison, serving as Adams's envoy, would be unable to accomplish anything in France. To Jefferson, Havre, May 14, 1797, in Moncure D.
Conway, *The Life of Thomas Paine*, 3rd ed. (2 vols., New York), II,
272.
28. William Patterson to Iredell, New Brunswick, March 7, 1797, in Grif-
fith J. McRee, *Life and Correspondence of James Iredell* (2 vols., New
York, 1858, reprinted in 1949), II, 459.
29. Adams to Dr. Walsh, March 10, 1797, Adams Papers, reel 117.
30. Adet to Minister of Foreign Relations, March 26, 1797, in Turner,
"Correspondence of French Ministers," pp. 1000–1001. Adet saw Adams
on March 13. See also Darling, *Rising Empire*, p. 250. At this time
another French observer also remarked on Adams's friendly attitude
toward France. Liancourt to Talleyrand, Phil., March 1797, in Jean
Marchand, ed., "Une lettre du Duc de Liancourt a Talleyrand (1797),"
Revue d'histoire diplomatique, XLIII (1929), 466–472.
31. The precise day on which Adams heard of Pinckney's rejection is not
clear. Marvin R. Zahniser, "The Public Career of Charles Cotesworth
Pinckney" (unpublished Ph.D. dissertation, University of California,
Santa Barbara, 1963), p. 206, says news of Pinckney's hostile reception
reached Charleston as early as Feb. 22, but that his rejection was not
officially known to the administration until March 21. For varying views
that place the arrival of the news early in March, see William Vans
Murray, Eastern Shore, Md., to McHenry, March 10, 1797, in Bernard
Steiner, *The Life and Correspondence of James McHenry, Secretary of
War under Washington and Adams* (Cleveland, 1907), p. 208; Mar-
shall Smelser, *The Congress Founds the Navy, 1787–1798* (Notre
Dame, Ind., 1959), p. 103; and Robert G. Harper to constituents,
Phil., March 13, 1797, in Donnan, "Bayard Papers," p. 37. When
Pinckney became Minister to France he did not consider himself a
firm Federalist. See Marvin Zahniser, "The First Pinckney Mission to

France," *The South Carolina Historical Magazine*, LXVI (Oct. 1965), 207.

32. The decree is printed in *ASP FR*, II, 30–31. The American government would not admit the right of any foreign government, or its agents, to prescribe arbitrary regulations for American commerce. Nonetheless, it would, if a merchant requested it, grant a certificate, or *rôle d'équipage*. John Steele, Comptroller, to all Collectors of Customs, Phil., Aug. 28, 1797, Rufus King Papers, Huntington Library, San Marino, California.

33. See Kurtz, *Presidency of John Adams*, p. 286; Bowers, *Jefferson and Hamilton*, pp. 342–343; and Adams, *Life of John Adams*, II, 225. Some Federalists were opposed to an embargo because it would injure Americans more than the French. George Cabot to Jeremiah Smith, Brookline, April 17, 1797, in Henry Cabot Lodge, *Life and Letters of George Cabot* (Boston, 1877), p. 130. But in Europe an embargo was expected. Bourne to Edward Gwinn, Hamburg, June 28, 1797, Sylvanus Bourne Papers, Manuscript Division, Library of Congress. The questions went to the department heads on March 14, 1797, according to Smith, *Adams*, pp. 924, 1145, note 18.

34. Adams's proclamation of March 25, 1797, is in Richardson, *Messages of the Presidents*, I, 222–223. The quotations are from Adams to Henry Knox, Phil., March 30, 1797, Adams, *Works of John Adams*, VIII, 535–536; Ames to Oliver Wolcott, Dedham, March 24, 1797, in Gibbs, *Wolcott Papers*, I, 477; and Robert Oliver to J. Gay, April 6, 1797, cited in Stuart W. Bruchey, *Robert Oliver, Merchant of Baltimore, 1783–1819* (Baltimore, 1956), p. 176.

35. Jefferson to James Madison, Phil., May 18, 1797, in Ford, *Writings of Jefferson*, VII, 124–127, and Jefferson to P. White, Phil., June 4, 1797, Jefferson Papers, Duke University Library, Durham, N.C.

36. Hamilton to Pickering, New York, March 29, and to Wolcott, March 30, 1797, in Henry Cabot Lodge, ed., *The Works of Alexander Hamilton* (9 vols., New York, 1885–86), VIII, 454–457. Basically, Federalist leaders in New England were divided over the sending of a new mission to France. For details see Winfred E. A. Bernhard, *Fisher Ames: Federalist and Statesman, 1758–1808* (Chapel Hill, N.C., 1965), pp. 285–286, 292–293.

37. Hamilton to Pickering, New York, March 22 and 29, 1797, in Lodge, *Hamilton's Works*, X, 454–455; and Steiner, *James McHenry*, pp. 212–213. Hamilton also pointed out that Federalists had sent an envoy, John Jay, to Britain in 1794. They could do no less for France, or they would be open to the charge of inconsistency. See Miller, *Hamilton*, p. 456.

38. Adet to Minister of Foreign Relations, Phil., March 31, 1797, and Instructions to Létombe, Phil., May 3, in Turner, "Correspondence of French Ministers," pp. 1004, 1011.

39. When an artillery company in Norfolk, Virginia, exchanged salutes with French frigates in the harbor, Federalists were upset. Daniel Bedinger to Edward Tiffin, Norfolk, June 3, 1797, Caroline Danske Dandridge

Papers, Duke University Library. The Boston *Independent Chronicle,*
April 6, 1797, predicted civil strife if there were war against France. It
denounced "warhawks." See also Donald H. Stewart, "Jeffersonian
Journalism: Newspaper Propaganda and the Development of the
Democratic-Republican Party, 1789–1801" (unpublished Ph.D. disser-
tation, Columbia University, 1950), pp. 522–523.

40. John B. McMaster, *A History of the People of the United States from
the Revolution to the Civil War* (8 vols., New York, 1886–1926), II,
318.

41. Samuel E. Morison, *The Maritime History of Massachusetts, 1783–1860*
(Boston, 1921), p. 168; Schachner, *Founding Fathers,* p. 417; Bruchey,
Robert Oliver, p. 177; and Smelser, *Congress Founds the Navy,* p.
105. These depredations in the West Indies heightened animosity
against France. "A spirit of disapprobation and resentment even begins
to prevail among the lower classes," the British Minister pointed out,
"who had hitherto been unanimous in an enthusiastic attachment to
France." Liston to Grenville, Phil., May 11, 1797, No. 20, PRO GB FO
5. The French sensed a similar reaction. Adet to Minister of Foreign
Relations, March 21, 1797, in Turner, "Correspondence of French
Ministers," pp. 999–1000.

42. Pickering to Rufus King, Phil., April 26, 1797, Rufus King Papers,
Huntington Library. Republican newspapers maintained that British
depredations were worse than those of the French, and they invariably
listed British seizures of American ships. Stewart, "Jeffersonian Journalism," pp. 436–437.

43. Grenville to Liston, Downing Street, Jan. 27, 1797, in Bernard Mayo,
ed., "Instruction to the British Ministers to the United States, 1791–
1812," in *Annual Report of the American Historical Association for the
Year 1936* (3 vols., Washington, D.C., 1941), III, 128–130 and Darling, *Rising Empire,* p. 271 n.

44. Liston to Grenville, Phil., April 18, 1797, No. 16, PRO GB FO 5.
Liston said that the American fear of war was exaggerated. The Directory would not likely declare war. Without the sanction of Congress,
moreover, it appeared that Adams's government could not take strong
measures against the French. Pickering, he said, had "become one of the
most violent antigallicans I have ever met with." Neither he nor the
other department heads would allow France any advantages over
Britain. See also Bradford Perkins, *The First Rapprochement: England
and the United States, 1795–1805* (Phil., 1955), p. 92; Pickering to
King, Phil., May 9, 1797, Rufus King Papers, Huntington Library.

45. Adams's fourteen questions, dated Phil., April 14, 1797, are in Adams,
Works of John Adams, VIII, 540–541.

46. Hamilton sent his advice to McHenry in two separate papers, the first
of which he wrote on April 29, 1797. See Steiner, *James McHenry,*
pp. 213–222. This sentiment for peace was evident in many parts of
the country. Freeholders in Virginia, for example, on April 26, 1797,
deprecated the possibility of war and urged negotiation. John Clopton

Papers, Duke University Library. See also Marston Watson to Cabot, Marblehead, April 14, 1797, in Lodge, *Cabot*, p. 127; John Randolph to Henry M. Rutledge, April 29, 1797, in Russell Kirk, *Randolph of Roanoke* (Chicago, 1951), p. 24; and Joseph Charles, *The Origins of the American Party System* (New York, Torchbook edition, 1961), p. 127.

47. Pickering to John Adams, May 1, 1797, Timothy Pickering Papers, Massachusetts Historical Society, Boston (Microfilm copy), and Octavius Pickering and Charles W. Upham, *The Life of Timothy Pickering* (4 vols., Boston, 1867–73), III, 367–370. Wolcott's reply, dated April 25, 1797, is in Gibbs, *Wolcott Papers*, I, 502–517. Pertinent data is also in Wolcott to King, Phil., April 17, in the Rufus King Papers.

48. Hamilton to Pickering, May 11, 1797, in Lodge, *Hamilton's Works*, VIII, 466 and George Cabot to Oliver Wolcott, Brookline, April 17, 1797, in Lodge, *Cabot*, p. 129. In later years Adams said Hamilton at this time tried to impose on him "a whole system of instruction for the conduct of the President, the Senate, and the House of Representatives." See the correspondence originally published in the Boston *Patriot*, 1809, in Adams, *Works of John Adams*, IX, 289.

49. Phil., April 24, 1797, in Adams, *Letters of John Adams Addressed to His Wife*, II, 254; Adams to Elbridge Gerry, Phil., May 3, 1797, Adams Papers, reel 117; and George Cabot's contributions to the *Columbian Centinel*, Boston (April 15 and May 3, 1797), in Lodge, *Cabot*, pp. 582–583.

50. See Iredell to Samuel Tredwell, Annapolis, May 12, 1797, in McRee, *James Iredell*, II, 504, and Bruchey, *Robert Oliver*, p. 177.

51. Létombe took over Adet's diplomatic functions in May 1797. See E. Wilson Lyon, "The Directory and the United States," *American Historical Review*, XLIII (April 1938), 518. Faÿ, in *Revolutionary Spirit*, p. 563, note 97, claimed that Létombe was a personal friend of John Adams, but other evidence does not support the claim.

52. The Mazzei letter had been translated from English into Italian, then into French, and finally from French back to English. The original letter of April 24, 1796, and the *Moniteur's* remarks of Jan. 25, 1797, are in Ford, *Writings of Jefferson*, VII, 72–78. For a full discussion of the episode, see Malone, *Jefferson and the Ordeal of Liberty*, pp. 302–308, and Harry R. Warfel, *Noah Webster* (New York, 1936), p. 231. Webster edited the *Minerva*. The quotation is from George Cabot to Oliver Wolcott, Brookline, May 15, 1797, in Lodge, *Cabot*, p. 138.

53. The speech is printed in Richardson, *Messages of the Presidents*, I, 223–229.

54. George Cabot to Oliver Wolcott, Brookline, May 24, 1797, in Gibbs, *Wolcott Papers*, I, 536.

55. John Clopton was shocked, for example, because the President had opened the special session with a "violent Philippic against the very nation with whom he was about to treat." Circular letters of June 19, 1797, and Jan. 11, 1798, from Phil., in Clopton Papers, Duke University Library. Gallatin to Joseph Nicholson, Phil., May 26, 1797, in Henry Adams, *The Life of Albert Gallatin* (Phil., 1879), p. 184.

56. Phil., May 25, 1797, in Robert G. Harper, *Select Works of Robert Goodloe Harper* . . . (Baltimore, 1814), I, 153.
57. To Col. Thomas Bell, Phil., May 18, 1797, in Henry A. Washington, ed., *The Writings of Thomas Jefferson* (9 vols., New York, 1854–56), IV, 174, and to Peregrine Fitzhugh, June 4, 1797, in Ford, *Writings of Jefferson*, VII, 134–138. George Washington urged firmness, believing it would avoid bloodshed. To William Heath, Mt. Vernon, May 20, 1797, William Heath and Joseph Curtis Papers, 1725–1864, Duke University Library.
58. Rush to John Montgomery, Phil., June 16, 1797, in Lyman H. Butterfield, ed., *Letters of Benjamin Rush* (2 vols., Princeton, 1951), II, 787.
59. The replies from Congress are printed in Richardson, *Messages of the Presidents*, I, 229–234. For details, sometimes conflicting, on the lineup of parties in Congress, see William Smith to Ralph Izard, Phil., May 23 and 29, 1797, from which the quotation is taken, in Ulrich B. Phillips, ed., "South Carolina Federalist Correspondence, 1789–1797," *American Historical Review*, XIV (July 1909), 786–789; Noble E. Cunningham, Jr., *The Jeffersonian Republicans: The Formation of Party Organization, 1789–1801* (Chapel Hill, N.C., 1957), pp. 122–123; and Dauer, *Adams Federalists*, pp. 303–309.
60. The quotations are from Steiner, *James McHenry*, p. 274, based on later recollection, and Gibbs, *Wolcott Papers*, I, 467, 469, and note to 530–531.
61. William Smith to Ralph Izard, Phil., May 29, 1797, in Phillips, "South Carolina Federalist Correspondence," pp. 788–789, and Robert G. Harper to constituents, Phil., July 24, 1797, in Donnan, "Bayard Papers," pp. 41–42.
62. Jefferson to Gerry, Phil., June 21, 1797, in Ford, *Writings of Jefferson*, VII, 149. Earlier, Jefferson said the nomination of the envoys did not prove the administration had been converted to a policy of peace. To Peregrine Fitzhugh, Phil., June 4, 1797, Jefferson Papers, Duke University Library. Gerry was approved on June 22. The negative votes are listed in Gallatin to wife, June 23, 1797, in Adams, *Life of Gallatin*, p. 185. For an analysis of the vote on Gerry's nomination, see Eugene F. Kramer, "John Adams, Elbridge Gerry, and the Origins of the X Y Z Affair," *Essex Institute Historical Collections*, XCIV (Jan. 1958), 57–68. At this time Gerry was generally considered a Federalist, Stewart, "Jeffersonian Journalism," p. 568.
63. Phillips, "Public Career of Timothy Pickering," pp. 286–287. The French Counsul in New York, Alexandre d'Hauterive, reported that Adams appeared sincere in his desire for peace, but unknown to him there existed a Federalist project for war. To Pierre A. Adet, New York, June 7, 1797, in *Archives des Affaires Étrangères, Correspondance Politique, États-Unis*, vol. 47, part v, ff. 344. The originals are in Paris and reproductions are deposited in the Library of Congress. Hereinafter cited as AAE CP EU. The quotation is from Adams to Dr. Walsh, Phil., March 10, 1797, Adams Papers, reel 117.
64. The quotations are from Smith, *Adams*, pp. 933–934, and Adams to

Gerry, Phil., July 17, 1797, in Adams, *Works of John Adams*, VIII, 549. See also the sentiments Gerry expressed to Adams on Jan. 30, Feb. 3, and March 7, 1797, in Eugene F. Kramer, "The Public Career of Elbridge Gerry" (unpublished Ph.D. dissertation, The Ohio State University, 1955), pp. 124–125.

65. See George C. Rogers, Jr., *Evolution of a Federalist: William Loughton Smith of Charleston, 1758–1812* (Columbia, S.C., 1962), pp. 300–301, and Dice R. Anderson, *William Branch Giles* (Menasha, Wis., 1914), p. 57. Smith's resolutions are in 5 Cong., 1 sess., *Annals of the Congress, 1789–1824* (42 vols., Washington, D.C., 1834–1856), VII, 239. For Hamilton's instructions to Smith, see his letters of April 10, 1797, in Hamilton, *Works of Hamilton*, VI, 237, 269–278, and 485. Republican newspapers said the mission would fail unless the government adopted a friendlier attitude toward France. The Philadelphia *Aurora*, June 17, 1797, and the Boston *Independent Chronicle*, July 10, 1797. See also Malone, *Jefferson and the Ordeal of Liberty*, p. 319.

66. Kurtz, *Presidency of John Adams*, p. 289; Smelser, *Congress Founds the Navy*, p. 118; Dauer, *Adams Federalists*, pp. 298–302, who has tabulated the voting in the House during the special session; and Liston to Grenville, Phil., Aug. 31, 1797, No. 38, PRO GB FO 5.

67. Theodore Sedgwick to King, Phil., June 24, 1797, and George Cabot to King, Brookline, Aug. 17, in Charles C. King, ed., *The Life and Correspondence of Rufus King* (6 vols., New York, 1894–1900), II, 192, 212. Hereinafter cited as King, *Correspondence of Rufus King*. See also Robert G. Harper to constituents, Phil., July 24, 1797, in Donnan, "Bayard Papers," p. 40. Adams's message of June 12, 1797, and related documents are in *ASP FR*, II, 20–27. The message of July 3 is on p. 66, and Blount's letter of April 21, is on pp. 76–77, also in John Wood, *A History of the Administration of John Adams . . .* (New York, 1802), pp. 75–77.

68. For background and details on the "Blount Conspiracy," see DeConde, *Entangling Alliance*, pp. 448–449; Thomas P. Abernethy, *The South in the New Nation, 1789–1819* (Baton Rouge, La., 1961), pp. 169–216; Frederick Jackson Turner, ed., "Documents on the Blount Conspiracy, 1795–1797," *American Historical Review*, X (April 1905), 574–606; and Arthur Preston Whitaker, *The Mississippi Question, 1795–1803* (New York, 1934), pp. 104–105. Some observers argued that the Blount affair widened the breach with France. Daniel Bedinger to Henry Bedinger, Norfolk, July 11, 1797, Dandridge Papers, Duke University Library.

69. Cunningham, *Jeffersonian Republicans*, p. 120; Malone, *Jefferson and the Ordeal of Liberty*, p. 324; and Rogers, *Evolution of a Federalist*, p. 302, from which the quotation is taken. In general, the Federalist press attacked Monroe almost as if he were a traitor. See Létombe to Charles Delacroix, Phil., July 16, 1797, in Turner, "Correspondence of French Ministers," p. 1045.

70. Monroe published his vindication in Philadelphia in December 1797

under the title, *A View of the Conduct of the Executive in the Foreign Affairs of the United States, Connected with the Mission to the French Republic during the Years 1794, 5 & 6.* The text, without documents, is in Stanislaus M. Hamilton, ed., *The Writings of James Monroe* (7 vols., New York, 1898–1903), III, 383–457.

71. For the Reynolds episode, see Broadus Mitchell, *Alexander Hamilton: The National Adventure, 1788–1804* (New York, 1962), pp. 399–422.

72. To Edward Rutledge, Phil., June 24, 1797, in Andrew A. Lipscomb and Albert E. Bergh, eds., *The Writings of Thomas Jefferson* (20 vols., Washington, D.C., 1903–04), IX, 411.

73. Jefferson to James Madison, Phil., June 15, 1797, and to Aaron Burr, Phil., June 17, 1797, in Lipscomb, *Writings of Jefferson*, X, 397–404. Létombe thought that war might result from the measures of the special session. To Charles Delacroix, Phil., July 17, 1797, in Turner, "Correspondence of French Ministers," pp. 1046–1047. Newspaper reaction is summarized in Stewart, "Jeffersonian Journalism," p. 526.

74. Smelser, *Congress Founds the Navy*, p. 397; Carroll, *Washington*, p. 479; Rush to Noah Webster, Phil., April 27, 1798, in Butterfield, *Letters of Benjamin Rush*, II, 798; and Kenneth R. Rossman, *Thomas Mifflin and the Politics of the American Revolution* (Chapel Hill, N.C., 1952), pp. 284–285.

〰〰 *Notes — Chapter II* 〰〰

1. For a critical analysis of the Directors and their political ideas, see Georges Dejoint, *La politique économique du Directoire* (Paris, 1951), pp. 31–50. See also Albert Mathiez, *Le Directoire* (Paris, 1934); John Holland Rose, *The Revolutionary and Napoleonic Era, 1789–1815* (Cambridge, 1901), pp. 95–96; Robert R. Palmer, *The Age of Democratic Revolution: A Political History of Europe and America, 1760–1800,* Vol. II, *The Struggle* (Princeton, 1964), pp. 215–217; Georges Lefebvre, *The Thermidoreans and the Directory,* trans. from the French (New York, 1964), pp. 239–461; and A. Godwin, "The French Executive Directory—A Revaluation," *History,* New Series, XXII (Dec. 1937), 201–218.

2. Louis Philippe de Ségur, for example, who had served in America during the Revolution, defended the United States in two vigorous articles in *Nouvelles Politiques,* April 25 and May 17, 1797, cited in Echeverria, *Mirage in the West,* p. 223, and Faÿ, *Revolutionary Spirit,* p. 392.

3. This analysis is based on documents which contain assessments of public opinion, dated April 6, 12, 21, 27 and June 9, 1797, in François V. A. Aulard, ed., *Paris pendant la réaction Thermidorienne et sous le Directoire: Recueil de documents pour l'histoire d'esprit public à Paris* (5 vols., Paris, 1898–1902), IV, 44, 57, 73, 84–85, and 162. See also Marshall to George Washington, The Hague, Sept. 15, 1797, in J. Franklin Jameson, ed., "Letters of John Marshall when Envoy to France, 1797–1798," *American Historical Review,* II (Jan. 1897), 296. Godwin, "The French Executive Directory," p. 211, says the Directors knew that the people desired peace.

4. Pastoret is quoted in C. C. Pinckney to Secretary of State, The Hague, June 28, 1797, Department of State, Diplomatic Dispatches, France, 24: 193, National Archives (microfilm copy), and in James A. James, "French Opinion as a Factor in Preventing War between France and the United States, 1795–1800," *American Historical Review,* XXX (Oct. 1924), 52. Observations on Pastoret's accusations in the *Conseil Cinq-*

Cents on June 2 [1797], for the Minister of Foreign Relations [Paris], June 25, 1797, in AAE CP EU, vol. 47, part VI, ff. 445–447. The shipowners and sailors of Nantes to the *Conseil Cinq-Cents,* June-July 1797, expressed agreement with Pastoret and urged a peaceful settlement with the United States, *ibid.,* ff. 440–442. Pickering had Pastoret's speech translated into English and published in John Fenno's *Gazette of the United States* (Phil.). Pickering to John Adams, Trenton, Sept. 16, 1797, Pickering Papers, Massachusetts Historical Society.

5. Bowman, "Struggle for Neutrality," pp. 321–322; Frédéric Masson, *Le Département des affaires étrangères pendant la révolution, 1787–1804* (Paris, 1877), p. 361, and Lyon, "The Directory and the United States," pp. 518–519. William Vans Murray cited the case of one member of the Ancients who opposed the government's policy toward the United States, not necessarily because the United States was right, but mainly because he hated the Executive Directory. To McHenry, July 14, 1797, in Steiner, *James McHenry,* p. 231.

6. Murray to George Washington, The Hague, Sept. 16, 1797, George Washington Papers, Library of Congress. For the effect of the *coup* on the legislators, see Pierre-François Henry, *Histoire du directoire exécutif de la république française* . . . (2 vols., Paris, 1801), II, 83–114; E. Wilson Lyon, *The Man Who Sold Louisiana: The Career of François Barbe-Marbois* (Norman, Okla., 1942), pp. 103–106; Albert Meynier, *Les coups d'état du Directoire* (3 vols., Paris, 1927–1928), I, *Le dix huit fructidor an V* (4 *Septembre 1797); Leo Gershoy, *The French Revolution and Napoleon* (New York, 1933), p. 331; Louis Madelin, *La France du Directoire* (Paris, 1934), pp. 174–176; and Palmer, *Age of Democratic Revolution,* II, 255–257. Reubell dominated the Executive Directory's foreign policy at this time. See Louis Marie Larévellière-Lépeaux, *Mémoires de Larévellière-Lépeaux* (3 vols., Paris, 1895), II, 125–160.

7. The quotations are from Marshall to Pickering, The Hague, Sept. 15, 1797, in Jack L. Cross, ed., "John Marshall on the French Revolution and on American Politics," *The William and Mary Quarterly,* 3rd Series, XII (Oct. 1955), 638, and J. Q. Adams to John Adams, London, Sept. 21, 1797, in Worthington C. Ford, ed., *The Writings of John Quincy Adams* (7 vols., New York, 1913–1917), II, 211. See also Samuel E. Morison, *The Life and Letters of Harrison Gray Otis, 1765–1848* (2 vols., Boston, 1913), I, 83 n.

8. Some Republicans felt that France had a long account against the United States, and to settle it Americans might have to purchase peace as they had with the Algerines of North Africa. Daniel Bedinger to Henry Bedinger, Norfolk, Aug. 15, 1797, Dandridge Papers, Duke University Library.

9. Skipwith to Talleyrand, Paris, July 20, 1797, AAE CP EU, vol. 48, part II, f. 117; Albert J. Beveridge, *The Life of John Marshall* (4 vols., Boston, 1916–1919), II, 253. From The Hague, William Vans Murray reported that the Directory wished to avoid war, and would be concilia-

tory toward the American commissioners. This attitude, he felt, was designed to keep Americans from arming. To McHenry, July 18, Aug. 7 and 11, 1798, in Steiner, *James McHenry*, pp. 224–248. Faÿ, in *Revolutionary Spirit*, p. 404, maintains, contrary to the documentary evidence, that Talleyrand's appointment "was the final blow to friendship between France and the United States."

10. William Smith in Lisbon made a sound assessment. Talleyrand, he said, "is a shrewd, and interested politician, he will probably pursue that course which he thinks will tend to his aggrandizement." To Pickering, Aug. 24, 1797, in Bernard C. Steiner, ed., "Correspondence of William Smith, American Minister to Portugal," *The Sewanee Review*, XIV (Jan. 1906), 79. While Talleyrand resided in the United States he devoted himself to acquiring money. See Richard M. Brace, "Talleyrand in New England: Reality and Legend," *New England Quarterly*, XVI (Sept. 1943), 397–406. See also Louis Madelin, *Talleyrand, A Vivid Biography of the Unscrupulous, and Fascinating French Statesman*, trans. from the French (New York, 1948), pp. 51–52, 57–58, 61, and 103–105. Felix Gilbert in "The 'New Diplomacy' of the Eighteenth Century," *World Politics*, IV (Oct. 1951), 35, says that under the Directory France returned to the usual methods of diplomacy.

11. The quotation is in Charles M. Talleyrand, *Memoir Concerning the Commercial Relations of the United States with England* (Boston, 1809), p. 6, and Alfred Schalck de la Faverie, *Napoléon et L'Amerique* (Paris, 1917), p. 104. See also Carl L. Lokke, *France and the Colonial Question* (New York, 1932), pp. 169–170. William Smith thought Talleyrand had treated Americans well in his essay. To James McHenry, Lisbon, Oct. 9, 1797, in Steiner, "Correspondence of William Smith," p. 87. For a detailed analysis of Talleyrand's stay in America and of his views on the United States, see George Lacour-Gayet, *Talleyrand, 1754–1883* (4 vols., Paris, 1928–1934), I, 181–206, and Charles Maurice Talleyrand, *Memoirs of the Prince de Talleyrand*, ed. by Duc de Broglie, trans. from the French (5 vols., London, 1891–1892), I, 173–186.

12. Louis-Guillaume Otto, *Considérations sur la conduite du gouvernement Américain envers la France, depuis le commencement de la révolution jusqu'en 1797*, with an introduction by Gilbert Chinard (Princeton, 1945), 31 pp. See also James, "French Opinion as a Factor in Preventing War," pp. 44–46.

13. Adet arrived in Paris late in May 1797 and had a conference with the Directors on July 10. Minister of Foreign Relations to Létombe, Paris, July 13, 1797, AAE CP EU, vol. 48, part I, ff. 41–42. Adet's report, dated Sept. 27, 1797, was received Oct. 13, Lyon, "The Directory and the United States," p. 520.

14. See *ibid.*, p. 521; Frances S. Childs, "French Opinion of Anglo-American Relations, 1795–1805," *French-American Review*, I (Jan.-March 1948), 30; and Frances S. Childs, "A Secret Agent's Advice on

America, 1797," in Edward Mead Earle, ed., *Nationalism and Inter-nationalism: Essays Inscribed to Carlton J. H. Hayes* (New York, 1950), pp. 18–44, which offers a perceptive analysis of Hauterive's ideas and advice. Hauterive to Adet, New York, June 19, 1797, July 2, 16, in AAE CP EU, vol. 47, part V, f. 344 (source of the quotation), part VI, ff. 393–397, and vol. 48, part I, f. 6. For a brief sketch of Hauterive see Masson, *Le Département des affaires étrangères pendant la révolution*, pp. 409–414; and for details on his career as it touched the United States, see Artaud de Montor, *Histoire de la vie et des travaux politiques du Comte d'Hauterive. . . .* , 2nd. ed. (Paris, 1839), pp. 68–104.

15. The quotation is from Talleyrand to Létombe, Paris, Aug. 4, 1797, AAE CP EU, vol. 48, part II, ff. 152–153. Bernard Faÿ, in *The Two Franklins: Father of American Democracy* (Boston, 1933), p. 329, maintains that Talleyrand followed Hauterive's advice. Raymond Guyot, in *Le Directoire et la paix de l'Europe des traités de Bâle à la deuxième coalition (1795–1799)* (Paris, 1911), p. 559, says the Directory itself put off an official reception for the American commissioners.

16. William Vans Murray explained the Federalist position on this point. "I sincerely hope," he wrote, "that, if the old treaty of 1778 is to be revived—the Free ships free goods may be omitted. The internal code of France has always contravened it & always will—& no nation will observe it, unless the neutrality be *armed*. If we can arm & enforce, it wd. be great for us—but that we can not be expected. In 20 years, we shall be equal to its *enforcement*." To McHenry, July 14, 1797, in Steiner, *James McHenry*, pp. 242–243.

17. The instructions, dated July 15, 1797, are printed in *ASP FR*, II, 153–157. Pickering and Upham, *Life of Pickering*, III, 371, call this one of Pickering's "celebrated State Papers." Henry J. Ford, "Timothy Pickering," in Samuel F. Bemis, ed., *The American Secretaries of State and Their Diplomacy* (10 vols., New York, 1927–29), II, 217, suggests, on the other hand, that Marshall wrote the instructions. Some Republicans, such as Daniel Bedinger, believed the commissioners would be rebuffed because they were not "furnished with powers sufficient to place the [French] Republic upon the same favorable footing with Great Britain." To Henry Bedinger, Norfolk, Aug. 15, 1797, Dandridge Papers, Duke University Library.

18. Sept. 9, 1797, in Beveridge, *John Marshall*, II, 232. Later, Marshall said the *coup d'état* "blasted every hope of an accommodation between the United States and France." See John Stokes Adams, ed., *An Autobiographical Sketch by John Marshall* (Ann Arbor, Mich., 1927), p. 23. Pinckney shared a similar view, Zahniser, "Public Career of Charles Cotesworth Pinckney," pp. 221–222.

19. Jefferson had asked the French to receive the envoys graciously and to listen to them. See Létombe to Delacroix, Phil., June 7, 1797, in Turner, "Correspondence of French Ministers," p. 1030. See also Alfred

O. Aldridge, *Man of Reason: The Life of Thomas Paine* (Phil., 1959),
pp. 251–254, and Paine to the Commissioners, Paris, Oct. 11, 1797,
Department of State, Diplomatic Dispatches, France, National Archives,
film 34, roll 8.

20. Envoys to Secretary of State, Paris, Oct. 22, 1797, in *ASP FR*, II, 158–
160. See also Ulane Bonnel, *La France, les États-Unis et la guerre
de course (1797–1815)* (Paris, 1961), p. 58. In the eighteenth century
and during the American Revolution, loans, such as the one the French
demanded, were not considered unneutral. See Charles S. Hyneman,
*The First American Neutrality: A Study of the American Understanding
of Neutral Obligations during the Years 1792 to 1815* (Urbana, Ill.,
1934), pp. 40–41.

21. Later Adams said even if a *douceur*, or bribe, would lead to a beneficial
treaty it should not be paid. He stressed that "the giving of the smallest
amount would be derogatory to America." Samuel Smith to James
Bayard, Baltimore, Aug. 3, 1738, reporting a conversation with Adams
on the "Topick . . . of a war with France," in Donnan, "Bayard
Papers," pp. 69–70. John Marshall, "General Marshall's Journal In
Paris From September 27, 1797, To April 11, 1798," Oct. 19, 1797,
manuscript in the Massachusetts Historical Society, Boston, with a
microfilm copy in the library, University of California, Santa Barbara.

22. Envoys to Secretary of State, Paris, Oct. 22, 1797, *ASP FR*, II, 159.
On the matter of the loan and the bribe, John Quincy Adams commented, "We have not even the benefit of choosing between extortion
and robbery. Both are pointed against us at once." To King, Berlin, Jan.
26, 1798, Rufus King Papers.

23. See Palmer, *Age of Democratic Revolution*, II, pp. 328, 536; J. Holland
Rose, *William Pitt and the Great War*, 2nd ed. (London, 1912), p.
325; Pierre Rain, *La diplomatie française: de Mirabeau à Bonaparte*
(Paris, 1950), p. 159; and Great Britain, Historical Manuscripts Commission Reports, *The Manuscripts of J. B. Fortescue, Esq., Preserved at
Dropmore*, ed. by Walter Fitzpatrick (No. 30, 10 vols., London, 1892–
1898), III, 356–359. Hereinafter cited as *Dropmore Papers*.

24. Marshall, "Journal in Paris," Oct. 20 and 21, 1797. The American
envoys did not expect to be received. They even made arrangements at
this time to return to America. Marshall to George Washington, Paris,
Oct. 24, 1797, in Jameson, "Letters of John Marshall when Envoy to
France," p. 302.

25. Mountflorence to Gerry and Gerry to Mountflorence, Paris, Nov. 5 and
6, 1797, Elbridge Gerry Papers, Manuscript Division, Library of Congress. Theodore Sizer, ed., *The Autobiography of Colonel John Trumbull*
(New Haven, 1953), p. 222.

26. The quotations are from Beveridge, *John Marshall*, II, 271–273. This
sequence of conversation differs from that in Zahniser, "Public Career
of Charles Cotesworth Pinckney," pp. 229–230, who says Hauteval
elicited Pinckney's outburst. A slightly different version appears in
Envoys to Pickering, Paris, Oct. 27, 1797, *ASP FR*, II, 161.

27. Marshall, "Journal in Paris," Oct. 29, 1797; Envoys to Secretary of State, Paris, Oct. 29, 1797, *ASP FR*, II, 163.
28. Envoys to Minister of Foreign Relations, Paris, Nov. 11, 1797, *ASP FR*, II, 166. Word had now spread that the envoys would be rejected, and then France would strike openly at the United States. William Vans Murray to King, Rotterdam, Nov. 4, 1797, and C. C. Pinckney to King, Nov. 26, Rufus King Papers; Murray to John Quincy Adams, The Hague, Nov. 4, 1797, in Worthington C. Ford, ed., "Letters of William Vans Murray to John Quincy Adams, 1797–1803," *Annual Report of the American Historical Association for the Year 1912* (Washington, D.C., 1914), p. 366; Marshall to Pinckney, Paris, Nov. 27, 1797, in Cross, "Marshall on the French Revolution," p. 642; and Marshall, "Journal in Paris," Dec. 17, 1797.
29. These quotations are from Zahniser, "Public Career of Charles Cotesworth Pinckney," p. 238, citing Mary Pinckney to Mrs. Gabriel Manigault, Paris, March 9, 1798, Manigault Papers, South Carolina Library, University of South Carolina. Later, Republicans accused Pinckney and Marshall of intimacies with the lady, suggesting that if they had been as successful in their mission as they were in Paris boudoirs, they would be remembered as America's greatest diplomats. See John C. Miller, *Crisis in Freedom: The Alien and Sedition Acts* (Boston, 1951), pp. 148–149.
30. Beveridge, *John Marshall*, II, 291–292, and Pinckney's note of Dec. 21, 1797, in *ASP FR*, II, 167.
31. The memorial is printed in *ASP FR*, II, 169–182. See also Adams, *Marshall's Autobiographical Sketch*, pp. 23–24 and Zahniser, "Public Career of Charles Cotesworth Pinckney," p. 237.
32. The decree is printed in *ASP FR*, III, 288–289. See also James D. Phillips, "Salem's Part in the Naval War with France," *New England Quarterly*, XVI (Dec. 1943), 543–566, and W. Allison Phillips and Arthur H. Reede, *Neutrality: Its History, Economics and Law*, Vol. II, *The Napoleonic Period* (New York, 1936), p. 83.
33. To John Rutledge, Paris, Jan. 25, 1798, The John Rutledge Papers, Southern Historical Collection, University of North Carolina Library, Chapel Hill.
34. William Vans Murray to King, The Hague, April 4, 1798, Rufus King Papers; C. C. Pinckney to Elbridge Gerry, Feb. 2, 1798, Pinckney Family Papers, Library of Congress, cited in Zahniser, "Public Career of Charles Cotesworth Pinckney," p. 241; Eli F. Heckscher, *The Continental System* (London, 1922), pp. 47–49; and Phillips and Reede, *Neutrality*, II, p. 85.
35. Marshall, "Journal in Paris," Feb. 3, 5, 26, and March 6, 13, 1798.
36. Talleyrand later denied any connection with Beaumarchais, except on the matter of Beaumarchais's claims against the American government. Minister of Foreign Relations to the Minister General of Police, Paris, April 26, 1798, AAE CP EU, vol. 49, p. 339.
37. Lyon, in "The Directory and the United States," p. 522, says the French

Foreign Office went over the memorial very carefully. Beveridge, in *John Marshall*, II, 310, says it was virtually ignored. The evidence suggests a careful perusal.

38. Talleyrand is quoted in Lyon, "The Directory and the United States," p. 523. Marshall maintained that France's fear of driving England and the United States together was the commissioners' main bargaining point, and therefore America's fate depended on England's power to resist the French. See Marshall to George Washington, March 8, 1798, in Jameson, "Letters of John Marshall when Envoy to France," pp. 303–304.

39. Talleyrand's reply, dated March 18, 1798, is translated and printed in *ASP FR*, II, 188–191.

40. The quotations are from Marshall, "Journal in Paris," March 23, 1798; Gerry to Mrs. Gerry, March 26, "Elbridge Gerry Letter Book," Library of Congress, cited in Beveridge, *John Marshall*, II, 327; and Zahniser, "Public Career of Charles Cotesworth Pinckney," p. 249.

41. A decree by the Directory, dated April 10, 1797, had nullified passports and visas issued by Americans. This meant that French authorities would not accept American passports. See Adam G. Gebhardt, comp., *State Papers Relating to the Diplomatick Transactions between the American and French Governments from the Year 1793 to the Conclusion of the Convention, on the 30th of September, 1800* (3 vols., London, 1816), III, 413. Marshall's note of April 3, 1798, is in *ASP FR*, II, 191–199.

42. See Gerry to Talleyrand, Paris, April 20, 1798, in James T. Austin, *The Life of Elbridge Gerry, with Contemporary Letters* (2 vols., Boston, 1828–29), II, 231–33. Gerry's decision infuriated extreme Federalists. They said he was a dupe, feebleminded, and deceitful. William Vans Murray considered him an honest, if misguided, man. Murray pointed out that Talleyrand's pressure on Gerry to remain in Paris at least indicated that the French wished to avoid a final rupture. Murray to King, April 2 and 13, 1798, Rufus King Papers, Huntington Library. Gerry believed he had a duty to prevent open war with France. Such a war would give the Hamiltonian extremists the opportunity they sought of adopting a militaristic policy, of making an alliance with England, and of discrediting republican institutions. See Samuel E. Morison, "Elbridge Gerry, Gentleman, Democrat," *New England Quarterly*, II (Jan. 1929), 23–27. Gerry also thought the American people would not support a war against France. See Eugene F. Kramer, "Some New Light on the X Y Z Affair: Elbridge Gerry's Reasons for Opposing War with France," *New England Quarterly*, XXIX (Dec. 1956), 512.

43. Marshall to C. C. Pinckney, Bordeaux, April 21, 1798, Pinckney Family Papers, cited in Zahniser, "Public Career of Charles Cotesworth Pinckney," p. 251. Gerry felt that Marshall's stand would lead to war, so he was pleased to see Marshall and Pinckney leave Paris. Kramer, "Public Career of Elbridge Gerry," p. 144.

44. See Lyon, "The Directory and the United States," pp. 523–524, and Thomas Jefferson to James Madison, Phil., Jan. 25, 1798, in Ford, *Writings of Jefferson*, VII, 191–194.

45. Timothy Pickering to King, Trenton, N.J., Oct. 31, 1797, Rufus King Papers, Huntington Library.

46. Adams thought that Talleyrand, "as a reasonable man," would accept the American mission. To Oliver Wolcott, Eastchester, Oct. 27, 1797, Adams Papers, Letter No. 8, reel 118. Also Adams to Pickering, Oct. 31, *ibid.*, reel 117. Létombe reported to Talleyrand that Americans considered war unlikely. Phil. Nov. 12, 1797, in Turner, "Correspondence of French Ministers," p. 1077.

47. The speech is printed in Richardson, *Messages of the Presidents*, I, 240–244, and in Adams, *Works of John Adams*, IX, 121–125.

48. See Dauer, *Adams Federalists*, p. 137; Albert Gallatin to Wife, Phil., Dec. 1, 1797, in Adams, *Life of Gallatin*, p. 188; Otis to Wife, Dec. 3, 1797, in Morison, *Harrison Gray Otis*, I, 76; and Morton Borden, *The Federalism of James A. Bayard* (New York, 1955), p. 27. The Senate and House replies, dated Nov. 27 and 28, 1797, are in Richardson, *Messages of the Presidents*, I, 244–248. Daniel Bedinger wrote that Congress was holding up legislation until it heard from the commissioners. To Henry Bedinger, Norfolk, Jan. 30, 1798, Dandridge Papers, Duke University Library.

49. Articles of impeachment were presented on Jan. 25, 1798; the Senate formed itself into a court of impeachment on Dec. 17; and the impeachment was dismissed on Jan. 14, 1799. For details, see Borden, *James A. Bayard*, pp. 47–61; David Y. Thomas, "The Law of Impeachment in the United States," *American Political Science Review*, II (May 1908), 382–383, 387–388. The quotation is in Morison, *Harrison Gray Otis*, I, 87. See also Miller, *Crisis in Freedom*, p. 104; Frank Van der Linden, *The Turning Point: Jefferson's Battle for the Presidency* (Washington, D.C., 1962), pp. 101–104; and J. Fairfax McLaughlin, *Matthew Lyon* (New York, 1900), pp. 225–305.

50. Gallatin to Wife, Jan. 2, 11 and 19, in Adams, *Life of Gallatin*, p. 189. Gallatin predicted that nothing would be done until the fate of the negotiation was known. The Boston *Independent Chronicle*, Jan. 19, Feb. 1, 15 and 19, 1798, claimed the administration wanted war, but that "True Americans" would pray for peace and the success of the mission.

51. There were in the House of Representatives, an extreme Federalist explained, "52 determined and rancorous Jacobins, and 54 who profess attachment to the government, or in other words, confidence in the Executive." Under Gallatin's control the Republicans were "a well organized and disciplined corps, never going astray, or doing right even by mistake." Theodore Sedgwick, to King, April 9, 1798, in King, *Correspondence of Rufus King*, II, 310–311. The quotation is from Oliver Wolcott, Jr., to Frederick Wolcott, Phil., Feb. 27, 1798, in Gibbs, *Wolcott Papers*, II, 13.

52. Pickering reported that private letters indicated failure of the mission, and "even present a prospect of war." To King, Phil., Jan. 13, 1798, Rufus King Papers. See also James Bayard to Richard Bassett, Phil., Dec. 30, 1797, in Donnan, "Bayard Papers," p. 46. The quotation is from Washington to McHenry, Mount Vernon, March 4, 1798, in John C. Fitzpatrick, ed., *The Writings of George Washington from the Original Manuscript Sources, 1745–1799* (39 vols., Washington, D.C., 1931–44), XXXVI, 179.

53. Malone, *Jefferson and the Ordeal of Liberty*, pp. 368–369.

54. The questions are in Adams, *Works of John Adams*, VIII, 561–562.

55. For details see E. H. Stuart Jones, *An Invasion That Failed: The French Expedition to Ireland, 1796* (Oxford, 1950), pp. 199–201; James Dugan, *The Great Mutiny* (New York, 1965); Rose, *William Pitt and the Great War*, pp. 299–364; Philip A. Brown, *The French Revolution in English History* (London, 1918), pp. 154–155; Palmer, *Age of Democratic Revolution*, II, pp. 491–505; and Lefebvre, *The Thermidoreans and the Directory*, p. 362. One journalist compared the Irish uprising with the American Revolution. *Carey's United States Recorder* (Phil.), May 17 and 19, 1798, cited in Stewart, "Jeffersonian Journalism," p. 458.

56. Jackson to James Robertson, Phil., Jan. 11, 1798, in John S. Bassett, ed., *Correspondence of Andrew Jackson* (7 vols., Washington, D.C., 1926–35), I, 42. An American, on the other hand, acted as an informer for the British on the French preparations. Dundas to Spencer, Somerset, April 27, 1798, in Second Earl Spencer, *Private Papers of George, Second Earl Spencer First Lord of the Admiralty, 1784–1801*, ed. by Julian S. Corbett and H. W. Richmond (3 vols., London, 1913–1924), II, 325–326.

57. Cabot wrote as "Political Monitor" in the *Massachusetts Mercury*, Jan. 30, 1798, reprinted in Lodge, *Cabot*, p. 593.

58. Otis to Wife, March 14, 1798, in Morison, *Harrison Gray Otis*, I, 69; Marshall to George Washington, Paris, March 8, 1798, in Jameson, "Letters of John Marshall when Envoy to France," p. 303.

59. McHenry's request and Hamilton's reply are in Steiner, *James McHenry*, pp. 291–295. McHenry to John Adams, Feb. 15, 1798, is in the Adams Papers, reel 387, and is summarized in Adams, *Works of John Adams*, VIII, 562–563. See also Darling, *Rising Empire*, pp. 308–309.

60. Grenville to Liston, Downing Street, Jan. 15, 1798, in Mayo, "Instructions to the British Ministers," pp. 148–149.

61. Adams to Congress, March 5, 1798, in Richardson, *Messages of the Presidents*, I, 253–254, and 5 Cong., 2 sess., *Annals of the Congress*, VII, 1201.

62. *Gazette of the United States* (Phil.), March 5, 1798.

63. See Robert G. Harper to Constituents, Phil., March 9, 1798, in Donnan, "Bayard Papers," p. 51 and Gallatin to Wife, March 6, 1798, in Adams, *Life of Gallatin*, p. 195.

64. Adams to Heads of Department, Phil., March 13, 1798, in Adams, *Works of John Adams,* VIII, 568.
65. Smith, *Adams,* pp. 953–954; Hamilton to Pickering, March 17, 25, and 27, 1798, in Hamilton, *Works of Hamilton,* VI, 278, 485; Lodge, *Hamilton's Works,* X, 275–278; and Pickering to J. Q. Adams, March 8, 1798, in Ford, *Writings of John Quincy Adams,* II, 267–270.
66. From two pages of undated notes, with some passages crossed out, titled "Message" in the Adams Papers, reel 387. It seems clear that these notes were written some time between March 15 and 19, 1798.
67. From two additional, but separate, pages of undated notes in *ibid.*
68. Smith, *Adams,* pp. 954–955, and Abigail Adams to Mary Cranch, Phil., March 20, 1798, in Stewart Mitchell, ed., *New Letters of Abigail Adams, 1788–1801* (Boston, 1947), pp. 146–167.
69. Message of March 19, 1798, crossed out passage, Adams Papers, reel 387.
70. Citizen Rozier to Minister of Foreign Relations, New York, March 13, 1798, *Archives nationales, relations extérieures,* U.S.A., AF, III, 64 dossier, no. 263. Photographed from the originals in Paris.
71. The message of March 19, 1798, is printed in Adams, *Works of John Adams,* IX, 156–157, and *ASP FR,* II, 152. After seeing a circular permitting American ships to arm, William Vans Murray said, for example, "It was all the President could authorize, but it is war. Congress must do the rest." To J. Q. Adams, June 1, 1798, in Ford, "Letters of William Vans Murray," p. 412.
72. Pickering to Envoys, March 23, 1798, in Pickering and Upham, *Life of Pickering,* III, 375–377.
73. See Jefferson to James Madison, March 21, 1798, in Ford, *Writings of Jefferson,* VII, 219; Schachner, *Founding Fathers,* pp. 449–450; Dauer, *Adams Federalists,* p. 141; *Augusta Chronicle* (Ga.), April 21, 1798, cited in Stewart, "Jeffersonian Journalism," p. 542; and Harry M. Tinkom, *The Republicans and Federalists in Pennsylvania, 1790–1801* (Harrisburg, Pa., 1950), p. 206, for sentiment against war.
74. 5 Cong., 2 sess., *Annals of the Congress,* VII and VIII, 1200–1327; and Dauer, *Adams Federalists,* p. 146.
75. Richard Sprigg, in 5 Cong., 2 sess., *Annals of the Congress,* VII and VIII, 1262–1373. One argument touched on whether the first resolution should read "resort to" or "declare" war. Adams's address, Republicans said, implied a state of war against France. See also William E. Dodd, *Life of Nathaniel Macon* (Raleigh, N.C., 1903), pp. 109, 120.
76. To Mary Cranch, Phil., March 27, 1798, in Mitchell, *New Letters of Abigail Adams,* pp. 147–149.
77. Giles, a Republican, asked for the correspondence, Anderson, *William Branch Giles,* p. 59. See also Pickering to William Vans Murray, March 27 and 30, 1798, in Ford, "Letters of William Vans Murray," p. 390 n, and Phillips, "Public Career of Timothy Pickering," p. 293. It was assumed, apparently, that the commissioners had departed, and hence

would not be endangered by a disclosure. For an interesting character-
ization of Allen, see Wood, *Administration of John Adams*, p. 141.

78. 5 Cong., 2 sess., *Annals of the Congress*, VIII, 1367–1371, and Dauer,
Adams Federalists, pp. 141–142, and Vote Chart No. IV, pp. 305–309.

79. Jonathan Mason, Jr., to Otis, Boston, March 30, 1798, in Morison,
Harrison Gray Otis, I, 93. In some circles men talked about war with
France now being inevitable. John Rutledge to Bishop [Robert] Smith,
Phil., April 1, 1798, John Rutledge Papers, Southern Historical Collec-
tion, University of North Carolina Library. The latter quotation is from
Sedgwick to Henry Van Schaack, Phil., March 17, 1798, Sedgwick
Papers, cited in Charles, *Origins of the American Party System*, p. 126.

80. Jefferson to James Madison, Phil., April 5, 1798, in Ford, *Writings of
Jefferson*, VII, 230–232, and Raymond Walters, Jr., *Albert Gallatin:
Jeffersonian Financier and Diplomat* (New York, 1957), p. 107.

81. Adams to Congress, April 3, 1798, in Adams, *Works of John Adams*, IX,
158. See also Smith, *Adams*, p. 959.

82. "The Jacobins in Senate and House were struck dumb," Abigail reported, "and opened not their mouths, not having their cue, not having
received their lessons" from Talleyrand's agents. To Mary Cranch, Phil.,
April 4, 1798, in Mitchell, *New Letters of Abigail Adams*, pp. 150–152.

83. 5 Cong., 2 sess., *Annals of the Congress*, VIII, 1379–1380.

84. Robert Troup to King, New York, June 3, 1798, in King, *Correspondence
of Rufus King*, II, 329. On the same day the Senate also ordered publication of the envoys' instructions. Pickering to John Adams, Phil., April
10, 1798, Pickering Papers, Massachusetts Historical Society. *Porcupine's Gazette* (Phil.) devoted the whole issue of April 9, 1798, to the
dispatches. William Cobbett, the editor, announced that he would have
the printed dispatches ready in pamphlet form in a few hours. Later he
wrote a satirical poem on the subject, calling it: "French Arrogance;
or 'The Cat let out of the Bag:' A Poetical Dialogue between the Envoys
of America, X.Y.Z. and Lady." See Mary E. Clark, *Peter Porcupine in
America: The Career of William Cobbett, 1792–1800* (Phil., 1939), pp.
126, 129. Even the Republican *Aurora* of Philadelphia, April 10–12,
printed the dispatches. The whole X Y Z episode is summarized in a
readable, popular style in Frederick T. Hill, "Adventures in Diplomacy:
The Affair of X, Y, and Z," *Atlantic Monthly*, CXIII (April 1914),
533–545.

85. Dispatches were coming in from Europe, for example, from Joseph Fen-
wick, the American Consul at Bordeaux, March 17, 1798, saying war
seemed inevitable. Pickering Papers, Massachusetts Historical Society.

Notes — Chapter III

1. Robert Liston reported that after publication of the X Y Z dispatches the Republicans in Congress met privately and decided "to give up for the moment all opposition to Government." To Grenville, Phil., April 12, 1798, No. 19, PRO GB FO 5. Liston thought the X Y Z affair would almost inevitably lead to war. George W. Kyte, "Robert Liston and Anglo-American Cooperation, 1796–1800," *American Philosophical Society Proceedings,* XCIII (1949), 263. See also Marshall Smelser, "The Jacobin Phrenzy: The Menace of Monarchy, Plutocracy, and Anglophilia, 1789–1798," *Review of Politics,* XXI (Jan. 1959), 255.

2. Jefferson's views are in letters to Madison, April 6, 1798, and Peter Carr, April 12, in Ford, *Writings of Jefferson,* VII, 234–240. Pickering's views are in letters to Washington, Phil., April 14, 1798, Pickering Papers, Massachusetts Historical Society, and to Rufus King, Aug. 29, 1798, in Pickering and Upham, *Life of Pickering,* III, 381. "It was anticipated," Pickering told King of the dispatches, "that their publication would do much good in Europe as well as in America." In Europe, William Vans Murray told Rufus King, the people were "charmed with this exhibition of villainy of X & Y & T." May 28, 1798, in Rufus King Papers, Huntington Library. John Jay thought publication of the dispatches would promote national unity. To Pickering, Albany, April 19, 1798, Pickering Papers, Massachusetts Historical Society.

3. Russell J. Ferguson, *Early Western Pennsylvania Politics* (Pittsburgh, 1938), pp. 144–145. That June, 1798, the New Hampshire legislature also approved a memorial saying that peace purchased at the expense of liberty "is a greater evil than war." See Lynn W. Turner, *William Plumer of New Hampshire, 1759–1850* (Chapel Hill, N.C., 1962), pp. 64–65; Delbert H. Gilpatrick, *Jeffersonian Democracy in North Carolina, 1789–1816* (New York, 1931), p. 82; and Mary E. Loughrey, *France and Rhode Island, 1686–1800* (New York, 1944), p. 59, for other evidence of anti-French sentiment.

4. Abigail Adams to Mary Cranch, April 13, 1798, in Mitchell, *New Letters of Abigail Adams,* pp. 155–157, and Abigail Adams to Mercy Warren, Phil., April 25, 1798, in [Worthington C. Ford, ed.], *Warren–Adams*

Letters, Being Chiefly a Correspondence among John Adams, Samuel Adams, and James Warren . . . 1743–1814 (2 vols., Boston, 1917–25), II, 336. Henrietta Liston to James Jackson, May 3, 1798, quoted in Perkins, *First Rapprochement*, p. 94. Earlier, Mrs. Liston had said the publication of the X Y X dispatches was a "dose too strong for the French party here to swallow." To Jackson, Phil., April 10, 1798, in Bradford Perkins, ed., "A Diplomat's Wife in Philadelphia: Letters of Henrietta Liston, 1796–1800," *William and Mary Quarterly*, Third Series, IX (Oct. 1954), 615.

5. Theodore Sedgwick to King, May 1, 1798, and Robert Troup to King, June 3, in King, *Correspondence of Rufus King*, II, 319, 329.

6. *The Gazette and Daily Advertiser* (Charleston), Nov. 9, 1798, with a dateline of London, Sept. 9.

7. "The Warning," Feb. 21, 1797, is in Lodge, *Hamilton's Works*, V, 374–378. For "The Stand," see Hamilton, *Works of Hamilton*, VII, 639–681. The latter quotation is from Hamilton to William Smith, April 10, 1797, in Charles, *Origins of the American Party System*, pp. 125–126.

8. See *American State Papers, Military Affairs*, I, 120; Dauer, *Adams Federalists*, pp. 146–147; and Adams, *Life of John Adams*, II, 243. See also Welch, *Theodore Sedgwick*, p. 615, where it is said that this difference over program marked the beginning of a clear-cut division among Federalists, and David H. Fischer, *The Revolution of American Conservatism: The Federalist Party in the Era of Jeffersonian Democracy* (New York, 1965), p. 10, who points out that Federalists did form a clear-cut socioeconomic interest group. Dauer, in *Adams Federalists*, pp. 6–7, from whom I have taken the label High Federalist, explains the Federalist differences in terms of agriculture versus commerce.

9. Ames to Harrison Gray Otis, Dedham, Mass., April 23, 1798, in Seth Ames, ed., *Works of Fisher Ames* (2 vols., Boston, 1854), I, 225. The latter quotation is from the *New York Gazette*, April 12, 1798, in James Morton Smith, *Freedom's Fetters: The Alien and Sedition Laws and American Civil Liberties* (Ithaca, N.Y., 1956), p. 15. "We are now wonderfully popular," Abigail told Mary Cranch, Phil., April 28, 1798, in Mitchell, *New Letters of Abigail Adams*, pp. 167–168. Robert Liston reported that "in no circumstance in the United States has so striking a change taken place as in the degree of popularity enjoyed by the President, Mr. Adams." To Grenville, Phil., May 2, 1798, No. 20, PRO GB FO 5.

10. Knox to Oliver Wolcott, Boston, May 2, 1798, The Henry Knox Papers, 1770–1825, Massachusetts Historical Society. Many High Federalists were pleased because the X Y Z imbroglio offered the occasion for striking at Republicans. "It will," Theodore Sedgwick wrote, for example, "afford a glorious opportunity to destroy faction." Quoted in Smith, *Freedom's Fetters*, p. 21.

11. To Mary Cranch, Phil., April 7, 1798, in Mitchell, *New Letters of Abigail Adams*, pp. 153–155.

12. The quotation is from Miller, *Crisis in Freedom*, p. 30. For a contemporary comment on the anti-French attitude of the press, see Althéa de Puech, ed. and trans., *My Odyssey: Experience of a Young Refugee from Two Revolutions, by a Creole of Saint Domingue* (Baton Rouge, La., 1959), p. 175. See also Faÿ, *Revolutionary Spirit*, p. 451, and Jefferson to Madison, April 26, 1798, in Ford, *Writings of Jefferson*, VII, 245–246. Jefferson urged Republicans to save their papers by subscribing to them. Otherwise, he said, "republicanism will be entirely brow beaten," and the "war hawks" would take over.

13. See Smith, *Freedom's Fetters*, pp. 192–193; Sawvel, *Complete Anas*, April 13, 1798, p. 194; Nathaniel Ames, diary entry of April 13, 1798, in Charles Warren, *Jacobin and Junto, or Early American Politics as Viewed in the Diary of Dr. Nathaniel Ames, 1758–1822* (Cambridge, Mass., 1931), p. 75; see also p. 75 n. Létombe reported that Quakers and others petitioned Congress to keep the peace. To Talleyrand, Phil., April 19, 1798, AAE CP EU, vol. 49, pp. 328–329.

14. Liston to Grenville, Phil., May 2, 1798, No. 21, PRO GB FO 5. Logan's speech of May 12, 1798, is quoted in Frederick B. Tolles, *George Logan of Philadelphia* (New York, 1953), pp. 150–151. Another critic, Henry Tazewell, complained that "every measure of defence" against France was "made the means of increasing the power of the Executive." May 9, 1798, quoted in Dunbar, *Monarchical Tendencies*, p. 122. James Monroe thought Adams wanted war. See Arthur Styron, *The Last of the Cocked Hats: James Monroe and the Virginia Dynasty* (Norman, Okla., 1945), p. 213.

15. "Mr. Adams spends the whole morning from 6 o'clock till 12 or 1," Liston reported, "in writing these answers, which are frequently as long as the addresses to which they apply." To Grenville, Phil., May 20, 1798, PRO GB FO 5. See also Smelser, *Congress Founds the Navy*, p. 160, and Walter R. Fee, *The Transition from Aristocracy to Democracy in New Jersey, 1789–1829* (Somerville, N.J., 1933), p. 83, which gives a local reaction to this national issue.

16. See Abigail to Mary Cranch, Phil., May 18, 1798, Mitchell, *New Letters of Abigail Adams*, pp. 174–176; Adams to the Inhabitants of the Town of Hartford, Conn., May 10, 1798, in Adams, *Works of John Adams*, IX, 192–193, to a Vermont Regiment, Quincy, Aug. 15, 1798, Adams Papers, reel 119; and Faÿ, *The Two Franklins*, p. 347.

17. See Smith, *Freedom's Fetters*, p. 192. Adams spoke to the Young Men of Philadelphia on May 7. The President's answer to the Young Men of Boston is in Adams, *Works of John Adams*, IX, 194. The newspaper comment is that of the Boston *Independent Chronicle*, and is cited in Smelser, *Congress Founds the Navy*, p. 161. Adams later told soldiers from Ohio that the Navy would protect American commerce, Quincy, Aug. 21, 1798, Adams Papers, reel 119.

18. The quoted editor was Benjamin Russell of the *Columbian Centinel* (Boston), July 4, 1798. See Warren, *Jacobin and Junto*, pp. 81–86;

Dauer, *Adams Federalists*, p. 151. Adams himself greeted the Philadelphians wearing a black cockade on his hat. In time, the black cockade
became a symbol of extreme Federalism. See William O. Lynch, *Fifty
Years of Party Warfare, 1789–1837* (Indianapolis, 1931), p. 177, and
Clark, *Peter Porcupine in America*, pp. 127–128.

19. The quotations are from John A. Davis, *Travels of Four Years and a
Half in the United States of America, 1798–1802* (London, 1803), p.
118; Tolles, *George Logan*, p. 149. Joseph Hopkinson, composer of
"Hail Columbia," was delighted to have "execrable french murder
shouts" replaced. See John C. Miller, *The Federalist Era, 1789–1801*
(New York, 1960), p. 213 n., and Abigail to Mary Cranch, Phil., April
26, 1798, in Mitchell, *New Letters of Abigail Adams*, pp. 164–
166.

20. See Warren, *Jacobin and Junto*, p. 82. Adams's proclamation, dated
March 23, 1798, is in Richardson, *Messages of the Presidents*, I, 258–
260. The "psalm" is from the Boston *Independent Chronicle*, April 30,
1798. A Republican churchman issued his own prayers against American
foreign policy. See Charles Crowe, "The War of 'Pure Republicanism'
against Federalism, 1794–1801: Bishop James Madison on the American
Political Scene," *West Virginia History*, XXV (July 1963), 360.

21. Gary B. Nash, "The American Clergy and the French Revolution,"
William and Mary Quarterly, Third Series, XIII (July 1965), 392–412.
For further details on the Illuminati, see Vernon Stauffer, *New England
and the Bavarian Illuminati* (New York, 1918), and Anson D. Morse,
The Federalist Party in Massachusetts to the Year 1800 (Princeton,
1909), pp. 169–173.

22. See Adams to Jefferson, Quincy, June 30, 1813, in Adams, *Works of
John Adams*, X, 47–48; Morison, *Harrison Gray Otis*, I, 65; North
Callahan, *Henry Knox: General Washington's General* (New York,
1958), p. 365; Bowers, *Jefferson and Hamilton*, p. 367; and Edward G.
Everett, "Some Aspects of Pro-French Sentiment in Pennsylvania, 1790–
1800," *Western Pennsylvania Historical Magazine*, XLIII (March,
1960), 39.

23. See 5 Cong., 2 sess., *Annals of the Congress*, May 8, 1798, VIII, 1640–
1641; *Gazette of the United States* (New York), June 9, 1798. Hamilton,
among others, was convinced "that the powerful faction which has for
years opposed the government, is determined to go to every length
with France." Republicans, he concluded, would aid a French invasion.
To Washington, New York, May 19, 1798, in Lodge, *Hamilton's Works*,
VIII, 483. See also Dauer, *Adams Federalists*, p. 150, and Smith,
Freedom's Fetters, pp. 19–20.

24. Pickering to Harper, March 21, 1798, quoted in Morison, *Harrison
Gray Otis*, I, 68, note 11. Otis had written the pamphlet. The last
quotation is from *Porcupine's Gazette* (Phil.), June 7, 1798; also cited
in Bowers, *Jefferson and Hamilton*, p. 370. When Negroes did plot a
revolt in 1800 in Virginia, in the "Gabriel Plot," they did hope for

French help. See Herbert Aptheker, *American Negro Slave Revolts* (New York, 1943), p. 225.

25. See Ulrich B. Phillips, "The South Carolina Federalists," *American Historical Review*, XIV (July 1909), 739–740; Charles Fraser, *Reminiscences of Charleston* (Charleston, 1854), pp. 46–48; Zahniser, "Public Career of Charles Cotesworth Pinckney," pp. 276–277; and Henry Knox to Adams, Boston, June 26, 1798, in Knox, *Quasi-War Documents*, I, 140. See also James, "French Opinion as a Factor in Preventing War," pp. 49–50.

26. See Hamilton to Washington, May 19, 1798, in Lodge, *Hamilton's Works*, VIII, 483–484; Washington to Hamilton and to Pickering, May 27 and June 11, 1798, in Fitzpatrick, *Washington's Writings*, XXXVI, 227–272; and Carroll, *Washington*, p. 509. Stephen Higginson, a Federalist merchant from Boston, called for open war, saying nothing less could save the country from revolution, in Phillips, "Public Career of Timothy Pickering," p. 358. See also Morison, *Harrison Gray Otis*, I, 110–111.

27. The American Philosophical Society even cut down on the number of Frenchmen invited to membership, Faÿ, *Revolutionary Spirit*, pp. 453–454. Nathaniel Ames recorded on June 17, 1798: "Frenchmen abused in Boston, their cockades torn off and trampled upon," in Warren, *Jacobin and Junto*, p. 75. See Jefferson to Madison and to Monroe, May 3 and 21, 1798, in Ford, *Writings of Jefferson*, VII, 248, 257.

28. *Porcupine's Gazette* (Phil.), June 22, 1798; also quoted in Gilbert Chinard, *Volney et L'Amérique, d'àpres des documents inédits et sa correspondance avec Jefferson* (Baltimore, 1923), pp. 98–99. Cobbett worked closely with Robert Goodloe Harper against any connection with France. See William Reitzel, "William Cobbett and Philadelphia Journalism, 1794–1800," *Pennsylvania Magazine of History and Biography*, LIX (July 1935), 223–244.

29. Jefferson to Madison, May 31 and June 7, 1798, in Ford, *Writings of Jefferson*, VII, 262, 267, and Chinard, *Volney et L'Amérique*, p. 92. Murray, on the other hand, reported from secondhand sources that Volney was angry over the lashing he had received in American newspapers, and was convinced the American people were bitter enemies who hated the French because of the maritime depredations. To John Q. Adams, Jan. 31, 1799, in Ford, "Letters of William Vans Murray," p. 514. Later, Volney did write "that there exists between the two people a conflict of customs and social forms which makes any close union very difficult." Quoted in Echeverria, *Mirage in the West*, p. 193. In October 1798 Liston told officials in Canada that Volney was plotting with the Directory for an attack on Upper Canada. See Benjamin Sulté, "Les Projets de 1793 à 1810," *Proceedings and Transactions of the Royal Society of Canada*, third series, V (1911), Section I, 56.

30. Létombe to Directors, Phil., June 5, 1798, *Archives nationales, relations extérieures, U.S.A., AF* III, 64, dossier 263, no p. no. Also, James C.

Mountflorence to King, July 14, 1798, Rufus King Papers, Huntington Library.

31. Moreau de St. Méry, for example, wrote in his diary on June 27, that the Federalist party "worked for war against us." See other entries in Kenneth and Anna M. Roberts, eds. and translators, *Moreau de St. Méry's American Journey, 1793–1798* (Garden City, N.Y., 1947), pp. 252–253. See also Smith, *Freedom's Fetters*, p. 161, and Frances S. Childs, *French Refugee Life in the United States, 1790–1800: An American Chapter of the French Revolution* (Baltimore, 1940), pp. 189–190.

32. Abigail to Mary Cranch, July 17, 1798, in Mitchell, *New Letters of Abigail Adams*, pp. 205–206. Still, some Republicans, such as Nathaniel Ames, persisted in favoring "Alliance with France, defiance to Britain." Diary entry of July 4, 1798, in Warren, *Jacobin and Junto*, p. 78. Years later Pickering maintained that "Mr. Adams, in his vigorous answers to numerous addresses presented to him, enforced by the weight of his official station, as president of the U. States contributed, doubtless, more than any other man to elevate the temper of the nation" to resistance to France. Memorandum of April 6, 1819, quoted in Smith, *Freedom's Fetters*, p. 20. See also Fischer, *The Revolution of American Conservatism*, p. 286, for Timothy Dwight; Wood, *Administration of John Adams*, p. 128; George Cabot to Oliver Wolcott, Jr., Brookline, June 9, 1798, in Gibbs, *Wolcott Papers*, II, 53; and Ames to Pickering, Dedham, July 10, 1798, in Ames, *Works of Fisher Ames*, I, 232.

33. Madison to Jefferson, May 13 and June 10, 1798, Madison Papers, quoted in Schachner, *Founding Fathers*, p. 457. See also Kurtz, *Presidency of John Adams*, p. 300.

34. The quotation is from Ames to Pickering, Dedham, June 4, 1798, in Ames, *Works of Fisher Ames*, I, 228. The pressure for war can be seen in statements such as this: "If it were known either that our envoys had left the territory of France, or were retained in the country against their will, or if it in any way be ascertained that this mission was at an end, . . . the honor, dignity, and interest of this country require that we should make war upon the French Republic, and . . . it would be the duty of Congress to declare it." Samuel Sitgreaves, May 25, 1798, 5 Cong., 2 sess., *Annals of the Congress*, VIII, 1806. Legislators, and others, differed as to how far the President could go in the use of force against France without the specific sanction of Congress. "In so delicate a case, in one which involves so important a consequence as that of War—," Hamilton said, for example, "my opinion is that no doubtful authority ought to be exercised by the President." To James McHenry, May 17, 1798, in Knox, *Quasi-War Documents*, I, 75–76.

35. To build up defenses in Charleston, Americans had to borrow cannons from the British. See George W. Kyte, ed., "Guns for Charleston: A Case of Lend-Lease in 1798–1799," *Journal of Southern History*, XIV (Aug. 1948), 401–408.

36. Details on the creation of the Navy Department, April 30, 1798, are in Smelser, *Congress Founds the Navy*, pp. 150–159. Stoddert was ap-

pointed on May 21, and took up his duties on June 24. Stoddert's personal traits are discussed in Murray to J. Q. Adams, Aug. 6, 1798, in Ford, "Letters of William Vans Murray," p. 450, and in Harriet S. Turner, "Memoirs of Benjamin Stoddert, First Secretary of the United States Navy," *Columbia Historical Society Records*, XX (Washington, 1917), 141–166. For Cabot's reasons for declining, see Cabot to Pickering, Brookline, May 11, 1798, in Lodge, *Cabot*, pp. 156–158.

37. See Carlos E. Godfrey, "Organization of the Provisional Army of the United States in the Anticipated War with France, 1798–1800," *Pennsylvania Magazine of History and Biography*, XXXVIII (April 1914), 129. The laws of April 27, May 4, and 28, 1798, are in *The Statutes at Large of the United States of America* (Boston, 1854), I, 552, 555 and 558. The Republican quoted is Edward Livingston of New York, in 5 Cong., 2 sess., *Annals of the Congress*, VIII, 1519.

38. Ames to Pickering, Dedham, June 4, 1798, in Ames, *Works of Fisher Ames*, I, 228. See also 5 Cong., 2 sess., *Annals of the Congress*, VIII, 1870–71; Jonathan Mason, Jr., Boston, May 28, 1798, in Morison, *Harrison Gray Otis*, I, 96. In Europe a minor American official expressed the view of many Federalists. The annulment of the treaties, he said, particularly "to be unfettered of the Treaty of alliance and its enslaving clauses of Guarantee," would be one of the great benefits of the French crisis. "I hope," he added, "we would then form no more Treaties of alliance with any Nation. . . ." James C. Mountflorence to King, The Hague, Aug. 18, 1798, Rufus King Papers, Huntington Library. See also "An Act to suspend the commercial intercourse between the United States and France, and the dependencies thereof," in *Statutes at Large*, I, 565.

39. Jefferson to Madison, Phil., March 29, 1798, in Ford, *Writings of Jefferson*, VII, 224–227. When another Republican suggested disunion as the answer to the Federalist program, Jefferson urged patience, saying the "reign of witches" would pass. To John Taylor, June 1, 1798, in *ibid.*, VII, 263–266. See also Timothy Pickering to John Pickering, Jr., June 16, 1798, Pickering Papers, Massachusetts Historical Society; Henrietta Liston to James Jackson, Phil., June 11, 1798, Liston Papers, Box III, National Library of Scotland; David J. Mays, *Edmund Pendleton, 1721–1803* (2 vols., Cambridge, Mass., 1952), II, 319, 324; Charles, *Origins of the American Party System*, p. 87; and McLaughlin, *Matthew Lyon*, pp. 331–333, for a strong protest against war.

40. "Let us not . . . act on speculative grounds," Gallatin said, "but examine our present situation, and, if better than war, let us keep it." In Adams, *Life of Gallatin*, pp. 200–201. Republicans objected to a "propensity to deify" Marshall. *Albany Register* (New York), June 29, 1798, cited in Stewart, "Jeffersonian Journalism," pp. 569–570.

41. For details, see Beveridge, *John Marshall*, II, 347–350, and Smith, *Freedom's Fetters*, pp. 3–5. A short time later Adams himself said that "of the three envoys, the conduct of Marshall alone has been entirely satisfactory and ought to be marked by the most decided approbation

of the public." To Pickering, Sept. 29, 1798, Adams Papers, "Letters," Massachusetts Historical Society. See also Bowman, "Struggle for Neutrality," p. 350, and the views expressed by important American merchants, in Bruchey, *Robert Oliver*, p. 189.

42. For details, see 5 Cong., 2 sess., *Annals of the Congress*, VIII, 1972–1973; Smith, *Freedom's Fetters*, pp. 58, 102, and 193; and Pickering and Upham, *Life of Pickering*, III, 379.

43. Otis, for example, had said that the French crisis could be imputed "to a desperate and misguided party, existing in the bosom of our own country, who are in league with other bad citizens resident in France, and with the French nation. . . ." March 2, 1798, in Morison, *Harrison Gray Otis*, I, 70. See also William N. Chambers, *Political Parties in a New Nation: The American Experience, 1776–1809* (New York, 1963), p. 136, and Miller, *Crisis in Freedom*, pp. 41, 72–73. The law is in *Statutes at Large*, I, 566–569, and is summarized in Smith, *Freedom's Fetters*, pp. 33–34. The American Society of United Irishmen, it was said, numbered about 50,000 at this time. See Carroll, *Washington*, p. 457. This society did favor peace with France. See, for example, Joseph I. Shulim, *John Daly Burk: Irish Revolutionist and American Patriot* (Phil., 1964), p. 25. In England similar coercive legislation had already been passed. See Brown, *French Revolution in English History*, pp. 152, 158.

44. Adams's message of June 21, 1798, is in Richardson, *Messages of the Presidents*, I, 256, and Adams, *Works of John Adams*, IX, 158–159. Jefferson to Madison, June 21, 1798, Jefferson Papers, Library of Congress, quoted in Smelser, *Congress Founds the Navy*, p. 174. See also William North to Jay, [Phil.], June 22, 1798, in Henry P. Johnston, ed., *The Correspondence and Public Papers of John Jay* (4 vols., New York, 1890–93), IV, 243, and Kurtz, *Presidency of John Adams*, p. 306.

45. The quotation is from Ames to Dwight Foster, Dedham, June 24, 1798, in Ames, *Works of Fisher Ames*, I, 230. The analysis in these paragraphs is based in large part on Smith, *Adams*, p. 971. James Morton Smith, in "Background for Repression: America's Half-War with France and the Internal Security Legislation of 1798," *Huntington Library Quarterly*, XVIII (Nov. 1954), p. 57, points out that the X Y Z affair was not the cause but the occasion for Federalists striking at political opposition.

46. Godfrey, "Organization of the Provisional Army," p. 130. An amendment to the Army Act on March 3, 1799, increased the enlisted strength of a regiment from 700 to 1000. See also James R. Jacobs, *The Beginning of the U.S. Army, 1783–1812* (Princeton, 1947), pp. 207–208, 222–223; White, *The Federalists*, pp. 243–245; Miller, *Federalist Era*, p. 218; and Adams, *Life of John Adams*, II, 245.

47. Adams to Washington, Phil., June 22, 1798, Adams, *Works of John Adams*, VIII, 573; Steiner, *James McHenry*, pp. 309–315; and Carroll, *Washington*, pp. 518–521. Later, it was reported that Washington's acceptance of the command carried great weight and had a brilliant

effect in Europe. William Vans Murray to Pickering, The Hague, Oct. 5, 1798, Dispatches, The Netherlands, Vol. 4, No. 61, Department of State, National Archives.

48. Abigail Adams to William Smith, Phil., July 7, 1798, quoted in Charles, *Origins of the American Party System*, p. 60, and Hamilton to McHenry, July 22, 1798, in Steiner, *James McHenry*, p. 315.

49. For a detailed account of the army issue that emphasizes this interpretation, see Kurtz, *Presidency of John Adams*, pp. 307–333. Congress expanded the army beyond what Adams had requested. He explained in later years that "the army was none of my work. . . . Hamilton's project of an army of fifty thousand, ten thousand of them to be horse, appeared to me to be proper only for Bedlam. His friends however in the Senate and the House embarrassed me with a bill for more troops than I wanted." Adams to Benjamin Rush, Quincy, Aug. 23, 1805, quoted in Dauer, *Adams Federalists*, p. 212.

50. For arguments that fear of French machinations and of French refugee activities led to passage of the Alien and Sedition laws, see Frank M. Anderson, "Contemporary Opinion of the Virginia and Kentucky Resolutions," *American Historical Review*, V (Oct. and Dec., 1899), 60; see also Smith, *Freedom's Fetters*, p. 37; Childs, *French Refugee Life in the United States*, p. 188; and Phillips, "Public Career of Timothy Pickering," p. 342. High Federalists, apparently, did not consult Adams on such legislation. June 19, 1798, 5 Cong., 2 sess., *Annals of the Congress*, VIII, 1973–1997.

51. Robert Goodloe Harper, June 19, 1798, in 5 Cong., 2 sess., *Annals of the Congress*, VIII, 1992. For a discussion of the precedent set by English laws on aliens, on sedition, and on treason, see Smith, *Freedom's Fetters*, p. 146, and note, and Dauer, *Adams Federalists*, pp. 157–159.

52. Senator Stevens Thomas Mason of Virginia, quoted in *Gazette of the United States* (Phil.), June 27, 1798.

53. For the texts of the laws, see *Statutes at Large*, I, 570–572, 577–578, and 596–597. For further details, see Smith, *Freedom's Fetters*, pp. 48–49, 61–62, and 176. The figures on French residents are from Carroll, *Washington*, p. 457. In later years John Adams tried to justify the Alien Friends Act, saying, "We were then at war with France: French spies then swarmed in our cities and the country. Some of them were intolerably turbulent, impudent, and seditious. To check these was the design of the law." To Jefferson, Quincy, June 14, 1813, in Cappon, *Adams-Jefferson Letters*, II, 329. Miller, in *Crisis in Freedom*, p. 67, points out that one version of the treason and sedition bill introduced into the Senate "was a virtual declaration of war against France." For the original draft of the sedition law and amendments, see Dauer, *Adams Federalists*, pp. 343–348.

54. *Gazette of the United States* (Phil.), Oct. 10, 1798. Adams's quotation is from "Correspondence Originally Published in the Boston Patriot," 1809, from notes prepared in 1801, Adams, *Works of John Adams*, IX, 291. For Hamilton's role in the turmoil, see James Morton Smith,

"Alexander Hamilton, the Alien Law, and Seditious Libels," *Review of Politics*, XVI (July 1954), 304–333. The pamphleteer is James T. Callendar, writing to Jefferson on June 16, 1798, and quoted in Kurtz, *Presidency of John Adams*, p. 338. The Federalist program, including the Alien and Sedition laws, silenced the French press in the United States, Allen J. Barthold, "French Journalists in the United States, 1780–1800," *The Franco-American Review*, I (Winter, 1937), 227.

55. For details on the naval legislation see Smelser, *Congress Founds the Navy*, pp. 169–192.

56. For the provisions of the law, called the Evaluation Act, see *Statutes at Large*, I, 597–605. For other details, see 5 Cong., 2 sess., *Annals of the Congress*, Appendix, 3758–3763, 3778–3786; Henry Carter Adams, *Taxation in the United States, 1789–1816* (Baltimore, 1884), pp. 55–57; McMaster, *History of the United States*, II, 388–389; William W. H. Davis, *The Fries Rebellion, 1798–99* . . . (Doylestown, Penn., 1899), p. 3; and Timothy Pitkin, *A Statistical View of the Commerce of the United States of America*, 2nd ed. (Hartford, Conn., 1817), p. 352.

57. For the provisions of the law abrogating the French treaties, see *Statutes at Large*, I, 578. For the proclamation of July 13, 1798, revoking the exequaturs of the French consuls, see Adams, *Works of John Adams*, IX, 170–172. Létombe remained in the country and continued to function as France's representative, much to Pickering's disgust. Pickering considered him corrupt and tried to force him out of the country, charging him with the payment of a bribe. See Pickering to Adams, Phil., Aug. 1, 1799, and Adams to Pickering, Quincy, Aug. 13, Adams, *Works of John Adams*, IX, 6, 14.

58. Pickering to Gerry, June 25, 1798, *ASP FR*, II, 204. Pickering had ordered Gerry home on March 13. Gerry had ignored those instructions which arived in Paris on May 12. See Carroll, *Washington*, pp. 535–536.

59. *Aurora* (Phil.), June 28, 1798, and 5 Cong., 2 sess., *Annals of the Congress*, VIII, 2084–2086.

60. See Smith, *Adams*, p. 979, and Dauer, *Adams Federalists*, pp. 168–169. Even in Europe some Federalists spoke with an eagerness for war. See, for example, Smith to James McHenry, Lisbon, June 23, 1798, Steiner, "Correspondence of William Smith," pp. 97–98.

61. Sedgwick to King, July 1, 1798, in King, *Correspondence of Rufus King*, II, 352. Welch, in *Theodore Sedgwick*, pp. 176–177, analyzes why Sedgwick, and Federalists like him, wanted war. The Speaker of the House was Jonathan Dayton of New Jersey. On July 4, 1798, the *Columbian Centinel* (Boston) in a long article asserted that a defensive war had been forced on the United States, and "that this day is fixed on in Congress for a declaration of war against France," quoted in Dauer, *Adams Federalists*, p. 169. For details on the Essex Junto and the men usually identified with it see Bernhard, *Fisher Ames*, p. 325; Morison, *The Maritime History of Massachusetts, 1783–1860*, p. 167; Miller, *Federalist Era*, pp. 261–262 n; and Cappon, *Adams-Jefferson Letters*, II, 300 n. According to David H. Fischer, in "The Myth of the Essex

Junto," *William and Mary Quarterly*, third series, XXI (April 1964), 220–221, 235, after 1797 the phrase "Essex Junto" ceased to have any real meaning.

62. Cabot to King, July 2, 1798, in King, *Correspondence of Rufus King*, II, 354.

63. This analysis includes a summary of Robert Liston's appraisal of Federalist sentiment as sent to Grenville, Phil., July 14, 1798, No. 41, PRO GB FO 5. See also advantages as stated by William Smith to Oliver Wolcott, Feb. 3, 1799, in Rogers, *Evolution of a Federalist*, pp. 319–320. For details on the war caucus see Chester M. Destler, *Joshua Coit: American Federalist, 1758–1798* (Middletown, Conn., 1962), p. 127; Kurtz, *Presidency of John Adams*, p. 310; Stoddert to Adams, Bladensburg, Oct. 12, 1800, in Lodge, *Cabot*, p. 202; and Morison, *Harrison Gray Otis*, I, 97. Jefferson claimed that a majority of five defeated the move for a declaration of war, in Sawvel, *Complete Anas*, pp. 197, 198, and 204. Senator James Lloyd of Maryland, who had sponsored the Sedition bill, expressed his own disappointment and that of other extreme Federalists. "I fear Congress will close the session without a declaration of War," he told George Washington, "which I look upon as necessary to enable us to lay our hands on traitors, and as the best means that can be resorted to, to destroy the effect of the skill of the Directory in their transactions with Mr. Gerry." Phil., July 4, 1798, Washington Papers, quoted in Smelser, *Congress Founds the Navy*, p. 196. Uriah Tracy, considered to be especially intimate with the President, had urged that Congress remain in session so as to keep the war spirit alive. See Jefferson to Madison, June 21, 1798, in Ford, *Writings of Jefferson*, VIII, 441.

64. July 6, 1798, 5 Cong., 2 sess., *Annals of the Congress*, VIII, 2116–2120. The quoted Congressman is Samuel Sitgreaves of Pennsylvania. Dauer, in *Adams Federalists*, pp. 169–170, maintains that the sequence of Federalist action in Congress, "ranging from the war caucus to the actual voting on a declaration of war, constitutes the most serious attempt in American history to declare war without a recommendation by the President." See also p. 225.

65. The act is in *Statutes at Large*, I, 578. Details on the voting are in Smelser, *Congress Founds the Navy*, pp. 188–191. The moderate Federalist is Coit, quoted from Destler, *Joshua Coit*, p. 124. See also Robert G. Albion and Jennie B. Pope, *Sea Lanes in Wartime: The American Experience, 1775–1942* (New York, 1942), pp. 80–81.

66. Most scholars who have dealt with John Adams, or with the history of his administration, have said, in effect, that Adams himself was opposed to a declaration of war, and for that reason did not request it. As a result, Congress did not vote such a declaration. An exception to this interpretation is advanced by Page Smith in his *Adams*, p. 979. Smith points out that Adams at this time desired a declaration of war. The evidence of Adams's own actions, his words, particularly as revealed in the unpublished Adams Papers, and those of his wife, who reflected his views, all suggest that the President did want, or at least favor, war

at this point. The quotation, Abigail to John Quincy Adams, July 14, 1798, is from Janet P. Whitney, *Abigail Adams* (Boston, 1955), p. 28.

67. To John Quincy Adams, July 20, 1798, Adams Papers, quoted in Smith, *Adams*, p. 979. Abigail's view of popular sentiment is in part supported by the observation of Robert Liston. He reported that Americans he knew agreed that in the United States there was "infinitely more unanimity against France than there was against Great Britain in the first stage of their successful Rebellion." To Grenville, Boston, Sept. 27, 1798, No. 57, PRO GB FO 5. John Jay, at the time governor of New York, on the other hand, indicated that public opinion was not yet ready for full-scale war. See Jay to William North, New York, June 25, 1798, in Johnston, *Correspondence of John Jay*, IV, 244–245.

68. Harper to Constituents, Phil., July 23, 1798, Donnan, "Bayard Papers," p. 58. Although uncertain as to what France's reaction to this policy might be, Harper thought that "her pride, the passions of her rulers, and perhaps their policy," would drive her to open war.

69. See Stoddert to John Adams, Bladensburg, Oct. 12, 1809, in Lodge, *Cabot*, p. 202. Hamilton, too, thought it best under the circumstances to allow France to force full-scale war. Miller, *Hamilton*, pp. 470–471. See also, Morison, *Harrison Gray Otis*, I, 98, and Anderson, *William Branch Giles*, p. 62.

70. Robert Troup to Rufus King, New York, Oct. 2, 1798, King, *Correspondence of Rufus King*, II, 432–433.

71. Charles Lee's opinion of Aug. 21, 1798, is in James Brown Scott, ed., *The Controversy over Neutral Rights between the United States and France, 1797–1800* . . . (New York, 1917), p. 98.

72. Ames to Pickering, Dedham, July 10, 1798, in Ames, *Works of Fisher Ames*, I, 234. Twenty days later Ames told Christopher Gore, "I do not rail at Congress for *not declaring* war, but then they ought to have gone farther in *waging* it," p. 237.

73. Several months later Robert Liston reported that many Federalists hoped France would attack the United States, and hence relieve them of embarrassment. To Grenville, Kingston, N.J., No. 63, PRO GB FO 5. Rufus King, on the other hand, had predicted that France would not launch a war against the United States, saying a war would give her no advantage and hence she would seek new negotiations. To Murray, London, Sept. 17, 1798, William Vans Murray Papers, Manuscript Division, Library of Congress.

74. George Cabot to Oliver Wolcott, Jr., Oct. 25, 1798, in Gibbs, *Wolcott Papers*, II, 109. Pinckney is quoted in Miller, *Federalist Era*, p. 215. For Adams's recollections on this matter of the war declaration see his "Correspondence Originally Published in the Boston Patriot," 1809, in Adams, *Works of John Adams*, IX, 304–305.

75. Pickering later admitted that he, and others, at this time deemed war with France practically inevitable. To Alexander Hamilton, Easton, Dec. 14, 1800, Pickering Papers, Massachusetts Historical Society.

ᛊᛊᛊ Notes—Chapter IV ᛊᛊᛊ

1. This was the third invasion of yellow fever in five years, and the worst. Within a month business in Philadelphia came virtually to a standstill. See Carroll, *Washington*, p. 543. See also Rush to William Marshall, Phil., Sept. 15, 1798, in Butterfield, *Letters of Benjamin Rush*, II, 806–807. Rush said the fever was "much more malignant than in 1793 and 1797. . . ."

2. Hamilton to McHenry, Phil., July 30, 1798, in Lodge, *Hamilton's Works*, VI, 90–92, and Steiner, *James McHenry*, pp. 320–321.

3. Adams to McHenry, Quincy, Aug. 14, 1798, in Adams, *Works of John Adams*, VIII, 580.

4. McHenry to Adams, Aug. 22, 1798, Sept. 6, in Steiner, *James McHenry*, pp. 325, 338; Adams to McHenry, Quincy, Aug. 29, 1798, Sept. 13, in Adams, *Works of John Adams*, VIII, 587–588, 593–594; and John Adams Letterbook, Quincy, Sept. 10, 1798, Adams Papers, reel 119.

5. See McHenry to Hamilton, Sept. 10, 1798, in Hamilton, *Works of Hamilton*, VI, 356, and Wolcott to Adams, Trenton, Sept. 17, 1798, in Gibbs, *Wolcott Papers*, II, 93–99; and Cabot to John Adams, Sept. 29, 1798, Brookline, Sept. 29, 1798, in Lodge, *Cabot*, p. 167.

6. Washington to Adams, Sept. 25, 1798, in Fitzpatrick, *Washington's Writings*, XXXVI, 453–462.

7. Adams to Washington, Oct. 9, 1798, Adams, *Works of John Adams*, VIII, 600–601. See also Steiner, *James McHenry*, 345–347; Callahan, *Henry Knox*, pp. 371–374; and Bernhard Knollenberg, "John Adams, Knox, and Washington," *American Antiquarian Society Proceedings*, LVI (Oct. 1946), 227–237.

8. This army issue has been interpreted as "the first decisive symptom of a schism in the Federal Party itself. . . ." See John Quincy Adams, *Parties in the United States* (New York, 1941), p. 25, and Kurtz, *Presidency of John Adams*, pp. 308, 324–325. This issue also cooled Adams's ardor for full-scale war against France, but it did not immediately make him a dove. "From this time," Adams's son and grandson wrote, "may be dated the beginning of his distrust of his ministers and

of his determination to resist their control." See Adams, *Life of John Adams,* II, 256.

9. McHenry to Adams, Oct. 15, 1798, Adams Papers, cited in Smith, *Adams,* p. 983, and Adams to McHenry, Quincy, Oct. 22, 1798, in Adams, *Works of John Adams,* VIII, 612–613. Later, Adams claimed that he prevented recruitment of the army "at the risque of his reputation and his office." See Zoltán Haraszti, *John Adams and the Prophets of Progress* (Cambridge, Mass., 1952), p. 264.

10. Adams to Adrian Van der Kemp, Quincy, April 25, 1808, Pennsylvania Historical Society, quoted in Charles, *Origins of the American Party System,* p. 61. For the Federalist desire to use the army politically, see also Dauer, *Adams Federalists,* p. 149; Miller, *Federalist Era,* p. 152; and Kurtz, *Presidency of John Adams,* p. 314. For Hamilton's ideas on a professional army, see Russell F. Weigley, *Towards an American Army: Military Thought from Washington to Marshall* (New York, 1962), pp. 23, 26.

11. For details, see Darling, *Rising Empire,* pp. 220–225, 263–266, and Whitaker, *Mississippi Question,* pp. 3–115. Except for the final decision on a matter such as war, Spain coordinated her policy toward the United States with French policy. Manuel de Godoy to Carlos de Yrujo, San Ildefonso, Aug. 14, 1797, Archivo del ministerio des estado (Madrid), in Whitaker, "The Retrocession of Louisiana in Spanish Policy," *American Historical Review,* XXIX (April 1934), 464.

12. See E. Wilson Lyon, *Louisiana in French Diplomacy, 1759–1804* (Norman, Okla., 1934), pp. 88–93. The recovery of Louisiana had been a major goal of French policy since 1795. See Whitaker, *Mississippi Question,* p. 102; Childs, "French Opinion of Anglo-American Relations," p. 31; and Frederick Jackson Turner, "The Policy of France toward the Mississippi Valley in the Period of Washington and Adams," *American Historical Review,* X (Jan. 1905), 278. The entire article stresses continuity in French policy toward Louisiana. For an analysis of the Directory's policy, see Mildred S. Fletcher, "Louisiana as a Factor in French Diplomacy from 1763 to 1800," *Mississippi Valley Historical Review,* XVII (Dec. 1930), 371–376.

13. Pickering to King, Feb. 15, 1797, Rufus King Papers, Huntington Library, and Liston to Grenville, March 16, 1797, cited in Darling, *Rising Empire,* p. 269.

14. Pickering to King, June 20, 1797, *ASP FR,* II, 68, and J. Q. Adams to King, June 26, Rufus King Papers, Huntington Library. Létombe reported the uneasiness such rumors concerning Louisiana caused in the United States. To Charles Delacroix, Phil., July 18, 1797, in Turner, "Correspondence of French Ministers," p. 1049.

15. Lyon, *Louisiana in French Diplomacy,* pp. 93–94. The quoted minister is Manuel de Godoy, Oct. 20, 1797, in Whitaker, *Mississippi Question,* p. 180.

16. See Guyot, *Le Directoire et la paix de l'Europe,* p. 409; James H. Malmesbury, *Diaries and Correspondence of James Harris, First Earl*

of Malmesbury, ed. by his grandson, the third earl (4 vols., London, 1844), III, 384–385; André Fugier, *La Révolution Française et l'empire Napoléonien* (Paris, 1954), p. 111; and Rain, *La diplomatie française*, pp. 151–160. For other details, see Charles Ballot, *Les négociations de Lille, 1797* (Paris, 1910).

17. Lyon, *Louisiana in French Diplomacy*, pp. 95–97. Létombe to Talleyrand, Phil., April 19, 1798, AAE CP EU, vol. 49, ff. 328–329.

18. See Talleyrand to Guillemardet, May 20–June 19, 1798, quoted in Darling, *Rising Empire*, p. 297, and Georges Pallain, ed., *Le ministère de Talleyrand sous le Directoire* (Paris, 1891), pp. 309–310.

19. Letter of Collot outlining purported American war plans, Phil., June 26, 1798, *Archives nationales, relations extérieures, U.S.A., AF III, 64*, dossier 263, pp. 5–6. Létombe to Directory, July 18, 1797, in Turner, "Correspondence of French Ministers," pp. 1048–1051. This dispatch arrived in Paris on Nov. 3, while Pinckney, Marshall, and Gerry were seeking a negotiation. For details on Collot, see Turner, "Policy of France toward Mississippi Valley," pp. 272–273. Later, Pickering tried to force Collot to leave the country by using the Alien laws against him. See Smith, *Freedom's Fetters*, pp. 164–169, and George W. Kyte, "The Detention of General Collot: A Sidelight on Anglo-American Relations, 1798–1800," *William and Mary Quarterly*, third series, VI (Oct. 1949), 628–630.

20. For details, see Whitaker, *Mississippi Question*, pp. 116–121, and Darling, *Rising Empire*, p. 322. In later years Adams discussed aspects of this plan of conquest in terms of a "Hamiltonian conspiracy." See Benjamin Waterhouse to Adams, Cambridge, Mass., July 8, 1811, and Adams to Waterhouse, Quincy, July 12, 1811, in Ford, *Statesman and Friend*, pp. 58–63, 64–66. The quotation is from William Cobbett, *Porcupine's Works* (12 vols., London, 1801), VI, 270, 273, dated July, 1797.

21. Hamilton commenting on a letter of Feb. 7, 1798, from Miranda. Quoted in William S. Robertson, *The Life of Miranda* (2 vols., Chapel Hill, N.C., 1929), I, 176–177.

22. Miranda had written to Hamilton on Feb. 7, 1798, for example, that "the entire Spanish-American Continent seems prepared to throw off the yoke . . . and to enter into an alliance with the United States and England." Quoted in Mitchell, *Hamilton: The National Adventure*, p. 724 n. Yrujo's quarrel with Pickering became so nasty that Adams wanted to have the Spaniard recalled. For the quotations and other details see Robertson, *Miranda*, I, 168; Hamilton to McHenry, Jan. 1798, in Steiner, *James McHenry*, p. 295; and Darling, *Rising Empire*, pp. 265, 316–317.

23. Pickering to King, April 2, 1798, quoted in Darling, *Rising Empire*, p. 310, and Cabot to Wolcott, Brookline, June 9, 1798, in Lodge, *Cabot*, p. 159.

24. Liston to Grenville, Phil., May 2, Aug. 31, 1798, Nos. 21 and 52, PRO GB FO 5. Grenville to Liston, Downing Street, June 8, 1798, No. 12,

in Mayo, "Instructions to British Ministers," pp. 155–160. In August 1798, *The Anti-Jacobin Review* of London, the administration's organ, publicly urged an alliance with the United States. Dauer, *Adams Federalists*, p. 181.

25. See Miranda to Adams, London, March 24, 1798, Aug. 17, 1798, Pickering to Adams, Trenton, Aug. 21, 1798, and enclosures, in Adams, *Works of John Adams*, VIII, 569–572, 581–582, and 583–587.

26. Hamilton to King, New York, Aug. 22, 1798, in Lodge, *Hamilton's Works*, VIII, 505–506.

27. Adams to Pickering, Quincy, Oct. 3, 1798, to James Lloyd, Quincy, March 5 and 29, 1815, in Adams, *Works of John Adams*, VIII, 600, X, 134–136, 146–149.

28. Adams's views are recorded in Liston to Grenville, Boston, Sept. 27, 1798, No. 55, PRO GB FO 5. At this time Adams told the grand jurors of Ulster County, N.Y., that Britain and the United States could not help being natural allies because they had a common enemy in France. Quincy, Sept. 26, 1798, Adams Papers, reel 119. See also Kyte, "Robert Liston and Anglo-American Cooperation," p. 264.

29. "Through the intervention of Mr. Liston," Pickering explained, "signals have been agreed on by which the British and American ships on our coast and in the West Indies, may know one another." To Rufus King, Jan. 2, 1799, in Pickering and Upham, *Life of Pickering*, III, 342. See also Pickering to Stoddert, Phil. and Trenton, July 20 and Oct. 6, 1798, and Capt. Charles W. Goldsborough to Capt. Thomas Tingey, Trenton, Nov. 2, 1798, in Knox, *Quasi-War Documents*, I, 227, 235, 288, 296, 499, 501, and II, 4–5. Some British statesmen wanted to loan warships to the United States to forestall the making of a rival navy. Duke of Gloucester to William Windham, Ashford, Oct. 31, 1798, in William Windham, *The Windham Papers* (2 vols., London, 1913), II, 80–81.

30. For details, see Gerard Clarfield, "Postscript to the Jay Treaty: Timothy Pickering and Anglo-American Relations, 1795–1797," *William and Mary Quarterly*, third series, XXIII (Jan. 1966), 106–120; Dauer, *Adams Federalists*, p. 184; Perkins, *First Rapprochement*, pp. 95–101, 112–115; Alice B. Keith, "Relaxations in the British Restrictions on the American Trade with the British West Indies, 1783–1802," *Journal of Modern History*, XX (March 1948), 14; and Kyte, "Robert Liston and Anglo-American Cooperation," pp. 260–264.

31. Liston to Grenville, Phil., Jan. 29, 1799, No. 4, PRO GB FO 5.

32. Hamilton to General Gunn, New York, Dec. 22, 1798, and to Harrison Gray Otis, Jan. 26, 1799, in Hamilton, *Works of Hamilton*, V, 184, VI, 390.

33. For details, see John C. Hamilton, *Life of Alexander Hamilton* (7 vols., New York, 1834), VII, 344; Jacobs, *The Beginning of the U.S. Army*, pp. 227–229; James R. Jacobs, *Tarnished Warrior: Major-General James Wilkinson* (New York, 1938), pp. 190–191; Miller, *Hamilton*, pp. 498–499; and Thomas R. Hay and M. R. Werner, *The Admirable Trumpeter:*

A *Biography of General James Wilkinson* (New York, 1941), pp. 183–184.

34. Hamilton to Washington, New York, June 15, 1799, Lodge, *Hamilton's Works*, VIII, pp. 534–535. See also Dale Van Every, *Ark of Empire: The American Frontier, 1784–1803* (New York, 1963), pp. 343–344. Washington also refused to become involved in a scheme advanced by John Trumbull, an artist and political dabbler, to liberate Spanish America as desired by Miranda. See Marshall Smelser, "George Washington Declines the Part of El Libertador," *William and Mary Quarterly*, third series, XI (Jan. 1954), 42–51.

35. Rufus King, whose own views were apparently embodied in the essay, advised publication. See King to Hamilton, March 4, 1799, in Hamilton, *Works of Hamilton*, VI, 402. The essay itself—142 manuscript pages—was enclosed in Gore to Hamilton, London, Feb. 27, 1799, Hamilton Papers, Library of Congress, cited in Mitchell, *Hamilton: The National Adventure*, p. 445, and in Dauer, *Adams Federalists*, pp. 191–192.

36. Louis-Guillaume Otto cited in Rayford W. Logan, *The Diplomatic Relations of the United States with Haiti, 1776–1891* (Chapel Hill, N.C., 1941), p. 60. At this time American ships were carrying over 90 per cent of the nation's foreign trade, and probably more in the West Indies. See Douglass C. North, *The Economic Growth of the United States, 1790 to 1860* (Englewood Cliffs, N.J., 1961), p. 41, and Anna C. Clauder, *American Commerce as Affected by the Wars of the French Revolution and Napoleon, 1793–1812* (Phil., 1932), p. 43.

37. See the chart on insurance notes in Nathan Sargeant, "The Quasi-War with France," *The United Service*, IX (July 1883), 11; Logan, *Haiti and the U.S.*, p. 60; Allen, *Our Naval War with France*, p. 84; and Albion, *Sea Lanes in Wartime*, p. 83. The rates cited were set as war premiums for ships bound for the British West Indies. Underwriters refused to insure ships bound for French ports. J. D. Forbes, in *Israel Thorndike, Federalist Financier* (New York, 1953), p. 45, cites an 80 per cent insurance premium in the case of the ship *Eliza* in Feb. 1798 bound fom Boston to England. See also Smelser, *Congress Founds the Navy*, p. 105. Even whale fishing declined because of the French raids. Robert A. Davison, *Issac Hicks: New York Merchant and Quaker, 1767–1820* (Cambridge, Mass., 1964), p. 83. *Carey's United States Recorder* (Phil.), April 7, 1798, among other gazettes, reported stories of seriously injured trade, in Stewart, "Jeffersonian Journalism," p. 560.

38. For details, see Smelser, *Congress Founds the Navy*, pp. 102–103, 179–180; Heckscher, *The Continental System*, p. 49; and Allen, *Our Naval War with France*, pp. 41–48.

39. Stoddert to Dale, Phil., June 27, 1798, in Knox, *Quasi-War Documents*, I, 145; Smelser, *Congress Founds the Navy*, pp. 178, 182; and Howard I. Chapelle, *The History of the American Sailing Navy* (New York, 1949), p. 140.

40. Adams to Stoddert, Quincy, Oct. 1, 1798, Adams Papers, reel 119.

The Secretary of the Navy, like the President, considered the Navy an instrument of defense and a protector of commerce. See Robert F. Jones, "The Naval Thought and Policy of Benjamin Stoddert, First Secretary of the Navy, 1798–1801," *American Neptune*, XXIV (Jan. 1964), 61–69.

41. *Columbian Centinel* (Boston), Aug. 8, 1798, and William Bainbridge to Stoddert, Guadeloupe, Jan. 3, 1799, in Knox, *Quasi-War Documents*, II, 122–124. See also Harold and Margaret Sprout, *The Rise of American Naval Power, 1776–1918* (Princeton, 1939), p. 41.

42. The quotation is from Allen, *Our Naval War with France*, p. 82. See also p. 133; Robert G. Harper to Constituents, Phil., Feb. 10, 1799, in Donnan, "Bayard Papers," p. 77; Schachner, *Founding Fathers*, pp. 505–506; and William Vans Murray to Pickering, The Hague, Oct. 23, 1798, Dispatches, The Netherlands, Vol. 4, No. 64, Department of State, National Archives.

43. Desfourneaux to Adams, Guadeloupe, Jan. 17, 1799, Knox, *Quasi-War Documents*, II, 248–249. See also Allen, *Our Naval War with France*, p. 87. Desfourneaux's appeal, promising fair treatment, protection, and justice to Americans was reproduced in French and English, and widely circulated in the United States. Liston to Grenville, Phil., Feb. 18, 1799, No. 11, PRO GB FO 5.

44. Truxtun to Stoddert, Feb. 9, 1799, Knox, *Quasi-War Documents*, II, 326–337. For details, see Eugene S. Ferguson, *Truxtun of the Constellation* . . . (Baltimore, 1956), pp. 160–169.

45. Truxtun to Stoddert, Feb. 9, 1799, Knox, *Quasi-War Documents*, II, 327, 357–358. The British offered Truxtun money and presents for his capture of the *Insurgente*. Baltimore *American*, July 2, 1799, cited in Stewart, "Jeffersonian Journalism," p. 444.

46. A decree of the Directory of Oct. 29, 1798, on the treatment of seamen as pirates, forwarded by Adams to Congress on Jan. 28, 1799, as well as Adams's letter of Feb. 15, 1799, announcing the suspension of the decree is in *ASP FR* II, 238. See also Circular Instructions from Secretary of Navy, Phil., March 12, 1799, in Knox, *Quasi-War Documents*, II, 447.

47. See Allen, *Our Naval War with France*, pp. 84, 103; Colonel H. de Poyen, *Les guerres des Antilles de 1793 à 1815* (Paris, 1896), pp. 185–186; Bonnel, *La France, les États-Unis et la guerre de course*, pp. 98–99; Robert G. Harper to Constituents, Phil., March 20, 1799, from Miscellaneous Papers, Maryland Historical Society, Baltimore; and Albion, *Sea Lanes in Wartime*, p. 83. In less than three years of Quasi-War the Navy captured one French frigate, defeated another, captured three privateers, sank four, recaptured more than seventy merchant ships, and reduced seizures drastically. Fletcher Pratt, in *The Navy, A History* (Garden City, N.Y., 1938), p. 106, summarizes the naval cost, and profit, of the Quasi-War. See also Dudley W. Knox, "Documents on Naval War with France," *United States Naval Institute Proceedings*, LXI (April 1935), 535–536.

48. The action of "our little glorious fleet," particularly the *Constellation's* victory over the *Insurgente,* made a deep impression on the French, and on other Europeans. William Vans Murray to King, April 22, 1799, Rufus King Papers, Huntington Library, and to Pickering, April 23, in Ford, "Letters of William Vans Murray," pp. 543–544. "The success of the American cruisers," Robert Liston reported, "has served gradually to habituate the people of the United States to the prospect of a French war, which is now contemplated without that dread and horror, which at first accompanied the idea." To Grenville, Phil., April 2, 1799, No. 26, PRO GB FO 5. See also John Spencer Bassett, *The Federalist System, 1789–1801* (New York, 1906), p. 239.

49. See Logan, *Haiti and the U.S.*, p. 101. For use and spelling of Saint Domingue, see p. 2 n. Saint Domingue also served as a valuable channel of communication for the United States with Latin America. Arthur P. Whitaker, *The United States and the Independence of Latin America* (Baltimore, 1941), p. 5.

50. See Mayer to Pickering, July 17, 1797, in Charles C. Tansill, *The United States and Santo Domingo, 1798–1873* (Baltimore, 1938), p. 13.

51. There were also other reasons for the British failure. See *ibid.,* p. 19. For background on Toussaint, see C. L. R. James, *The Black Jacobins: Toussaint L'Ouverture and the San Domingo Revolution,* 2nd ed., rev. (New York, 1963); Alfred Zimmermann, *Die Kolonialpolitik Frankreichs von den Anfängen bis zur Gegenwart* (Berlin, 1901), pp. 261–285; and a contemporary piece of British propaganda, James Stephen, *Buonaparte in the West Indies; or, The History of Toussaint Louverture, the African Hero* (London, 1803).

52. To the Minister of War, Oct. 15, 1796, quoted in T. Lothrop Stoddard, *The French Revolution in San Domingo* (Boston, 1914), p. 262.

53. Robert G. Harper, Phil., March 20, 1799, told his constituents that Hédouville had been prepared to launch an invasion of the South "with an army of blacks." Miscellaneous Papers, Maryland Historical Society.

54. Toussaint did obtain authority from Hédouville to negotiate. James, *Black Jacobins,* pp. 208–210. The convention is printed in Logan, *Haiti and the U.S.,* pp. 65–66.

55. See Mary W. Treudley, "The United States and Santo Domingo, 1789–1866," *Journal of Race Development,* VII (July 1916), 129–130, and Tansill, *United States and Santo Domingo,* p. 34.

56. The quotations are from Tansill, *United States and Santo Domingo,* pp. 14, 33, and 34. See also Treudley, "United States and Santo Domingo," p. 95. The President's son also believed that the French islands in the Caribbean should be "free and independent, in close alliance and under the guarantee of the United States." John Quincy Adams to William Vans Murray, July 14, 1798, Ford, *Writings of John Quincy Adams,* II, 336.

57. The quotation is from Stephen Alexis, *Black Liberator: The Life of Toussaint Louverture,* trans. from the French (New York, 1949), p. 131. Roume arrived at Cap Français on Jan. 12, 1799, as Hédouville's

successor, p. 132. See also James, *Black Jacobins*, pp. 218–220. Antoine Michel, *La mission du General Hédouville à Saint-Domingue* (Port-au-Prince, 1929), stresses that Hédouville's mission began war between Toussaint and Rigaud.

58. Toussaint to Adams, Cap Français, Nov. 6, 1798, Rufus King Papers, Huntington Library. See also J. Franklin Jameson, ed., "Letters of Toussaint Louverture and of Edward Stevens, 1798–1800," *American Historical Review*, XVI (Oct. 1910), 66–67.

59. Pickering to Mayer, Nov. 30, 1798, quoted in Tansill, *United States and Santo Domingo*, p. 15. See also Logan, *Haiti and the U.S.*, p. 75.

60. Stoddert to Barry, Jan. 16, 1799, quoted in Tansill, *United States and Santo Domingo*, p. 17. John Quincy Adams summed up the administration's attitude at this time. "I have long been convinced," he wrote, "that the blacks must eventually remain masters of St. Domingo." The consequences of this are threatening, he continued, for other slave societies, "but may perhaps be guarded against at least upon our Continent. As far as the Events in that quarter have tended to prepare the total expulsion of the french from all American possessions, they may be considered as favourable." To King, Berlin, Jan. 18, 1799, Rufus King Papers, Huntington Library.

61. The law is in Scott, *Controversy over Neutral Rights between the United States and France*, pp. 68–72. Jefferson's comments to James Madison, Feb. 5, 1799, are quoted in Tansill, *United States and Santo Domingo*, pp. 17–18 n. Although phrased in general terms, "Toussaint's clause" was intended only for Saint Domingue. Pickering, for example, rebuffed an emissary from Guadeloupe who sought to have it applied there. See Perkins, *First Rapprochement*, p. 108, and Pickering to General Etienne Desfourneaux, Commander in Chief at Guadeloupe, Phil., March 16, 1799, in Knox, *Quasi-War Documents*, II, 480–481. Pickering stressed that depredations, regardless of French laws, must wholly cease before the United States would resume trade. See also Cabot to Wolcott, Brookline, Feb. 22, 1799, in Lodge, *Cabot*, pp. 222–223. To secure trade with the French islands, Cabot said, "we must perhaps forbear to supply them until their dependence on the Jacobin parent is entirely destroyed."

62. Jefferson to Madison, Phil., Feb. 19, 1799, in Lipscomb,*Writings of Jefferson*, X, 110–113; Pickering to Toussaint, Phil., March 4, 1799, Rufus King Papers, Huntington Library; and Oliver Wolcott to Samuel Smith, Phil., March 20, 1799, in Gibbs, *Wolcott Papers*, II, 228–229.

63. Pickering to Stevens, Phil., March 4, 1799, Rufus King Papers, Huntington Library.

64. Hamilton to Pickering, New York, Feb. 21, 1799, in Lodge, *Hamilton's Works*, VIII, 528–529. Charles, in *Origins of the American Party System*, p. 134, argues that American dealings with Saint Domingue were in Pickering's hands, that Pickering took his orders from Hamilton, and that much of this policy was carried on behind Adams's back. Charles's interpretation overlooks the President's direct responsibilities

for what went on and also Adams's own feelings on Saint Domingue, which were consistent with his policy.

65. See Pickering to King, Phil., March 12, 1799, in King, *Correspondence of Rufus King*, II, 557.

66. King to Grenville, Great Cumberland Place, Dec. 1, 1798, in *ibid.*, 447. Dundas to King, Dec. 9, 1798, and Memorandum of Dec. 6, cited in Perkins, *First Rapprochement*, p. 107. When Americans saw the Maitland-Toussaint Convention they shed their fears. It "amounts to no more than a Truce for the War," Stoddert explained to Samuel Smith on March 16, 1799, cited in Tansill, *United States and Santo Domingo*, p. 46 n.

67. For details see Logan, *Haiti and the U.S.*, pp. 69–71; Perkins, *First Rapprochement*, pp. 107–108; and King to Secretary of State, London, Jan. 10, 1799, in King, *Correspondence of Rufus King*, II, 499–503.

68. The details and quotations are from Tansill, *United States and Santo Domingo*, pp. 47–48, 54–55, 56, and 57; and Logan, *Haiti and the U.S.*, p. 95.

69. Pickering to Stevens, Phil., April 20, 1799, in Knox, *Quasi-War Documents*, III, 70–72.

70. See Cabot to Pickering, Brookline, Feb. 21, 1799, in Lodge, *Cabot*, p. 219; James, "French Opinion as a Factor in Preventing War," p. 51; and Childs, "French Opinion of Anglo-American Relations," pp. 21–22.

71. At this time the British had established a free port system in the Caribbean which permitted the enemy, France and Spain, to trade in designated ports, such as Kingston, Jamaica, and Port of Spain, Trinidad. See Dorothy B. Goebel, "British Trade to the Spanish Colonies, 1796–1823," *American Historical Review*, XLIII (Jan. 1938), 288–320. See also Lefebvre, *The Thermidoreans and the Directory*, p. 358.

72. For details, see Lyon, "The Directory and the United States," pp. 525–526, and Faÿ, *Revolutionary Spirit*, p. 428, who said the Directory had nothing to fear or expect from the United States but respected it for its moral force in the world.

ᔐᔑᓭ Notes—Chapter V ᔐᔑᓭ

1. Quoted in Lyon, "The Directory and the United States," p. 525.
2. William Vans Murray to King, May 18, 1798, Rufus King Papers, Huntington Library. *Arrêté* of May 15, 1798, signed by Talleyrand, is in AAE CP EU, vol. 49, p. 364. See also Faÿ, *Revolutionary Spirit*, pp. 425–427, and Paul A. Varg, *Foreign Policies of the Founding Fathers* (East Lansing, Mich., 1963), pp. 132–133.
3. For insights on *Floréal*, see Palmer, *Age of Democratic Revolution*, II, pp. 255–260, 370, and 550; Lefebvre, *The Thermidoreans and the Directory*, pp. 373–386; and Meynier, *Coup d'état du Directoire*, II, *Le vingt-deux floréal an VI (11 mai 1798) et le trente Prairial an VII (18 juin 1799)*.
4. Samuel E. Morison, "DuPont, Talleyrand and the French Spoliations," *Massachusetts Historical Society Proceedings*, XLIX (1915–16), 76.
5. Louis André Pichon told this to Murray. Commonplace Book, June 28, 1798, II, 227, in William Vans Murray Papers, Princeton University Library (microfilm copy). See also Guyot, *Le Directoire et la paix de l'Europe*, p. 562.
6. For details see, Gerry to Talleyrand, [Paris], June 4, 1798, AAE CP EU, vol. 49, p. 429; Crane Brinton, *The Lives of Talleyrand* (New York, 1936), p. 109; Faÿ, *Revolutionary Spirit*, p. 428, who points out that Talleyrand circulated a pamphlet protesting his innocence and moderation; Guyot, *Le Directoire et la paix de l'Europe*, pp. 563–564; George Duruy, ed., *Memoirs of Barras: Member of the Directorate*, trans. from the French (4 vols., London, 1895–96), III, 270–271; and Austin, *Life of Gerry*, II, 233. Even small American newspapers published Talleyrand's denials and his letters to Gerry. See, for example, *The Green Mountain Patriot* (Peacham, Vt.), Sept. 7 and 14, 1798.
7. Talleyrand, "Report to the Executive Directory," Paris, June 1, 1798, AAE CP EU, vol. 49, pp. 393–404. The semiofficial *Gazette Nationale ou Le Moniteur Universel* (Paris), June 9, 1798, said Americans were foolish to make a fuss over an error. All the French wanted was an act of goodwill to offset the Jay Treaty. The *Décade philosophique* expressed

hope that Adams would not allow the X Y Z incident to stir up the American nation against France. Cited in Childs, "French Opinion of Anglo-American Relations," pp. 23–26. See also Lyon, "The Directory and the United States," p. 525.

8. John Quincy Adams to King, July 11, 1798, Rufus King Papers, Huntington Library. Talleyrand admitted to Gerry that the agents worked for him, Haraszti, *Adams and the Prophets of Progress*, p. 346, note 9. See also Carl L. Lokke, "The Trumbull Episode: A Prelude to the 'X Y Z' Affair," *New England Quarterly*, VII (March 1934), 111.

9. Murray to John Quincy Adams, June 5, 1798, in Ford, "Letters of William Vans Murray," p. 414; Murray to King, June 8, 1798, in Rufus King Papers, Huntington Library. At this time Talleyrand told the Spanish ambassador in Paris that France would leave no stone unturned in an effort to prevent open war with the United States, but said he was uncertain about success in the effort. See Whitaker, "The Retrocession of Louisiana in Spanish Policy," p. 467.

10. Talleyrand to Gerry, June 27, 1798, quoted in Lyon, "The Directory and the United States," p. 527. Gerry always insisted that if he had not been in Paris when the published X Y Z dispatches arrived, full-scale war would have followed. See Miller, *Federalist Era*, p. 212.

11. Quoted from Lyon, "The Directory and the United States," p. 527.

12. Talleyrand's report to the Directory, July 10, 1798, on relations with the United States in G. Pallain, *Le Ministère de Talleyrand*, pp. 302–310.

13. Pichon's official title was "Secretary of the Legation of the French Republic near Batavia." For details see, James, "French Opinion as a Factor in Preventing War," p. 54 n; Samuel F. Bemis, *John Quincy Adams and the Foundations of American Foreign Policy*, second printing with corrections (New York, 1956), p. 91; Alexander DeConde "William Vans Murray and the Diplomacy of Peace: 1797–1800," *Maryland Historical Magazine*, XLVIII (March 1953), 8–9.

14. Commonplace Book, June 30, 1798, II, 227, William Vans Murray Papers, Princeton University Library, and Murray to Pichon, The Hague, Sept. 23, 1798. Dispatches, The Netherlands, Department of State, National Archives, Microcopy 42, Roll No. 5.

15. July 3, 1798, in Ford, "Letters of William Vans Murray," pp. 426–427. See also Darling, *Rising Empire*, p. 302, and Bowman, "Struggle For Neutrality," pp. 372–374.

16. DuPont sent his first dispatch to Talleyrand from Bordeaux on July 7, 1798, AAE CP EU, vol. 50, ff. 8–9. See also James, "French Opinion as a Factor in Preventing War," p. 53.

17. Talleyrand to DuPont, Paris, July 21, 1798, AAE CP EU, vol. 50, ff. 68 and 99. For details, see Lyon, "The Directory and the United States," pp. 528–529.

18. Morison, in "Dupont, Talleyrand and the French Spoliations," p. 66 n., points out that Talleyrand already knew about the spoliations, but he wanted more reliable information on which he could base an appeal to

the Executive Directory to restrain the corsairs, a step he considered necessary in order to avoid an enlarged war.

19. Victor DuPont's influence with the Directory is analyzed in Pierre Jolly, *DuPont de Nemours, soldat de la liberté* (Paris, 1956), pp. 189–194.

20. Adet to Directors, July 16, 1798, *Archives nationales, relations extérieures, U.S.A., AF* III, dossier 263. Hauteval to Minister of Foreign Relations, July 23, 1798, cited in James, "French Opinion as a Factor in Preventing War," pp. 51–54. "DuPont . . . gave it as his opinion," John Quincy Adams wrote, "that a rupture would only strengthen the English party and English influence in America, and that the true patriots, French and American, wished for conciliatory measures on the part of France. From that moment, the French government have affected a friendly disposition towards the United States." To Abigail Adams, Sept. 14, 1798, in Ford, *Writings of John Quincy Adams*, II, 361–362. See also Morison, "Du Pont, Talleyrand and the French Spoliations," p. 76, and Jolly, *DuPont de Nemours*, p. 194.

21. Quoted in Darling, *Rising Empire*, p. 300. See also *Le Moniteur Universel* (Paris), July 27, 1798.

22. Commonplace Book, entry of July 17, 1798, William Vans Murray Papers, Princeton University Library.

23. See Murray to John Adams, The Hague, July 17, 1798, and Talleyrand to Pichon, July 9, in Adams, *Works of John Adams*, VIII, 680–684.

24. See Lyon, "The Directory and the United States," p. 528, and Gerry to Talleyrand, Paris, July 20, 1798, Dispatches, France, Department of State, National Archives, Film No. 34, Roll 8. This letter was published in *Le Rédacteur* (Paris).

25. Commonpace Book, entry of July 25, 1798, William Vans Murray Papers, Princeton University Library.

26. The quotation is from Pinckney to Pickering, July 26, 1798, in Zahniser, "The Public Career of Charles Cotesworth Pinckney," p. 259. Talleyrand's appeal is printed in Morison, "Du Pont, Talleyrand and the French Spoliations," pp. 76–78.

27. Kramer, "Public Career of Elbridge Gerry," pp. 148–149, who says that Talleyrand did not allow Gerry to depart until he knew Murray was receptive to peace feelers. See also Austin, *Life of Gerry*, II, 234; Phillips, "Public Career of Timothy Pickering," p. 311; and Talleyrand to Fulwar Skipwith, Paris, Aug. 6, 1798, in Gebhardt, *Diplomatick Transactions between the American and French Governments*, III, 352.

28. Murray to King, Aug. 4, 1798, Rufus King Papers, Huntington Library, and Murray to Pickering, Aug. 7, in Ford, "Letters of William Vans Murray," p. 452.

29. Aug. 15, 1798, quoted in Lyon, "The Directory and the United States," p. 530.

30. Quoted in Phillips and Reede, *Neutrality*, II, p. 87. See also Bonnel, *La France, les États-Unis et la guerre de course*, pp. 92–93, and Gebhardt, *Diplomatick Transactions between the American and French Governments*, III, 358.

31. Murray to King, Aug. 21, 1798, Rufus King Papers, Huntington Library, and Murray to Pickering, Aug. 23, in Ford, "Letters of William Vans Murray," pp. 458–459.
32. For details, see Miecislaus Haiman, *Kosciuszko: Leader and Exile* (New York, 1946), pp. 73–74, 80, and 85–86. Charles B. Todd, for example, in *Life and Letters of Joel Barlow, LL.D. . . .* (New York, 1886), p. 155, ascribes the change to Barlow's private influence with the Directors and to his public influence with the French people through articles he wrote for the French press. See also Murray to John Quincy Adams, Aug. 31, 1798, in Ford, "Letters of William Vans Murray," p. 462, and Adams to Pitcairn, Berlin, Sept. 7, 1798, in "Letters of Thomas Boylston Adams to Joseph Pitcairn," *Quarterly Publication of the Historical and Philosophical Society of Ohio*, XII (Jan.–March, 1917), 20.
33. Commonplace Book, entry of August 5, 1798, William Vans Murray Papers, Princeton University Library, and Murray to King, Aug. 6, Rufus King Papers, Huntington Library. Logan arrived in Amsterdam on Aug. 3.
34. A ship captain, Gideon Gardner, attributed the Directory's decision to Logan's intercession, and so did *Le Moniteur Universel* (Paris), Aug. 28, 1798. For details, see Tolles, *George Logan*, pp. 165–167, and Georgia Robison, *Revèlliére-Lépeaux, Citizen Director, 1753–1824* (New York, 1938), p. 218.
35. Morison, "Elbridge Gerry, Gentleman, Democrat," p. 24.
36. Frederick B. Tolles, "Unofficial Ambassador: George Logan's Mission to France, 1798," *William and Mary Quarterly*, Third Series, VII (Jan. 1950), 10–20.
37. Bemis, *John Quincy Adams and the Foundations of American Foreign Policy*, pp. 99–100. Earlier, the President had asked his son to write to him freely and directly concerning affairs in Europe, particularly on how to preserve peace and friendship with the Europeans. See Smith, *Adams*, p. 935. The quotation is from *Décade philosophique*, in Echeverria, *Mirage in the West*, p. 226.
38. Murray to John Quincy Adams, Aug. 31, 1798, in Ford, "Letters of William Vans Murray," p. 463. In private letters Murray kept President Adams, Pickering, John Quincy Adams, and Rufus King informed of the general drift of his conversations with Pichon. Murray to John Quincy Adams, Sept. 6, in *ibid.*, p. 466. The American Consul General in Paris, Fulwar Skipwith, reported that the French were releasing American seamen from jail. Darling, *Rising Empire*, p. 301.
39. The letter of Aug. 28, 1798, is in *ASP FR*, II, 241–242.
40. Commonplace Book, entries of Sept. 6 and 7, 1798, William Vans Murray Papers, Princeton University Library.
41. Mountflorence to King, Sept. 8, 1798, Rufus King Papers, Huntington Library.
42. *The Gazette and Daily Advertiser* (Charleston, S.C.), Nov. 9, 1798, but the source is dated London, Sept. 9.
43. King to Hamilton, London, Sept 23, 1798, in Hamilton, *Works of Ham-*

ilton, VI, 359–360. The marginal comments are in Charles, *Origins of the American Party System,* p. 126.

44. Murray to Pichon, The Hague, Sept. 23, 1798, Dispatches, The Netherlands, Vol. 4, Department of State, National Archives.

45. Talleyrand's letter of Sept. 28 is in *ASP FR,* II, 239–240, and Adams, *Works of John Adams,* VIII, 690–691.

46. Murray to Pickering, The Hague, Oct. 5, 1798, Dispatches, The Netherlands, Vol. 4, No. 61, Department of State, National Archives.

47. Morison, "Elbridge Gerry, Gentleman, Democrat," pp. 28–29, and Austin, *Life of Gerry,* II, 237. The quotation is from Gerry to Pickering, Nantucket Road, Oct. 1, 1798, Dispatches, France, Department of State, National Archives, Film No. 34, Roll No. 8.

48. See Austin, *Life of Gerry,* II, 301.

49. Correspondence Originally Published in the Boston *Patriot,* 1809, in Adams, *Works of John Adams,* IX, 287. In private Adams also defended Gerry's stay in Paris after the publication of the X Y Z dispatches. John Adams Letterbook, Quincy, Aug. 3, 1799, Adams Papers, reel 120, also Adams to William Cunningham, Nov. 4, 1808, *ibid.*

50. Murray to John Quincy Adams, Oct. 5, 1798, in Ford, "Letters of William Vans Murray," p. 479, and Murray to Pickering, Oct. 12, Dispatches, The Netherlands, Vol. 4, Department of State, National Archives.

51. The timing here is important. The quarrel over rank had not only cooled Adams's ardor for building up the nation's military power, but it also apparently caused him to take a new look at the French crisis. He now became receptive to the possibility of an accommodation with France if such news came from men he knew and trusted, such as Gerry and Murray. A similar point is stressed in Phillips, "Public Career of Timothy Pickering," p. 335. See Adams to Pickering, Quincy, Oct. 29, 1798, and Murray to Adams, The Hague, July 1, 1798, in Adams, *Works of John Adams,* VIII, 614–615, 677–680, and Kurtz, *Presidency of John Adams,* p. 342.

52. Adams to Pickering, Quincy, Oct. 20, 1798, Adams, *Works of John Adams,* VIII, 609–610.

53. Codman to Otis, Paris, Aug. 26, 1798, is in Morison, *Harrison Gray Otis,* I, 168–170. Nathaniel Cutting wrote to Jefferson on Aug. 27, expressing similar sentiments. "The present," Cutting wrote, "is perhaps the most favorable moment we can ever expect to adjust our differences, and to define our political relation with France." Most of the Directors, he said, were emerging from the "cloud of error" that had enveloped them. Quoted in Malone, *Jefferson and the Ordeal of Liberty,* p. 432.

54. See Pickering to Adams, Trenton, Nov. 5, 1798, and Adams to Gerry, Phil., Dec. 15, 1798, in Adams, *Works of John Adams,* VIII, 616–617; Phillips, "Public Career of Timothy Pickering," p. 335; Carroll, *Washington,* pp. 550–552; Darling, *Rising Empire,* pp. 334–337; and Dauer, *Adams Federalists,* p. 229.

55. Charleston *City Gazette*, Nov. 3, 10, and 21, 1798, quoted in Zahniser, "Public Career of Charles Cotesworth Pinckney," p. 271.

56. The first quotation is from Tolles, *George Logan*, p. 176, and the second is from Fitzpatrick, *Washington's Writings*, XXXVII, 18–20.

57. Smith to McHenry, Lisbon, Nov. 18, 1798, in Steiner, "Correspondence of William Smith," pp. 98–99.

58. For details, see Smith, *Adams*, pp. 986–988, and Kurtz, *Presidency of John Adams*, pp. 346–347. For Adams's account of the meeting, recollected later, see Correspondence Originally Published in the Boston *Patriot*, 1809, in Adams, *Works of John Adams*, IX, 244.

59. The quotation is from Tolles, *George Logan*, p. 180. William Branch Giles was a prominent Republican from Virginia. See also Darling, *Rising Empire*, p. 334.

60. See Phillips, "Public Career of Timothy Pickering," p. 351; Gibbs, *Wolcott Papers*, II, 186–187; and Hamilton, *Works of Hamilton*, VI, 359.

61. For details, see Dauer, *Adams Federalists*, p. 225; Wood, *Administration of John Adams*, p. 171; Adams, *Life of John Adams*, II, 263–267; Varg, *Foreign Policies of the Founding Fathers*, p. 139; Bowers, *Jefferson and Hamilton*, p. 430; Charles R. Brown, *The Northern Confederacy According to the Plans of the "Essex Junto," 1796–1814* (Princeton, 1916), pp. 22–23; and Correspondence Originally Published in the Boston *Patriot*, 1809, from notes of 1801, in Adams, *Works of John Adams*, IX, 304–305. Adams's modification of Wolcott's draft was not only important but also apparently quite unexpected. On Nov. 29, 1798, for example, Wolcott wrote to William Smith, "We shall not declare war against France nor shall we send any new ministers," but, he finished, we will continue the Quasi-War. Quoted in Rogers, *Evolution of a Federalist*, p. 320.

62. *Porcupine's Gazette* (Phil.), Dec. 4, 1798, quoted in Clark, *Peter Porcupine in America*, pp. 135–136.

63. Second annual address, Dec. 8, 1798, printed in Richardson, *Messages of the Presidents*, I, 261–265.

64. The quotations are from Mason to Otis, Jan. 12, 1799, in Dauer, *Adams Federalists*, p. 227; Gallatin to Wife, Dec. 14, 1798, in Adams, *Life of Gallatin*, p. 223; and John Dawson to Madison, Dec. 9, 1798, in Kurtz, *Presidency of John Adams*, p. 344. See also Murray to John Quincy Adams, Feb. 8, 1799, in Ford, "Letters of William Vans Murray," p. 517, and David M. Erskine to father, Phil., Dec. 9, 1798, in Patricia H. Menk, "D. M. Erskine: Letters from America, 1798–1799," *William and Mary Quarterly*, Third Series, VI (April 1949), 257. Erskine said Adams had offered the possibility of peace when "Americans consider themselves to be at War at present."

65. See Senate to Adams, Dec. 11, 1798, and Adams to Senate, Dec. 12, in Richardson, *Messages of the Presidents*, I, 265–267. The Paris newspapers attributed Adams's moderation to the influence of the Republican opposition, which they maintained was growing stronger. Murray to

John Quincy Adams, Feb. 18, 1799, in Ford, "Letters of William Vans Murray," p. 519.

66. See Otis to Hamilton, Phil., Dec. 21, 1798, and Adams to Otis, no precise date, in Morison, *Harrison Gray Otis*, I, 158–160, 162, and Hamilton to Otis, Dec. 27, 1798, and Jan. 26, 1799, in Hamilton, *Works of Hamilton*, VI, 379–380, 390–392.

67. To Abigail, Phil., Jan. 1, 1799, Adams Papers, reel 393.

68. Details are from Tolles, *George Logan*, pp. 185–204; Walters, *Albert Gallatin*, pp. 115–117; Charles Warren, *History of Laws Prohibiting Correspondence with a Foreign Government and Acceptance of a Commission*, 64th Cong., 2nd sess., Senate Document No. 696 (Washington, 1917), pp. 4–12; and 5 Cong., 3 sess., *Annals of the Congress*, IX, 2496–2545, 2583–2626. Ford, "Timothy Pickering," in Bemis, *American Secretaries of State*, II, 231, says Pickering suggested "Logan's Law."

69. Quoted in Smith, *Adams*, p. 994. See also Bemis, *John Quincy Adams and the Foundations of American Foreign Policy*, pp. 99–100.

70. For details see Phillips, "Public Career of Timothy Pickering," p. 354; Wood, *Administration of John Adams*, p. 181; and Adams to Pickering, Jan. 15, 1799, in Adams, *Works of John Adams*, VIII, 621. Thomas had posted his dispatches from New York. They may have reached his father before he did. In any case, Thomas and his dispatches moved the President to action. See Bemis, *John Quincy Adams and the Foundations of American Foreign Policy*, pp. 99–101.

71. Pickering's report, dated Jan. 18, 1799, is in *ASP FR*, II, 229–238. See also Pickering and Upham, *Life of Pickering*, III, 387.

72. Murray to Adams, The Hague, Oct. 7, 1798, Adams, *Works of John Adams*, VIII, 688–690, and dispatch of Oct. 12, Dispatches, The Netherlands, Department of State, National Archives, Microcopy 42, Roll 5.

73. Pickering to Murray, Phil., Feb. 1, 1799, Ford, "Letters of William Vans Murray," p. 515. The Dutch Minister in the United States had approached Adams with the offer. The italics are Pickering's.

74. Barlow's letter is in Todd, *Life and Letters of Joel Barlow*, pp. 156–160. This was Barlow's third letter to the United States in behalf of improved relations with France. See Joel Barlow, *Two Letters to Citizens of the United States and One to General Washington* (New Haven, 1800), and James Woodress, *A Yankee's Odyssey: The Life of Joel Barlow* (Phil., 1958), pp. 187–203.

75. Quoted in Darling, *Rising Empire*, p. 341. Washington himself had never been a war hawk. Even during the X Y Z frenzy he had hoped that "the Despots of France" would come to their senses and keep the peace. To William Vans Murray, Mount Vernon, Aug 10, 1798, Washington Papers, Manuscript Division, Library of Congress. Although Washington believed in the existence of a French plot to overthrow the government, and had approved of Adams's war program, he had always been willing to support a fair negotiation with the French. For

an astute analysis, see Marshall Smelser, "George Washington and the Alien and Sedition Acts," *American Historical Review,* LIX (Jan. 1954), 333–334.

76. See, for example, Jean Antoine Rozier, "Mémoire sur la relation des États-Unis d'Amérique avec le gouvernement directorial addressé par Rozier, consul-général à New York, au directeur Larévellière-Lépeaux," in Larévellière-Lépeaux, *Mémoires de Larévellière-Lépeaux,* III, 179–189.

77. Quoted in Lyon, "The Directory and the United States," pp. 531–532. The Executive Directory came to recognize the need for repressing the violence and rapacity of the French privateers. See Fulwar Skipwith to Secretary of State, Paris, Jan. 23, 1799, in Knox, *Quasi-War Documents,* II, 272–273.

78. Faÿ, *Revolutionary Spirit,* p. 428. The new French friendliness was important in helping to overcome American hostility, for, as Federalists realized, "the proper temper of the nation cannot be revived without new and open outrages on the part of France." Cabot to Pickering, Brookline, Feb. 14, 1799, in Lodge, *Cabot,* p. 217. Republican newspapers were pleased to publish Gerry's and Talleyrand's letters because that correspondence showed there had been no treason in it, merely a desire to preserve peace. *Massachusetts Spy* (Worcester), Feb. 6, 13, and 20, 1799, among others, carried the correspondence. Cited in Stewart, "Jeffersonian Journalism," p. 570.

79. Jefferson to Madison, Feb. 5, 1799, Ford, *Writings of Jefferson,* VII, 342–345.

80. See Smith, *Adams,* p. 999, and Zahniser, "Public Career of Charles Cotesworth Pinckney," pp. 279–281.

81. Murray pointed this out several months later. "To go on in the *middle state,* with such a constitution, was hazardous. It laid it and the nation bare to TREASON, for the very word *'enemy'* is technical with us, and there was no ENEMY technically, under the half way measures." To John Quincy Adams, June 17, 1799, in Ford, "Letters of William Vans Murray," p. 564. Extreme Federalists still wanted Congress to declare war. Stephen Higginson to Timothy Pickering, Jan. 31, 1799, Pickering Papers, Massachusetts Historical Society.

82. Adams's message of Feb. 18, 1799, is in Adams, *Works of John Adams,* IX, 159–160. See also pp. 245–247, Correspondence Originally Published in the Boston *Patriot,* 1809; Robert L. Hilldrup, *The Life and Times of Edmund Pendleton* (Chapel Hill, N.C., 1939), p. 317; John Quincy Adams to Pickering, Berlin, Oct. 6, 1798, in Ford, *Writings of John Quincy Adams,* II, 372–373, in which young Adams urges the appointment of Murray to enter preliminary discussions with the French; Bemis, *John Quincy Adams and the Foundations of American Foreign Policy,* pp. 100–102, who maintains that young Adams's advice was decisive in the President's own decision to negotiate; Pickering and Upham, *Life of Pickering,* III, 392; and Murray to McHenry, Jan. 30, 1799, in Steiner, *James McHenry,* pp. 371–374.

83. Henrietta Liston to James Jackson, Phil., March 13, 1799, Liston Papers, National Library of Scotland. See also Adams, *Life of John Adams*, II, 274. Adams called the war hawks in his party "the Hyper-federalists or the Ultrafederalists," and in later years he claimed: "Their *Summum bonum* is a war with France, an Alliance with England, and a dependence on the British Navy for the protection of their Commerce." To Benjamin Waterhouse, Quincy, March 16, 1813, in Ford, *Statesman and Friend*, p. 93.

84. Adams to Washington, Phil., Feb. 19, 1799, and Washington to Adams, March 3, 1799, in Adams Papers, reels 117 and 393. Létombe to Talleyrand, Feb. 15 and 25, 1799, is cited in Logan, *Haiti and the U.S.*, p. 90. In "The French Mission of 1799–1800: Concluding Chapter in the Statecraft of John Adams," *Political Science Quarterly*, LXXX (Dec. 1965), 543–557, Stephen G. Kurtz argues that the intrigue of cabinet officers had nothing to do with Adams's decision to use Murray. That decision to negotiate, Kurtz maintains, "was dictated largely by concern over internal unrest. . . ."

85. Some historians have considered Adams's act one of the truly important decisions in the history of the new nation. John Quincy and Charles Francis Adams in Adams, *Life of John Adams*, II, 283, called it "the most noted event of Mr. Adams's administration." It has also been analyzed as terminating Adams's connection with the war program of the High Federalists, as destroying Hamilton's dream of military glory, as beginning the breakup of the Federalist party, and as marking the end of the Quasi-War, or at least of easing the French crisis. Charles, in *Origins of the American Party System*, p. 162, calls it "an act of political suicide for Adams" whereas Kurtz, in *Presidency of John Adams*, p. 353, says "it was politically intelligent." For some other judgments, see Darling, *Rising Empire*, p. 341; Dauer, *Adams Federalists*, p. 230; Adams, *Life of Gallatin*, p. 222; and Smith, *Adams*, p. 1002, who says the President acted "with little or no regard for . . . practical political consequences."

Notes — Chapter VI

1. Historians have also been puzzled by Adams's motivation. Most of those dealing with the subject have accepted Adams's own later explanations that he acted from patriotic concerns for the good of his country. See, for example, Adams, *Life of John Adams*, II, 296, and the latest biographer, Smith, in *Adams*, pp. 1001–1002. Kurtz, in *Presidency of John Adams*, pp. 348–353, 375, 378, and 383, stresses political motivation. Robert Liston believed that letters from John Quincy Adams had prompted the President to act. To Grenville, March 14, 1799, No. 17, PRO GB FO 5. See also Steiner, *James McHenry*, p. 370.
2. Samuel Dexter to Murray, Phil., Feb. 19, 1799, William Vans Murray Papers, Library of Congress, and Liston to Grenville, Phil., Feb. 22, 1799, No. 14, PRO GB FO 5.
3. Higginson to Pickering, March 3, 1799, in J. Franklin Jameson, ed., "Letters of Stephen Higginson, 1783–1804," *Annual Report of the American Historical Association for the Year 1896* (Washington, 1897), I, 819–820; Sedgwick to Hamilton, Feb. 19, 1799, in Hamilton, *Works of Hamilton*, VI, 396; and the anonymous letter quoted in Adams, *Works of John Adams*, VIII, 452–453 n. The italics are in the original.
4. George Cabot to Pickering, Brookline, March 7, 1799, Pickering Papers, Massachusetts Historical Society; Jonathan Mason to Otis, Boston, Feb. 27, 1799, in Morison, *Harrison Gray Otis*, I, 172; and Jefferson to Madison, Pendleton, and Monroe, Feb. 19, 1799, in Ford, *Writings of Jefferson*, VII, 361–367. Although pleased, Jefferson believed that Adams had taken the step grudgingly and tardily, had not meant to meet France's "overtures effectively," had been forced to make the nomination, and hoped the senators "would take on their own shoulders the odium of rejecting it." To Madison, Feb. 26, 1799, in *ibid.*, p. 370.
5. The quotations are from Pickering and Upham, *Life of Pickering*, III, 439. In later years Pickering accused Adams of allowing the French to nominate his minister for him, and called the nomination the result of a corrupt bargain with Republicans. To McHenry, Phil., May 7,

1810, in Steiner, *James McHenry*, pp. 557–558. See also Phillips, "Public Career of Timothy Pickering," pp. 352–353.

6. Washington to Adams, Mount Vernon, March 3, 1799, in Fitzpatrick, *Washington's Writings*, XXXVII, 143–144; Knox to John Adams, Boston, March 5, 1799, Adams, *Works of John Adams*, VIII, 627; and Stoddert to Adams, Bladensburg, Oct. 12, 1809, in Lodge, *Cabot*, p. 202.

7. The *Aurora* (Phil.), Feb. 20, 1799, quoted in Schachner, *Founding Fathers*, p. 504; John Clopton, circular letter, Phil., Feb. 22, 1799, Clopton Papers, Duke University Library; T. B. Adams to Joseph Pitcairn, Quincy, March 2, 1799, in "Letters of Thomas Boylston Adams to Joseph Pitcairn," pp. 25–26.

8. Abigail to John Adams, Quincy, Feb. 27, and March 30, 1799, in the Adams Papers, reel 393.

9. Liston to Grenville, Phil., Feb. 22, 1799, No. 14, PRO GB FO 5.

10. The other members of the committee are discussed in Pickering to Cabot, Phil., Feb. 21, 1799, in Lodge, *Cabot*, p. 221; Gibbs, *Wolcott Papers*, II, 204; and Welch, *Theodore Sedgwick*, pp. 186–187. Some senators felt that Paris was the "Focus of every species of intrigue," and that the negotiations, if they must be held, should take place in some neutral city such as Berlin. John Rutledge to ————, Phil., Feb. 27, 1799, Rutledge Papers, Southern Historical Collection, University of North Carolina Library.

11. The quotations are from a note to Pickering from one of the members of the committee, dated Jan. 1, 1822, and printed in part in Pickering and Upham, *Life of Pickering*, III, 440–441. What actually took place at the conference has been the subject of dispute. For an analysis, see Welch, *Theodore Sedgwick*, pp. 186–188.

12. For details, see Adams, *Works of John Adams*, I, 547–549; Darling, *Rising Empire*, p. 342; and Miller, *Federalist Era*, p. 245. The letter of nomination is in *ASP FR*, II, 240. Pickering said that Ellsworth disliked the mission, but accepted the post "from the necessity of preventing a greater evil," such as the appointment of James Madison or Aaron Burr. To Cabot, Feb. 26, 1799, in Lodge, *Cabot*, p. 273. William Vans Murray, at this juncture, praised Ellsworth because of his reputation and great experience in government. Murray to John Luzac, The Hague, April 15, 1799, Rufus King Papers, Huntington Library.

13. The quotations are from Ames to Timothy Dwight, Boston, Feb. 27, 1799, Ames, *Works of Fisher Ames*, I, 252, and Cabot to Pickering, Brookline, March 7, 1799, in Lodge, *Cabot*, p. 224. See also Elisha P. Douglass, "Fisher Ames, Spokesman for New England Federalism," *Proceedings of the American Philosophical Society*, CIII (Oct. 1959), 710, and Elizabeth Cometti, "John Rutledge, Jr., Federalist," *Journal of Southern History*, XIII (May 1947), 190–191.

14. Pickering to Murray, Phil., March 6, 1799, Dispatches, The Netherlands, Vol. 4, Department of State, National Archives.

15. Phillips, "Public Career of Timothy Pickering," p. 363; Pickering to King, March 12, 1799, in King, *Correspondence of Rufus King*, II, 558;

Carroll, *Washington,* 597 n; Patrick Henry to Pickering, Charlotte County, Va., April 10, 1799, *ASP FR,* II, 241; and Henry to Adams, Charlotte County, April 16, 1799, in William W. Henry, ed., *Patrick Henry: Life, Correspondence, and Speeches* (3 vols., New York, 1891), II, 323.

16. Ellsworth to Pickering, Halifax, March 25, 1799, and Pickering to Davie, Phil., June 1, 1799, in William R. Davie Papers, 1778–1819, North Carolina Department of Archives and History, Raleigh. See also Blackwell P. Robinson, *William R. Davie* (Chapel Hill, N.C., 1957), pp. 321–322.

17. Even Murray in Europe was aware of the political danger. He warned that "this splitting of the Fed [1]. party . . . will do immense mischief—unless stopped in time—for the Jacobins are & will be united & agt. Govt.—whether success or defeat attend this [peace mission] or any Govt. measure—" To King, May 20, 1799, Rufus King Papers, Huntington Library. The mission also contributed to a sectional split. "Unhappily," Cabot told Christopher Gore, "the Federalists of the North do not agree with those of the South." Jan. 21, 1800, in Lodge, *Cabot,* pp. 268–269. The quotation is from Adams to Charles Lee, Quincy, March 29, 1799, Adams, *Works of John Adams,* VIII, 629.

18. Tracy to McHenry, Sept. 2, 1799, in Steiner, *James McHenry,* pp. 416–417.

19. Barlow to Dr. Lemuel Hopkins, Paris, April 12, 1799, in Pickering Papers, Massachusetts Historical Society.

20. Since Congress scrupled at unequivocal war, John Quincy Adams, for example, considered negotiation necessary for internal as well as external reasons. Both Britain and France sought to use American politics to advance their own interests. They took for granted, he said, "that we have no such thing as an American party among us." To King, April 26, 1799, Rufus King Papers, Huntington Library. See also the letter to King of April 15, in Ford, *Writings of John Quincy Adams,* II, 409–412.

21. Robert Troup to King, April 19, 1799, in King, *Correspondence of Rufus King,* II, 596–597, and James Iredell, April 11, 1799, in McRee, *James Iredell,* II, 552, are the sources for the quotations. This letdown, followed by a rise in Republicanism, was evident even in Federalist strongholds such as New Hampshire. See Turner, *William Plumer,* p. 68. See also Margaret Woodbury, "Public Opinion in Philadelphia, 1789–1801," *Smith College Studies in History,* V, Nos. 1–2 (Northampton, Mass., 1919–1920), p. 91; Bowers, *Jefferson and Hamilton,* p. 418.

22. Ames to Dwight Foster, Dedham, June 24, 1798, in Ames, *Works of Fisher Ames,* I, 230. Callender reported to Jefferson, Raspberry Plain, Oct. 26, 1798, that "already, the X. Y. Z. mania is greatly cooled." Worthington C. Ford, ed., *Thomas Jefferson and James Thomson Callender, 1798–1802* (Brooklyn, 1897), p. 14.

23. The Philadelphia *Gazette,* March 6, and the *Aurora* (Phil.), March 7, 21, and April 1, 1799, are quoted in Miller, *Crisis in Freedom,* pp. 148–149.

24. For details on the "Tub Plot," see *ibid.*, pp. 146–150; McMaster, *History of the United States*, II, 441; Wood, *Administration of John Adams*, pp. 186–187; and Zahniser, "Public Career of Charles Cotesworth Pinckney," pp. 281–283. Papers in England carried the story of the "Tub Plot," according to Murray to John Quincy Adams, April 30, 1799, in Ford, "Letters of William Vans Murray," p. 547.

25. In August 1800 the total population of the United States was 5.3 million, Pitkin, *A Statistical View of the Commerce of the United States*, pp. 286–287. Expenditures and receipts are summarized in Davis R. Dewey, *Financial History of the United States*, 12th ed. (New York, 1939), pp. 110–113. See also Washington to Hamilton, Mount Vernon, Feb. 25, 1799, in Fitzpatrick, *Washington's Writings*, XXXVII, 136–138; Kurtz, *Presidency of John Adams*, pp. 307, 359–360; Miller, *Federalist Era*, pp. 218–219; Beard, *Economic Origins of Jeffersonian Democracy*, p. 355, who points out that for the year 1800 government expenditure was $10.8 million. In July 1800 Albert Gallatin published, as a campaign document, an attack on Federalist spending during the Quasi-War. He called it *Views of the Public Debt, Receipts, and Expenditures of the United States*. For details, see Walters, *Albert Gallatin*, pp. 122–123. According to Lynton K. Caldwell, *The Administrative Theories of Hamilton and Jefferson* (Chicago, 1944), p. 76, Hamilton had hoped to overcome public antipathy to military service, in part at least, through efficient organization of the Army. Obviously, he failed. Lynch, in *Fifty Years of Party Warfare*, p. 88, says inefficiency in the War Department was a basic factor in the failure to recruit the Army.

26. These comments are as Adams recalled them in later years, to James Lloyd, Quincy, Feb. 21, 1815, in Adams, *Works of John Adams*, X, 130.

27. *Time Piece* (New York), May 18, 1798, quoted in Bowers, *Jefferson and Hamilton*, p. 372. The editor of the *Time Piece* consistently urged peace and called war reckless and impractical, Shulim, *John Daly Burk*, pp. 27–28.

28. John Gardner to Otis, Boston, March 24, 1798, in Morison, *Harrison Gray Otis*, I, 90–91. In one Massachusetts town, for example, Federalist merchants supported the President, but they opposed war. See Benjamin W. Labaree, *Patriots and Partisans: The Merchants of Newburyport, 1764–1815* (Cambridge, Mass., 1962), p. 115. The item on the college students is from Stewart, "Jeffersonian Journalism," p. 556. See also Smith, *Freedom's Fetters*, pp. 247–248.

29. The freeholders' petition is dated Aug. 21, 1798. Details, and Pickering's letter, are in Pickering and Upham, *Life of Pickering*, III, 471–478. See also the protest against war, "lavish expenditure," and other parts of the Federalist program in Dodd, *Life of Nathaniel Macon*, pp. 113–114.

30. Dispatch of Arcambal, French Vice Consul in Newport, Rhode Island, Nov. 21, 1798, forwarded to the Directory on Feb. 19, 1799, *Archives nationales, relations extérieures, U.S.A., AF III, 64, Dossier 263, no p. no.*

31. Otis in "The Envoy," *J. Russell's Gazette* (Boston), in Morison, *Harrison Gray Otis*, I, 165. George Cabot expressed admiration for last year's war spirit and lamented that "the proper temper of the nation cannot be revived without new & open outrages on the part of France." To Pickering, Brookline, Feb. 14, 1799, Pickering Papers, Massachusetts Historical Society.

32. The *Independent Chronicle* (Boston), April 4, 1799; also quoted in Warren, *Jacobin and Junto*, pp. 89–90, and Bassett, *Federalist System*, p. 277.

33. Jefferson is quoted in Lynch, *Fifty Years of Party Warfare*, p. 84. There has always been a vagueness about Jefferson and Madison's purpose in drawing up their manifestos, but Adrienne Koch and Harry Ammon, in "The Virginia and Kentucky Resolutions: An Episode in Jefferson's and Madison's Defense of Civil Liberties," *William and Mary Quarterly*, Third Series, V (April 1948), 174, argue that the purpose was concern for liberty, whereas Leonard Levy, in *Jefferson and Civil Liberties: The Darker Side* (Cambridge, Mass., 1963), p. 56, says the purpose was defense of states' rights.

34. The Federalist campaign against the resolutions began early, and never let up. See Anderson, "Contemporary Opinion of the Virginia and Kentucky Resolutions," p. 239. Koch and Ammon, "Virginia and Kentucky Resolutions," p. 176, suggest that the resolutions were successful in rallying Republicans.

35. See Anderson, "Contemporary Opinion of the Virginia and Kentucky Resolutions," pp. 48–49, 241. Many critics implied that the resolutions stemmed from French influence. John Ward Fenno, Jr., in the *Gazette of the United States* (Phil.), reprinted in the *Albany Centinel*, Dec. 18, 1798, presented the resolutions to his readers under the heading, "Fruits of French Diplomatic Skill." See also the Salem *Gazette*, March 29, 1799, quoted in Warren, *Jacobin and Junto*, p. 110. For a refutation of the Federalist charge, see Philip G. Davidson, "Virginia and the Alien and Sedition Acts," *American Historical Review*, XXXVI (Jan. 1931), 336–342.

36. William Heth to Hamilton, Jan. 14, 1799, quoted in Dauer, *Adams Federalists*, p. 208. The *Aurora* (Phil.), Jan. 22, 1799, quoted in Kurtz, *Presidency of John Adams*, p. 336. In February another petition containing over a thousand signatures went to Congress in protest of the Federalist war measures. For the time, this was an unusually large number of protesters. See Eugene P. Link, *Democratic-Republican Societies, 1790–1800* (New York, 1942), p. 205. In the spring of 1799 Thomas Cooper also expressed concern over the Federalist attitude of "treating fair, open, decent and argumentative opposition" as evidence of hostility to the Union and "of preference to French interests. . . ." Quoted in Dumas Malone, *The Public Life of Thomas Cooper, 1783–1839* (New Haven, 1926), p. 103.

37. Diary entry of Jan. 20, 1799, in Warren, *Jacobin and Junto*, p. 123.

38. The assessors were not required by law to count windows. They could

have used some other means of assessment. See Davis, *Fries Rebellion,*
p. 37.

39. The proclamation is in Richardson, *Messages of the Presidents,* I, 276–
277. In later years Adams told Jefferson, "You certainly never realized
the terrorism of Fries's most outrageous Riot and Rescue, as I call it.
. . ." Quincy, June 30, 1813, in Cappon, *Adams-Jefferson Letters,* 346.

40. The quotation is from Miller, *Hamilton,* p. 505. For other details, see
Davis, *Fries Rebellion,* pp. 78–79.

41. See Warren, *Jacobin and Junto,* p. 125; Bowers, *Jefferson and Hamilton,*
pp. 419–423; Darling, *Rising Empire,* p. 353; and Francis Wharton,
*State Trials of the United States during the Administrations of Wash-
ington and Adams* (Phil., 1849), pp. 458–684. If, as the extremists
claimed, it became evident that the French were involved in the rebellion, Murray expected the peace negotiations to be abandoned. To John
Quincy Adams, May 3, 1799, in Ford, "Letters of William Vans Murray," p. 548.

42. See Adams's exchange with his department heads, May 20 and 21,
1800, in Adams, *Works of John Adams,* IX, 57–61, and Smith, *Adams,*
p. 1033. The proclamation of pardon is in Richardson, *Messages of the
Presidents,* I, 294–295.

43. See Phillips, "Public Career of Timothy Pickering," pp. 367–368; Tolles,
George Logan, pp. 208–211; and Davis, *Fries Rebellion,* pp. 137–138.

44. Even High Federalists admitted that hostility toward Britain had not
died. See, for example, Cabot to Pickering, Brookline, March 18, 1799,
in Lodge, *Cabot,* p. 226. Discontent over some aspects of commercial
relations with Britain, for example, was increased because of the war
taxes and additional duties the British imposed on American imports.
A convoy tax, for instance, was considered as discriminatory against
the United States. See Vernon G. Setser, *The Commercial Reciprocity
Policy of the United States, 1774–1829* (Phil., 1937), p. 145. The
newspaper is the *Columbian Museum* (Savannah, Ga.), July 6, 1798,
quoted in Stewart, "Jeffersonian Journalism," pp. 437–438. Stewart also
has gathered evidence of people holding public meetings in port cities
to petition Congress to take steps to prevent British seizures.

45. See Herbert W. Briggs, *The Doctrine of Continuous Voyage* (Baltimore,
1926), pp. 17–18; Perkins, *First Rapprochement,* pp. 88–89; William
E. Lingelbach, "England and Neutral Trade," *Military Historian and
Economist,* II (1917), 156–157; and Malcolm Lester, "Anglo-American
Diplomatic Problems Arising from British Naval Operations in American Waters, 1793–1802" (unpublished Ph.D. dissertation, University
of Virginia, 1954), pp. 358–359.

46. See Cabot to Oliver Wolcott, Brookline, Feb. 22, 1799, in Lodge,
Cabot, p. 222; Keith, "American Trade with the British West Indies,"
pp. 15–16; and Paul Goodman, *The Democratic-Republicans of Massachusetts* (Cambridge, Mass., 1964), pp. 102, 104–105, and 112, which
stresses the point of urban and merchant groups opposing war with
France. See also John H. Reinoehl, "The Impact of the French Revolu-

tion and Napoleon upon the United States as Revealed by the Fortunes of the Crowninshield Family of Salem" (unpublished Ph.D. dissertation, Michigan State College of Agriculture and Applied Science, 1953), pp. 35–37.

47. *Columbian Museum* (Savannah, Ga.), Jan. 28, 1796. On Aug. 12, 1796, this paper reported that about 2000 American seamen were serving in the British navy under duress. Cited in Stewart, "Jeffersonian Journalism," p. 435. For other details, see Miller, *Federalist Era*, p. 222.

48. Quoted in Darling, *Rising Empire*, p. 304.

49. See Liston to Pickering, Phil., Dec. 31, 1798, Stoddert to Phillips, and Phillips to Pickering, Jan.–Feb. 1799, in Knox, *Quasi-War Documents*, II, 29–34. For a detailed account of the episode, see John F. Campbell, "The Havana Incident," *American Neptune*, XXII (Oct. 1962), 264–276.

50. David M. Erskine to Father, Phil., Jan. 1, 1799, in Menk, "D. M. Erskine: Letters from America," p. 279.

51. *Connecticut Courant* (Hartford), March 18, 1799, quoted in Campbell, "Havana Incident," p. 275.

52. Pickering to King, Jan. 8, 1799, Rufus King Papers, Huntington Library, and Adams to Pickering, Quincy, June 7, 1799, in Adams, *Works of John Adams*, VIII, 655–656.

53. King to Pickering, July 15, 1799, in King, *Correspondence of Rufus King*, III, 53–59. King spent almost all of 1799 trying to reach an agreement with Lord Grenville on the main issue of impressment on the high seas. See James F. Zimmerman, *Impressment of American Seamen* (New York, 1925), p. 82. William Savage, the seamen's agent, also pointed out that impressments from American ships were so extensive as to decimate the crews of some vessels. To Pickering, Kingston, Jamaica, Sept. 17, 1799, and Feb. 26, 1800, in Knox, *Quasi-War Documents*, IV, 196, and V, 248.

54. In 1799 another case in which the captain and crew of the British packet *Chesterfield* attacked American authorities in Philadelphia with "half-pikes" stimulated resentment against the "arrogance" of British officers. See Darling, *Rising Empire*, pp. 304–305.

55. Before being executed Robbins confessed that he was Nash, but Republicans ignored the confession. Stewart, "Jeffersonian Journalism," p. 445. For details, see Dudley Pope, *The Black Ship* (New York, 1964), pp. 274–285, and Wharton, *State Trials of the United States*, pp. 392–457. Jefferson is quoted in Beveridge, *John Marshall*, II, 459. See also Miller, *Federalist Era*, p. 224; Schachner, *Founding Fathers*, pp. 506–507; and Perkins, *First Rapprochement*, pp. 124–125.

56. Adams to Pickering, Quincy, Aug. 6, 1799, in Adams, *Works of John Adams*, IX, 10–12, and Stevens to Pickering, Cap Français, May 3, 1799, in Jameson, "Letters of Toussaint Louverture and of Edward Stevens," p. 71. See also Treudley, "United States and Santo Domingo," pp. 138–139.

57. The arrangement Stevens had made with Toussaint on April 25, as a

result of Maitland's arrival, was not carried out. See Logan, *Haiti and the U.S.*, p. 97. See also Henry Dundas to Lord Grenville, Tunynghame, Jan. 23, 1800, *Dropmore Papers*, VI, 107.

58. Stevens did not sign because he did not yet know if Adams had approved the arrangement. *Le Moniteur Universel* (Paris), Oct. 18, 1799, states that Roume had concluded a commercial treaty with the United States. See also Ludwell Lee Montague, *Haiti and the United States, 1714–1938* (Durham, N.C., 1940), pp. 39–40.

59. Quoted in Tansill, *United States and Santo Domingo*, p. 66. Aptheker, in *American Negro Slave Revolts*, pp. 43–44, points out that another objective of the agreement was to keep revolutionaries out of American and British slave territories.

60. Adams to Pickering, Quincy, June 15, 1799, in Adams, *Works of John Adams*, VIII, 658. For other details, see Stevens to Pickering, L'Arcahaye, June 23, 1799, in Jameson, "Letters of Toussaint Louverture and of Edward Stevens," p. 74, and Tansill, *United States and Santo Domingo*, p. 69.

61. Adams's proclamation of June 23, 1799, is in *ASP FR*, II, 240–241, and Treasury documents are in Knox, *Quasi-War Documents*, III, 408–410. See also Stevens to Pickering, L'Arcahaye, June 24, 1799, in Jameson, "Letters of Toussaint Louverture and of Edward Stevens," p. 80, and Létombe to the Consuls of the Republic, Phil., Aug. 24, 1799, *Archives nationales, relations extérieures, U.S.A., AF* III, 64, Dossier 263, no p. no.

62. Létombe reported on the extent of American intervention in behalf of Toussaint. He thought Americans sought control of St. Domingue. To Talleyrand, Phil., June 13, 1800, AAE CP EU, vol. 52, pp. 66–69. See also Timothy Pickering to Edward Stevens, July 12, 1799, Pickering Papers, Massachusetts Historical Society.

63. For details, see Ferguson, *Truxtun of the Constellation*, pp. 187–202; Allen, *Our Naval War with France*, pp. 163–177; the *Aurora* (Phil.), Feb. 25 and 26, 1800; Sargent, "Quasi-War with France," pp. 17–19; Knox, "Documents on the Naval War with France," p. 537; and DuPont to Jefferson, near New York, Aug. 24, 1800, in Dumas Malone, ed., *Correspondence between Jefferson and Pierre Samuel du Pont de Nemours, 1798–1817* (Boston, 1930), pp. 22–23. The report of the Captain of *La Vengeance* is printed in Edgar S. Maclay, *A History of the United States Navy from 1775 to 1894* (2 vols., New York, 1897), I, 197–198.

64. The Stevens quotation is from Henry Adams, *History of the United States of America during the Administrations of Jefferson and Madison* (9 vols., New York, 1889–91), I, 386. See also Stevens to Pickering, Leogane, Jan. 16, 1800, in Jameson, "Letters of Toussaint Louverture and of Edward Stevens," p. 90, and Treudley, "United States and Santo Domingo," p. 137. For Toussaint's acknowledgment of American assistance, see his letters of March 16 and 21, 1800, in Knox, *Quasi-War Documents*, V, 309–310, 336–337. Adams's proclamation dated May 9, 1800, is in Richardson, *Messages of the Presidents*, I, 292.

65. This proclamation is also in Richardson, *Messages of the Presidents*, I, 294–295. For additional details on American aid to Toussaint against Rigaud, see Logan, *Haiti and the U.S.*, pp. 109–110.

66. The quotation is from William Smith, Lisbon, June 21, 1799, Rufus King Papers, Huntington Library. John Quincy Adams was among those who had expected losses. To King, Jan. 18, 1799, in *ibid*. For other details, see Dauer, *Adams Federalists*, pp. 31, 233–234, and 237; Chambers, *Political Parties in a New Nation*, p. 143; and Fee, *Transition in New Jersey*, pp. 233–234.

67. See Robinson, *William R. Davie*, pp. 299–300; Adams, *Marshall's Autobiographical Sketch*, pp. 25–26; and Beveridge, *John Marshall*, II, 411–413.

68. The quotations are from King to James C. Mountflorence, London, June 7, 1799, Rufus King Papers, Huntington Library; John Ward Fenno, Jr., to Pickering, Phil., Oct., 16, 1799, Pickering Papers, Massachusetts Historical Society; and Uriah Tracy to Oliver Wolcott, Pittsburgh, Aug. 7, 1800, in Gibbs, *Wolcott Papers*, II, 399. For details see Sanford W. Higginbotham, *The Keystone in the Democratic Arch: Pennsylvania Politics, 1800–1816* (Harrisburg, Pa., 1952), pp. 16, 25, and 26. Despite their gains, the Federalists did not carry Virginia. See David K. McCarrell, "The Formation of the Jeffersonian Party in Virginia" (unpublished Ph.D. dissertation, Duke University, 1937), pp. 236–237.

69. Murray to Talleyrand, May 5, 1799, Dispatches, The Netherlands, Vol. 4, Department of State, National Archives.

70. See Darling, *Rising Empire*, p. 347, and Murray to King, The Hague, July 14, 1799, Rufus King Papers, Huntington Library. The Marquis de Lafayette, who was pleased with the appointment of the new mission, also considered the timing appropriate. "I have every Reason to think the French Government are Earnestly wishing for a reconciliation," he wrote to Jefferson. Vianen, near Utrecht, April 19, 1799, in Gilbert Chinard, ed., *The Letters of Lafayette and Jefferson* (Baltimore, 1929), p. 182.

71. The quotations are from E. Wilson Lyon, "The Franco-American Convention of 1800," *Journal of Modern History*, XII (Sept. 1940), 306–307.

72. See Fugier, *La Révolution Française et l'empire Napoléonien*, p. 119; Meynier, *Coups d'état du Directoire*, II; Rose, *The Revolutionary and Napoleonic Era*, pp. 112–114; and Lacour-Gayet, *Talleyrand*, I, 343.

73. Lyon, "Convention of 1800," pp. 307–308; Bowman, "Struggle for Neutrality," pp. 407–410; Masson, *Département des affaires étrangères*, pp. 432–442; and Forrest to Adams, Georgetown, April 28, 1799, and Adams to Forrest, Quincy, May 13, 1799, in Adams, *Works of John Adams*, VIII, 637–638, 645–646.

74. General Gunn to Hamilton, Dec. 19, 1798, and Jan. 23, 1799, Hamilton, *Works of Hamilton*, V, 182–183, 195, and 274–275, and Miller, *Hamilton*, pp. 501–502.

75. John Adams Letterbook, Quincy, Aug. 6, 1799, Adams Papers, reel 120,

and Adams to Pickering, Quincy, Aug. 6, 1799, in Adams, *Works of John Adams,* IX, 10–12.

76. McHenry to Robert Goodloe Harper, Phil., Aug. 1, 1799, in the Elbridge Gerry Papers, Manuscript Division, Library of Congress.

77. Liston to Grenville, New York, June 17, 1799, PRO GB FO 5. In August Ellsworth said he had to go. "There is nothing in politics he [Ellsworth] more detests than this mission," Pickering wrote, "and nothing in nature he more dreads than the voyage across the wide Atlantic." To Cabot, Trenton, Sept. 13, 1799, in Lodge, *Cabot,* p. 237. For news of the *coup,* see Robert E. Reeser, "Rufus King and the Federalist Party" (unpublished Ph.D. dissertation, University of California, Los Angeles, 1948), pp. 189–190.

78. Lafayette said the French Directors sincerely desired a *rapprochement* with the United States. See Lafayette to Washington, Wittmold, April 20, 1798, Vianen, May 9, 1799, to Hamilton, Wittmold, Aug. 12, 1798, Washington to Lafayette, Mount Vernon, Dec. 25, 1798, and Hamilton to Lafayette, New York, April 28, 1798, in Marquis de Lafayette, *Mémoires, Correspondance et Manuscrits du Général Lafayette* (6 vols., Paris, 1837–1838), IV, 410–411, 426, 431–437, 438–444, and V, 40. William Vans Murray said it was administration policy to keep Lafayette in Europe. To King, Aug. 9, 1799, Rufus King Papers, Huntington Library. See also Lafayette to Jefferson, La Grange, Feb. 10, 1800, in Chinard, *Letters of Lafayette and Jefferson,* p. 209, also p. 162.

79. James C. Mountflorence reported that a majority in the new Executive Directory desired an accommodation, but that a powerful minority interested in privateering wished to prevent all negotiations. To King, The Hague, Aug. 10, 1799, Rufus King Papers, Huntington Library. See also Phillips, "Public Career of Timothy Pickering," p. 370, and Stoddert to Adams, Trenton, Aug. 29, 1799, and Adams to Stoddert, Quincy, Sept. 4, 1799, in Adams, *Works of John Adams,* IX, 18–20.

80. Pickering to King, Trenton, Oct. 4, 1799, Rufus King Papers, Huntington Library. Fisher Ames urged Pickering to oppose the mission. Until it could be abandoned, he said, "the schism among the friends of government cannot be healed." Good men were against the mission, but he feared the masses favored it, "for a time" anyway. To Pickering, Dedham, Oct. 19, 1799, in Ames, *Works of Fisher Ames,* I, 257–258.

81. Stoddert to Adams and Adams to Stoddert, Trenton and Quincy, Sept. 13 and 21, 1799, in Adams, *Works of John Adams,* IX, 25–29, 33–34. Earlier, extreme Federalists had also complained of Adams's retreat to Quincy, commenting that "all measures of government are retarded by this kind of abdication." Robert Troup to King, April 19, 1799, in King, *Correspondence of Rufus King,* II, 596–597.

82. See Adams to Pickering and Pickering to Adams, Quincy and Trenton, Sept. 21 and 24, 1799, and Adams to Ellsworth, Quincy, Sept. 22, in Adams, *Works of John Adams,* IX, 33–37. Adams had told Ellsworth he would postpone the mission, and Ellsworth had informed Pickering.

Ellsworth expressed his views on the mission to Pickering, in Hartford, Sept. 19, 20, and Windsor, Oct. 5, 1799, and in other letters, Pickering Papers, Massachusetts Historical Society. Adams stopped at Windsor on Oct. 4, 1799, Brown, *Oliver Ellsworth*, pp. 276–278.

83. Lee to Adams, Winchester, Oct. 6, 1799, Adams, *Works of John Adams*, IX, 38. Pickering was so upset by the President's determination to go ahead with his peace policy that he reprimanded Murray for dealing with the French. Hurt, Murray defended his actions, saying the assurances he had extracted *"from a haughty and insolent government* will add to *the glory* of my country when the manner of my letters and of your critique shall be in oblivion." Murray also decried what he called "federal jacobinism," explaining that there were "disloyal Jacobinical federalists," as well as Republican ones. See Pickering to Murray (Private), Trenton, Oct. 4, 1799, Murray to Pickering, The Hague, Dec. 1, 1799, and Murray to John Quincy Adams, Dec. 6, 1799, in Ford, "Letters of William Vans Murray," pp. 600–602, 623–627, and 629–630. Italics are in the original.

84. This is how Abigail Adams reported the conversation to her sister, Mary Cranch, Phil., Dec. 30, 1799, in Mitchell, *New Letters of Abigail Adams*, pp. 224–225. See also Miller, *Hamilton*, pp. 501–502, and Correspondence Originally Published in the Boston *Patriot*, 1809, in Adams, *Works of John Adams*, IX, 254–255.

85. Adams to Pickering, Trenton, Oct. 16, 1799, Adams, *Works of John Adams*, IX, 39. See also the *Autobiography of Charles Biddle, 1745–1821* (Phil., 1883), p. 282, and Kurtz, "The French Mission of 1799–1800," pp. 544, 555, where it is argued that Adams deliberately delayed the departure of Ellsworth and Davie for eight months in order to build up naval strength in the Caribbean.

86. Pickering to George Cabot, Trenton, Oct. 22 and 24, 1799, Pickering Papers, Massachusetts Historical Society, and Pickering to Murray, Trenton, Oct. 25, 1799, in Ford, "Letters of William Vans Murray," pp. 610–612. For Adams's later defense of his decision as the result of "full and dispassionate consideration of the whole subject," see Adams, *Works of John Adams*, IX, 255–256 n.

87. Jay to Parsons, Albany, July 1, 1800, in *Memoir of Theophilus Parsons* . . . (Boston, 1859), pp. 474–475, and Leven Powell, Dec. 11, 1799, in William E. Dodd, ed., "Correspondence of Col. Leven Powell, M.C., Relating to the Election of 1800," *The John P. Branch Historical Papers of Randolph-Macon College*, I (Richmond, Va., 1901), 232.

88. See Miller, *Hamilton*, p. 503, and Higginson to Pickering, Boston, Nov. 24, 1799, in Jameson, "Letters of Stephen Higginson," pp. 831–832. For details on the British reaction, see Benjamin Stoddert to Adams, Trenton, Sept. 13, 1799, and William Smith to Pickering, Lisbon, Sept. 14, 1799, in Knox, *Quasi-War Documents*, IV, 179–182, 185.

89. Liston to Grenville, Phil., Nov. 4, 1799, No. 59, PRO GB FO 5; Kyte, "Robert Liston and Anglo-American Cooperation," p. 265; and Steiner,

James McHenry, p. 420, the source of the first quotation. The last quotation, and similar sentiments, are in John Rutledge to Bishop Smith, Phil., Dec. 7, 1799, and Harrison Gray Otis to Rutledge, Boston, Nov. 12, 1799, Rutledge Papers, Southern Historical Collection, University of North Carolina Library.

Notes—Chapter VII

1. Ellsworth and Davie to Secretary of State, Lisbon, Dec. 7, 1799, Dispatches, The Netherlands, Department of State, National Archives, Film No. 34, Reel No. 9. Pickering thought this precaution would not only delay the negotiation, but it also would make completion of the mission unnecessary. To King, Phil., Nov. 6, 1799, in Rufus King Papers, Huntington Library. Ellsworth, whose health was poor, had expected to be sick the entire voyage. His fears were justified, for he emerged from his voyages practically a broken man. See Brown, *Oliver Ellsworth*, p. 281, and also Robinson, *William R. Davie*, pp. 324, 319–358, for a discussion of the mission.

2. Murray to Pickering, Dec. 9, 1799, Dispatches, The Netherlands, Vol. 4, No. 107, Department of State, National Archives, and Murray to John Quincy Adams, Dec. 10, 1799, in Ford, "Letters of William Vans Murray," p. 630. See also Robert G. Harper to Constituents, Phil., May 15, 1800, Donnan, "Bayard Papers," p. 104, and Adams, *History of the United States*, I, 361, who maintains, contrary to Murray and others, that Bonaparte did not want prompt negotiations. According to Henry Adams the First Consul favored a peace settlement in Europe first so that he could deal with the United States when it stood alone and he could dictate his own terms. Some Americans felt the change in the French government would damage the negotiations. See Chipman to ———, Phil., Feb. 28, 1800, in Daniel Chipman, *The Life of Hon. Nathaniel Chipman* . . . (Boston, 1846), pp. 130–131. Pickering wrote on Feb. 14, 1800, that the problem of credentials should not impede the proposed negotiation if the French wanted it, but the commissioners did not receive these instructions until May 16. Pickering and Upham, *Life of Pickering*, III, 444. For other details, see Rose, *The Revolutionary and Napoleonic Era*, pp. 119–123, and Meynier, *Coups d'état du Directoire*, III, *Le dix-huit brumaire an VIII (9 Novembre 1799) et le fin de la République.*

3. Murray to John Quincy Adams, [Jan. 26, 1800], and Feb. 17, 1800, in Ford, "Letters of William Vans Murray," pp. 637–638, 643, and Murray

to Pickering, The Hague, Feb. 17, 1800, Dispatches, The Netherlands, Vol. 4, No. 117, Department of State, National Archives. See also Echeverria, *Mirage in the West*, p. 226.

4. *Correspondance de Napoléon Ier . . .* , ed. by a commission headed by J. B. P. Vaillant (32 vols., Paris, 1858–70), XXX, 330. Talleyrand was reappointed on Nov. 22, 1799. He had been in close touch with Bonaparte preceding the *coup*. Bonaparte believed Talleyrand had sought money during the X Y Z affair, *ibid.*, p. 465. See also Lacour-Gayet, *Talleyrand*, I, 360; Madelin, *Talleyrand*, pp. 72–73; and Dard, *Napoléon et Talleyrand*, p. 37. At this time Napoleon was called Bonaparte. In Aug. 1802, when he became First Consul for life he was called Napoleon Bonaparte, and later, in 1804 when he became Emperor, the world came to know him simply as Napoleon.

5. Lyon, "Convention of 1800," pp. 307–308. Bonaparte appeared to have a good grasp of affairs in the United States according to an American who had spoken to him. See Hulbert Footner, *Sailor of Fortune: The Life and Adventures of Commodore Barney, U.S.N.* (New York, 1940), p. 228.

6. Talleyrand, Report to the Consuls of the Republic, Paris, *Archives nationales, relations extérieures, U.S.A., AF IV, 1681 IA, Dr. No. 1, pp. 1–3.

7. James, "French Opinion as a Factor in Preventing War," pp. 54–55; Faÿ, *Revolutionary Spirit*, p. 430; Bowman, "Struggle for Neutrality," p. 412; and Lyon, "Convention of 1800," p. 308.

8. Murray to John Quincy Adams, Feb. 14, 1800, Ford, "Letters of William Vans Murray," pp. 641–642, and Lacour-Gayet, *Talleyrand*, II, 57–59. The First Consul's decree is in *Correspondance de Napoléon Ier*, XXX, 467.

9. "Éloge funèbre de Washington, prononcé dans le temple de mars, par Louis Fontanes, le 20 pluviôse an 8," in supplément au *Le Moniteur Universel* (Paris), Feb. 19, 1800. The translated quotation is from Echeverria, *Mirage in the West*, p. 254. Ironically, in an oration before the Massachusetts legislature Fisher Ames, the leading Federalist spokesman of the region, used the occasion of Washington's death to make a severe attack upon "French Politicks." See Bernard, *Fisher Ames*, pp. 319–321.

10. Commissioners to Secretary of State, Paris, April 18, 1800, Dispatches, France, Department of State, National Archives, Film No. 34, Reel 9, and Brown, *Oliver Ellsworth*, pp. 283–284. Since Murray was the only envoy who could speak a little French, he acted as spokesman for the commissioners. Murray to John Quincy Adams, March 7, 1800, Ford, "Letters of William Vans Murray," p. 644.

11. See Bonnel, *La France, les États-Unis et la guerre de course*, p. 123, and Murray to John Quincy Adams, Paris, Oct. 10, 1800, in Ford, "Letters of William Vans Murray," pp. 656–657. One of the French commissioners, Roederer, had written a book in which he attributed France's rupture with the United States to the depredations of French privateers. He wanted to revive American friendship and divide "the

Anglo-Americans." Charles Herries, the translator, in the introduction to Frederick Gentz, *On the State of Europe Before and After the French Revolution* . . . , trans. from the German, 3rd ed. (London, 1803), pp. xliii–xliv.

12. Murray to John Quincy Adams, The Hague, Nov. 7, 1800, in Ford, "Letters of William Vans Murray," p. 659, and Memorandum Book, April 24, 1801, William Vans Murray Papers, Library of Congress.

13. American to French commissioners, Paris, April 3, 1800, *ASP FR*, II, 312, and Albert du Casse, *Histoire des négociations diplomatiques relatives aux traités de Mortfontaine, de Lunéville, et d'Amiens* (3 vols., Paris, 1855), I, 224–228. The American commissioners were eager to get on with their task because their instructions said that if they were not received promptly they should demand their passports and leave France without listening to fresh overtures. See Richard Hildreth, *The History of the United States of North America* (6 vols., New York, 1849), V, 322–323.

14. Paine to Jefferson, Oct. 1, 1800, in Moncure D. Conway, ed., *The Writings of Thomas Paine* (4 vols., New York, 1894–96), II, 284–285. See also Aldridge, *Man of Reason*, p. 265.

15. The instructions, dated Oct. 22, 1799, are printed in *ASP FR*, II, 301–306. The administration did not want the negotiation to go beyond April 1, except for special circumstances, because it wished the present Congress to be able to act upon any agreement that resulted from the mission. Benjamin Stoddert reported that the instructions were such "that if the Directory have any disposition to reconciliation, a treaty will be made." Jan. 12, 1800, in Sawvel, *Complete Anas*, p. 198.

16. In his original draft of the instructions Pickering had wanted to go beyond this demand. He had insisted that the French must acknowledge the actions of their corsairs to have been piratical. Ellsworth had objected, saying that such a condition was "unusually degrading," and would probably defeat the negotiation "and place us in the wrong." Brown, *Oliver Ellsworth*, p. 289.

17. The commercial treaty with Prussia, signed July 11, 1799, was negotiated by the President's son, and did not mention free ships, free goods. See Bemis, *John Quincy Adams and the Foundations of American Foreign Policy*, p. 94. The treaty is in *ASP FR*, II, 244–249.

18. Bonnel, *La France, les États-Unis et la guerre de course*, p. 141, and Heckscher, *The Continental System*, p. 50.

19. The French instructions are in du Casse, *Négociations diplomatiques relatives aux traités de Mortfontaine*, I, 186–213, and are summarized in Lyon, "Convention of 1800," pp. 312–313. These instructions were in such opposition to American objectives that a successful negotiation hardly seemed possible. Yet Republicans such as Jefferson believed the Consulate was so favorably disposed toward an accommodation that the American envoys would be unable to avoid a settlement. See Joseph Shulim, *The Old Dominion and Napoleon Bonaparte: A Study in American Opinion* (New York, 1952), p. 89.

20. The French government repeatedly admitted that many cruisers in the West Indies that flew its flag were not controlled by lawful commissioners, were sailed by foreigners and pirates, and habitually used excessive violence. Brooks Adams, "The Convention of 1800 with France," p. 422.

21. The exchanges between the commissioners of April 9, 11, 14, and 17, 1800, and the draft treaty articles are in *ASP FR*, II, 314–317. A report by Oliver Wolcott on the suspension of commercial intercourse, dated Feb. 14, 1800, is on pp. 285–286.

22. Commonplace Book, April 9, 1800, also entry of April 18, in William Vans Murray Papers, Princeton University Library.

23. Brown, *Oliver Ellsworth*, pp. 292–293.

24. The commissioners to Pickering, Paris, May 17, 1800, in *ASP FR*, II, 325.

25. Murray to John Quincy Adams, May 11, 1800, in Ford, "Letters of William Vans Murray," p. 646. The French position is stated in French commissioners to [American commissioners], Paris, May 6, 1800, AAE CP EU, Vol. 52, pp. 7–8.

26. See George A. King, "The French Spoliation Claims," *American Journal of International Law*, VI (April 1912), 370. For a brief modern discussion of the discharge of treaties, see J. L. Brierly, *The Law of Nations . . .* , ed. by Sir Humphrey Waldock, 6th ed. (New York, 1963), pp. 327–345, and Lord McNair, *The Law of Treaties* (Oxford, 1961), pp. 553–571, which points out that there is a vague right of unilateral abrogation following a fundamental breach of a treaty.

27. Murray to John Quincy Adams, March 23, 1801, Ford, "Letters of William Vans Murray," pp. 690–691. International law assumes that war kills a treaty because both parties elect to destroy it.

28. Commonplace Book, May 15, 1800, William Vans Murray Papers, Princeton University Library.

29. A. M. Roederer, ed., *Oeuvres du comte P. L. Roederer . . .* (8 vols., Paris, 1853–59), III, 337, and Commonplace Book, May 23, 1800, William Vans Murray Papers, Princeton University Library.

30. See Joseph to Napoleon Bonaparte, Paris, May 24, 1800, in du Casse, *Négociations diplomatiques relatives aux traités de Mortfontaine*, I, 273–274.

31. French commissioners to Talleyrand, Paris, May 26, June 5, 1800, and [Talleyrand] to French commissioners, Paris, June 5, in AAE CP EU, Vol. 52, ff. 36–49, 64–65. See also Lyon, "Convention of 1800," pp. 316–317.

32. Commonplace Book, May 15 and 25, 1800, William Vans Murray Papers, Princeton University Library.

33. Bonaparte to Talleyrand, Paris, July 22, 1800, *Correspondance de Napoléon Ier*, VI, 415–416.

34. Brown, *Oliver Ellsworth*, pp. 286–287.

35. See commissioners to Pickering, Paris, July 15, 1800, *ASP FR*, II, 327–328.

36. Commonplace Book, July 15, 1800, William Vans Murray Papers, Princeton University Library. For a summary of Mably's views, see Ernest A. Whitfield, *Gabriel Bonnot de Mably* (London, 1930), p. 120.
37. Talleyrand, Report to the First Consul, Paris, June [1800], *Archives nationales, relations extérieures, U.S.A. Serie I AF IV,* 16181 IA, Dr. No. 1, pp. 5–19. Two other reports of July [?] and 13, 1800, are quoted in Lyon, "Convention of 1800," pp. 318–319.
38. July 20 and 21, 1800, Commonplace Book, William Vans Murray Papers, Princeton University Library. Henry Adams maintains that Joseph, anxious to succeed in his first diplomatic effort, persuaded the First Consul to end the crisis and go ahead with the negotiation. Adams, *History of the United States,* I, 361.
39. Commonplace Book, July 23 and 25, 1800, William Vans Murray Papers, Princeton University Library. In his *History of the United States,* I, 362, Henry Adams says Bonaparte cared nothing for the guarantee in the Franco-American treaties. He used this provision as a bargaining point, merely to offset claims by the United States that he was determined not to pay. See also Bonnel, *La France, les États-Unis et la guerre de course,* pp. 132–133.
40. Commonplace Book, July 27, 1800, William Vans Murray Papers, Princeton University Library.
41. Quoted in Alfred Thayer Mahan, *The Influence of Sea Power upon the French Revolution and Empire, 1793–1812,* 4th ed. (2 vols., Boston, 1894), II, 27.
42. Quoted in Phillips and Reede, *Neutrality,* II, p. 94.
43. Details are in Francis T. Piggott and G. W. T. Omond, *Documentary History of the Armed Neutralities: 1780 and 1800 . . .* (London, 1919), pp. 380–381, 398–403; Mahan, *Sea Power and the French Revolution,* II, 32–33; J. Holland Rose, *The Life of Napoleon I* (2 vols., New York, 1918), I, 98–99, 240; Fugier, *Révolution Française et l'empire Napoléonien,* p. 129; Driault, *La politique extérieure du premier consul,* pp. 83–84, 143, 152; and M. A. Thiers, *The History of the Consulate and the Empire of France under Napoleon,* trans. from the French (2 vols., London, 1875), I, 140–142.
44. Commonplace Book, Aug. 1, 1800, William Vans Murray Papers, Princeton University Library. See also Driault, *La politique extérieure du premier consul,* p. 155.
45. The details and quotations are from Commonplace Book, Aug. 6, 1800, William Vans Murray Papers, Princeton University Library.
46. Ira Allen, in an article in the *Journal of Commerce,* Paris, Aug. 6, 1800, in James B. Wilbur, *Ira Allen: Founder of Vermont, 1751–1814* (2 vols., Boston, 1928), II, 517–519. The *Times* (London), Aug. 6, 1800, 2:3, also reported that the American negotiators were making no progress.
47. Arthur A. Richmond, "Napoleon and the Armed Neutrality of 1800: A Diplomatic Challenge to British Sea Power," *Journal of the Royal United Service Institution,* CIV, No. 614 (May 1959), 189.
48. The French note of Aug. 11, 1800, is in du Casse, *Négociations diplo-*

matiques relatives aux traités de Mortfontaine, I, 292–296, and *ASP FR*, II, 330–332.

49. Commonplace Book, Aug. 11 and 12, 1800, William Vans Murray Papers, Princeton University Library.

50. Journal of Negotiations at Paris, Aug. 14, 1800, William Vans Murray Papers, Library of Congress. Yet, the envoys agreed "that the negotiations must be abandoned or our instructions deviated from." See commissioners to Pickering, Paris, Aug. 20, 1800, *ASP FR*, II, 333–334.

51. Journal of Negotiations at Paris, Aug. 15 and 18, 1800, William Vans Murray Papers, Library of Congress. These terms are in the note of the American commissioners to French commissioners, Paris, Aug. 20, 1800, *ASP FR*, II, 333–334.

52. Memorandum Book containing diary notes, Aug. 20, 1800, William Vans Murray Papers, Library of Congress.

53. Journal of Negotiations, Aug. 25, 1800, in *ibid.* See also French to American commissioners, Paris, Aug. 25, 1800, in du Casse, *Négociations diplomatiques relatives aux traités de Mortfontaine*, I, 304–306, and in *ASP FR*, II, 333–336.

54. Journal of Negotiations, Aug. [30], 1800, William Vans Murray Papers, Library of Congress.

55. The best account of the earlier neutral combination is Isabel de Madariaga, *Britain, Russia, and the Armed Neutrality of 1780* (New Haven, 1962). See also Paul Fauchille, *La diplomatie Française et la ligue des neutres de 1780* (Paris, 1893), and Phillips and Reede, *Neutrality*, II, 100–101. Paul's declaration and decree of Aug. 27 and 29, 1800, are in James Brown Scott, ed., *The Armed Neutralities of 1780 and 1800* (New York, 1918), pp. 489–492, 493–494.

56. Journal of Negotiations, Sept. 4, 5, and 11, 1800, William Vans Murray Papers, Library of Congress.

57. Murray to John Quincy Adams, Dec. 22, 1800, Ford, "Letters of William Vans Murray," pp. 664–666.

58. Brown, *Oliver Ellsworth*, pp. 297–298. Journal of Negotiations, Sept. 12, 1800, William Vans Murray Papers, Library of Congress.

59. Journal of Negotiations, Sept. 13 and 20, 1800, in *ibid.* See the notes of Sept. 13 and 19, 1800, exchanged by the American and French commissioners, *ASP FR*, II, 339. "Our negotiators," Gouverneur Morris explained later, "huddled up a treaty because there was to be a general peace. . . ." To Alexander Hamilton, Jan. 16, 1801, in Anne C. Morris, ed., *The Diary and Letters of Gouverneur Morris* (2 vols., New York, 1888), II, 399–400.

60. Journal of Negotiations, Sept. 24, 1800, William Vans Murray Papers, Library of Congress. "They apply the principle of free bottoms free goods from the *signature* for the purpose of extricating a great number of our ships, uncondemned." Murray to McHenry, Paris, Oct. 3, 1800, in Steiner, *James McHenry*, pp. 495–496.

61. See Heckscher, *The Continental System*, p. 78.

62. Thus the agreement brought Bonaparte's and Paul's maritime policies

into harmony. See Driault, *La politique extérieure du premier consul,* p. 156.

63. Journal of Negotiations, Sept. 24, 1800, William Vans Murray Papers, Library of Congress.

64. French commissioners to Talleyrand, Paris, at midnight, Sept. 26, 1800, AAE CP EU, Vol. 52, p. 320, and Murray to John Quincy Adams, The Hague, Nov. 7, 1800, Ford, "Letters of William Vans Murray," p. 659.

65. Murray to John Quincy Adams, Sept. 27, 1800, and Dec. 22, 1800, in *ibid.,* pp. 653–654, 666, where Murray also points out that the American negotiators made every motion, and pulled the French along the whole way.

66. Murray to Secretary of State, Paris, Oct. 1, 1800, Dispatches, The Netherlands, Vol. 4, Department of State, National Archives.

67. Journal of Negotiations, Oct. 1, 1800, at night, William Vans Murray Papers, Library of Congress.

68. Pierre Louis Roederer, *Mémoires sur la Révolution, le Consulat et l'Empire,* ed. by Octave Aubry (Paris, 1942), p. 136; Maurice Vitrac, ed., *Journal du Comte P.-L. Roederer . . .* (Paris, 1909), pp. 23–24; and Brown, *Oliver Ellsworth,* pp. 307–308. Earlier, in February 1798, the Prussian government had asked if the United States would join in a a new armed neutrality directed against France as well as England. John Adams and Timothy Pickering made it clear then that they would not join any neutral concert that would hamper England in her fight against France. See Bemis, *John Quincy Adams and the Foundations of American Foreign Policy,* pp. 91–92.

69. To John Quincy Adams, Paris, Oct. 5, 1800, in Ford, "Letters of William Vans Murray," pp. 654–655. The fête is also described in *Le Moniteur Universel* (Paris), Oct. 6, 1800; the *Maryland Gazette* (Annapolis), Dec. 11, 1800, p. 1; Brown, *Oliver Ellsworth,* pp. 305–308; and George F. Hoar, "A Famous Fête," *Proceedings of the American Antiquarian Society,* New Series, XII (1899), 240–259.

70. Thiers, *Consulate and Empire,* I, 171–172, and Driault, *La politique extérieure du premier consul,* p. 156.

71. Ellsworth to Pickering, Le Havre, Oct. 16, 1800, Pickering Papers, Massachusetts Historical Society, and to Wolcott, in Gibbs, *Wolcott Papers,* II, 434.

ᚱᚱᚱᚱᚱ Notes — Chapter VIII ᚱᚱᚱᚱᚱ

1. Liston to Grenville, Phil., Nov. 4, 1799, No. 59, PRO GB FO 5.
2. For Washington's reaction to a possible draft, see Carroll, *Washington,* pp. 595–596, and Dauer, *Adams Federalist,* p. 249. Darling, in *Rising Empire,* p. 372, views Adams's decision to send Ellsworth and Davie off as a key one in domestic politics, as well as in foreign policy, saying that decision "set the Federalist clique at once to the business of throwing the President out of the party."
3. To Fisher Ames and William Bingham, Oct. 24 and 29, 1799, quoted in Dauer, *Adams Federalists,* p. 246.
4. McHenry to Washington, Nov. 10, 1799, in Steiner, *James McHenry,* p. 420, and Morris to Washington, Dec. 9, 1799, in Jared Sparks, *The Life of Gouverneur Morris, with Selections from His Correspondence and Miscellaneous Papers* (3 vols., Boston, 1823), III, 123.
5. Smith to McHenry, Lisbon, Dec. 26, 1799, in Steiner, "Correspondence of William Smith," p. 103.
6. Washington to Jonathan Trumbull, Mount Vernon, July 21, 1797, Fitzpatrick, *Washington's Writings,* XXXVII, 313.
7. To Mary Cranch, Phil., Dec. 4, 1799, in Mitchell, *New Letters of Abigail Adams,* pp. 217–219.
8. Message of Dec. 3, 1799, in Richardson, *Messages of the Presidents,* I, 270–282.
9. Abigail to Mary Cranch, Phil., Dec. 11, 1799, in Mitchell, *New Letters of Abigail Adams,* pp. 219–222, and Dodd, "Correspondence of Col. Leven Powell," pp. 231–233.
10. Oliver Wolcott to Fisher Ames, Phil., Dec. 29, 1799, in Gibbs, *Wolcott Papers,* I, 313. Some orthodox Federalists assumed that Adams had not, in fact, changed his policy toward France, believing "that the mission was a fit and indispensable preliminary to a declaration of war." In effect, they chose to think that he was calling the Directory's bluff. See also Kurtz, *Presidency of John Adams,* p. 360.
11. See Adams, *Life of John Adams,* II, 302–304, and Richard B. Morris, "Washington and Hamilton: A Great Collaboration," *Proceedings of the*

American Philosophical Society, CII (April 1958), 116, for an example of Washington's restraint. Henrietta Liston remarked that "the Magic of his [Washington's] name kept all parties right. . . ." To James Jackson, Phil., Dec. 19, 1799, Liston Papers, National Library of Scotland.

12. To Tobias Lear, New York, Jan. 2, 1800, in Lodge, *Hamilton's Works,* VIII, 538.

13. Adams to Senate, Dec. 23, 1799, in Richardson, *Messages of the Presidents,* I, 289. Nonetheless, in later years Adams could write that High Federalists had used Washington as a façade to cover their own objectives, saying they "puff'd Washington like an air-balloon to raise Hamilton." To Benjamin Rush, Sept. 23, 1805, quoted in Parsons, "Continuing Crusade," p. 47.

14. Dec. 12, 1799, quoted in Miller, *Federalist Era,* pp. 250–251.

15. 6 Cong., 1 sess., *Annals of the Congress,* X, 247, 249–250, 252–253, 271, and 369. This John Nichols should not be confused with John Nichols, the clerk of Albermarle County, Virginia, an ardent Federalist.

16. Cabot to Wolcott, Jan. 16, 1800, in Gibbs, *Wolcott Papers,* II, 322. See also 6 Cong., 1 sess., *Annals of the Congress,* X, 522–527.

17. The Provisional Army was disbanded on June 15, 1800. See Godfrey, "Organization of the Provisional Army," p. 132. Kathryn Turner, in "Federalist Policy and the Judiciary Act of 1801," *William and Mary Quarterly,* Third Series, XXII (Jan. 1965), 31–32, suggests that as a substitute for the army Federalists tried to strengthen the power of the national judiciary.

18. Schachner, *Founding Fathers,* pp. 526–527. For a report, dated Jan. 23, 1800, on the effectiveness of the Non-Intercourse Act, see Knox, *Quasi-War Documents,* V, 121–124.

19. The Richmond *Examiner,* March 21, 1800, had commented that the loan would enrich speculators, but bring the people nothing more than increased taxes. Cited in Donald H. Stewart, "The Press and Political Corruption during the Federalist Administrations," *Political Science Quarterly,* LXVII (Sept. 1952), 433–434.

20. Jefferson to Madison and to T. M. Randolph, Phil., Feb. 2 and May 12, 1800, in Lipscomb, *Writings of Jefferson,* X, 150–153, 165–166, and Warren, *Jacobin and Junto,* p. 150. The diary entry is dated May 16, 1799, but should be 1800.

21. Quoted in Gilbert Chinard, *Honest John Adams* (Boston, 1933), p. 296.

22. Wolcott to Fisher Ames, Phil., Dec. 29, 1799, in Gibbs, *Wolcott Papers,* II, 314–315.

23. Phillips, "Public Career of Timothy Pickering," p. 333.

24. See Higginson to Pickering, April 26, 1800, in Jameson, "Letters of Stephen Higginson," p. 863; Morse, *Federalist Party in Massachusetts,* pp. 178–179; and Goodman, *The Democratic-Republicans of Massachusetts,* p. 104.

25. For the December caucus, see Kurtz, *Presidency of John Adams,* p. 392. See also Theodore Sedgwick to Henry Van Schaack, Feb. 9, 1800, in Welch, *Theodore Sedgwick,* p. 214. See Abigail to Mary Cranch, Phil.,

May 5, 1800, in Mitchell, *New Letters of Abigail Adams,* p. 251, and Charles, *Origins of the American Party System,* p. 64.

26. Troup to King, New York, March 9, 1800, in King, *Correspondence of Rufus King,* III, 207–209.

27. See Matthew L. Davis to Gallatin, New York, March 29, April 15, and May 1, 1800, in Adams, *Life of Gallatin,* pp. 232–238. Here the candidates, with the occupations of the Federalists, are listed.

28. Consul of New York [name unreadable] to Talleyrand, New York, May 5, 1800, AAE CP EU, Vol. 52, pp. 5–6.

29. See James McHenry to John McHenry, Phil., May 20, 1800, in Gibbs, *Wolcott Papers,* II, 347. The Republican caucus chose Burr on May 11, 1800, Malone, *Jefferson and the Ordeal of Liberty,* p. 474, and Borden, *James A. Bayard,* p. 75. Federalist members of Congress had been in the habit of holding these caucuses, or semiofficial meetings, to plan strategy on important issues. See M. Ostrogorski, "The Rise and Fall of the Nominating Caucus, Legislative and Congressional," *American Historical Review,* V (Jan. 1900), 259–261.

30. See Cunningham, *Jeffersonian Republicans,* pp. 165, 185, and 392. Hamilton did not accept defeat easily. On May 7, 1800, he asked Governor John Jay to call the lame duck Federalist legislature into special session so that it would redistrict the state for the purpose of choosing presidential electors by popular election. This tactic would take the choosing of electors out of the hands of the Republican legislature, probably give the state to the Federalist presidential candidate, and nullify the recent Republican victory. Jay refused to adopt such "a measure for party purposes." For details, see Frank Monaghan, *John Jay, Defender of Liberty* (New York, 1935), pp. 419–421, and Miller, *Hamilton,* pp. 513–514.

31. Quoted in Smith, *Adams,* pp. 1027–1028.

32. Abigail to Mary Cranch, Phil., Dec. 11, 1799, in Mitchell, *New Letters of Abigail Adams,* pp. 219–221. White, in *The Federalists,* p. 251, points out that Adams had decided on the cabinet change earlier, but he had postponed action to avoid "a turbulent session in Congress."

33. The exchange of letters is reproduced in Pickering and Upham, *Life of Pickering,* III, 486–488. Adams gave various reasons for his action, but stressed Pickering's efforts to undermine the Ellsworth mission. See Phillips, "Public Career of Timothy Pickering," p. 392; Pickering to McHenry, Washington, July 27, 1813, in Steiner, *James McHenry,* p. 606; and Pickering to Charles C. Pinckney, Phil., May 25, 1800, in Henry Adams, ed., *Documents Relating to New England Federalism* (Boston, 1906), pp. 331–337. According to some Hamiltonians, McHenry and Pickering were sacrificed on the altar of peace so that Adams could gain favor in the South and thus help his election campaign. See Brown, *The Northern Confederacy,* pp. 18–19. Pickering claimed that the dismissals were unexpected. To Timothy Williams, Phil., May 19, 1800, Pickering Papers, Massachusetts Historical Society.

34. *Aurora* (Phil.), May 9, 1800. For a sample of Federalist reaction against the dismissal, see William Bristol to Daggett, New Haven, June 30, 1800, in Franklin B. Dexter, ed., "Selections from Letters Received by David Daggett, 1786–1802," *Proceedings of the American Antiquarian Society*, New Series, IV (1885–87), 375.

35. See Lodge, *Cabot*, p. 279. Adams sent Marshall's nomination to the Senate on May 12, 1800, and it was confirmed on the next day, but Marshall did not take up his new duties until June 6. Andrew J. Montague, "John Marshall: Secretary of State," in Bemis, ed., *American Secretaries of State*, II, 247.

36. *Aurora* (Phil.), May 27, 1800, and Pinckney to McHenry, June 10, 1800, quoted in Beveridge, *John Marshall*, II, 490, 492. Cabot felt that Marshall had accepted the post "from good motives, and with a view of preserving union . . . ," Sept. 30, 1800, in Lodge, *Cabot*, p. 291.

37. Van der Linden, *The Turning Point*, p. 167, and Bayard to [John Rutledge, Jr.?], Wilmington, June 8, 1800, in Donnan, "Bayard Papers," p. 112.

38. Adams's quotation, from notes in 1800, is from Howe, *Changing Political Thought of John Adams*, p. 207, and the Virginia quotation of May 26, 1800, is from Cunningham, *Jeffersonian Republicans*, p. 228.

39. Quoted in Smith, *Freedom's Fetters*, pp. 339–340. See also Shulim, *The Old Dominion and Napoleon Bonaparte*, p. 90.

40. The *Aurora* (Phil.), May 19, 1800, listed three parties in the campaign —the Republicans, the Friends of the President, and the Followers of Hamilton. It called the last two party groups "Adamites" and "Pickeroons," indicating that Pickering was responsible for much of the Federalist hysteria of 1798–1800. Kurtz, in *Presidency of John Adams*, p. 333, points out that Adams thought peace could be a more potent political issue than the threat of war had been in 1797–98. For other details, see Smith, *Adams*, p. 1040, and Beveridge, *John Marshall*, II, 512–518.

41. Hamilton to Charles Carroll, New York, July 1, 1800, in Lodge, *Hamilton's Works*, VIII, 554–556, and Cabot to Hamilton, Brookline, Aug. 21, and 23, 1800, in Lodge, *Cabot*, pp. 285, 286. On Aug. 27 Carroll reported to Hamilton that Republicans were making gains in Maryland, but that the masses were friendly to Adams's government, in Ellen H. Smith, *Charles Carroll of Carrollton* (Cambridge, Mass., 1942), p. 259. Moderate Federalists were distressed to learn that Hamiltonians were deserting Adams. See, for example, Murray to Samuel Dexter, Paris, July 12, 1800, in Ford, "Letters of William Vans Murray," p. 648.

42. Several newspapers carried Adams's alleged remarks. He did not contradict any of them. Some of the papers were the *Aurora* (Phil.), Feb. 6, 1800; *Centinel of Freedom* (Newark, N.J.), Sept. 9, 1800; and the Richmond *Examiner* (Va.), Nov. 7, 1800. Cited in Stewart, "Jeffersonian Journalism," p. 479. In later years Adams continued to speak of "the British faction" aided "by Alexander Hamilton and his satellites."

See Correspondence Originally Published in the Boston *Patriot*, 1809, Adams, *Works of John Adams*, IX, 281, and Parsons, "Continuing Crusade," p. 47.

43. Republicans criticized Federalists for not taking strong action against the British. *Independent Chronicle* (Boston), Jan. 28, Feb. 18, and 21, 1799. In 1800 it was estimated that the number of Americans in the British fleet had risen to more than 3,000. *Impartial Journal* (Stonington, Conn.), April 1, 1800, cited in Stewart, "Jeffersonian Journalism," pp. 441, 586–587, and 689. The quotation is from Hamilton to Pickering, April 15, 1800, in Knox, *Quasi-War Documents*, V, 418.

44. The first quotation, dated March 1, 1799, is from Borden, *James A. Bayard*, p. 33, and the second is from Cabot to Hamilton, Brookline, Aug. 10, 1800, in Lodge, *Cabot*, p. 283.

45. For details see Smith, *Adams*, p. 1042; Miller, *Hamilton*, p. 519; and Hamilton to Adams, New York, Aug. 1 and Oct. 1, 1800, in Lodge, *Hamilton's Works*, VI, 391–446. Hamilton wrote two letters to the President demanding an explanation of the alleged remarks about the "British faction."

46. Hamilton to Wolcott, New York, Sept. 26, 1800, in Gibbs, *Wolcott Papers*, II, 441–442, and in Lodge, *Hamilton's Works*, VIII, 563. Presidential electors were chosen as the state legislatures saw fit. See Dumas Malone, *Thomas Jefferson as a Political Leader* (Berkeley, Calif., 1963), p. 44.

47. Cabot to Hamilton, Brookline, Nov. 29, 1800, in Lodge, *Cabot*, pp. 298–300. The public feud between Adams and Hamilton made front-page news in Paris, notably in *Le Moniteur Universel* of Dec. 21, 1800. In laters years Adams asked in reference to Hamilton's disclosures: "Had Mr. Hamilton a spy in the cabinet, who transmitted to him, from day to day, the confidential communications between the President and heads of department?" Correspondence Originally Published in the Boston *Patriot*, 1809, reprinted in Adams, *Works of John Adams*, IX, 303.

48. Noah Webster, *A Letter to General Hamilton Occasioned by His Letter to President Adams, by a Federalist* ([New York], 1800), 8 pp., and Webster to Wolcott, New Haven, Sept. 17, 1800, in Harry R. Warfel, ed., *Letters of Noah Webster* (New York, 1953), pp. 220–221. Murray to John Quincy Adams, Dec. 30, 1800, in Ford, "Letters of William Vans Murray," p. 670. Later, Murray reported to young Adams that he heard Hamilton's letter had been directed against the Ellsworth mission. Jan. 20, 1801, in *ibid.*, pp. 674–675.

49. Robert Troup to King, Oct. 1 and Nov. 9, 1800, in King, *Correspondence of Rufus King*, III, 315, 331.

50. See Beveridge, *John Marshall*, II, 522 n, and Rush to Jefferson, Phil., Aug. 22, 1800, in Butterfield, *Letters of Benjamin Rush*, II, 820.

51. The *Aurora* (Phil.), Oct. 4, 1800, and also the *Temple of Reason* (New York), Nov. 29, 1800, in Stewart, "Jeffersonian Journalism," p. 620.

52. Rutledge to Bishop Smith, Oct. 8, 1800, quoted in Cometti, "John Rutledge, Jr.," pp. 194–195.

53. The *Aurora* (Phil.), Oct. 14, 1800, and the Pittsfield *Sun* (Mass.), Oct. 21, 1800, quoted in Cunningham, *Jeffersonian Republicans*, pp. 213, 219.

54. Henrietta Liston wrote that everyone waited impatiently for news from the envoys. To James Jackson, Phil., Liston Papers, Box XIV, National Library of Scotland.

55. Commonplace Book, Aug. 1, 1800, William Vans Murray Papers, Princeton University Library.

56. Fisher Ames to John Rutledge, Jr., Dedham, Oct. 16, 1800, Rutledge Papers, Southern Historical Collection, University of North Carolina Library.

57. Commonplace Book, Aug. 11, 1800, William Vans Murray Papers, Princeton University Library.

58. Murray also pointed out that Ellsworth, who had been opposed to the mission, was now committed heart and soul to its success. To John Quincy Adams, Aug. 20, 1800, in Ford, "Letters of William Vans Murray," p. 651.

59. Harrison Gray Otis to John Rutledge, Jr., Boston, Aug. 25, 1800, Rutledge Papers, Southern Historical Collection, University of North Carolina Library.

60. Some Federalists maintained that Jefferson would revolutionize America, in the style of France, and bring on war against Britain. They revived the issue of the Mazzei letter to prove Jefferson's pro-French bias, and claimed that he would clamp a dictatorship on the country, using French troops. See Charles O. Lerche, "Jefferson and the Election of 1800: A Case Study in the Political Smear," *William and Mary Quarterly*, third series, V (Oct. 1948), 478–479, 480, 485, and Carroll to Hamilton, Brooklandwood, Aug. 27, 1800, in Kate M. Rowland, *The Life of Charles Carroll of Carrollton, 1737–1832* (2 vols., New York, 1898), II, 241. The latter quotation is from Harper to McHenry, Baltimore, Aug. 2, 1800, Robert Goodloe Harper Papers, Manuscript Division, Library of Congress.

61. See Adams to Marshall, Quincy, Aug. 30 and Sept 4, 1800, and Marshall to Adams, Aug. 25, 1800, in Adams, *Works of John Adams*, IX, 80–81, and 81 n. See also Montague, "John Marshall," pp. 253–254. Here the chronology of the exchange of ideas is garbled.

62. These quotations, dated Sept. 13 and 17, 1800, are from Beveridge, *John Marshall*, II, 523. See also Adams to Pitcairn, Phil., Feb. 18, 1800, Sept. 5 and Oct. 17, in "Letters of Thomas Boylston Adams to Joseph Pitcairn," pp. 34, 40–44.

63. Adams to Marshall, Quincy, Sept 27, 1800, Adams Papers, reel 283.

64. Murray to John Quincy Adams, Sept. 27, 1800, in Ford, "Letters of William Vans Murray," pp. 653–654. Earlier, young Adams had hoped for an accommodation before the elections took place so that the results would not be of any great consequence in the question of war or peace. John Quincy Adams to King, Aug. 12, 1800, in Rufus King Papers, Huntington Library. Morison, in *Harrison Gray Otis*, I, 191 n, suggests

that Bonaparte hastened the conclusion of the convention in order to influence the elections, and then adds, mistakenly, that the peace agreement probably did influence them.

65. The Baltimore *Telegraph and Daily Advertiser*, Nov. 7, 1800, had just a news item on the signing. It did not carry the text of the convention. On Nov. 13 the *Maryland Gazette* (Annapolis) carried the same news with a Baltimore dateline of Nov. 7. It explained that the information had arrived from London in the very short passage of fourteen days. This was, the gazette announced, "the most important news (to Americans) that we have received for a length of time."

66. Memorandum Book, March 15, 1801, William Vans Murray Papers, Library of Congress.

67. Gallatin to Wife, Washington, Jan. 15, 1801, in Adams, *Life of Gallatin*, p. 252. For a description of Washington in November 1800, see Constance M. Green, *Washington: Village and Capital, 1800–1878* (Princeton, 1962), pp. 19–23.

68. The message is in Richardson, *Messages of the Presidents*, I, 295–298, and Adams, *Works of John Adams*, IX, 143–146. Beveridge, in *John Marshall*, II, 530–531, points out that Marshall wrote "every word of the speech."

69. Pinckney to Jefferson, Columbia, S.C., Nov. 22, 1800. Two years earlier Pinckney had pledged himself "to use every Exertion in my power to make a peace with France." J. Franklin Jameson, ed., "South Carolina in the Presidential Election of 1800," *American Historical Review*, IV (Oct. 1898), 119, 121.

70. The vote is tabulated in Rogers, *Evolution of a Federalist*, p. 351. Phillips, in "The South Carolina Federalists," p. 741, maintains that the Federalists in South Carolina allowed the election to go mainly by default. Zahniser, in "Public Career of Charles Cotesworth Pickney," pp. 301–302, points out that by repudiating Hamilton's plans to subvert Adams, C. C. Pinckney reduced the chances for a Federalist victory in the state. The work of Charles Pinckney and Peter Freneau is usually credited for the Republican victory. See Richard B. Davis and Milledge B. Seigler, "Peter Freneau, Carolina Republican," *Journal of Southern History*, XIII (Aug. 1947), 398–399, and John H. Wolfe, *Jeffersonian Democracy in South Carolina* (Chapel Hill, N.C., 1940), pp. 137–165.

71. The quotation is from Adams to John Trumbull, Quincy, Sept. 10, 1800, in Adams, *Works of John Adams*, IX, 83–84. Historians have disputed the causes of Adams's defeat, and the precise effect of each cause. Anson D. Morse, in "Causes and Consequences of the Party Revolution of 1800," *Annual Report of the American Historical Association for the Year 1894* (Washington, 1895), p. 531, argues that foreign policy, particularly as reflected in preparations for war, injured the Federalists. Kurtz, in the *Presidency of John Adams*, pp. 406–407, gives a careful analysis of the defeat. He is in general agreement with Bemis, in *John Quincy Adams and the Foundations of American Foreign Policy*, p. 106, who says foreign policy actually aided Adams, for he ran ahead of his

party. Haraszti, in *Adams and the Prophets of Progress,* pp. 346–347, note 13, concludes that Adams attributed his defeat to Hamilton's machinations, whereas Smith, in *Adams,* p. 1067, says that Adams attributed his downfall to the sending of the Ellsworth mission. Stewart, in "The Press and Political Corruption," p. 446, maintains that the charges of political corruption against Federalist officeholders contributed to Adams's defeat.

72. Murray to John Quincy Adams, Nov. 7, 1800, in Ford, "Letters of William Vans Murray," pp. 660–661.

73. Moderates, however, were not frightened. Oliver Ellsworth commented that now the Republicans would have their turn at "rolling stones up hill." He thought that Jefferson would not deviate from established Federalist policy. William Smith said that "we must reconcile ourselves . . . to what is unavoidable." Ellsworth to King, Bath, Eng., Jan. 21 and 24, 1801, and Smith to King, Lisbon, Feb. 18, 1801, Rufus King Papers, Huntington Library.

74. See Bayard to [Bassett?] and to [Rodney?] Washington, Jan. 3 and 5, 1801, in Donnan, "Bayard Papers," pp. 117–118, and Colonel Francis Peyton to Powell, Loudoun, Feb. 20, 1801, in Dodd, "Correspondence of Col. Leven Powell," p. 63, who expressed fear of armed violence if Jefferson or Burr was not chosen. See also Miller, *Federalist Era,* p. 269; Van der Linden, *The Turning Point,* p. 178; and Welch, *Theodore Sedgwick,* pp. 221–235.

75. The quotations are from Miller, *Hamilton,* p. 526, and Douglass, "Fisher Ames, Spokesman for New England Federalism," p. 711.

76. Bayard's crucial role, as well as the intricate bargaining in the House, are analyzed in Morton Borden, "The Election of 1800: Charge and Countercharge," *Delaware History,* V (March 1952), 42–62. See also Gallatin to Wife, Feb. 17, 1801, in Adams, *Life of Gallatin,* p. 262, and Lynch, *Fifty Years of Party Warfare,* pp. 99–115.

77. Quoted in Perkins, *First Rapprochement,* p. 130. For a French reaction, see Larévellière-Lépeaux, *Mémoires de Larévellière-Lépeaux,* II, 260.

78. Adams's message of Dec. 15, 1800, and the text of the convention, at this point, in English and in French, are in *ASP FR,* II, 295–301. "The patriots are not too well pleased with the Treaty," Murray learned. "The moderates & good men are." To Sylvanus Bourne, Feb. 18, 1801, William Vans Murray Papers, Princeton University Library. See also Otis to Hamilton, Dec. 17, 1800, in Morison, *Harrison Gray Otis,* I, 205; Ralston Hayden, *The Senate and Treaties, 1789–1817* (New York, 1920), p. 126 ff.; Shulim, *The Old Dominion and Napoleon Bonaparte,* pp. 94–95; Beveridge, *John Marshall,* II, 524; and Robinson, *William R. Davie,* pp. 356–357.

79. William Smith to King, Lisbon, Nov. 25, 1800, in Rufus King Papers, Huntington Library.

80. Moderates, too, considered the treaty a personal triumph for the President. "He has done a great thing," Murray believed, "by great management of small means & by a judicious observance of times & causes. He

has settled a quarrel between two nations—his own & France! & on
terms better than any other nation has settled with France." Memoran-
dum Book, Jan. 10, 1801, William Vans Murray Papers, Library of
Congress. See also Marshall to C. C. Pinckney, Dec. 18, 1800, in Cross,
"Marshall on the French Revolution," p. 644, and Welch, *Theodore
Sedgwick,* p. 210.

81. Hayden, *The Senate and Treaties,* p. 114.
82. Leven Powell to Major Burr Powell, Phil., Dec. 23, 1800, in Dodd,
"Correspondence of Col. Leven Powell," p. 239. On the point of the
restoration of ships, see Stoddert to Chairman of the Committee on
Naval Affairs, Washington, Feb. 15, 1801, in Knox, *Quasi-War Documents,* VII, 122.
83. The quotations are from Beveridge, *John Marshall,* II, 524.
84. Diary entry of Dec. 31, 1800, and to Hamilton, Jan. 5, 1801, in Morris,
Gouverneur Morris, II, 397–398.
85. John Rutledge, Jr., to Hamilton, Jan. 10, 1801, in Hamilton, *Works of
Hamilton,* VI, 511.
86. See King to Secretary of State, London, Oct. 31 and Nov. 22, 1800, in
ASP FR, II, 343–344, and Brown, *Oliver Ellsworth,* p. 312. King told
Murray that the British saw no cause for complaint in the convention,
and Murray wrote that "it is a glorious thing for the administration to
have put an end to hostilities with France, and yet have extorted the
satisfaction of Great Britain." Murray to John Quincy Adams, The
Hague, Nov. 18, 1800, in Ford, "Letters of William Vans Murray," pp.
661–662, and to King, Nov. 19, 1800, in Rufus King Papers, Huntington
Library.
87. Thornton to Grenville, Washington, Jan. 16, 1801, No. 3, PRO GB
FO 5. Gallatin to Wife, Washington, Jan. 15, 1801, in Adams, *Life of
Gallatin,* p. 254, also stresses merchant support.
88. Believing there would be no general peace in Europe, Gouverneur
Morris, for example, saw no necessity for gulping down the convention.
To Hamilton, Jan. 16, 1801, in Morris, *Gouverneur Morris,* II, 399–400.
The quotation, dated Jan. 20, 1801, is from Kathryn Turner, "The
Appointment of Chief Justice Marshall," *William and Mary Quarterly,*
third series, XVIII (April 1960), 159.
89. Adams to Senate, Jan. 21, 1801, *ASP FR,* II, 295. See also Murray to
John Quincy Adams [March 10, 1801] in Ford, "Letters of William
Vans Murray," p. 689; Hayden, *The Senate and Treaties,* p. 118; and
Thornton to Grenville, Washington, Feb. 5, 1801, No. 6, PRO GB FO 5.
90. Morris, *Gouverneur Morris,* II, 399; James A. Bayard to Andrew
Bayard, Washington, Jan. 23, 1801, Donnan, "Bayard Papers," p. 120;
John Quincy Adams to King, Berlin, March 7, 1801, Rufus King Papers,
Huntington Library; and Memorandum Book, March 15, 1801, William
Vans Murray Papers, Library of Congress.
91. Theophilus Parsons to Otis, Boston, Jan. 23, 1801, in Morison, *Harrison
Gray Otis,* I, 214; Gallatin to Wife, Jan. 29, Feb. 5, 1801, in Adams,
Life of Gallatin, pp. 258, 259. For the influence of public opinion, see

Charles Pinckney to Jefferson, Jan. 8, 1801, [probably wrong date] in Jameson, "South Carolina in the Presidential Election of 1800," p. 127. An example of a rising merchant who was concerned and wanted peace in early 1801 was Robert Oliver, a wholesaler in Baltimore. He had come to the United States from Ireland with little or no money and was accumulating one of the nation's large fortunes on profits from foreign trade. See Bruchey, *Robert Oliver,* pp. 19–20, 217. Trade with France and her colonies had dropped from $20.2 million in 1795 to $3.2 million in 1799, Pitkin, *A Statistical View of the Commerce of the United States,* pp. 250–252.

92. Létombe to Minister of Foreign Relations, Phil., Feb. 9, 1801, AAE CP EU, Vol. 53, pp. 14–140.

93. Morris to James Leray, Feb. 3, 1801, in Morris, *Gouverneur Morris,* II, 403.

94. For Bayard's reasoning, see Borden, *James A. Bayard,* pp. 97–98; Van der Linden, *The Turning Point,* pp. 316–317; and Bayard to Adams, Washington, Feb. 19, 1801, in Donnan, "Bayard Papers," pp. 129–130. See Adams to Senate, March 2, 1801, in Knox, *Quasi-War Documents,* VII, 132, and *ASP FR,* II, 344. See also Sargeant, "Quasi-War with France," p. 23. In later years Adams blamed the High Federalists for the prolongation of the Quasi-War and delay in the peacemaking. "Had Mr. Murray's nomination been approved," Adams wrote for instance, "he would probably have finished the business long before, and obtained compensation for all spoliations." Correspondence Originally Published in the Boston *Patriot* in 1809, in Adams, *Works of John Adams,* IX, 256.

95. Thornton to Grenville, Washington, March 4, 1801, No. 15, PRO GB FO 5.

🙟🙟🙟 *Notes—Chapter IX* 🙞🙞🙞

1. Talleyrand, Sept. 27, 1800, is quoted in Lyon, "Convention of 1800," p. 326. Earlier, the First Consul had given Roederer and Fleurieu 15,000 francs apiece. See Roederer, *Oeuvres*, III, 338.

2. James, in "Louisiana as a Factor in French Diplomacy," pp. 44–56, argues that France's desire to regain Louisiana was her main reason for consummating the Convention of Môrtefontaine.

3. Charles Jean Marie Alquier to Talleyrand, Aug. 20, 1800, in Lyon, *Louisiana in French Diplomacy*, p. 107.

4. For details, see *ibid.*, pp. 107–110, and Adams, *History of the United States*, I, 369–370. The treaty is in Frances G. Davenport, ed., *European Treaties Bearing on the History of the United States and Its Dependencies* (4 vols., Washington, 1917–1937), IV, 181–182.

5. Whitaker, *Mississippi Question*, pp. 176–186. Whitaker shows that Spain wanted to get rid of Louisiana because it was costly to hold. See his "The Retrocession of Louisiana in Spanish Policy," pp. 454–476. For Bonaparte's stress on secrecy, see Paul Gaffarel, *La politique coloniale en France de 1789 à 1830* (Paris, 1908), pp. 168–169.

6. Gentz, *On the State of Europe Before and After the French Revolution*, in which the translator, John Charles Herries, argues that American cooperation "was of the greatest consequence" to French plans for destroying Britain's commerce. See also Haraszti, *Adams and the Prophets of Progress*, p. 272; Fugier, *Révolution Française et l'Empire Napoléonien*, p. 147; and Louis Madelin, in *Le Consulat et l'Empire, 1799–1815* (2 vols., Paris, 1932–33), I, 88, who maintains that the Convention of Môrtefontaine was directed against Britain's maritime practices.

7. Memorandum Book, March 15, 1801, William Vans Murray Papers, Library of Congress.

8. See Richmond, "Napoleon and the Armed Neutrality of 1800," p. 191, and Lawrence S. Kaplan, "Jefferson's Foreign Policy and Napoleon's Idéologues," *William and Mary Quarterly*, third series, XIX (July 1962), 348–349.

9. *Le Moniteur Universel* (Paris), Oct. 3 and 22, 1800. Arthur A. Rich-

mond, "The United States and the Armed Neutrality of 1800" (unpublished Ph.D. dissertation, Yale University, 1951), p. 129, and Lyon, "Convention of 1800," p. 332. Sweden and Denmark were pleased with the maritime principles embodied in the Convention of 1800. William Smith to King, Lisbon, Nov. 25, 1800, in Rufus King Papers, Huntington Library.

10. The quotations are from Murray to John Luzac, The Hague, Oct. 28, 1800, William Vans Murray Papers, Library of Congress, and Murray to King, Nov. 13, 1800, Rufus King Papers, Huntington Library.

11. Quoted in Richmond, "Napoleon and the Armed Neutrality of 1800," p. 191.

12. Within a few weeks Lewis Goldsmith translated and published d'Hauterive's book under the title *State of the French Republic at the End of the Year VIII* (London, 1801). A short time later Frederick von Gentz, a brilliant and cynical Prussian writer hired by the British government for the task, published a reply to d'Hauterive called *Von dem Politischen Zustande von Europa von und nach der Französischen Revolution* which was quickly translated into English by John Charles Herries and published in London as *On the State of Europe Before and After the French Revolution*. Bonaparte was so pleased with d'Hauterive's book that he gave him a present of 25,000 francs. See Haraszti, *Adams and the Prophets of Progress*, pp. 259, 261.

13. See Kazimierz Waliszewski, *Paul the First of Russia*, trans. from the French (London, 1913), pp. 348–349; Louis A. F. de Bourrienne, *Memoirs of Napoleon Bonaparte*, ed. by R. W. Phipps, Rev. ed. (4 vols., New York, 1891), I, 345–348; Talleyrand, *Memoirs*, I, 210; and Phillips and Reede, *Neutrality*, II, 101.

14. Murray wrote: "I knew nothing of that promise." Journal of Negotiations, Oct. 6, 1800, William Vans Murray Papers, Library of Congress. In his first "Report to the Consuls of the Republic" on American affairs, Paris, Nov. 30, 1799, Talleyrand had expressed concern over the status of Saint Domingue and of American policy there. *Archives nationales, relations extérieures, U.S.A., Serie I, AF IV, 1681, IA Dr. No. I, p. 3.

15. Carl L. Lokke, "Jefferson and the Leclerc Expedition," *American Historical Review*, XXXIII (Jan. 1928), 322, and Logan, *Haiti and the U.S.*, pp. 112–113.

16. *Ibid.*, p. 124; Stoddard, *The French Revolution in San Domingo*, pp. 286–287; Tansill, *United States and Santo Domingo*, p. 86; and Bonaparte to Toussaint, Paris, Nov. 4, 1800, *Correspondance de Napoléon Ier*, VI, 497.

17. For an American estimate of Pichon, see Murray to John Quincy Adams, Jan. 3, 1801, Ford, "Letters of William Vans Murray," pp. 671–672. For the quotation, see Lyon, "Convention of 1800," p. 328. The *Maryland Gazette* (Annapolis), Jan. 8, 1801, carried the news of Pichon's appointment.

18. Pichon told Murray this. He also said the French government considered it "very strange" that the United States had not left a Minister

in Paris. Murray himself did not want a French Minister sent to the United States until after the convention had been ratified. Journal of Negotiations, Oct. 6 and 7, 1800, William Vans Murray Papers, Library of Congress.

19. Lokke, "Jefferson and the Leclerc Expedition," p. 323, and Kaplan, "Jefferson's Foreign Policy and Napoleon's Idéologues," p. 349, and n 20.

20. Lyon, "Convention of 1800," p. 329, and du Casse, *Négociations diplomatiques relatives aux traités de Mortfontaine*, I, 330–334.

21. The texts of the conventions are in Scott, *Armed Neutralities*, pp. 531–549. For details, see Phillips and Reede, *Neutrality*, II, 103–105, and Adams to Murray, Berlin, Jan. 27, 1801, and to Rufus King, Feb. 1, in Ford, *Writings of John Quincy Adams*, II, 494–499.

22. Quoted in Madelin, *Le Consulat et l'Empire*, I, 100. For details, see Driault, *La politique extérieure du premier consul*, pp. 157–158.

23. Bonaparte believed the Convention of Môrtefontaine had been important in persuading the northern neutrals to band together. Richmond, "The United States and the Armed Neutrality of 1800," p. 151. Paul's declaration was directed to neutral powers whereas the declaration of 1780 was addressed to belligerents. See Francis T. Piggott, "The Freedom of the Seas, Historically Treated," *International Affairs*, XXIII (London, 1920), No. 148 of Peace Handbooks, p. 77.

24. Memorandum Book, Dec. 20, 1800, William Vans Murray Papers, Library of Congress.

25. Smith to King, Lisbon, Feb. 14, 1801, Rufus King Papers, Huntington Library. When Paul turned against England, Federalists who had praised Russia for fighting revolutionary France suddenly became harsh critics of the Russians. See Joseph I. Shulim, "The United States Views Russia in the Napoleonic Age," *Proceedings of the American Philosophical Society*, CII (April 1958), 149.

26. Madison to Jefferson, Jan. 10, 1801, in Gaillard Hunt, ed., *The Writings of James Madison* (9 vols., New York, 1900–1910), VI, 414–415. See also Thiers, *Consulate and Empire*, I, 214, on the League's naval power.

27. Richmond, "Napoleon and the Armed Neutrality of 1800," p. 193, and Darling, *Rising Empire*, p. 421.

28. Létombe to Minister of Foreign Relations, Phil., March 15, 1801, AAE CP EU, Vol. 53, pp. 40–42.

29. Talleyrand to Pichon, Paris, Jan. 24, 1801, in *ibid.*, pp. 6–7. James Madison was confirmed as Secretary of State on March 5, 1801, but did not take over until May 2.

30. "Sketches on the State of Europe," March 1801, The *Palladium*, in Ames, *Works of Fisher Ames*, II, 149, and Alfred W. Crosby, Jr., *America, Russia, Hemp, and Napoleon: American Trade with Russia and the Baltic, 1783–1812* (Columbus, Ohio, 1965), p. 85.

31. The quotations are from Perkins, *First Rapprochement*, p. 131. See Rufus King to Lord Grenville, Private, Great Cumberland Place, Feb.

12, 1801, *Dropmore Papers*, VI, 445. Pichon said the Federalist gazettes made much of King's note. To Minister of Foreign Relations, Georgetown, May 1, 1801, AAE CP EU, Vol. 53, pp. 115–118.

32. In later years Jefferson wrote of Bonaparte: "I had supposed him a great man until his entrance into the Assembly des cinq cens, 18, Brumaire (an. 8)." To John Adams, Monticello, July 5, 1814, in Cappon, *Adams-Jefferson Letters*, II, 431. See also Echeverria, *Mirage in the West*, p. 274.

33. For details, see Kaplan, "Jefferson's Foreign Policy and Napoleon's Idéologues," pp. 349–351.

34. Pichon to Minister of Foreign Relations, Georgetown, May 1, 1801, AAE CP EU, Vol 53, pp. 115–118.

35. Darling, *Rising Empire*, p. 146, and Richmond, "The United States and the Armed Neutrality of 1800," pp. 125, 144, and 155.

36. King to Madison, March 26, 1801, in King, *Correspondence of Rufus King*, III, 411–413. The British sailed on March 12, 1801. See Phillips and Reede, *Neutrality*, II, 106.

37. Quoted in Mahan, *Sea Power and the French Revolution*, II, 46. The English, understandably, were pleased with Paul's removal. See Driault, *La politique extérieure du premier consul*, p. 170.

38. Murray to [Sylvanus] Bourne, The Hague, April 23, 1801, William Vans Murray Papers, Library of Congress.

39. Scott, *Armed Neutralities*, pp. 595–609; Phillips and Reede, *Neutrality*, II, 106–107; Piggott, *Armed Neutralities: 1780 and 1800*, pp. 389–390, 504–516.

40. Jefferson to Lafayette, Washington, March 13, 1801, in Chinard, *Letters of Lafayette and Jefferson*, p. 212.

41. Létombe had also been informed of the resumption of commercial relations. Létombe to Minister of Foreign Relations, March 15, 1801, AAE CP EU, Vol. 53, pp. 40–42. Although orders for American cruisers to cease hostilities were given to Captain Charles C. Russell of the warship *Herald* on March 23, 1801, it was not until April 11 that he sailed out of Boston harbor for the cruising stations in the West Indies with his message of peace. Allen, *Our Naval War with France*, p. 221.

42. Jefferson had offered Livingston the post on Feb. 24, 1801. George Dangerfield, *Chancellor Robert R. Livingston of New York, 1746–1813* (New York, 1960), p. 304. See also Irving Brant, *James Madison: Secretary of State, 1800–1809* (Indianapolis, 1953), p. 67.

43. Jefferson to Paine, March 18, 1801, in Ford, *Writings of Jefferson*, VIII, 18.

44. John Dawson to Ellsworth, U.S.S. *Maryland* in the English Channel, April 25, 1801, Rufus King Papers, Huntington Library. The *Maryland Gazette* (Annapolis), March 19, 1801, reported that Livingston would not proceed immediately to France, and that Murray would negotiate the supplementary arrangements of the convention.

45. Memorandum Book, Feb. 17, May 15, and 20, 1801, William Vans Murray Papers, Library of Congress. Murray received official instruc-

tions from Acting Secretary of State Levi Lincoln, dated March 18, 1801, on May 20. See also Murray to John Quincy Adams, Feb. 17 and May 16, 1801, in Ford, "Letters of William Vans Murray," pp. 683, 697–698.

46. Richmond, "The United States and the Armed Neutrality of 1800," p. 145; Commonplace Book, May 24, 1801, William Vans Murray Papers, Princeton University Library; and Murray to Robert Gilmour, The Hague, May 27, 1801, Pennsylvania Historical Society, Phil. (Mss. Microfilm 259, Huntington Library).

47. In the summer, to escape Washington's stifling heat, Jefferson retired to Monticello, his estate in Virginia. For two months, therefore, it seemed as if the government practically ran itself. Edward Channing, *The Jeffersonian System* (New York, 1906), p. 6.

48. Brant, *James Madison: Secretary of State*, p. 63, and Logan, *Haiti and the U.S.*, p. 114, 120 n, and Tansill, *United States and Santo Domingo*, p. 81. Lear arrived at Saint Domingue on July 4, 1801, in a merchant ship.

49. Adams, *History of the United States*, I, 389, and Tansill, *United States and Santo Domingo*, pp. 82–83.

50. Jefferson to James Monroe, May 26, 1801, in Ford, *Writings of Jefferson*, VIII, 58; The *Times* (London), March 29, 1801; and King to Secretary of State, London, March 9, 1801, King, *Correspondence of Rufus King*, III, 414. Jefferson did not obtain a copy of the second Treaty of San Ildefonso until late in 1801. Rufus King sent him a copy from London on Nov. 20, 1801. See 7 Cong., 2 sess., *Annals of the Congress*, Appendix, p. 1016. See also Mary P. Adams, "Jefferson's Reaction to the Treaty of San Ildefonso," *Journal of Southern History*, XXI (May 1955), 173–188, for military precautions taken.

51. Pichon to Talleyrand, Georgetown, May 1, 1801, AAE CP EU, Vol. 51, pp. 115–118, and Brant, *James Madison: Secretary of State*, p. 66.

52. Murray to Levi Lincoln, The Hague, May 20, 1801, Dispatches, The Netherlands, Vol. 4, No. 134, Department of State, National Archives.

53. Murray to Lincoln, Paris, June 1, 1801, *ibid.*

54. *Ibid.*, June 9, 1801. Pichon had not liked what the Senate had done to the convention, but he had advised Talleyrand, as a matter of sound policy, to consider the treaties of 1778 "as gone forever." Washington, March 3, 1801, AAE CP EU, Vol. 53, pp. 79–82.

55. Commonplace Book, June 14 and 17, 1801, William Vans Murray Papers, Princeton University Library.

56. *Ibid.*, June 21 and 23, 1801, and Murray to James Madison, Paris, June 23, 1801, Dispatches, The Netherlands, Vol. 4, No. 3, Department of State, National Archives.

57. "Report to the First Consul" by [Talleyrand], Paris, June 22, 1801, AAE CP EU, Vol. 53, pp. 110–112. Commonplace Book, June 24, 25, and 27, 1801, William Vans Murray Papers, Princeton University Library, and Murray to Madison and to the French Commissioners, Paris, June

26 and 27, 1801, Dispatches, The Netherlands, Vol. 4, Nos. 5 and 14, Department of State, National Archives.

58. Quoted in Lyon, "Convention of 1800," p. 332.

59. Commonplace Book, July 1 and 3, 1801, William Vans Murray Papers, Library of Congress, and Murray to Madison, Paris, July 1, 1801, Dispatches, The Netherlands, Vol. 4, No. 6, Department of State, National Archives.

60. Commonplace Book, July 5, 1801, William Vans Murray Papers, Princeton University Library.

61. Murray to James Madison, Paris, July 11, 1801, Dispatches, The Netherlands, Vol. 4, No. 17, Department of State, National Archives.

62. Joshua Barney to Samuel Smith, Paris, July 11, 1801, Thomas Jefferson Papers, Manuscript Division, Library of Congress.

63. Murray to John Quincy Adams, Paris, July 15, 1801, in Ford, "Letters of William Vans Murray," p. 701.

64. Murray to King, Paris, July 16, 1801, Rufus King Papers, Huntington Library.

65. Murray to James Madison, Paris, July 23 and Aug. 3, 1801, Dispatches, The Netherlands, Vol. 4, Nos. 10 and 13, Department of State, National Archives. Bonaparte's act of ratification of July 31 is printed in *ASP FR*, II, 344.

66. Commonplace Book, Aug. 4 and 5, 1801, William Vans Murray Papers, Princeton University Library.

67. Jefferson to William C. Claiborne, Governor of the Mississippi Territory, July 13, 1801, in Ford, *Writings of Jefferson*, VIII, 71–72. For details, see Brant, *James Madison: Secretary of State*, pp. 70–71, and Shulim, *The Old Dominion and Napoleon Bonaparte*, p. 99.

68. Jefferson to Albert Gallatin, Monticello, Sept. 5 and 18, 1801, and to William Short, Washington, Oct. 3, 1801, in Ford, *Writings of Jefferson*, VIII, 94–99.

69. The *Maryland Gazette* (Annapolis), Oct. 8, 1801, carried the news, dated Phil., Sept. 29.

70. To John Parrish, Oct. 5, 1801, in Morris, *Gouverneur Morris*, II, 407. Later, on Dec. 14, Pichon apparently told Morris that Bonaparte would not have ratified the amended convention if he had not suffered defeats in Egypt and at Copenhagen, *ibid.*, p. 416.

71. Lyon, *Louisiana in French Diplomacy*, p. 147, and François P. Renaut, *La question de la Louisiane, 1796–1806* (Paris, 1918), p. 62.

72. Echeverria, *Mirage in the West*, p. 255.

73. The text of the armistice is in Davenport, *European Treaties Bearing on the History of the United States*, IV, 185–186. For details, see Mahan, *Sea Power and the French Revolution*, II, 70–72; *Official Papers, Relative to the Preliminaries of London and the Treaty of Amiens*, published at Paris by Authority of the French Government, 2nd ed. (London, 1803), which is a piece of French propaganda; and

Driault, *La politique extérieure du premier consul,* pp. 189–204. Murray believed this peace agreement was important to the United States because "it settles all our disputes," meaning it foreclosed probable difficulties with France and England over interpretations of provisions in the Convention of Môrtefontaine. Memorandum Book, c. Nov. 17, 1801, William Vans Murray Papers, Library of Congress.

74. Lyon, *Louisiana in French Diplomacy,* pp. 118–119, and Carl L. Lokke, ed., "The Leclerc Instructions," *Journal of Negro History,* X (Jan. 1925), 81–84.

75. Logan, *Haiti and the U.S.,* pp. 114–115, and Stoddard, *The French Revolution in San Domingo,* p. 301.

76. Logan, *Haiti and the U.S.,* pp. 117–120, 125–126, and Lokke, "Jefferson and the Leclerc Expedition," pp. 325, 327, which questions the view that Jefferson offered to assist Bonaparte's effort to reconquer Saint Domingue. Apparently Jefferson did suggest to Pichon that France declare Saint Domingue independent under the protection of France, Britain, and the United States.

77. Logan, *Haiti and the U.S.,* pp. 121–122; Lokke, "The Leclerc Instructions," p. 93. Those instructions were first printed in Gustav Roloff, *Die Kolonialpolitik Napoleons I* (Munich, 1899), pp. 244–254. Despite the British willingness to go along with Bonaparte, the British did not know of Spain's cession of Louisiana to France when they signed the Preliminaries to peace. Some Englishmen were alarmed by the session. See Hugh C. Bailey and Bernard C. Weber, "A British Reaction to the Treaty of San Ildefonso," *William and Mary Quarterly,* third series, XVIII (April 1960), 242–248.

78. Livingston to Rufus King, Dec. 30, 1801, is quoted in Adams, *History of the United States,* I, 392, and Lyon, *Louisiana in French Diplomacy,* p. 119. For other details, see *ibid.,* pp. 119–120, 125, and 130–131. On Jan. 6, 1802, the First Consul told his brother Joseph that he might send General Carl Johan Bernadotte on an expedition to take possession of Louisiana. Napoléon Bonaparte, *The Confidential Correspondence of Napoléon Bonaparte with His Brother Joseph . . .* (2 vols., New York, 1856), I, 57.

79. Two additional squadrons sailed from Rochefort and L'Orient. Leclerc's time of sailing and the figures on his troops are taken from Stoddard, *The French Revolution in San Domingo,* pp. 307–308. For other details, see Antoine Métral, *Histoire de l'expédition des français à Saint-Domingue, sous le Consulat de Napoléon Bonaparte . . .* (Paris, 1825), pp. 24–32; Mahan, *Sea Power and the French Revolution,* II, 78–79; and Henry Adams, "Napoléon Ier et Saint-Domingue," *Revue Historique,* XXIV (1884), 92, 93, and 102. Adams's dates and figures differ from those used herein.

80. Livingston landed at L'Orient on Nov. 12. His instructions, dated Sept. 28, 1801, are summarized in Darling, *Rising Empire,* pp. 423–424. Dangerfield, in *Robert R. Livingston,* pp. 309–311, says Livingston sailed before he received word of the exchange of ratifications. News of the

exchange arrived in Phil. as early as Sept. 29, and Livingston did not sail from New York until Oct. 15. So it appears likely he knew of the exchange before departing. See also Brant, *James Madison: Secretary of State*, p. 73.
81. Jefferson to Robert R. Livingston and to James Madison, Monticello, Sept. 9 and 12, 1801, in Ford, *Writings of Jefferson*, VIII, 88–94, and Jefferson to Senate, Dec. 11, 1801, *ASP FR*, II, 345.
82. Diary entry of Dec. 18, 1801, in Morris, *Gouverneur Morris*, II, 416.
83. *Journal of the Executive Proceedings of the Senate*, I, 365–398; *ASP FR*, II, 345; and Hayden, *The Senate and Treaties*, p. 124. The text of the convention, in French and in English, and in final form with supporting documents and useful notes, is in David Hunter Miller, ed., *Treaties and Other International Acts of the United States of America* (7 vols., Washington, 1931———), II, 457–487. The text of the original Convention of Môrtefontaine is reproduced, in English and French, on pages 351–372.
84. Edward Thornton to Lord Hawkesbury, Washington, Dec. 26, 1801, No. 60, PRO GB FO 5. For a critical appraisal of the convention, see Gibbs, *Wolcott Papers*, II, 438–439.

ᴊᴠᴠᴠᴠᴠᴠ᷍ᶳ Notes—Chapter X ᶜᶺᴠᴠᴠᴠᴠᴠᴠ

1. For a perceptive analysis that carries suggestions for a similar theme for the entire Federalist period, but mainly on domestic issues, see Marshall Smelser, "The Federalist Period as an Age of Passion," *American Quarterly*, X (Winter 1958), 391–419. On key issues of the day, both in public and in private, Smelser says, men were "blinded by emotion."

2. See Georges-Nestler Tricoche, "Une page peu connue de l'histoire de France: La guerre franco-américaine, 1798–1801," *La Revue Historique*, LXXXV (May–Aug. 1904), 288, who also points out that the Quasi-War is much less known in France than in the United States. The question of whether or not the Quasi-War was a true war is taken up in *Gray v. United States*, decided on May 17, 1886. Although the question is treated here in judicial rather than political terms, the legal opinions are worth noting. Since neither France nor the United States declared war or recognized the existence of a state of war, the court held that there was no general public war. The court called the conflict a limited maritime war, in effect, a prolonged series of reprisals. Opinions in this case are reproduced in Scott, *Controversy over Neutral Rights between the United States and France*, pp. 227–293. King, in "The French Spoliation Claims," especially pp. 373–377, cites various legal and diplomatic documents to show that a true war did not exist. On the nature of war and peace, see Raymond Aron, *Paix et guerre entre les nations*, 3rd ed. (Paris, 1962), pp. 33–37, 157–161. Talleyrand stressed the point of no formal war in his "Report to the First Consul," Paris, June [1800], *Archives nationales, relations extérieures, U.S.A., Serie I, AF IV, 1681, IA Dr. No. I*, pp. 5–19.

3. Gibbs, *Wolcott Papers*, II, 216. For an arch-Federalist's reasons for war, see Rogers, *Evolution of a Federalist*, pp. 319–320.

4. The point on nationalism is stressed in Dexter Perkins, *The American Approach to Foreign Policy* (Cambridge, Mass., 1952), p. 116; Robert R. Palmer, "A Neglected Work: Otto Vossler on Jefferson and the Revolutionary Era," *William and Mary Quarterly*, third series, XII (July 1955), 466–467; Charles, *Origins of the American Party System*, pp.

137–138; Childs, "A Secret Agent's Advice on America," p. 22; and Brown, *The Northern Confederacy*, pp. 23–24. Echeverria, *Mirage in the West*, p. 207, suggests that a new sense of nationalism, cultural as well as political, produced the "great schism between France and America." See also Norman K. Risjord, *The Old Republicans: Southern Conservatism in the Age of Jackson* (New York, 1965), p. 23, and Monaghan, *John Jay*, p. 413, where Jay is quoted in Oct. 1797. "I wish to see our people more *Americanized*," he said, and independent of foreign intrigue.

5. Commonplace Book, Aug. 25, 1798, William Vans Murray Papers, Princeton University Library.

6. See Brooks Adams, "The Convention of 1800 with France," p. 407, and Adams to John Marshall, Quincy, Sept. 4, 1800, in Adams, *Works of John Adams*, IX, 81. The opinions in *Bas v. Tingy* are in Scott, *Controversy over Neutral Rights between the United States and France*, pp. 104–115.

7. The *Aurora* (Phil.) for Aug. 22, 23, and 25, 1800, is quoted in Charles Warren, *The Supreme Court in United States History*, Rev. ed. (2 vols., Boston, 1926), I, 157. See also the *Virginia Argus* (Richmond), Sept. 2, 1800, quoted in Stewart, "Jeffersonian Journalism," pp. 603–604.

8. *The Gazette and Daily Advertiser* (Charleston), Nov. 9, 1798, with a dateline of London, Sept. 9.

9. Quoted in Logan, *Haiti and the U.S.*, p. 91.

10. July 27, 1798, quoted in Childs, "French Opinion of Anglo-American Relations," p. 33. See also Adet's comments in Gebhardt, *Diplomatick Transactions between the American and French Governments*, III, 460.

11. In later years, with possible overstatement, Adams explained that his decision for peace and Jefferson's victory were "better than following the fools who were intriguing to plunge us into an alliance with England, an endless war with all the rest of the world, and wild expeditions to South America and St. Domingo; and, what was worse than all the rest, a civil war, which I knew would be the consequence of the measures the heads of that [Federalist] party wished to pursue." To James Lloyd, Quincy, March 31, 1815, in Adams, *Works of John Adams*, X, 154–155. See also Adams's letter of Feb. 14, 1815, to Lloyd, p. 122, where he says, "What strength, what power, what force, had such a party [High Federalist] to support a war against France, when she held the olive branch to us, with both hands, upon our own terms?" Bonaparte thought that Adams had to yield to public opinion when he decided to send the Ellsworth mission to France. Bonaparte, *Mémoires*, III, 318.

12. Hamilton to John Marshall, Oct. 2, 1800, quoted in Clinton Rossiter, *Alexander Hamilton* (New York, 1964), p. 313, no. 170.

13. Morison, in "Du Pont, Talleyrand and the French Spoliations," p. 63, says that since the extreme Federalists were not strong enough to carry off a war in which the United States might appear the aggressor, they needed an acceptance of their challenge by the Directory. Merle Curti, in *The Growth of American Thought*, 2nd ed. (New York, 1951), pp.

186, 187, explains the Quasi-War as a "political victory for conservative interests and ideas."

14. Samuel E. Morison, in "Squire Ames and Doctor Ames," *The New England Quarterly*, I (Jan. 1928), p. 19, hinted at the cause of peace. The French, he wrote, "were more cunning than profligate. They cried peace before Congress had made up its mind to declare war."

15. For a fuller treatment of this theme, see Robert R. Palmer, "The World Revolution of the West, 1763–1801," *Political Science Quarterly*, LXIX (March 1954), 1–14. The Quasi-War marked the end of the first cycle, or epoch, in Franco-American relations. See Léonie Villard, *La France et les États-Unis: échanges et rencontres* (1524–1800) (Lyons, 1952), p. 348. The Quasi-War may also be seen in the context of an important watershed in the history of the Western World. See Franklin L. Ford, "The Revolutionary-Napoleonic Era: How Much of a Watershed?" *American Historical Review*, LXIX (Oct. 1963), 18–29.

16. To Joseph Pitcairn, Germantown, Pa., Oct. 23, 1799, in "Letters of Thomas Boylston Adams to Joseph Pitcairn," p. 29.

17. To John Quincy Adams, [Paris], June 10, 1801, in Ford, "Letters of William Vans Murray," pp. 698–699. At about this time John Adams himself commented: "The fate of the U.S. seems likely to be decided in future entirely by the conduct of their foreign affairs." Haraszti, *Adams and the Prophets of Progress*, p. 265.

18. For discussion of this point as a principle of conduct, see Harold D. Lasswell, *Power and Personality* (New York, 1948), pp. 176–177.

19. Thornton to Lord Hawkesbury, Washington, Dec. ?, 1801, No. 57, PRO GB FO 5.

20. Adams blamed the High Federalists for his loss in 1800. See, for example, his letter to John Jay, Washington, Nov. 24, 1800, in Adams, *Works of John Adams*, IX, 90–91. Years later, in a letter to James Lloyd, Quincy, Jan. 1815, *ibid.*, p. 113, he expressed the opinion that the Federalist party would have suffered a greater defeat if he had not sought peace, or as he put it, "the house would have fallen with a greater explosion." See also his defense of his peace with France in his letter to Benjamin Waterhouse, Quincy, March 16, 1813, in Ford, *Statesman and Friend*, pp. 92–94. For other appraisals of Adams's decision for peace and its influence on American politics, see Morse, "Causes and Consequences of the Party Revolution of 1800," p. 531; Darling, *Rising Empire*, p. 372; Handler, *America and Europe*, p. 181; Lyon, "Convention of 1800," pp. 305–306; Kurtz, *Presidency of John Adams*, p. 353; Morison, *Harrison Gray Otis*, II, 161; Koch, *Power, Morals, and the Founding Fathers*, p. 74; and Fischer, *The Revolution of American Conservatism*, pp. 18, 26, and 52–53.

21. *Maryland Gazette* (Annapolis), Feb. 11, 1802, p. 1, and Gebhardt, *Diplomatick Transactions between the American and French Governments*, III, 481.

22. This interpretation differs from that of Henry Adams, who calls the Convention of Môrtefontaine a diplomatic triumph for Bonaparte. See

Adams's *History of the United States,* I, 362, 370. See also Lyon, "Convention of 1800," p. 305, who points out that despite the importance of the agreement, few scholars have studied it carefully; Allen, *Our Naval War with France,* p. 251; and William H. Trescot, *The Diplomatic History of the Administrations of Washington and Adams, 1789–1801* (Boston, 1857), pp. 221–223.

23. Lyon, *Louisiana in French Diplomacy,* pp. 222, 225.
24. Brooks Adams, in "The Convention of 1800 with France," says that in effect the United States gave France a forced loan. The American government itself became obligated to its own citizens for their claims against France, and the government did not finally settle those French "spoliation claims" until 1915. For details, see Albion, *Sea Lanes in Wartime,* p. 84; Scott, *Controversy over Neutral Rights between the United States and France,* pp. 102–438; Clauder, *American Commerce as Affected by the Wars of the French Revolution,* p. 47; and George A. King, "The French Spoliation Claims," *American Journal of International Law,* VI (Oct. 1912), 830–857.
25. May 31, 1801, quoted in Smith, *Adams,* pp. 1054–1055.
26. To James Lloyd, Quincy, Jan. 1815, in Adams, *Works of John Adams,* X, 113. A month later, on Feb. 6, Adams told Lloyd that "My own 'missions to France' . . . I esteem the most splendid diamond in my crown." *Ibid.,* p. 115. Earlier, before the peace of 1800, Adams said he liked this epitaph for himself:

> "Who British, French & Moorish wiles withstood
> Not for his own but for his Country's good"

To James McHenry, Phil., Jan. 3, 1798, in Adams Papers, reel 117. Adams's later evaluations of the events of his Presidency, it should be kept in mind, are not as trustworthy as his appraisals contemporary to the events. In his long life he sought to justify himself and his record to posterity, and especially to future historians. In his judgment, for example, the War of 1812 suffered in comparison to the Quasi-War, "a glorious and triumphant war." This campaign of self-justification lasted until his death. See Parsons, "Continuing Crusade," pp. 45, 48, and Sargent, "Quasi-War with France," pp. 26–27.
27. Lyon, in "Convention of 1800," p. 308, says Talleyrand deserves the main credit for restoring peace between France and the United States, and Bowman, in "Struggle for Neutrality," p. 450, argues that "almost single-handedly" Talleyrand prevented full-scale war. Even if these scholars overstate the case for Talleyrand, their basic theme is a sound one.

Index

973.45
D35

42809

DeConde, Alexander
        The Quasi-War

Mitchell College Library
New London, CT 06320

A2240 028499 9

DATE DUE

GAYLORD   PRINTED IN U.S.A.

Mitchell College Library
New London, Conn.

FLORIDA

85°   80°   75°

25°

STRAITS OF FLORIDA

B A H A M A

I S L A N D S

⑧

Havana   Matanzas

Old Bahama Channel

Caicos Pass.

CUBA

ISLA DE PIÑOS

GREAT INAGUA

Nuevitas

G R E A T E R

20°

GRAND CAYMAN

Baracoa

St. Yago (Santiago)

Windward Passage

Môle St. Nicolas

Bight of Léogane   Cap Frar (Cap H

SAINT   Gon

GONAIVES I.   DOMINC (Haiti)

Jeremie   Jacmel

Lucea   C. Tiburon

JAMAICA   Kingston   Les Cayes   Port Republica

Port Royal   (Port-au-Prin

C A R I B B E A N

S E A

15°

C E N T R A L

A M E R I C A

Cartagena

10°

N E W   G R A N A D A

(COLOMBIA)

PANAMA   S O T

80°   75°